MUSICALS IN FILM

A Guide to the Genre

MUSICALS IN FILM

A Guide to the Genre

Thomas S. Hischak

An Imprint of ABC-CLIO, LLC
Santa Barbara, California • Denver, Colorado

Library of Congress Cataloging-in-Publication Data

Names: Hischak, Thomas S. author.
Title: Musicals in film : a guide to the genre / Thomas S. Hischak.
Description: Santa Barbara : Greenwood, 2017. | Includes bibliographical references and index.
Identifiers: LCCN 2016019986 (print) | LCCN 2016034331 (ebook) | ISBN 9781440844225
    (hard copy : alk. paper) | ISBN 9781440844232 (ebook)
Subjects: LCSH: Musical films—History and criticism.
Classification: LCC PN1995.9.M86 H58 2016 (print) | LCC PN1995.9.M86 (ebook) |
    DDC 791.43/6—dc23
LC record available at https://lccn.loc.gov/2016019986

ISBN: 978-1-4408-4422-5
EISBN: 978-1-4408-4423-2

21 20 19 18 17   1 2 3 4 5

This book is also available as an eBook.

Greenwood
An Imprint of ABC-CLIO, LLC

ABC-CLIO, LLC
130 Cremona Drive, P.O. Box 1911
Santa Barbara, California 93116-1911

www.abc-clio.com

This book is printed on acid-free paper ∞

Manufactured in the United States of America

For my mother,
who has always loved movie musicals

CONTENTS

BIOGRAPHIES LIST

INTRODUCTION: WHO NEEDS TALKING?

The unique art form known as the movie musical is an American invention. In fact, it is among the very few totally original contributions to the arts that were developed in the United States. Its beginnings in Hollywood were, like many new ideas, partially matters of chance and circumstance. But once the concept of a movie musical was born, the genre rapidly developed and grew and became one of Hollywood's most popular exports around the world.

In order to understand how this new art form was born, it is important to realize that silent movies were never totally silent. Just about every showing of a silent film short or feature was accompanied by music, whether it was a rickety piano in a small neighborhood movie house or a full symphonic orchestra in a large movie palace in a major metropolis. Such background music was expected by moviegoers to add to the drama, romance, or comedy that was appearing on the screen. What the audience was not expecting was for film actors to speak. Not only was the public not waiting for sound movies, they didn't really want to hear dialogue in a film. One's imagination was able to make the screen stars sound as you wished. It was part of the exotic and magical quality of going to the movies. Experiments in adding sound to film stock had been made years before 1927, but the Hollywood studios were not interested because they believed the public was not interested.

That all changed with *The Jazz Singer* in 1927. There had been some short films made with talking and even singing but they were curiosities at best. Warner Brothers, a studio that had long been financially unsteady, decided to sink all of its money into *The Jazz Singer*, the first talking movie. Yet it wasn't a talking picture. It was a silent movie except when the star Al Jolson burst into song. The

Warners reasoned that audiences didn't want to hear Jolson talk but they sure wanted to hear him sing. He was a famous song-and-dance man on Broadway and, aside from some early records, you had to go to Broadway to hear him. When Jolson sang a handful of popular songs on-screen in *The Jazz Singer*, the audience loved it. So the first "talking" film was really a "singing" film; that is, a musical.

Yet Jolson did something odd when they were filming the musical numbers. After he finished a song, and while the sound cameras were still running, he spoke. "Wait a minute," he said to the patrons at a nightclub. "Wait a minute! You ain't heard nothing yet!" This was talking, not singing. Later in the film, he sat down at the parlor piano and sang two songs to his mother. In between, while the camera was still rolling and the microphone was still live, he ad- libbed some affectionate endearments to her. More talking. Then that was it. The rest of *The Jazz Singer* is vocally silent unless Jolson was singing. The movie public loved hearing Jolson sing and, to the surprise of Warner Brothers and all of Hollywood, the audience also liked the talking. Soon sound movies were all the rage. Every studio switched to sound and what did they make? Musicals. Many of these early "talkies" were still mostly silent, the sound turned on only for singing and dancing numbers. The birth of the movie musical and the advent of sound movies are one and the same.

There were problems from the start that Hollywood had to solve. Film is basically a realistic medium. It is essentially photographs that move. And being a realistic art form, one has to give plausible reasons for what happens on the screen. In a Broadway theater, a character can be on a ranch and break out in song. But in a movie, the studios worried, it is not realistic to sing on the prairie. Why is he singing? Where is the orchestra? That is a real cactus and a real cloud and real sagebrush but the character is not behaving realistically. He is singing! Hollywood was so worried about this supposedly odd mixture of movie reality and musical theater reality that the studios insisted that all musical numbers on-screen take place in a nightclub, cabaret, theater, saloon, restaurant, or any place where an orchestra could be seen and the song be part of a "show." As much variety as those places could provide, it was still very limiting. What if you wanted the lovers to sing to each other on a beach in the moonlight? Then the music must come from an orchestra playing in a nearby nightclub or perhaps a carousel not far away. What if you wanted the leading man to sing to his sweetheart in a living room? Then the parlor radio might provide the music, or perhaps he would put a record on the phonograph to accompany his crooning. In one film, the star was required to sing a song on a golf course. How does one find music on a golf course? The studio solved the problem by having the caddy pull out his harmonica and start playing. Dancing was another problem. You couldn't have a dance number in an early musical unless you could explain the source of the music. Onstage no one looked for such a source. It was time to dance so the chorus or the characters danced. But you cannot do that on-screen. Today we find such restrictions silly and meaningless. But to a Hollywood just discovering sound, it was a real concern.

It took a few years before the filmmakers trusted the moviegoer's imagination and let song and dance naturally occur as on the stage. That is why so many early musicals are about show business. They were called "backstagers," and they were the most practical solution to this problem of making a musical in a realistic medium. The first time Hollywood broke this unwritten rule was in the MGM musical *The Broadway Melody* (1929). The film was a backstager, and most of the musical numbers took place on the stage of a theater. But in one scene, the leading man (Charles King) is in a room with the girl (Anita Page) he loves and he sings the love song "You Were Meant for Me." No orchestra is present, the radio is not on, and there's not a harmonica in sight. He just sings to her with the accompaniment heard on the soundtrack. This was quite a risk to take. But MGM played it safe. After King finishes singing, he tells Page that he wrote that love song just for her. That is realistic. He was not just breaking out in song but singing something he wrote. That is logical. But the question remained: Where was the orchestra? To the surprise of MGM executives, the audience didn't care. Moviegoers were not concerned about the source of the music because they quickly adjusted their expectations and accepted a new reality with a movie musical.

Today we are so used to the musical form on-screen that we wonder what all the fuss was about. But one has to remember that in the late 1920s the film musical was a new idea. There were no rules, guidelines, or proven methods to making such movies. Hollywood had no sound engineers, no cinematographers who were expert with sound cameras, no singing actors, and no songwriters. It was a brand-new kind of show business and the studios quickly came up with new ways to make movie musicals. For example, in 1929 someone at MGM came up with the idea of prerecording musical numbers. Instead of having the orchestra on the set and the actor delivering the song with the microphones picking up both singer and musicians, it was thought more practical to record the vocal tracks in a sound studio then replay the track on the sound stage. This way of handling musical numbers on-screen quickly caught on. It was cheaper, more efficient, and worked like a charm. Of course, the actors had to lip-sync to their own recorded voices but it was a task that they quickly picked up. Soon prerecording musical numbers was the only way to make a musical. Then eight decades after the system was introduced, the film version of *Les Misérables* was made and the director Tom Hooper came up with a brilliant idea. In order to make the acting and singing more spontaneous, the performers sang live on the studio set as they were being filmed. This was announced as an important innovation. In reality, it was a return to the beginning.

Perhaps the first major Hollywood musical to totally disregard the need to explain the source of music is the popular fantasy musical *The Wizard of Oz* (1939).

The film is filled with songs but there is never a stage, saloon, nightclub, orchestra, phonograph, radio, or harmonica. Granted, *The Wizard of Oz* is a fantasy and not at all worried about realism. But just 10 years after *The Broadway Melody* first broke the rule, Hollywood could make a whole film without worrying about the source of the music. The same thing happened five years later in another Judy Garland film, *Meet Me in St. Louis* (1944). None of the songs took place on a stage with an orchestra unless you count the parlor piano when Garland and Margaret O'Brien sang and danced at a party. Three decades later, director Bob Fosse did a bold thing with the movie *Cabaret* (1972): All of the musical numbers were in a nightclub except one at a beer garden. Another innovation? No, just another return to the beginning.

Dancing on-screen had its own particular difficulties. Whether there was an orchestra visible or not, dance is not realistic. Professional dancers on a stage made sense but dancing cowboys or dancing street gangs was a bit risky. Even after characters started singing to each other off a stage, dancing in Hollywood musicals remained theater-bound. There was also the question of how to film dancers in a movie. On a stage the dancers face the audience. So all the dances in the earliest musicals kept dancing on a stage and the camera took the audience's point of view. This was very limiting and, from the moviegoers' point of view, often uninteresting. It was the movie *Whoopee!* (1930) that broke the rule. For the dance number "Stetson," choreographer Busby Berkeley had a chorus of pretty cowgirls dancing outside in the desert rather than on a stage. Even more radical, he did not have the girls dance in a chorus line as in a theater. Instead the camera moved about, picking up one girl here, another there, and even doing close-ups of some of them. It was a kind of dancing that would not work in a theater but it certainly worked in a movie. Berkeley would further develop his idea of how to film dance in several spectacular musicals in the 1930s. No longer did chorus lines dominate movie dancing. By the time *Moulin Rouge!* (2001) was made, dance was created in the editing room and not on the set. The performers danced but the camera focused on a leg, a shoulder, or a facial gesture and it was all put together after the fact. From *Whoopee!* to *Moulin Rouge!*, dance on-screen had come a long way, yet both films utilized the same concept.

As we will see throughout the history of movie musicals, Hollywood would change and rethink the new art form as the times and the public demanded. The studios would also alter the kind of music heard in musicals as swing, jazz, Big Band, rock, and other forms of popular music were introduced. Part of the fascination of watching a movie musical from the past is to experience the sound and look of another era, knowing that the new movie musicals we enjoy today will one day be records of how we sounded and looked to future generations.

TIMELINE OF MOVIE MUSICALS

Year	Notable Film Musicals	Historical and Cultural Events
1927	*The Jazz Singer*	Charles Lindbergh flies across the Atlantic.
		Show Boat opens on Broadway.
1928	*The Singing Fool*	Alexander Fleming discovers penicillin.
1929	*The Broadway Melody*	St. Valentine's Day massacre wipes out seven Chicago gangsters.
	Sunny Side Up	Ernest Hemingway's *A Farewell to Arms* is published.
	Rio Rita	The stock market crashes and sets off the Depression.
1930	*Paramount on Parade*	Hoagy Carmichael's song "Georgia on My Mind" is published.
	Whoopee!	Comic strip *Blondie* debuts in newspapers.
1931	*The Smiling Lieutenant*	Scottsboro Boys trial is held in Alabama.
1932	*Love Me Tonight*	*The Jack Benny Show* debuts on radio.
	The Big Broadcast	FDR wins the presidential election.
1933	*42nd Street*	New Deal programs to ease Depression begin.
	Flying Down to Rio	Hitler becomes dictator of Germany.
	Gold Diggers of 1933	Duke Ellington's "Sophisticated Ladies" is recorded.

Year	Notable Film Musicals	Historical and Cultural Events
1934	*Evergreen*	Gangster John Dillinger is gunned down.
	The Gay Divorcee	*It Happened One Night* wins the five top Oscars.
1935	*Naughty Marietta*	Social Security is established in the United States.
	Top Hat	*Porgy and Bess* premieres on Broadway.
1936	*Rose Marie*	Spanish Civil War against Franco begins.
	The Great Ziegfeld	Prokofiev's *Peter and the Wolf* premieres.
	Show Boat	Greta Garbo stars on-screen in *Camille*.
	Swing Time	Thomas Jefferson's head is completed at Mt. Rushmore.
1937	*High, Wide and Handsome*	J. R. R. Tolkien's *The Hobbit* is published.
	Snow White and the Seven Dwarfs	Flyer Amelia Earhart is lost in the Pacific Ocean.
	One Hundred Men and a Girl	Picasso's *Guernica* is unveiled in Paris.
1938	*The Goldwyn Follies*	Orson Welles' *War of the Worlds* radio broadcast causes a panic.
	Carefree	Germany annexes Austria.
	Alexander's Ragtime Band	Thornton Wilder's *Our Town* opens on Broadway.
1939	*Babes in Arms*	*Gone with the Wind* is released.
	The Wizard of Oz	Germany invades Poland and World War II begins.
1940	*Pinocchio*	Rockefeller Center opens in New York City.
	Road to Singapore	Winston Churchill becomes Britain's prime minister.
	Strike Up the Band	Richard Wright's *Native Son* is published.
1941	*Sun Valley Serenade*	Pearl Harbor is attacked and the United States enters World War II.
	Moon Over Miami	Billie Holiday records "God Bless the Child."
1942	*Yankee Doodle Dandy*	*Casablanca* is released.
	Holiday Inn	The Battle of Midway is fought in the Pacific Ocean.
	The Fleet's In	The Battle of Stalingrad is waged in Russia.
1943	*Cabin in the Sky*	Mussolini is deposed by his own troops.

Year	Notable Film Musicals	Historical and Cultural Events
	Girl Crazy	The Jews in the Warsaw Ghetto rise up in defiance of the Nazis.
	The Gang's All Here	Bing Crosby records "I'll Be Home for Christmas."
		Oklahoma! opens on Broadway
1944	*Going My Way*	Normandy invasion (D-Day) in France begins.
	Meet Me in St. Louis	Aaron Copland's ballet *Appalachian Spring* premieres.
	Cover Girl	FDR is elected to unprecedented fourth term.
1945	*Anchors Aweigh*	Tennessee Williams' *The Glass Menagerie* opens on Broadway.
	Meet Me in St. Louis	The atom bomb is dropped on Hiroshima, Japan.
1946	*The Harvey Girls*	*The Best Years of Our Lives* wins the top Oscars.
	The Jolson Story	Carson McCullers' *The Member of the Wedding* is published.
	Blue Skies	Nuremberg war-crimes trials begin in Germany.
1947	*Good News*	Anne Frank's diary is published.
1948	*Easter Parade*	The LP (long-playing) record is introduced.
1949	*On the Town*	Arthur Miller's *Death of a Salesman* opens on Broadway.
	Cinderella	George Orwell's *1984* is published.
	Neptune's Daughter	Gene Autry records "Rudolph the Red-Nosed Reindeer."
1950	*Annie Get Your Gun*	The Korean War begins.
	Summer Stock	Charles Schultz's comic strip *Peanuts* debuts.
1951	*The Great Caruso*	J. D. Salinger's *The Catcher in the Rye* is published.
	An American in Paris	Nat King Cole records "Unforgettable."
1952	*Hans Christian Andersen*	Jonas Salk develops the polio vaccine.
	Singin' in the Rain	The TV series *Gunsmoke* premieres.
1953	*The Band Wagon*	Samuel Beckett's *Waiting for Godot* premieres in France.
	Kiss Me, Kate	The structure of DNA is discovered.

Year	Notable Film Musicals	Historical and Cultural Events
1954	*Seven Brides for Seven Brothers*	A civil war begins in Vietnam.
	White Christmas	Jasper Johns' painting *Flag* is unveiled.
	A Star Is Born	The Miles Davis Quintet is formed.
	The Glenn Miller Story	William Golding's *Lord of the Flies* is published.
1955	*Love Me or Leave Me*	Rosa Parks is arrested in Alabama and the Civil Rights Movement begins.
	Oklahoma!	Boris Pasternak's *Doctor Zhivago* is rejected for publication in the Soviet Union.
	Guys and Dolls	James Dean stars in *Rebel Without a Cause.*
1956	*The King and I*	Eugene O'Neill's *Long Day's Journey Into Night* opens on Broadway.
	High Society	The Hungarian uprising in Budapest is crushed by Soviet troops.
1957	*Funny Face*	Elvis Presley records "All Shook Up."
	The Pajama Game	The Soviet satellite *Sputnik* orbits the Earth.
1958	*Gigi*	The TV series *Rawhide* debuts.
	South Pacific	Pete Seeger records "Where Have All the Flowers Gone?"
1959	*Porgy and Bess*	Hawaii becomes a U.S. state.
1960	*Bells Are Ringing*	Harper Lee's *To Kill a Mockingbird* is published.
		Alfred Hitchcock's *Psycho* is released.
1961	*West Side Story*	Patsy Cline records "I Fall to Pieces."
1962	*The Music Man*	Nuclear war averted with the Cuban Missile Crisis.
		Ken Kesey's *One Flew Over the Cuckoo's Nest* is published.
1963	*Bye Bye Birdie*	John F. Kennedy is assassinated in Dallas.
		Hello, Dolly! opens on Broadway.
1964	*A Hard Day's Night*	The Beatles' first American tour begins.
	Mary Poppins	*Dr. Strangelove* is released.
	My Fair Lady	Marc Chagall's Paris Opera House murals are unveiled.
		The New York World's Fair opens.
1965	*The Sound of Music*	Simon and Garfunkel record "Sounds of Silence."
		The Autobiography of Malcolm X is published.

Year	Notable Film Musicals	Historical and Cultural Events
1966	*How to Succeed in Business . . .*	*Cabaret* opens on Broadway.
		The new Metropolitan Opera House opens in New York's Lincoln Center.
1967	*Thoroughly Modern Millie*	*The Graduate* is released.
	Doctor Dolittle	*Hair* opens on Broadway.
1968	*Funny Girl*	Martin Luther King, Jr. and Robert F. Kennedy are assassinated.
	Oliver!	The Beatles record "Hey Jude."
	Chitty Chitty Bang Bang	*Rowan & Martin's Laugh-In* debuts on TV.
1969	*Hello, Dolly!*	The rock festival Woodstock is held in Bethel, New York.
		Apollo 11 lands on the moon.
	Darling Lili	Vonnegut's *Slaughterhouse-Five* is published.
1970	*On a Clear Day You Can See Forever*	Student war protestors are killed at Kent State in Ohio.
		Gary Trudeau's comic strip *Doonesbury* debuts.
1971	*Fiddler on the Roof*	*The French Connection* is released.
1972	*Cabaret*	Stevie Wonder records "You Are the Sunshine of My Life."
	Lady Sings the Blues	*The Godfather* is released.
	1776	The burglary of Democratic headquarters in DC erupts into the Watergate scandal.
1973	*Charlotte's Web*	Judy Collins records "Send in the Clowns."
	Godspell	Native Americans occupy Wounded Knee in South Dakota.
	Jesus Christ Superstar	*The Sting* is released and revives interest in Scott Joplin's ragtime music.
1974	*Phantom of the Paradise*	Richard Nixon resigns the presidency.
		All the President's Men is published.
1975	*Nashville*	Saigon falls to North Vietnam as U.S. troops evacuate Vietnam.
	Rocky Horror Picture Show	Altair, first personal computer, is put on the market.

Year	Notable Film Musicals	Historical and Cultural Events
1976	*A Star Is Born*	Alex Haley's *Roots* is published.
	Bugsy Malone	Earth, Wind and Fire record their *Spirit* album.
1977	*Saturday Night Fever*	*Star Wars* is released.
	New York, New York	First cases of AIDS are reported in the United States.
1978	*Grease*	John Irving's *The World According to Garp* is published.
	The Buddy Holly Story	Billy Joel records his *52nd Street* album.
1979	*Hair*	*Sweeney Todd* opens on Broadway.
	The Rose	Woody Allen's *Manhattan* is released.
1980	*Fame*	Willem de Kooning's painting *Untitled I* is unveiled.
	Coal Miner's Daughter	Carl Sagan's *Cosmos* is published.
1981	*Pennies from Heaven*	The first U.S. space shuttle *Columbia* is launched.
		Phil Collins records his *Face Value* album.
1982	*Victor/Victoria*	Alice Walker's *The Color Purple* is published.
	Flashdance	Michael Jackson's *Thriller* album is released.
1983	*Yentl*	The TV miniseries *The Winds of War* is broadcast.
1984	*Footloose*	The Soviet Union boycotts the Los Angeles Olympics.
	This Is Spinal Tap	David Mamet's *Glengarry Glen Ross* opens on Broadway.
1985	*Follow That Bird*	*The Oprah Winfrey Show* debuts on TV.
1986	*Little Shop of Horrors*	Van Halen records his *5150* album.
1987	*La Bamba*	Tom Wolfe's *The Bonfire of the Vanities* is published.
	Dirty Dancing	*Moonstruck* is released.
1988	*Bird*	Bobby McFerrin records "Don't Worry, Be Happy."
	Oliver and Company	Stephen Hawking's *A Brief History of Time* is published.
1989	*The Little Mermaid*	Spike Lee's *Do the Right Thing* is released.
		I. M. Pei's glass Pyramid opens in Paris.

Year	Notable Film Musicals	Historical and Cultural Events
1990	*Dick Tracy*	East and West Germany are reunited.
		Garth Brooks records his *No Fences* album.
1991	*The Doors*	The Soviet Union disbands and Communism ends in Russia.
	Beauty and the Beast	*The Silence of the Lambs* is released.
1992	*Newsies*	Bill Clinton is elected president.
	Aladdin	Bruce Springsteen records his *Human Touch* album.
1993	*The Nightmare Before Christmas*	Tony Kushner's *Angels in America* opens on Broadway.
1994	*The Lion King*	The Channel Tunnel between England and France opens.
	The Swan Princess	*Pulp Fiction* is released.
1995	*Pocahontas*	A bomb devastates Oklahoma City's federal building.
		Windows 95 is released by Microsoft.
1996	*The Preacher's Wife*	Summer Olympics are held in Atlanta, Georgia.
	Evita	E-bay starts online sales.
	The Hunchback of Notre Dame	The Spice Girls record "Wannabe."
1997	*Anastasia*	*The Lion King* opens on Broadway.
	Hercules	*Titanic* is released.
		The UK gives Hong Kong back to China.
1998	*Mulan*	European Union nations adopt the Euro.
	The Prince of Egypt	The TV series *Will and Grace* debuts.
1999	*Tarzan*	Napster is introduced.
2000		Tiger Woods is the youngest golfer to win the Grand Slam.
2001	*Moulin Rouge!*	Attacks made on the World Trade Center and the Pentagon paralyze the nation.
		Wikipedia goes online.
		The first *Harry Potter* film is released.
2002	*Chicago*	The Winter Olympics are held in Salt Lake City, Utah.
2003	*Camp*	*Wicked* opens on Broadway.
		Apple introduces iTunes.

Year	Notable Film Musicals	Historical and Cultural Events
2004	*Ray*	Pixar's *The Incredibles* is released.
	The Phantom of the Opera	Facebook begins at Harvard University.
2005	*Walk the Line*	*Doubt* opens on Broadway.
	Rent	Hurricane Katrina devastates the South.
2006	*Dreamgirls*	The final part of *Lord of the Rings* film cycle is released.
		Christina Aguilera records "Ain't No Other Man."
2007	*Hairspray*	Apple introduces the iPhone.
	Enchanted	*Spider-Man 3* is released.
	Sweeney Todd	*Radio Golf*, the final drama in August Wilson's 10-play cycle, opens on Broadway.
2008	*High School Musical 3*	*Billy Elliot* opens on Broadway.
		The Dark Knight is released.
2009	*Nine*	Black Eyed Peas records "Boom Boom Pow."
	The Princess and the Frog	The TV series *Glee* debuts.
		Barack Obama is inaugurated as first African American U.S. president.
2010	*Tangled*	*American Idiot* opens on Broadway.
2011	*The Muppets*	Adele records "Rolling in the Deep."
		The Occupy Wall Street protest spreads to other U.S. cities.
2012	*Les Misérables*	The science laboratory named *Curiosity Rover* lands on Mars.
		Lincoln is released.
2013	*Frozen*	Bombings occur during the Boston Marathon.
2014	*Into the Woods*	Lady Gaga records "Do What U Want."
	Jersey Boys	The Apple Watch is introduced.
2015		*Jurassic World* is released.
		Hamilton opens on Broadway.
		Taylor Swift records "Blank Space."

Movie Musical Terms

The following movie musical terms are used throughout the book. They are presented here to help the reader understand the various descriptions of Hollywood musicals.

B movie   When movie houses used to show double features, the B movie was the secondary film. It usually had a lower budget and fewer stars than the A attraction.

ballad   In modern popular music, a ballad is a sentimental or romantic song about love, home, or any other heartfelt subject. Most often the hit songs from movies are ballads.

character song   Any song that helps reveal a character's thoughts, hopes, or personality is labeled a character song. They can range from the comic to the tragic.

charm song   A musical number that charms the audience by having the character tug at the heartstrings is considered a charm song. Often they are sung by children in movie musicals.

composer   The person or persons who write the music heard in film musicals is the composer. Usually one composer writes the music for the songs and another writes the soundtrack scoring heard between songs.

crooner   A singer who uses the microphone to sing softly and intimately is said to be crooning. This is the opposite of a *belter*, a singer who blasts out the song at high volume.

dubbing   When a studio adds or replaces an actor's singing and/or speaking voice, the process is known as dubbing. For most film musicals, the singers record their vocals in a recording studio then "dub" themselves on the shooting set.

feature   A full-length movie is called a feature, as opposed to a movie "short." When movie theaters played two long movies together, it was called a "double feature."

integrated musical   When the songs and dances are carefully tied into the plot and characters, that stage or screen musical is described as integrated. The Broadway musical *Oklahoma!* (1943) is considered the first fully integrated musical.

interpolation   If a song is added to a movie musical but not written by the songwriters who wrote the rest of the score, the number is said to be interpolated. Often famous old songs are interpolated into film musicals.

lyric   The words to a song are called the lyric. The person who writes those words is known as a *lyricist.*

pastiche song   Any new musical number that copies or echoes the music of a past style is said to be pastiching. Such songs are used to re-create a past period by suggesting the time through music, such as using jazz in a movie set in the 1920s.

remake   When a studio takes the story and characters from a past movie and makes a new film with them, the movie is called a remake. This is different from a *sequel* in which the characters and situation of one film are used to make a new movie with a different story and score.

reprise   The repeating of all or part of a song later in a film musical, either by the same or different characters, is said to be a reprise. These are particularly used in movies based on Broadway musicals, which often use reprises.

specialty   In older Hollywood musicals, it was common practice to add a star of radio, records, or Broadway to the movie without giving that performer a character or any lines. Considered a specialty spot, the singer or dancer usually performed on-screen in a nightclub and was not part of the plot.

standard   A song that remains popular over the decades and has been recorded by many different singers is considered a standard. A song standard can be interpolated into a film or a new song from a movie can become so popular it eventually becomes a standard.

studio A film studio was not only the place in Hollywood where movies were made, it also referred to the film company. The expression "the studios" came to mean the moviemaking business.

Tin Pan Alley Up until the 1950s, the music business was often called Tin Pan Alley. It referred back to the days when many of the song publishers had their offices on a street in Manhattan that reverberated with the sounds of pianos plucking away at songs.

Tinseltown A slang expression for Hollywood, it was originally used as a sarcastic term but today refers to the studios and moviemaking in general.

torch song In popular music, a sentimental ballad about lost love is labeled a torch song. Singing about a lover who does not return one's affection has served as the basis of many famous torch songs.

MOVIE MUSICAL GENRES

Before looking at movie musicals decade by decade, it is useful to describe the different kinds of film musicals past and present. Some types are products of their time, such as escapist backstage musicals during the Depression and patriotic musicals made during World War II. Other types are perennial favorites, returning decade after decade, such as the biographical musical or the fantasy musical. Of course there are many films that are more than just one type, such as a biographical backstager or a fantasy rock musical. Defining the possible type(s) of musical helps one understand the purpose behind the film and who the audience is for such a movie. As we shall see, the nature of one type of musical can change from decade to decade. A Mickey Rooney-Judy Garland "let's put on a show" musical like *Babes in Arms* (1939) and a gritty urban musical like *Fame* (1980) can both be described as youth backstagers, but the two movies could not be more different. Similarly, Disney's *Snow White and the Seven Dwarfs* (1937) and the Beatles' *Yellow Submarine* (1968) can both be labeled animated musicals but one would never be mistaken for the other. Finally, one must keep in mind that movie genres go in and out of fashion over time. Operetta musicals were very popular in the 1930s, fell from favor in the 1940s, then came back in a new form in the 1960s. What follows is an historical look at the various musical movie genres. Their story is the story of the Hollywood musical.

BACKSTAGE MUSICALS

As we have seen, many of the early film musicals were set in a location where singing and dancing were not only possible but expected. Hollywood felt that musical numbers on-screen only made logical sense if they took place on some kind of stage. The backstage musical is often about putting on a show, be it a Broadway extravaganza or a rock concert. The term "backstage" is used because the plot of the movie revolves around the people putting on the show; the music and the spectacle come from the performance itself. *The Jazz Singer*, the first "talkie," is a backstage musical and much of it takes place in cabarets, nightclubs, and theaters. *The Broadway Melody* in 1929 was not only about putting on a big Broadway production but there were a few times in the script when the characters sang to each other offstage. This was an important breakthrough because now the backstage movie musical could have songs outside of the context of the big show. As in the theater, there now could be character songs. These are songs that are sung by a character in the story that reveal something going on inside the person. Such songs do not take place on a stage or in a nightclub. They are personal moments, often sung when the character is by herself or himself. Backstage musicals involve characters who are performers so it is more logical for a chorus girl or leading man to express themselves offstage with a song. A rock singer may sing one kind of song in a concert but a very different kind of song to his girlfriend after the show. When backstage musicals were able to include character songs, the stories and the characters became much richer.

So many backstagers were made during the first decade of talking movies that it often seemed it was the only kind of musical. The focus of all these early backstage musicals was the big show at the end of the movie. More often than not, that show was a Broadway show. Hollywood, like much of America, thought that a big dazzling Broadway production was the highest form of entertainment so most of the backstage musicals involved Broadway. In *The Jazz Singer*, the title character's career reaches its peak when he stars in a Broadway show. All the subsequent backstagers followed the same pattern. Most moviegoers across America had never seen a Broadway production and, more than likely, never would. So America's vision of a Broadway hit was what they saw in the movies. This was ironic because few stage productions on Broadway or anywhere else ever looked like the lavish extravaganzas that Hollywood made. All the same, the studios insisted that the big show should be a Broadway show and not a movie. Some of this reasoning came from the inferiority complex Hollywood had about Broadway and the stage. The theater being the older and more established form of entertainment, the studios thought that plays and musicals on Broadway were a higher art form than the movies. Broadway was expensive and catered to an audience of sophisticated urbanites. Movies were inexpensive and were made for the everyday Americans. Broadway meant great playwrights, literate plays and musicals, and renowned acting. Talking movies were new, primitive, and struggling to establish an identity. In short, theater was upper class, movies were lower class. This, of course, was a gross exaggeration but the Hollywood studios felt that way all the same. That is why a movie musical, which could outspend and outdazzle any stage show, still had to take place on Broadway.

The 1933 classic *42nd Street* is considered the quintessential backstage film musical in the old style. The film was not only popular in itself, it was copied over and over again until the audience came to expect a backstager to be like *42nd Street*. The most copied part of the formula was that the star (whom no one likes) cannot go on and do the show on opening night so a younger, more talented singer-dancer from the chorus (whom everyone likes) takes her place and becomes a star. This contrived but useful plot device could be found in many backstage musicals in the 1930s. Sometimes it got ridiculous, as in *The Cat and the Fiddle* (1934) when the girlfriend (Jeanette MacDonald) of the composer had nothing to do with the big show but on opening night replaced the star (Vivienne Segal) all the same. This backstage cliché was used so often that audiences began to expect it. Imagine their surprise in *Music in the Air* (1934) when the inexperienced singer (June Lang) replaced the star (Gloria Swanson) on opening night and failed miserably. Embarrassed by her failure, she left the big city and went home with her boyfriend. Were the filmmakers being sarcastic? Or were they just tired of the cliché as well?

Warner Brothers, which had produced both *The Jazz Singer* and *42nd Street*, made the best backstage musicals of the 1930s. Its popular series of "Gold Digger" movies usually returned to the Broadway backstage setting. In *Gold Diggers of 1933*, the big Broadway show could not go on because of the Depression and lack of financing. So the movie concerns the way the chorus girls managed to get money from a rich Bostonian so that they will all have jobs. That big show also had a last-minute cast replacement, but this time it was an unknown guy (Dick Powell) who went on for the male star (Clarence Nordstrom). Warner made so many backstagers that it ran out of ways to tell the same story over and over again. In *Footlight Parade* (1933), the writers broke tradition and the big show was not a Broadway musical but a series of prologues. These were live stage shows that were presented in movie houses before the feature film was shown. Of course the prologues in *Footlight Parade* were as big (actually bigger) than Broadway productions so it came down to the same thing.

During the Depression, audiences loved the excessive, spectacular quality of the big shows in backstage musicals. It was escapism of the highest order. But in the 1940s, when financial hard times eased considerably, the backstage musical changed. Some films still went overboard during the big show, but most films in the genre put on more modest shows. Instead of Broadway, the climatic entertainment was more often in a nightclub or other more intimate venue. Take *Holiday Inn* (1942) as an example. There are a few numbers staged in a classy Manhattan night spot, but most of the numbers are presented at the inn, which has a smaller stage and fewer chorus members. In some films the big show taking place in a nightclub is so big that one wonders where the patrons sit. But, by and large, the 1940s backstage musical offered a more realistic version of live entertainment.

Also, the location of the show often left the urban night life and found intimacy elsewhere. The show is at a resort in *Sun Valley Serenade* (1941) and *Springtime in the Rockies* (1942), on a boat in *The Fleet's In* (1942), on the midway in *State Fair* (1945), in an ice cream parlor in *Good News!* (1947), at a high school dance in *A Date with Judy* (1948), and in a swimming pool in *Neptune's Daughter* (1949).

In the 1950s, Hollywood seemed to go back to Broadway. Most musicals were now in color so the spectacle was often more a matter of glittering costumes and colorful lighting than huge production numbers with lots of extras. Also, when a number took place on the stage of a Broadway theater, it looked like it could actually fit on a normal-sized stage. The Broadway shows in *The Band Wagon* (1953), *Kiss Me, Kate* (1953), *The Country Girl* (1954), *Deep in My Heart* (1954), *My Sister Eileen* (1955), and other backstagers of the 1950s were accurate representations of a New York stage production. None of the musicals just mentioned went in for big spectacle. The entertainment value was determined by the high quality of the songs and the performers. The same was true when the show did not take place in a theater. Just as the shows at *Holiday Inn* were modest, so too were those at another inn in *White Christmas* (1954). The nightclub entertainment in musicals such as *Young Man with a Horn* (1950), *Pete Kelly's Blues* (1955), *The Joker Is Wild* (1957), *Pal Joey* (1957), and *The Five Pennies* (1959) were sometimes less than modest. The musical numbers often took place in outright dives. The backstager lost some of its glamour in the 1950s as the seamier side of show business was explored. The stories were more realistic (many were based on real people), and the tinsel of show business was more tawdry. Even in the more glossy musicals, such as *A Star Is Born* (1954) and *There's No Business Like Show Business* (1954), there is more heartbreak backstage than glitter onstage. One could not describe most of the 1950s backstage musicals as forms of escapism.

Fewer backstagers were made in the 1960s and 1970s. Perhaps Hollywood (or moviegoers) were not as interested in what went on behind the scenes as they were in earlier decades. But the genre was far from dead. There were period pieces that went backstage with success, such as *Gypsy* (1962), *Funny Girl* (1968), *Cabaret* (1972), *Lady Sings the Blues* (1972), and *The Buddy Holly Story* (1978). There were even a few contemporary backstage musicals that found an audience, such as *Nashville* (1975), the remake of *A Star Is Born* (1976), *All That Jazz* (1979), and *The Rose* (1979). Just about all of these were brutally realistic, showing the dark and lonely side of celebrity. All of the preceding musicals also have something else in common: None end with the big show. The idea of turning the climax of a backstage musical into a glorious production number had been abandoned some years before. These films end with abandonment or death. Actually, there is a big show at the end of *Nashville*, but it climaxes with the star not being replaced at the last minute but instead gets shot. It looked like the *42nd Street* formula was indeed gone and forgotten.

Very few backstage musicals were made during the last two decades of the century that it is not possible to make many generalizations about them. But one thing is clear: They were not about Broadway. When one went behind the scenes in show business, that business was the recording industry. The big show was replaced by recording sessions and rock concerts. Whether fiction or based on actual performers, these backstagers were usually contemporary or at least relatively recent. Country music was explored in *Coal Miner's Daughter* (1980) and jazz music in *Bird* (1988), but the rest were more interested in various forms of rock and roll. *La Bamba* (1987), *The Commitments* (1991), *The Doors* (1991), and *That Thing You Do* (1996) all went behind the scenes of the rock industry. Even the satiric rockumentary *This Is Spinal Tap* (1984) got its energy from the rock scene as it made fun of *Woodstock* (1970) and other documentaries covering rock stars. It seemed that moviegoers were still interested in musicals that were about show business but that business was not Broadway or nightclubs.

The backstage musical may not be as plentiful or as popular as it was in the 1930s, but it is far from dead. The new century saw movies go behind the scenes in *Hedwig and the Angry Inch* (2001), *Ray* (2004), *Walk the Line* (2005), *Dreamgirls* (2006), *Once* (2006), and *Jersey Boys* (2014). Again, they are all about the music business and, whether fiction or fact, they do not paint a very rosy picture of backstage. The genre has moved from ridiculous escapism in the early Warner musicals to a much more sobering depiction of the world of show business. But the backstage musical will never disappear because audiences are always curious about what goes on behind the scenes.

FRONTIER MUSICALS

Perhaps the kind of musical that would be the opposite of a backstager is the frontier musical. Movies about show business usually take place in the city. Frontier musicals are rural and, most often, set in the past. Another way of defining the frontier musical is a combination of two of Hollywood's favorite genres: musicals and westerns. That is not to say that all frontier musicals are about the Wild West. The locale can be the Mississippi River towns, such as *Show Boat* (1936); the hills of Western Pennsylvania, the setting for *High, Wide and Handsome* (1937); the Badlands in the Dakotas, as seen in *Calamity Jane* (1953); a New Mexico desert town, as in *The Harvey Girls* (1946); the cattle land of Oklahoma Territory in *Oklahoma!* (1955); or the untamed forests of Virginia in *Pocahontas* (1995). The true frontier musical concerns the rugged pioneer spirit of America and the way people live with the land. While the backstage musical was usually about urban characters who are slick or sophisticated, the people in the frontier musicals are less polished and more rustic. The music in the city is modern, utilizing ragtime, jazz, swing, or whatever is the most recent trend. The rural musicals tend toward folk songs, cowboy ballads, or square dance tunes. Just as many of the backstagers were not very realistic about show business, the frontier musicals often romanticized life in the country. Exaggerated stereotypes can be found in both genres, usually for comic effect. For every wisecracking chorus girl there was a country rube or a backwoods hick. In frontier musicals there was no big show in the finale so the love story usually got more attention.

As we have seen, early talkies had to deal with the logic of singing and dancing in lifelike settings. This was even trickier in the frontier musicals where there were no nightclubs, cabarets, ballrooms, or theaters to explain the musical numbers. Therefore, frontier films had to rely on saloon entertainment, town socials, weddings, country dances, and other kinds of gatherings. Before long these musicals allowed duets on the prairie and dancing in the barnyard. Instead of a chorus line, there were the townsfolk. Replacing the dance orchestra was the fiddler or small hoedown band. Because most frontier musicals were set in the past, there was a sense of nostalgia for the simple country life. Both urban and rural moviegoers found a kind of comfort watching the frontier musicals because they presented an America that was mostly imagination.

Few frontier musicals were made during the early years of the talkies. Those first movie musicals were preoccupied with the big show. Yet a few exceptions are worth pointing out. *Hallelujah* (1929) was far ahead of its time, not only as a frontier musical but as an honest depiction of African Americans. It was set in the South where sharecroppers picked cotton for their meager living. The music heard was mostly gospel hymns and work songs that the laborers sang as they picked the cotton and brought the bales to market. It was far from a rose-colored version of the truth. Quite the opposite was *Whoopee!* (1930), which was a musical farce set on a California ranch. The jokes came from putting a city hypochondriac (Eddie Cantor) on a dude ranch where he had to deal with Wild West bad guys and stereotypic tribesmen. Both *Mississippi* (1935) and *Show Boat* (1936) were more serious and took place along the famous river. The popular operetta *Rose Marie* (1936) was set in the Canadian Rockies but still had an American spirit in its main characters. The next year saw one of Hollywood's finest frontier musicals, *High, Wide and Handsome* (1937), which was about the pioneering men who drilled oil wells and ran pipelines in Western Pennsylvania in 1859. Because the story included a barn dance, medicine show, circus, girly saloon, and wedding, there was plenty of opportunity for musical numbers.

The movie musicals of the 1940s were more interested in Latin American settings and patriotic morale boosters in big cities, but a handful of excellent frontier musicals came out of the decade. Perhaps the best one was *The Harvey Girls* (1946) about girls from the East who work as waitresses in Harvey's Restaurant in Sandrock, New Mexico, in the 1880s. There were some musical numbers in the local saloon but the most memorable songs were performed in other locations about the town. Like the earlier *Whoopee!*, *Girl Crazy* (1943) put a city kid (Mickey Rooney) in the desert, this time in the Arizona town of Custerville. Since Tommy Dorsey and his orchestra was also in town, it made for some great music. *Can't Help Singing* (1944) painted a more realistic picture of the West. Most of the musical took place on a wagon train heading over the prairie to California in 1847. There was no Big Band but with Deanna Durbin as the heroine there was lovely music all the same. More a parody of a frontier musical was *The Paleface* (1948) and its sequel *Son of Paleface* (1952). It used a familiar format: city dentist (Bob Hope) stuck out West where he gets involved with bandits and sharpshooters.

Some of Hollywood's best frontier musicals were made in the 1950s. Irving Berlin's Broadway hit *Annie Get Your Gun* was filmed in 1950 and it included all the elements needed for a top-notch rural musical. The action traveled all over the continent (and in Europe too) but the venue was Buffalo Bill's Wild West Show and the heroine was sharpshooter Annie Oakley (Betty Hutton) so there was always a frontier feeling about the film. *Calamity Jane* (1953) was about another gal (Doris Day) good with a gun, but the action mostly took place in the town of Deadwood in the Dakota Territory. *The Farmer Takes a Wife* (1953) was a romance set on the Erie Canal in 1850. The frontier musical favorite, *Seven Brides for Seven Brothers* (1954), was set in the backwoods of Oregon in 1850, and it found plenty of opportunity for song and dance without once going to a saloon. The same was true of *Oklahoma!* (1955), which was about the rivalry between farmers and cowhands in the Oklahoma Territory right before it becomes a state in 1907. There was a picnic social and a wedding but most of the musical numbers came from characters who were tied to the land. At the end of the decade came a satiric frontier musical, *L'il Abner* (1959), set in the fictional town of Dogpatch somewhere in the backwoods of the Ozarks. Based on a comic strip and still very cartoonish on the screen, *L'il Abner* mocked the frontier spirit and got away with it.

Fewer westerns appeared on television and in movie theaters in the 1960s and 1970 so perhaps that is why there were much fewer frontier musicals. *The Unsinkable Molly Brown* (1964) featured a strong frontier girl (Debbie Reynolds) as *Annie Get Your Gun* and *Calamity Jane* had. The film mostly took place in Colorado, the nearby mountains and Denver, but Molly retained her fighting spirit even when she went to Europe and when she survived the sinking of the *Titanic*. *Finian's Rainbow* (1968), a musical fantasy with an agenda, was set in "Missitucky" and spoofed everything from Irish leprechauns to Jim Crow laws. This was perhaps the frontier musical for the turbulent 1960s. *Paint Your Wagon* (1969) concerned the California gold rush of 1853. There was not much pioneer spirit on display but plenty of dancing in the mud. By the 1980s, the frontier musical was nowhere to be found unless one saw *Footloose* (1984) as a modern version of the genre. The big city kid (Kevin Bacon) moves to a small Utah town where dancing is not allowed and turns everyone on their heads. In the 1980s, that counted as pioneer spirit.

Disney's *Pocahontas* (1995) was one of the few animated frontier musicals, and it was exceptionally well done. The conflict between the Native Americans and the British settlers in the colony of Virginia was portrayed with sincerity and even some accuracy. Another Disney animated musical, the overlooked *Home on the Range* (2004), was much lighter but contained all the elements of the Old West right down to a yodeling cattle rustler. It was so much fun that one hopes the frontier musical, serious or not, is not gone forever.

AMERICANA MUSICALS

Similar to the frontier musical but distinct in its goal is the film that celebrates Americana. When a movie musical is about a past time (recent or long past) in American history and life in that time is lovingly re-created on-screen, it is an example of Americana. Whether it is the big city, a small town, or on the prairie, such musicals take a nostalgic look at the past and attempt to portray all-American values. Few of these musicals are very realistic, preferring to take a romanticized point of view. As each generation discovers a different past era, there is sometimes a fad-like interest in the period. A good example is the rediscovery of the 1950s by Americans in the 1970s. The television show *Happy Days* (1974 to 1984) and the movie musical *Grease* (1978) were not very accurate, but they had the look and the sound of the 1950s and that was enough. Sometimes the Americana musical reminds older moviegoers of their youth, but, just as often, these films paint such a heartwarming or exciting picture of the past that memory has nothing to do with it. Once in a while an Americana musical will look at the not-so-pretty aspects of the past, but usually the audience is comforted with a happy ending or at least hope for a better tomorrow. Such is the case with *New York, New York* (1977) and *Newsies* (1992).

We are so used to period musicals today that it comes as a surprise that just about all of the early musical talkies were contemporary. Movies were considered a modern invention and so they usually showed modern things. There had been many silent films that were period pieces but musicals preferred to be up to date. The first notable costume movies with singing were the picturesque operetta films featuring Jeanette MacDonald and Nelson Eddy but they were rarely set in America. *Alexander's Ragtime Band* (1938) looked back to the early decades of the century and used songs from that period so it might be labeled an Americana musical. *Tin Pan Alley* (1940), *Birth of the Blues* (1941), and *For Me and My Gal* (1942) were set in the same time period and also used old songs but those films were more about the music than nostalgia. For the first classic Americana musical, one has to look at *Meet Me in St. Louis* (1944). It re-creates life in the midwestern city of the title in 1904 as seen through one family. Life was simpler then and, according to the film, happier. *Meet Me in St. Louis* is still regarded as one of Hollywood's best period pieces, but it must be remembered that in 1944 moviegoers over the age of 45 could distinctly recall that year of the fair. It is a credit to the power of the film that modern audiences watching an America of over 100 years ago are still enthralled. *Centennial Summer* (1946), about the 1876 exposition in Philadelphia celebrating the 100th anniversary of the Declaration of Independence, is a pale copy of *Meet Me in St. Louis* but an Americana musical as well. One had to be a very old moviegoer to be able to recall that year, and the rest of the audience could not get involved with the problematic film.

A much-loved (but often misunderstood) Americana musical was *Song of the South* (1946), which was set on a plantation and the nearby countryside in the Deep South in the late 1800s. With animation and live action brilliantly mixed together, the film portrayed a nostalgic view of southern country life. While some in the 1960s thought the movie racist for its depiction of African Americans, most now view *Song of the South* as the warmhearted and nostalgic musical that was intended. *Mother Wore Tights* (1947) and *The Shocking Miss Pilgrim* (1947), two period musicals starring Betty Grable, were filled with Americana in the clothes and settings of the turn of the century and they even included some songs from the era. *Summer Holiday* (1948) was a gentle look at growing pains within a New England family living in the first decade of the new century. The score consisted of new songs so the nostalgia had to come from the characters and the story. *In the Good Old Summertime* (1949), on the other hand, was chock full of turn-of-the-century tunes and, as sung by Judy Garland, the songs conjured up a feeling for the past. Disney's animated *Lady and the Tramp* (1955) takes place during the same period in a small town filled with Americana touches. The setting that the artists created would later inspire the look of Main Street at the Disney theme parks. Another small town was featured in *The Music Man* (1962). River City, Iowa, in the 1910s was as important as the townspeople in conveying what life was like at the time. A Boston family moves to a little town in Maine in *Summer Magic* (1963) and all the homespun touches are there in the characters and their small-town doings.

The Roaring Twenties were revisited in *Thoroughly Modern Millie* (1967). Most of the songs were new but they were such accurate pastiches of 1920s tunes that they ended up charming audiences all the same. The musical exaggerated and even spoofed the era but *Thoroughly Modern Millie* was so much fun it didn't matter. Hardly a picture postcard version of Manhattan in the late 1940s, *New York, New York* (1977) nevertheless re-created the era accurately. Far from heartwarming, the musical sounded right. *Grease* (1978), on the other hand, wanted to be a naughty version of the 1950s but was so likable that it became a social phenomenon. *Grease* opened on Broadway in 1972 and many credit it for the new fascination Americans had for the 1950s. By the time the movie *Grease* opened, the fad was in full swing. *Newsies* (1992), a musical that took a while to find an audience, was set during a newsboys strike in New York in 1899. Certainly no one in the movie theater could recall that time so it didn't matter if the pop songs made no attempt to sound like the period. That was not a problem in *Across the Universe* (2007), a musical about the volatile 1960s, because all the songs were Beatles numbers from that decade. The popular *Hairspray* (2007) looked at the early 1960s, a time before the turmoil of *Across the Universe,* and came up with a slaphappy version of life in segregated Baltimore in 1962. The Americana musical has certainly changed since *Meet Me in St. Louis* but it is still with us. Someday there might even be a nostalgic musical about the turn of the 21st century.

BROADWAY ADAPTATIONS

When sound came in, Hollywood recruited writers, composers, lyricists, directors, choreographers, and performers from Broadway to make musicals for the screen. Just as important, the studios also bought the rights to Broadway musicals, particularly the long-run shows with hit songs. Ironically, the studios often changed the storyline, characters, and even the songs when the musical was adapted to the screen. In many cases famous songs were cut and the studios' own songwriters wrote new ones, though they were rarely as good as the stage songs. Hollywood had its own opinion as to what worked on the screen and thought nothing of making such changes. No wonder so many Broadway songwriters were not happy working in the movies.

Broadway has produced hundreds of musicals over the years and many of them were made into films. A successful Broadway musical provided the studio with a plot, characters, and songs. Even when these were changed for the screen, the Broadway musical was Hollywood's single most important source for material. Before 1927, some stage works were turned into silent films. The concept of a "silent" musical seems very odd but one has to recall that it was never totally quiet in a pretalkie movie house. Sometimes the studio bought the Broadway show, filmed it with necessary dialogue titles, and the piano or organ or full orchestra played the familiar melodies from the stage score. Perhaps the best of these adaptations was *The Student Prince in Old Heidelberg* (1927), based on the 1924 Broadway hit. The story and the characters were so strong that the romantic tale played beautifully without the songs. Yet many moviegoers heard sections of the popular "Deep in My Heart, Dear" and "The Drinking Song" coming from the movie house musicians.

The first Broadway musical to be filmed with sound was *The Desert Song* in 1929, based on the 1926 exotic operetta set in French Morocco. The sound and even the cinematography were pretty primitive and the movie was not a success at the box office. But later that year RKO's film version of *Rio Rita* opened and it was a resounding hit. Based on the 1927 romantic adventure musical set along the Mexican border, *Rio Rita* had better cinematic qualities and some sections were even in two-strip Technicolor. Its success prompted RKO and other studios to buy up stage shows and turn them into movie musicals. Among the first were the Marx Brothers' musicals *The Cocoanuts* (1929) and *Animal Crackers* (1930), which were basically the Broadway shows reconstructed in a film studio. They are accurate copies and very entertaining but cinematically rather stagnant. Much livelier visually was *Whoopee!* (1930), which was based on the 1928 Eddie Cantor stage hit. The fact that Cantor reprised his Broadway performance helped make this one of the better adaptations of the time. In the 1930s, few of the screen adaptations were very faithful to the original Broadway products. *Show Boat* (1936) was among the few exceptions. *The Cat and the Fiddle* (1934) kept the entire Broadway score, a true rarity in Hollywood. But *The Merry Widow* (1934), *The Gay Divorcee* (1934), *Music in the Air* (1934), *Sweet Adeline* (1935), *Roberta* (1935), *Naughty Marietta* (1935), *Rose Marie* (1936), *Anything Goes* (1936), *Maytime* (1937), *The Firefly* (1937), *Rosalie* (1937), *Sweethearts* (1938), and *Babes in Arms* (1939) saw major changes in the stage script and/or score that, sometimes, the movie barely resembled the Broadway original. Yet many of these films were very good and were very popular. And, in some cases, the screen version was an improvement over the stage work.

Hollywood continued to tinker with its Broadway purchases throughout the 1940s. *Strike Up the Band* (1940), for instance, kept only the title and the title song from the 1930 stage hit. The rest of the movie was original. For some reason, Hollywood made fewer Broadway adaptations in the 1940s. *Too Many Girls* (1940), *Cabin in the Sky* (1943), *Best Foot Forward* (1943), *Girl Crazy* (1943), and *Good News* (1947) were the only other notable ones but some of them were gems. By the 1950s, Hollywood made many more adaptations and the studios learned to trust the stage musicals they bought and brought them to the screen with most of the plot and score intact. Also, powerful songwriters learned to yield their power by refusing to allow screen versions of their work unless they were faithful to the original. This was certainly true with the decade's first adaptation, Irving Berlin's *Annie Get Your Gun* (1950). It was also true of the film versions of the Rodgers and Hammerstein musicals, such as *Oklahoma!* (1955), *Carousel* (1956), *The King and I* (1956), and *South Pacific* (1958). Other 1950s adaptations that were close to the stage works include *Show Boat* (1951), *Where's Charley?* (1952), *Call Me Madam* (1953), *Kiss Me, Kate* (1953), *The Student Prince* (1954), *Brigadoon* (1954), *Carmen Jones* (1954), *Guys and Dolls* (1955), *Kismet* (1955), *Silk Stockings* (1957), *The Pajama Game* (1957), and *Damn Yankees* (1958). Less faithful were *Gentlemen Prefer Blondes* (1953) and *Pal Joey* (1957), which dropped most of the stage songs and big hunks of the plot.

By the 1960s and 1970s, just about the only movie musicals being made were ones based on Broadway hits. *West Side Story* (1961), *The Music Man* (1962), *Bye Bye Birdie* (1963), *My Fair Lady* (1964), *The Sound of Music* (1965), *Oliver!* (1968), *Funny Girl* (1968), *Cabaret* (1972), and *Grease* (1978) all paid off big time, but there were expensive and embarrassing flops like *Paint Your Wagon* (1969), *Song of Norway* (1970), *Man of La Mancha* (1972), and *The Wiz* (1978), which raised the question of whether Hollywood had forgotten how to make musical adaptations. In between were many satisfying musicals based on Broadway hits, such as *Bells Are Ringing* (1960), *Can-Can* (1960), *Flower Drum Song* (1961), *Jumbo* (1962), *Gypsy* (1962), *The Unsinkable Molly Brown* (1964), *A Funny Thing Happened on the Way to the Forum* (1966), *How to Succeed in Business without Really Trying* (1966), *Camelot* (1967), *Finian's Rainbow* (1968), *Hello, Dolly!* (1969), *Sweet Charity* (1969), *On a Clear Day You Can See Forever* (1970), *Fiddler on the Roof* (1971), *1776* (1972), *Godspell* (1973), *Jesus Christ Superstar* (1973), and *Hair* (1979). By this time the old Hollywood system had broken down and the studios no longer had whole departments devoted to making big musicals. This made the costs escalate, and too many movies taken from Broadway shows lost money. In the 1980s and 1990s, it was difficult for *any* movie musical to make money unless it was geared to the youth market, and those films were not coming from Broadway. The number of shows that opened on Broadway drastically declined in and after the 1960s, and the Hollywood musical suffered. A great source for musicals dried up and by the 1990s the movie musical was nearly extinct. The few state adaptations included the financial fiasco *Annie* (1982), the clever *Little Shop of Horrors* (1986), and the impressive *Evita* (1996).

Matters started to improve in the new century and Broadway musicals are again being made into films. Much of this can be credited to *Chicago* (2002), which was a surprise hit. It opened the doors for such accomplished musical adaptations as *Dreamgirls* (2006), *Hairspray* (2007), *Sweeney Todd, The Demon Barber of Fleet Street* (2007), *Les Misérables* (2012), and *Into the Woods* (2014). But the success of *Chicago* also prompted studios to make such misguided adaptations as *The Phantom of the Opera* (2004), *The Producers* (2005), *Rent* (2005), *Mamma Mia!* (2008), *Nine* (2009), and *Jersey Boys* (2014). The Broadway scene improved greatly in the 1990s and in the new century so more musicals have been produced, which means a wider field for possible film adaptations. As we have seen, Hollywood has always turned to Broadway for quality products and it is likely to do so in the future. The studios might be more cautious than they were during the Golden Age of musicals but a popular Broadway musical still has the makings of a successful movie.

BIOGRAPHICAL MUSICALS

When a backstage musical is about a real person, it combines the genres of backstager and biography. Most biographical movie musicals are about people in show business such as performers, producers, and songwriters, in particular. Generally inaccurate and romanticized versions of the truth, musicals based on famous people have always had an appeal to both Hollywood and the public. While the

life of a songwriter may not have been terribly exciting in reality, the screen version will add drama to hold the audience's interest in between the songs, which
are the real reason for the movie. Most biographical musicals tell the same story:
The artist struggles to find success, eventually achieves it, but has to go through
some personal crisis before he or she gets there. These films are often described
as "rags to riches" tales.

Hollywood had been making biographical films since the silent days, but the
studios did not consider making a biographical musical until MGM wagered a lot
of money on *The Great Ziegfeld* in 1937 and it was a huge hit. The inaccurate plot
was about Florenz Ziegfeld, who went from a small-time carnival promoter to Broadway's most flamboyant producer. The film was dramatically powerful, had interesting characters, was filled with lavish production numbers in the Ziegfeld style, and
the audiences loved it. The musical "bio-pic," as they were called in Tinseltown, was
born. But copying *The Great Ziegfeld* was not going to be easy because producers
generally are not known to the public. Ziegfeld was the notable exception. So the
studios turned to other artists in show business, and the most obvious choice was
the performer. Ziegfeld and other producers did not sing and dance, but performers certainly did. And if they were stage performers, chances are moviegoers knew
their names and their hit songs so it was easy to have someone, usually a film
star, impersonate the Broadway star. The only problem was many of the most
known stage names were still alive and might not agree to a film about their lives,
accurate or not. Al Jolson willingly cooperated with the making of *The Jolson Story*
(1946) and *Jolson Sings Again* (1949), even providing his singing voice on the
soundtrack. Eddie Cantor played himself in *The Eddie Cantor Story* (1953). Others
were not so willing. The popular comic Fanny Brice held on to her privacy so Fox
changed the name and the details and made *Rose of Washington Square* (1939).
Brice was furious, sued the studio, and made a bundle. Years after her death, *Funny
Girl* (1968) told the story without disguises. Of course, it was usually safe to make
a bio-pic of a performer long gone. Alice Faye was *Lillian Russell* (1940), Betty
Grable and June Haver were *The Dolly Sisters* (1946), Haver was dancing star
Marilyn Miller in *Look for the Silver Lining* (1949), Mario Lanza was *The Great
Caruso* (1951), Frank Sinatra played singer-turned-comic in *The Joker Is Wild* (1957),
Ann Blyth starred in *The Helen Morgan Story* (1957), and Julie Andrews portrayed
Gertrude Lawrence in *Star!* (1968).

Hollywood did not restrict itself to only Broadway stars. Singers, dancers,
comics, and even musicians from every medium were considered. Among some of
the most memorable musical bio-pics about performers over the years include
The Story of Vernon and Irene Castle (1939) with Fred Astaire and Ginger Rogers,
Susan Hayward as Jane Froman in *With a Song in My Heart* (1952), James Stewart
in *The Glenn Miller Story* (1954), Susan Hayward as Lillian Roth in *I'll Cry Tomorrow*
(1955), Steve Allen in *The Benny Goodman Story* (1955), Doris Day as Ruth Etting

in *Love Me or Leave Me* (1955), Natalie Wood as Gypsy Rose Lee in *Gypsy* (1962), George Hamilton as Hank Williams in *Your Cheatin' Heart* (1965), Diana Ross as Billie Holiday in *Lady Sings the Blues* (1982), Gary Busey in *The Buddy Holly Story* (1978), Sissy Spacek as Loretta Lynn in *Coal Miner's Daughter* (1980), Lou Diamond Phillips as Ritchie Valens in *La Bamba* (1987), Forest Whitaker as Charlie Parker in *Bird* (1988), Val Kilmer as Jim Morrison in *The Doors* (1991), Jamie Foxx as Ray Charles in *Ray* (2004), and Joaquin Phoenix as Johnny Cash and Reese Wither-spoon as June Carter in *Walk the Line* (2005).

After performers, the most popular subject for a musical bio-pic is the songwriter. Few songwriters were singers or dancers but the biography of a famous composer and/or lyricist provided plenty of opportunities for song and dance that were performed by others. The lives of most songwriters were less than dramatic so a fictitious biography was created and the songs fell into place. A good example of such bio-pics is *Till the Clouds Roll By* (1946) about the great composer Jerome Kern. Robert Walker played Kern in the fictional and dull story, but there were over two dozen superb musical numbers so the musical was first-rate entertainment. Other bio-pics with less-than-thrilling stories about renowned songwriters include *The Great Victor Herbert* (1939), *My Gal Sal* (1942) with the songs of Paul Dresser, *Rhapsody in Blue* (1945) featuring George Gershwin music, *Stars and Stripes Forever* (1952) with John Phillip Sousa marches, *Deep in My Heart* (1954) with Sigmund Romberg music, *St. Louis Blues* (1958) about W. C. Handy, *Scott Joplin* (1977), and *Bound for Glory* (1976) about folksinger Woody Guthrie. The songwriter whose life has been dramatized the most is the pioneering American Stephen Foster. His story was told in *Harmony Lane* (1935), *Swanee River* (1939), and *I Dream of Jeanie* (1952).

Sometimes the true story about a songwriter could not be told because the Hollywood censor would not allow it. This happened to homosexual composers and lyricists like Cole Porter and Lorenz Hart. So a totally fictitious script provided a greatly sanitized tale, such as *Words and Music* (1948) about Richard Rodgers and Hart and *Night and Day* (1946) about Porter. Years later the bio-pic *De-Lovely* (2004) was able to include Porter's gay lifestyle but even it was filled with inaccura-cies. In the opinion of many, the best of all songwriter bio-pics is *Yankee Doodle Dandy* (1942) about George M. Cohan. It helped that Cohan was also a performer so one got to enjoy the terrific songs and James Cagney's dynamic performance of them. But even the screenplay for *Yankee Doodle Dandy* was frequently fiction. It seems to be the one unifying element in the genre.

OPERETTAS

An operetta is a particular kind of stage musical that originated in Europe and was very popular on Broadway from the 1880s through the 1920s. By definition, an operetta is a light form of opera that uses dialogue, songs, a fanciful setting, and a lot of romance. The plots tend to be contrived and the characters one-dimensional because the music is the most (and sometimes the only) important thing. After years of importing French, Viennese, and British operettas, America produced its own form of the genre in the works by Victor Herbert. He composed over 40 operettas between 1894 and 1924, including such Broadway favorites as *The Fortune Teller* (1898), *Babes in Toyland* (1903), *Mlle. Modiste* (1905), *The Red Mill* (1906), *Naughty Marietta* (1910), and *Sweethearts* (1913). Several of Herbert's musicals were later turned into movies. The other two famous American composers for the genre were Rudolf Friml and Sigmund Romberg, both scoring many Broadway operettas between 1912 and 1954. Among their most beloved shows are *The Firefly* (1912), *The Blue Paradise* (1915), *Maytime* (1917), *Blossom Time* (1921), *The Student Prince in Heidelberg* (1924), *Rose-Marie*, (1924), *The Vagabond King* (1925), *The Desert Song* (1926), *The Three Musketeers* (1928), *The New Moon* (1928), and *Up in Central Park* (1945). Several of these were also filmed after sound came in. The American operetta on Broadway reached its Golden Age in the 1910s and 1920s, many of the musicals returning to Broadway frequently. The Depression pretty much killed off the old-time operettas on Broadway. Even the word "operetta" was box office poison, so when Jerome Kern and other composers wrote musicals that emphasized operetta singing, they called them musicals. *Show Boat* (1927), *Sweet Adeline* (1929), *The Cat and the Fiddle* (1931), *Music in the Air* (1932), and *Roberta* (1933) are good examples of the "new" operettas that Broadway produced during that time. The Gershwin brothers even came up with a comic operetta, *Of Thee I Sing* (1931), which spoofed the genre's style even as it used it for its jazzy score.

Oddly, just as operetta died in New York, Hollywood discovered it and many operetta movies were made during the 1930s. There were some operetta movies early on but the trend really began with a film adaptation of Herbert's *Naughty Marietta* in 1935. The 1910 operetta was given a spruced-up story and the old song favorites were delivered with style by Jeanette MacDonald and Nelson Eddy. The popular singing couple, in their first movie together, single-handedly revived interest in operetta. The duo re-teamed for seven more movies, including such major hits as *Rose Marie* (1936), *Maytime* (1937), *Sweethearts* (1938), and *New Moon* (1940), all of which were operettas from Broadway's golden days. Other stage operettas with other singers that Hollywood brought to the screen during the first decade of talkies include *Rio Rita* (1929), *The Desert Song* (1929), *Music in the Air* (1934), *The Cat and the Fiddle* (1934), *The Merry Widow* (1934), *Sweet Adeline* (1935), *Roberta* (1935), *Show Boat* (1936), *The Firefly* (1937), and *The Great Waltz* (1938). Hollywood was not going to be confined to just adaptations of stage operettas. The studios made their own original movie operettas in the 1930s, some of them rivaling the Broadway products in quality. The most memorable were *Love*

Me Tonight (1932), *One Night of Love* (1934), *I Dream Too Much* (1935), *High, Wide and Handsome* (1937), and *Balalaika* (1939). Even the animated movies *Snow White and the Seven Dwarfs* (1937) and *Gulliver's Travels* (1939) were musically in the operetta style.

During the 1940s and 1950s, both Broadway and Hollywood seemed to have abandoned operettas because very few were made. Perhaps audiences found the artificiality of operetta unappealing during wartime. Also, musical tastes changed and swing and Big Band were not the sounds of operetta. Yet a new kind of operetta arrived on Broadway with Rodgers and Hammerstein's *Oklahoma!* in 1943. These new forms had more realistic settings, plots, and characters. And rather than take place in exotic locales, the musicals were often set in America. Rodgers and Hammerstein's *Carousel* (1945) and *The Sound of Music* (1959) were good examples of operettas that no one thought of as operettas. Other similar Broadway shows with operetta-like qualities include *Carmen Jones* (1943), *Song of Norway* (1944), *Street Scene* (1947), *Brigadoon* (1947), *Lost in the Stars* (1949), *Kismet* (1953), *The Golden Apple* (1954), *My Fair Lady* (1956), *The Most Happy Fella* (1956), and *Candide* (1956). Some of these were made into effective movies; others were too stage-bound to work on the screen. In addition, Hollywood stopped making original operettas once World War II broke out so it looked like operetta, at least in the old sense of the word, was gone forever.

The genre was revived in the most unlikely way: the "invasion" of British sung-through musicals on Broadway. London hits such as *Evita* (1979), *Cats* (1982), *Les Misérables* (1987), *The Phantom of the Opera* (1988), *Miss Saigon* (1991), and *Sunset Boulevard* (1994) had all the qualities of old-time operetta: lots of singing, an exotic setting, and a romantic nature. Of course the music was not in the mode of Herbert, Friml, or Romberg, but the operetta mentality was still there. These musicals encouraged other composers to return to the operetta format even if the music was rock or Latino. Broadway and Off Broadway saw shows that overflowed with music, such as *Sweeney Todd, the Demon Barber of Fleet Street* (1979), *Tommy* (1993), *Rent* (1996), *Floyd Collins* (1996), *Ragtime* (1998), *Caroline or Change* (2004), *The Light in the Piazza* (2005), *The Color Purple* (2005), *In the Heights* (2008), and *Hamilton* (2015). Yet very few of these musicals have been picked up by Hollywood. Perhaps the new kind of operetta is not meant for the screen. More likely, a new way to film such musicals has yet to be developed.

TEEN MUSICALS

For many years, a teen movie meant one about teenagers; by the 1970s it meant a film about and *for* teenagers. The difference is significant. Today movie audiences are so segmented and films are made to appeal to a particular audience group that one forgets that for decades all movies were made for everyone. The features, the shorts, the newsreels, the travelogues, even the cartoons were made for one big general audience. One of the few times Hollywood aimed for a target audience was when it made the weekly cowboy or adventure serials shown on Saturday mornings for kids. Of course people picked and chose the films they wanted to see but movie marketing was broad, not the target kind of approach used today. Teen movies in the 1930s and 1940s were aimed at everyone, from those not yet teens to those who could barely remember their teen years. A teen musical had even broader appeal in the 1930s. Bright, talented, energetic teenagers singing and dancing (and, of course, falling in and out of puppy love) was highly appealing to moviegoers during the Depression.

Yet this idea of a musical featuring a youthful cast did not come about until the Depression was mostly over. The origin can be traced to the 1937 Broadway show *Babes in Arms*. It was an unusual show in that the cast was comprised of performers in their teens or early twenties. The score was by Richard Rodgers (music) and Lorenz Hart (lyrics), who also wrote the original script. The musical started with a gimmick but developed into a very satisfying show. A group of teens, the children of out-of-work vaudeville entertainers, don't want to be sent to a work farm so they gang together to write, produce, and perform a big show to raise money to save their families. There were some romantic tangles and production setbacks along the way but everyone knew how it would turn out. Thanks to a score filled with hits and an amiable cast, *Babes in Arms* enjoyed a long-run on Broadway. Hollywood took notice and two years later MGM released the screen version. The film dropped much of the superb Rodgers and Hart score (including the hits "My Funny Valentine," "The Lady Is a Tramp," "Johnny One Note," and "I Wish I Were in Love Again") and altered the plot a little but they got the basic idea right. It helped that Mickey Rooney and Judy Garland, in their first movie together, captured the spirit of this idea and that the musical numbers were staged with zest by director Busby Berkeley. *Babes in Arms* was a novelty and a very popular one at that. MGM teamed Rooney and Garland in three more teen musicals, all with basically the same plot. Nevertheless, *Strike Up the Band* (1940), *Babes on Broadway* (1941), and *Girl Crazy* (1943) were just as entertaining (and as popular) and the series might have gone on much longer if the two stars hadn't outgrown their teen roles.

Other studios planned teen musicals but they didn't have Rooney and Garland under contract. Universal did have Deanna Durbin, a singing teenager with an opera-quality voice. She was featured as one of three conniving sisters in the musical *Three Smart Girls* (1936) and the camera liked her. More important, the moviegoers took to her. In 1937, two years before *Babes in Arms*, Durbin was starred in *One Hundred Men and a Girl* and again was a meddling teen who this time managed to save an entire orchestra from unemployment. She also got to sing some trilling songs and even opera selections. Universal cast Durbin as a teen in 11 subsequent musicals and audiences wanted more. By the time she made *Can't Help*

Singing in 1944, the 23-year-old soprano had to graduate to slightly older characters. The public went along with her for a few films but then her popularity dropped so Durbin retired in 1948. Jane Powell and Debbie Reynolds had better luck. They played teenagers on-screen as well but managed to keep their careers alive into adulthood. Powell was delightful in eight teen musicals, including *Three Daring Daughters* (1948), *A Date with Judy* (1948), and *Two Weeks with Love* (1950). Reynolds was also in *Two Weeks with Love* and a handful of other teen films. Interestingly, she was able to shift back and forth from adult to teen roles. For example, Reynolds played teens in *The Affairs of Dobie Gillis* (1952), *I Love Melvin* (1952), and *Athena* (1953) after she had made *Singin' in the Rain* (1952).

Collegiate musicals might be considered teen movies even though the characters were moving out of their teenage years. Both *Too Many Girls* (1940) and *Good News* (1947) had the spirit of a teen musical and were quite enjoyable even though the actors were fearfully too old to be in college, even in a postgraduate program. One could say the same thing about Ann-Margaret in *Bye Bye Birdie* (1963), perhaps the last teen musical of the old school. Teenagers in the later 1960s were nothing like Rooney and Garland, and when the teen film returned in the 1970s the genre had changed. Perhaps it was *Saturday Night Fever* (1977) that made that change. These discontented teens were not bright and optimistic even if they were energetic and talented. Even the escapist musical *Grease* (1978) was filled with restless teens who had some demons to work out. Although both musicals were extremely popular with a wide audience, it was clear that they were aimed at the youth market. Some of the later entries in the genre had limited appeal to older moviegoers but were very popular with the musicals' target audience. *Fame* (1980), *Flashdance* (1983), *Footloose* (1984), *Dirty Dancing* (1987), *The Commitments* (1991), *That Thing You Do* (1996), *Camp* (203), *Hairspray* (2007), and *High School Musical 3* (2008) may have stretched the teen years a bit at times but all were teen musicals at heart. The popularity of the television musical series *Glee* (2009 to 2015) makes it clear that the teen musical is alive and likely to be around as long as there are teens to sing and dance and other teens to watch them.

ANIMATED MUSICALS

Walt Disney and other pioneering animators had been using music and even songs in cartoons and shorts long before the first feature-length animated musical came along with *Snow White and the Seven Dwarfs* (1937). Disney was America's most recognized innovator with music and animation, presenting his Mickey Mouse shorts and his *Silly Symphony* cartoons, which had elaborate musical soundtracks. Warner Brothers offered *Looney Tunes* shorts with Bugs Bunny and his friends animated with songs, Universal had Oswald the Rabbit, Paramount its *Puppetoon* flicks, Columbia offered *Color Rhapsodies*, and independent animators such as Max Fleischer created Popeye and Betty Boop, all of them using music to some degree. The idea of a feature-length cartoon was ridiculous to most studio executives. A cartoon was meant to be a brief but pleasing diversion to be shown between longer films. Hollywood scoffed when Disney announced that his Snow White movie would be a feature. It was a risk, to be sure. Would moviegoers sit for a cartoon that lasted more than six minutes? Could animated characters sing serious love song or ballads and be accepted by the audience? Could some of those characters be humans who moved realistically and had life-like facial gestures? Disney strongly believed that the answer to all of the concerns was yes. Not until *Snow White and the Seven Dwarfs* opened and audiences were enthralled did Hollywood stop sneering.

When Disney broke new ground by giving the public full-length animated musicals, the other studios were hesitant to follow in his footsteps. Dave Fleischer produced *Gulliver's Travels* (1939) through Paramount but most studios were content to stick to shorts. Hollywood saw animated musicals as a novelty that would soon wear out. Also, a feature cartoon was very expensive and time-consuming to make. Only the Disney studio had a decade of experience with animated movies and the staff and resources to continue making long animated films. The other studios did not. It turned out that *Snow White and the Seven Dwarfs* was not just a novelty. Keeping the quality and craftsmanship very high, Disney continued to offer animated features and had success with *Pinocchio* (1940), *Dumbo* (1941), *Bambi* (1942), *Song of the South* (1946), *Ichabod and Mr. Toad* (1949), *Cinderella* (1950), *Alice in Wonderland* (1951), *Peter Pan* (1953), *Lady and the Tramp* (1955), *Sleeping Beauty* (1959), *One Hundred and One Dalmatians* (1961), *The Sword in the Stone* (1963), and *The Jungle Book* (1967). Not quite as popular but still profitable were Disney's musical anthology movies: *Salads Amigos* (1943), *The Three Caballeros* (1945), *Make Mine Music* (1946), *Fun and Fancy Free* (1947), and *Melody Time* (1948). The only outright financial failure the studio had to endure was the innovative *Fantasia* (1940), which took years to be recognized as the cinema masterwork that it is.

Music was integral to all these features, some films having extensive scores and providing songs hits, others just a few tunes. Soon the idea of an animated feature sounded normal and hearing love songs or torch songs sung by cartoon characters seemed natural. And all through these decades of excellent animated musicals, Disney had no competition. Even as the studio had hit after hit and the movies were periodically rereleased with further success, the rest of Hollywood shied away from cartoon features. After the death of Walt Disney in 1966, even his own studio was reluctant to continue sinking so much money into animated musicals. Instead they concentrated on television, theme parks, and live-action comedies. Yet still some commendable cartoon musicals were made. They may not have compared favorably to the earlier classics, but there was much to enjoy in such musicals as

The Aristocats (1970), *Robin Hood* (1973), *The Rescuers* (1977), *The Fox and the Hound* (1981), *The Great Mouse Detective* (1986), and *Oliver & Company* (1988). Occasionally another studio ventured into the animated musical arena and ended up with a success, such as *Gay-Purr-ee* (1962), *Yellow Submarine* (1968), and *Charlotte's Web* (1973). The craftsmanship of the Disney movies may have been missing, but these films demonstrated that Disney was not the only studio that could make an animated musical.

Everything changed in 1989 with Disney's *The Little Mermaid*. In the late 1980s the studio had been building up its animation department and its younger artists were gaining experience as well as opportunities to revive the glory days of Disney animation. *The Little Mermaid* was a runaway hit and was followed by a series of superb animated musicals, including *Beauty and the Beast* (1991), *Aladdin* (1992), *The Lion King* (1994), *Pocahontas* (1995), *The Hunchback of Notre Dame* (1996), *Hercules* (1997), and *Mulan* (1998) as well as the stop-action animated musicals *The Nightmare Before Christmas* (1993) and *James and the Giant Peach* (1996). Known in Hollywood as the Disney Renaissance, it was a decade of outstanding films that rivaled the days of Walt Disney. This time the other studios did not sit back and watch with envy. Tentatively at first, other studios started making animated musicals. *The Swan Princess* (1994), *Thumbelina* (1994), *The Pebble and the Penguin* (1995), *A Troll in Central Park* (1994), *Cats Don't Dance* (1996), *Anastasia* (1997), *The Prince of Egypt* (1998), and *The Road to El Dorado* (2000) varied in quality and popularity but they were significant signs that the Disney studio would not have the animation field all to itself.

With the new century, the Disney studio moved away from musical animation to action animation with such pictures as *Dinosaur* (2000) and *The Incredibles* (2004). Other studios followed suit and, during the first decade of the 21st century, more animated features were being made than at any other previous time but rarely were they musicals. Happily, the musical format returned with such Disney films as *Home on the Range* (2004), *The Princess and the Frog* (2009), *Tangled* (2010), and *Frozen* (2013), so the animated musical is alive and well. Hopefully the other studios will return to animated musicals as well. It is an art form whose possibilities have hardly been exhausted.

FANTASY MUSICALS

While most animated films use fantasy, a number of live-action movie musicals also employ an imagined, unreal existence to tell a story. The most famous of these is probably *The Wizard of Oz* (1939), a stunning film that contrasts the realistic life in Kansas with the surreal world in Oz. Sometimes such fantasies use sections of animation, as in *Mary Poppins* (1964) and *Enchanted* (2007), but most fantasy musicals create imaginary worlds through creative scenery and special effects. Today fantasy films, musical or not, use a lot of computer techniques to create their stunning effects. But before the computer, fantasy movies were very labor intensive to make. It is one thing to create a new world on paper for animation, but it is quite a different task to actually build this new world on a studio set. Musicals, because they are not real, have a bit of fantasy already instilled in them. Singing and dancing outside of an entertainment venue are fantastical. But a true fantasy musical goes far beyond this. Such projects are so expensive that it is little wonder why there are so few live-action fantasy musicals. But the ones that work are magical indeed.

Fantasy and science fiction movies go back to the silents. When sound came in, a few fantasy films were made but the 1930s and the Depression era was not conducive to fantastical elements. A few of the early musicals had dream sequences that might qualify them as fantasies but the genre does not begin until 1939 and *The Wizard of Oz*, the first major (and possibly still the best) live-action fantasy musical. The MGM film was one of the most complicated and expensive that the studio had yet made because the fantastical world of Oz had to be created on mammoth sound stages. A lot of matte painting was used for the backgrounds but all the trees, houses, castle locales, poppies, corn stalks, and the yellow brick road itself had to be made in a three-dimensional form in order to register well on film. The fact that *The Wizard of Oz* looks so impressive today is a credit to the artists who manufactured this new reality.

One would think that every studio would want to rush out and make a fantasy musical after the success of *The Wizard of Oz* but they didn't. Hollywood knew how costly such films were and the chance of coming up with another *The Wizard of Oz* was a long shot. It would not be until the 1950s that another notable fantasy musical was made. That decade was filled with science fiction films ranging from the sensational to the thought provoking. Most had to do with aliens from outer space coming to Earth with dire consequences for all. In the midst of all this, the celebrated children's author Theodore Geisel, better known by his pen name Dr. Seuss, worked on a live-action fantasy musical, *The 5,000 Fingers of Dr. T* (1953). There were no invaders from space but the villain, the diabolical Dr. Terwilliger (Hans Conreid), was just as evil. The world the filmmakers had to create was Dr. T's cavernous lair with a piano hundreds of feet long, a dungeon filled with captive creatures, and bizarre rooms and passageways in the surreal Seussian style, the very architecture defying logic and gravity. It was indeed a wondrous film with first-rate songs, but *The 5,000 Fingers of Dr. T* was too odd for most audiences and the movie was not a success at the box office. The next year, a romantic fantasy, *Brigadoon* (1954), was more popular. It was a screen version of a Broadway musical fantasy about a Scottish village that defies time by going to sleep for a hundred years each sunset. There were no fantastical sets to build for *Brigadoon* and the musical came across as more romantic than fantastic. *Tom Thumb* (1958), on the other hand, had plenty of fantastical elements. The thumb-sized Tom (Russ Tamblyn) was placed in a realistic medieval setting but there was a magical Forest Queen (June Thorburn), a comic puppet creature, and Tom himself. A British-Hollywood production based on a Brothers Grimm tale, *Tom Thumb* required lots of trick photography and some oversized props rather than the construction of giant houses and such. It is a playful fantasy and the songs are equally light-hearted but the movie was marketed to kids so most adults never saw it.

The 1960s saw a handful of musical fantasies, the crowning one being Disney's *Mary Poppins* (1964). Although the most fantastical parts of the movie were animated, there was still plenty of magic in the live-action portion of the film. The fantastical elements were more whimsical than spectacular but difficult to achieve all the same. Mary (Julie Andrews) pulling large objects out of her carpet bag, a line of nannies blowing away in the wind, and a tea party with the celebrants floating in the air were among the many fantasy touches that made *Mary Poppins* so memorable. Two non-Disney fantasy musicals followed, both costing staggering amounts of money. 20th Century Fox nearly went bankrupt making *Doctor Dolittle* (1967), a fantasy about a cockeyed veterinarian (Rex Harrison) who can talk to animals. The doctor sets off on a worldwide journey to find and converse with unusual animals, including the bizarre Great Pink Sea Snail, the Giant Lunar Moth, and a two-headed llama called Pushmi-Pullyu. Before the development of computer animation, such creatures were very difficult to create but they ended up being very impressive on the screen. *Doctor Dolittle* cost a whopping $18 million but received such poor notices when it opened that it made only half that at the box office on its first release. But the film later found fans on video and DVD. The British musical fantasy *Chitty Chitty Bang Bang* (1968) fared much better. The most fantastical element in this tuneful musical was the title automobile that could also float and fly. It was a magical piece of technology but the rest of the movie was more musical fairy tale than outright fantasy. The movie had strong production values and a delightful score, helping it find an audience and modest profits. *Finian's Rainbow* (1968), on the other hand, found neither. Based on the satirical Broadway musical of 1947, this awkward movie musical had a mischievous leprechaun (Tommy Steele) and a magic spell that turned a bigoted white senator (Keenan Wynn) into an African American so that he could experience the Jim Crow laws of the South. It was an uncomfortable musical, to say the least.

There were a few fantasy musicals in the 1970s and 1980s, though in some cases the fantastical touches were minor. For example, *Scrooge* (1970) was a musical version of *A Christmas Carol* with the requisite spirits and such, and *The Boy Friend* (1971) had musical fantasy sequences that were surreal at times. But *Willy Wonka and the Chocolate Factory* (1971) was a full-scale musical fantasy and it quickly became an audience favorite. Based on Roald Dahl's popular children's book *Charlie and the Chocolate Factory*, the movie had a quixotic magician in the person of chocolate manufacturer Wonka (Gene Wilder), a gang of odd creatures called Oompa Loompas, and a fantastical factory with chocolate rivers and other amazing effects. The setting for *Pete's Dragon* (1977) was a realistic seaside town in Maine and the fantasy was found in an animated dragon called Elliott who befriends the orphan Pete (Sean Marshall). The most ambitious musical fantasy of the decade was *The Wiz* (1978), based on the successful 1975 Broadway musical that retold the story of *The Wizard of Oz* in a funky, clever style with an expert Motown-inspired score. There were high hopes for this African American vision of the famous fantasy story but the film version was botched beyond recognition. *The Wiz* did more damage to the future of musical fantasies (and movie musicals) than anyone suspected at the time.

While we too often associate fantasy with children's stories, there are also darker and more adult fantasy musicals. *Little Shop of Horrors* (1986) is a good example. It too was based on a stage musical, the 1982 Off-Broadway hit that was based on a campy 1960 film. The offbeat tale, about an evil plant that lives off human blood, had a delicious 1960s pastiche score and a macabre sense of humor. The screen version was expertly done, making it the best musical fantasy of its era. Hollywood would not attempt another movie in the genre until 2004 when the screen version of *The Phantom of the Opera* was released. The London and Broadway musical sensation seemed like an ideal candidate for a first-rate movie. After all, both silent and sound versions of the famous tale had been filmed with success. But this *The Phantom of the Opera* seem lifeless and tired on the screen and one of the world's greatest fantasy stories was reduced to an inert music video.

Like *Mary Poppins, Enchanted* (2007) used animation in sections but was mostly a live-action fantasy. Cartoon characters from an animated kingdom find themselves in contemporary New York City in this clever and ultimately charming modern fairy tale. There were only a few songs and one major production number but *Enchanted* felt like a full-fledged musical. *Into the Woods* (2014) was a Broadway hit that took nearly three decades to come to the screen. The musical is a series of interrelated fairy tales with some sober conclusions. The success of these two films demonstrated that moviegoers were still interested in musical fantasy. That's fortunate because more are on the way. In 2017, the live-action version of Disney's musical *Beauty and the Beast* will be ready. And following that there are likely to be movie versions of such popular stage fantasy musicals as *Wicked* (2003) and *Matilda* (2013).

PATRIOTIC MUSICALS

When patriotism runs high, it shows up in the American musical. Fundraising shows and flag-waving musical numbers in revues on Broadway were common during World War I and again in the 1940s. Patriotic movie musicals during World

War II were more than entertainment, they were morale boosters. But patriotic musicals are not confined to times of war. In Hollywood they can show up at any time when the feeling of nationalism is strong. During the Depression, for instance, movies sometimes tried to offer encouragement and the hope for a better day. During *Gold Diggers of 1933*, one of the musical numbers was a salute to President Franklin Roosevelt and supported his national recovery programs. The American troops were glorified in *Footlight Parade* (1933) as sailor James Cagney disguised his sweetheart Ruby Keeler as a fellow sailor and they marched off to their ship together at the end of the "Shanghai Lil" number.

Little Shirley Temple did her part when she sang and danced to "Military Man" in *Poor Little Rich Girl* (1936). Mickey Rooney and Judy Garland led the cast of *Strike Up the Band* (1940) in singing the patriotic title number during the film's finale. The Andrews Sisters harmonized on "Boogie Woogie Bugle Boy" and "You're a Lucky Fellow, Mr. Smith" in *Buck Privates* (1941) and "We're in the Navy" in *In the Navy* (1941). Fred Astaire sang and tapped to "Shootin' the Works for Uncle Sam" in *You'll Never Get Rich* (1941). All of these were made and released before the United States entered the war on December 8, 1941. The true patriotic musical, in which the entire movie is devoted to boosting the American spirit, quickly followed that date.

Yankee Doodle Dandy (1942), the musical bio-pic about songwriter-performer George M. Cohan (James Cagney), had been in production for some time and was released five months after the attack on Pearl Harbor. Although not planned as a patriotic musical, the film was filled with American spirit because Cohan had written "Over There," "You're a Grand Old Flag," "Yankee Doodle Boy" and other flag-waving tunes. The first Hollywood musical to be made as a morale booster during wartime was the tuneful *Star Spangled Rhythm* (1942). Like the succeeding patriotic musicals, the story was set stateside so none of the war was shown. But the story always involved GI characters and a lot of celebrities (sometimes playing themselves) who contributed to a full assortment of musical numbers. These musicals were also big on comedy, making them escapist by nature, and sometimes even the patriotic numbers were less than reverent. In *Star Spangled Rhythm*, Betty Hutton rode in a jeep full of GIs and sang "I'm Doing It for Defense." On a more serious note, Bing Crosby led a chorus in singing "Old Glory." In many ways these World War II patriotic movies were actually revues, plotless musicals with lots of song and dance. But Hollywood did not like revues so a thin storyline was always used to connect the many musical numbers.

A half dozen of the most notable patriotic musicals were released during the next two years. *This Is the Army* (1943) was a screen version of a 1942 Broadway fundraiser for the Army Emergency Relief Fund. Irving Berlin organized the musical revue on Broadway and wrote the songs. The cast consisted entirely of enlisted men. The limited engagement of *This Is the Army* sold out and raised lots of money.

Warner Brothers made a screen version but insisted on a flimsy plot about putting on a wartime benefit. What mattered were the songs and the stars, including Berlin himself singing "Oh, How I Hate to Get Up in the Morning." The title of *Thank Your Lucky Stars* (1943) referred to the stars and stripes on the American flag, but for moviegoers it was the Hollywood stars that were the attraction. Just about every celebrity under contract to Warner Brothers was in this lively patriotic musical. Again the plot was a laborious affair but the cast and the songs made it all seem like gold. *Stage Door Canteen* (1943) was about the famous Manhattan gathering spot for GIs that offered food and entertainment for free. It was sponsored by the American Theatre Wing, which encouraged stage celebrities to stop by and do everything from dancing with the soldiers to washing dishes in the kitchen. United Artists made a film about the place, creating an unexciting romance about a canteen hostess and a GI for the plot. In addition to the fine musical numbers, the film included cameos by all the major Broadway stars of the day, some of whom never appeared in any other movie. *Hollywood Canteen* (1944) was the West Coast version of a similar institution in Los Angeles. Again there was a forgettable story but lots of stars and wonderful songs.

Since MGM had more stars than any other studio, its patriotic musical *Thousands Cheer* (1943) was indeed celebrity packed. Also being an MGM product, the production numbers were more elaborate. The plot involved a romance between a colonel's daughter (Kathryn Grayson) and a circus-performer-turned-soldier (Gene Kelly) but they often took a backseat to a series of terrific musical numbers. In the movie's extended finale, the screen was crowded with so many stars that one got bleary-eyed. The title *Two Girls and a Sailor* (1944) referred to two sisters (June Allyson and Gloria DeHaven) who turn a warehouse into a servicemen's canteen with the help of a GI (Van Johnson). The MGM film was much more modest than *Thousands Cheer* but just about as entertaining. Universal's entry in the patriotic musical parade was *Follow the Boys* (1944) about Hollywood celebrities going overseas to entertain the troops. The celebrities were real and the songs and dances were top-notch. All of the preceding were popular box office attractions but in most cases the money went to various war relief causes. Adding to these examples were several other wartime musicals full of patriotism, among them *True to the Army* (1942), *Private Buckaroo* (1942), *When Johnny Comes Marching Home* (1943), *Reveille with Beverly* (1943), *Johnny Doughboy* (1943), *Four Jills in a Jeep* (1944), *Pin-Up Girl* (1944), and *Here Come the Waves* (1944).

These kinds of movie musicals dropped off quickly in the late 1940s when many Americans wanted to forget the war and move on with their lives. From that point on, a Hollywood musical that had a patriotic theme tended to be more nostalgic, as in the musical bio-pic *The Glenn Miller Story* (1954) and the holiday favorite *White Christmas* (1954). During the Korean War there was an effort to revive the patriotic musical but the only notable entry was *Starlift* (1951) about some air force fliers who scheme to meet a movie star (Janice Rule). Warner Brothers gathered a number of big names and song standards for the musical and it is well done. But audiences were still war-weary from the 1940s and cared little about the Korean conflict. There were no patriotic musicals made during the 1960s and the Vietnam War and rarely since then. Instead one found antiwar musicals such as *Hair* (1978) and *Across the Universe* (2007). Perhaps the patriotic musical is a genre that is not destined to survive.

ROCK MUSICALS

Broadway was slow to pick up on rock and roll. Hollywood was not so hesitant. It was over a decade after the new sound was heard on radio, television, and in some films that a rock musical made it to Broadway. *Hair* opened Off Broadway in 1967 and the next year was on Broadway; it was controversial, abrasive, satirical, and (most importantly) a hit. By its very nature, a rock musical tends to be unconventional and more experimental than traditional shows, not only in subject matter but also in structure and presentation. The music is often more pounding, with more emphasis on the beat and less on the lyrics, and the musical itself usually is a free-flowing celebration or protest, or both. The rock shows are usually less literary and more anachronistic and rely on a variety of audiovisual effects. Most significantly, the orchestrations for rock musicals require a good deal of electronic instruments so mechanical amplification is a must. Broadway was slow to embrace the rock sentiment but *Hair* opened the floodgates and the rock sound popped up everywhere. Within a short time the theater saw such successes as *Jesus Christ Superstar* (1971) and *Godspell* (1971) and flops like *Dude* (1972) and *Via Galactica* (1972). By the mid-1970s, rock shows were dwindling but not the rock sound. Touches of the rock sound are predominant in such stage works as *The Wiz* (1975), *Evita* (1979), *Dreamgirls* (1981), *Starlight Express* (1987), *The Phantom of the Opera* (1988), *Miss Saigon* (1991), *Aida* (2000), *Hairspray* (2002), and even *Tarzan* (2006), though few of those could rightfully be called a rock musical. Other Broadway musicals were true rock shows, such as *The Who's Tommy* (1993), *Rent* (1996), *Hedwig and the Angry Inch* (1998), *Spring Awakening* (2006), *Next to Normal* (2009), *Rock of Ages* (2009), *American Idiot* (2010), and *Hamilton* (2015). After *Hair*, even conventional Broadway musicals started using electronic instruments and amplified sound, and the timbre of the traditional musical score was altered. The violin may have been the primary instrument in the operetta days and the woodwinds and brass in the musical comedy days, but the guitar was the key instrument in rock. Today that has been replaced by the electric keyboard, which is often used to artificially create the sounds needed for a Broadway score. Like it or not, Broadway sounds different because of rock musicals.

Rock and roll was heard in the movies almost from the very start of the new form. In fact, the film drama *Rock Around the Clock* (1956), featuring Bill Haley and the Comets, the Platters, and other rock pioneers heard on the soundtrack, was greatly responsible for spreading the new sound. Early rock films such as *Rock Rock Rock* (1956), *Don't Knock the Rock* (1957), *Carnival Rock* (1957), and *Mr. Rock 'n' Rock* (1957) were cheaply made movies that were addressed directly to the youth market, but the Elvis Presley musicals were mainstream hits and Hollywood realized before television and theater that there was money to be made from the new sound. Many of the rock movie musicals over the years have been screen versions of stage works, such as *Jesus Christ Superstar* (1973), *The Rocky Horror Picture Show* (1975), *Hair* (1979), *Hedwig and the Angry Inch* (2001), *Rent* (2005), and *Hairspray* (2007). To these the studios added their own versions of rock musicals, often in a format that did not resemble a stage piece. Among those that relied heavily on rock music were *A Hard Day's Night* (1964), *Help!* (1965), *Head* (1968), *Yellow Submarine* (1968), *Phantom of the Paradise* (1974), *A Star Is Born* (1976), *I Wanna Hold Your Hand* (1978), *American Hot Wax* (1978), *The Buddy Holly Story* (1978), *Thank God It's Friday* (1978), *Rock 'n' Roll High School* (1979), *Quadrophenia* (1979), *The Rose* (1979), *Fame* (1980), *The Jazz Singer* (1980), *Flashdance* (1983), *Footloose* (1984), *Labyrinth* (1986), *Dirty Dancing* (1987), *La Bamba* (1987), *The Commitments* (1991), *The Doors* (1991), *That Thing You Do* (1996), *Spice World* (1998), *The Road to El Dorado* (2000), *Moulin Rouge!* (2001), and *Across the Universe* (2007). Add to those the many nonmusical films that utilize a rock soundtrack and one can see that Hollywood has done very well by rock and roll.

ROCKUMENTARIES

Film documentaries covering a rock concert, festival, tour, or recording session were dubbed "rockumentaries" in the 1970s because the distinctive genre needed a label. These behind-the-scenes movies go back to the 1950s when rock was gaining a foothold. *Rockin' the Blues* (1956) chronicled performances by several African American artists (the Hurricanes, the Miller Sisters, Flournoy Miller, the Harptones) who were just starting to popularize the rock and roll sound. Films focusing on rock groups were common by the late 1950s, but a major documentary about them would not come along until the *T.A.M.I. Show* (1964), which covered the Teenage Awards Music International in California and featured the Rolling Stones, Lesley Gore, Marvin Gaye, the Beach Boys, the Supremes, Gerry and the Pacemakers, and others. Among the similar films were *The Big T.N.T. Show* (1966), *You Are What You Eat* (1968), and *Monterey Pop* (1969). The rockumentary that would prove the most effective (and influential to subsequent films of the genre) was *Woodstock* (1970), Michael Wadleigh's coverage of the legendary 1969 festival in Bethel, New York. Other notable rockumentaries during the 1970s included *Gimme Shelter* (1970), about a Rolling Stones tour; *Mad Dogs and Englishmen* (1970), with Joe Cocker and entourage touring America; *Let It Be* (1970), covering the Beatles' last recording session; *The Concert for Bangladesh* (1972), featuring George Harrison and various performers at a Madison Square Garden benefit concert; *Let the Good Times Roll* (1973), with a nostalgic look at rock artists from the 1950s; *The Grateful Dead* (1977); and *The Last Waltz* (1978), Martin Scorsese's vivid coverage of a farewell tour by The Band. By the 1980s, MTV and other television outlets were covering the rock scene pretty thoroughly and patrons were not as willing to pay to see a film about the rock stars they could see for free on TV. All the same there were rockumentaries such as *Black Flag Live* (1984), *Madonna: Truth or Dare* (1991), and *1991: The Year Punk Broke* (1992). With the new century, a flood of rockumentaries arrived, including *Festival Express* (2003), *KISS Loves You* (2004), *Metallica: Some Kind of Monster* (2004), *No Direction Home: Bob Dylan* (2006), and *Party at Ground Zero* (2007). There have also been a handful of television and movie spoofs of rockumentaries over the years, most notably *The Rutles: All You Need Is Cash* (1978) and *This Is Spinal Tap* (1984). Just as rock is here to stay, rockumentaries also seem to be perennial favorites with young moviegoers.

MUSICAL REVUES

A musical revue is a program of songs, dances, and sketches that offers a plotless evening of stage entertainment. Rather than just a bill of acts as in vaudeville, the musical revue was planned, designed, scored, directed, and choreographed with the same kind of integrity used in book musicals on Broadway. Although there were some early revues in the late 19th century, the American theater revue reached some kind of highpoint with the *Ziegfeld Follies*, which producer Florenz Ziegfeld presented on Broadway between 1907 and 1931. His lavish, star-studded shows had the most expensive tickets on Broadway but they were very popular until the Depression hurt business and the costly revue went out of fashion. Ziegfeld was not alone in the field. Other revues series included the *George White Scandals*, *Earl Carroll's Vanities*, the *Music Box Revues*, *Greenwich Village Follies*, *Garrick Gaieties*, and *Artists and Models*. The nature of the revue changed during the Depression. Instead of a spectacular show, the new kind of revue was more literate, had high-quality songs, and often had a theme. This golden age for the Broadway revue began with *The Little Show* (1929) and lasted into the early 1940s. Among the superior revues from this period were *Three's a Crowd* (1930), *The Band Wagon* (1931), *As Thousands Cheer* (1933), *Life Begins at 8:40* (1934), *At Home Abroad* (1935), *The Show Is On* (1936), *Pins and Needles* (1938), *Hellzapoppin'* (1938), and *This Is the Army* (1942). The genre started to wane after World War II and by the 1950s and 1960s revues with original scores were usually to be found Off Broadway, if anywhere at all. In the 1970s, a new breed of musical revue became popular: the nostalgic recollection of the work of former greats. The music of "Fats" Waller was collected for *Ain't Misbehavin'* (1977), *Eubie* (1978) celebrated composer Eubie Blake, *Sophisticated Ladies* (1981) honored Duke Ellington, and the pop music songs by the team of Leiber and Stoller provided the score for the long-running *Smokey Joe's Cafe* (1995). Other shows, such as *Bubbling Brown Sugar* (1976), *Sugar Babies* (1979), *Tintypes* (1980), *Black and Blue* (1989), *Five Guys Named Moe* (1992), *Swing!* (1999), and *Motown* (2015) concentrated on a particular culture or on a period of music from the past. Also, dance has sometimes been the format for a revue, as with *Dancin'* (1978), *Fosse* (1999), *Contact* (2000), and *Movin' Out* (2002). But the full-scale Broadway revue with original songs and top-class production numbers is a thing of the past.

Movie revue musicals had a brief but potent life during the early days of sound. Each studio gathered their talent on contract and put together a revue of songs, sketches, dances, dramatic scenes, and ballet and tied the whole program together with one or more master of ceremonies. Because the novelty of talking pictures was still fresh and the spectacle could be impressive (some even had color sections), these revues were popular for a few years. MGM offered *The Hollywood Revue of 1929*, Warner Brothers made *On with the Show* (1929) and *The Show of Shows* (1929), Universal had *King of Jazz* (1930), and *Paramount on Parade* (1930) showed off that studio's stars. When the appeal of these musicals declined in the early 1930s, the studios abandoned the revue format and later disguised their variety shows as *The Big Broadcast* (1932), *The Broadway Melody of 1936* (1935), and other films that offered a parade of talents but tied them together with the thinnest of plots. The titles of the famous Broadway revues such as *Ziegfeld Follies*, *George White's Scandals*, *Earl Carroll Vanities*, *Artists and Models*, and *Greenwich Village Follies* were all used by Hollywood for movie musicals that had a plot that was an excuse for a series of production numbers, but a true movie revue would be a rare thing. The few exceptions include *Ziegfeld Follies* (1946), *New Faces* (1954), and *Jacques Brel Is Alive and Well and Living in Paris* (1975) as well as the animated anthology musicals such as *Saludos Amigos* (1943), *The Three Caballeros* (1945), *Make Mine Music* (1946), *Fun and Fancy Free* (1947), and *Melody Time* (1948).

A different kind of revue showed up during World War II. These patriotic musicals had slender plots that barely held together a first-class lineup of stars and songs. Although they were not billed as revues, these musicals were more of a big show than a story. *Star Spangled Rhythm* (1942) was the first notable entry and it was followed by such entertaining films as *This Is the Army* (1943), *Thank Your Lucky Stars* (1943), *Thousands Cheer* (1943), *Stage Door Canteen* (1943), *Hollywood Canteen* (1944), *Two Girls and a Sailor* (1944), *Four Jills in a Jeep* (1944), and *Here Come the Waves* (1944). For many years television took up the musical revue in the form of weekly variety shows that featured stars, songs, sketches, and production numbers. *The Hollywood Palace, The Ed Sullivan Show, The Carol Burnett Show*, and many others were very popular and offered shows that were a cross between vaudeville and the opulent Broadway revue, but by the 1980s such programs lost their appeal and the revue faded away in another medium.

RADIO MUSICALS

While Broadway only used radio as its subject in a few musicals, Hollywood seemed obsessed with the air waves, and film after film was made in the 1930s and 1940s about radio and radio stars. This is ironic when one considers that radio was Tinseltown's biggest competition for audiences in those decades. Radio shows were broadcast nationally in the 1920s but it was during the 1930s that radio became a huge entertainment empire. The nature of radio then was much different from that of contemporary radio. Music was its predominant element but there were news programs, sports broadcasts, soap operas, adventure series, situation comedies, original dramas, variety shows, quiz programs, and even live broadcasts of scenes from movies with the original stars reprising their screen roles. While listeners knew what most radio celebrities looked like, most of the actors on radio were just voices and it was the audience who filled in the details with their imagination. Just as moviegoers had to imagine what their silent screen stars sounded like, so too radio demanded some creativity on its audience.

Many popular movie stars began in and found fame on the radio, including Rudy Vallee, Bob Hope, Frances Langford, Jack Benny, Jane Frazee, Bing Crosby, Edgar Bergen, Kate Smith, Kenny Baker, Dinah Shore, Russ Columbo, and George Burns and Gracie Allen. Also, all the popular Big Band conductors—Glenn Miller, Benny Goodman, Jimmy and Tommy Dorsey, Count Basie, Harry James, Kay Kyser, and others—found fame on the radio before being featured in the movies. When all the preceding were first put on-screen, they usually played themselves or fictional radio stars, the thinking of the studios being that moviegoers would most easily accept them in films if the milieu was a familiar one. Some of these radio personalities became movie stars with no problem; others struggled on the screen and eventually returned to the medium that proved more successful for them. Hollywood wagered that moviegoers wanted to see radio stars on the screen. They also guessed correctly that the public wanted to see behind the scenes of the radio business.

Paramount was the first studio to gather a lot of radio talent and make a musical about radio. *The Big Broadcast* (1932) had a silly plot about a radio crooner (Bing Crosby) competing with a Texas millionaire (Stuart Erwin) over a girl. It was a feeble tale but the movie was filled with top-ranking singers and comics and the audience loved it so Paramount made three more "broadcast" musicals.

The Big Broadcast of 1936 (1935) was about a radio crooner (Jack Oakie) who cannot sing but he fools the public by having a "ghost' singer (Henry Wadsworth) secretly go on the air for him. Crosby and other radio favorites were also in the film. *The Big Broadcast of 1937* (1936) had a very impressive lineup of famous and little-known-today radio singers and comics. The plot, about a struggling radio station and a gimmick to try and save it, was negligible but the music was terrific, particularly the swing music by Benny Goodman. Most agree that *The Big Broadcast of 1938* is the best of the series. It certainly had the best song, "Thanks for the Memory," sung by Bob Hope and Shirley Ross. The screenplay was about a trans-Atlantic race with broadcasts coming from one of the two competing ocean liners. With W. C. Fields playing twin brothers and Martha Raye as the comic foil, the movie was as funny as it was musical.

While no other studio offered a series of radio musicals, all of them made films about broadcasting. Some of the Shirley Temple vehicles at 20th Century Fox were about radio entertainment, including *Poor Little Rich Girl* (1936) and *Rebecca of Sunnybrook Farm* (1938). Several musicals involved putting on a big radio show, just as backstagers had revolved around a big Broadway show. Some films spoofed the radio business and a lot made fun of the sponsors behind radio programs. Over the years, other films dealing with broadcast entertainment included *Say It with Songs* (1929), *Hello Everybody* (1933), *Torch Singer* (1933), *Myrt and Marge* (1934), *Twenty Million Sweethearts* (1934), *Strictly Dynamite* (1934), *Gift of Gab* (1934), *Millions in the Air* (1935), *Sing, Baby, Sing* (1936), *With Love and Kisses* (1937), *Wake Up and Live* (1937), *Mr. Dodd Takes the Air* (1937), *Love and Hisses* (1937), *The Hit Parade* (1937), *Melody and Moonlight* (1940), *A Little Bit of Heaven* (1940), *Love Thy Neighbor* (1940), *The Great American Broadcast* (1941), *Reveille with Beverly* (1943), *I'll Tell the World* (1945), *Ladies' Man* (1947), and *My Dream Is Yours* (1949). When television came in, radio gradually changed from a wide entertainment medium to a music, sports, and talk show medium and few movies were made about this new venue. Perhaps the fondest and most nostalgic tribute to the old-style medium was Woody Allen's film *Radio Days* (1987), which was not a musical but was filled with memorable songs one heard on the radio in the 1940s.

SPECIALTY MUSICALS

The word "specialty" is used in various ways in Hollywood. If a famous singer appears in a film singing one song and in no other scenes, it is considered a "specialty spot." Many African American performers, such as Louis Armstrong, Billie Holiday, or the Nicholas Brothers, were often featured in specialty spots. Sadly, this was done so that their spots could be edited out when the movie played to white audiences in the South. If a song is written with a performer's special talents in mind, it is called a "specialty number." Danny Kaye, for instance, could talk-sing very, very fast so songwriters wrote such wordy songs for him to sing in his movie musicals. Then there is the "specialty musical." This is an entire movie musical built around a star with a very specific talent. Instead of a performer being cast in movie that has been written and scored, the musical is created to fit a star's novelty. Such movies go back to the Depression and continued to be made into the 1970s.

The most popular movie star of the Depression years was Shirley Temple, a surprisingly gifted singer, actress, and dancer who starred in her first movie at the age of eight. Temple was the first musical star in Hollywood who required specialty musicals. 20th Century Fox did not cast the popular tot in just any musical. The film had to be written and scored specifically to show off Temple's considerable talents. Not only did the leading character have to be a little girl, the script and songs had to give her opportunities to tap dance, sing a cheer-up song, be neglected or even abused, help some adults out of their problems, sing a cute little ditty or two, and tug on the audience's heartstrings. After Temple's sensational debut in *Stand Up and Cheer* (1934), Fox manufactured a series of musicals in which she could do all of these. The plots varied, as did the songs, but the requirements remained the same. During the Depression, Temple made 15 specialty musicals, among them such popular favorites as *Little Miss Marker* (1934), *Baby Take a Bow* (1934), *Curly Top* (1935), *The Littlest Rebel* (1935), *Captain January* (1936), *Poor Little Rich Girl* (1936), *Rebecca of Sunnybrook Farm* (1938), and *The Little Princess* (1939). Her supporting cast changed from film to film, though the great African American tap dancer Bill "Bojangles" Robinson appeared in five Temple movies, allowing the little dancer to match taps with the Master. Part of Temple's tremendous popularity was the way she cheered up audiences during the Depression. When Temple outgrew child roles, she turned to playing teenagers in nonmusicals. Of course every studio wanted to have its own version of Shirley Temple, and several kid performers were cast in musicals, hoping to cash in on the moviegoers' fascination with young talent. Only one performer managed to come close. Bobby Breen wasn't a dancer and his acting was routine but he had a high, bird-like singing voice that appealed to the public. Nine-year-old Breen starred in his first specialty musical, *Let's Sing Again*, in 1936 and RKO featured him in six subsequent films, most memorably *Rainbow on the River* (1936), *Make a Wish* (1937), *Fisherman's Wharf* (1939) and *Way Down South* (1939). When Breen reached his teen years, he retired from Hollywood and had a long career singing in nightclubs.

Republic Pictures, one of Hollywood's minor studios, found something of a gold mine in Judy Canova. She was not a child star but a 20-year-old comic singer who played hillbilly characters with a flourish. After making a good impression in the musical *Going Highbrow* (1935), Canova was featured in 20 specialty musicals, just about all of them low-budget B movies. The character she played was usually a hick named Judy and in every film she got to clown around, do some yodeling, and sing songs with her siren voice. Among her notable musicals were *Thrill of a*

Lifetime (1937), *True to the Army* (1942), *Joan of Ozark* (1942), *Hit the Hay* (1945), *Singin' in the Corn* (1946), *Oklahoma Annie* (1952), *The WAC from Walla Walla* (1952), and *Carolina Cannonball* (1955). She may not have been a star like those at MGM and the other major studios, but Canova was a top performer at Republic and the musicals built around her were popular enough to make money. Republic's bigger star was cowboy singer Roy Rogers and the studio many dozens of specialty musicals for the "King of the Cowboys." These films were westerns and included the required action of that genre. But music was an important part of the Rogers movies and some of the songs he sang became standards. His character was usually named Roy Rogers and he always played a soft-spoken, mild-mannered lawman or rancher. Among his most popular movies were *Under Western Stars* (1938), *In Old Caliente* (1939), *The Arizona Kid* (1939), *Red River Valley* (1941), *Romance on the Range* (1942), *Hands Across the Border* (1944), *Man from Oklahoma* (1945), *Rainbow Over Texas* (1946), *Under Nevada Skies* (1946), *Apache Rose* (1947), *Down Dakota Way* (1949), *Heart of the Rockies* (1951), and *In Old Amarillo* (1951). On occasion, Republic loaned Rogers out to bigger studios and he appeared in some big-budget musicals, such as *Melody Time* (1948) and *Son of Paleface* (1952). Many of his musicals also featured his wife Dale Evans, and, later, the two found success on radio and television together.

Esther Williams and Sonja Henie, two Hollywood stars with unconventional talents, each inspired a series of specialty musicals that were very popular in their day and are still enjoyable. Henie was a three-time Olympic figure skating champion from Norway who was put under contract at 20th Century Fox. She did not sing and could barely speak English but Fox built 10 specialty musicals around her dazzling skating abilities. While the singing and dancing were left to others, Henie was the major character, usually a Scandinavian, and took to the ice in each film, the skating sequences usually staged by top Hollywood choreographers. She made her debut in *One in a Million* (1936) and was an immediate favorite with audiences. Among her most notable musicals were *Second Fiddle* (1939), *Sun Valley Serenade* (1941), *Iceland* (1942), and *Wintertime* (1943). Henie retired from films in 1948 to star in a series of popular ice shows, which she usually produced herself. MGM searched for a skating star of its own but failed to find one with cinematic potential. Instead it created Hollywood's only swimming star with Esther Williams. A swimming champ since her teen years, Williams had starred in aquacades where she was discovered by the studio. She was featured in *Bathing Beauty* (1944) and was such a novelty that MGM made 17 more specialty musicals for her. Williams could sing and act so it was easier to come up with scripts and songs for her. But each Williams film had to have at least one spectacular aquatic number so the stories had to take place where a giant swimming pool was nearby. Williams had a longer movie career than Henie, starring in musicals until 1960. Her most popular films include *Thrill of a Romance* (1945), *Fiesta* (1947), *Take Me Out to the Ball Game* (1949), *Neptune's Daughter* (1949), *Million Dollar Mermaid* (1952), *Dangerous When Wet* (1953), and *Jupiter's Darling* (1955). Appropriately, when Williams retired from Hollywood she ran a swimming suit business.

Two comedy teams required specially made movies, the Marx Brothers in the 1930s and Abbott and Costello in the 1940s and 1950s. Groucho, Chico, Harpo, and Zeppo Marx were unique comics who began in vaudeville and graduated to Broadway where they were starred in three musical comedies. Two of them—*The Cocoanuts* (1929) and *Animal Crackers* (1930)—were filmed pretty much as they were on the stage. But when Hollywood wanted to make further movies featuring the foursome, they had to create specialty musicals that catered to the team's wacky comedics. Although each brother was given a new name and a new situation in each film, each comic retained the same character. Groucho was the wisecracking shyster, Chico the lame-brained Italian, Harpo the silent but expressive clown, and Zeppo the straight man. The writers outlined new adventures for each Marx Brothers film, but sometimes there was so much ad-libbing that the movies often seemed like high-flying chaos. While the singing and dancing were often relegated to other characters or the chorus, in every movie Groucho sang comic songs, Chico played the piano with hilarious finger work, and Harpo plucked beautiful melodies on the harp. The brothers' first four original movies are considered their best: *Horse Feathers* (1932), *Duck Soup* (1933), *A Night at the Opera* (1935), and *A Day at the Races* (1937). Yet there are inspired moments in their less-satisfactory musicals *At the Circus* (1939), *Go West* (1940), *The Big Store* (1931), and *Love Happy* (1949). Bud Abbott and Lou Costello were a comedy team onstage and on the radio who were given small roles in the musical *One Night in the Tropics* (1940). The twosome stole the show from the stars so Universal gave them their own vehicle, *Buck Privates* (1941). Neither comic sang or danced but, like the Marx Brothers, always played the same character even though their names changed from film to film. Abbott was always the fast-talking con man who took advantage of the innocent, frustrated Costello. The duo made 36 features, 18 of them musicals in which the singing and dancing were left to others. These specialty musicals found clever ways to put the two comics in the U.S. Army, the Navy, the Air Corps, out West, in Alaska, at college, and elsewhere. The Abbott and Costello wartime musicals are perhaps their best films, as with *In the Navy* (1941), *Hold That Ghost* (1941), *Keep 'Em Flying* (1941), *Ride 'Em Cowboy* (1942), *Rio Rita* (1942), *Pardon My Sarong* (1943), and *In Society* (1944). They continued to work in Hollywood and on television until Costello's death in 1959.

A specialty musical star who definitely did his own singing was Elvis Presley, the rock and roll pioneer who had a 14-year Hollywood career. Presley had established himself as a major recording star and concert attraction before he was signed by Hollywood to star in movie musicals. After proving his screen appeal in the musical drama *Love Me Tender* (1956), various studios starred Presley in 30 musicals over the next two decades. All of these movies were especially tailored to his throaty, expressive singing voice and his conspicuous sex appeal. Not only did the scores in his films all resemble each other, Elvis played basically the same character in each. The characters' names changed but he usually ended up playing a loose-living free spirit who indulges in thrilling jobs in between singing and getting involved with one of many adoring females who are more than willing. As much as the writers changed the locales (Hawaii, Las Vegas, New Orleans, the Ozark Mountains, Acapulco, and so on) and the jobs (race car driver, roustabout, rodeo rider, seaman, boxer, even a doctor), it was always the same Elvis. This was unfortunate because Presley was obviously capable of more variety. But his management and the studios insisted that young moviegoers wanted more of the same so that is what they got. Just about all of the Presley musicals were box office hits but most would consider his best films to be *Jailhouse Rock* (1957), *King Creole* (1958), *Blue Hawaii* (1961), *Kid Galahad* (1962), *Fun in Acapulco* (1963), *Viva Las Vegas* (1964), *Girl Happy* (1965), *Frankie and Johnny* (1966), *Spinout* (1966), *Double Trouble* (1967), *Clambake* (1968), and *The Trouble with Girls* (1970). Presley left Hollywood in 1970 and for the last seven years of his life he concentrated on concert performing.

At the same time that Presley was portraying a seductive, less-than-wholesome leading man in movies, Annette Funicello and Frankie Avalon were the very picture of wholesomeness in a series of "beach" musicals. Funicello had found fame as one of the youngsters on television's *The Mickey Mouse Club*. After making her film debut in the Disney live-action musical *Babes in Toyland* in 1961, she was signed by American International Pictures (AIP), a small Hollywood studio that specialized in low-budget, high-profit films. Funicello was teamed with 24-year-old Frankie Avalon, a popular singer who had made some movies, including the musical *Jamboree* (1957). The two played supporting roles in the sunny musical *Beach Party* (1963) and were an immediate hit so AIP starred them in *Muscle Beach Party* (1964), which was an even bigger success. This was followed by *Bikini Beach* (1964), *Beach Blanket Bingo* (1965), *Fireball 500* (1966), and *How to Stuff a Wild Bikini* (1967). These specialty musicals resembled each other a lot. Avalon usually played Frankie, a good-looking, genial beach bum, and Funicello was often named DeeDee, his ongoing love interest. Although they spent much of their movies in bathing suits (but no bikini for her), the twosome were clean-cut and as American as apple pie. Funicello and Avalon handled most of the songs and some dancing on the beach, leaving others to carry the plot and provide the comedy. The series might have lasted longer but Avalon didn't want to be typecast and went on to other projects. The two were reunited in 1987 when they played a married couple in the musical *Back to the Beach*.

At the same time Funicello and Avalon were frolicking on the beach, the Beatles were making a short (three films) series of specialty musicals for United Artists. The Fab Four had taken America by storm in 1964 and that same year the low-budget, black-and-white film *A Hard Day's Night* was released. Since the Beatles had no acting or dancing experience, the movie concentrated not on character but on the rehearsal and performance of a television special. In between they ran all over London where they were chased by girls. It was a carefree, silly film but was surprisingly entertaining. In an innovative move, Beatles recordings were heard behind whole sections of *A Hard Day's Night*, giving the film an early music video look. Coming up with a plot for a second Beatles movie was not going to be easy because the foursome insisted on playing themselves again. *Help!* (1965) was a spy spoof, a travelogue, and another music video. The group's many fans did not complain even though *Help!* was not as much fun as *A Hard Day's Night* and hinted that the talented singer-songwriters were rather limited as movie stars. The Beatles did not enjoy making movies so refused any future offers. United Artists did convince them to let them use recordings of their songs for the score for the animated *The Yellow Submarine* in 1968. The four main animated characters were again the Beatles but their speaking voices were done by others. *Yellow Submarine* is a merry fable filled with pop art and wonderful songs. Yet it too was a specialty musical and, like other movies in that genre, was inspired and limited by the unique talents of its stars.

FOREIGN MUSICALS

As stated earlier, the movie musical is an American invention. But that doesn't mean other countries have not tried to copy the art form, sometimes succeeding very well. Hollywood turned out so many musicals during the Golden Age that Americans forget that there was a thriving film industry in Great Britain producing English musicals, very few of which came to the United States. *Evergreen* (1934) was one of the exceptions and it was based on a West End show with a score by Americans Richard Rodgers and Lorenz Hart. In the 1960s, British and American studios started to coproduce movie musicals with plans for wide distribution in both countries. Many of these were big-budget musicals filmed in England with American-British casts and were often set in Britain and based on English sources. Some of them were purely British products that were financed and promoted in America. *A Hard Day's Night* (1964), *Help!* (1965), *Doctor Dolittle* (1967), *Half a Sixpence* (1967), *Chitty Chitty Bang Bang* (1968), *Goodbye, Mr. Chips* (1969), *Scrooge* (1970), *The Boy Friend* (1971), *Tommy* (1975), and *The Rocky Horror Picture Show* (1975) were among the British or British-American musicals to find a wide audience on American screens. The French cinema has attempted the musical form on occasion but with varied success. Three French musicals that found an audience in the United States are *The Umbrellas of Cherbourg* (1964) and *The Girls of Rochefort* (1967), both made by Jacques Demy, and the revue musical *Jacques Brel Is Alive and Well and Living in Paris* (1975). When it comes to the number of movie musicals made each year, no country produces more than India. The Bollywood films are filled with singing and dancing and, although only a handful ever make it to American movie screens, they are produced by the dozens every year and are seen by a huge Hindu population.

HISTORY OF THE MOVIE MUSICAL

THE 1920s: LEARNING TO SING ON-SCREEN

Although the Hollywood musical didn't appear until the last years of the 1920s, the new art form was an innovation that was typical of the decade. Often called the Roaring Twenties or the Jazz Age, the decade was a time of booming business, a new freedom in several areas, and a period of bold advances. After World War I, the United States embarked on a period of progress unseen before. Cities grew (literally) because of the advanced structure of skyscrapers. Industry grew, particularly in the manufacture of automobiles and household products. Both transportation and communication grew as ocean liners and railroad systems got more efficient and the telephone and the radio became more prevalent. One might even say that the American spirit grew as the country became the most powerful nation on earth after a war that had diminished most other countries. Historians point to the 1920s as a bold departure from the Victorian and Puritan thinking of the prewar years. Life on the farm and in small rural communities may have held on to the old ways but in the cities everything was "modern." The way people dressed, cut their hair, entertained each other, and even courted each other changed. Women were given the right to vote in 1920 and throughout the decade more women worked than before and there were more women in government, education, business, and social causes. New newspapers and magazines flooded the growing market, and many other kinds of business were started and flourished as the stock market soared and people were making money faster than ever thought possible.

The 1920s was also a fertile period for the arts in America. More plays opened on Broadway, more novels were sold, and more phonograph records were bought than the previous two decades combined. Some of America's greatest writers, composers, artists, and performers were very active in the 1920s because there was money for the arts and people had money to spend. Writers such as Carl Sandberg,

Edith Wharton, F. Scott Fitzgerald, Eugene O'Neill, Sinclair Lewis, Robert Frost, Langston Hughes, O. Henry, William Faulkner, Dorothy Parker, Ernest Hemingway, Edna Ferber, and Thomas Wolfe all wrote some of their greatest works in the 1920s. The same can be said for such composers as Charles Ives, Jerome Kern, Aaron Copland, Irving Berlin, Virgil Thomson, Eubie Blake, and George Gershwin, and artists Georgia O'Keefe, Grant Wood, and Edward Hopper. It was possible to find outstanding singers, dancers, and actors in different media: vaudeville, radio, Broadway, phonograph records, and, of course, the movies. Giants in American entertainment were everywhere in the 1920s. Al Jolson, Mary Pickford, Louis Armstrong, Greta Garbo, Rudolph Valentino, Gloria Swanson, Ethel Barrymore, Paul Robeson, Martha Graham, Helen Hayes, Buster Keaton, Lillian Gish, Sophie Tucker, John Barrymore, and Bessie Smith were among the performers who reached a wider public than previously thought possible. The 1920s was also the period of the Harlem Renaissance, the Art Deco Movement, the proliferation of jazz, the Theatre Guild, and other movements that aimed to broaden the range of the American arts.

Hollywood and the movies came of age in the 1920s. The pioneering little companies that established the industry in Southern California in the 1910s grew to become major studios with enormous resources and a multitude of popular stars. It was also the decade that saw the construction of the great movie palaces. In large and even small cities across the nation, mammoth theaters were built that seated over a thousand moviegoers in a palatial setting. These architectural wonders were usually designed in an exotic style, such as the Bush Egyptian Theatre (opened in 1923) in San Diego, Grumman's Chinese Theatre (1926) in Los Angeles, and the Spanish-flavored Loew's Valencia Theatre (1929) in New York. Although built to show movies, they were equipped with elaborate theater organs, an orchestra pit on an elevator stage large enough to hold a live symphony, and state-of-the-art backstage technology for live stage shows presented between films. Such palaces open to the public was a uniquely American invention and illustrated the power and the appeal of the movies in the 1920s. The "studio system," as it is called, was formed and solidified in the 1920s. The studios were run like efficient factories with different people working in different departments and everything scheduled so tightly that each studio could turn out dozens of films each year. Not only actors but writers, songwriters, and designers were on contract to ensure that there would be no lack of personnel to keep the factory operating. Also, the studios owned hundreds of movie theaters, both the palaces and the little neighborhood movie houses, to guarantee that there were plenty of venues for their products. The system worked so well in the 1920s and 1930s that Hollywood was able to produce hundreds of new films each year and make significant profits on most of them.

Charles Lindbergh made history by flying solo over the Atlantic five months before *The Jazz Singer* opened in 1927. The flight and the movie can be considered symbols of American technological prowess. But all that optimism was crushed two years later when the stock market crashed. In October 1929, with only two months left to the jazz decade, the entire economic structure of America collapsed. Both the rich and the poor lost everything, and the catastrophe triggered a series of economic setbacks that dug the nation deeper into despair. It would take decades before the optimism of the 1920s was restored. Hollywood would survive the Depression rather well. Both radio and movies prospered during these hard times. As for the film musical, it was just coming into its own as the 1920s ended. The introduction of sound movies was very much in the spirit of the Roaring Twenties. It was an exciting new development but Hollywood had to change the system to include many new jobs, from sound technicians to studio orchestra musicians. Sound created new screen stars and saw some old favorites fall from celebrity because their voices were a disappointment to moviegoers. Hollywood turned to Broadway for actors who could speak well, offering more money than the stage could ever pay them. Also, songwriters, orchestrators, conductors, choreographers, and other musical-related personnel were recruited from Broadway. The talkies changed Hollywood and most studios quickly learned to adjust to the change and keep the system going even as it added new kinds of products for the public. As for the movie musical, it was such a novelty that the early films in the new genre were all successful. It didn't stay that way for long but for the moment the musical was king. As Al Jolson told the audience in *The Jazz Singer*, "You ain't heard nothing yet!"

The history of the film musical may start with Warner Brothers' 1927 movie *The Jazz Singer* but one must go back one year earlier to get the whole story. The same studio had been experimenting with the Vitaphone process for a few years. This early system allowed a recorded soundtrack to be played concurrently with the movie so that the audio matched the visuals. In 1926 Warner Brothers made the first feature-length movie in Vitaphone, the swashbuckling romantic adventure *Don Juan*. The New York Philharmonic recorded the musical score and then sound effects were added to the Vitaphone process. The result was a silent movie with music and sound effects. Although no actors spoke on the soundtrack, audiences were thrilled with the action movie, which included such novelties as hearing the swords clash during the fight scenes. It was the success of *Don Juan* that prompted the studio to make *The Jazz Singer*.

.The reaction to this singing (with a little talking) musical was overwhelming. The public's response to *The Jazz Singer* was so great that every studio in Hollywood ceased production and switched to sound. Getting a hold of sound cameras and operators was no small problem. And the sound cameras that existed were primitive and clumsy. Because the grinding noise of the camera was so loud, the camera and the operator had to be enclosed in a glass box so that its noise was not picked up by the microphones. Both the camera and the operators could last only a short time because the boxes got so hot. But the studios persevered and in

1928 a handful of movie musicals were made. Jolson returned in *The Singing Fool* and it was even more popular than *The Jazz Singer*. Broadway favorite Fanny Brice made *My Man* and the nation got to see and hear what the famous comedienne-singer was like on stage. Sadly, most of these early musicals are lost today. The sound film stock was highly flammable and too brittle to withstand many showings. In some cases the film survived without the sound.

In 1929 over 60 movie musicals were made, including the landmark *The Broadway Melody*, which introduced several innovations. The first musical with an original score, the first to use prerecorded singing, and the first to include spoken dialogue rather than titles was billed as "All Talking! All Singing! All Dancing!" It was indeed all that plus more. *The Broadway Melody* set a pattern to be used by dozens of backstage musicals over the decades. Also, by 1929 most of the movie houses across the country were equipped for sound and the first big attraction they booked was *The Broadway Melody*. So for most Americans it became the first movie musical they saw. The other 1929 musicals were rather a diverse lot. Some were also backstagers, such as *Gold Diggers of Broadway, Syncopation, Applause*, and *Broadway Scandals*. Others were film versions of Broadway hits, as with *The Cocoanuts, The Desert Song*, and *Rio Rita*. Most studios offered a musical revue using their contract players to create a star-studded entertainment. Among the most notable of these were *On with the Show, Hollywood Revue of 1929, The Show of Shows*, and *King of Jazz*. Some of the musicals were in the European operetta style, as with *Innocents of Paris, The Love Parade*, and *Devil May Care*. Then there were some very individual musicals that made important innovations, such as the African American drama *Hallelujah* and the early Gershwin brothers film *Sunny Side Up*. Again, many musicals from 1929 are partially or completely lost. While the quality of these early musical efforts may vary, they generally make for very interesting viewing today. Consider the limitations under which they were made. The sound and music departments in each studio were new. There was no set pattern or method for how to make a movie musical. Performers had no experience on how to sing in a movie musical. Even the experienced actors from Broadway had to learn to adjust their delivery. Some did so with polish; others came across as overblown or just plain corny. Some silent screen stars possessed pleasing speaking and even singing voices; others were out of their league in both areas. Directors who had made dozens of silent films found themselves confused and frustrated when they had to deal with the complications that sound created. And, as we have already seen, Hollywood still hadn't figured out how to put song and dance into a realistic medium like the movies.

The first three years of the Hollywood musical were trial by fire. It was a difficult yet exciting time for Hollywood. After making every kind of movie imaginable for the past two decades, the studios were suddenly confronted with a brand-new genre: the musical. Yet by the end of the decade, the movie musical had established itself as a powerful and popular new art form. But the question was: Will it last or is the movie musical just a fad? No one in Hollywood could foresee what would happen.

What follows are descriptions of some notable examples of film musicals of the 1920s, presented in the order in which they were released. The same format is used for each subsequent decade. These may not be generally considered the best movie musicals but they offer, we believe, a good representation of this unique art form.

THE JAZZ SINGER

Studio and release date: Warner Brothers; October 1927
Producer: Darryl F. Zanuck
Screenplay: Alfred A. Cohn, based on the play by Samson Raphaelson
Songwriters: Irving Berlin, Gus Kahn, James Monaco, Louis Silvers, Grant Clarke, Ted Fiorito, Sam Lewis, Walter Donaldson, Joe Young, Edgar Leslie, Robert King (music and lyrics)
Director: Alan Crosland
Musical Director: Louis Silvers
Cinematographer: Hal Mohr
Cast: Al Jolson, Warner Oland, May McAvoy, Eugenie Besserer, Bobby Gordon
Principal Songs: "Toot Toot Tootsie"; "My Mammy"; "Dirty Hands, Dirty Face"; "Blue Skies"; "Mother of Mine, I Still Have You"

There is very little talk in this very important movie generally known as the first talking feature film. Yet *The Jazz Singer* is actually a silent movie with sound added for the songs only. All the same, *The Jazz Singer* is a major landmark and is still surprisingly effective. The story is a typical backstage tale. The young Jakie Rabinowitz (Bobby Gordon), who lives in the Jewish immigrant community on Manhattan's Lower East Side, upsets his parents when he is caught singing jazz and ragtime songs in a local saloon. Not wishing to become a synagogue cantor like his father and four generations of Rabinowitzs before him, Jakie runs away from home and, calling himself Jack Robin (Al Jolson), goes into show business. Thanks to the love and encouragement of dancer May (May McAvoy), Jakie finds success, singing in nightclubs and eventually returning to New York to be in a Broadway show. When he hears that his father is dying, Jakie goes to the local synagogue and sings the Yom Kippur service in the old man's place. Jakie then opens on Broadway and, with his mother sitting in the front row, sings "My Mammy" to her.

How the movie came about was a mixture of innovation and desperation. The Warner Brothers studio was in substantial debt and had gambled a lot of money on its Vitaphone process, adding music and sound effects to its 1926 adventure film *Don Juan*. Encouraged by the audience acceptance of that movie, the studio

The Jazz Singer (1927), Hollywood's first musical, made a film star out of Broadway star Al Jolson (pictured). Here he sings to his mother (Eugenie Besserer) in one of the movie's musical sequences, the only times that sound was used in the film. Alan Crosland directed the landmark movie. (Warner Bros. Pictures/Photofest)

decided to take the next logical step and add singing. The studio bought the rights to Samson Raphaelson's 1925 play *The Jazz Singer,* which had starred comic-singer George Jessel on Broadway. They signed Jessel for the screen version, but when the star insisted on more money for filming the singing sequences, the studio dropped him and signed Jolson. While some sections of *The Jazz Singer* are dated, there is still much to enjoy. Director Alan Crosland shot the exteriors on location in Manhattan and the depiction of the Lower East Side, the smoke-filled saloons and nightclubs, and the backstage world of the theater have a tawdry realism to them. The story is solid, character development is not complex but clear, and, of course, there is the dazzling presence of Al Jolson. In both the silent and sound sections of the movie, the stage entertainer grabs one's attention and holds it with confidence and charm. In the more serious scenes he avoids melodramatics and lets a simple frown or the turn of the head say it all. It was Jolson's first feature film and he took to the camera like a silent film veteran. The studio planned for sound to be used only when the actors started singing, either the popular songs or

Al Jolson (1886–1950)   One of the top entertainers on stage, on-screen, and records during the first half of the 20th century, the dynamic singer-actor was the cinema's first singing star. He was born in present-day Lithuania, the son of a cantor, was brought to America as a youngster, and lived in Washington, DC. He was onstage from childhood, singing in vaudeville and minstrel shows, before making his Broadway bow in 1911 in *La Belle Paree*. Often appearing in black face and singing sentimental songs, Jolson soon became an audience favorite and was featured in a series of popular shows on Broadway, including *The Honeymoon Express* (1913), *Robinson Crusoe, Jr.* (1916), *Sinbad* (1918), *Bombo* (1921), and *Big Boy* (1925). He made movie history when he starred in the early talkie *The Jazz Singer* (1927). Other movie musicals followed, such as *The Singing Fool* (1928), *Mammy* (1930), *Big Boy* (1930), *Hallelujah, I'm a Bum* (1933), *Wonder Bar* (1934), *Go Into Your Dance* (1935), *The Singing Kid* (1936), *Rose of Washington Square* (1939), and *Swanee River* (1939). Jolson usually played broad, sentimental characters on the screen as he had done onstage. He enjoyed a revival of popularity with the biopics *The Jolson Story* (1946) and *Jolson Sings Again* (1949) in which he provided his singing voice for actor Larry Parks. Jolson remained a major recording star up to his death. Biography: *Jolson: The Story of Al Jolson*, Michael Freedland (1995).

the Hebrew chants. Yet Jolson was used to inserting phrases and comments during his stage performances so when he did the same on film, the audience actually heard his speaking voice as well as his singing. It wasn't very much dialogue but it was enough to start a revolution.

All the songs used in *The Jazz Singer* but one were numbers already familiar to audiences. "Blue Skies" and "Toot, Toot Tootsie!" were already Jolson favorites from the stage so moviegoers got to experience a little bit of Jolson's Broadway shows. The sentimental ballad "Mother of Mine, I Still Have You" was written for the film by Louis Silvers and Grant Clarke, and Jolson sang it in blackface at a rehearsal while his mother watched tearfully from the wings. It has the distinction of being the first true movie song. The birth of the movie musical also meant a whole new music industry: the selling of popular songs through the movies. But Warner Brothers was not concerned with Jolson talking or the selling of songs when it gambled everything on the risky Vitaphone process. Audience responded favorably to the singing, which was expected, but moviegoers also were thrilled by the few lines of spoken dialogue in the film. This was a surprise to everyone in the movie industry. *The Jazz Singer* saved Warner Brothers and changed the course of film history.

In 1953, the same studio remade *The Jazz Singer* with Danny Thomas as Jerry Golding, who returns from serving in the Korean War and decides to go into show business. The singer Judy Lane (Peggy Lee) provided the love and support, and again Jerry went to the synagogue at the last moment. As with the original film, the songs were mostly recognized standards ("Birth of the Blues," "Just One of Those Things," "Lover," and "I'll String Along With You"). A third version of *The Jazz Singer* (1980) updated the story to the 1980s. Yussel Rabinovitch (Neil Diamond) forsakes his Jewish heritage and becomes the rock singer Jess Rabinovitch. Molly Bell (Lucie Arnaz) was his girlfriend, and in this version the cantor father (Laurence Olivier) doesn't die but lives to accept his son's calling and is seen at a rock concert cheering the boy on. Neither of these remakes has the sincerity and impact of the 1927 original and neither was a box office hit.

See also: *The Jolson Story*; Al Jolson biography box

FURTHER READING

Barrios, Richard. *A Song in the Dark: The Birth of the Musical Film*. 2nd ed. New York: Oxford University Press, 2010.
Bingen, Steven. *Warner Bros.: Hollywood's Ultimate Backlot*. Lanham, MD: Taylor Trade Publishing, 2014.
Geduld, Harry M. *The Birth of the Talkies*. Bloomington: Indiana University Press, 1975.
Hirschhorn, Clive. *The Warner Bros. Story*. New York: Crown Publishers, 1979.

THE BROADWAY MELODY

Studio and release date: Metro-Goldwyn-Mayer; February 1929
Producer: Irving Thalberg
Screenplay: Sarah Y. Mason, Norman Houston, James Gleason, Edmund Goulding
Songwriter: Nacio Herb Brown (music), Arthur Freed (lyrics)
Director: Harry Beaumont
Choreographer: George Cunningham
Cinematographer: John Arnold
Cast: Charles King, Anita Page, Bessie Love, Jed Prouty, Kenneth Thomson, Mary Doran, Eddie Kane, James Gleason
Songs: "Broadway Melody"; "You Were Meant for Me"; "Harmony Babies from Melody Lane"; "The Wedding of the Painted Doll"; "Boy Friend"; "Truthful Parson Brown"; "Love Boat"

MGM's first musical was a tentative venture. Producer Irving Thalberg insisted that *The Broadway Melody* be filmed as a silent movie at the same time as the talking picture so that, should talkies be a fad that quickly died out, the studio would still have a conventional silent offering. As it turned out, the sound version was very popular, and *The Broadway Melody*, as the ads proclaimed, was the "first all talking, all dancing, all singing" Hollywood musical. The legendary movie also boasts a series of other cinema firsts: the first use of Technicolor (for the lavish "The Wedding of the Painted Doll" sequence), the first score (by Nacio Herb Brown and Arthur Freed) written specifically for a film, the first original screenplay written for a musical, the first production that was filmed with some of the music prerecorded, and the first musical to win the Oscar for best picture. In addition, it had a tough-as-nails backstage story, interesting characters, and clever production numbers that still entertain. The plot is about vaudeville performing sisters Queenie (Anita Page) and Harriet "Hank" Mahoney (Bessie Love) who find that their act (and their friendship) are broken by song-and-dance man Eddie Kerns (Charles King); he is engaged to Hank but leaves her when he falls in love with Queenie. All three characters are involved in a Broadway production called *The Broadway Melody*, so there are plenty of opportunities for musical numbers. Yet it is the few songs sung outside of the context of a show that were groundbreaking, such as "You Were Meant for Me" becoming a musical scene. Both it and the title number became very popular, demonstrating that Hollywood could create song hits just as Broadway and records had. The songwriting team of Arthur Freed and Nacio Herb Brown became famous, and Hollywood realized that every studio needed to have songwriters on staff so they could turn out song hits with the studio owning the song and sharing in the profits. Because of the success of *The Broadway Melody,* just about every studio created a music department and wooed Broadway and Tin Pan Alley songwriters to come west and write for the movies.

Watching *The Broadway Melody* today, the film seems primitive in some ways. The scenery looks like stage scenery, the dancing is a bit awkward and unoriginal, and the sound quality for the dialogue is often murky. Yet much of the movie still works. The backstage scenes are not glamorized and there is a sassiness in the dialogue that foreshadows the tough *Gold Diggers* movies and other Depression films. Wisecracking humor, difficult to convey in a silent movie, becomes very potent in *The Broadway Melody*. Some performances lack excitement but Bessie Love is a sharp-tongued "Hank" and she gives the film energy. She had been acting in silent films since 1915 and would never become a first-class screen star but she continued to work in movies and television into the 1980s. Charles King, as the song-and-dance man Eddie, is very personable in *The Broadway Melody* and the camera takes to him. The vaudeville hoofer never got as good a movie role as this, and his subsequent film career was sketchy. Anita Page, as the naive Queenie, is a classic blonde beauty who made several silent films and early talkies but her performance in *The Broadway Melody* disappoints. She is clearly uncomfortable with dialogue (it was her first talkie) and is the weak link in the romantic triangle.

In the landmark film *The Broadway Melody* (1929), a Broadway production actually looked like a real Broadway show. Just as the characters and plot were close to reality, so too were the on-stage scenes. Pictured are Anita Page, Charles King, and Bessie Love (center) with the chorus in the title number. (MGM/Photofest)

Harry Beaumont directed the problematic production, which faced many difficulties. The sound cameras were large, noisy, and clunky and the placement of microphones was a continual headache. (Two decades later the early difficulties with movie sound were presented comically and accurately in the film *Singin' in the Rain*.) Having the orchestra, singers, and cameras all together in the studio was clumsy and expensive. So someone came up with the idea of prerecording the singing voices in a sound studio with the musicians. The recording was then played on the stage studio and the singers lip-synced their own voices. The system worked so well that before long all movie musicals used prerecorded soundtracks for the songs and dances. Hollywood had been experimenting with color for some time (there were primitive color sequences in the 1925 silent *The Phantom of the Opera*) and the decision was made at MGM to do one musical number in the new Technicolor process. They chose the spectacle dance number "The Wedding of the Painted Doll" to show off the colorful sets and costumes. The sequence was impressive but there was little interest in color on the audience's part. It was also very expensive. It would be 10 years later, with *The Wizard of Oz*, that a color musical would grab the audience's attention.

Arthur Freed and **Nacio Herb Brown** Hollywood's first notable song-writing team, they concentrated on the movies before any other songwriters chose the screen over the stage. Lyricist Freed (1894–1973) was born in Charleston, South Carolina, and began his career writing songs for music publishers and for vaudeville. He then went to Hollywood where he directed silent films. With the coming of sound, MGM hired him to write lyrics for original songs to be featured in the talkies. With composer Nacio Herb Brown, he wrote the scores for such early film musicals as *The Broadway Melody* (1929), *Hollywood Revue of 1929* (1929), *Good News!* (1930), *Going Hollywood* (1933), *Broadway Melody of 1936* (1935), and *Broadway Melody of 1938* (1937). Brown (1896–1964) was born in Deming, New Mexico, and studied at the Musical Arts High School in Los Angeles before working as a tailor and a real estate agent. He wrote popular songs, but instead of going to Broadway as most songwriters did, he elected to stay in California where he was teamed up with Freed. The collaboration ended when Freed served as coproducer for the classic *The Wizard of Oz* (1939) and he abandoned lyric writing for producing. He established the celebrated "Freed Unit" at MGM and for the next 20 years presented some of the greatest of all Hollywood musicals, including *Babes in Arms* (1939), *Strike Up the Band* (1940), *For Me and My Gal* (1942), *Cabin in the Sky* (1943), *DuBarry Was a Lady* (1943), *Girl Crazy* (1943), *Meet Me in St. Louis* (1945), *The Harvey Girls* (1946), *Till the Clouds Roll By* (1947), *Good News!* (1947), *Summer Holiday* (1948), *Easter Parade* (1948), *Words and Music* (1948), *Take Me Out to the Ball Game* (1949), *The Barkleys of Broadway* (1949), *On the Town* (1949), *Annie Get Your Gun* (1950), *Royal Wedding* (1951), *Show Boat* (1951), *An American in Paris* (1951), *The Belle of New York* (1952), *Singin' in the Rain* (1952), *The Band Wagon* (1953), *Brigadoon* (1954), *It's Always Fair Weather* (1955), *Silk Stockings* (1957), *Gigi* (1958), and *Bells Are Ringing* (1960). For what is arguably his greatest achievement, *Singin' in the Rain*, the catalogue of Freed's old songs with Brown was used. Brown worked with various lyricists on other movies but, unfortunately, none were memorable.

The Broadway Melody was the first talkie that most Americans at the time saw because it was given such a wide release. Although the title would be reused for other backstage musicals, the only movie that is an actual remake of *The Broadway Melody* is MGM's *Two Girls on Broadway* (1940). In this version the renamed sisters Pat (Lana Turner) and Molly Mahoney (Joan Blondell) are driven apart by dancer Eddie Kerns (George Murphy). Some of the original songs were used and numbers by various songwriters were added. *Two Girls on Broadway* was not nearly as popular as *The Broadway Melody*, though some of the later "Broadway Melody" musicals were box office hits.

See also: *Broadway Melody of 1940*; Arthur Freed and Nacio Herb Brown biography box

FURTHER READING

Barrios, Richard. *A Song in the Dark: The Birth of the Musical Film*. 2nd ed. New York: Oxford University Press, 2010.
Crowther, Bosley. *The Lion's Share: The Story of an Entertainment Empire*. New York: E. P. Dutton & Co., 1957.
Eames, John Douglas. *The MGM Story*. New York: Crown Publishers, 1975.

HOLLYWOOD REVUE OF 1929

Studio and release date: Metro-Goldwyn-Mayer; June 1929
Producer: Harry Rapf
Screenplay: Al Boasberg, Robert Hopkins, Joe Farnham
Songwriters: Gus Edwards, Nacio Herb Brown, Louis Alter, and others (music), Joe Goodwin, Arthur Freed, and others (lyrics)
Director: Charles F. Reisner
Musical Director: Arthur Lange
Choreographers: Sammy Lee, Albertina Rasch, Natasha Natova
Cinematographers: John Arnold, Irving Reis, Maximilian Fabian
Cast: Jack Benny, Conrad Nagel, Cliff Edwards, John Gilbert, Norma Shearer, Joan Crawford, Buster Keaton, Marie Dressler, William Haines, Bessie Love, Charles King, Anita Page, Lionel Barrymore, Stan Laurel, Oliver Hardy
Principal Songs: "Got a Feelin' for You"; "Singin' in the Rain"; "You Were Meant for Me"; "Nobody But You"; "Tommy Atkins on Parade"; "Your Mother and Mine"; "Orange Blossom Time"; "Low-Down Rhythm"; "While Strolling Through the Park One Day"

One of the earliest and best of the musical revues that Hollywood turned out during the early years of sound, this lavish but uneven movie gave MGM a chance to show off its roster of stars, both new and established names. The musical revue took Broadway by storm in the early years of the 20th century and by the 1920s had become a popular fixture in New York. Unlike a vaudeville show, which was a series of unrelated acts, the revue was a program of songs, comedy, and dance that was tied together, either thematically or visually, to create a plotless but balanced evening of high-class entertainment. Although the first notable revue was *The Passing Show* in 1894, the genre found its form in 1907 with the annual *Ziegfeld Follies* revues, which producer Florenz Ziegfeld presented up through 1931. These were the most spectacular revues on Broadway and the inspiration for MGM's *Hollywood Revue of 1929*. Because all of its players were on contract, the studio could crowd as many stars as it wanted without paying additional sums for the performers. Instead, the money went toward the production, particularly the sets and costumes. The revue resembled a stage revue with a curtain and two hosts (actor Conrad Nagel and comic Jack Benny) addressing the movie audience as if in a theater. But the production numbers often included visuals that would have been difficult onstage, in particular the torrents of rain during the movie's most famous number, "Singin' in the Rain." The song was sung by comic actor-singer Cliff Edwards, billed as "Ukelele Ike," strumming his ukulele and singing with the chorus, all dressed in raincoats and rain hats as the water came tumbling down. It remains a silly but memorable moment in screen history and the song itself became very popular not only on records but in later MGM movies. When Gene Kelly sang and danced to the number 23 years later in *Singin' in the Rain* (1952), another classic moment in movie musicals was created.

"Singin' in the Rain" was written by Nacio Herb Brown (music) and Arthur Freed (lyrics), who also contributed the military number "Tommy Atkins on Parade" and the hit song "You Were Meant for Me," which had recently been introduced in *The Broadway Melody* (1929). Much of the rest of the score was written by Gus Edwards (music) and Joe Goodwin (lyrics), most memorably the lullaby-like "Your Mother and Mine," the cheery "Nobody But You," and the romantic "Orange Blossom Time." In all, 36 songs were used in the movie, ranging from opera selections to the period standard "While Strolling Through the Park One Day." It took three choreographers—Sammy Lee, Albertina Rasch, Natasha Natova—to stage all the numbers but only one director—Charles F. Reisner—to keep the show running. Parts of the film lag because some scenes do not hold up as well as others. The musical numbers come off the best, though seeing silent screen stars Norma Shearer and John Gilbert enact a scene from *Romeo and Juliet* is of interest. Audiences heard their voices for the first time and careers were defined; Shearer's lovely, smooth voice ensured a long career in talkies but Gilbert's voice came across as strident and falsetto in the primitive sound recording and his future in talking pictures was doomed. The comic sketches are uneven, comedy being the first thing that dates. Jack Benny (in his first screen appearance) is more effective than his cohost Conrad Nagle in their scenes with various comics. The silent comedy stars Stan Laurel and Oliver Hardy do not seem to be hampered by sound and still please. A delightful surprise is silent actress Marian Davies, often cast in serious romantic roles, who shines here letting loose with the number "Tommy Atkins on Parade." Among the many other MGM stars to make appearances in *The*

Hollywood Revue of 1929 are Joan Crawford, Buster Keaton, Lionel Barrymore, Marie Dressler, Bessie Love, and Charles King.

Like the Ziegfeld revues, the most impressive aspect of *The Hollywood Revue of 1929* is the spectacle. Because Hollywood had bigger budgets than even Ziegfeld, the studio could dazzle on a larger scale on-screen than anyone could on the stage. The dozens of chorus girls, the sparkling sets, and the ability to change scenery instantly meant movie musicals could rival Broadway. Two of the sequences in *The Hollywood Revue of 1929*—the *Romeo and Juliet* scene and the production number "Orange Blossom Time"—were even filmed in an early two-color Technicolor format. MGM put a lot of money into the movie and, as the title suggests, other screen revues were to follow. But public reaction was only favorable rather than enthusiastic and *Hollywood Revue of 1929* did only modest business. To audiences, movies were a narrative art form and revues had no story or characters to focus on. So *The Hollywood Revue of 1930* was never made and within a few years no studios were making musical revues. When the genre returned two decades later in patriotic revues, the films were always given some kind of story, no matter how slim, to hold together the musical. Yet these early revues put out by various studios have their particular charm even for modern audiences. Warner Brothers' *On with the Show* (1929) and *The Show of Shows* (1929), Universal's *King of Jazz* (1930), Paramount's *Paramount on Parade* (1930) and *The Big Broadcast* (1932), and other Hollywood revues were like family affairs, each studio proudly putting all its performing talent in one big show. It's a kind of movie musical long gone today and unlikely ever to return.

See also: *Star Spangled Rhythm*

FURTHER READING

Grant, Barry Keith. *The Hollywood Film Musical*. Hoboken, NJ: Wiley-Blackwell, 2012.
Thomas, Lawrence B. *The MGM Years*. New York: Arlington House, 1971.

HALLELUJAH

Studio and release date: Metro-Goldwyn-Mayer; August 1929
Producer: King Vidor
Screenplay: Ransom Rideout, Richard Schayer, Wanda Tuchock, King Vidor
Songwriters: Irving Berlin, W. C. Handy, Nacio Herb Brown, Arthur Freed, etc.
Director: King Vidor
Musical Director: Eva Jessye
Cinematographer: Gordon Avil

Cast: Daniel L. Haynes, Nina Mae McKinney, Victoria Spivey, William
   Fontaine, Harry Gray, Fanny Belle DeKnight, Everett McGarrity
Principal Songs: "Cotton"; "St. Louis Blues"; "Swanee Shuffle"; "Waiting at the
   End of the Road"; "(Gimme Dat) Old Time Religion"; "Go Down Moses";
   "Sometimes I Feel Like a Motherless Child"; "Goin' Home"

This early talkie about southern African Americans is noteworthy not only because
of its all-black cast, but the semi-musical is also a powerful drama that still holds
up. Much of the credit is due to producer-director King Vidor, who had long wanted
to make a sympathetic and honest film that portrayed the African American sharecroppers in the rural South. Vidor couldn't convince MGM to make the movie
until sound came in and he argued that the use of Negro spirituals heard on the
soundtrack would make an appealing musical. The studio would not okay the project until Vidor offered to forgo his director salary and promised to produce *Hallelujah* on a very limited budget. The screenplay, by Vidor and others, centered on
the poor cotton farm worker Zeke Johnson (Daniel L. Haynes) who is in love with
the sweet innocent Missy Rose (Victoria Spivey). After the family's cotton crop is
picked, he sells it for $100. The seductive Chick (Nina Mae McKinney) knows Zeke
has so much cash and so, working with her lover Hot Shot (William Fontaine), she
lures Zeke into a crooked crap game where he is cheated out of all the money. In his
anger and frustration, Zeke returns home and, in a family argument, accidentally
shoots his younger brother Spunk (Everett McGarrity) then runs away. When Zeke
later returns to his home county, he has been saved and is now the preacher Brother
Zekiel who moves the crowd with his spiritual strength. He asks Missy Rose to marry
him but when Chick comes to Zekiel to be saved, he is again ensnared in her seductive power, forsaking his girl and his religion. But when Chick goes back to Hot Shot,
Zeke chases after them; Chick dies when the buggy overturns and Zeke kills Hot
Shot in a swamp. Arrested and sentenced to a chain gang, Zeke finally finds salva-
tion and, when he is released from prison, returns to the faithful Missy Rose.

Hallelujah was highly melodramatic and was filled with several black stereotypes, yet there is a sincerity in the characters and situations that make the film
very moving at times. To save time and money, Vidor shot the film on location in
Tennessee and Arkansas with no sound equipment so the camerawork is more fluid
and moves a great deal more than in other early talkies. The actors and singers
later did all the dialogue and songs in the Los Angeles sound studio and, while
the synchronization is not always perfect, there is a gritty, documentary feel to
Hallelujah that is still enthralling. As promised, Vidor filled the music soundtrack
with many Negro spirituals (dubbed by the celebrated Dixie Jubilee Singers), turning the movie into a sort of opera, six years before George Gershwin did just that
with *Porgy and Bess*. The studio insisted on some nonspiritual songs to make the
film more commercial so, against Vidor's wishes, two new Irving Berlin songs were

added to the traditional numbers. Both were very effective and provided memorable cinematic moments. "Waiting at the End of the Road" was sung by Zeke and the other plantation workers as they waited in line to sell their bales of cotton, comparing it to waiting to get into heaven. "Swanee Shuffle" was the steamy number Chick sang to tempt Zeke and it is indeed seductive. Nina Mae McKinney was so convincing as Chick that she was signed to a studio contract, the first female African American to be offered such a contract. Haynes went on to make 10 other Hollywood movies but none offered him such a challenging role as Zeke.

Although the little-known Fox musical *Hearts in Dixie* (1929) was the first all-black musical film, it is *Hallelujah* that remains the early classic in African American cinema. MGM debuted the film in two places in New York City: up in Harlem and downtown in Times Square. Both white audiences and northern African American moviegoers found the movie rather foreign yet very involving. Southern audiences were better able to identify with *Hallelujah* though many southern theaters refused to show the film. MGM lost money on the movie but was proud enough of it that it rereleased it in 1932 with 10 minutes of footage removed. Today the original *Hallelujah* is available and its status as an early film classic is more recognized. That said, it must be pointed out that over the years, the musical did perpetuate many black stereotypes, from the crocked gambler to the saloon floozy. Because many moviegoers across the country did not encounter African Americans in everyday life, movies like *Hallelujah* prejudiced them into thinking that black Americans were indeed like the types seen on-screen. Of course, none of this was the intent of Vidor, who wanted to present southern blacks in a sympathetic and understanding light.

See also: *Cabin in the Sky*

FURTHER READING

Bloom, Ken. *Hollywood Musicals: The 101 Greatest Song-and-Dance Movies of All Time*. New York: Black Dog and Leventhal, 2010.

Knight, Arthur. *Disintegrating the Musical: Black Performance and the American Musical Film*. Durham, NC: Duke University Press, 2002.

THE 1930S: SINGING AND DANCING THROUGH A DEPRESSION

At the beginning of the 1930s, not only was the country deep into financial chaos but the Hollywood musical faced extinction. The stock market crash of 1929 was the cause of the money woes but the reasons for the decline in musicals were quite different. While the dark shadow of the Depression affected most aspects of life in America during the 1930s, Hollywood enjoyed a Golden Age. The other arts continued on, if on a smaller scale. The number of shows to open on Broadway in the 1930s was noticeably less than the previous decade. The cost of putting on a play or musical was prohibitive, especially when producers had to reduce ticket prices to keep their theaters full. Yet there were many memorable stage productions during the decade, including such notable musicals as *The Band Wagon* (1931), *Of Thee I Sing* (1931), *Anything Goes* (1934), *Porgy and Bess* (1935), *On Your Toes* (1936), *Babes in Arms* (1937), and *The Boys from Syracuse* (1938). Not all of these made money but are today considered classics of the American musical theater. If the Depression took a bite out of Broadway, it swallowed up vaudeville. This form of variety entertainment, which had flourished from the start of the century, experienced a slow death during the Depression. The famous vaudeville circuits, which had included hundreds of theaters across the nation, went out of business and thousands of performers joined the growing ranks of the unemployed. Audiences who had frequented the vaudeville houses turned to cheaper and more accessible entertainment: the movies. Symphony orchestras, dance troupes, and opera companies also suffered in the 1930s, some going bankrupt and others struggling to present even a reduced season of performances.

The darkest days of the Depression were 1931 and 1932. Every day more businesses folded, more people were out of work, and the future looked bleak indeed. A reversal of sorts began when Franklin D. Roosevelt was elected president in 1932 and took office the next year. FDR put an end to the panic if not the hard times. He instituted several work programs, which gave thousands of unemployed Americans jobs building parks, dams, roads, and bridges. In a series of "fireside chats" on the radio, FDR was able to instill a sense of hope in America. His programs took a while to take effect and they could not cure all the ills in the financial crisis but there was some progress. In Europe, where the Depression hit Germany particularly hard, the clouds of war were forming. A civil war in Spain, the rise of Mussolini in Italy, and Hitler's growing military power could not be ignored, yet most Americans were too concerned about domestic cares to worry about other countries. FDR promised his fellow countrymen that the United States would keep out of any war developing in Europe. It was a promise impossible to keep in the next decade. The 1930s ended with optimism and tragedy. In New York, a world's fair demonstrated how the future would be much better. It demonstrated air conditioning, electric typewriters, a modern highway system, 3-D movies, electric razors, the first television broadcasts, and even an early form of the computer. Such hopefulness turned sour on September 1 when Hitler invaded Poland and World War II began.

For many Americans, going to the movies was an escape from the grim reality of their world. Tickets were inexpensive enough that most Americans found the money to go to the local movie house at least once a week. Sitting in the dark they were able to go to a Long Island mansion with frivolous and wealthy people unaware of hard times or to the Land of Oz where goodness and evil were clearly presented. Even a tearful melodrama was soothing to the soul because it offered the chance to enter another world and forget one's own troubles. As one might expect, comedies and musicals were the most popular. But adventure stories, mysteries, westerns, historical dramas, and romances flourished as well. Not only were more movies made in the 1930s than previously or since, the quality of those movies was surprisingly high. In 1939, over two dozen films that we rank as classics opened. That year saw everything from *The Hound of the Baskervilles* and *Gunga Din* to *The Wizard of Oz* and *Gone with the Wind*. No year before or since has seen such a flourish of exceptional filmmaking. As for the movie musicals of the 1930s, they were as varied as they were numerous. Yet at the beginning of the decade it looked like the musical genre was just a passing fad. After the success of the early musicals of the late 1920s, every studio started making musicals. Many of them were made quickly and without much concern for quality. Most used the predictable backstage setting and climaxed with a big show. With so many similar musicals flooding the market, moviegoers got bored and restless. The public, it seemed, was getting tired of the same backstage plot and the same kind of production numbers. Attendance for musicals dropped radically by 1932 and the studios panicked and pulled back on production. Some musicals were released without their songs and sold to moviegoers as comedies or melodramas. Musicals already in production were rewritten as nonmusicals. It looked like the Hollywood musical was just a flash in the pan, a novelty that had worn out its welcome.

Two musicals released in 1933 are credited with saving the Hollywood musical. RKO's *Flying Down to Rio* introduced the dancing team of Fred Astaire and Ginger Rogers as they danced to "The Carioca." Just as importantly, the movie was not stage bound. The big finale of the film involved airplanes loaded with chorus girls standing on the wings and flying over the hotel where the big show was taking place. This was not Broadway staging but a uniquely cinematic way of looking at song and dance. Even more influential was Warner Brothers' *42nd Street* that same year. In some ways it was another routine backstage musical, but the way choreographer Busby Berkeley handled the big production numbers was also uniquely cinematic. Using his camera to do close-ups of chorus girls or shoot a dance from overhead was refreshingly new and not at all what one would find on Broadway. These two musicals gave the genre a shot in the arm. Audiences loved them and wanted more so Hollywood obliged. For the next three decades the movie musical was safe and secure.

Approximately 400 musicals were made during the decade. The glittering backstagers continued to appeal to audiences, but also popular were frontier musicals, nostalgic Americana musicals, animated musicals, and even a few British musicals. Warner Brothers seemed to dominate the genre during the early years of the Depression. This was due to the popularity of its "Gold Digger" musicals. These were backstagers about putting on a Broadway show and usually involved a scheming chorus girl or two who manage to ensnare a wealthy man. All the plots resembled each other but the production numbers, also choreographed by Berkeley, were dazzling. No other series of musicals offered such gleeful excess as Warners' Gold Digger films. Some of them even concerned the Depression and hard times. It was risky to remind moviegoers about such things when they came to see an escapist musical. But the Gold Digger movies were able to pull it off and every entry in the series was a hit at the box office. There were other commendable Warners musicals during the decade and, not surprisingly, they often looked like the Gold Digger musicals. *Footlight Parade* (1933), *Dames* (1934), *Go Into Your Dance* (1935), and *Varsity Show* (1937) were among the most notable.

Child star Shirley Temple single-handedly kept 20th Century Fox afloat during the 1930s with a series of specialty musicals that were audience favorites. More than any other Hollywood personality, Temple offered an optimistic philosophy that was comforting to Depression moviegoers. In musicals such as *Baby Take a Bow* (1934), *Curly Top* (1935), *Poor Little Rich Girl* (1936), and *Rebecca of Sunnybrook Farm* (1938), she demonstrated a lively skill for keeping up America's spirit. It is little wonder that she ended up being the top movie star of the decade. Fox made other musicals during the decade, including such accomplished films as *Thanks a Million* (1935), *King of Burlesque* (1935), *On the Avenue* (1937), and *Alexander's Ragtime Band* (1938). The studio was also starting to feature singers Alice Faye and Betty Grable, who would dominate Fox's musicals in the 1940s. After their sensational debut in *Flying Down to Rio*, Astaire and Rogers continued to keep RKO financially solvent by making seven more musicals together. Such sterling musical romances as *Roberta* (1935), *Top Hat* (1935), *Swing Time* (1936), *Follow the Fleet* (1936), and *Shall We Dance* (1937) have come to represent the romantic musical at its best. With their sleek decor, shimmering costumes, famous songs, and superb dancing, these black-and-white films marked a high point for the Hollywood musical. Every studio wanted its own version of Shirley Temple but none succeeded. RKO came close with the boy singer Bobby Breen, who sang like a bird and also managed to tug on America's heartstrings. Though not nearly as popular as Temple, Breen's seven films in the 1930s were very successful, in particular *Let's Sing Again* (1936), *Rainbow on the River* (1936), *Make a Wish* (1937), *Hawaii Calls* (1938), and *Fisherman's Wharf* (1939). Also, RKO made a wise decision when it agreed to distribute Walt Disney's feature-length animated musical. Most of Hollywood scoffed at the idea but *Snow White and the Seven Dwarfs* (1937) ended up being one of the most profitable movies of the decade.

By 1936 MGM became the most prolific and prestigious of the Hollywood studios but its Golden Age for musicals didn't come until the 1940s and 1950s. All the same, there were some superior MGM musicals in the 1930s, including *Going Hollywood* (1933), *The Merry Widow* (1934), *A Night at the Opera* (1935), *The Great Ziegfeld* (1936), *San Francisco* (1936), *Born to Dance* (1936), *The Wizard of Oz* (1939), and *Babes in Arms* (1939). MGM struck gold when it teamed singers Jeanette MacDonald and Nelson Eddy together in *Naughty Marietta* (1935). The musical was a surprise hit and launched a series of operetta films starring the duo. Among the most memorable of their seven subsequent movies together were *Rose Marie* (1936), *Maytime* (1937), *Sweethearts* (1938), *New Moon* (1940), *Bitter Sweet* (1940), and *I Married an Angel* (1942). Even studios not particularly known for making musicals came up with some classics in the 1930s, such as Universal, which produced one of the finest of all 1930s musicals, *Show Boat* (1936). Universal also had a leading musical star in the teenager singer Deanna Durbin. After she shone in *Three Smart Girls* (1936), the studio starred her in a series of musicals in which she played spunky teens and sang popular and classical selections in her crystal-clear soprano voice. Among her most successful 1930s films were *One Hundred Men and a Girl* (1937), *Mad About Music* (1938), *That Certain Age* (1938), and *First Love* (1939). Her limited but impressive screen career carried into the 1940s.

Other studios that were somewhat reluctant to embark on musical movies in the 1920s surprised themselves by producing many such films in the 1930s. United

Artists, for example, presented such first-class movies as *Whoopee!* (1930), *Hallelujah, I'm a Bum* (1933), *Kid Millions* (1934), and *The Goldwyn Follies* (1938). Paramount was prompted to put more money into musicals after its *The Big Broadcast* (1932) was so successful. The public's fascination with radio and radio stars led to a series of "Big Broadcast of" musicals by Paramount. Also, the studio signed young singer Bing Crosby to the studio early in the decade and it paid off tenfold with such popular Crosby musicals as *We're Not Dressing* (1934), *Mississippi* (1935), *Anything Goes* (1936), *Double or Nothing* (1937), and *Sing You Sinners* (1938). Paramount also offered such splendid (and diverse) 1930s musicals as *Paramount on Parade* (1930), *Monte Carlo* (1930), *One Hour with You* (1932), *Love Me Tonight* (1932), *The Phantom President* (1932), *Duck Soup* (1933), *Murder at the Vanities* (1934), *Every Night at Eight* (1935), *High, Wide and Handsome* (1937), *Artists and Models* (1937), *St. Louis Blues* (1938), and *Man About Town* (1939). Great Britain produced many movie musicals in the 1930s as well, though few were shown in the United States and even fewer found an audience here. The notable exception was the delightful *Evergreen* (1934) featuring England's favorite singing-dancing star, Jessie Matthews. All in all, it was a robust and exciting decade for the movie musical.

WHOOPEE!

Studio and release date: Goldwyn/United Artists; September 1930
Producers: Samuel Goldman, Florenz Ziegfeld
Screenplay: William Conselman, based on the 1928 stage script by William Anthony McGuire, which was based on the play *The Nervous Wreck* by Owen Davis
Songwriters: Walter Donaldson (music), Gus Kahn (lyrics)
Director: Thornton Freeland
Music Director: Alfred Newman
Choreographer: Busby Berkeley
Cinematographers: Lee Garmes, Ray Rennahan, Gregg Toland
Cast: Eddie Cantor, Paul Gregory, Eleanor Hunt, Ethel Shutta, John Rutherford, Chief Caupolican, Betty Grable, Spencer Charters
Songs: "Makin' Whoopee"; "My Baby Just Cares for Me"; "I'll Still Belong to You"; "Stetson"; "Cowboy Number"; "A Girl Friend of a Boy Friend of Mine"; "Song of the Setting Sun"

While not nearly as much fun as the 1928 Broadway hit, *Whoopee!* on the screen was filled with delightful performances and some innovative camerawork. Comic Eddie Cantor had one of his greatest stage triumphed in the Broadway hit *Whoopee!* Cantor was a short, singing comic known for his big eyes that seemed to pop out,

Eddie Cantor (1892–1964)   A distinctive American comic of stage and screen, he was recognized by his skipping, leering personality and rolling his "banjo" eyes as he sang suggestive lyrics. Cantor was born in Manhattan's Lower East Side, the son of Russian immigrants who died when he was a child. By the age of 15 he was performing on vaudeville stages across America and in England. Cantor made his Broadway debut in Florenz Ziegfeld's *The Midnight Frolic* (1917), and the cartoonish little comic went over so well he was featured in five editions of the *Ziegfeld Follies* and introduced several song standards. His other Broadway musicals include *Whoopee!* (1928), *Make It Snappy* (1922), *Kid Boots* (1923), and *Banjo Eyes* (1941). When Cantor reprised his stage performance in the 1930 film version of *Whoopee!* his screen career was launched and he played comic heroes in such musicals as *Palmy Days* (1931), *The Kid from Spain* (1932), *Roman Scandals* (1933), *Kid Millions* (1934), *Strike Me Pink* (1936), *Ali Baba Goes to Town* (1937), and *Forty Little Mothers* (1940). He played himself or Cantor-like roles in *Thank Your Lucky Stars* (1943), *Hollywood Canteen* (1944), *Show Business* (1944), *If You Knew Susie* (1948), and *The Story of Will Rogers* (1952) as well as providing the singing vocals for Keefe Brasselle in *The Eddie Cantor Story* (1953). He was also very popular on the radio in the 1930s, and he had his own television show in the 1950s. Autobiographies: *My Life in Your Hands* (1928); *Take My Life* (1957); *The Way I See It* (1959); *As I Remember Them* (1962); biography: *Banjo Eyes: Eddie Cantor and the Birth of Modern Stardom,* Herbert G. Goldman (1997).

his leering grin, and his bouncy athletics when he sang and danced. He had been in vaudeville for two decades before he got one of his best roles as the hypochondriac Henry Williams in *Whoopee!* The show's producer, Florenz Ziegfeld, who had lost all his money in the stock market crash of 1929, sold the movie rights to Samuel Goldwyn on the condition that Ziegfeld serve as coproducer of the film. In this capacity, Ziegfeld was able to see that the film version was relatively faithful to the stage work. He also insisted that Cantor reprise his stage performance on-screen even though the comic had not come across very well in three previous films. The result was a musical that made Cantor a Hollywood star and *Whoopee!* one of the most popular movies of the year.

Much of the stage plot made it to the screen. Neurotic Henry leaves the East Coast and settles in the wilds of California for health reasons. But his nerves fall apart when he gets involved with the local tribe, the damsel Sally Morgan (Eleanor Hunt) on the run from an amorous sheriff (Jack Rutherford), and other Wild

Betty Grable (1916–1973)   A blonde singer-dancer who was queen of Technicolor musicals in the 1940s, she was the American GI's favorite pinup girl during World War II. She was born in St. Louis and began dance lessons at the age of three. Her ambitious stage mother brought her 13-year-old daughter to Hollywood in 1930 and, lying about the girl's age, got her cast in the chorus or in minor roles in 30 movie musicals before finding fame in *Down Argentine Way* (1940). The leggy star managed to remain popular throughout the war years and into the 1950s with such musicals as *Tin Pan Alley* (1940), *Moon Over Miami* (1941), *Springtime in the Rockies* (1942), *Coney Island* (1943), *Four Jills in a Jeep* (1944), *Pin-Up Girl* (1944), *The Dolly Sisters* (1945), *The Shocking Miss Pilgrim* (1947), *Mother Wore Tights* (1947), *Wabash Avenue* (1950), *Call Me Mister* (1951), and *The Farmer Takes a Wife* (1953). Grable also made many nonmusical films and appeared on Broadway and in nightclubs before her premature death from lung cancer. Admired for her feisty screen characters and chipper singing voice, she was most known for her shapely legs, which 20th Century Fox insured for $1 million in a crafty publicity stunt. Biographies: *Betty Grable: The Girl with the Million Dollar Legs,* Tom McGee (1995); *Betty Grable: The Reluctant Movie Queen,* Doug Warren (1981).

West antics. Adding to the fun was Henry's wisecracking nurse, Mary (Ethel Shutta), who loved Henry and was not shy about chasing him across the desert. The thin plot stopped frequently to allow Cantor to do one of his comic bits or sing a song in his own distinctive way. The Broadway score by Walter Donaldson (music) and Gus Kahn (lyrics) was mostly cut for the film but it did have two of the best stage songs, the suggestive "Makin' Whoopee" and the cowboy ditty "Stetson." Added to the screen score was the daffy, romantic "My Baby Just Cares for Me," which Cantor sang as a black-faced waiter trying to escape from his many pursuers. (The show's famous torch song "Love Me or Leave" was sung by Ruth Etting on Broadway; both the song and Etting were not used in the film version.) Just as important as the songs themselves was the way in which they were presented on-screen. Thornton Freeland was the director but it was Broadway choreographer Busby Berkeley, in his film debut, who changed the way musical numbers were filmed in Hollywood. Berkeley promised Goldwyn that he would break away from the static way production numbers in movie musicals were usually filmed. He made good on his claim, getting rid of multiple cameras so that each number had one specific point of view, filming the chorus girls in close-up for the first time, and putting the camera overhead and creating the first of his famous kaleidoscope shots of women making geometric patterns. "Stetson," for example, was ingeniously filmed by Berkeley with the girls popping up in front of the camera sporting cow-boy hats. For the "Cowboy Number," the camera captured Betty Grable and the chorus from above, the girls' native headdresses swirling in an almost surreal pat-tern. Also innovative about *Whoopee!* was a new two-color Technicolor process that was impressive then and remains so today. Few early color films have sur-vived but *Whoopee!* illustrates how effective the early color process was.

Because *Whoopee!* was fairly faithful to the stage work and much of the Broad-way cast was used in the film, the movie is of historic importance as a record of a 1920s Broadway musical. At the same time, *Whoopee!* is more than a filmed ver-sion of a stage piece. It is cinematic in its attitude and a breakthrough in the approach Hollywood would take in putting Broadway shows on-screen. The studios soon learned that what worked in a Broadway theater was not necessarily the best way to put it on-screen. This led to a rather superior attitude that Holly-wood took in later years, buying Broadway hits then decimating the scores, reject-ing the stage stars, and sometimes altering the original beyond recognition. But on occasion the changes the studios made worked and *Whoopee!* is one of those cases.

See also: Eddie Cantor, Busby Berkeley, Betty Grable biography boxes

FURTHER READING

Bloom, Ken. *Hollywood Musicals: The 101 Greatest Song-and-Dance Movies of All Time*. New York: Black Dog and Leventhal, 2010.
Grant, Barry Keith. *The Hollywood Film Musical*. Hoboken, NJ: Wiley-Blackwell, 2012.
Spivak, Jeffrey. *Buzz: The Life and Art of Busby Berkeley*. Lexington: University Press of Ken-tucky, 2010.

LOVE ME TONIGHT

Studio and release date: Paramount; August 1932
Producer: Rouben Mamoulian
Screenplay: Samuel Hoffenstein, Waldemar Young, George Marion, Jr., based on the play *Tailor in the Chateau* by Leopold Marchand, Paul Armont
Songwriters: Richard Rodgers (music), Lorenz Hart (lyrics)
Director: Rouben Mamoulian
Music Director: Nathaniel Finston
Cinematographer: Victor Milner
Cast: Maurice Chevalier, Jeanette MacDonald, Charles Ruggles, Myrna Loy, C. Aubrey Smith, Charles Butterworth, Elizabeth Patterson, Ethel Griffies

Principal Songs: "Isn't It Romantic?"; "Lover"; "Mimi"; "That's the Song of Paree"; "Love Me Tonight"; "A Woman Needs Something Like That"; "The Son of a Gun Is Nothing But a Tailor"; "The Poor Apache"

Arguably the finest film score by songwriters Richard Rodgers (music) and Lorenz Hart (lyrics) can be found in this sophisticated musical fairy tale for adults. Rodgers and Hart were the toast of Broadway from the late 1920s into the early 1940s with over a dozen hit musicals and many popular songs that became standards. When the Depression hit and fewer Broadway musicals were produced in the 1930s, Rodgers and Hart were persuaded by Hollywood's big money to go West and write songs for the movies. The studios did not treat songwriters with the same kind of respect that they got on Broadway and most stage songwriters were not happy in Hollywood. Neither were Rodgers and Hart, yet they turned out a handful of superior scores that were often as innovative as they were pleasing. *Love Me Tonight* is not only a cinema masterwork but a landmark film in the way it blended song, background music, character, plot, camerawork, and editing in an enchanting manner never seen before and only rarely accomplished since. Much of the credit must go to producer-director Rouben Mamoulian who broke new ground in finding cinematic ways to present a musical tale. Yet one cannot underestimate the Rodgers and Hart score, which was just as ingenious.

The plot, based on a little-known French play, concerned the Paris tailor Maurice Courtelin (Maurice Chevalier) who follows the Vicomte de Vareze (Charles Ruggles) to his country chateau to collect an unpaid debt. When he arrives, Maurice is mistaken for a baron and, after rescuing the haughty Princess Jeanette (Jeanette MacDonald) from a runaway carriage, falls in love with her. The princess' man-hungry friend Countess Valentine (Myrna Loy) suspects that Maurice is not a baron but she is too busy chasing after him to give him away. When everyone at the chateau finds out the truth about Maurice's lowly social position, he boards the first train back to Paris. Jeannette chases after him on horseback, bravely stands in front of the oncoming train to stop it, and claims her lover regardless of rank. Although this was not the first pairing of MacDonald and Chevalier in a film musical, *Love Me Tonight* provided them with the team's best score. The delightful Rodgers and Hart songs are so tightly woven into the witty story line that the movie sometimes resembles a cockeyed operetta that bounces along in a slaphappy manner. Often Rodgers and Hart's rhythmic dialogue led into and out of songs, also adding to the operetta flavor. Yet such hits as the rhapsodic "Lover," the suggestive "Mimi," the funny-romantic "Isn't It Romantic?", and the gushing title number all became song standards outside of the movie. The clever ways Mamoulian moved the camera to comment on the action made the songs even more fun. MacDonald sang the operatic "Lover" as she bounced along in a carriage, the music rising and falling with her movements. Leering Chevalier delivered "Mimi" to MacDonald but as filmed he delivered most of

Maurice Chevalier (1888–1972)   A French entertainer who usually played charming dandies on the screen, he was very popular in Europe and America. He was born in poverty in Paris and as a child worked in a factory and then as a teenager performed as an acrobat onstage. During World War I, Chevalier spent time in a German prisoner-of-war camp and learned his broken English from the British soldiers. He first became popular in Paris cafes and then was the star of the famous *Folies Bergere*. Chevalier made a few films in France but it was his Hollywood debut in *Innocents of Paris* (1929) that made him an international star. His other musical films of the period were *The Love Parade* (1929), *Paramount on Parade* (1930), *The Big Pond* (1930), *The Smiling Lieutenant* (1931), *One Hour With You* (1932), *Love Me Tonight* (1932), *The Merry Widow* (1934), and *Folies Bergere* (1935). Chevalier left films in the 1940s and concentrated on concerts, nightclubs, and, later, television specials. He made a triumphal return to the musical screen in *Gigi* (1958) and was featured in the film musicals *Can-Can* (1960), *Pepe* (1960), *Jessica* (1962), and *I'd Rather Be Rich* (1964), as well as lending his voice to the animated *The Aristocats* (1970). Chevalier was a unique talent in that he always played himself in every role he played, much to the pleasure of his many fans. Autobiographies: *The Man in the Straw Hat* (1949), *With Love* (1960), *I Remember It Well* (1970); biography: *Maurice Chevalier*, David Bret (2003).

it to her horse. A deer hunt in the woods became a slow-motion ballet of people, horses, and stags. Perhaps the most memorable of the many thrilling sequences was near the opening of the film in which the song "Isn't It Romantic?" was used to introduce characters and propel the movie forward. The song was first sung by tailor Chevalier on a Paris street, then was picked up by a whistling taxi driver who is driving a composer to a train station. The composer jots the melody down on paper before they arrive at the station. The song continued on a train that passed by a marching regiment of soldiers who then sang it. When they pass by the Vicomte's chateau, the princess MacDonald hears the song and sings it as well. Although they are miles apart, the story's two lovers are musically linked even before they meet. Among the other treats that Mamoulian employed in *Love Me Tonight* was the use of a zoom lens in certain scenes, one of the first times that cinema technique shows up in a Hollywood movie.

While the entire cast of the musical is excellent, including wonderful character parts led by Charles Ruggles and Myrna Loy, it is the unusual chemistry between MacDonald and Chevalier that holds much of the movie together. His French accent and wide grin that is both silly and sexy are matched by her innocent but knowing attitude and forceful delivery of the high notes. The twosome made only four movies together and this chemistry is evident in them all. Oddly, MacDonald became even more beloved for her eight musicals with Nelson Eddy and rarely was there such chemistry in any of them. That is why such gems as *Love Me Tonight* are so fondly remembered by so many moviegoers.

See also: Hallelujah, I'm a Bum; Maurice Chevalier, Jeanette MacDonald, Richard Rodgers biography boxes

FURTHER READING

Eames, John Douglas. *The Paramount Story*. New York: Crown Publishers, 1985.
Hirschhorn, Clive. *The Hollywood Musical*. 2nd ed. New York: Crown Publishers, 1983.
Spergel, Mark. *Reinventing Reality: The Art and Life of Rouben Mamoulian*. Lanham, MD: Scarecrow Press, 1993.

HALLELUJAH, I'M A BUM

Studio and release date: United Artists; January 1933
Producer: Joseph M. Schenck
Screenplay: S. N. Behrman
Songwriters: Richard Rodgers (music), Lorenz Hart (lyrics)
Director: Lewis Milestone
Music Director: Alfred Newman
Cinematographer: Lucien Andriot
Cast: Al Jolson, Madge Evans, Frank Morgan, Chester Conklin, Harry Langdon, Edgar Connor
Principal Songs: "You Are Too Beautiful"; "Hallelujah, I'm a Bum"; "My Pal Bumper"; "What Do You Want with Money?"; "I Gotta Get Back to New York"; "Bumper Found a Grand"; "Dear June"

Al Jolson, Hollywood's first musical star, got his most demanding screen role in this unusual movie, and he gave a low-key but heartbreaking performance with none of the gushing he often used when singing "Mammy" songs. Yet *Hallelujah, I'm a Bum* was perhaps too unusual and reminded audiences too much of the current Depression to become popular, and it took many years before the musical was recognized as a Hollywood classic. Today's audiences marvel at the distinctive look of the film, its cockeyed use of rhymed dialogue, and its freewheeling spirit that seems far ahead of its time.

The bittersweet tale centers on the many homeless in the Depression who lived in Central Park. When New York City mayor John Hastings (Frank Morgan) has a quarrel with his fiancée June Marcher (Madge Evans), she tries to commit suicide by jumping off a bridge in the park. She is rescued by Bumper (Jolson), a tramp in the park who rules as "mayor" of the homeless. Both mayors are acquaintances of each other and actually respect each other's position. June suffers from amnesia and cannot recall her past and she and Bumper fall in love. He finds out that she is Hastings' girl yet he does not interfere in reuniting the two. Bumper is heartbroken when June regains her memory and she leaves him for the real mayor. He returns to his fellow hobos, his buoyant spirit strong as ever. The songs by Richard Rodgers (music) and Lorenz Hart (lyrics) had extended sections of rhythmic dialogue so the movie often sounded like a comic-romantic operetta. Yet this was far from the usual operetta escapism. Jolson got to sing "You Are Too Beautiful" to Evans, a restrained ballad that he delivered with perfection. Other numbers included the sly "What Do You Want With Money?," the jovial "I've Got to Get Back to New York," and the philosophical title song that had to be recorded twice—the word "tramp" substituted for the England release because "bum" refers to buttocks in British slang. (The musical was retitled *Hallelujah, I'm a Tramp* in Great Britain.) The sterling supporting cast included the great silent comic Harry Langdon and the marvelous African American character actor Edgar Connor. Lewis Milestone directed with a semidocumentary look and feel that is still impressive.

Hallelujah, I'm a Bum was an expensive movie to make because of Jolson's hefty salary ($25,000 a week) and the last-minute casting of Morgan, who also demanded a top salary. Also expensive was the need to film dialogue and songs twice, one version using the word "bum" and the other with the substitute "tramp." Yet what appears on the screen is a small movie with little spectacle or glamour. Moviegoers wishing to escape the Depression were not comforted by this stylized view of poverty and acceptance of bad times. There was also something anti-American about Bumper and his friends who ignored the system and survived nicely all the same. It would be decades before such an attitude was thought to be appealing. In the same year as *Hallelujah, I'm a Bum* there was another unconventional musical scored by Rodgers and Hart, *The Phantom President*. It also starred a beloved Broadway star, George M. Cohan, and again rhymed dialogue and song were used to tell a story about politics. It also was a box office failure despite a commanding performance by Cohan and an innovative score. It seemed that Depression audiences preferred to see aristocratic people wearing lovely clothes in lavish settings on the screen, particularly in musicals. Being reminded of the Depression was a sure sign of failure, though Warner Brothers soon found a way to mix Depression angst with Tinseltown glamour in its *Gold Digger* musicals, exemplified by *Gold*

Diggers of 1933. Today's audience finds both kinds of 1930s musicals enjoyable, either as nostalgia for a past America or for their downright silliness. Oddball movie musicals like *Hallelujah, I'm a Bum* may have been box office failures but they were triumphs in inventive musical filmmaking.

See also: *Gold Diggers of 1933;* Al Jolson, Richard Rodgers biography boxes

FURTHER READING

Balio, Tino. *United Artists.* Madison: University of Wisconsin Press, 1976.
Freedland, Michael. *Jolson: The Story of Al Jolson.* London: Virgin Books, 1995.
Grant, Barry Keith. *The Hollywood Film Musical.* Hoboken, NJ: Wiley-Blackwell, 2012.

42nd STREET

Studio and release date: Warner Brothers; February 1933
Producer: Darryl F. Zanuck
Screenplay: James Seymour, Rian James, based on the novel by Bradford Ropes
Songwriters: Harry Warren (music), Al Dubin (lyrics)
Director: Lloyd Bacon, Mervyn LeRoy (uncredited)
Choreographer: Busby Berkeley
Music Director: Leo F. Forbstein
Cinematographer: Sol Polito
Cast: Warner Baxter, Ruby Keeler, Bebe Daniels, Dick Powell, George Brent, Ginger Rogers, Una Merkel, Guy Kibbee
Songs: "Forty-Second Street"; "Shuffle Off to Buffalo"; "You're Getting to Be a Habit with Me"; "Young and Healthy"

Perhaps no other single movie played such a pivotal role in the history of the musical film, because *42nd Street* revitalized the genre after two years of declining interest by the moviegoing public. It is also the ultimate backstager and almost every aspect of *42nd Street* later became a cliché from overuse in later movies and stage works. The film is based on a tough and uncompromising novel by Bradford Ropes. In the novel, the homosexual director Julian Marsh lives with the young actor Tommy Lawlor and puts him in the leading male role of his new Broadway musical *Pretty Baby* starring the veteran, alcoholic star Dorothy Brock. When Brock is jilted by her lover Pat Denning, Dorothy gets so drunk she falls down a staircase and breaks her leg. Without a leading lady, it looks like *Pretty Lady* will not open on Broadway. Then Tommy recommends that the unknown

The quintessential backstage musical, *42nd Street* was often tough and even gritty in its characters and dialogue. In this scene, the Broadway producer Julian Marsh (Warner Baxter, right center) has some harsh words for the chorus girls in his latest show. His assistant Andy (George E. Stone, center left) is also a strict taskmaster. Also pictured are Ruby Keeler (second from the left) and Ginger Rogers (fifth from the right). (Warner Bros./Photofest)

chorus girl Peggy Sawyer from Maine take Dorothy's place. Peggy goes on, becomes a star, and is soon acting as temperamental and difficult as Dorothy. This was an unsentimental view of show business and much of the story could not be filmed in 1933. Yet the Warner Brothers musical managed to be tough and sarcastic even as the characters were softened and the ending was more upbeat. In the screenplay by Rian James and James Seymour, Julian Marsh (Warner Baxter) is a moody producer who has lost all his money in the stock market crash. The money for *Pretty Lady* comes from wealthy Abner Dillon (Guy Kibbee), and the Broadway star Dorothy Brock (Bebe Daniels) is the box office draw. The innocent Peggy Sawyer (Ruby Keeler) from Sioux City, Iowa, comes to New York to be on Broadway and is cast in the chorus. Peggy befriends dancer-singer Billy Lawlor (Dick Powell) and chorus girl "Anytime" Annie (Ginger Rogers) who rehearse with her and soon realize she has a lot of talent. When Dorothy gets drunk and breaks her ankle, the backer Dillon insists that his girlfriend Annie take over the lead, but Annie convinces Julian that Peggy is the girl to save the show. After Julian tells Peggy, "Sawyer, you're going out a youngster, but you've got to come back a star," she plays the lead in *Pretty Lady* and indeed becomes a star. As everyone celebrates, the loner Julian sits in the alley and quietly smokes his cigarette.

42nd Street didn't look like the many Hollywood musicals that had been glutting the market in the preceding few years. Busby Berkeley's choreography did not recall a Broadway staging at all; his use of the camera to follow individuals in a production number or to view performers from angles not possible in a theater made the film a true Hollywood musical rather than a film of a stage-like show. Lloyd Bacon directed briskly and there is a fast-paced urgency in the film that comes across in the rapid, wisecracking dialogue as well as in the production numbers. It was Keeler's first sizable part on-screen, and the movie made her a bigger star than "Peggy Sawyer." The movie was the first of 23 films scored by Harry Warren (music) and Al Dubin (lyrics), the songwriters most associated with Warner Brothers musicals. Although they wrote only four songs for the movie, it can be considered their masterwork for it captures both the anxiety and carefree abandon of the Depression. The spirited "Young and Healthy" is full of optimism, there is a plaintive matter-of-fact quality in "You're Getting to Be a Habit with Me," a slyness creeps into "Shuffle Off to Buffalo," and there is something downright sinister about the joyful decadence of the title number. This last number was staged by Berkeley as a mini-musical in which the hedonistic life of a flapper was followed from dawn to midnight when she falls to her death during a wild party in a high-rise apartment. Depression audiences loved both the gritty texture of *42nd Street* as well as its escapism, and the score reflects this. The success of the movie prompted Warner Brothers to produce a series of similar backstagers with Berkeley creating more elaborate showpieces with each film. Few in the series would match the overall impact of *42nd Street* but it would be a golden age for the ridiculously joyous backstage movie musical.

When many of the 1930s Warner Brothers musicals were rediscovered by arthouse audiences in the 1960s, *42nd Street* stood out as a classic, and today it is considered the quintessential Warners musical and the granddaddy of all backstage musicals. In 1980, Broadway producer David Merrick presented a lavish stage version of *42nd Street* and it too was a hit. Much of the tough quality of the movie was lost and the characters were not as well defined because much of the show was spectacular production numbers. Songs by Warren and Dubin from other Warner Brothers films were added to the score so the show was a musical and visual feast. Also memorable was the direction and choreography by Gower Champion. *42nd Street* ran over four years on Broadway, was successfully revived in 2001, and is often produced by various theater groups.

Busby Berkeley (1895–1976)   A former Broadway choreographer-director who began working in Hollywood in 1930, he redefined the art of filming musical numbers. He was born in Los Angeles, the son of a stage director and a film actress, and moved with his family to New York City when he was three years old. He was on the stage as a youth, later performing in stock and in small roles on Broadway before turning to choreography in the 1920s. Berkeley did the dances for several Broadway shows before *Whoopee!* (1928) was turned into a film and he went to Hollywood to restage his dances. Instead of repeating the same stage choreography, Berkeley rethought each number in a cinematic way, using one camera to focus on one aspect of the dance. He created similar effects for such screen musicals as *The Kid from Spain* (1932), *42nd Street* (1933), *Gold Diggers of 1933*, *Footlight Parade* (1933), *Roman Scandals* (1933), *Wonder Bar* (1934), and *Dames* (1934). Starting with *Gold Diggers of 1935*, Berkeley sometimes also directed, doing both jobs for such musicals as *Hollywood Hotel* (1937), *Babes in Arms* (1939), *Strike Up the Band* (1940), *Babes on Broadway* (1941), *For Me and My Gal* (1942), *The Gang's All Here* (1943), and *Take Me Out to the Ball Game* (1949). Among the many other movie musicals he worked on are *Go Into Your Dance* (1935), *In Caliente* (1935), *The Singing Marine* (1937), *Gold Diggers in Paris* (1938), *Ziegfeld Girl* (1941), *Lady, Be Good* (1941), *Cabin in the Sky* (1943), *Girl Crazy* (1943), *Romance on the High Sea*s (1948), *Call Me Mister* (1951), *Million Dollar Mermaid* (1952), *Small Town Girl* (1953), *Rose Marie* (1954), and *Jumbo* (1962). Biography: *Showstoppers: Busby Berkeley and the Tradition of Spectacle*, Martin Rubin (1993).

See also: *Footlight Parade, Born to Dance*; Busby Berkeley, Dick Powell, and Al Dubin and Harry Warren biography boxes

FURTHER READING

Bloom, Ken. *Hollywood Musicals: The 101 Greatest Song-and-Dance Movies of All Time*. New York: Black Dog and Leventhal, 2010.

Hoberman, J. *42nd Street*. (BFI Film Classics). London: British Film Institute, 1993.

Spivak, Jeffrey. *Buzz: The Life and Art of Busby Berkeley*. Lexington: University Press of Kentucky, 2010.

Thomas, Tony. *Harry Warren and the Hollywood Musical*. New York: Lyle Stuart, Inc., 1975.

GOLD DIGGERS OF 1933

Studio and release date: Warner Brothers; May 1933
Producer: Hal B. Wallis
Screenplay: Erwin Gelsey, James Seymour, David Boehm, Ben Markson, based on the 1919 play *The Gold Diggers* by Avery Hopwood
Songwriters: Harry Warren (music), Al Dubin (lyrics)
Director: Mervyn LeRoy
Choreographer: Busby Berkeley
Musical Director: Leo F. Forbstein
Cinematographer: Sol Polito
Cast: William Warren, Joan Blondell, Ruby Keeler, Dick Powell, Aline MacMahon, Ginger Rogers, Guy Kibbee, Ned Sparks, Sterling Holloway
Principal Songs: "We're in the Money"; "Shadow Waltz"; "Pettin' in the Park"; "Remember My Forgotten Man"; "I've Got to Sing a Torch Song"

Warner Brothers' most successful series of musicals in the 1930s, the *Gold Digger* films, reach some kind of crazy climax in this 1933 musical, which managed to mix the tough reality of the Depression with the escapist magic of the musical genre. The series started in 1929 with *Gold Diggers of Broadway*, a musical based on a play and a silent film. A "gold digger" was an old expression for an enterprising girl (usually a chorus line beauty) who snags a rich husband. The original story centered on three chorus girls (Winnie Lightner, Nancy Welford, and Ann Pennington) who trick a Boston snob (Conway Tearle) who comes to New York into paying off the gold digger who is after his nephew. After a night on the town, during which the stuffy uncle is put in a compromising position, all ends happily as each girl gets the guy of her choice. The first film in the series was far from the best but it did offer two songs by Joe Burke (music) and Al Dubin (lyrics), "Tip Toe Through the Tulips" and "Painting the Clouds with Sunshine," which became popular. *Gold Diggers of Broadway* was successful enough at the box office that sequels were planned, but by 1930 there were too many mediocre movie musicals being released and the public's interest in the genre was declining. It was the success of *42nd Street* (1933) that prompted Warner Brothers to make *Gold Diggers of 1933*, generally considered the best in the series. In fact, the sequel was going to be a nonmusical but after the terrific score Harry Warren (music) and Al Dubin (lyrics) wrote for *42nd Street*, they were hired to write songs for *Gold Diggers of 1933*.

The thin plot dealt with backstage again but this time it was Broadway during the depths of the Depression. The film was one of the few musicals to deal with the economic condition that had so affected audiences watching the movie. Some of the 1929 plot remained with Ginger Rogers, Joan Blondell, Ruby Keeler, and Aline MacMahon as chorus girls whose show is closed down in rehearsal because the producer (Ned Sparks) has run out of money. Their neighbor, the struggling song-writer Brad Roberts (Dick Powell), is a millionaire in disguise so he not only writes the songs for the show but bankrolls it himself. On opening night the leading man cannot go on so Brad fills in with his sweetheart Polly Parker (Keeler) as his costar. But Brad's snobbish family finds out about the show and Polly and they threaten to cut him off without a cent. The couple is helped by the fellow chorines, who trick Brad's dour brother Lawrence (William Warren) into a compromising position and all ends well for Polly and her gold digger friends. If the plot was sus-piciously close to that of *42nd Street*, it was no accident. In fact, much of the cast of that movie, along with much of the artistic staff, were reunited for *Gold Diggers of 1933*. With such an already familiar plot, more emphasis was put on the pro-duction numbers, and choreographer Busby Berkeley turned each one of the songs into a visual as well as a musical feast. Rogers and the chorines were dressed in outfits made of coins for the optimistic "We're in the Money"; lovers cuddled and kissed in "Pettin' in the Park" until a sudden thunder shower sent the girls scurry-ing for cover and they were shown changing out of their wet clothes in silhouette; and violin-playing chorus girls formed patterns and even glowed in the dark for "The Shadow Waltz." The finale was a tribute to war veterans out of a job during the Depression. As Etta Moten and Blondell sang "Remember My Forgotten Man," flashbacks of soldiers marching off to war dissolved into scenes of the same men now in bread lines. It was musical comedy at its most socially conscious and yet was still enormously entertaining.

The rest of the *Gold Digger* series was entertaining if not inspired. The Broad-way backstage locale was abandoned for *Gold Diggers of 1935*, which was both directed and choreographed by Berkeley. The musical was set in a New Hamp-shire summer resort where the gold digging is done by a Russian con man (Adol-phe Menjou) who is trying to fleece a society matron (Alice Brady). At the same time a secretary (Glenda Farrell) is blackmailing a wealthy snuff box collector (Hugh Herbert), and a struggling medical student (Dick Powell) is falling in love with an heiress (Gloria Stuart). The songs were again by Warren and Dubin and it was the large production numbers that counted, such as having 56 pianos played by 56 girls for "The Words Are in My Heart," the pianos moving about to create designs and patterns. The "Lullaby of Broadway" sequence was the most ambitious. It was a narrative ballet that showed 24 hours in the life of a carefree New York cho-rus girl. A long shot of Winifred Shaw's face grew from a distant speck of light into a facial close-up that dissolved into the Manhattan skyline. What followed was a montage of the city's nightlife that climaxed with the chorine being pushed out a window to her death. It is perhaps Berkeley's most dramatic film sequence and relied on precision dancing and dynamic camerawork rather than gimmicks.

Character actress Joan Blondell finally got to play the leading lady in *Gold Diggers of 1937* (1936). An insurance salesman (Dick Powell) tries to sell a

Al Dubin and **Harry Warren**   One of Hollywood's most successful song-writing team, they are unusual in that they wrote mostly for the movies rather than the stage or Tin Pan Alley. Composer Warren (1893–1981) was born in Brooklyn and began his career as a drummer in a carnival band. After providing songs for a few Broadway shows, he went to Hollywood where he teamed up with lyricist Dubin and began a long and fabled career in the movies. Dubin (1891–1945) was born in Zurich, Switzerland, and emigrated to America with his family two years later. He worked for different music publishers in New York and contributed songs to a few Broadway musicals before heading West where he first wrote film songs with composer Joe Burke. It was his collaboration with Warren that led to a successful string of movie musicals with memorable scores, including *Gold Diggers of 1933*, *Footlight Parade* (1933), *Roman Scandals* (1933), *Moulin Rouge* (1934), *Wonder Bar* (1934), *Dames* (1934), *Gold Diggers of 1935*, *Go Into Your Dance* (1935), *Colleen* (1936), *Gold Diggers of 1937* (1936), *The Singing Marine* (1937), *Gold Diggers in Paris* (1938), and *Garden of the Moon* (1938). After Dubin's premature death, Warren wrote with various lyricists, turning out hit songs decade after decade. Among his many later film musicals scored with various lyricists were *Down Argentine Way* (1940), *That Night in Rio* (1941), *Sun Valley Serenade* (1941), *Weekend in Havana* (1941), *Orchestra Wives* (1942), *Iceland* (1942), *Springtime in the Rockies* (1942), *The Gang's All Here* (1943), *Yolanda and the Thief* (1945), *Ziegfeld Follies* (1946), *The Harvey Girls* (1946), *The Barkleys of Broadway* (1949), *Summer Stock* (1950), *The Belle of New York* (1952), *The Caddy* (1953), *Artists and Models* (1955), *Cinderfella* (1960), and *Ladies Man* (1961). Biographies: *Harry Warren and the Hollywood Musical*, Tony Thomas (1975); *Lullaby of Broadway: The Life of Al Dubin*, Patricia Dubin McGuire [his daughter] (1983).

theatrical producer (Victor Moore) a huge policy so that his cronies could have enough money to produce a Broadway show after he dies. The old man continues to live but the show goes on anyway, featuring a military finale, "All's Fair in Love and War" by Warren and Dubin, in which Blondell led dozens of goose-stepping chorus girls in a battle of the sexes. The same songwriters also came up with the catchy "With Plenty of Money and You," while Harold Arlen (music) and E. Y. Harburg (lyrics) wrote "Let's Put Our Heads Together," which 50 couples sang as they rocked to the rhythm of the music in giant rocking chairs. The popular series ended with *Gold Diggers of Paris* (1938), a less satisfying musical in which Rudy Vallee and his nightclub dancing girls are invited to a Paris festival with the misunderstanding that they are a ballet troupe. Berkeley again staged the musical numbers, though on a much less lavish scale than earlier in the series. Warren and Dubin's "The Latin Quarter" was a breezy song about the Left Bank of Paris and Berkeley choreographed it with grace. Warren and Johnny Mercer wrote the ballad "Day Dreaming (All Night Long)," which Vallee and Rosemary Lane sang together. The movie did so poorly at the box office that *Gold Diggers* sequels were discontinued. Years later the series returned somewhat with *Painting the Clouds with Sunshine* (1951), a remake of the original *Gold Diggers of Broadway*, with Virginia Mayo, Lucille Norman, and Virginia Gibson as the three showgirls, and some old standards (including two from the 1929 film) were dusted off and used again.

See also: *42nd Street*, Dick Powell, Busby Berkeley, Al Dubin and Harry Warren biography boxes

FURTHER READING

Bergman, Andrew. *We're in the Money: Depression America and Its Films*. New York: Harper & Row, 1971.
Bingen, Steven. *Warner Bros.: Hollywood's Ultimate Backlot*. Lanham, MD: Taylor Trade Publishing, 2014.
Hirschhorn, Clive. *The Warner Bros. Story*. New York: Crown Publishers, 1979.
Thomas, Tony. *The Busby Berkeley Book*. New York: New York Graphics Society, 1973.

FOOTLIGHT PARADE

Studio and release date: Warner Brothers; September 1933
Producer: Hal B. Wallis
Screenplay: Manuel Seff, James Seymour
Songwriters: Harry Warren, Sammy Fain (music), Al Dubin, Irving Kahal (lyrics)
Director: Lloyd Bacon
Choreographer: Busby Berkeley
Music Director: Leo F. Forbstein
Cinematographer: George Barnes
Cast: James Cagney, Ruby Keeler, Dick Powell, Joan Blondell, Guy Kibbee, Frank McHugh, Ruth Donnelly, Hugh Herbert, Billy Barty
Principal Songs: "By a Waterfall"; "Shanghai Lil"; "Sittin' on a Backyard Fence"; "Honeymoon Hotel"; "Ah, the Moon Is Here"

This tuneful escapist musical is sometimes linked to the *Gold Digger* series of musicals because so many Warner Brothers talents from those films show up here. Yet there is something distinctive about *Footlight Parade* that makes it a musical classic in its own right. Instead of being about putting on a Broadway show, this backstager was about the production of "prologues," mini-musicals presented in movie theaters as preshow entertainment. The hyperactive producer Chester Kent (James Cagney in his first screen musical) produces prologues for a chain of Manhattan movie houses but all his ideas are being stolen by the competition. His secretary, Nan Prescott (Joan Blondell), loves her boss so she finds out who the culprit is. The performers Scotty Blair (Dick Powell) and Bea Thorn (Ruby Keeler) were featured in the prologues and their songs often parallel their offstage romance. In order to outwit the competition, Chester rehearses three prologues at the same time behind closed doors and premieres them in three different theaters on the same night. That fact that these mini-musicals were so huge and lavish that no one theater could accommodate any of them just adds to the ridiculousness of *Footlight Parade*. When the three prologues are finally unveiled, reality has quite disappeared. For the "By a Waterfall" number, dozens of girls dive and swim for nearly 15 minutes while Powell and Rudy dream away in each other's arms. "Honeymoon Hotel" shows groups of newlyweds checking in to a Jersey City hotel and preparing for bed, with a lot of singing and smirking about the activities to follow. The final prologue is "Shanghai Lil" in which a melancholy sailor (Cagney) searches through a Chinese saloon and an opium den looking for (and eventually finding) his long-lost Lil (Keeler) before they both set out for sea. Even though it has a dynamite score by Harry Warren (music) and Al Dubin (lyrics) and others and vintage performances by Cagney and company, the musical is most remembered for those fantastical Busby Berkeley production numbers that seem to top themselves in the film's last reel. On the other hand, many feel that the movie really belongs to Cagney, who propels the action, sings with no-nonsense bite, and dances with the determination of an athlete. He would not get such an opportunity again until nine years later with *Yankee Doodle Dandy* (1942).

Footlight Parade is perhaps the movie musical at its dizziest. It reaches heights of ridiculousness rarely equaled, yet audiences had no trouble accepting it then. Today we laugh at such excesses but, like those Depression audiences, we are drawn into the far-fetched nature of the production numbers. Ironically, the book scenes are somewhat realistic and the hard work and sweat that goes into song and dance is accurately captured. Cagney/Chester is a high-energy dynamo who is so driven that one has to admire him even if he seems possessed. (A similar kind of driven director was seen decades later in Bob Fosse's autobiographical movie musical *All That Jazz* in 1979.) From such excess comes these outlandish production numbers that do not worry about reality. The movies can do things not

Dick Powell (1904–1963)   A youthful-looking leading man of 1930s musicals and a dramatic actor in 1940s melodramas, the versatile actor-singer had a long and varied career in movies but he is best remembered for a series of Warner Brothers musicals, usually paired with Ruby Keeler. He was born in Mountain View, Arkansas, and began his career as a band vocalist. Powell made his screen debut in 1932 and the next year rose to stardom with *42nd Street* (1933). His 1930s musical credits include *Gold Diggers of 1933*, *Footlight Parade* (1933), *Dames* (1934), *Wonder Bar* (1934), *Flirtation Walk* (1934), *Gold Diggers of 1935*, *Broadway Gondolier* (1935), *Shipmates Forever* (1935), *Thanks a Million* (1935), *Gold Diggers of 1937* (1936), *On the Avenue* (1937), *The Singing Marine* (1937), *Varsity Show* (1937), *Hollywood Hotel* (1937), *Cowboy From Brooklyn* (1938), *Going Places* (1938), and *Naughty But Nice* (1939). Although he wearied of playing the same part over and over, audiences wanted more so even as he turned to dramatic roles in the 1940s, he still was seen in such musicals as *In the Navy* (1941), *Star Spangled Rhythm* (1942), *Happy Go Lucky* (1943), *True to Life* (1943), and *Meet the People* (1944). By the end of the decade Powell was accepted in detective roles, and by the 1950s he eased out of acting altogether and produced and directed television series, making an appearance on occasion up into the 1960s, as with his own television show. Biography: *The Dick Powell Story*, Tony Thomas (1992).

possible onstage and no film makes that point more overtly than *Footlight Parade*. The movie also illustrates choreographer Busby Berkeley at his most extreme. After only three years of staging musical numbers in Hollywood, Berkeley had become the master of cinematic surrealism. Using a single camera and providing a single point of view, the Berkeley dances are journeys for the eye. He reveals people and scenery in the manner of a magician, controlling what you see and when. One might even say that the camera is the true dancer in a Berkeley production number. Surely it is rarely the human dancer. Cagney is so magnetic in *Footlight Parade* that you watch the performer. But in many of the other Berkeley extravaganzas in various films, the actual dancing is not very impressive. Pianos move and water falls and crowds converge and disappear but the true art of dance is often lost. No wonder so many later movie choreographers and dancers disparaged Berkeley's kind of production number. But audiences adored it then and still do in a cockeyed way.

See also: *Gold Diggers of 1933*, *42nd Street;* James Cagney, Busby Berkeley, Harry Warren and Al Dubin biography boxes

FURTHER READING

Bingen, Steven. *Warner Bros.: Hollywood's Ultimate Backlot*. Lanham, MD: Taylor Trade Publishing, 2014.

Spivak, Jeffrey. *Buzz: The Life and Art of Busby Berkeley*. Lexington: University Press of Kentucky, 2010.

Thomas, Tony. *Harry Warren and the Hollywood Musical*. New York: Lyle Stuart, Inc., 1975.

FLYING DOWN TO RIO

Studio and release date: RKO Radio Pictures; December 1933
Producer: Louis Brock
Screenplay: Cyril Hume, H. W. Hannemann, Erwin Gelsey
Songwriters: Vincent Youmans (music), Edward Eliscu, Gus Kahn (lyrics)
Director: Thornton Freeland
Choreographers: Dave Gould, Hermes Pan
Cinematographer: J. Roy Hunt
Cast: Dolores Del Rio, Gene Raymond, Fred Astaire, Ginger Rogers, Raul Roulien, Blanche Friderici, Eric Blore
Principal Songs: "The Carioca"; "Music Makes Me"; "Flying Down to Rio"; "Orchids in the Moonlight"

Hollywood's favorite dancing couple, Fred Astaire and Ginger Rogers, were first teamed together in this South American–set film, which was so popular that it created a nationwide interest in Latin-flavored music. *Flying Down to Rio* is also, along with *42nd Street* (1933), credited with saving the movie musical at a time when interest in the genre was dwindling. The story line is far from gripping but there were so many wonderful moments in the musical that it still enthralls. The American Roger Bond (Gene Raymond), a bandleader who is also an aviator, meets the Brazilian beauty Belinha De Rezende (Dolores Del Rio) in Miami and realizes it is true love. But Belinha is engaged to dashing Julio Ruberio (Raul Roulien) from her own country and she can't decide which of the two men she loves. Roger's band, the Yankee Clippers, is hired to open a new hotel in Rio de Janeiro so Roger pursues Belinha in her native country. Frankly, audiences were not too concerned about her dilemma or his pursuit and found the secondary couple more enticing. The American hoofer Fred Ayres (Astaire) comes up with a sensational number to open the hotel. While he sings "Flying Down to Rio" in the hotel plaza, a fleet of airplanes fly overhead, each one with scantily clad chorus girls dancing on the wings. The outlandish show is a great success and Roger wins Belinha's hand. The

Fred Astaire (1899–1987)   A Broadway hoofer who became a Hollywood song-and-dance star, he symbolized the elegant, romantic leading man in screen musicals even though he had a thin but pleasing singing voice. Yet as a dancer, he was versatile, experimental, and a master at various kinds of dance. Astaire was born in Omaha, Nebraska, and was on the vaudeville stage with his elder sister Adele Astaire for some years before the team was on Broadway in 1917. After such stage successes as *Lady, Be Good* (1924), *Funny Face* (1927), and *The Band Wagon* (1931), Adele gave up show business to marry an English lord and Fred continued on, starring in *Gay Divorce* (1932) before going to Hollywood. He was featured in *Dancing Lady* (1933) but didn't become a screen favorite until he was teamed up with Ginger Rogers in *Flying Down to Rio* (1933), dancing "The Carioca" together and giving birth to Hollywood's most famous dancing couple. The twosome were reunited for nine more musicals, most of them major hits: *The Gay Divorcee* (1934), *Roberta* (1935), *Top Hat* (1935), *Follow the Fleet* (1936), *Swing Time* (1936), *Shall We Dance* (1937), *Carefree* (1938), *The Story of Vernon and Irene Castle* (1939), and *The Barkleys of Broadway* (1949). Although moviegoers and studio heads preferred Astaire with Rogers, he did find other dancing partners in *A Damsel in Distress* (1937), *Broadway Melody of 1940*, *You'll Never Get Rich* (1941), *You Were Never Lovelier* (1942), *The Sky's the Limit* (1943), *Ziegfeld Follies* (1946), *Blue Skies* (1946), and *Easter Parade* (1948). In the 1950s, many of Astaire's musicals did not do as well at the box office, yet he still managed to shine in *Three Little Words* (1950), *Royal Wedding* (1951), *The Belle of New York* (1952), *The Band Wagon* (1953), *Daddy Long Legs* (1955), *Funny Face* (1957), and *Silk Stockings* (1957). He turned to dramatic roles on occasion and did many television specials in the 1960s and 1970s, returning to Hollywood for his last screen musical *Finian's Rainbow* (1968). Astaire excelled in all manner of dance (tap, soft shoe, ballet, jazz, modern) while maintaining a distinctive persona of wit and romance that has never been equaled. Autobiography: *Steps in Time* (1959); biographies: *Fred Astaire*, Sarah Giles (1988); *The Fred Astaire-Ginger Rogers Book*, Arlene Croce (1972).

high-flying finale is the most remembered scene because it is so ridiculously delightful. But the musical highlight of the movie came earlier when Astaire and Rogers danced to "The Carioca" on top of seven white pianos in a nightclub. The sleek, attractive new couple and the romantic strains of the Latin music changed the history of movie dancing. Astaire and Rogers had secondary roles but they caught the attention of moviegoers and the studio heads. Edward Eliscu, Gus Kahn, and

Vincent Youmans collaborated on the film's four songs that were also innovative. The rhythm number "Music Makes Me" and the warm ballad "Orchids in the Moonlight" did not have the brash, Broadway sound of *42nd Street*, that year's other landmark film. Youmans' music was not only Latin but it introduced a more serene, fox-trot pattern that would dictate much of the dance music in the 1930s. Also, "The Carioca" started a rage for the samba and other south-of-the-border dances. Much of *Flying Down to Rio* is preposterous and silly, particularly to contemporary viewers, yet it was one of the most important movie musicals of the decade.

Like many Hollywood miracles, the teaming of Astaire and Rogers was an accident. Now-forgotten dancer Dorothy Jordan was originally cast as Honey Hale, Astaire's dancing partner who did not figure into the plot very much and had only one important dance number, "The Carioca." When film producer Merian C. Cooper proposed marriage to Jordan, she dropped out of the film to get married and go on a honeymoon. Ginger Rogers, a Broadway dancer-singer who had so far only gotten secondary roles in films, was cast as Honey. When she and Astaire took to the dance floor for "The Carioca," something special happened. Many have tried to describe the dancing chemistry between Astaire and Rogers but the most satisfying explanation is the observation that he gave her class and she gave him sex appeal. During filming, director Thornton Freeland noticed this chemistry and Rogers was given more lines with Astaire. The executives at RKO must have noticed something in the film footage and tried to feature the couple in the final print. In the finale of the movie, it is not the stars Del Rio and Raymond who are featured but it was Astaire and Rogers. Audiences immediately noticed and were taken with the dancing couple, and it was clear to RKO that the two should have the leading roles in their own movie. Ironically, Astaire was not anxious to work with Rogers again. For many years he had been part of a dance team onstage with his sister Adele Astaire. He wanted to be recognized as a solo dancer and not part of another team. But the studio prevailed and Astaire and Rogers went on to make nine more movies together.

See also: *Roberta, Top Hat*; Fred Astaire, Ginger Rogers, Hermes Pan biography boxes

FURTHER READING

Bordman, Gerald. *Days to Be Happy, Years to Be Sad: The Life and Music of Vincent Youmans*. New York: Oxford University Press, 1982.

Jewell, Richard B., and Vernon Harbin. *The RKO Story*. New York: Arlington House, 1982.

Lasky, Betty. *RKO: The Biggest Little Major of Them All*. Englewood Cliffs, NJ: Prentice-Hall, 1984.

EVERGREEN

Studio and release date: Gaumont (Great Britain); June 1934

Producer: Michael Balcon

Screenplay: Marjorie Gaffney, Emlyn Williams, based on the 1930 London script *Ever Green* by Benn W. Levy

Songwriter: Richard Rodgers, Harry Woods, Joseph Tabrar (music), Lorenz Hart, Harry Woods (lyrics)

Director: Victor Saville

Choreographer: Buddy Bradley

Musical Director: Louis Levy

Cinematographer: Glen MacWilliams

Cast: Jessie Matthews, Sonnie Hale, Ivor McLaren, Betty Balfour, Barry Mackay

Principal Songs: "Dancing on the Ceiling"; "Daddy Wouldn't Buy Me a Bow-Wow"; "When You've Got a Little Springtime in Your Heart"; "I Give in to You"; "Over My Shoulder"; "Just By Your Example"; "Tinkle Tinkle Tinkle"; "Dear Dear"

One of the most beloved of all British movie musicals, *Evergreen* is basically a vehicle for singing-dancing star Jessie Matthews, England's leading musical star at the time. While many Broadway musicals in the 1920s and 1930s transferred to London, few of the many British musicals of that time made it to New York. The same could be said for the movies. Great Britain turned out many screen musicals but few found popularity in the United States. *Evergreen* is the exception. The piece started as a 1930 London stage musical titled *Ever Green*, which starred Matthews. The inspiration for the story came from the popular Music Hall singer Lottie Collins, whose theme song was "Ta-Ra-Ra-Boom-de Ray." She had a daughter, Jose Collins, who also became a stage star. The London musical, spelled *Ever Green*, told the far-fetched story about a fictitious performer who tricks the public into thinking that she is a beloved star from the past. Hoping to break into show business, Harriet Green (Matthews) pretends to be her 60-year-old grandmother, a London actress of some repute before she moved to Australia many years before. Harriet tells her public that her secrets of cosmetology have kept her so young looking and, becoming a sort of freak attraction, she is starred in a musical show. Although she is falling in love with the young Tommy Thompson, Harriet does not tell him the truth until her deception is revealed. By that time Tommy loves her and the public adores her onstage so all ends happily. The London musical was a huge hit and one of Matthews' greatest successes. American songwriters Richard Rodgers (music) and Lorenz Hart (lyrics), in their third and most successful London musical, wrote 15 songs for the show, the most popular being the dreamy ballad "Dancing on the Ceiling," which became a song standard in England and later in the United States.

Despite its success in Britain, *Ever Green* was deemed too British for Broadway so it never made it to the United States. The British movie version made one significant change in the plot. Harriet pretends to be her mother, a beloved music hall star who had vanished from public view years before. Her sweetheart Tommy (Barry Mackay) is a press agent who aids her in her deception. Also in on the hoax is the flamboyant director Leslie Benn (Sonnie Hale). Only three of the Rodgers and Hart songs were retained for the newly titled *Evergreen* film. Because the two Americans were under contract in Hollywood and couldn't return to London to provide new songs, new numbers by various English songwriters filled out the score. The most memorable were the sprightly "When You Have a Little Springtime in Your Heart" and the silly "Daddy Wouldn't Buy Me a Bow-Wow." The nonsensical story was saved by Matthews' charming performance and some excellent production values. Matthews was primarily a dancer, a petite but energetic performer who was equally adept with ballet as she was with hoofing and tapping. Her porcelain beauty and thin but pleasing singing voice were also assets. One can see why Matthews was so beloved in Great Britain. Victor Saville directed with a sense of lavishness and an eye on promoting his star for moviegoers on both sides of the Atlantic. It worked, for *Evergreen* became one of the few British film musicals to find an audience in America.

The difference between successful shows and films in America and those found in Great Britain has long puzzled producers. Because we both speak the same language, it is assumed that what works in one country will work in another. The list of stage musicals that triumphed in one nation only to fail in the other is long and puzzling. In the case of movies, the problem was that very few British films, particularly musicals, were ever released in the United States. Hollywood products were thought to be the best in the world so why waste movie houses on foreign films. This superior and narrow-minded attitude kept Americans from seeing many British screen musicals until decades later when some became available on video and DVD. Few of these movies were as fine as *Evergreen* but, all the same, some top-notch entertainment was hidden from view.

See also: Richard Rodgers biography box

FURTHER READING

Mundy, John. *The British Film Musical*. Manchester, UK: Manchester University Press, 2007.

ROBERTA

Studio and release date: RKO Radio Pictures; February 1935

Producer: Pandro S. Berman

Screenplay: Jane Murfin, Sam Mintz, Gen Tyron, Allan Scott, based on Otto Harbach's 1933 stage script, which was based on the novel *Gowns By Roberta* by Alice Duer Miller

Songwriters: Jerome Kern (music), Otto Harbach, Dorothy Fields (lyrics)

Director: William A. Seiter

Music Director: Max Steiner

Choreographer: Hermes Pan

Cinematographer: Edward Cronjager

Cast: Irene Dunne, Fred Astaire, Ginger Rogers, Randolph Scott, Helen Westley

Principal Songs: "Smoke Gets in Your Eyes"; "I Won't Dance"; "Yesterdays"; "I'll Be Hard to Handle"; "Lovely to Look At"; "Let's Begin"

Although it lost much of its terrific score in the transition from Broadway to Hollywood, this "modern operetta" is still great fun and is filled with great music. The 1933 Broadway musical was something of a slipshod affair with a tired plot but first-class songs by Jerome Kern (music) and Otto Harbach (lyrics). The reviews were unenthusiastic and box office was tepid until one song from the show, the haunting "Smoke Gets in Your Eyes," received a lot of radio play and became a hit. Billed as "the Smoke Get in Your Eyes musical," *Roberta* managed to become a Broadway success. The story, based on a popular novel, asked the audience to believe that the exiled Russian Princess Stephanie is disguised as a dressmaker's assistant at the Paris shop named Roberta run by the aged American Minnie. When Minnie dies, the shop is inherited by her nephew John Kent, an all-American fullback, who comes to claim possession of the shop. Stephanie begins quarreling with John over how the shop should be run but soon they are in love, she reveals her aristocratic background, and the two end up both a romantic and business couple. The comedy was provided by John's wisecracking bandleader friend Huckleberry Haines, played by Bob Hope in his first major Broadway role, and his dizzy Polish girlfriend Clementina Scharwenka (Lyda Roberti). In addition to "Smoke Gets in Your Eyes," the score also included the jazzy "Let's Begin," the nostalgic "Yesterdays," the flowing "The Touch of Your Hand," and the clever dance number "I'll Be Hard to Handle." *Roberta* has long been forgotten with very few revivals but many of the songs have remained standards.

RKO bought the screen rights for *Roberta* as a vehicle for Fred Astaire and Ginger Rogers (their third movie together) and reworked the story so that Huckleberry and Clementina were as prominent as John and Stephanie. Somewhat improving on the stage script, the plot now concerned football player John Kent (Randolph

Ginger Rogers (1911–1995)   A glamorous, funny blonde whose dancing and singing could be romantic or silly, she had a varied career but is most remembered for her movie musicals with Fred Astaire. She was born in Independence, Missouri, and took singing and dancing lessons as a young child. After appearing in vaudeville and winning some dance contests, Rogers made her Broadway debut in 1929 and the next year gained recognition for her performance in *Girl Crazy* (1930). Hollywood signed her up to play wisecracking blondes in a series of B pictures before getting noticed in supporting roles in *42nd Street* (1933), *Gold Diggers of 1933*, and *Sitting Pretty* (1933). Rogers was first teamed with Astaire in *Flying Down to Rio* (1933) and when the two danced "The Carioca" together, the public was enthralled and they soon became the most famous dance team in the history of the movies. Rogers was partnered with Astaire in *The Gay Divorcee* (1934), *Roberta* (1935), *Top Hat* (1935), *Follow the Fleet* (1936), *Swing Time* (1936), *Shall We Dance* (1937), *Carefree* (1938), *The Story of Vernon and Irene Castle* (1939), and *The Barkleys of Broadway* (1949). Her musicals with other leading men include *Twenty Million Sweethearts* (1934), *In Person* (1935), *Having Wonderful Time* (1938), and *Lady in the Dark* (1944). She also appeared in many comedies and dramas through the 1950s before retiring from films and doing concerts and nightclubs. Autobiography: *Ginger: My Story* (1991); biography: *Shall We Dance: The Life of Ginger Rogers*, Sheridan Morley (1995).

Scott) who decides to visit his Aunt Minnie (Helen Westley) who owns a dress shop in Paris called Roberta. So he goes to France with his pal, bandleader Huckleberry Haines (Astaire), where he falls in love with his aunt's able assistant Stephanie (Irene Dunne). Minnie dies, leaving the shop to John instead of Stephanie, who turns out to be a Russian princess who had to flee her homeland. In the second plot, Haines woos and wins a phony Russian countess (Ginger Rogers) and they were much more fun than the leading roles played by Dunne and Scott. It was still far from a satisfying story but, as on Broadway, the musical was saved by the fine performances and the superior songs. "Smoke Gets in Your Eyes" and other hits from Broadway were retained and lyricist Dorothy Fields collaborated with Kern on two splendid new songs for the film, the gushing "Lovely to Look At" and the sassy "I Won't Dance." *Roberta* was directed with pizazz by William A. Seiter with choreography by Astaire and Hermes Pan. It is one of the better Astaire-Rogers musicals and their dancing to "Smoke Gets in Your Eyes" and "I'll Be Hard to Handle" is unforgettable. The couple seems to be having a great deal of fun, even breaking each other up at times. This might be because Astaire and codirector Pan convinced the studio to let the couple dance on a wooden floor rather than the shiny, hard surface usually used in musicals. Consequently, their tapping sounds are more vibrant (the sound of taps was dubbed in their other movies) and there is a spring to their dancing that comes with a wooden dance floor. *Roberta* was so successful that MGM bought the rights from RKO and planned to do its own version someday.

In 1952 MGM released its remake, now titled *Lovely to Look At*. The movie went back to the Broadway plot and told of American comic Al Marsh (Red Skelton) who inherits the Paris dress shop. He goes to France with his buddies Tony Naylor (Howard Keel) and Jerry Ralby (Gower Champion) to find that the store is run by sisters Stephanie (Kathryn Grayson) and Clarisse (Marge Champion) and facing bankruptcy. The boys help put on a big fashion show, save the shop, and win the hearts of the sisters and the provocative Bubbles Cassidy (Ann Miller). It was not as solid as the earlier film but there was still much to enjoy, including two Kern-Harbach songs—"You're Devastating" and "The Touch of Your Hand"—from the original stage score not used in the 1935 film, and a daffy new number called "Lafayette." Mervyn LeRoy directed the lush production, which was filled with talented players and 42 gowns by Adrian for the fashion show finale.

See also: *Flying Down to Rio*; Jerome Kern, Fred Astaire, Ginger Rogers, Irene Dunne, Dorothy Fields biography boxes

FURTHER READING

Franceschina, John. *Hermes Pan: The Man Who Danced with Fred Astaire*. New York: Oxford University Press, 2012.

Grant, Barry Keith. *The Hollywood Film Musical*. Hoboken, NJ: Wiley-Blackwell, 2012.

Jewell, Richard B., and Vernon Harbin. *The RKO Story*. New York: Arlington House, 1982.

Lasky, Betty. *RKO: The Biggest Little Major of Them All*. Englewood Cliffs, NJ: Prentice-Hall, 1984.

NAUGHTY MARIETTA

Studio and release date: Metro-Goldwyn-Mayer; March 1935
Producer: Hunt Stromberg
Screenplay: John Lee Mahin, Frances Goodrich, Albert Hackett, based on the 1910 stage script by Rida Johnson Young
Songwriters: Victor Herbert (music), Rida Johnson Young (lyrics)
Director: W. S. Van Dyke
Music Director: Herbert Stothart
Cinematographer: William Daniels

Cast: Jeanette MacDonald, Nelson Eddy, Frank Morgan, Elsa Lanchester, Douglas Dumbrille, Joseph Cawthorn

Principal Songs: "Ah! Sweet Mystery of Life"; "Italian Street Song"; "Tramp! Tramp! Tramp!"; "I'm Falling in Love with Someone"; " 'Neath the Southern Moon"; "Chansonette"

The singing team of Jeanette MacDonald and Nelson Eddy was introduced to moviegoers in this operetta film and it was love at first sight. The movie not only inspired seven more movie musicals with the pair but also paved the way for the popularity of film operettas through the rest of the decade. One of the ironies of Hollywood musicals is the sudden interest in operetta in the 1930s. The genre had been steady fare on Broadway since the 1890s and reached a climax in the 1920s with such stage classics as *Rose-Marie* (1924), *The Student Prince* (1924), *The Vagabond King* (1925), *The Desert Song* (1926), *Rio Rita* (1927), and *The New Moon* (1928). But when the stock market crashed in 1929, there was a sudden shift away from operetta on Broadway. Perhaps this romantic, exotic kind of musical felt out of place during the Depression. Or perhaps the old-fashioned music found in operetta did not appeal to theatergoers who were still discovering jazz and other forms of music. The few stage operettas that opened in the 1930s failed and the genre seemed dead. At about the same time, moviegoers discovered operetta and liked it. Or at least they liked it when MacDonald and Eddy sang. *Naughty Marietta* opened the door for operetta on-screen and it stayed well into the 1950s.

Naughty Marietta opened on Broadway in 1910 with a luscious score by composer Victor Herbert (music) and Rida Johnson Young (lyrics), who also wrote the script. French New Orleans in the 1780s is being terrorized by the pirate Bras Pique whose true identity is unknown, and Captain Dick Warrington and his rangers are sent by the king of France to find the culprit. The peasant girl Marietta, who is really the Countess d'Altena in disguise, has fled France because she was being forced to wed a man she didn't love. In New Orleans, Marietta is drawn to Etienne Grandet, the son of the governor, but then her affections fall on Dick, the two expressing themselves in a handful of gushing duets. Dick is ordered to return Marietta to France, but she is kidnapped by Etienne, who turns out to be the pirate Bras Pique. Dick rescues Marietta, Etienne escapes with his pirates, and the lovers reprise the score's most famous duet, "Ah, Sweet Mystery of Life." It was all melodramatic nonsense, but Herbert's soaring music made it all seem believable. The score also included such operetta favorites as the vivacious "Italian Street Sing," the rousing march "Tramp! Tramp! Tramp!," the waltzing "I'm Falling in Love with Someone," the dreamy ballad " 'Neath the Southern Moon," and the flowing title number. *Naughty Marietta* is considered Herbert's masterpiece, and it was frequently revived onstage over the next half century.

Jeanette MacDonald and **Nelson Eddy**   The most popular singing duo in the history of American movies, their performance style may seem dated today but they were much beloved in the 1930s. MacDonald (1901–1965) was born and educated in Philadelphia and studied voice in New York before landing her first jobs in the chorus of Broadway musicals. Soon the elegant blonde soprano was playing leading roles in operettas and musical comedies, yet she never became a stage star. MacDonald fared much better in Hollywood where her first film, *The Love Parade* (1929) with Maurice Chevalier, was a hit. After costarring with Chevalier again in *One Hour with You* (1932), *Love Me Tonight* (1932), and *The Merry Widow* (1934), she was teamed with Nelson Eddy in *Naughty Marietta* (1935), and audiences demanded more films starring the twosome. Eddy (1901–1967) was born in Providence, Rhode Island, and was a boy soprano in church choirs. As an adult he toured in operettas until he was signed to a Hollywood contract in 1933. After the movie musicals *Broadway to Hollywood* (1933), *Dancing Lady* (1933), and *Student Tour* (1934), Eddy found wider fame with MacDonald, the couple also starring in *Rose Marie* (1936), *Maytime* (1937), *The Girl of the Golden West* (1938), *Sweethearts* (1938), *New Moon* (1940), *Bitter Sweet* (1940), and *I Married an Angel* (1942). With other leading men, MacDonald starred in the musicals *The Vagabond King* (1930), *Monte Carlo* (1930), *The Cat and the Fiddle* (1934), *San Francisco* (1936), *The Firefly* (1937), *Smilin' Through* (1941), *Cairo* (1942), *Three Darling Daughters* (1948), and others. Eddy sang opposite other leading ladies in *Rosalie* (1937), *Let Freedom Ring* (1939), *Balalaika* (1939), *The Chocolate Soldier* (1941), *The Phantom of the Opera* (1943), *Knickerbocker Holiday* (1944), and *Northwest Outpost* (1947). While MacDonald was sometimes dubbed the "Iron Butterfly" for her icy beauty and superhuman voice, she was beloved by audiences and her partnership with Eddy was movie musical gold. Biography: *The Jeanette MacDonald Story*, Robert Parish (1976).

The screenplay for the 1935 screen version is perhaps more satisfying than the 1910 script, but it still overflows with romance and adventure. In the movie, Marietta (MacDonald) is sailing to the New World when her ship is attacked by pirates, but she is rescued by Dick (Eddy). By the time they arrive in New Orleans, the two are in love. There were a lot of contrived complications as she continued to hide her true identity, but all was resolved in an illogical but romantic fashion. The highlights from the Herbert-Young score were retained and, as sung by the two stars, the songs were so thrilling that audiences embraced the old favorites all over again. The recurring "Ah, Sweet Mystery of Life" was used effectively throughout the movie and the duo's gushing rendition of the song was later the stuff of parody. W. S. Van Dyke directed with efficiency, and the movie looked as beautiful as it sounded.

MGM had owned the screen rights to *Naughty Marietta* since the 1920s, and an early talking-singing version was planned in 1930 with Marion Davies as the title heroine. But movie musicals were losing favor at the time and the project was abandoned. It was studio head Louis B. Mayer who thought that the popular MacDonald just might be able to pull off the operatic heroine and teamed her with studio contract singer Eddy who had limited screen experience but a powerful baritone singing voice. He also had limited acting experience, often struggling with the dialogue scenes but finding confidence with the songs. Mayer's hunch that the two singers might appeal to the public was risky, but audiences immediately took to the new team and Hollywood's most famous singing duo was born.

While the eight MacDonald-Eddy musicals still have charm, they have dated much more than other 1930s film musicals. Audiences today do not like their heroines to have high soprano voices. Neither do they feel that a stiff, handsome baritone is the ideal hero. Also, operetta music is not easily grasped and appreciated by modern moviegoers. Yet, despite these difficulties, *Naughty Marietta* and the other operetta movies of the period can still entertain and even enthrall. Operettas were always romantic fantasies with exotic locations, pretty costumes, melodramatic plots, and lush music. Moviegoers in the 1930s must have found them the ultimate escape from the grim reality of the time. Today they are reminders of a time when a musical created its own romantic reality and let the music dictate everything else.

See also: *Rose Marie;* Jeanette MacDonald and Nelson Eddy biography box

FURTHER READING

Eames, John Douglas. *The MGM Story*. New York: Crown Publishers, 1975.
Rich, Sharon. *Sweethearts: The Timeless Love Affair . . . Between Jeanette MacDonald and Nelson Eddy*. 3rd ed. New York: Bell Harbour Press, 2014.

TOP HAT

Studio and release date: RKO Radio Pictures; August 1935
Producer: Pandro S. Berman
Screenplay: Dwight Taylor, Allan Scott, based on the play *The Girl Who Dared* by Alexander Farago, Aladar Laszlo
Songwriter: Irving Berlin (music and lyrics)

Director: Mark Sandrich

Musical Director: Max Steiner

Choreographers: Hermes Pan, Fred Astaire

Cinematographer: David Abel

Cast: Fred Astaire, Ginger Rogers, Edward Everett Horton, Helen Broderick, Eric
Blore, Erik Rhodes

Principal Songs: "Cheek to Cheek"; "Isn't This a Lovely Day?"; "Top Hat,
White Tie and Tails"; "No Strings"; "The Piccolino"

Fred Astaire wears white tie, tails, and a top hat for much of this musical classic, so in many ways it feels like the ultimate Astaire and Ginger Rogers movie. The fact that the twosome have five dances together, more than in any other of their films, also adds to the argument that this is their finest movie. *Top Hat* was the first film to be written with Astaire and Rogers in mind; their previous musicals had been adapted to fit their talents. The musical is a treasure trove of entertainment for its many memorable scenes and indelible Irving Berlin score. The script, loosely based on a Hungarian play, takes the device of mistaken identity and sustains it for nearly all of the movie's running time. The American hoofer Jerry Travers (Astaire) is in London to do a show and falls in love with the American tourist Dale Tremont (Rogers) at first sight, following her and wooing her. Dale mistakenly finds out that his name is Horace Hardwicke, the husband of her dear friend Madge Hardwicke (Helen Broderick), so she leaves London and joins Marge at the Lido in Venice. Jerry and the real Horace (Edward Everett Horton), Jerry's fussy producer, follow, and, Dale, feeling guilty over starting to love her friend's husband, marries the Italian dress designer Alberto Beddini (Erik Rhodes). The mistaken identity continues until Jerry and Horace are finally together in one place and Dale realizes her mistake. She can now let her true feelings of affection for Jerry surface, and it turns out her wedding to Beddini is invalid because the ceremony was performed by Horace's valet Bates (Eric Blore) posing as a preacher. The expert players were so adept at this sort of thing that the story almost seemed to make logical sense. The romantic yet hesitant (on her part) relationship between Astaire and Rogers was one of their most amusing as well as romantic. Horton was delightful as always but here his character is more entrenched in the plot, and Broderick shines as the deadpan wife who is disbelieving and a little pleased to hear that her fussbudget husband is such a ladies' man.

Because of the complicated plotting, there are only five songs in *Top Hat* but they are by Berlin at his best. Perhaps the most unforgettable one is "Cheek to Cheek" sung by Astaire and danced with Rogers, a classic moment of musical romance. In the famous number she wears a dress covered with feathers that float and billow with every move. What the moviegoer doesn't see is all the difficulty the feathers caused during shooting, calling for endless retakes as feathers kept getting

Hermes Pan (1905?–1990)   One of the most sought-after choreographers during Hollywood's golden age of musicals, his career was closely tied to that of dancer Fred Astaire. Little is known about Pan's early years except that he was born either in Nashville or Memphis, Tennessee, and was an experienced dancer by the time he arrived in Hollywood when sound came in. After working as assistant dance director on *Flying Down to Rio* (1933), *The Gay Divorcee* (1934), and *Roberta* (1935), he found fame for his choreography in such beloved musicals as *Top Hat* (1935), *Follow the Fleet* (1936), *Swing Time* (1936), *Shall We Dance* (1937), *A Damsel in Distress* (1937), *Carefree* (1938), *The Story of Vernon and Irene Castle* (1939), *That Night in Rio* (1940), *Sun Valley Serenade* (1941), *Weekend in Havana* (1941), *Springtime in the Rockies* (1942), *Blue Skies* (1946), *The Barkleys of Broadway* (1949), *Three Little Words* (1950), *Lovely to Look At* (1952), *The Student Prince* (1954), *Hit the Deck* (1955), *Silk Stockings* (1956), *Porgy and Bess* (1959), *Can-Can* (1960), *Flower Drum Song* (1961), *My Fair Lady* (1964), *Finian's Rainbow* (1968), and *Darling Lili* (1969). Pan was also a featured dancer in several films he choreographed, such as *Moon Over Miami* (1941), *My Gal Sal* (1942), *Coney Island* (1943), *Sweet Rosie O'Grady* (1943), *Pin-Up Girl* (1944), *Kiss Me, Kate* (1953), and *Pal Joey* (1957). He physically resembled Astaire and was called the star's alter ego, the two working together on 17 films and several television specials. Biography: *Hermes Pan: The Man Who Danced with Fred Astaire*, John Franceschina (2012).

into Astaire's eyes and mouth. Astaire sang and tapped the slaphappy "No Strings" and wooed Rogers with the intoxicating "Isn't This a Lovely Day (To Be Caught in the Rain)?" when they were caught in a London park during a rain shower. Astaire sang and danced the debonair "Top Hat, White Tie and Tails" even as he "shot" down tuxedoed chorus boys with his cane, and just about everyone in the cast joined in singing and dancing the festive "The Piccolino" at the Lido. Not only was each number radiant but the songs actually had something to do with the plot, a rarity in 1930s musicals. Mark Sandrich directed with a light touch and Hermes Pan and Astaire did the choreography, which ranged from precision tapping to gliding fox-trot to Busby Berkeley-like formations by the dancing couples on the Lido.

Another distinctive feature of *Top Hat* is the look of the film. With its implausibly sleek art deco sets and highly stylized clothes and furniture, *Top Hat* is a fantasy of musical comedy and exists in its own wonderful reality. For the Venice waterfront called the Lido, RKO built the largest set yet constructed by the studio. It included a canal, bridges, waterside restaurants, and gondolas gliding by. The

Irving Berlin (1888–1989)   No one wrote more song standards than this durable and diverse composer-lyricist whose career spanned six decades. Berlin was born in Temun, Russia, the son of a cantor, and as a child came to America where he grew up on New York's Lower East Side. While working as a teenage singing waiter, he started writing songs though he had no musical education. His first major hit was "Alexander's Ragtime Band" in 1911, followed by hundreds of songs for Broadway, Hollywood, and Tin Pan Alley. Berlin's first of 20 Broadway scores was *Watch Your Step* (1914), followed by such noteworthy musicals as *Ziegfeld Follies* (1919, 1920, 1927), *Music Box Revue* (1922, 1923, 1924), *The Cocoanuts* (1925), *Face the Music* (1932), *As Thousands Cheer* (1933) *Louisiana Purchase* (1940), *This Is the Army* (1942), *Annie Get Your Gun* (1946), and *Call Me Madam* (1950). Only a few of his stage musicals were filmed but the songs were frequently used in Hollywood musicals. Berlin wrote original songs for such memorable screen musicals as *Hallelujah* (1929), *Puttin' on the Ritz* (1930), *Top Hat* (1935), *Follow the Fleet* (1936), *On the Avenue* (1937), *Alexander's Ragtime Band* (1938), *Carefree* (1938), *Holiday Inn* (1942), *Blue Skies* (1946), *Easter Parade* (1948), *White Christmas* (1954), and *There's No Business Like Show Business* (1954). Among Berlin's many talents was his ability to capture the feelings and concerns of America through different eras, even as musical styles changed. Memoir: *Irving Berlin: A Daughter's Memoir*, Mary Ellen Barrett (2004); biographies: *Irving Berlin*, Jeffrey Magee (2008); *As Thousands Cheer: The Life of Irving Berlin*, Laurence Bergren (1996).

water in the canal was dyed black so that it would contrast with the white buildings and bridges. Similar efforts were made in creating the art deco hotel, the fanciful gazebo in a London park, and the stuffy British men's club. Visually, the film is as luscious as the music and the dancing. Although Pan was the credited choreographer, Astaire worked out many of the movie's dance sequences on his own. His box office popularity gave him plenty of clout at the studio and, being a perfectionist, he insisted on days of rehearsing before filming began. Rogers had to have several pairs of shoes made because the strenuous dancing caused her feet to bleed and the blood was spotted by the camera. Astaire also insisted that there be as few cuts as possible, making sure the focus was on the dancer and not the camerawork. The movie is filled with long takes; sometimes the dancing filmed continuously for extended periods of time. For example, the dancing in "The Picolino" was all filmed in one two-minute take, unheard of in musical cinematography. This attention to details and striving for perfection is what makes the Astaire-Rogers musicals so special. Everything looks frothy and easy, all the hard work hidden from view. The magic of Hollywood musicals of the 1930s was not magic at all but well-planned craftsmanship mixed with superb talent and whimsical inspiration.

See also: Roberta, Shall We Dance; Irving Berlin, Hermes Pan, Fred Astaire, Ginger Rogers biography boxes

FURTHER READING

Bloom, Ken. *Hollywood Musicals: The 101 Greatest Song-and-Dance Movies of All Time*. New York: Black Dog and Leventhal, 2010.

Croce, Arlene. *The Fred Astaire and Ginger Rogers Book*. New York: Dutton, 1987.

Jewell, Richard B., and Vernon Harbin. *The RKO Story*. New York: Arlington House, 1982.

A NIGHT AT THE OPERA

Studio and release date: Metro-Goldwyn-Mayer; November 1935
Producer: Irving Thalberg
Screenplay: George S. Kaufman, Morrie Ryskind
Songwriters: Nacio Herb Brown, Bronislau Kaper, Walter Jurmann (music), Arthur Freed, Ned Washington (lyrics)
Directors: Sam Wood, Edmund Goulding
Choreographer: Chester Hale
Cinematographer: Merritt B. Gersvad
Cast: Marx Brothers, Margaret Dumont, Kitty Carlisle, Allan Jones, Walter Woolf King, Sig Ruman
Principal Songs: "Cosi-Cosa"; "Alone"; "All I Do Is Dream of You"; opera selections

A delicious mashup of high-brow opera and low-brow comedy, this is the favorite Marx Brothers movie for many fans. Groucho, Chico, Harpo, and Zeppo Marx had started in vaudeville and eventually starred in three Broadway comedies that had enough songs to be labeled as musicals. Two of them—*The Cocoanuts* (1929) and *Animal Crackers* (1930)—were brought to the screen with success. After three more features that did not do so well at the box office, Paramount decided to not renew the brothers' contract. MGM producer Irving Thalberg thought the brothers' needed a strong plot to hold together their antics. He hired them to make a movie for his studio, the result being a kind of comic climax to the brothers' film careers with *A Night at the Opera*. The siblings don't sing much in the movie but, being about an opera company, the film is filled with music. In some ways, the songs (particularly

In the Hollywood classic *A Night at the Opera* (1935), the Marx Brothers turned a performance of *Il Trovatore* into a madcap farce. At one point in the merriment, Harpo and Chico (far left) literally attack the orchestra pit musicians. Sam Wood directed the still-popular movie favorite. (MGM/Photofest)

the opera selections) are respites from the zany, fast-paced comedy so the film is pleasingly balanced.

Playwrights George S. Kaufman and Morrie Ryskind, who had written for the Marx Brothers on Broadway, concocted the wacky screenplay in which the four brothers stow away on an ocean liner to New York, disguise themselves as Russian aviators to get ashore, and wreak havoc on a performance of the opera *Il Trovatore*. The story also concerned the struggling tenor Ricardo Baroni (Allan Jones) and his sweetheart Rosa Castaldi (Kitty Carlisle) and their efforts to sing opera. Except for a few duets, the lovers didn't get in the way too much and there was enough screen time for the famous stateroom scene: for Otis B. Driftwood (Groucho Marx) to woo and insult Mrs. Claypool (Margaret Dumont), for Fiorello (Chico Marx) to play "All I Do Is Dream of You" on the piano, and for Tomasso (Harpo Marx) to pluck out "Alone" on the harp. This last was written for the film by Nacio Herb Brown (music) and Arthur Freed (lyric) and was sung beautifully by Jones and Carlisle. Another laudable number was the sing-along ditty "Cosi Cosa" by Bronislaw Kaper, Walter Jurmann, and Ned Washington. Irving Thalberg devised a way to gauge how well the brother's comedy came across to audiences. Instead of showing the completed film to preview audiences and consulting their reactions through comment cards, he arranged for cast members to tour vaudeville houses doing scenes from the

The **Marx Brothers**   A successful comedy team onstage and on-screen, they are perhaps even more popular today because of their anarchic and sometimes surreal sense of humor. The brothers were Leonard "Chico" Marx (1886–1961) who spoke with a fractured Italian accent; Milton "Gummo" Marx (1893–1977) who gave up performing early on to become a manager; Adolph "Harpo" Marx (1888–1964) who wore a blond curly wig, played the harp, and never spoke; Julius "Groucho" Marx (1890–1977) who wore a painted mustache, sported a cigar, and made lewd wisecracks; and Herbert "Zeppo" Marx (1901–1979) who was the straight man for the others. The brothers were all born in New York and began in vaudeville together in 1917. One of their acts was expanded into the Broadway show *I'll Say She Is* (1924), followed by the musicals *The Cocoanuts* (1925) and *Animal Crackers* (1928), both of which were filmed more or less as they appeared onstage. The brothers concentrated on movies during the 1930s, turning out the musical comedies *Horse Feathers* (1932), *Duck Soup* (1933), *A Night at the Opera* (1935), *A Day at the Races* (1937), and *At the Circus* (1939) as well as such nonmusicals as *Monkey Business* (1931) and *Room Service* (1938). Because their later films—*Go West* (1940), *The Big Store* (1941), *A Night in Casablanca* (1946), and *Love Happy* (1949)—were not successful, the brothers fell out of favor. By 1949 they separated and only Groucho enjoyed a continued career on radio and then television. By the 1960s there was a revival of interest in the Marx Brothers and their movies became cult favorites. Only Groucho was still performing and found himself in demand for concerts and personal appearances. With their zany, physical humor, outrageous puns and verbal jokes, and touches of inspired chaos, the Marx Brothers were unique even as they represented the best of old-time vaudeville comedy. Autobiographies: *Harpo Speaks*, Harpo with Rowland Barber (1961); *Groucho and Me*, Groucho (1959); *Memoirs of a Mangy Lover*, Groucho (1964); *The Secret Word Is Groucho*, Groucho with Hector Arce (1976). Biography: *Monkey Business: The Lives and Legends of the Marx Brothers*, Simon Louvish (2000).

script. The reactions of the live audience were then used to finalize the shooting script before production even began. Thalberg also gave the Marx Brothers the most lavish production of their Hollywood careers. His gamble paid off; *A Night at the Opera* was a smash hit and soon recognized as a musical comedy classic. Sadly, Thalberg died soon after the film was released and the brothers never again were treated with much respect by the studios.

Defining the unique appeal of the Marx Brothers is not easy. There were many loud and frantic comedy teams in vaudeville early in the century but there was something different about the brothers. Their humor was both verbal and physical but, more significantly, there was a sense of anarchy in their humor as well. Nothing was sacred in their quest to lampoon or destroy bastions of civility and convention. Groucho's insults, Chico's charming stupidity, and Harpo's childlike innocence as he acted in an outrageous manner were unique. Onstage, they were allowed to be spontaneous, even out of control. This was harder to do in a film studio but on occasion they did it anyway. During the 1920s such behavior was applauded because there was a sense of freedom and wild abandon at the time. This was harder to sustain in the Depression 1930s, but the Marx Brothers were able to pull it off. By the end of that decade and during the war years, the foursome were pretty much forgotten. Their kind of comedy seemed unpatriotic, even un-American. But in the turbulent 1960s young audiences rediscovered the team and the old movies were favorites in art film houses and then later on video and DVD. Today, the Marx Brothers' movies that were dismissed on first release—in particular *Duck Soup* (1933)—are now considered comic masterworks. *A Night at the Opera* also falls within that description.

See also: Marx Brothers biography box

FURTHER READING

Crowther, Bosley. *The Lion's Share: The Story of an Entertainment Empire*. New York: E. P. Dutton & Co., 1957.

Grant, Barry Keith. *The Hollywood Film Musical*. Hoboken, NJ: Wiley-Blackwell, 2012.

Louvish, Simon. *Monkey Business: The Lives and Legends of the Marx Brothers*. New York: Thomas Dunne Books, 2000.

ROSE MARIE

Studio and release date: Metro-Goldwyn-Mayer; January 1936
Producer: Hunt Stromberg
Screenplay: Frances Goodrich, Albert Hackett, Alice Duer Miller, based on the 1924 stage script by Oscar Hammerstein, Otto Harbach
Songwriter: Rudolf Friml, Herbert Stothart, and others (music), Otto Harbach, Oscar Hammerstein, and others (lyrics)
Director: W. S. Van Dyke
Music Director: Herbert Stothart
Choreographer: Chester Hale
Cinematographer: William Daniels

Cast: Jeanette MacDonald, Nelson Eddy, James Stewart, Reginald Owen, Allan Jones, Una O'Connor, Alan Mowbray

Principal Songs: "Indian Love Call"; "Rose Marie"; "The Mounties"; "Totem Tom Tom"; "Just for You"; "Dinah"; "Pardon Me Madame"; "Some of These Days"

One of the biggest Broadway hits of the 1920s became a movie hit as well, a film that many consider the best of the eight operettas featuring Jeanette MacDonald and Nelson Eddy. The 1924 stage work was spelled *Rose-Marie* and was a breakthrough in the way the songs, by Rudolf Friml (music), Oscar Hammerstein, and Otto Harbach (lyrics), were integrated into the plot. The complicated story centered on Rose-Marie la Flame, a singer at Lady Jane's Hotel high up in the Canadian Rockies. She is wooed by the fur trapper Jim Kenyon and the slick Edward Hawley from the big city. Rose-Marie prefers Jim so when the drunken tribesman Black Eagle is murdered, Hawley makes it look like Jim is the culprit. Thinking Jim is a murderer, Rose-Marie agrees to marry Hawley. Jim's friend, the comic Hard-Boiled Herman, finds out that the half-breed Wanda accidentally killed Black Eagle in a domestic quarrel. He convinces Wanda to go to the authorities and, just as the wedding of Rose-Marie and Hawley is about to start, Jim is freed and is able to marry Rose-Marie. Hammerstein and Harbach broke several conventions when writing the stage script, such as including a murder in the story and letting the songs continue the plot. For example, the famous duet "Indian Love Call" is sung by Jim to tell Rose-Marie the story of a legendary Native romance, the song then turning into a duet for the modern romance. Other outstanding songs in the score include the sweeping "The Door of My Dreams," the vigorous march "The Mounties," the sprightly "Pretty Things," the rhythmic "Totem Tom-Tom," and the rhapsodic title song. *Rose-Marie* was not only one of the most successful operettas of the 1920s, it was one of the first Broadway musical to have long runs in London and Paris.

A silent version of *Rose-Marie* was made in 1928 with Joan Crawford as the title character. Unfortunately, the film is believed to be lost. MGM still owned the film rights and planned a talkie version with opera singer Grace Moore as Rose-Marie, but her opera house schedule at the time did not allow her to make the movie. So the leading role went to MGM's favorite soprano, Jeanette MacDonald. After the success of *Naughty Marietta* (1935), Nelson Eddy was the obvious choice for her leading men. The screen version changed the title to the unhyphenated *Rose Marie* and reworked the plot considerably but the best of the score made it to the screen. The famous Canadian opera singer Marie de Flor (MacDonald) hears that her brother John (James Stewart) has committed a murder and is now a fugitive from the law. She suspects her brother is hiding out in the Rockies so she sets off to find him, followed by the Canadian Mountie Sergeant Bruce (Eddy). Unaware that the sergeant is after John, Rose Marie accepts his help as she tries to get through the wilderness. Of course the two fall in love and sing some ravishing duets together before both love and justice are served. The four best songs from the stage were heard in the movie version. The rest of the music came from familiar standards ("Dinah" and "Some of These Days"), two new numbers ("Pardon Me, Madame" and "Just for You" by Herbert Stothart and Gus Kahn), and established opera arias for MacDonald. Director W. S. Van Dyke shot much of *Rose Marie* on location in the California mountains, and "Indian Love Call" was even more effective in a realistic, rural setting. All of the production values are top-notch, both in the city scenes and in the country settings. The "Totem Tom-Tom" number had stopped the show on Broadway as a chorus line of girls dressed as totem poles made geometric patterns. On-screen the number was a spectacular tribal dance choreographed by Chester Hale. *Rose Marie* was one of the most expensive MGM films of its era, but it was also one of the most popular. The studio even brought the musical back to movie houses a few years later, a move rarely done in Hollywood at the time.

In 1954 MGM remade *Rose Marie* in color CinemaScope and the scenery often outshone the story, which was a mixture of the stage script and the 1936 movie. Ann Blyth was Rose Marie, a Mountie named Mike Malone (Howard Keel) was the hero, and Rose Marie ends up in the arms of the fur trapper Duval (Fernando Lamas). The low-caste Wanda from the stage became a ravishing Indian princess (Joan Taylor), the daughter of the chief of the tribe. The one improvement in the movie was a delightful turn by Bert Lahr singing "I'm a Mountie Who Never Got His Man" by George Stoll and Herbert Baker. Other new numbers by Hammerstein, Paul Francis Webster, and others included "The Right Place for a Girl," "Free to Be Free," "I Have the Love," and "Love and Kisses." The film, produced and directed by Mervyn LeRoy and choreographed by Busby Berkeley, was not a success at the box office, and by the 1960s the musical *Rose Marie* was little more than a corny relic from the past and "Indian Love Call" the stuff of parody.

See also: *Naughty Marietta*; Jeanette MacDonald and Nelson Eddy, Oscar Hammerstein biography boxes

FURTHER READING

Druxman, Michael B. *The Musical from Broadway to Hollywood.* New York: Barnes, 1980.
Grant, Barry Keith. *The Hollywood Film Musical.* Hoboken, NJ: Wiley-Blackwell, 2012.
Rich, Sharon. *Sweethearts: The Timeless Love Affair . . . Between Jeanette MacDonald and Nelson Eddy.* 3rd ed. New York: Bell Harbour Press, 2014.

THE GREAT ZIEGFELD

Studio and release date: Metro-Goldwyn-Mayer; April 1936
Producer: Hunt Stromberg
Screenplay: William Anthony McGuire
Songwriters: Irving Berlin, Walter Donaldson, Harold Adamson, Nora Bays,
    Jack Norworth, Anna Held, and others (music and lyrics)
Director: Robert Z. Leonard
Choreographer: Seymour Felix
Musical Director: Arthur Lange
Cinematographers: Oliver T. Marsh, George Folsey, Karl Freund, Ray June
Cast: William Powell, Luise Rainer, Myrna Loy, Frank Morgan, Fanny Brice,
    Virginia Bruce, Reginald Owen, Ray Bolger, Joseph Cawthorn
Principal Songs: "A Pretty Girl Is Like a Melody"; "It's Delightful to Be
    Married"; "Shine on Harvest Moon"; "Won't You Come and Play with Me?";
    "My Man"; "If You Knew Susie"

Although it was not the first biographical movie musical to come out of Hollywood, this early entry in the new genre was certainly one of the most opulent and, surprisingly, involving. The movie, built around the life and career of Broadway producer Florenz Ziegfeld, has rarely been topped for pure showmanship and glamour. Ziegfeld was a Broadway producer who was known for his lavish musical productions. In 1907 he presented the first of his annual *Follies*, elaborate shows with singing, dancing, and comedy done on a grand scale. Ziegfeld's shows were the most expensive Broadway had ever seen but they were also among the most popular. Ziegfeld spent money carelessly but often brought in enough money that he was able to keep presenting such shows until the stock market crash of 1929 ended his spectacular career. A colorful character who was always in the news, Ziegfeld was known to people across the country even if they had never seen any of his shows. All the same, a movie about his life was going to be a bit risky and, by nature of the subject, expensive. Yet MGM was in a financial and artistic position to make such a film and it proceeded with confidence.

Previous to *The Great Ziegfeld,* most film biographies were about famous and/or legendary people in history. Some movies about Abraham Lincoln and Napoleon, for example, had demonstrated how effective the film medium could be in bringing biography alive. Show business bio-pics were rare until the success of *The Great Ziegfeld*. Its popularity prompted just about every studio in Hollywood to make musicals out of the lives of songwriters, performers, and producers. One thing they all had in common was a willingness to stretch, bend, or even change the facts in order to make for a pleasing and dramatic story. The result was a tendency to keep telling the same rags-to-riches story and so the musical bio-pics started to all look alike. Not so with *The Great Ziegfeld*, which, while altering facts, was realistically dramatic with interesting characters and terse dialogue between the many production numbers.

The screenplay by William Anthony McGuire is long (176 minutes), detailed, and intriguing. At the midway at the 1893 Chicago World's Fair, sideshow barker Florenz Ziegfeld (William Powell) promotes his attraction, strong man The Great Sandow (Nat Pendleton), and sharpens his showmanship skills. Soon he is producing revues on Broadway and is known for his celebrated *Follies*. Ziegfeld brings the provocative French singer Anna Held (Luise Rainer) to New York on a wave of publicity then marries her. But the marriage is a difficult one and Ziegfeld divorces her when he meets and falls in love with actress Billie Burke (Myrna Loy). The artistic high point in Ziegfeld's Broadway career is the night in 1927 when his production of *Show Boat* opens. But soon the Depression wipes him out financially and Ziegfeld dies in 1932 thinking back on all his past triumphs. The show business bio-pic genre was new in 1936 so *The Great Ziegfeld* was a novelty. The script was a mixture of fact and fiction with plenty of celebrities from the past portrayed by themselves or by others. Seymour Felix choreographed the musical numbers, the most famous being Irving Berlin's "A Pretty Girl Is Like a Melody" staged on a giant spiral staircase with 180 singers, dancers, and musicians posed on the 175 steps. The sequence was the single most expensive musical number Hollywood had ever filmed. The circular curtain alone cost $200,000 in 1936 dollars. So many memorable songs came from Ziegfeld productions that the score was a treasure trove of standards and they were performed with taste and panache by the large cast. Surprisingly, many of the book scenes were also excellent and the performances by the leading players were outstanding. Luise Rainer's Oscar-winning performance as Ziegfeld's first wife is riveting and heartbreaking, something quite uncommon in a musical. Also superior was the musical direction, the decor and costumes, and the direction by Robert Z. Leonard. The Hunt Stromberg production was a major hit at the box office and the film also won the Academy Award for best picture. Its success spawned a string of show biz musical biographies for decades and they are still being made on occasion. But *The Great Ziegfeld* is the grandaddy of them all and still one of the best.

FURTHER READING

Bloom, Ken. *Hollywood Musicals: The 101 Greatest Song-and-Dance Movies of All Time*. New York: Black Dog and Leventhal, 2010.

Eames, John Douglas. *The MGM Story*. New York: Crown Publishers, 1975.

Mordden, Ethan. *Ziegfeld: The Man Who Invented Show Business*. New York: St. Martin's Press, 2008.

SHOW BOAT

Studio and release date: Universal; April 1936

Producer: Carl Laemmle, Jr.

Screenplay: Oscar Hammerstein, based on his 1927 stage script that was based on Edna Ferber's 1926 novel

Songwriters: Jerome Kern (music), Oscar Hammerstein (lyrics)

Director: James Whale

Music Director: Adolph Deutsch

Choreographer: LeRoy Prinz

Cinematographers: John Mescall, John Fulton

Cast: Irene Dunne, Allan Jones, Helen Morgan, Paul Robeson, Charles Winninger, Helen Westley, Hattie McDaniel, Queenie Smith, Sammy White, Donald Cook

Principal Songs: "Ol' Man River"; "Can't Help Lovin' Dat Man"; "Bill"; "Make Believe"; "You Are Love"; "Gallivantin' Around"; "After the Ball"; "Goodbye, My Lady Love"; "I Have the Room Above Her"; "Ah Still Suits Me"; "Cotton Blossom"

The first masterpiece of the Broadway musical stage, *Show Boat* was filmed three times but this version from 1936 is considered the best, a cinema classic that still enthralls. The 1927 Broadway success was the first show that was a "musical play" as opposed to a "musical comedy." *Show Boat* had a script and score with a larger scope and a more complex temperament than any work before it, bringing to fruition the dream of Jerome Kern (music) and Oscar Hammerstein (book and lyrics) to create a piece of serious music-theater. It also had the most complex plot of any musical yet seen. In the 1880s, Cap'n Andy Hawkes pilots the show boat *Cotton Blossom* up and down the Mississippi River, bringing stage melodramas to the riverside towns and cities. His wife Parthy doesn't like raising her daughter Magnolia among show people and river riffraff so she is particularly suspicious of Gaylord Ravenal, a dashing-looking gentleman who she (rightly) suspects is a river gambler. When the local sheriff learns that Julie La Verne, the featured actress on the *Cotton Blossom*, is a mulatto and is married to the white man Steve, the couple is forced to flee and Gaylord and Magnolia take over the leading roles in the show boat's repertoire. The two fall in love and, with Cap'n Andy's help, elope and move to Chicago. Ravenal's gambling luck deserts him and, unable to face his failure, he abandons Magnolia and their little girl Kim. Magnolia gets a job singing in a Chicago nightclub after the star of the show quits; that star is the alcoholic Julie and, unknown to Magnolia, she hears Magnolia's audition and quits so that her friend can get the job. On New Year's Eve the Cap'n and Parthy are reunited with Magnolia at the nightclub where she is such a success that her singing career is launched. Years pass and Kim has grown up and is now a Roaring Twenties singing and dancing star. Magnolia decides to retire from performing and, joining her parents and Kim back on the *Cotton Blossom*, she is reunited with the aged Ravenal once again. Throughout the years, the African American riverboat worker Joe and his wife, the cook Queenie, remain on the *Cotton Blossom* and observe the changes that occur in the Hawkes family. As much as life on the Mississippi may change, Joe knows that the river itself is unaware of the plight of humans and it continues on regardless of people's fortunes or failures.

Hammerstein's adaptation of Edna Ferber's sprawling novel was a masterwork of storytelling and character development. He not only condensed and clarified the book's many events and characters, but he rethought them in terms of a musical theater production. The Kern-Hammerstein score was richer and more varied than any other yet heard, filled with operetta numbers, folk and blues music, and bright musical comedy songs. *Show Boat* is also the first musical to hold together so well thematically, the song "Ol' Man River" linking the score just as the Mississippi ties together the plot and characters. Several standards came out of the score, including the playful but romantic duet "Make Believe," the rhapsodic "You Are Love," the rhythmic torch song "Can't Help Lovin' Dat Man," the ballad "Why Do I Love You?," and the folk song "Ol' Man River," but *Show Boat* is much more than a string of hit songs. Each number comments on the action or the characters, even if it is part of the show being presented on the boat or in a nightclub. Never before had a Broadway score taken its characters (and the audience) to so many places emotionally and thematically. Over the years the musical has not only been revived but revised so that there is no one definite version of *Show Boat* onstage. The three movie versions also differ considerably.

The first film of *Show Boat* (1929) was a silent film version of Ferber's book that Universal had in production when the musical opened on Broadway. The studio added sound to some scenes, put Negro spirituals in the background, and filmed an 18-minute prologue in which members of the Broadway company sang some of the hits from the musical. The result is an odd, disjointed movie, but it does have those historic clips of the original players. Laura La Plante and Joseph Schildkraut are Magnolia and Ravenal in the nonmusical story and they are often quite effective, but the supporting characters are mostly stereotypic and melodramatic. The movie was produced by Carl Laemmle; it was his son Carl Laemmle, Jr., who produced the first talkie version of the musical seven years later. Directed with skill and sensitivity by James Whale with choreography by LeRoy Prinz, the film is a masterwork of striking visuals and lyrical music. Helen Morgan (Julie), Charles Winninger (Cap'n Andy), and others from the original cast were reunited for this superb sound version, beautifully filmed, acted, and sung. Irene Dunne and Allan Jones shine as Magnolia and Ravenal, Paul Robeson is a towering Joe,

Jerome Kern (1885–1945)   A pioneering composer who was instrumental in creating the sound of the American musical, he worked in movies only during the last decade of his life but left some unforgettable songs. He was born in New York City, the son of a German-born merchandiser and an American-born mother of Bohemian descent who taught the boy piano. Kern studied at the New York College of Music before his songs were interpolated into other songwriters' shows on Broadway. By 1915 he was famous for his music for the Princess musicals, a series of contemporary musical comedies that helped define the new sound of stage music. Among his dozens of Broadway shows are *Very Good Eddie* (1915), *Oh, Boy!* (1917), *Leave It to Jane* (1917), *Sally* (1920), *Sunny* (1925), *Show Boat* (1927), *Sweet Adeline* (1929), *The Cat and the Fiddle* (1931), *Music in the Air* (1932), *Roberta* (1933), and *Very Warm for May* (1939). During the Depression when there were fewer shows on Broadway, Kern went to Hollywood where he scored such notable movies as *I Dream Too Much* (1935), *Swing Time* (1936), *High, Wide and Handsome* (1937), *Joy of Living* (1938), *One Night in the Tropics* (1940), *You Were Never Lovelier* (1942), *Cover Girl* (1944), *Can't Help Singing* (1944), and *Centennial Summer* (1946). Kern's remarkable melodic gifts and his experimenting with the ballad form and the musical play cannot be overestimated and his music is still potent today. Biographies: *Jerome Kern: His Life and Music*, Gerald Bordman (1980); *Jerome Kern*, Stephen Banfield (2006).

Hattie McDaniel is superb as Queenie, and every player down to the smallest role is excellent. Some songs from the stage score had to be cut and Hammerstein and Kern wrote three new ones: the charm ballad "I Have the Room Above Her," the wry character number "Ah Still Suits Me," and the spirited "Gallivantin' Around," some of which were later incorporated into stage revivals of the show. Hammerstein's screenplay made changes in the later part of the story and the ending is closer to a Hollywood finale rather than the bittersweet conclusion of the play. But all in all this *Show Boat* is a film classic and is still powerful and pleasing.

The 1946 Kern bio-pic *Till the Clouds Roll By* opens with a 15-minute sequence in which the opening night of *Show Boat* is illustrated. It is a beautifully edited and sung condensation featuring Kathryn Grayson as Magnolia, Tony Martin as Gaylord, Lena Horne as Julie, Caleb Peterson as Joe, and Virginia O'Brien as Ellie. In some ways the sequence was a screen test by MGM in preparation for a full-length, color remake of the entire musical, though only Grayson was used in the subsequent film. The 1951 *Show Boat* was produced by Arthur Freed, directed by George Sidney, and choreographed by Robert Alton. The use of color and location shooting distinguished the MGM remake but, some fine performances aside, it is disappointing. Grayson and Howard Keel as Magnolia and Ravenal are in top form vocally but neither performance is totally convincing. Ava Gardner (dubbed by Annette Warren) is effective in the enlarged part of Julie, but too many of the other supporting cast are only superficially entertaining. The screenplay by John Lee Mahin also made many changes in the latter half of the plot, some of which work well. Julie, for instance, is instrumental in bringing Magnolia and Ravenal back together at the end of the film. Yet after the outstanding 1936 version, this *Show Boat* seems unnecessary.

See also: Hide, Wide and Handsome, Till the Clouds Roll By, Oklahoma!; Jerome Kern, Oscar Hammerstein, Irene Dunne biography boxes

FURTHER READING

Decker, Todd. *Show Boat: Performing Race in an American Musical*. New York: Oxford University Press, 2012.

Fitzgerald, Michael G. *Universal Pictures: A Panoramic History*. Westport, CT: Arlington House, 1977.

Gehring, Wes. D. *Irene Dunne: First Lady of Hollywood*. 2nd ed. Lanham, MD: Scarecrow Press, 2006.

Kreuger, Miles. *Show Boat: The Story of a Classic American Musical*. Boston: Da Capo Press, 1990.

SAN FRANCISCO

Studio and release date: Metro-Goldwyn-Mayer; June 1936
Producers: John Emerson, Bernard Hyman
Screenplay: Anita Loos, Robert Hopkins
Songwriter: Bronislau Kaper, Nacio Herb Brown, and others (music), Gus Kahn, Arthur Freed, and others (lyrics)
Director: W. S. Van Dyke
Music Director: Herbert Stothart
Choreographer: Val Raset
Cinematographer: Oliver T. Marsh
Cast: Jeanette MacDonald, Clark Gable, Spencer Tracy, Jack Holt, Ted Healy, Jessie Ralph, Shirley Ross
Principal Songs: "San Francisco"; "Would You?"; "A Heart That's Free"; "At the Georgia Camp Meeting"; "A Hot Time in the Old Town Tonight"; "The Battle Hymn of the Republic"; opera selections

Today this movie would be labeled a "disaster movie," yet it is still a musical and one in which the characters and the story are as intriguing as the special effects. It is arguably the best musical disaster movie to come out of Hollywood, which is a silly statement because Tinseltown has produced only two notable films in the oddball genre. Nonmusical disaster movies had proven to be audience pleasers in the 1930s, so MGM spent a lot on the special effects and gave the whole production top-of-the-line sets and costumes as well. The musical aspects of *San Francisco* were not slighted either. Only a few new songs were written for the movie, but many familiar favorites were added to make the musical sections of the film highly accessible. With soprano Jeanette MacDonald cast as the heroine, it was clear to audiences that *San Francisco* was a musical, but most patrons came to see Clark Gable and the earthquake.

The screenplay by Anita Loos and Robert Hopkins offered interesting characters and ample opportunity for songs. Opera singer Mary Blake (MacDonald) from the Midwest travels to San Francisco's notorious Barbary Coast district in 1906 to sing in a saloon run by Blackie Norton (Gable). She begins a romance with the tough but charming proprietor, but soon high society calls and Mary is singing at the Tivoli Opera House to the delight of all the swells on Nob Hill. Blackie refuses to turn genteel to keep Mary, and their relationship is at an impasse when the earthquake strikes and the two lovers, surviving the disaster and looking at life differently now, are reunited. Spencer Tracy, in a career-boosting performance as the priest Fr. Mullin who runs a Barbary Coast mission, led the strong supporting cast that included Jack Holt, Ted Healy, Shirley Ross, Edgar Kennedy, and Al Shean. W. S. Van Dyke directed, Val Raset choreographed, and James Basevi did the spectacular earthquake sequence that is still stunning to behold. Bronislau Kaper (music) and Gus Kahn (lyrics) wrote the title song, which was used as both a rousing anthem and a tender hymn, and Nacio Herb Brown (music) and Arthur Freed (lyrics) provided the waltzing "Would You?" The rest of the score was comprised of either old standards (such as "At the Georgia Camp Meeting" and "Battle Hymn of the Republic") or selections from classical operas (*La Traviata* and *Faust*). *San Francisco* outlives most disaster movies because the story is interesting even without the destruction. As they watched buildings crumble and fall, moviegoers were still interested in what happened to the major characters that had intrigued them so. That is a sign of expert filmmaking. *San Francisco* still holds the attention of viewers because the entertainment value is not merely about destruction.

Hollywood's other disaster musical, *In Old Chicago* (1938), also holds up well even though the characters are less complex and the melodramatics are a bit thick at times. 20th Century Fox obviously tried to copy the success of *San Francisco* in this musical starring the studio's leading female singer, Alice Faye. Fox even tried (without success) to borrow Gable from MGM for the male lead.

The Great Chicago Fire of 1871 provided the disaster this time. Saloon singer Belle Fawcett (Faye) and the enterprising, slick Dion O'Leary (Tyrone Power) have a complicated love-hate relationship while Dion's goodhearted brother Jack (Don Ameche) runs for mayor and tries to clean up the corruption in Chicago. Faye and the chorus sang old favorites like "How Many Miles Back to London Town?" and new songs such as the waltzing "I've Taken a Fancy to You" by Lew Pollock (music) and Sidney Clare (lyrics) and the vivacious title number by Harry Revel (music) and Mack Gordon (lyrics). The story reached a crisis point and the brothers are about to destroy each other when the O'Leary's family cow knocks over a lantern in the barn and the great fire breaks out. From that point the music stopped and the film became a catastrophic spectacle. Alice Brady, as Mrs. O'Leary, was a standout in the supporting cast, which also featured Andy Devine, Brian Donlevy, Phyllis Brooks, Sidney Blackmer, and Burton Churchill. Producer Darryl F. Zanuck spent $1.8 million on *In Old Chicago*, one of the most expensive films of the decade, and director Henry King made sure it all showed up on the screen. *In Old Chicago* still impresses but not on the level that *San Francisco* does.

See also: Jeanette MacDonald biography box

FURTHER READING

Grant, Barry Keith. *The Hollywood Film Musical*. Hoboken, NJ: Wiley-Blackwell, 2012.
Thomas, Lawrence B. *The MGM Years*. New York: Arlington House, 1971.
Turk, Edward Baron. *Hollywood Diva: A Biography of Jeanette MacDonald*. Oakland: University of California Press, 2000.

SWING TIME

Studio and release date: RKO Radio Pictures; August 1936
Producer: Pandro S. Berman
Screenplay: Howard Lindsey, Allan Scott, based on the story *Portrait of John Garnett* by Erwin Gelsey
Songwriter: Jerome Kern (music), Dorothy Fields (lyrics)
Director: George Stevens
Music Director: Nathaniel Shilkret
Choreographer: Hermes Pan, Fred Astaire
Cinematographer: David Abel
Cast: Fred Astaire, Ginger Rogers, Helen Broderick, Victor Moore, Eric Blore
Principal Songs: "The Way You Look Tonight"; "A Fine Romance"; "Never Gonna Dance"; "Pick Yourself Up"; "Bojangles of Harlem"

Some argue that this is the classiest of the Fred Astaire and Ginger Rogers musicals. It certainly has an outstanding score, and the two leading players were at the peak of their talents when *Swing Time* was made. The plot, on the other hand, was nothing exceptional. If *Swing Time* is still highly rated, it is because the stars and Jerome Kern's score make mediocre material look like gold. The irresponsible gambler "Lucky" Garnett (Astaire) leaves his fiancée Margaret Watson (Betty Furness) at the altar while he's partying with his pal Pop Cardetti (Victor Moore). Her infuriated father, Judge Watson (Landers Stevens), tells Lucky he has to earn $25,000 before he can marry his daughter. Lucky and Pop go to New York to try and raise the cash but he is sidetracked by the

As the title suggests, the dancing in *Swing Time* (1936) moves away from ballroom dance and embraces the new sound of swing when Fred Astaire and Ginger Rogers (pictured) take to the dance floor. Yet even with this jazzier sound, the beloved dance couple still has plenty of class. George Stevens directed this classic "Fred and Ginger" musical. (RKO/Photofest)

beautiful dance instructor Penny Carroll (Rogers). He takes lessons just to be near her but she's engaged to bandleader Ricardo Romero (Georges Metaxa). Before you know it the quarreling Lucky and Penny have a successful dance act and are falling in love, though Ricardo and Margaret present a major obstacle until the final reel. The contrived screenplay at least had some sparkling dialogue for the lovers and comic bits for the secondary couple made up of Moore and Helen Broderick. It also left plenty of room for dance and all of it was superb. The couple's effervescent instrumental "Waltz in Swing Time," allowed for some clever choreography, which alternated between waltzing and swing music. Astaire put on blackface makeup in the rhythmic "Bojangles of Harlem," which was a tribute to the great African American tap dancer Bill Robinson, nicknamed Bojangles. The seductive dance duet "Never Gonna Dance" is a minor-key number that looks effortless but took 47 takes before Astaire thought it was right. In the tongue-in-cheek number "Pick Yourself Up," Astaire pretends he cannot dance very well in order to keep getting lessons from Rogers. Astaire and Hermes Pan devised the choreography for the film and it was quintessential Astaire and Rogers magic. George Stevens directed the Pandro S. Berman production, which was originally

Dorothy Fields and **Jimmy McHugh**   A stage and screen songwriting team that had many hits in both media, they had an accomplished career together and also with other artists. Lyricist Fields (1904–1974) was the daughter of the celebrated stage comic and producer Lew Fields and as a boarding school student wrote light verse. In the late 1920s she teamed up with composer McHugh, and some of their songs were heard at the Cotton Club in Harlem and on Broadway. McHugh (1892–1969) was born in Boston and worked as an office boy at the Boston Opera House, later plugging, writing, and publishing songs. He first gained attention when he teamed up with Fields, the two of them going to Hollywood in 1930 and scoring such musicals as *Love in the Rough* (1930), *Cuban Love Song* (1931), *Hooray for Love* (1935), and *Every Night at Eight* (1935). Fields worked with composer Jerome Kern on *Roberta* (1935), *I Dream Too Much* (1935), *Swing Time* (1936), *Joy of Living* (1938), and *One Night in the Tropics* (1940). She was the first woman to win an Oscar for best song with "The Way You Look Tonight" from *Swing Time*. Fields also had a very long career on Broadway, writing the script and/or the lyrics for such notable musicals as *Let's Face It!* (1941), *Something for the Boys* (1943), *Annie Get Your Gun* (1946), *A Tree Grows in Brooklyn* (1951), *Sweet Charity* (1966) and *Seesaw* (1973). McHugh's other frequent collaborator was lyricist Harold Adamson, the two scoring the films *Top of the Town* (1937), *Mad About Music* (1938), *That Certain Age* (1938), *Higher and Higher* (1943), *Four Jills in a Jeep* (1944), *Nob Hill* (1945), *Doll Face* (1945), *If You Knew Susie* (1948), and others. With various lyricists he also wrote songs for such films as *Buck Benny Rides Again* (1940), *You're the One* (1941), *Seven Days' Leave* (1942), and *Happy Go Lucky* (1943). Fields biography: *On the Sunny Side of the Street*, Deborah Grace Winer (1977).

titled *I Won't Dance* and then *Never Gonna Dance* until the studio, worried that the public would not come and see an Astaire-Rogers picture with no dancing, changed it to *Swing Time* (though there is only one swing number in the film). Although the movie is remembered as one of the great dance musicals, it also boasts one of the best film scores of the 1930s. Jerome Kern (music) and Dorothy Fields (lyrics) wrote the delectable songs that, in addition to the dance numbers already mentioned, included two outstanding numbers that were presented with perfection. "A Fine Romance" was a wry musical conversation with the lovers quarreling in a snow-covered wood, the song itself becoming a complete musical scene. In addition, Astaire sang the Oscar-winning "The Way You Look Tonight" to Rogers as she lathered her head with shampoo. The offbeat way of setting the number made it all the more romantic.

This being the sixth Astaire and Rogers musical, one would expect that the formula was getting old and that the two stars had done just about all they could when it came to dance duets. Yet there is nothing tired about *Swing Time* when the twosome sing and dance. During two of the film's most memorable musical moments, "The Way You Look Tonight" and "A Fine Romance," the couple does not dance at all. Audiences had so fully accepted the team as full-fledged stars that they found them interesting even when no footsteps were involved. As popular as the duo was, both Astaire and Rogers wanted to make movies with other partners. Rogers did a series of comedies and dramas while Astaire played opposite Joan Fontaine in *Damsel in Distress* (1937) and Eleanor Powell in *Broadway Melody of 1940*. But audiences demanded to see their favorite dancing couple again and again so after *Swing Time* Astaire and Rogers made four more musicals together.

See also: *Top Hat, Roberta*; Jerome Kern, Dorothy Fields, Fred Astaire, Ginger Rogers biography boxes

FURTHER READING

Bordman, Gerald. *Jerome Kern: His Life and Music*. New York: Oxford University Press, 1980.

Croce, Arlene. *The Fred Astaire and Ginger Rogers Book*. New York: Dutton, 1987.

Winer, Deborah Grace. *On the Sunny Side of the Street: The Life and Lyrics of Dorothy Fields*. New York: Schirmer Books, 1997.

BORN TO DANCE

Studio and release date: Metro-Goldwyn Mayer; November 1936
Producer: Jack Cummings
Screenplay: Jack McGowan, Sid Silvers
Songwriter: Cole Porter (music and lyrics)
Director: Roy Del Ruth
Choreographer: Dave Gould
Musical Director: Alfred Newman
Cinematographer: Ray June
Cast: Eleanor Powell, James Stewart, Sid Silvers, Virginia Bruce, Frances Langford, Una Merkel, Buddy Ebsen, Raymond Walburn, Alan Dinehart
Songs: "Easy to Love"; "I've Got You Under My Skin"; "Swingin' the Jinx Away"; "Rap Tap on Wood"; "Rolling Home"; "Hey, Babe, Hey"; "Love Me, Love My Pekinese"

One of the first sailors-on-leave musicals, this overblown but contagiously silly movie is filled with riches, most importantly terrific dancing and memorable Cole Porter songs. Only three years had passed since *42nd Street* had capitalized on the plot turn in which the young unknown performer goes on for the leading lady on opening night and becomes a star, yet during that time it had been used so often by Hollywood that it was not only familiar to audiences but even expected. If moviegoers were weary of the cliché, they didn't complain. And in the case of *Born to Dance*, what preceded the cliché was so contrived that no one expected this kind of musical to make sense. In the plot, the sailor-buddies Ted Barker (James Stewart), Gunny Saks (Sid Silvers), and Mush Tracy (Buddy Ebsen) get shore leave in New York City and get involved with the career of Nora Paige (Eleanor Powell), a struggling dancer who understudies the temperamental Broadway star Lucy James (Virginia Bruce). Gunny's wife Jenny (Una Merkel) is not sure she is happy to find out that she married such a goofy looking guy and doesn't tell him about their little girl Sally (Juanita Quigley). To keep the secret, Jenny passes Sally off as Nora's child, which certainly puts a dent in Nora's romance with Ted. Also adding complications is Lucy's predatory interest in Ted. To no one's surprise, Nora becomes a star when she steps in for Lucy on opening night and the sweethearts are reconciled.

Although some Cole Porter's songs had been heard in earlier film musicals, *Born to Dance* was his first screen assignment and he did not disappoint, writing his first Hollywood standard, "I've Got You Under My Skin." The number was sung by Bruce and danced to by the team of Georges and Jalna at a fancy nightclub. The film's other hit ballad, "Easy to Love," had been written for Porter's Broadway show *Anything Goes* two years earlier but was cut when the leading man couldn't hit the song's demanding high notes. Ironically, it was sung in the film by Stewart who couldn't sing *any* of the notes but his sincere rendition was so touching that the studio decided not to dub him. (The role of Ted had originally been cast with operatic singer Allan Jones; the two performers could not be more different.) The rich and varied score also included the rhythmic "Rap Tap on Wood" in which Powell did some furious tapping, the silly "Love Me, Love My Pekinese," which Bruce sang to a group of sailors onboard their ship, and the playful sailors' ditty "Rolling Home." For an odd but agreeable bit of whimsy, a Central Park cop (Reginald Gardiner) conducted an invisible orchestra in a rousing rendition of Ponchielli's "Dance of the Hours," spoofing the famous conductor Leopold Stokowski's style with frenzied hair and erratic gestures. The most famous (and later most parodied) musical number in the film was the nautical finale "Swingin' the Jinx Away" set on an all-white battleship deck with Powell dancing down from the crow's nest to tap her way across the shiny deck surrounded by a Navy orchestra.

Eleanor Powell was considered the Queen of Tap in Hollywood (though later Ann Miller gave her a run for her money) and many believe that her finest tapping

Eleanor Powell (1912–1982)   In the opinion of many, the best female tap dancer on-screen, the tall, leggy performer demonstrated her machine-like tapping on Broadway but didn't become famous until Hollywood called. Born and educated in Springfield, Massachusetts, Powell started dancing professionally at the age of 11 and by the time she was 17 was tapping away in Broadway shows. Yet she never quite became a Broadway star, so Powell went to Hollywood in 1935 where she found fame with her performances in a series of musicals, most memorably *Broadway Melody of 1936* (1935), *Born to Dance* (1936), *Broadway Melody of 1938* (1937), *Rosalie* (1937), *Broadway Melody of 1940*, and *Lady, Be Good* (1941). She continued to dance on-screen until 1944, and then performed in nightclubs and for charity benefits. Biography: *Eleanor Powell: First Lady of Dance*, Alice Levin (1998).

was in *Born to Dance*. Because she had no dance partner in the movie, her dazzling footwork is not hampered by the limitations of another. Her solo dancing is energetic but sexless and even a bit cold. It wasn't until four years later in *Broadway Melody of 1940* that Powell demonstrated her ability to connect with a partner who equaled her tapping ability: Fred Astaire. Yet Powell had always been more than just a dance technician. She exuded a warmth on-screen even if her acting was limited and her singing always had to be dubbed. Her chemistry with Stewart in *Born to Dance* is noticeable even though it was never expressed in dance. The other outstanding dancer in *Born to Dance* is the tall, thin Buddy Ebsen who was given specialty spots in some of the numbers. With his rubber limbs and lanky frame, Ebsen is both funny and mesmerizing. He was featured in a dozen Hollywood movies before hanging up his dance shoes and then enjoyed 50 years as a popular character actor. His presence in *Born to Dance* reminds us of the wealth of talented hoofers Hollywood had on contract during the Golden Age of musicals.

See also: *Broadway Melody of 1940, 42nd Street*; Eleanor Powell, Cole Porter biography boxes

FURTHER READING

Bloom, Ken. *Hollywood Musicals: The 101 Greatest Song-and-Dance Movies of All Time*. New York: Black Dog and Leventhal, 2010.
McBrien, William. *Cole Porter*. New York: Vintage Press, 2011.
Schwartz, Charles. *Cole Porter: A Biography*. New York: Dial Press, 1977.

SHALL WE DANCE

Studio and release date: RKO Radio Pictures; April 1937
Producer: Pandro S. Berman
Screenplay: Allan Scott, Ernest Pagano, based on the story *Watch Your Step* by Lee Loeb, Harold Buchman
Songwriters: George Gershwin (music), Ira Gershwin (lyrics)
Director: Mark Sandrich
Music Director: Nathaniel Shilkret
Choreographers: Hermes Pan, Harry Losee, Fred Astaire
Cinematographer: David Abel
Cast: Fred Astaire, Ginger Rogers, Edward Everett Horton, Eric Blore, Jerome Cowan, Ketti Gallian, Harriet Hoctor
Songs: "They All Laughed"; "They Can't Take That Away from Me"; "Let's Call the Whole Thing Off"; "(I've Got) Beginner's Luck"; "Slap That Bass"; "Shall We Dance"

Most agree that the finest score that George and Ira Gershwin wrote for Hollywood was for this delectable, though uneven, Fred Astaire and Ginger Rogers musical that manages to be very touching in a way few musical comedies are. The Gershwin brothers had been wooed by the studios for some time, but the songwriters managed to find projects on Broadway even during the dark days of the Depression. After their opera *Porgy and Bess* (1935) failed to run very long, both men got discouraged with the New York critics and decided to take up Tinseltown's offer. They scored *Damsel in Distress* (1937), which reunited them with Astaire, whom they had worked with on Broadway in the 1920s, then the brothers wrote the songs for *Shall We Dance*. George Gershwin was the leading jazz composer in America since his sensational "Rhapsody in Blue" debuted in 1924. Astaire wanted to incorporate more jazz into his dancing, so in *Shall We Dance* the brothers were able to accommodate him with not only songs but some instrumental selections. Both the songs and the dance music are exceptional, making this a Hollywood classic despite its contrived story line.

The American ballet dancer Pete Peters (Fred Astaire) has been booked for an engagement in London but he prefers jazz and modern dance. This is very distressing for his fussy, worrisome manager Jeffrey Baird (Edward Everett Horton). When Peter catches sight of the American musical comedy star Linda Keene (Rogers), he falls head over heels. But instead of approaching her as himself, Peter puts on a phony Russian accent and pretends to be an affected ballet star named Petrov. The disguise doesn't last long, and soon the two are aboard a ship returning to New York when rumors circulate that Peter and Linda are married. Unable to refute the stories in the press, the couple decides to wed then have a very public divorce.

George and **Ira Gershwin**   An outstanding songwriting team on Broadway and Tin Pan Alley, their movie career was limited yet exceptional. Ira Gershwin (1896–1983) was often overshadowed by his composer brother George Gershwin (1898–1937) yet he was one of America's finest lyricists. The brothers were born to a poor immigrant family in Brooklyn where Ira started writing light verse and lyrics while a student at Columbia University. George showed musical abilities at an early age, studying piano and composition with some respected teachers. While George had an early hit with the song "Swanee" and was in demand for songs for Broadway revues, Ira did not find fame until the brothers' jazz-flavored stage musicals such as *Lady, Be Good!* (1924), *Tip-Toes* (1925), *Oh, Kay!* (1926), *Funny Face* (1927), *Rosalie* (1928), *Strike Up the Band* (1930), *Girl Crazy* (1930), *Of Thee I Sing* (1931), and the unique American opera *Porgy and Bess* (1935) with DuBose Heyward. The Gershwins went to Hollywood in 1936 but scored only three musicals—*Shall We Dance* (1937), *Damsel in Distress* (1937), *The Goldwyn Follies* (1938)—before George's early death from a brain tumor. Songs by the brothers were later heard in such screen musicals as *Rhapsody in Blue* (1945), *The Shocking Miss Pilgrim* (1947), *An American in Paris* (1951), *Funny Face* (1957), and *When the Boys Meet the Girls* (1965) as well as on Broadway in *My One and Only* (1983), *Crazy for You* (1992), and *An American in Paris* (2015). Ira Gershwin collaborated with various composers on such movie musicals as *Cover Girl* (1944), *Lady in the Dark* (1944), *The Barkleys of Broadway* (1949), *Give a Girl a Break* (1953), *A Star Is Born* (1954), and *The Country Girl* (1954). Ira Gershwin's lyrics are known for their unique use of slang and an ingenious turn of phrase in his romantic songs. George Gershwin is considered one of America's best composers for the stage, concert hall, and the movies, opening up new musical forms and taking jazz in new and exciting directions. Biographies: *Fascinating Rhythm: The Collaboration of George and Ira Gershwin*, Deena Ruth Rosenberg (1998); *George Gershwin: A New Biography*, William G. Hyland (2003); *George Gershwin: His Life and Work*, Howard Pollack (2006).

Once ashore and married, they realize they love each other and drop the idea of the divorce. The nonsensical screenplay seemed to search for improbable complications just to keep the plot going. Director Mark Sandrich did his best to help the picture make sense but all he could do was film it with style. The same could be said for the unmotivated production numbers choreographed by Astaire, Harry Losee, and Hermes Pan. The whole musical is a trivial nothing, yet the characters still enchant. When it looks like they must go through with the divorce and part, singing the indelible ballad "They Can't Take That Away From Me," there is genuine empathy. Every number in the Gershwins' score is pure gold right down to the instrumental piece "Walking the Dog" that has its own cockeyed charm: Astaire and Rogers sing and dance to the title number in a sleek ballroom high up in a skyscraper, Astaire taps all over the white art deco engine room of the ocean liner with "Slap That Bass," the couple roller skate in Central Park as they playfully admonish "Let's Call the Whole Thing Off," Astaire performs the bouncy "(I've Got) Beginner's Luck," Rogers has fun with the musical words in "They All Laughed," and their duet version of "They Can't Take That Away From Me" is restrained yet unforgettable. Rarely have so many beloved standards come from one Hollywood musical. Pandro S. Berman was the lucky producer, though moviegoers were even luckier.

George Gershwin died of a brain tumor three months after *Shall We Dance* was released. He had completed most of the music for the film musical *The Goldwyn Follies*, and Vernon Duke had to compose a few additional sections before the movie was released in 1938. Thus ended Gershwin's short but remarkable career in Hollywood. In less than three years in Tinseltown, Gershwin had made quite an impact. Although none of his three films were runaway hits, the songs they introduced included a dozen timeless classics. Fortunately, Gershwin's movie career extended far beyond his lifetime. Among the later Hollywood musicals to have Gershwin scores were *Lady, Be Good* (1941), *Girl Crazy* (1943), *Rhapsody in Blue* (1945), *The Shocking Miss Pilgrim* (1947), *An American in Paris* (1951), *Funny Face* (1957), *Porgy and Bess* (1959), *Kiss Me, Stupid* (1964), and *When the Boys Meet the Girls* (1965). Gershwin's legacy may concentrate on the theater, the opera house, and the concert hall, but his contribution to the movies cannot be ignored.

See also: *Flying Down to Rio, Swing Time*; George and Ira Gershwin, Fred Astaire, Ginger Rogers biography boxes

FURTHER READING

Croce, Arlene. *The Fred Astaire and Ginger Rogers Book*. New York: Dutton, 1987.
Franceschina, John. *Hermes Pan: The Man Who Danced with Fred Astaire*. New York: Oxford University Press, 2012.
Jewell, Richard B., and Vernon Harbin. *The RKO Story*. New York: Arlington House, 1982.

HIGH, WIDE AND HANDSOME

Studio and release date: Paramount; July 1937
Producer: Arthur Hornblow, Jr.
Screenplay: Oscar Hammerstein
Songwriters: Jerome Kern (music), Oscar Hammerstein (lyrics)
Director: Rouben Mamoulian
Music Director: Boris Morros
Choreographer: LeRoy Prinz
Cinematographers: Victor Milner, Theodore Sparkuhl
Cast: Irene Dunne, Randolph Scott, Dorothy Lamour, Raymond Walburn, Akim
    Tamiroff, Charles Bickford, Ben Blue, Elizabeth Patterson
Songs: "The Folks Who Live on the Hill"; "High, Wide and Handsome";
    "Allegheny Al"; "The Things I Want"; "Can I Forget You?"; "Will You Marry
    Me Tomorrow, Maria?"

One of Hollywood's finest pioneer musicals, this sprawling musical adventure has only recently become available on DVD, so now everyone can enjoy this broad panorama of frontier life that includes a medicine show, a backwoods saloon, a carnival sideshow, a barn dance, a rural wedding celebration, and a circus. Oscar Hammerstein wrote the screenplay (and the lyrics to Jerome Kern's music), and one can find traces of his earlier *Show Boat* and his later *Oklahoma!* in the film. Paramount had high hopes for the epic tale and spent plenty of money on the on-location shooting in the California Hills and the large cast, some scenes requiring hundreds of extras. The studio also took a risk in hiring stage director Rouben Mamoulian, who had only directed three small-scale movie musicals. Yet Mamoulian, who was known for the striking visuals in his stage and screen projects, captured the look and feel of Americana, making *High, Wide and Handsome* a unique film musical.

Hammerstein's original screenplay was set in the western hills of Pennsylvania in 1859. The farmer Peter Cortlandt (Randolph Scott) toils on his farm and tinkers with a contraption that will draw oil out of the ground. Peter takes in the itinerant medicine man Doc Waterson (Raymond Walburn), his daughter Sally (Irene Dunne), and their sidekick Mac (William Frawley) when their wagon catches fire and the trio are left homeless and jobless. Peter's grandmother (Elizabeth Patterson) is not happy about having such riffraff in her house, but she agrees to the arrangement while Doc and Mac build a new wagon. By the time the wagon is finished and Doc is ready to set out on the road selling his "mineral oil" cure, Peter and Sally have fallen in love. Not until the wagon leaves the farm does Peter find the resolve to chase after it and propose marriage to Sally. On their wedding day, Peter's newfangled drilling contraption strikes oil on his farm, setting off an

Irene Dunne (1898–1990)   A multi-talented actress-singer with an operatic soprano range, she was not only successful in musicals but also in comedies and dramas. She was born in Louisville, Kentucky, the daughter of a steamship inspector and a musician, and studied at the Indianapolis Conservatory and the Chicago Musical College to train as an opera singer. When she failed to get accepted by the Metropolitan Opera in New York in 1920, she turned to musical theater, making her Broadway debut in 1922 and was featured in a half dozen forgettable musicals before getting attention in the 1929 tour of *Show Boat*. Dunne was so effective as the heroine Magnolia that she got to reprise her performance in the 1936 screen version of the musical. Dunne never returned to Broadway but was seen in over 40 movies, including the musicals *Sweet Adeline* (1935), *Roberta* (1935), *High, Wide and Handsome* (1937), *Joy of Living* (1938), and *Love Affair* (1939). Dunne was also a bankable movie star in nonmusicals, praised for her fine performances in *Cimarron* (1931), *The Age of Innocence* (1934), *The Awful Truth* (1937), *Anna and the King of Siam* (1946), *Life with Father* (1947), *I Remember Mama* (1948), *The Mudlark* (1950), and other films. Dunne retired in 1952 and concentrated on politics, diplomacy (she was a UN delegate), charities, and business. Biography: *Irene Dunne: First Lady of Hollywood*, Wes D. Gehring (2003).

oil rush in the area. The railroad robber baron Walter Brennan (Alan Hale) raises his shipping rates until the farmers cannot afford to bring their crude oil to the refinery, so Peter proposes building a pipeline that bypasses the railroad. Brennan opposes him every step of the way, hiring goons to destroy the finished sections of the pipeline. Peter's marriage to Sally is also threatened when the neglected Sally runs off to join a circus troupe with her father. When Brennan's henchmen try to destroy the final link in the pipeline, Sally returns and brings along the personnel from the circus, dwarfs and elephants included, to drive away the railroad goons and allow Peter to complete his pipeline. While most musicals suffered from thin and nonsensical plots, *Hide, Wide and Handsome* had a strong story, gripping action, and interesting supporting characters, such as Dorothy Lamour as the saloon singer Molly who is befriended by Sally and who warns her of Brennan's devious plans. The story resembled a sprawling novel, not unlike Hammerstein's previous adaptation of Edna Ferber's *Show Boat*.

Mamoulian brought the epic-like tale to the screen with a visually stunning look and a sure hand for both the romantic and the action scenes. Both the studio scenes and the location sequences have a rustic and poetic sensibility. Hammerstein often romanticized nature in his musicals, and *High, Wide and Handsome* is one of the most bucolic. While the story itself did not require songs, the movie is richer because of the way music enhances this romanticism. The original score by Kern-Hammerstein was the best the team ever wrote for Hollywood, and the songs were more integrated into the story than in most previous movie musicals. The gentle domestic ballad "The Folks Who Live on the Hill" was the standout number but also laudable were the simple but sincere ballad "Can I Forget You?," the frolicking frontier ditty "Allegheny Al," the bluesy "The Things I Want," and the rollicking title number. Producer Arthur Hornblow, Jr., the creators of the film, and the studio were all very proud of the expensive and classy movie and the reviews were favorable, yet *High, Wide and Handsome* did modest box office and never paid off its high price tag. It seriously hurt Hammerstein's career and he suffered a series of stage and screen disappointments until he teamed up with Richard Rodgers six years later and created the Broadway classic *Oklahoma!* It took decades before *High, Wide and Handsome* was fully appreciated and today it is considered a frontier musical classic.

See also: *Show Boat, Oklahoma!*; Irene Dunne, Jerome Kern, Oscar Hammerstein biography boxes

FURTHER READING

Eames, John Douglas. *The Paramount Story.* New York: Crown Publishers, 1985.
Freedland, Michael. *Jerome Kern: A Biography.* New York: Stein and Day Pub., 1981.
Gehring, Wes. D. *Irene Dunne: First Lady of Hollywood.* 2nd ed. Lanham, MD: Scarecrow Press, 2006.

ONE HUNDRED MEN AND A GIRL

Studio and release date: Universal; September 1937
Producers: Charles Rogers, Joe Pasternak
Screenplay: Bruce Manning, Charles Kenyon, James Mulhauser
Songwriters: Frederick Hollander and others (music), Sam Coslow and others (lyrics)
Director: Henry Koster
Music Director: Leopold Stokowski
Cinematographer: Joseph Valentine
Cast: Deanna Durbin, Leopold Stokowski, Adolphe Menjou, Alice Brady, Eugene Pallette, Mischa Auer
Principal Songs: "A Heart That's Free"; "It's Raining Sunbeams"; orchestral and opera selections

Teenage singing star Deanna Durbin, with her energetic smile and heavenly soprano voice, was the impetus behind this modern yet charming fairy tale. Durbin had begun her screen career the same time as Judy Garland, yet the two singing voices couldn't be more different. While Garland had a full, throaty mature voice even as a child, Durbin had a crystal clear voice ideal for opera and operetta. Durbin had been featured in a musical short and the full-length *Three Smart Girls* (1936) and was widely noticed. Universal took a chance and starred the 17-year-old in *One Hundred Men and a Girl* with the hope of creating a new teen singing star. The movie did exactly that and for the next 10 years Durbin was a musical favorite on-screen.

The tailor-made script was both a modern Cinderella tale and a "Depression chaser," a movie created to cheer up Depression-weary moviegoers. Symphony trombonist John Cardwell (Adolphe Menjou) and dozens of other classical musicians find themselves out of work when hard times force many symphony orchestras to fold. Cardwell tries to get a job at Carnegie Hall in the orchestra of the renowned conductor Leopold Stokowski but keeps getting kicked out by the doorman. Cardwell's's spunky teenage daughter Patsy (Durbin) decides to find work for her father and 99 out-of-work musicians by forming a new symphony and getting them a radio contract. She manages to meet the wealthy Mrs. Frost (Alice Brady), who promises that the orchestra will perform on her husband's radio program. But the absentminded Mrs. Frost goes off to Europe without telling her husband about the orchestra. The 100 musicians rehearse in a garage but when Patsy finally meets Frost (Eugene Pallette) and tries to set up a broadcast date, he knows nothing about it and believes the whole thing is a practical joke played on him by his friend Tommy Bitters (Jed Prouty). Undeterred, the optimistic Patsy manages to meet Stokowski (playing himself) and explain the plight of the new orchestra. After all the musicians show up at Stokowski's house and audition for him, the maestro agrees to conduct them in a concert. At the opening night concert, the orchestra is a sensation and Patsy is called forth by Stokowski and asked to sing. She launches into an opera aria from *La Traviata* and wows the audience as well as moviegoers. Durbin got to sing some other numbers as well, and classical pieces by Tchaikovsky, Liszt, Mozart, and Berlioz were performed by the orchestra so the movie was filled with music. Coproducer Joe Pasternak made the decision to have more classical music than popular songs in the film, trusting that the audiences would enjoy them. His hunch was correct and audiences found the classical music and opera selections surprisingly entertaining.

One Hundred Men and a Girl was one of the first films to feature a high-quality recording of classical music. Pasternak insisted that the concert selections be recorded by a respected symphony orchestra rather than the in-house Universal musicians. He also wanted the music conducted by a famous maestro. Stokowski was one of the world's most acclaimed conductors at the time and he took the film project very seriously. (Three years later Stokowski would return to the movies in Disney's *Fantasia*.) Pasternak hired the Philadelphia Orchestra and the music was recorded at the Philadelphia Academy of Music on a new multichannel sound system, the first time such a system was used for a film. The 100 musicians seen in the film were not the ones who recorded the soundtrack but were California musicians who were able to accurately simulate playing to the recorded track.

Since Durbin was not an experienced actress, much of the dialogue scenes focused on the other characters. Some of Hollywood's favorite character actors played members of the orchestra, and there were delicious comic turns by Alice Brady and Eugene Pallette as the Frosts. Also memorable in a small part was Frank Jenks as a singing cab driver who breaks into arias on occasion. Director Henry Koster kept the Cinderella story light and frothy and the movie never gets bogged down with sentimentality. All the same, *One Hundred Men and a Girl* was a breath of optimism during the Depression, and audiences responded favorably to it. While the movie launched Durbin's career, few of her subsequent musicals were as expert as this. Only *Can't Help Singing* (1944) comes close. By the end of the 1940s, Durbin was no longer a teen and her popularity dropped. Rather than struggle to reinvent herself in Hollywood, she retired in 1938 and lived in Europe, hidden from the public eye, for the next 66 years.

See also: *Can't Help Singing;* Deanna Durbin biography box

FURTHER READING

Fitzgerald, Michael G. *Universal Pictures: A Panoramic History*. Westport, CT: Arlington House, 1977.
Hirschhorn, Clive. *The Universal Story*. New York: Crown Publishers, 1981.
Mills, W. E. *The Deanna Durbin Fairy Tale*. Baltimore: Images, Ltd., 1996.

SNOW WHITE AND THE SEVEN DWARFS

Studio and release date: Disney/RKO; December 1937
Producer: Walt Disney
Screenplay: Ted Sears, Otto Englander, Earl Hurd, Dorothy Ann Blank, and others, based on the story *Little Snow White* by Jacob and Wilhelm Grimm
Songwriters: Frank Churchill (music), Larry Morey (lyrics)
Directors: David Hand, Perce Pearce, Ben Sharpsteen, Larry Morey, William Cottrell, Wilfred Jackson
Music Directors: Leigh Harline, Frank Churchill, Paul J. Smith

Voices: Andriana Caseletti, Harry Stockwell, Lucille LaVerne, Roy Atwill, Pinto Colvig, Billy Gilbert, Moroni Olsen, Scott Mattraw

Songs: "Some Day My Prince Will Come"; "Heigh-Ho"; "Whistle While You Work"; "I'm Wishing"; "One Song"; "Isn't This a Silly Song?"; "With a Smile and a Song"

Among the many remarkable aspects of this legendary animated musical filled with "firsts' is that it is so polished and doesn't look like the primitive first of anything. It was the first feature-length animated movie, the first cartoon to use live models to simulate human movement, the first animated feature to use a multiplane camera to achieve depth, the first movie musical to produce (in 1944) a best-selling soundtrack, and the first Hollywood film to earn over $6 million on its initial release. The story, based on the Grimm brothers' tale, was familiar to audiences but many details had to be filled in to sustain a full-length movie. The dwarfs, for example, have no names or distinct characters in the original story. Producer Walt Disney

Disney's first animated feature, *Snow White and the Seven Dwarfs* (1937) is filled with unforgettable moments. Who can possibly forget the evil Queen turning herself into an old hag so that she can offer Snow White a poisoned apple? The film is so beautifully done that it is difficult to believe it was the first of its kind. (RKO Radio Pictures/Photofest)

Walt Disney (1901–1966)   Internationally famous for producing cartoon shorts, animated features, live-action adventure film, television programs, nature documentaries, and theme parks, he also produced some of the best animated and live-action movie musicals during his long career. Disney was born in Chicago and studied at the Kansas City Art Institute. In the early 1920s, he set up his own animation studio and found success with the creation of Mickey Mouse and other beloved cartoon characters. He experimented with ways to coordinate music with animation in a series of cartoon shorts, then produced the first feature-length animated musical, *Snow White and the Seven Dwarfs* (1937). Disney then offered a series of animated classics, most of which had full musical scores, such as *Pinocchio* (1940), *Dumbo* (1941), *Cinderella* (1950), *Alice in Wonderland* (1951), *Peter Pan* (1954), *The Lady and the Tramp* (1955), *Sleeping Beauty* (1959), and *The Jungle Book* (1967). He also presented anthology musicals, such as *Fantasia* (1940), *The Three Caballeros* (1945), *Make Mine Music* (1946), *Fun and Fancy Free* (1947), and *Melody Time* (1948) as well as films that mixed animation and live action, as with *Song of the South* (1946) and *Mary Poppins* (1964). Biographies: *Walt Disney: The Triumph of the American Imagination*, Neal Gabler (2006); *Walt Disney: An American Original*, Bob Thomas (1994).

and his writers built on the Grimms' tale and created a highly original screenplay, which today is better known than its source material.

Every time the queen asks her magic mirror who is the fairest in the land, it replies that she is. But when Snow White grows up and the mirror tells the queen that the young orphan is the fairest, the jealous monarch orders the huntsman to take the girl deep into the forest and kill her. Unable to carry out her wishes, he tells Snow White to flee and never return to the castle. The lost Snow White stumbles upon the cottage of the seven dwarfs, whom she befriends. When the queen learns from the mirror that Snow White lives, she swallows a potion, turning her into an aged old crone, and goes to the cottage offering Snow White a poisoned apple. One bite and Snow White falls into a coma. The dwarfs return and chase the queen/crone to the edge of a ravine where she falls and dies while trying to destroy the dwarfs with a boulder. The dwarfs do not have the heart to bury the still-lovely Snow White and are kneeling in reverence before her body when a prince, whom Snow White had once met and spoken to, comes into the forest. He kisses the sleeping Snow White and she awakes to see that her prince has truly come.

Disney and hundreds of artists spent four years working on the project, which the film community saw as a grand folly. The very idea of a cartoon lasting 83 minutes of animated characters singing love songs to each other and of artists creating a complex and detailed art decor for a kids' movie was laughable. Yet the film changed the way audiences thought about cartoons, children's movies, and Disney. Although the script softened some of the original story's more gruesome aspects, the film was still frightening and powerful at times, yet warm-hearted and fanciful in other spots. Never had moviegoers been so caught up in an animated tale, and the public, both children and adults, liked the experience.

Frank Churchill (music) and Larry Morey (lyrics) wrote the songs, several of which became hits, and just about all of them are now part of American musical folklore. The songwriters turned to operetta for the romantic numbers, such as "One Song," "I'm Wishing," and "Someday My Prince Will Come," then used musical comedy for the dwarfs, as with "Heigh-Ho," "and "The Dwarfs' Yodeling Song." Also very effective was the music background score by Leigh Harline and Paul J. Smith, adding suspense and drama throughout. It is interesting that Disney saw his initial animated feature as a musical, but then he had been experimenting with music in cartoons for some time and always saw music and action linked. *Snow White and the Seven Dwarfs* started a tradition of animated features being musicals, and very few Disney products over the decades would offer animation without songs. To celebrate the 50th anniversary of the film, the studio rereleased it in 1987 with 4,000 prints seen in 58 countries on the same day, the largest opening day in the history of the movies.

See also: *Pinocchio, The Little Mermaid, Pocahontas*; Walt Disney biography box

FURTHER READING

Kaufman, J. B. *Snow White and the Seven Dwarfs: The Art and Creation of Walt Disney's Classic Animated Film.* San Francisco: Walt Disney Family Foundation Press, 2012.
Maltin, Leonard. *The Disney Films.* 4th ed. Glendale, CA: Disney Editions, 2000.
Thomas, Bob. *Walt Disney: An American Original.* Glendale, CA: Disney Editions, 1994.

THE BIG BROADCAST OF 1938

Studio and release date: Paramount; February 1938
Producer: Harlan Thompson
Screenplay: Walter DeLeon, Francis Martin, Ken Englund
Songwriters: Ralph Rainger (music), Leo Robin (lyrics)
Director: Mitchell Leisen
Choreographer: LeRoy Prinz

Music Director: Boris Morros
Cinematographers: Harry Fishbeck, Gordon Jennings
Cast: W. C. Fields, Bob Hope, Dorothy Lamour, Shirley Ross, Martha Raye,
   Lynne Overman, Ben Blue
Principal Songs: "Thanks for the Memory"; "You Took the Words Right Out of
   My Mouth"; "Mama, That Moon Is Here Again"; "The Waltz Lives On";
   "Don't Tell a Secret to a Rose"; "This Little Ripple Had Rhythm"; "Truckin'
   (They're Going Hollywood in Harlem)"

During the Depression, radio was very popular and new singers and comics were
being discovered by the public all the time. In 1932, Paramount decided to let radio
fans see what some of their favorite stars looked like, so they hired a number of
popular "voices" and fitted them into a nearly plotless film called *The Big Broadcast.*
It was successful enough to launch a series of Paramount "Broadcast" musicals,
and soon radio musicals were made by other studios. The first musical centered
on the rivalry between airwaves singer Bing Crosby (playing himself) and Texas
millionaire Leslie McWhinney (Stuart Erwin) over the affections of Anita Rogers
(Leila Hyams), but the story was happily interrupted by a dozen radio stars. Kate
Smith sang "It Was So Beautiful" and her theme song "When the Moon Comes
Over the Mountain," Cab Calloway delivered "Minnie the Moocher" and "Kickin'
the Gong Around" with his orchestra, the Mills Brothers harmonized through "Tiger
Rag" and "Goodbye Blues," Vincent Lopez and his orchestra played their trade-
mark "Nola," and Crosby got to sing his theme song "Where the Blue of the Night
Meets the Gold of the Day" as well as "Please," " Dinah," and "Here Lies Love."
The movie was so successful that in 1935 Paramount released *The Big Broadcast of
1936.* The sequel dealt with both radio and the newfangled invention of the "radio
eye" (an early form of television). Broadcast singer Spud Miller (Jack Oakie) goes by
the name "Lochinvar" on the airwaves, but his singing is actually dubbed by Smiley
(Henry Wadsworth, whose actual singing was provided by Kenny Baker). When
the rich Countess Ysobel de Naigila (Lyda Roberti) comes to woo Lochinvar, complications arise involving comics George Burns and Gracie Allen (playing themselves). Crosby was on hand again to sing "I Wished on the Moon" and also
featured were the Nicholas Brothers, Bill Robinson, Ethel Merman, Amos and Andy,
Charles Ruggles, and even the Vienna Boys Choir. *The Big Broadcast of 1937* (1936)
was also about radio rivalry. Small-town radio announcer Gwen Holmes (Shirley
Ross) battles against tenor star Frank Rossman (Frank Forest), while radio net-
work owner Jack Carson (Jack Benny) had to deal with Mr. and Mrs. Platt (Burns
and Allen), sponsors of the station's *Platt Golf Ball Hour.* Benny Goodman provided the swing music, conductor Leopold Stokowski led the orchestra in some
classical music, and Ralph Rainger (music) and Leo Robin (lyrics) supplied such

delightful songs as "Vote for Mr. Rhythm" (sung by comedienne Martha Raye), "I'm Talking Through My Heart," and "You Came to My Rescue." Raye also sang a swing version of "Here Comes the Bride" at a wedding.

The Big Broadcast of 1938 was the last entry in the series and it was perhaps the best one. The plot was about two ocean liners, the *S.S. Gigantic* and the *S.S. Colossal*, that race each other across the Atlantic trying to break a new record. W. C. Fields provided the laughs as both the shipping tycoon J. Frothingale Bellows and his twin brother S. B. Bellows, and Martha Raye played Frothingale's siren-mouth daughter Martha Bellows. A series of broadcasts from the ships allowed for the musical numbers and most were introduced by radio emcee Buzz Fielding (Bob Hope in his screen debut). What little plot there was revolved around Buzz being pursued by three ex-wives for their alimony money, while Buzz's fiancée Dorothy (Dorothy Lamour) falls in love with the engine inventor Bob Hayes (Leif Erickson). The comedy in the movie was both physical and verbal, as with Fields' golf cart turning into a small airplane and Raye's bombastic one-liners. Yet it is the musical sequences that are the most memorable. Lamour sang the warm ballad "You Took the Words Right Out of My Mouth," Shep Fields and his Rippling Rhythm Orchestra had fun with "This Little Ripple Had Rhythm," opera diva Kirsten Flagstad bellowed Brunnhilde's "Battle Cry" from *Die Walkuere*, Mexican crooner Titio Guitar sang the lush "Don't Tell a Secret to a Rose," and Raye clowned around with "Mama, That Moon Is Here Again" as she was tossed about the deck by sailors. The elaborate production number "The Waltz Lives on" was the most complex musical sequence in the whole series. Dozens of singers and dancers illustrated different dancing styles over the ages, the waltz always cropping up in each era. The number, staged by LeRoy Prinz, involved many costumes, sets, and lighting changes but it flowed along seamlessly as only a movie can do. The undisputed high point of the film (and the whole series) was when Buzz joined his ex-wife Cleo (Shirley Ross) in the ship's bar and the two sang the Oscar-winning duet "Thanks for the Memory" by Rainger and Robin, one of the decade's most touching musical scenes. Hope used the number as his theme song for the next six decades.

See also: *Road to Utopia*; Bob Hope biography box

FURTHER READING

Curtis, James. *W. C. Fields: A Biography*. Curtis eBook Edition, 2011.
Eames, John Douglas. *The Paramount Story*. New York: Crown Publishers, 1985.
Zoglin, Richard. *Bob Hope: The Entertainer of the Century*. New York: Simon & Schuster, 2014.

REBECCA OF SUNNYBROOK FARM

Studio and release date: 20th Century Fox; March 1938

Producers: Darryl F. Zanuck, Raymond Griffith

Screenplay: Karl Tunberg, Don Ettlinger, based on the 1903 novel by Kate Douglas Wiggin

Songwriters: Mack Gordon, Jack Yellen, Arthur Lange, Sidney D. Mitchell, Lew Pollack, Harry Revel, Raymond Scott, Samuel Pokrass (music and lyrics)

Director: Allan Dwan

Choreographers: Nick Castle, Geneva Sawyer

Musical Director: Arthur Lange

Cinematographer: Arthur C. Miller

Cast: Shirley Temple, Randolph Scott, Jack Haley, Gloria Stuart, Helen Westley, Bill Robinson, Phyllis Brooks, Slim Summerville, William Demarest

Principal Songs: "Come and Get Your Happiness"; "Alone with You"; "An Old Straw Hat"; "Parade of Wooden Soldiers"; "You've Got to Eat Your Spinach, Baby"; "Happy Endings"; "On the Good Ship Lollipop"; "Animal Crackers in My Soup"; "When I'm with You"

Kate Douglas Wiggin's 1903 tale about the orphaned Rebecca had been turned into several plays and movies before 20th Century Fox decided it was ideal musical material for child star Shirley Temple. For many, this is the dancing-singing tot's best movie. Temple was the most popular movie star of the 1930s bar none. After making a dozen shorts and appearing in small roles in some features, Temple burst on the scene in 1934 with *Stand Up and Cheer!* The title was prophetic. Audiences in the darkest days of the Depression found the cheerful, optimistic little performer to be like a breath of fresh air. And it was more than just a surface gloss. Temple really could sing, act, and dance. She was even able to keep up with the master tap dancer Bill Robinson on five films. By 1938, when she made *Rebecca of Sunnybrook Farm*, the 10-year-old Temple had been starred in 16 films so she was a seasoned Hollywood veteran. In fact, she already had such a notable career that at one point in the film she sat down at the piano and sang a medley of her past hits, such as "Animal Crackers in My Soup," "When I'm With You," and "On the Good Ship Lollipop." Moviegoers were enthralled.

This musical version was far from faithful to the original story of *Rebecca of Sunnybrook Farm* but it turned out to be one of Temple's best movies. The original tale, set in Maine at the beginning of the 20th century, had an episodic plot in which a widow with seven children cannot make ends meet and asks the family aunts, Miranda and Jane, to take young Rebecca. Miranda would rather have an older child who can help out with the chores on Sunnybrook Farm. But the widow needs help as well, and the stern, humorless Miranda reluctantly agrees to take in

Shirley Temple (1928–2014)   The curly blonde little girl who carried several movie musicals in the 1930s with her considerable singing and dancing talents, she remains the most popular child star in the history of Hollywood. She was born in Santa Monica, California, the daughter of a bank teller, and started taking dance lessons at the age of three. Before she was four, Temple was featured in a series of film shorts and bit parts in features. She first caught the attention of moviegoers singing "Baby Take a Bow" in *Stand Up and Cheer* (1934) and was a star by the time she made *Little Miss Marker* (1934). Temple's other childhood musicals are *Baby Take a Bow* (1934), *Bright Eyes* (1934), *The Little Colonel* (1935), *Curly Top* (1935), *The Littlest Rebel* (1935), *Captain January* (1936), *Poor Little Rich Girl* (1936), *Dimples* (1936), *Stowaway* (1936), *Rebecca of Sunnybrook Farm* (1938), *Little Miss Broadway* (1938), *Just Around the Corner* (1938), *The Little Princess* (1939), *The Blue Bird* (1940), and *Young People* (1940). While much of her appeal had to do with Depression-weary audiences seeing Temple as a symbol of innocence and optimism, there was no question she was one of the most talented kids ever put on the screen. When she outgrew kiddie roles, her popularity dropped so she left Hollywood in 1947. Temple resurfaced on television for a time then she retired from acting for good and went into politics in the 1960s, where she had more success serving as a congresswoman and later an ambassador. Autobiography: *Child Star* (1988); biography: *The Little Girl Who Fought the Great Depression: Shirley Temple and 1930s America*, John F. Kasson (2014).

Rebecca. While the spinster Miranda disciplines the child, Aunt Jane is more loving and teaches Rebecca to cook and sew. When Rebecca grows up, she wants to become a teacher but her mother's poverty stands in the way. A happy ending is achieved when the railroad buys land on Sunnybrook Farm, Aunt Miranda gets rich, and she dies and leaves the farm to Rebecca's family. The independent, cheerful character of Rebecca was particularly appealing to female readers, and the book soon became a beloved favorite. *Rebecca of Sunnybrook Farm* first appeared on the stage in 1910, and the first of several movie and TV versions was a silent movie in 1917 starring Mary Pickford, a youthful blonde who was billed as "America's Sweetheart."

The sunny disposition of the character Rebecca was very close to the persona Temple exuded on-screen so it seemed like a good idea to musicalize the material for 20th Century Fox's little star. Several concessions and changes were made in the story to allow for plenty of musical numbers. Audiences liked Temple when her acting tugged the heartstrings, but they loved her when she sang and danced.

Bill Robinson (1878–1949)   An outstanding tap dancer onstage and on-screen, the smiling African American hoofer, nicknamed "Bojangles," often stole a movie in a small supporting role. He was born in Richmond, Virginia, where he performed for pennies on the streets as a child. Robinson went into vaudeville as a teenager and was eventually a headliner in the best variety houses and then was featured in the Broadway musicals *Blackbirds of 1928*, *Brown Buddies* (1930), *Blackbirds* (1933), *The Hot Mikado* (1939), *All in Fun* (1940), and *Memphis Bound* (1945). He made his movie debut as a specialty act in *Dixiana* (1930) then was cast as minor characters in seven more musicals, four of them—*The Little Colonel* (1935), *The Littlest Rebel* (1935), *Rebecca of Sunnybrook Farm* (1938), and *Just Around the Corner* (1938)—opposite Shirley Temple, who danced with him in some unforgettable tap numbers. Robinson was also featured in *Hooray for Love* (1935), *Big Broadcast of 1936* (1935), and *Stormy Weather* (1943). He choreographed most of his dances onstage and on-screen and frequently returned to vaudeville and nightclubs. Robinson was an activist for black performers, being a founding member of the Negro Actors Guild of America. He had a genius for making tap dancing look effortless and was instrumental in changing the form from a heavy, flat-footed kind of dance to a light, on the toes or on the heels kind of style. In a joint 1989 resolution, Congress designated his birthday (May 25) as National Tap Dancing Day. Biography: *Mr. Bojangles: The Biography of Bill Robinson*, James Haskins, N. R. Mitgang (2014).

In the Temple film, city girl Rebecca joins her Aunt Miranda (Helen Westley) on Sunnybrook Farm to get away from show business. But radio producer Tony Kent (Randolph Scott) finds out where the little tyke is and sets up a radio broadcast from the farm. The broadcast is widely heard, and Rebecca's greedy Uncle Harry Kipper (William Demarest) shows up on the farm hoping to cash in on Rebecca's success. The complications that follow are resolved by the cheerful tot, who even arranges for Tony to get together with local girl Gwen (Gloria Stuart). Six different songwriters contributed to the score, and the film is filled with wonderful musical numbers, particularly two with farmhand Aloysius (Bill Robinson): the freewheeling "An Old Straw Hat" and the march tune "Parade of the Wooden Soldiers." Other new songs included "Come and Get Your Happiness," Happy Endings," "You've Gotta Eat Your Spinach, Baby"; and "Alone With You." The movie was directed in a no-nonsense manner by Allan Dwan, who knew how far to go with Temple's cuteness. The supporting cast is strong and the production values expert. But everything comes down to one factor: Temple. She is in just about every scene and her personality drives the movie. Few Hollywood stars carried an entire musical as Temple did in the 1930s. And because she was handed an established story and some first-class songs, *Rebecca of Sunnybrook Farm* is a Temple highpoint.

See also: Shirley Temple, Bill Robinson biography boxes

FURTHER READING

Allvine, Glendon. *The Greatest Fox of Them All.* New York: Lyle Stuart, 1969.

Kasson, John F. *The Little Girl Who Fought the Great Depression: Shirley Temple and 1930s America.* New York: W. W. Norton & Co., 2014.

Thomas, Tony, and Aubrey Solomon. *The Films of 20th Century-Fox.* Secaucus, NJ: Citadel Press, 1979.

THE WIZARD OF OZ

Studio and release date: Metro-Goldwyn-Mayer; August 1939
Producer: Mervyn LeRoy
Screenplay: Noel Langley, Florence Ryerson, Edgar Allan Woolf, John Lee Mahin, based on the book *The Wonderful Wizard of Oz* by L. Frank Baum
Songwriters: Harold Arlen (music), E. Y. Harburg (lyrics)
Directors: Victor Fleming, King Vidor
Choreographer: Bobby Connolly
Musical Director: Herbert Stothart
Cinematographers: Harold Rosson, Allen Darby
Cast: Judy Garland, Ray Bolger, Jack Haley, Bert Lahr, Margaret Hamilton, Billie Burke, Frank Morgan, Charley Grapewin, Clara Blandick
Songs: "Over the Rainbow"; "We're Off to See the Wizard"; "Ding-Dong! The Witch Is Dead"; "Follow the Yellow Brick Road"; "If I Only Had a Brain/ Heart, Courage"; "If I Were King of the Forest"; "Merry Old Land of Oz"

There are many stage, screen, and television versions of Frank Baum's 1900 story *The Wonderful Wizard of Oz* but the one that always comes first to mind is that this timeless Hollywood classic, which has become such a part of American pop culture, seems to have been created by magic. Yet the troublesome movie went through a dozen scriptwriters, four directors, several cast changes (some after filming began), and one of the most complicated and difficult production histories on record. The first *Wizard of Oz* musical arrived on Broadway two years after the first Oz book appeared in print. The 1903 stage spectacular used the Baum story as an excuse for musical numbers and lavish pageantry. Although Baum himself wrote the stage script and the lyrics, the Broadway version differed a great deal from *The*

Much of *The Wizard of Oz* (1939) is a dream that Dorothy (Judy Garland) has after being knocked on the head during a tornado. Near the end of the film, the good witch Glinda (Billie Burke, right) gives Dorothy the knowledge and power to leave her dream and return to reality. This journey between the real and the imagined world is one of the many beguiling aspects of this classic film. (MGM/Photofest)

Wonderful Wizard of Oz. The musical ran 293 performances and inspired other large-scale family shows, most notably *Babes in Toyland* (1903). After silent film versions in 1910 and 1925, MGM decided to turn the tale into a full-scale musical. Several scripts by several writers were written and discarded before an acceptable one was agreed on, also taking liberties with Baum's original. In the MGM version, orphaned farm girl Dorothy Gale (Judy Garland) lives with her Uncle Henry (Charley Grapewin) and Aunt Em (Clara Blandick) on a drab farm in Kansas and she dreams of a world that is full of color and magic. When the local harridan Miss Gulch (Margaret Hamilton) gets a sheriff's order to have Dorothy's troublesome dog Toto destroyed, Dorothy runs away with Toto, only to return home after visiting the traveling fortune teller Professor Marvel (Frank Morgan) who tells her that her aunt needs her. A tornado lifts the farmhouse with Dorothy and Toto inside and it lands in Munchkinland, killing the Wicked Witch of the East.

The pint-sized Munchkins are thrilled and celebrate the witch's death but the appearance of the deceased's sister, the Wicked Witch of the West (Hamilton again), convinces Dorothy that she needs to return home to Kansas. The Good Witch Glinda (Billie Burke) instructs Dorothy to take the yellow brick road to the Emerald City where the mighty Wizard of Oz will grant her wish. On the way Dorothy befriends the Scarecrow (Ray Bolger), Tin Man (Jack Haley), and Lion (Bert Lahr) who accompany her to the Wizard in order to ask favors of their own. The Wizard (Morgan again) will not see the four friends at first and when he does grant them an audience, he demands the broomstick of the Wicked Witch as payment for their wishes. After being captured and rescued from the Witch's clutches, Dorothy accidentally melts the old crone by throwing water on her. With the broomstick in hand, Dorothy and her friends return to the Wizard only to find out that he is a fraud. Glinda reappears and tells Dorothy she only needs to wish herself home and the magic slippers she wears will make her wish come true. Dorothy awakes in Kansas, the whole experience in Oz being a dream she had after the tornado winds had knocked her unconscious, and she has a new appreciation of home.

Luckily the movie that studio head Louis B. Mayer envisioned, with Shirley Temple as Dorothy and W. C. Fields as the Wizard, never materialized, and Garland shot to stardom for her innocent, sincere performance. Bolger, Haley, and Lahr had the best screen roles of their careers as the Scarecrow, Tin Man, and Lion, and the rest of the cast was equally expert, including Morgan, who played a variety of roles, giving the cockeyed dream a kind of unity. The production began filming with Buddy Ebsen as the Tin Man but he got skin poisoning from the silver makeup and was hospitalized; Haley took over and a new makeup mixture was used. During filming, Hamilton was burnt during one of the fiery explosions manufactured on the set. Trouble persisted even after filming because the length of the picture worried the executives and musical numbers were cut, including the expensive, elaborate "The Jitterbug" dance as well as song verses and dances by Dorothy's friends. Harold Arlen (music) and E. Y. Harburg (lyrics) wrote one of filmdom's greatest scores, led by the Oscar-winning "Over the Rainbow," which was nearly left on the cutting room floor until wiser minds prevailed. Yet even that lovely song lost its introductory verse and much of the rest of the score was cut or abridged by the studio. Harburg foresaw a film with long extended musical scenes, a sort of fantasy operetta, and one can see how effectively it worked in the long Munchkinland sequence and during the preparations in the Emerald City before Dorothy and her friends see the Wizard. Similar musical scenes were lost and the film ended up having no songs at all during its last 20 minutes. Yet what is there is marvelous, from the jubilant "Ding-Dong! The Witch Is Dead" to the character numbers "If I Only Had a Brain/a Heart/ the Nerve" to the farcical "If I Were King of the Forest." All of the numbers have become part of American folklore, just as every line in the screenplay is widely recognized even out of context. Victor Fleming, King Vidor, George

Harold Arlen and **E. Y. Harburg.**   Two songwriters who worked together and with others on many stage and screen musicals, they are most remembered for their memorable songs for *The Wizard of Oz* (1939). The composer Arlen (1905–1986) was born in Buffalo, New York, the son of a cantor, and as a teenager sang in the synagogue. After playing piano in New York nightclubs, his songs were added to some Broadway revues. Among his stage scores with various lyricists are *9:15 Revue* (1928), *Earl Carroll's Vanities* (1930), *You Said It* (1931), *Life Begins at 8:40* (1934), *St. Louis Woman* (1946), *House of Flowers* (1954), and *Saratoga* (1959), but his most successful collaborations were with Harburg, the two of them scoring the Broadway musicals *Hooray for What!* (1937), *Bloomer Girl* (1944), and *Jamaica* (1957). Harburg was born in New York City and educated at City College of New York where he wrote light verse and submitted it to local newspapers. His first collaborator was Jay Gorney, the two of them writing "Brother, Can You Spare a Dime?," a song that had a major impact on Americans during the Depression with its musical cry of desperation heard in his lyrics. Other Harburg stage scores include *Earl Carroll's Sketchbook* (1929), *Americana* (1932), *Walk a Little Faster* (1932), *Ziegfeld Follies* (1934), *Life Begins at 8:40* (1934), *Finian's Rainbow* (1947), and *Flahooley* (1951). Harburg and Arlen began working together in 1937 and wrote songs for such movie musicals as *The Singing Kid* (1936), *Gold Diggers of 1937* (1936), *At the Circus* (1939), *Cabin in the Sky* (1943), the animated *Gay Purr-ee* (1962), as well as *The Wizard of Oz*. Working with other lyricists, Arlen scored the films *Let's Fall in Love* (1934), *Strike Me Pink* (1936), *Blues in the Night* (1941), *Star Spangled Rhythm* (1942), *The Sky's the Limit* (1943), *Up in Arms* (1944), *Here Come the Waves* (1944), *Casbah* (1948), *Mr. Imperium* (1951), *The Farmer Takes a Wife* (1953), *A Star Is Born* (1954), and *The Country Girl* (1954). Arlen was a masterful creator of blues and jazz songs with a particular feel for African American music. Harburg's scripts and lyrics are playful and clever, and he often used fantasy and satire to write about weighty issues. Biographies: *Harold Arlen: Happy With the Blues*, Edward Jablonski (1986); *Who Put the Rainbow in The Wizard of Oz?* Yip Harburg, Lyricist, Harold Myerson, Ernest Harburg [his son] (1993).

Cukor, and Richard Thorpe each directed different sections of the film, with Bobby Connolly doing the choreography, Cedric Gibbons and William Horning the imaginative sets, and Adrian the costumes. Using 29 sound stages, and 65 different sets, the movie was one of the most expensive in the studio's record books. But even acknowledging the high quality of all the movie's elements doesn't quite explain why *The Wizard of Oz* is so special. Billed as a treat for "children of all ages," it goes beyond anyone's idea of a children's movie. It is very adult in many ways, from its expressionistic look (the change from black and white in Kansas to color for Oz was a bold idea) to its difficult themes of friendship and home. Arriving at the end of the Depression may have impacted the film, for it was immediately a hit with audiences and went far beyond MGM's high hopes. Yet the movie has been equally enjoyed by many generations since. Perhaps *The Wizard of Oz* is the great American fantasy, a dream that still prevails within the hearts of moviegoers.

See also: *Broadway Melody of 1940*, *Babes Arms*; Judy Garland, Ray Bolger, Harold Arlen and E. Y. Harburg biography boxes

FURTHER READING

Clarke, Gerald. *Get Happy: The Life of Judy Garland*. Crystal Lake, IL: Delta, 2009.
Harmetz, Aljean. *The Making of The Wizard of Oz*. Chicago: Chicago Review Press, 2013.
Hirschhorn, Clive. *The Hollywood Musical*. 2nd ed. New York: Crown Publishers, 1983.
Myerson, Harold, and Ernie Harburg. *Who Put the Rainbow in The Wizard of Oz?* E. Y. Harburg, Lyricist. Ann Arbor: University of Michigan Press, 1995.
Rushdie, Salman. *The Wizard of Oz*. (BFI Film Classics). London: British Film Institute, 2012.

BABES IN ARMS

Studio and release date: Metro-Goldwyn Mayer; October 1939
Producer: Arthur Freed
Screenplay: Jack McGowan, Kay Van Riper, based on the 1937 stage script by Richard Rodgers and Lorenz Hart
Songwriter: Richard Rodgers, Nacio Herb Brown, and others (music), Lorenz Hart, Arthur Freed, and others (lyrics)
Director/Choreographer: Busby Berkeley
Musical Director: George Stoll
Cinematographer: Ray June
Cast: Mickey Rooney, Judy Garland, Guy Kibbee, Charles Winninger, June Preisser, Douglas McPhail, Betty Jaynes, Grace Hayes, Ann Shoemaker, Rand Brooks
Principal Songs: "Where or When"; "Babes in Arms"; "You Are My Lucky Star"; "Good Morning"; "Broadway Rhythm"; "God's Country"; "I'm Just Wild About Harry"; Daddy Was a Minstrel Man"; "I Cried for You"

This youthful and tuneful film is considered the granddaddy of all "let's put on a show!" movie musicals. Although it has often been imitated and parodied, the movie was considered refreshingly original in its day. *Babes in Arms* had been a surprise hit on Broadway in 1937. It had no stars, the cast was young and mostly inexperienced, and the plot was serviceable at best. But the show boasted more hit songs than any other Richard Rodgers (music) and Lorenz Hart (lyrics) musical, including such standards as "My Funny Valentine," "The Lady Is a Tramp," "Johnny One-Note," "I Wish I Were in Love Again," "Where or When," and the marching title number. In the Broadway script, some out-of-work vaudevillians take to the road during the Depression, leaving their teenage kids to fend for themselves and avoid the work farm. Led by the young songwriter Val "Valentine" La Mar, his adoring sweetheart Billie Smith, and the would-be socialist Peter, the pack of "babes in arms" puts on a show to raise money and save their parents and themselves. But the revue they stage loses money and the kids are sent to the work farm. Then a French aviator crossing the Atlantic makes an emergency landing at the farm and brings enough publicity to turn the teens' show into a hit. With the money, the "babes" are able to pay off their families' debt. It was a bright and optimistic musical and played well on Broadway to Depression-era audiences.

MGM bought the screen rights to *Babes in Arms* but then did a curious thing: The studio cut most of the brilliant score and retained most of the contrived story. The young songwriter was now named Mickey Moran and he was played by Mickey Rooney. In an inspired bit of casting, Judy Garland (whose performance in *The Wizard of Oz* had yet to be seen by moviegoers) was given the role of his sweetheart, now named Patsy Barton. The teaming was immediately electric. The two teens played off each other's energy and together exuded innocent romance. While the "babes" prepared a show to save their families, they are joined by Hollywood child star Rosalie Essex (June Preisser), patterned after Shirley Temple, who comes between the two teen lovers. The plot culminated in a big musical revue put on by the kids, and the "let's put a show on!" film musical was born. Of all the glorious songs from the Broadway show, only two made it to the screen: the haunting ballad "Where or When" and the marching title numbered. Nacio Herb Brown, Arthur Freed, and others wrote some new songs, including the sprightly "Good Morning," the jazzy "Broadway Rhythm," and the patriotic "God's Country." Among the old favorites used were "You Are My Lucky Star," "Moonlight Bay," "Oh, Susannah," "I'm Just Wild About Harry," and "Ida, Sweet as Apple Cider." The film overflowed with music and optimism, much of which is still contagious today.

Babes in Arms was director-choreographer Busby Berkeley's first movie at MGM, and the musical numbers started to take on a different look from those he had staged at Warner Brothers. The glitzy spectacle was replaced somewhat by cleverness and even character development. The movie was not only the first teaming of Rooney and Garland (who would go on to appear in 10 other movies together), it was also the first musical produced by lyricist-producer Arthur Freed and the beginning of the historic Freed Unit. This mini-organization within MGM presented

Mickey Rooney (1920–2014)   Short in stature but a bigger-than-life star in movie musicals, comedies, and dramas, he enjoyed one of the longest careers in show business—from 1926 to 2014. He was born in Brooklyn, the son of vaudevillian Joe Yule, was on the stage by the time he was 15 months old, and was soon singing, dancing, and telling jokes as part of the family act. Rooney made his first silent movie short in 1926 and appeared in over 50 film shorts before sound came in. Although he was cast in many early talkies, true stardom did not come until he played adolescent Andy Hardy in the B picture *A Family Affair* (1937); it was so popular Rooney starred in 14 more Hardy films, including the musicals *Love Finds Andy Hardy* (1938) and *Andy Hardy Meets Debutante* (1940). Equally popular were the "let's put on a show" musicals with Judy Garland, including *Babes in Arms* (1939), *Strike Up the Band* (1940), *Babes on Broadway* (1941), *Girl Crazy* (1943), and *Thousands Cheer* (1943). At the same time, Rooney also appeared in many famous nonmusical films. As an adult he made fewer musicals, yet he still shone in *Summer Holiday* (1948), *Words and Music* (1948), *The Strip* (1951), *All Ashore* (1958), *Pete's Dragon* (1977), and *The Magic of Lassie* (1978). He appeared on hundreds of TV programs and specials over the years and was still making films when he was in his nineties. Autobiographies: *i.e.* (1965); *Life Is Too Short* (1991); biographies: *The Life and Times of Mickey Rooney*, Richard A. Lertzman, William J. Birnes (2015).

some of the greatest movie musicals of the 1940s and 1950s. The Freed films were known for their polish, integrity, and inspired craftsmanship. *Babes in Arms* may have been intended as a "Depression chaser," but it also opened the door for the next decade and a new kind of Hollywood musical.

See also: *Beach Blanket Bingo*; Mickey Rooney, Judy Garland, Arthur Freed, Busby Berkeley biography boxes

FURTHER READING

Bloom, Ken. *Hollywood Musicals: The 101 Greatest Song-and-Dance Movies of All Time*. New York: Black Dog and Leventhal, 2010.

Fordin, Hugh. *MGM's Greatest Musicals: The Arthur Freed Unit*. Boston: Da Capo Press, 1996.

Lertzman, Richard A., and William J. Birnes. *The Life and Times of Mickey Rooney*. New York: Gallery Books, 2015.

THE 1940S: MUSICALS DURING A WORLD WAR

Just as the Depression cast a shadow over all of the 1930s, World War II and its aftermath dominated the lives of Americans in the 1940s. War began in Europe at the end of 1939 when Hitler's troops invaded Poland and each European nation took sides when Britain declared war. The United States didn't enter the war until the Japanese attack on Pearl Harbor in the Hawaiian Islands in late 1941. Unlike the European and Asian nations involved in World War II, the United States saw no battles or bombings on the home front. It was always a war far away. Yet it affected every man, woman, and child in the United States. Most families had at least one member fighting in Europe or the Pacific. Various foods and products were in short supply and were rationed. Items that had been imported from overseas were no longer available. Factories, trains, housing, and food were all given over to the war effort, making sure the American GIs were well equipped, clothed, and fed. There was a positive side to these changes. Businesses with war contracts expanded and there were many more jobs available. Women and African Americans, who were usually denied well-paying factory jobs, were hired because so many men were away at war. The economy in the United States recovered from the hard times and business was once again robust and profitable. World War II did something that FDR and all his programs had tried to do: end the Depression.

Even the Hollywood studios, which were in effect factories, were affected by the war. The government commissioned the studios to make training films and propaganda movies to keep up the morale of the country. Just as Hollywood had offered relief from the Depression in the 1930s, it provided patriotic films to lift spirits in the 1940s. Because there was no television, newsreel shorts about the war were shown in theaters and the public got to see footage of the war, though what they saw was heavily censored. The studios were affected in negative ways too. Many of the male staff, including movie stars, served during the war and had to be released from their contracts. There were shortages of supplies, particularly film stock. The biggest difficulty the war presented for Hollywood was the loss of foreign markets. Americans films had been shown in all the European countries and accounted for a sizable portion of the studios' profits. But during the war the only place where Hollywood films could be shown was Great Britain. All the other nations were occupied by German troops, and American films were not welcome there. So the studios turned to Central and South America. Hollywood films had always been shown in major cities in Mexico and other Latin countries, but distribution was increased during World War II, and movies (particularly musicals) were made specially to appeal to people who lived south of the United States. Luckily for Hollywood, these films were popular in the United States as well, and Americans of the north started to embrace Latin music and dance.

While most nations involved in World War II were devastated financially and physically by the time peace was declared, the United States was not. None of the 48 states had been bombed, very few civilians had been killed, and the economy was stronger than it had been in 16 years. The country's only loss, and it was a significant one, was the death of so many men and women who had served overseas. Although hostilities ended in 1945, the rest of the decade was preoccupied with the war in terms of recovery and efforts to return to some form of peace. Ironically, the end of World War II introduced the Cold War with the world again divided, this time between communist and democratic nations. The Soviet Union, who had been an ally of the United States during the war, quickly became the enemy in the undeclared rivalry and suspicion between the two countries. (American movies made before 1945 showed the Soviets in a kinder light than those later in the decade.) Because so many Americans wanted nothing to do with war and wished to rebuild their domestic lives, the Cold War was ignored by many. It was not until the 1950s that this communist-democratic rivalry would escalate and affect more Americans. For most, the postwar 1940s were a time for returning to work, buying a car, getting married, having children, finding housing (preferably in the growing suburbs), and enjoying the benefits of living in the strongest nation on earth. Of course, this plan did not come true for many Americans. Women who had prospered in the workplace were dismissed and their jobs given to returning GIs. The same thing happened to African American men and women who had worked in factories and other areas that flourished during the war effort. No car or suburbs for them. Several minority groups would not see economic or civic progress for another 20 years.

While moviegoing decreased somewhat during the 1940s, most American still went to the local movie house frequently. Added to the musicals, westerns, romances, and melodramas that were still popular was a new category: the war movie. A number of films about World War II were made and released while that conflict was still going on. The war melodrama *Thirty Seconds Over Tokyo* (1944), about General Doolittle's daring bombing mission, was in movie theaters less than two years after the actual raid. While many of these war films were to boost morale and inspire the sale of war bonds, some were surprisingly sobering about the consequences of war. *The Fighting Sullivans* (1944), about four brothers all killed in action in the Pacific, was so upsetting to watch that many communities would not allow the film to be shown there. Once the war was over, the war films continued because some of the public was still fascinated about the details of the four-year conflict. A few melodramas about GIs returning home from the war were also uncomfortable for some audiences because every homecoming was not a happy one. The finest of these truthful depictions of postwar times was *The Best Years of Our Lives* (1946).

When it came to musicals, a new and popular kind of movie was introduced: the patriotic musical. Broadway, vaudeville, and Hollywood had produced some patriotic shows during World War I, but the first war to inspire screen musicals was World War II. The aim of such musicals was to boost morale and sell war bonds. Since each studio had a number of stars under contract, it was deemed practical and financially prudent to put as many of these stars as possible into a patriotic musical. The ideal format for such entertainment was the revue, but Hollywood didn't like the plotless variety show that was prevalent on Broadway. Instead, these star-studded musicals had a thin plot that could be easily interrupted for songs, dances, comedy sketches, dramatic scenes, or even just a cameo appearance by a star. The first major studio to offer such a show was Paramount with *Star Spangled Rhythm* (1942). The apt title referred to the stars on the American flag but there were far more than 13 Hollywood stars in the film. The musical was a resounding success and other studios jumped on the band wagon. *This Is the Army* (1943), *Thank Your Lucky Stars* (1943), *Stage Door Canteen* (1943), *Thousands Cheer* (1943), *Follow the Boys* (1944), *Hollywood Canteen* (1944), *Four Jills in a Jeep* (1944), and *Here Come the Waves* (1944) were among the most popular of the patriotic musicals. Interest in this kind of entertainment dropped off when the war was over and the likes of it have never been seen again.

The show business bio-pic musical cropped up several times in the 1940s. The two most outstanding examples were *Yankee Doodle Dandy* (1942), in which James Cagney portrayed the Broadway showman George M. Cohan, and *The Jolson Story* (1946), in which Jolson provided the singing voice for Larry Parks who played Jolson. Both men returned for the sequel *Jolson Sings Again* (1949), which was almost as good (and as popular at the box office) as the original. Other bio-pics during the decade include *Lillian Russell* (1940) with Alice Faye as the-turn-of-the-century performer; *My Gal Sal* (1942), in which Victor Mature played the songwriter Paul Dresser; *Rhapsody in Blue* (1945), about George Gershwin's life and music; *The Dolly Sisters* (1946) with Betty Grable and June Haver as the celebrated Hungarian sister act on Broadway; *Till the Clouds Roll By* (1946), about the life and music of composer Jerome Kern; *Night and Day* (1946), in which Cary Grant impersonated songwriter Cole Porter; June Haver as dancer Marilyn Miller in *Look for the Silver Lining* (1949); and *Words and Music* (1949), in which Tom Drake and Mickey Rooney played songwriters Richard Rodgers and Lorenz Hart. While most of these musicals were nostalgic for the songs of the past, the various Americana musicals in the 1940s were nostalgic about life in the past. During the war, Americans were anxious to see films in which life was simpler and free from war. This kind of musical was best represented by *Meet Me in St. Louis* (1944), which presented idyllic family life in 1904. Similarly, musicals about the unhurried rural life were appealing to wartime audiences. The best example of this kind of musical was *State Fair* (1945).

Because many European markets for American films were closed during the war, Hollywood turned to South America and made several musicals set in Latin America that were meant to appeal to moviegoers both in the United States and south of the border. *Down Argentine Way* (1940) was the first and it was quickly followed by *One Night in the Tropics* (1940), *That Night in Rio* (1941), and *Weekend in Havana* (1941). 20th Century Fox made the most Latin-flavored musicals during the decade and that studio's *The Gang's All Here* (1943) is considered by many to be the best of the genre. The 1940s was a prodigious period for Fox, thanks to two blonde stars—Alice Faye and Betty Grable—and the Latin comedienne Carmen Miranda. With and without these ladies, the studio offered a variety of commendable musicals, including *Tin Pan Alley* (1940), *Moon Over Miami* (1941), *Sun Valley Serenade* (1941), *Orchestra Wives* (1942), *Springtime in the Rockies* (1942), *Hello, Frisco, Hello* (1943), *Coney Island* (1943), *Stormy Weather* (1943), *Three Little Girls in Blue* (1946), and *Mother Wore Tights* (1947). Columbia Pictures didn't have two blondes but it had redheaded Rita Hayworth. She was at her peak in the 1940s and gave the studios such musical hits as *You'll Never Get Rich* (1941), *My Gal Sal* (1942), *You Were Never Lovelier* (1942), and *Cover Girl* (1944).

Less popular in the 1940s than in the previous decade were operettas and backstage musicals. Perhaps both were considered just too frivolous during such trying times. MGM dominated the movie musical genre throughout the 1940s with such memorable films as *The Broadway Melody of 1940*, *Ziegfeld Girl* (1941), *Cabin in the Sky* (1943), *Girl Crazy* (1943), *Meet Me in St. Louis* (1944), *Anchors Aweigh* (1945), *The Harvey Girls* (1946), *Good News* (1947), *Easter Parade* (1948), *The Barkleys of Broadway* (1949), and *On the Town* (1949). Thanks to Bing Crosby, Paramount had giant hits with *Birth of the Blues* (1941), *Holiday Inn* (1942), *Going My Way* (1944), and *Blue Skies* (1946). Paramount was also very lucky when it teamed Crosby with Bob Hope in *Road to Singapore* (1940). The successful musical comedy prompted six more "road" movies, including *Road to Zanzibar* (1941), *Road to Morocco* (1942), *Road to Utopia* (1945), and *Road to Rio* (1947). Each of the major Hollywood studios made some first-class contributions to the art of the movie musical during the 1940s. With television in its infancy, Hollywood's only real competition was radio but, as in the 1930s, it was not a major threat. Also, many

Americans who did not have jobs in the Depression were working during the 1940s so there was more money to spend on entertainment. So the 1940s were prosperous years for movies and the Hollywood musical was no exception.

PINOCCHIO

Studio and release date: Disney/RKO; February 1940
Producer: Walt Disney
Screenplay: Ted Sears, Otto Englander, Webb Smith, and others, based on the
   1883 story *The Adventures of Pinocchio* by Carlo Collodi
Songwriters: Leigh Harline (music), Ned Washington (lyrics)
Directors: Ben Sharpsteen, Hamilton Luske, Bill Roberts, Norman Ferguson,
   Jack Kenney, Wilfred Jackson, T. Hee
Musical Directors: Leigh Harline, Paul J. Smith
Voices: Dickey Jones, Cliff Edwards, Christian Rub, Evelyn Venable, Walter
   Catlett, Charles Judels, Frankie Darro
Songs: "When You Wish Upon a Star"; "Hi-Diddle-Dee-Dee (An Actor's Life for
   Me)"; "Give a Little Whistle"; "I've Got No Strings"

The artistry of *Snow White and the Seven Dwarfs* (1937) was even more polished in this second animated feature musical from Walt Disney. The gripping story, unforgettable characters, catchy songs, and superb animation have rarely been equaled by Disney or anyone else. The plot, loosely based on the famous children's story by Carlo Collodi, is narrated by Jiminy Cricket who is also in the plot as Pinocchio's conscience. The goodhearted toymaker Gepetto carves the marionette Pinocchio and prays on the "wishing star" that the puppet might become a real boy. The Blue Fairy arrives that night and magically brings the puppet to life but tells Pinocchio that he must prove himself before becoming human. Pinocchio and Jiminy head off to school the next day but are sidetracked by the conniving J. Worthington Foxwell, thereby setting up a series of misadventures that include the greedy puppeteer Stromboli, the horrors of Pleasure Island, and rescuing Gepetto from inside Monstro the whale. The trials prove Pinocchio to be worthy and he becomes a real boy. As in the original tale, Pinocchio's nose grows every time he tells a lie. Collodi's character is much more mischievous than Disney's. In fact, the original puppet got into so much trouble that in an earlier version of the book Pinocchio was hung by the neck and died. Collodi's fictional creation has been seen by various cultures in many ways. Pinocchio is an epic figure to some, a legendary figure who battles all the evils of the world (and his own imperfections) that his being turned into a human is a triumph for the human spirit. Disney's take on the tale is not so grandiose and his Pinocchio retains the innocence of a little boy, his lies and mistakes being the natural actions of an exuberant youth.

The efficient screenplay is a marvelous blending of comedy, suspense, and warmth with both the villainous and lovable characters vividly coming to life. Certain scenes, once viewed, can never be forgotten, such as the stringless Pinocchio dancing with marionettes in Stromboli's theater, the frantic chase escaping from the whale, and the horrifying transition of the boy Lampwick into a donkey at Pleasure Island. This last scene is brilliantly done, showing the beginning of the transition then letting the moviegoer see its completion in silhouette. The animation is outstanding throughout and the masterly background art captures the cozy, continental European village as effectively as the garish, almost surreal Pleasure Island. The detail work by the Disney artists surpasses even that in *Snow White and the Seven Dwarfs*. Gepetto's workshop, for example, is a wonderland of toys and clocks. The scenes underwater have a look influenced by the impressionist artists while the waves and splashes recall those celebrated Japanese etchings of the sea. Some feel that Disney art and animation reached its peak in *Pinocchio*.

The songs by Leigh Harline (music) and Ned Washington (lyrics) are not only memorable in themselves but also fit nicely into the narrative. The Oscar-winning "When You Wish Upon a Star" sets the mood and theme of the movie and foreshadows Gepetto's wish, which sets the action in motion. "Honest" John's tuneful ditty "Hi Diddle Dee Dee" is a merry persuasion song that is so tuneful that there's no question of its working on Pinocchio. Jiminy's jaunty "Give a Little Whistle" is a contagious song that cements the friendship between the "conscience" and his young charge. The character of Jiminy Cricket (a Disney creation not in the original tale) was immediately embraced by moviegoers and the studio used him for decades in other features and on television, the spry little fellow becoming an unofficial host for the world of Disney. Also a signature of sorts was the song "When You Wish Upon a Star," which has become the unofficial theme song for everything Disney, from films and television to theme parks and cruise liners. It is a simple but potent ballad with a lullaby quality. Its lyric has been imitated so often that the song's sentiment may seem like a cliché to some. But like the movie, "When You Wish Upon a Star" is a timeless expression of optimism. *Pinocchio* has dated perhaps less than any other animated film; what was frightening then still is, and what was once joyous still soars.

See also: *Snow White and the Seven Dwarfs*; Walt Disney biography box

FURTHER READING

Gabler, Neal. *Walt Disney*. New York: Vintage Press, 2006.

Kaufman, J. B. *Pinocchio: The Making of the Disney Epic*. San Francisco: Walt Disney Family Foundation Press, 2015.

Maltin, Leonard. *The Disney Films*. 4th ed. Glendale, CA: Disney Editions, 2000.

BROADWAY MELODY OF 1940

Studio and release date: Metro-Goldwyn-Mayer; February 1940
Producer: Jack Cummings
Screenplay: Leon Gordon, George Oppenheimer
Songwriter: Cole Porter (music and lyrics)
Director: Norman Taurog
Choreographer: Bobby Connolly
Musical Director: Alfred Newman
Cinematographers: Oliver T. Marsh, Joseph Ruttenberg
Cast: Fred Astaire, Eleanor Powell, George Murphy, Frank Morgan, Ian Hunter, Florence Rice
Songs: "Begin the Beguine"; "I Concentrate on You"; "I've Got My Eyes on You"; "Please Don't Monkey with Broadway"; "Between You and Me"

Because of the success of MGM's *The Broadway Melody* in 1929, the studio returned to the title and presented a series of three "Broadway Melody" musicals. Most consider *Broadway Melody of 1940* to be the best of the series. While none of the trio of musicals can be considered a sequel, each uses a backstage setting and climaxes in a big show. *Broadway Melody of 1936* (1935), the first of the trio, centered on Broadway producer Bob Gordon (Robert Taylor), who is being bribed by a vicious gossip columnist Bert Keeler (Jack Benny) but is saved by newcomer Irene Foster (Eleanor Powell), who goes on in the leading lady's part at the last minute. Just as the show within the movie made Foster a stage star, the film made dancer-actress Powell a screen star. The movie also boasted another marvelous score by Nacio Herb Brown (music) and Arthur Freed (lyrics), who had scored the original *The Broadway Melody*. Highlights include the entrancing ballad "All I Do Is Dream of You," the jaunty "I've Got a Feeling You're Fooling," and wistful "You Are My Lucky Star." Roy Del Ruth directed, Dave Gould and Albertina Rasch choreographed, and the movie was such a hit that another "Broadway Melody" musical was inevitable.

That film, *Broadway Melody of 1938* (1937), also starred Powell and Taylor, who played performer Sally Lee and producer Steve Raleigh. While he strains to find the money to produce his next show, she has her hopes pinned on her race horse Stargazer who is inspired by opera music. After hearing an opera aria, Stargazer dashes off and wins a grand prize so Sally can save the show, play the leading lady, and win the heart of Steve. The veteran vaudeville favorite Sophie Tucker played Alice Clayton who runs a boarding house for actors and hopes to get her daughter Betty (Judy Garland) into show business. Betty is infatuated with Clark Gable, and the most memorable scene in the movie is when Garland sang "You Made Me Love You" to his photograph. The tender ballad by James Monaco (music) and Joseph McCarthy (lyrics) had been introduced on Broadway by Al Jolson in 1913 and had been a hit for him and many others. But Garland's rendition, once heard, is never forgotten and the scene demonstrated that the young Garland was a talent to be reckoned with. In the big show that concludes *Broadway Melody of 1938*, Tucker led the cast in singing "Your Broadway and My Broadway" and sang her signature song "Some of These Days." George Murphy joined Powell and Buddy Ebsen for "Follow in My Footsteps," and Garland was joined by the ensemble for "Everybody Sing."

The series ended with *Broadway Melody of 1940*, which again starred Powell but this time opposite Fred Astaire. The musical also boasted a top-notch Cole Porter score. What it didn't have was a top-notch screenplay. The struggling dance team of Johnny Brett (Astaire) and King Shaw (George Murphy) finally get a break when producer Bob Casey (Frank Morgan) hears of their act and is told that Johnny might be an ideal dancing partner for Casey's star Clare Bennett (Powell). When Casey mistakenly hires King, thinking he is Johnny, King gets to be Clare's leading man and the discouraged Johnny is left out in the cold. He accidentally meets Clare and the two hit it off on the dance floor and in each other's hearts. King finds out about the budding romance and feels guilty about stealing Johnny's chance for stardom so he pretends to be drunk on opening night and Johnny has to go on in his place. The contrived plot did not stand in the way of the terrific musical numbers. Astaire, in his first screen duet with a male, sang and danced with Murphy to the funny number "Please Don't Monkey with Broadway." Astaire and Powell created magic together dancing to "Begin the Beguine" on a shiny black floor and surrounded by stars. The intoxicating Porter standard had been introduced on Broadway in 1935 and had been recorded by many but this dance version seemed new and exciting. The film introduced two romantic numbers that also found popularity, "I Concentrate on You" and " I've Got My Eyes on You." *Broadway Melody of 1940* was Astaire's first film in which he danced extensively with someone else than Ginger Rogers. Legend has it that Astaire was nervous about performing with Powell because he felt she was a better tap dancer than he was. The chemistry between Powell and Astaire was different from the Astaire-Rogers teaming but the movie proved that Astaire could create sparks with others. In succeeding years he would do it again on-screen with Rita Hayworth, Vera-Ellen, Marjorie Reynolds, Judy Garland, Ann Miller, Cyd Charisse, Leslie Caron, and Audrey Hepburn. It was becoming quite clear that the key to a successful Astaire team was Fred Astaire.

See also: *The Broadway Melody;* Cole Porter, Fred Astaire, Eleanor Powell biography boxes

FURTHER READING

Astaire, Fred. *Steps in Time: An Autobiography*. New York: Dey Street Books, 2008.
Levin, Alice. *Eleanor Powell: First Lady of Dance*. Las Vegas, NV: Empire Publishers, 1998.
Schwartz, Charles. *Cole Porter: A Biography*. Boston: Da Capo Press, 1979.

SUN VALLEY SERENADE

Studio and release date: 20th Century Fox; July 1941
Producer: Milton Sperling
Screenplay: Robert Ellis, Helen Logan
Songwriters: Harry Warren (music), Mack Gordon (lyrics)
Director: H. Bruce Humberstone
Choreographer: Hermes Pan
Musical Directors: Emil Newman, Glenn Miller
Cinematographer: Edward Cronjager
Cast: Sonja Henie, John Payne, Milton Berle, Glenn Miller, Lynn Bari, Joan Davis, Dorothy Dandridge, Nicholas Brothers
Songs: "Chattanooga Choo-Choo"; "In the Mood"; "It Happened in Sun Valley"; "I Know Why (and So Do You)"; "The Kiss Polka"

Ice skating star Sonja Henie made 10 films and most consider this vibrant Big Band musical her best. It helped that bandleader Glenn Miller and his musicians were featured and that there was an outstanding score by Harry Warren (music) and Mack Gordon (lyrics). Henie was a curious Hollywood star. After winning medals at three different Olympics, the wholesome-looking Norwegian blonde was signed by Fox even though she was not a singer, a dancer, or an actress. She also had a thick Scandinavian accent that many found endearing. In her films Henie always played a Scandinavian, never sang, and always skated. Obviously the writers had to bend over backwards to come up with plots and characters that conformed to the skating star's strengths and limitations. In the case of *Sun Valley Serenade*, they managed to do so with great success.

The screenplay had an interesting twist that fit the war years' time frame. In order to get some needed publicity, band leader Phil Carey (Miller) and his boys sponsor a Norwegian child refugee to come to America. But when Karen Benson (Henie) shows up, she turns out to be not only full-grown but attractive as well. Against his wishes, pianist Ted Scott (John Payne) is put in charge of Karen, which causes trouble with the women he is wooing. When the band gets a gig at a resort in Sun Valley, Idaho, Ted brings Karen along. The complications arise from Karen's falling in love with Ted while he tries to juggle the affections of the other women in his life. It was a contrived plot but it seemed harmless enough when set on the snow-covered slopes. The cast also featured Milton Berle, Lynn Bari, Joan Davis, and Martha Tilton, as well as Glenn Miller's vocalists Ray Anthony, Bill May, Tex Beneke, Paula Kelly, Hal McIntyre, and the Modernaires. The Warren-Gordon songs were all first rate. Lynn Bari (dubbed by Pat Friday) sang the freewheeling "It Happened in Sun Valley" and the romantic "I Know Why (And So Do You)," and the lively "The Kiss Polka" was used for a cheery dance number. Two of Miller's signature tunes, "In the Mood" and "Moonlight Serenade," were added to the score to satisfy the many Miller fans who flocked to the movie. The musical high-light of *Sun Valley Serenade* was the Warren-Gordon swing classic "Chattanooga Choo-Choo." The number was played and vocalized by Miller and his band singers as part of a rehearsal, then it was sung by teenage Dorothy Dandridge and danced by the flying Nicholas Brothers. The sequence is among the most electric musical numbers of the 1940s. The movie's finale was a stunning ice skating sequence choreographed by Hermes Pan that had Henie gliding across black ice. H. Bruce Humberstone directed *Sun Valley Serenade* and it is still first-class fun.

Producer Darryl F. Zanuck had "discovered" Henie and put her in her first Hollywood film in 1936. By the time she made *Sun Valley Serenade*, the skating star had made six movies and both her English and acting had improved noticeably. Billing her with bandleader Miller was an odd but inspired bit of casting. Skating fans and Big Band fans were both drawn to the film and neither was disappointed. *Sun Valley Serenade* was a box office hit. A similar combination was used in *Iceland* (1942) when Henie was teamed with Sammy Kaye and his band, and in *Wintertime* (1943) with bandleader Woody Herman. But neither works as well as *Sun Valley Serenade*. Miller and Henie barely had screen time together in the film but the billing combination was still magical. Both stars shone brightly in the 1940s but their movie careers did not survive into the 1950s. After a few lackluster films, Henie left Hollywood and performed in ice shows before retiring from skating in 1960. A shrewd businesswoman, she invested her Hollywood money wisely, married a shipping magnate, and became one of the wealthiest women in the world by the time she died in 1969. Miller was only 40 years old when he died in a plane crash in 1944 while traveling to entertain Allied troops in Europe.

FURTHER READING

Allvine, Glendon. *The Greatest Fox of Them All.* New York: Lyle Stuart, 1969.

Henie, Sonja. *Wings on My Feet.* Upper Saddle River, NJ: Prentice-Hall, 1940.

Thomas, Tony. *Harry Warren and the Hollywood Musical.* New York: Lyle Stuart, 1975.

Thomas, Tony, and Aubrey Solomon. *The Films of 20th Century-Fox.* Secaucus, NJ: Citadel Press, 1979.

BIRTH OF THE BLUES

Studio and release date: Paramount; September 1941
Producers: B. G. DeSylva, Monta Bell
Screenplay: Harry Tugend, Walter DeLeon
Songwriters: W. C. Handy, Lew Brown, B. G. DeSylva, Ray Henderson, Gus Edwards, Ernie Burnett, Johnny Mercer, and others (music and lyrics)

Director: Victor Schertzinger
Musical Director: Robert Emmett Dolan
Cinematographer: William Mellor
Cast: Bing Crosby, Mary Martin, Brian Donlevy, Eddie Anderson, Jack Teagarden, J. Carroll Naish, Carolyn Lee, Ruby Elzy
Principal Songs: "Birth of the Blues"; "St. Louis Blues"; "My Melancholy Baby"; "Cuddle Up a Little Closer"; "The Waiter and the Porter and the Upstairs Maid"; "By the Light of the Silvery Moon"; "Wait 'til the Sun Shines, Nellie"; "Memphis Blues"; "Tiger Rag"

The history of jazz and blues is the subject of this intriguing Bing Crosby musical, which is as informative as it is entertaining, despite some liberties taken with the facts. In 1915 a white clarinet player named Alcide "Yellow" Nunez founded the first non-African blues-jazz group in New Orleans. They called themselves the Original Dixieland Jazz Band and became very popular, introducing jazz to mainstream audiences and opening doors for later white jazz musicians like Benny Goodman, the Dorsey Brothers, and Gene Krupa. The movie was inspired by the band but names and details were changed. In the screenplay, boy clarinetist Jeff Lambert (Ronnie Cosbey) is taught classical music but he prefers listening to and copying the jazz and blues performed by African American musicians in New Orleans. As an adult (Crosby) he forms the Basin Street Hot Shots, incorporating a trumpeter named Memphis (Brian Donlevy), the trombonist Pepper (Jack Teagarden, who did is own playing), and singer Betty Lou Cobb (Mary Martin). The group fights for recognition but the white citizens in town are content with the waltz. The musicians finally get a break when Betty Lou gets a job singing at a new club run by the gangster Blackie (J. Carroll Naish) and she insists that the band accompany her. Both the Hot Shots and Betty Lou are a hit, so popular that Blackie won't let them work for anyone else. They cut a record, which they send to an agent in Chicago, hoping to get work there. When the musicians try to leave town, Blackie's goons stop them but Jeff uses their record to trick Blackie's men into thinking they are rehearsing, giving the band a chance to catch a boat going north. The film ends with a tribute to the many jazz and blues musicians, both white and African American, who followed in the band's footsteps. There was a romantic triangle involving Jeff, Mary Lou, and Memphis but it was not very interesting. On the other hand, the character of Louey (Eddie Anderson billed simply as "Rochester") was one of the more defined African American roles in a Hollywood musical.

Birth of the Blues is routine in its plotting but catches fire in the musical numbers. Martin gives what is arguably her finest movie performance, singing "Cuddle Up a Little Closer," joining Crosby on "Wait 'til the Sun Shines, Nellie," and letting loose with Teagarden and Crosby on the sly number "The Waiter and the Porter and the

Upstairs Maid," written for the film by Johnny Mercer. This last number tells of a guest at a posh party who finds more fun when he goes downstairs into the kitchen and mixes with the hired help. Most of the numbers were song standards and were given exciting interpretations by the cast, such as Ruby Elzy's impassioned rendition of "St. Louis Blues," Crosby's mournful crooning of "My Melancholy Baby," and the title song, also sung by Crosby. The film may not have been accurate when it came to the story and characters but it was the genuine thing when the music started.

Birth of the Blues was the first Hollywood movie about jazz and blues, which is remarkable when you consider that these forms of music had been popular for three decades before the film was made. The musical revue *King of Jazz* (1930) was the only previous movie of note to feature such music but the musicians and singers were all white. (Incidentally, Crosby made his screen debut as one of the singing Rhythm Boys in that film.) Perhaps Hollywood was cautious about blues and jazz because they were most associated with African American performers. Or it might have been that jazz was not mainstream music in much of the nation. The impetus behind *Birth of the Blues* was Crosby himself. He loved blues and jazz and had enough influence on Paramount to get the movie made. (Many years later, Crosby stated that *Birth of the Blues* was one of his favorite films.) Paramount did not regret its concession to the popular singer because *Birth of the Blues* was very successful and actually prompted other studios to make musicals using blues and jazz. The two most noteworthy ones were Warner Brothers' *Blues in the Night* (1941) and RKO's *Syncopation* (1942). Songwriters Harold Arlen (music) and Johnny Mercer (lyrics) wrote a wailing blues song for a scene in a jail in *Blues in the Night*, a melodrama about the tough times of jazz musicians in the early years. The studio was so impressed with "Blues in the Night" that they used it for the title of the film. Today it is a blues standard, as is another Arlen-Mercer song from the movie, "This Time the Dream's on Me." *Blues in the Night* is weak in its plotting and characters but the music is spot on the mark. *Syncopation* was even less satisfying as a story but again the music is first class, especially when performed by such greats as Benny Goodman, Harry James, Charlie Barnett, Connee Boswell, Joe Venuti, and Gene Krupa.

See also: *High Society*; Bing Crosby, Johnny Mercer biography boxes

FURTHER READING

Eames, John Douglas. *The Paramount Story*. New York: Crown Publishers, 1985.

Prigozy, Ruth, and Walter Raubicheck, eds. *Going My Way: Bing Crosby and American Culture*. Rochester, NY: University of Rochester Press, 2007.

WEEKEND IN HAVANA

Studio and release date: 20th Century Fox; September 1941
Producer: William LeBaron
Screenplay: Karl Tunberg, Darrel Ware
Songwriters: Harry Warren (music), Mack Gordon (lyrics)
Director: Walter Lang
Choreographer: Hermes Pan
Musical Director: Alfred Newman
Cinematographer: Ernest Palmer
Cast: Alice Faye, John Payne, Carmen Miranda, Cesar Romero, Cobina Wright, Jr.
Songs: "Tropical Magic"; "A Week-End in Havana"; "The Nango"; "Romance and Rumba"; "When I Love I Love"

One of the many Fox musicals from the 1940s with a south-of-the-border setting, this Alice Faye and Carmen Miranda vehicle may have been rather predictable, but that doesn't make it any less enjoyable. During World War II, Hollywood wasn't able to export its movies to Europe and the loss of revenue hurt the studios deeply. After mostly ignoring its southern neighbors for so many years, Tinseltown realized that they were missing a valuable market. Hollywood movies (especially musicals) had been shown in Central and South America, but the studios never geared the films to that particular audience. So in the 1940s many movie musicals had a Latin setting and offered "south-of-the-border" music, which was also appealing to moviegoers in the United States. One of the best of these tailor-made musicals was *Weekend in Havana* (sometimes spelled *Week-End in Havana*).

The contrived plot featured Nan Spencer (Faye), a Macy's Department Store salesgirl, who takes a cruise to Cuba but her ship runs aground. She threatens to sue the steamship company so the executive Jay Williams (John Payne) takes Nan on an all-expenses-paid trip to Havana to get her to sign a release form. To no one's surprise, he falls head over heels in love with her. Cesar Romero was the Brooklyn-born Cuban Monte Blanca who was after the fortune he thinks Nan has, and Miranda was his jealous sweetheart Rosita Rivas. It was all agreeable nonsense that was interrupted by some fine Latin-flavored songs by Harry Warren (music) and Mack Gordon (lyrics). The rhythmic title song was sung by Miranda over the opening credits then was heard in spots throughout the film. Its evocative, romantic music gave the movie its flavor and effectively reminded moviegoers of the distinctive south-of-the-border locale. Even more romantic was "Tropical Magic," also heard at various points in the movie. More sassy was the spirited "When I Love I Love," which Miranda sang with comic, sexy gestures in a nightclub. "Romance and Rhumba" (music by James Monaco) was a dance number that Faye and Romero sang as they danced with others in a festive setting. Miranda also sang "The Nango," a swinging tango that Hermes Pan staged with Miranda and the chorus girls doing a kind of fusion of the two different styles of swing and the tango. *Weekend in Havana* was mostly filmed in the California studio, but a camera crew went to Cuba for some location shooting with doubles standing in for the stars. This colorful footage was edited into the final print, resulting in an exotic musical with plenty of Latin atmosphere.

Miranda represents Hollywood's wooing Latin American more than any other performer. The Portuguese-born singer grew up in Brazil where she first found fame on the radio and then in Spanish-language films. An American agent brought her to New York City where she performed in clubs and in Broadway revues. While still in Manhattan, Miranda was filmed singing three numbers, and the footage was added to *Down Argentine Way* (1940). Audiences were immediately thrilled with the funny, ribald singer, and she was brought to Hollywood where she appeared in 13 subsequent films. Never the star but always stealing the movie with her broad theatrics, Miranda remained popular until the 1950s, then returned to nightclubs in 1953. She died two years later of a heart attack at the age of 46. Today some Hispanics consider Miranda an outrageous stereotype who perpetuated demeaning clichés about Latin Americans. Others see her as a bold pioneer who was not afraid to be what she was rather than conform to the standards of the accepted movie star. Either way, Miranda appeared on the scene at exactly the right moment and was an audience favorite when Hollywood suddenly decided to go Latino.

See also: *You Were Never Lovelier, The Gang's All Here*; Alice Faye, Harry Warren biography boxes

FURTHER READING

Elder, Jane Lenz. *Alice Faye: A Life Beyond the Silver Screen.* Jackson: University Press of Mississippi, 2002.

Thomas, Tony. *Harry Warren and the Hollywood Musical.* New York: Lyle Stuart, 1975.

Thomas, Tony, and Aubrey Solomon. *The Films of 20th Century-Fox.* Secaucus, NJ: Citadel Press, 1979.

YANKEE DOODLE DANDY

Studio and release date: Warner Brothers; May 1942
Producer: Hal B. Wallis
Screenplay: Robert Bruckner, Edmund Joseph, Julius and Philip Epstein
Songwriter: George M. Cohan (music and lyrics)

Director: Michael Curtiz
Choreographers: LeRoy Prinz, Seymour Felix, John Boyle
Musical Director: Leo F. Forbstein
Cinematographer: James Wong Howe
Cast: James Cagney, Joan Leslie, Walter Huston, Richard Whorf, Rosemary DeCamp, Irene Manning, S. Z. Sakall, Jeanne Cagney, George Tobias, Frances Langford
Principal Songs: "Give My Regards to Broadway"; "Over There"; "The Yankee Doodle Boy"; "You're a Grand Old Flag"; "Forty-Five Minutes from Broadway"; "So Long, Mary"; "Harrigan"; "Mary's a Grand Old Name"

Of the dozens of biographical movie musicals about famous performers, this film about Broadway song-and-dance man George M. Cohan is one of the very best. The facts about the show business giant Cohan may have been altered, but the spirit of the man was certainly alive in this splendid musical in which James Cagney gives his finest musical performance. Cohan was a one-man dynamo who reigned on Broadway for nearly 40 years. As part of a family act in vaudeville, Cohan dreamed of going to Broadway. By 1904, that dream came true with *Little Johnny Jones*, a musical for which he wrote the book, music, and lyrics and also coproduced, directed, and starred in the show. He gave Broadway a truly American musical comedy style when the norm was European operetta. His songs were brash, unpoetic, and very catchy. In a series of musicals (which never changed even though the times did), Cohan introduced many standards that are still heard today. In the opinion of many, he invented the American musical. Putting all this into a bio-pic was a challenge and risky because most moviegoers had never seen Cohan onstage. He had appeared in five films, none of which was very successful. But producer Hal B. Wallis knew that Cohan's songs lived on and hoped they would help sell the movie. Casting Cagney as the great showman was inspired, and his plucky, energetic performance is the backbone of the film.

The literate (if inaccurate) screenplay introduced Little Georgie (Douglas Croft) who is born into a family of vaudeville performers and is on the stage at a young age, singing and dancing in variety with his parents (Walter Huston and Rosemary DeCamp) and sister Josie (Jeanne Cagney) and appearing in kid roles in plays. As a young man (Cagney), he is already writing songs and sketches for the family act but dreams of going to Broadway, which he does in 1904 with *Little Johnny Jones*. After a string of hits over several years, George finds that the newfangled musical theater is not for him so he retires to the country with his wife Mary (Joan Leslie). But the hyperactive performer cannot sit still so he returns to Broadway and has a triumph playing President Roosevelt in the musical *I'd Rather Be Right*. Having received the Congressional Medal of Honor from the real Roosevelt, George dances out of the White House and into history. The tight and efficient screenplay for

James Cagney (center) captured the magnetic charm of showman George M. Cohan in the musical biography *Yankee Doodle Dandy* (1942). Here he sells one of his songs while Joan Leslie looks on. *Yankee Doodle Dandy* remains one of Hollywood's finest bio-musicals. (Warner Bros./Photofest)

Yankee Doodle Dandy eliminates Cohan's unhappy first marriage and condenses his career so that the song hits just kept on coming. Michael Curtiz directed with flair and plenty of humor, none of the characters falling into historical blandness. The supporting cast was vibrant but the movie was really all Cagney's, making Cohan brash, funny, stubborn, and invigorating. His dancing was contagious and his showmanship in the stage sequences illustrated how one man could actually dazzle Broadway for years. The movie's most effective numbers were the two scenes from *Little Johnny Jones* in which Cagney got to sing the cocky "Yankee Doodle Boy" and the celebratory farewell song "Give My Regards to Broadway." Both numbers were actually very accurate to the original Broadway staging; there was no Hollywood excess here. These numbers actually looked like they were on a Broadway stage. Seymour Felix, LeRoy Prinz, and John Boyle shared the choreography chores and each one showed restraint, letting the performers shine brightly. Other notable Cohan songs featured in the movie were the adoring ballad "Mary's a Grand Old Name," the patriotic march "Over There," the celebratory "You're a Grand Old Flag," the gushing "Oh, You Wonderful Girl," the rousing

---

James Cagney (1899–1986)   A versatile leading man in Hollywood for four decades, he played everything from nimble song-and-dance characters to gangsters. Cagney was born in New York City to an Irish bartender and a Norwegian immigrant. He worked in restaurants and pool halls to earn tuition money for Columbia University. After gaining stage experience on the vaudeville circuit, he was cast in his first play on Broadway in 1925. Although he sang and danced in a handful of Broadway musicals, Cagney was brought to Hollywood to play toughies in melodramas. He found stardom with *The Public Enemy* (1931) and appearing in dozens of gritty gangster films over the next three decades. Cagney's first screen musical was *Footlight Parade* (1933), followed by singing and dancing in *Something to Sing About* (1937), *Yankee Doodle Dandy* (1942), *West Point Story* (1950), *Starlift* (1951), *The Seven Little Foys* (1955), and *Never Steal Anything Small* (1959). But most of Cagney's screen career was not in musicals, remaining a top box office star because of such movies as *A Midsummer Night's Dream* (1935), *Angels with Dirty Faces* (1938), *The Roaring Twenties* (1939), *The Strawberry Blonde* (1941), *White Heat* (1949), *Love Me or Leave Me* (1955), *Mister Roberts* (1955), *Man of a Thousand Faces* (1957), and *Ragtime* (1981). Autobiography: *Cagney on Cagney* (1975); biography: *Cagney*, John McCabe (1999).

"So Long Mary," the waltzing "Forty-five Minutes From Broadway," and the Irish ditty "Harrigan." *Yankee Doodle Dandy* was one of the first Hollywood pictures about an American songwriter and its success launched many others, few coming even close to this original in quality.

See also: *Footlight Parade*; James Cagney biography box

FURTHER READING

Bingen, Steven. *Warner Bros.: Hollywood's Ultimate Backlot*. Lanham, MD: Taylor Trade Publishing, 2014.

Bloom, Ken. *Hollywood Musicals: The 101 Greatest Song-and-Dance Movies of All Time*. New York: Black Dog and Leventhal, 2010.

Cagney, James. *Cagney By Cagney*. New York: Knopf Group, 2010.

HOLIDAY INN

Studio and release date: Paramount; August 1942
Producer/Director: Mark Sandrich
Screenplay: Claude Binyon
Songwriter: Irving Berlin (music and lyrics)
Choreographer: Danny Dare
Musical Director: Robert Emmett Dolan
Cinematographer: David Abel
Cast: Bing Crosby, Fred Astaire, Marjorie Reynolds, Virginia Dare, Walter Abel,
  Louise Beavers
Songs: "White Christmas"; "You're Easy to Dance With"; "Happy Holiday"; "I'll
  Capture Your Heart Singing"; "Let's Say It with Firecrackers"; "Let's Start the
  New Year Right"; "Lazy"; "Easter Parade"; "Abraham"; "Be Careful, It's My
  Heart"; "Song of Freedom"; "I Can't Tell a Lie"; "Plenty to Be Thankful For";
  "Holiday Inn"

This Christmas season favorite will always be remembered as the film in which
Bing Crosby introduced Irving Berlin's "White Christmas," but there is so much
else to enjoy in this treasure chest of a movie.

The screenplay has its preposterous moments but it certainly works as a vehicle to carry a bouquet of old and new Berlin songs. Song-and-dance partners Ted
Hanover (Fred Astaire) and Jim Hardy (Crosby) break up over a girl, singer-dancer
Lila Dixon (Virginia Dale), so Jim moves to the country and turns an old Connecticut homestead into an inn that's only open on holidays. When he falls for aspir-
ing singer Linda Mason (Marjorie Reynolds), Jim tries to keep her identity hidden
from Ted so as not to lose her too. Each holiday brings a new show to the inn and
another opportunity to keep the wolf-like Ted at bay. Ted eventually discovers Linda
and whisks her off to Hollywood to make a movie about the inn. After licking his
wounds, Jim finally goes to the California studio and, in the setting of the artificial
inn, wins her back. It is a stretch of the imagination to believe that a business
that's only open for the holidays could survive, but part of the charm of the film is
the carefree way it goes about its way to entertain. What is unusual in the story is the
fact that Astaire, for the first time in his movie career, does not get the girl; but then
his is not a very likable character. Only Astaire's charm allows him to carry it off.
The setting for the musical is also unique. The homey Connecticut inn seemed idyllic to wartime audiences, and the mood and setting for introducing the song "White
Christmas" make for one of the most cozy and romantic scenes in the history of
movie musicals. Berlin's holiday standard "Easter Parade" was the only song in
the score not written for the film. (It had been introduced on Broadway in 1933.) The
new holiday songs have been overshadowed by the tremendous popularity of the

The romantic triangle in *Holiday Inn* (1942) involved Marjorie Reynolds being pursued by Bing Crosby (at piano) and Fred Astaire (dancing). The rivalry between the two men was quite determined and for the only time in his career, Astaire did not get the girl. Mark Sandrich directed the holiday classic. (Paramount Pictures/Photofest)

Oscar-winning "White Christmas," but the others are also quite good and are given effective introductions. Crosby sang "Be Careful, It's My Heart," a warm ballad for Valentine's Day; "Let's Start the New Year Right," a chipper New Year's ditty; and the Fourth of July is celebrated with Astaire tapping to "Let's Say It With Firecrackers" as dozens of tiny explosions erupted at his feet. The most problematic number in the film, of course, is the revival-like song "Abraham" for Lincoln's birthday, which Crosby and Marjorie Reynolds performed as two black-faced minstrels. While it is a tribute to Abraham Lincoln, its use of minstrel singers is very difficult for modern viewers. The non-holiday songs were also given memorable treatments, such as Crosby attempting to dance like Astaire while Astaire tries to croon like Crosby in "I'll Capture Your Heart Singing," and Virginia Dale and Astaire gliding across the dance floor with "You're Easy to Dance With." Danny Dare and Astaire did the inventive choreography, Mark Sandrich produced and directed the film with a breezy style, and the movie was a giant hit.

Holiday Inn remains a familiar favorite because of its reappearance every December on television, video, and DVD. Ironically, the movie was not planned or released as a Christmas treat. It opened in August in New York City as a benefit

Bing Crosby (1903–1977)   The durable singer-actor who had more song hits than any other entertainer, he played an easy-going romantic figure in over 60 Hollywood musicals between 1930 and 1964. Her was born in Tacoma, Washington, and studied at Gonzaga University where he started singing with a campus band. Conductor Paul Whiteman teamed him with two other singers, billed them as the Rhythm Boys, and featured them in his concerts and in the film *King of Jazz* (1930). By the next year Crosby was performing solo, got his own radio show, and started his remarkable recording career. After doing specialty bits in a handful of movie musicals, he progressed to character parts with *College Humor* (1933). Among his most notable film musicals are *Going Hollywood* (1933), *We're Not Dressing* (1934), *Mississippi* (1935), *Anything Goes* (1936 and 1956), *Rhythm on the Range* (1936), *Pennies From Heaven* (1936), *Double or Nothing* (1937), *Sing You Sinners* (1938), *Birth of The Blues* (1941), *Holiday Inn* (1942), *Going My Way* (1944), *Here Come the Waves* (1944), *The Bells of St. Mary's* (1945), *Blue Skies* (1946), *A Connecticut Yankee in King Arthur's Court* (1949), *Here Comes the Groom* (1951), *White Christmas* (1954), *The Country Girl* (1954), *High Society* (1956), and *Robin and the Seven Hoods* (1964). Crosby first teamed up with Bob Hope in *Road to Singapore* (1940) and the duo was so popular together they went on to make six more *Road* pictures. Crosby appeared in several nonmusicals during his long career and but rarely did his public accept him unless he was singing. The original crooner, Crosby was one of the first singers to use the radio microphone effectively, offering an easygoing style of singing. Autobiography: *Call Me Lucky*, with Gary Giddins, Pete Martin (1953); memoirs: *Bing and Other Things*, Kathryn Crosby, his wife (1967); *Going My Own Way*, Gary Crosby, his son (1983); biography: *Going My Way: Bing Crosby and American Culture*, Ruth Prigozy, Walter Raubicheck (2007).

for the Navy Relief Society. Berlin thought up the idea of a movie musical that celebrated several holidays and pitched it to Paramount. The Christmas sequence was to be just one of many holiday sections of the story. During filming, Crosby sensed that "White Christmas" had the makings of a hit and sang it on his radio show on Christmas Day, 1941. Interest in the song grew then exploded after the film was released. "White Christmas" not only won the Oscar for best song but went on to break Tin Pan Alley records—the highest-selling nonreligious song of all time with over 50 million copies of records sold (the Crosby recording alone sold over 30 million records) and over 400 different versions in different languages. It is understatement to say that "White Christmas" is the most popular song ever to come out of Hollywood.

See also: *White Christmas*; Irving Berlin, Bing Crosby, Fred Astaire biography boxes

FURTHER READING

Crosby, Bing, and Pete Martin. *Call Me Lucky*. Boston: Da Capo Press, 2001.
Eames, John Douglas. *The Paramount Story*. New York: Crown Publishers, 1985.
Thomas, Bob. *The Man, the Dancer: The Life of Fred Astaire*. New York: St. Martin's Press, 1987.

YOU WERE NEVER LOVELIER

Studio and release date: Columbia Pictures; October 1942
Producer: Louis F. Edelman
Screenplay: Michael Fessier, Ernest Pagano, Delmer Daves
Songwriters: Jerome Kern (music), Johnny Mercer (lyrics)
Director: William A. Seiter
Choreographer: Val Raset
Musical Director: Leigh Harline
Cinematographer: Ted Tetzlaff
Cast: Fred Astaire, Rita Hayworth, Adolphe Menjou, Xavier Cugat, Leslie Brooks
Songs: "I'm Old Fashioned"; "Dearly Beloved"; "You Were Never Lovelier"; "Wedding in the Spring"; "Shorty George"

During World War II, Hollywood's desire to appeal to Latin countries sometimes forced them to make some odd changes. *You Were Never Lovelier* was set in Argentina even though the plot, characters, and even the music had nothing "south-of-the-border" about them. But with such a terrific cast and top-notch songs, the movie would have pleased no matter what the locale. The basic plot for the musical came from a Brazilian film titled *Carnival in Rio*. The studio, for some unknown reason, placed its version in Buenos Aires, Argentina. Fred Astaire and Rita Hayworth had first been teamed in *You'll Never Get Rich* (1941) and the two set off sparks, especially when they danced together. So Columbia wasted no time reteaming them, this time putting the twosome in a Latin setting. The wealthy Argentine mogul Edouardo Acuña (Adolphe Menjou) has four marriageable daughters and insists that they marry in order of their birthdates. When the eldest daughter weds, both father and youngest sisters scheme to find an eligible mate for the second born daughter, Maria (Hayworth). Acuña goes so far as to send flowers and love letters from a mysterious admirer to Maria, getting her primed for when he finds the right man for her. Instead, she falls for Manhattan nightclub hoofer Robert Davis (Astaire). He has come to Argentina for the horse racing but has lost all his

> **Johnny Mercer** (1909–1976)   A popular lyricist, singer, and sometime com-
> poser, he was an expert in writing songs filled with regional slang and folksy
> familiarity. He was born in Savannah, Georgia, and from his youth had ambi-
> tions to be a singer. Mercer got some singing jobs in New York, was a vocalist
> with bands touring the country, and started writing lyrics. While a few of his
> songs were heard in some Broadway revues, he had better luck in Hollywood
> writing lyrics for such musicals as *Old Man Rhythm* (1935), *Ready, Willing
> and Able* (1937), *Varsity Show* (1937), *Hollywood Hotel* (1937), *Cowboy From
> Brooklyn* (1938), *Garden of the Moon* (1938), *Going Places* (1938), *Blues in the
> Night* (1941), *Star Spangled Rhythm* (1942), *The Fleet's In* (1942), *You Were
> Never Lovelier* (1942), *The Sky's the Limit* (1943), *Here Come the Waves* (1944),
> *The Harvey Girls* (1946), *Dangerous When Wet* (1953), *Seven Brides for Seven
> Brothers* (1954), *Daddy Long Legs* (1955), *Merry Andrew* (1958), *You Can't
> Run Away From It* (1956), and *Darling Lili* (1969). Mercer's Broadway scores
> include *St. Louis Woman* (1946), *Top Banana* (1951), *Li'l Abner* (1956), *Sara-
> toga* (1959), and *Foxy* (1964). He also wrote many memorable theme songs
> for nonmusical films such as "Moon River" and "The Days of Wine and
> Roses." Mercer never gave up on his singing, making many recordings over
> the years of his own and others' songs, and in 1942 cofounded Capitol Rec-
> ords. Biographies: *Portrait of Johnny: The Life of John Herndon Mercer*, Gene
> Lees (2006); *Skylark: The Life and Times of Johnny Mercer*, Philip Furia (2004).

money gambling on them. So he seeks a job at a ritzy hotel owned by Acuña. Of course the father does not approve of the relationship so complications set in, such as Maria thinking the flowers and letter are from Robert and her disappointment when she finds out the truth. While the plot came to its inevitable conclusion, Astaire and Hayworth had some sensational dance duets to fill in the dull stretches.

There were some superb songs by Jerome Kern (music) and Johnny Mercer (lyrics) in the musical, such as the flowing title number, which Astaire and Hayworth danced to beautifully. The snappy wedding number "Dearly Beloved" was more swinging than reverent and Hayworth cut loose with a ditty called "Shorty George." But the undisputed musical highlight of *You Were Never Lovelier* was the disarming ballad "I'm Old Fashioned." Astaire and Hayworth sang it then did a sublime dance in a moonlit garden; it is one of the era's most romantic sequences. None of these songs were particularly Latin so Xavier Cugat and his orchestra were on hand to provide the only authentic Hispanic touch, unless you count 15-year-old Fidel Castro who, according to legend, was one of the extras in the film.

Rita Hayworth was one of Hollywood's brightest dancing stars. Many feel that she was Astaire's finest partner, able to match him in the steps and in style. She was certainly Astaire's sexiest dancing partner. Not only did Hayworth exude sex, she did it without overtly trying. Perhaps that is why she and Astaire sizzle even though she is playing a down-home, "old-fashioned" kind of girl. Hayworth was also an accomplished actress, being able to play sultry, as in *Gilda* (1946), or wholesome, as with *You Were Never Lovelier*. What Hayworth could not do was sing and in all her musicals she was dubbed. Oddly, the studios were never consistent in the way they dubbed her. Sometimes she has a mezzo-soprano chirping voice; in other films she has a throaty alto singing voice. Usually the singing voice did not match her warm speaking voice, making the dubbing even more ludicrous. Of course Hollywood never disclosed that Hayworth was dubbed. It was an industry secret that many of the stars in musicals were dubbed. Nan Wynn, one of Hollywood's busiest dubbing artists, provided Hayworth's singing voice in *You Were Never Lovelier* and it is one of the better matches in her career. It is another reason the movie is so satisfying.

See also: *Cover Girl*; Jerome Kern, Johnny Mercer, Fred Astaire, Rita Hayworth biography boxes

FURTHER READING

Dick, Bernard, ed. *Columbia Pictures: Portrait of a Studio*. Lexington: University of Kentucky Press, 1991.

Hirschhorn, Clive. *The Columbia Story*. 2nd ed. London: Hamlyn Press, 2001.

Leaming, Barbara. *If This Was Happiness: A Biography of Rita Hayworth*. New York: Viking Press, 1989.

STAR SPANGLED RHYTHM

Studio and release date: Paramount; December 1942
Producer: Joseph Sistrom
Screenplay: Harry Tugend
Songwriters: Harold Arlen (music), Johnny Mercer (lyrics)
Director: George Marshall
Choreographers: Danny Dare, George Balanchine
Musical Director: Robert Emmett Dolan
Cinematographer: Leo Tover
Cast: Eddie Bracken, Betty Hutton, Victor Moore, Mary Martin, Johnnie Johnston, Vera Zorina, Dorothy Lamour, Veronica Lake, Paulette Goddard, Dick Powell, Eddie Anderson, William Bendix, Jerry Colonna, Fred MacMurray, Bing Crosby, Bob Hope, Franchot Tone, Ray Milland, Dona Drake

Songs: "Hit the Road to Dreamland"; "That Old Black Magic"; "I'm Doing It for Defense"; "On the Swing Shift"; "Old Glory"; "A Sweater, a Sarong, and a Peek-a-Boo Bang"; "Sharp as a Tack"

Hollywood contributed to the war effort during World War II in many ways—from sponsoring war bond drives to making training films for the military. Each studio had dozens of stars on contract but fewer movies were being made so Hollywood turned to the musical revue, just as it had at the beginning of the talkies. Revues were excellent ways to employ a lot of contract performers for a short period of time with different directors and choreographers working on different scenes. The problem was audiences didn't respond well to revues, so these films always had a thin plot to hold together the different acts. Paramount's *Star Spangled Rhythm* was the first of these wartime revues and, in the opinion of many, the very best.

It seemed that every actor on the Paramount lot showed up in this wartime entertainment in which a slender plot was needed only as an excuse for a patriotic bonanza of celebrities. G.I. Johnny Webster (Eddie Bracken) wants to impress his shipmates so he schemes with switchboard operator Polly Judson (Betty Hutton) to pass off Johnny's father Billy (Victor Moore), a gatekeeper at Paramount, as a studio executive. The plan goes smoothly at first but soon Billy finds himself in charge of a huge stage show for servicemen. After some annoying complications, the big show begins and all is forgiven. Harold Arlen (music) and Johnny Mercer (lyrics) wrote the score and struck gold twice with the hypnotic ballad "That Old Black Magic," sung by Johnny Johnston and danced by Vera Zorina, and "Hit the Road to Dreamland," introduced by Mary Martin, Dick Powell, and the gospel-singing Golden Gate Quartet while riding on a train. The outstanding score also included Paulette Goddard, Dorothy Lamour, and Veronica Lake, each spoofing her image with "A Sweater, a Sarong, and a Peek-a-Boo Bang"; Marjorie Reynolds, Betty Jane Rhodes, and Dona Drake as "Rosie the Riveter" types singing about working "On the Swing Shift"; Hutton riding in a jeep full of sailors and slyly singing "I'm Doing It for Defense"; and Eddie "Rochester" Anderson and other African American performers jiving it up with "Sharp as a Tack" as he shows off his zoot suit, only to find that the best dressed men of 1942 were wearing military uniforms. The big patriotic finale of the film was Bing Crosby leading a giant chorus in "Old Glory" in front of Mount Rushmore and images of American history.

The comic highlight in the movie had nothing to do with the plot. It was a comedy sketch, "If Men Played Cards as Women Do," that George S. Kaufman had written decades ago for a Broadway revue. On-screen Fred MacMurray, Franchot Tone, and Ray Milland were hilariously droll playing bridge with a female attitude. Among the other Paramount stars stopping by the set were Bob Hope, Susan Hayward, Alan Ladd, Jerry Colonna, William Bendix, Arthur Treacher,

Sterling Holloway, Walter Catlett, and even directors Ralph Murphy, Preston Sturges, and Cecil B. DeMille. *Star Spangled Rhythm* was so successful that it was followed by other star-stuffed wartime musicals from various studios. Warner Brothers released *Thank Your Lucky Stars* in 1943, and it was almost as good as *Star Spangled Rhythm*. The shaky plot concerned an arrogant movie star and a look-alike fan (both played by Eddie Cantor) and two studio heads (Edward Everett Horton and S. Z. Sakall) trying to put on a charity show. Again, the film was packed with stars, songs, and dance, but the moment most viewers remember was a wry Bette Davis singing "They're Either Too Young or Too Old" about the male shortage on the home front. The same studio offered *This Is the Army* (1943), inspired by a Broadway revue, and featuring a score of old and new numbers by Irving Berlin. Perhaps the highlight of that film was Berlin himself in World War I uniform singing the 1917 hit "Oh, How I Hate to Get Up in the Morning." MGM offered a huge wartime revue titled *Thousands Cheer* (1943) and, because the studio had more stars than any other, the cast was impressive. But the movie itself has dated poorly, as have Universal's *Follow the Boys* (1944), United Artists' *Stage Door Canteen* (1943), and Warner's *Hollywood Canteen* (1944). With the end of the war, these patriotic "disguised" movie revues faded away and never returned.

See also: *The Hollywood Revue of 1929*; Harold Arlen, Johnny Mercer, Betty Hutton biography boxes

FURTHER READING

Bloom, Ken. *Hollywood Musicals: The 101 Greatest Song-and-Dance Movies of All Time*. New York: Black Dog and Leventhal, 2010.

Eames, John Douglas. *The Paramount Story*. New York: Crown Publishers, 1985.

Woll, Allen L. *The Hollywood Musical Goes to War*. Chicago: Nelson-Hall, 1983.

CABIN IN THE SKY

Studio and release date: Metro-Goldwyn-Mayer; April 1943
Producer: Arthur Freed
Screenplay: Joseph Schrank, based on the 1940 stage script by Lynn Root
Songwriters: Vernon Duke, Harold Arlen (music), John Latouche, E. Y. Harburg (lyrics)
Director: Vincente Minnelli
Choreographer: Busby Berkeley
Musical Director: George Stoll

Cinematographer: Sidney Wagner
Cast: Ethel Waters, Eddie Anderson, Lena Horne, Louis Armstrong, Rex Ingram, Kenneth Spencer, Duke Ellington, John Bubbles, Ford Buck
Principal Songs: "Taking a Chance on Love"; "Happiness Is a Thing Called Joe"; "Honey in the Honeycomb"; "Cabin in the Sky"; "Life's Full of Consequence"; "Li'l Black Sheep"; "Shine"

The major studios rarely made mainstream films about African Americans during the Golden Age, and musicals were no exception. At the same time, Hollywood knew that there was a significant black audience who went to the movies. So many of the studios made "race films," shorts and features cast with African Americans and they were shown in ethnic neighborhoods. *Cabin in the Sky* is that exceptional case when a first-class movie musical with an African American cast was given a general release so it could be enjoyed by all kinds of audiences. Producer Arthur Freed insisted that no shortcuts be taken and that the project be given the highly polished MGM touch. The result is a superb film and a cinematic record of some of the greatest African American performers of the time.

Closely based on the 1940 Broadway success, the movie is in the style of a "Negro" folk tale. Luckless Little Joe Jackson (Eddie Anderson) gets shot in a crap game fight. His faithful wife Petunia (Ethel Waters) prays to God to give her mis-led husband another chance. Joe survives his wounds and is given six months to prove himself a good soul, helped in the venture by the Lawd's General (Kenneth Spencer). His efforts are hindered by Lucifer Jr. (Rex Ingram) who tempts Joe with the sultry beauty Georgia Brown (Lena Horne). It looks like Joe is lost forever, and when Petunia goes to the Paradise Dancehall to bring him home, she is shot during a brawl. As she is dying, Petunia asks God to take both her and Little Joe to heaven. Unlike the Broadway version, it turns out the whole tale was a dream. In his screen directing debut, Vincente Minnelli gave the film a rustic yet dreamlike quality about it that is ideal for the fable it tells. Minnelli was a Broadway designer before coming to Hollywood and his movies often had a stylish, painterly feel to them. This black-and-white film is indeed a visual treat. It is also a musical feast even though only three of the stage songs by Vernon Duke (music) and John Latouche (lyrics) made it to the screen: the warm, domestic title song; the sexy "Honey in the Honeycomb" delivered sensuously by Horne; and the gently swinging ballad "Taking a Chance on Love," which had already become a song standard. Harold Arlen (music) and E. Y. Harburg (lyrics) wrote three new songs for the movie and they were also excellent. Waters sang the lullaby-like "Li'l Black Sheep," Anderson and Horne had fun with the philosophical "Life's Full of Consequence," and Waters did a beautiful rendition of the beloved ballad "Happiness Is a Thing Called Joe." Also heard were some Duke Ellington jazz and some gospel singing so music seems to flow throughout the rural community. Apart from

Ethel Waters (1896–1977)   A formidable African American actress-singer who broke many racial barriers during her stage and screen career, she and her velvet flowing voice were featured in a handful of musicals. She was born in poverty in Chester, Pennsylvania, and worked as a servant until someone who heard her sing suggested she try vaudeville. Waters made her stage debut in 1917 and became one of the few black performers to succeed in both "colored" and mainstream variety. Soon she rose to become a recognized singer of jazz and blues in supper clubs and cabarets, some of which had never featured African Americans before. Waters first appeared on Broadway in the "all-Negro" revues *Africana* (1927), *Lew Leslie's Blackbirds* (1930), and *Rhapsody in Black* (1931). Then in 1933, Waters became the first black performer to get star billing alongside whites in the popular revue *As Thousands Cheer.* Two years later she starred in the musicals *At Home Abroad* and *Cabin in the Sky* (1940). Waters reprised her performance in the 1943 film version of *Cabin in the Sky* and also appeared on-screen in the musicals *On with the Show* (1929), *Gift of Gab* (1934), *Cairo* (1942), and *Stage Door Canteen* (1943). She returned to Broadway in the musicals *Laugh Time* (1943), *Blue Holiday* (1945), *At Home With Ethel Waters* (1953), and *An Evening With Ethel Waters* (1959). Her finest nonmusical performances were in the stage and screen drama *The Member of the Wedding* (1952). Waters was the first African American to have her own national radio show, and in the 1950s she had her own television series, *Beulah*, and made guest appearances on all the top variety shows. She is most remembered for her expressive eyes, infectiously radiant smile, and flowing voice. Autobiographies: *His Eye Is on the Sparrow* (1951); *To Me It's Wonderful* (1972); biography: *Heat Wave: The Life and Career of Ethel Waters*, Donald Bogle (2011).

being enjoyable in itself, *Cabin in the Sky* is an archival treasure, preserving the performances of so many gifted players for future generations.

Both producer Freed and director Minnelli were very familiar with the way African Americans were portrayed onstage and in movies. One had to go back to 1929 and *Hallelujah* to find a major studio movie that looked at the African American culture with accuracy and compassion. Freed insisted that *Cabin in the Sky* avoid the overt stereotyping and underlying prejudice found in most movies with black characters. Yet even *Cabin in the Sky* relied on such types as obsessive gamblers and sexy sirens that too often appeared in African American stories. The fact that this film is told as a folk tale certainly helps one get past these types and enjoy the wonderful performances. Many African American activists praised the movie when it came out in 1943, pleased to see a major effort made by a top studio. Today one can still applaud *Cabin in the Sky*, not only for what it tried to do but for what it did so splendidly.

See also: Hallelujah; Ethel Waters, Vincente Minnelli biography boxes

FURTHER READING

Bogle, Donald. *Heat Wave: The Life and Career of Ethel Waters*. New York: HarperCollins, 2011.

Knight, Arthur. *Disintegrating the Musical: Black Performance and the American Musical Film*. Durham, NC: Duke University Press, 2002.

Waters, Ethel, and Charles Samuels. *His Eye Is on the Sparrow: An Autobiography*. Boston: Da Capo Press, 1992.

THE GANG'S ALL HERE

Studio and release date: 20th Century Fox; November 1943
Producer: William LeBaron
Screenplay: Walter Bullock
Songwriters: Harry Warren (music), Leo Robin (lyrics)
Director/Choreographer: Busby Berkeley
Musical Directors: Charles Henderson, Alfred Newman
Cinematographer: Edward Cronjager
Cast: Alice Faye, Carmen Miranda, Phil Baker, Charlotte Greenwood, Benny Goodman, Eugene Palette, Edward Everett Horton
Principal Songs: "The Lady in the Tutti-Frutti Hat"; "No Love, No Nothin'"; "A Journey to a Star"; "The Polka Dot Polka"; "Paducah"; "Minnie's in the Money"

Although it was not set in Latin America, this musical fits in with the other south-of-the-border films of the 1940s because of Carmen Miranda and the outrageous production numbers with a Caribbean decor. Perhaps the best example of a colorful 1940s musical, *The Gang's All Here* was low on content but overflowing with visual and musical thrills. The fact that the songs and dances had nothing to do with the story didn't seem to bother anyone at the time. It was probably because the studio and audiences were bleary-eyed from all the color. The plot centered on the showgirl Edie Allen (Faye) at a Manhattan nightclub who is romanced by the playboy soldier Andy Mason (James Ellison). He tells her his name is Casey then is shipped off to the Pacific. Not until he returns a war hero and Edie is hired with other chorus girls to entertain at Andy's family mansion do they meet again, and she makes him forget the fiancée Vivian Potter (Sheila Ryan) his family has chosen for him. It was far from a gripping story and it was relieved when Charlotte Greenwood, Edward Everett Horton, Phil Baker, and Eugene Palette wandered in and out of the plot to grab laughs when comedienne Miranda was occupied elsewhere. When Miranda was on the set, little sense mattered. To say the comic singer was bigger than life is an understatement. Only Betty Hutton got away with such broad comic acting and singing, though Miranda was not as shrill as Hutton. Although she barely enters the plot, Miranda steals the movie and in every scene she is not in, moviegoers missed her.

The musical values in *The Gang's All Here* are upstaged by the production values. The silly extravaganza was 20th Century Fox's most expensive musical of the war years, and one only has to look at director-choreographer Busby Berkeley's production numbers to see where the money went. It was Berkeley's first film in Technicolor and he vigorously embraced the new color palate. "The Lady in the Tutti-Frutti Hat" number featured Miranda, wagon-loads of colorfully dressed peasants on a plantation, and thousands of bananas all combined to form geometric patterns. For the finale, "The Polka Dot Polka," Faye, a gang of children from different time periods, and a nightclub chorus all performed in front of revolving mirrors that made dizzying kaleidoscopic images. The effect was practically psychedelic. Harry Warren (music) and Leo Robin (lyrics) wrote most of the score, which had its quieter moments, such as the two hit ballads "No Love, No Nothin'" and "A Journey to a Star," both sung by Faye in her last film for 19 years. Benny Goodman provided the required band needed to fill out the production numbers, and there were some Spanish ditties to add to the Latin atmosphere. William LeBaron produced and stopped worrying about the expense once the movie opened and was a hit.

The use of color in movie musicals has an odd history. Color techniques had been developed in the 1920s and some silent features had color sections in them, but it was considered just a novelty by the audiences and too expensive by the studios. Hence, just about every musical to come out of Hollywood before 1940 is in black and white. One recalls the *Gold Digger* musicals, the Fred Astaire and Ginger Rogers vehicles, and even the spectacle films like *The Great Ziegfeld* (1936) and *San Francisco* (1936) as black-and-white experiences. One didn't need color to convey class, realism, romance, or even disaster. The drama *Becky Sharp* (1935) was the first Technicolor movie but its colors were muted and fuzzy, giving the screen an impressionist look that did not please moviegoers. They preferred black and white. The musical that changed everything was *The Wizard of Oz* (1939). When Dorothy opened the door and walked into Munchkinland, the new Technicolor process was dazzling. The audience discovered real color and liked it. In the 1940s, most musicals were in color. Ironically, just when the public wanted color, the film stock for the color process was hard to come by because of war shortages. Walt Disney delayed his animated feature *Dumbo* for four years, waiting for color film to become available. Too often the Technicolor musicals lose much of

Alice Faye (1915–1998)   A unique leading lady of 1930s and 1940s film musicals, she possessed a husky speaking voice and a deep contralto singing voice. She was born in New York, the daughter of a policeman, and was singing and dancing professionally as a teenager. Faye had experience on Broadway and singing with Rudy Vallee's band before she made her film debut in *George White's Scandals* (1934), followed by major roles in *She Learned About Sailors* (1934), *Every Night at Eight* (1935), *King of Burlesque* (1936), *Poor Little Rich Girl* (1936), *Sing, Baby, Sing* (1936), *Stowaway* (1936), *On the Avenue* (1937), *Wake Up and Live* (1937), *In Old Chicago* (1938), *Alexander's Ragtime Band* (1938), *Rose of Washington Square* (1939), *Lillian Russell* (1940), *Tin Pan Alley* (1940), *That Night in Rio* (1941), *Weekend in Havana* (1941), *Hello, Frisco, Hello* (1943), *The Gang's All Here* (1943), and *Four Jills in a Jeep* (1944). Faye was at the peak of her popularity when she retired in 1945, but she returned two decades later to play maternal roles in the film musicals *State Fair* (1962) and *The Magic of Lassie* (1978). Biography: *Alice Faye: A Life Beyond the Silver Screen*, Jane Lenz Elder (2002).

their luster on the small TV screen or on DVD. Watching *The Gang's All Here* today is not quite what audiences saw on the big screen in 1943. Progress is not always a friend to the Golden Age of Hollywood musicals.

See also: *Weekend in Havana*; Busby Berkeley, Alice Faye, Harry Warren biography boxes

FURTHER READING

Allvine, Glendon. *The Greatest Fox of Them All.* New York: Lyle Stuart, 1969.
Elder, Jane Lenz. *Alice Faye: Life Beyond the Silver Screen.* Jackson: University of Mississippi Press, 2002.
Thomas, Tony. *Harry Warren and the Hollywood Musical.* New York: Lyle Stuart, 1975.

GOING MY WAY

Studio and release date: Paramount; February 1944
Producer/Director: Leo McCarey
Screenplay: Frank Butler, Frank Cavett
Songwriters: James Van Heusen and others (music), Johnny Burke and others (lyrics)

Musical Director: Robert Emmett Dolan
Cinematographer: Lionel Lindon
Cast: Bing Crosby, Barry Fitzgerald, Risë Stevens, Frank McHugh, Gene
    Lockhart, Jean Heather, William Frawley, Stanley Clements
Songs: "Swinging on a Star"; "Going My Way"; "The Day After Forever";
    "Too-Ra-Loo-Ra-Loo-Ral"; "Silent Night"; "Habanera"

Bing Crosby was the top box office attraction for several years running in the 1940s, and this heart-tugging musical drama demonstrates why the crooner's warm, easy-going style of acting and singing was a comfort to wartime audiences. Crosby played the gentle priest Fr. Chuck O'Malley who is sent to St. Dominic's, a run-down urban parish in New York City where aging, conservative Fr. Fitzgibbon (Barry Fitzgerald) is pastor. Attendance at church services is falling, the local toughs are making the neighborhood unsafe, and Fr. Fitzgibbon is 40 years behind the times. Fr. O'Malley and Fr. Fitzgibbon clash many times but the younger priest wins out. He organizes a boys choir out of the riffraff on the street, brings a young couple together, raises money for the poor parish, and even brings Fr. Fitzgibbon's 90-year-old mother (Adeline DeWalt Reynolds) from Ireland for Christmas. It was all very sentimental but the movie was handled with taste by director Leo McCarey and the cast. The supporting players included opera's Risë Stevens as opera singer Genevieve Linden who helps Fr. O'Malley get the choir heard by record producer Max Dolan (William Frawley). What he heard was the gentle title ballad and the hit novelty number "Swinging on a Star," both by James Van Heusen (music) and Johnny Burke (lyrics). "Going My Way" got some play later but it was "Swinging on a Star" that was the runaway hit. The film collected a choir loft full of Oscars (including one for "Swinging on a Star") and has remained an audience favorite over the years.

Crosby appeared as Fr. O'Malley again in RKO's *The Bells of St. Mary's*, another sentimental (and popular) film. Although it feels like a sequel to *Going My Way*, *The Bells of St. Mary's* was actually made first but *Going My Way* was released first. When Fr. O'Malley is sent to help at a poor parochial school, he finds himself up against the not-so-understanding Sister Mary Benedict (Ingrid Bergman). Again the antagonism between the two melts and a happy ending is ensured. The movie was tamer and more tired than the earlier work and there were only four songs, one of them a hymn, so *The Bells of St. Mary's* didn't feel much like a musical. Van Heusen and Burke again provided Crosby with a hit song, "Aren't You Glad You're You?" The understanding Fr. O'Malley sang it to the dejected Patsy Gallagher (Joan Carroll), one of the students in the parish school. Audiences loved *The Bells of St. Mary's* and it was also a box office hit.

Neither film would have amounted to much if it hadn't been for Crosby. Between 1944 and 1948, he was the number one box office attraction in the nation. He was

Johnny Burke and **James Van Heusen**   Two Hollywood songwriters who worked with various partners, their most remembered scores were written together. The lyricist Burke (1908–1964) was born in Antioch, California, and educated at the University of Wisconsin and Crane College, then performed in vaudeville as a song-and-dance man. He appeared in some Broadway revues and made several film shorts when talkies came in, then concentrated on writing lyrics for Hollywood. With composer Arthur Johnston, he scored *Go West, Young Man* (1936), *Pennies From Heaven* (1936), and *Double or Nothing* (1937) then teamed with James V. Monaco for *Doctor Rhythm* (1938), *Sing You Sinners* (1938), *East Side of Heaven* (1939), *The Star Maker* (1939), *Road to Singapore* (1940), *If I Had My Way* (1940), and *Rhythm on the River* (1940)—all starring Bing Crosby. But Burke's most frequent collaborator was composer Van Heusen (1913–1990), the team scoring 20 musicals together as well as dozens of songs for nonmusicals. Van Heusen was born in Syracuse, New York, and played piano professionally as a teenager then studied music at Syracuse University before getting a job as a local radio announcer. In 1940 he went to Hollywood and was partnered with Burke, the twosome scoring such notable musicals as *Love Thy Neighbor* (1940), *Dixie* (1943), *Going My Way* (1944), *And the Angels Sing* (1944), *Belle of the Yukon* (1944), *The Emperor Waltz* (1948), *A Connecticut Yankee in King Arthur's Court* (1949), and *Mister Music* (1950) as well as four of the *Road* pictures with Crosby and Bob Hope. (No one wrote more song hits for Crosby than Burke and Van Heusen.) The two also collaborated on such Broadway musicals as *Swingin' the Dream* (1939), *Nellie Bly* (1946), *Carnival in Flanders* (1953), and *Donnybrook!* (1961), all of which had bright scores but disappointing runs. The Burke-Van Heusen song catalogue was celebrated in the 1995 Broadway musical revue *Swinging on a Star*. Burke was an agile writer who could turn an everyday phrase into an intoxicating lyric and his work is very diverse. Van Heusen's music was similarly varied and often very catchy even on first hearing.

on the list of most popular film stars for 15 years (1934 to 1949), a record for a musical performer. What was it that made Crosby so important? He began as a crooner and excelled at a smooth, casual kind of singing that was unique. Never a stage performer, Crosby didn't sing out to the crowd. Rather, he sang to the microphone, delivering a quiet kind of intimacy that came off so well on records and radio. When Crosby began making movies, he didn't alter his style much. He didn't consider himself an actor and only played roles that were close to his own persona. He disliked costume roles, preferring to play contemporary characters who took life as it came. No shouting or heavily dramatic scenes for this crooner! For this very reason, Crosby was so effective in movies such as *Going My Way*.

See also: *Holiday Inn, Road to Utopia*; Bing Crosby, Johnny Burke and James Van Heusen biography boxes

FURTHER READING

Coppula, Christopher A. *Jimmy Van Heusen: Swinging on a Star*. Nashville, TN: Twin Creek Books, 2014.

Eames, John Douglas. *The Paramount Story*. New York: Crown Publishers, 1985.

Prigozy, Ruth, and Walter Raubicheck, eds. *Going My Way: Bing Crosby and American Culture*. Rochester, NY: University of Rochester Press, 2007.

COVER GIRL

Studio and release date: Columbia; March 1944
Producer: Arthur Schwartz
Screenplay: Virginia Van Upp, Sidney Buchman
Songwriters: Jerome Kern (music), Ira Gershwin (lyrics)
Director: Charles Vidor
Choreographers: Val Raset, Seymour Felix, Gene Kelly, Stanley Donen
Musical Director: Morris Stoloff
Cinematographers: Rudolph Maté, Allen Davey
Cast: Rita Hayworth, Gene Kelly, Phil Silvers, Lee Bowman, Eve Arden, Leslie Brooks, Jinx Falkenberg, Otto Kruger
Songs: "Long Ago and Far Away"; "Make Way for Tomorrow"; "Put Me to the Test"; "Sure Thing"; "Cover Girl"; "Who's Complaining?"; "The Show Must Go On"; "Poor John"

Gene Kelly and Rita Hayworth really clicked in this superior movie musical so it is surprising that this is their only film together. *Cover Girl* was created as a colorful vehicle for Hayworth, letting her play two characters, wear lots of stunning clothes, and do some sensuous dancing. Her singing voice, as usual, was dubbed (this time by Martha Mears) but everything else was for real. And, appearing in a color film for the first time, Hayworth looked better than ever. Columbia tried to get various leading men for her but had to settle for Kelly, who was just beginning to establish himself in Hollywood. Studio head Harry Cohn thought Kelly was too short for the tall, leggy Hayworth and that their dancing together would not work.

Rita Hayworth (1918–1987)   A redheaded beauty whose singing had to be dubbed, she was one of Hollywood's favorite dancing stars of the 1940s. She was born in Brooklyn, the daughter of professional dancers from Spain who had danced in the *Ziegfeld Follies,* and made her professional dance debut when she was 12 years old. While performing in nightclubs, Hayworth was signed by Hollywood and made her screen debut in 1935 but did not find fame until the 1940s in dramas, comedies, and musicals. Her best musicals were *You'll Never Get Rich* (1941), *My Gal Sal* (1942), *You Were Never Lovelier* (1942), *Cover Girl* (1944), *Gilda* (1946), and *Pal Joey* (1957). Hayworth was able to exude a sensual persona even as she played wholesome "girl next door" characters. Biographies: *Being Rita Hayworth: Labor, Identity, and Hollywood Stardom,* Adrienne L. McLean (2004); *If This Is Happiness: A Biography of Rita Hayworth,* Barbara Leaming (1991).

But he also sensed that Kelly was much more than a hoofer and gave the dancer control over some of the musical numbers. It was a wise decision because what is special about *Cover Girl* was provided by Kelly and Stanley Donen.

The screenplay was far from inspired but, as predictable as much of the plotting was, it offered lots of opportunities for song and dance. Hayworth played dancer Rusty Parker who works in a Brooklyn nightclub run by Danny McGuire (Kelly) but she dreams of moving into the big time. Danny is in love with her and, with his sidekick Genius (Phil Silvers), they do what they can to promote Rusty's career. When she wins a contest to be the cover girl for a popular magazine, Rusty becomes famous, forgets her old friends, and nearly marries the Broadway producer Noel Wheaton (Lee Bowman) before coming to her senses and returning to her Brooklyn buddies. In one section of the movie, the magazine publisher John Coudair (Otto Kruger) recalls Rusty's grandmother, Maribelle Hicks, whom he idolized, and Hayworth got to play her in a flashback, singing the old-fashioned ballad "Sure Thing" and the turn-of-the century vaudeville hit "Poor John." Jerome Kern (music) and Ira Gershwin (lyrics) wrote the film's score, which was rich with variety. In addition to the pastiche number "Sure Thing," the score included the jaunty "Put Me to the Test," the bouncy "Make Way for Tomorrow" (with co-lyricist E. Y. Harburg), and the dreamy ballad "Long Ago and Far Away," which became an oft-recorded standard.

Seymour Felix and Val Raset choreographed much of *Cover Girl,* as with the title number, which featured actual cover-girl celebrities from glamour magazines of the day. The number climaxed with Hayworth running down a seemingly endless ramp, her hair and dress blowing seductively in the wind, a scene ripe for parody over the years. More impressive were two numbers that Kelly and Donen staged. For the song "Make Way for Tomorrow," Kelly removed studio walls and had a long street set constructed so that he, Hayworth, and Silvers could dance down a Brooklyn street using trash cans, a mailbox, and other set pieces in their celebratory hoofing. Many see this number as an early version of what Kelly would so with the song "Singin' in the Rain" eight years later. Even more innovative was the "alter ego" dance devised by Kelly and Donen. Danny sauntered down a New York street all by himself then noticed his reflection in a store window. Using some clever double exposure, the reflection seemed to jump off the glass and joined Kelly in a *pas de deux* in which they, at first, hoofed in unison then launched into a competitive dance. The choreography made it clear that the reflection was Danny's alter ego and the two fought it out with footwork until Danny destroys his other self and ends the number, quietly moving on. It was a brilliant scene that took days of preparation and filming and the scene still impresses. It was clear that Kelly was much more than just another dancer and that he and Donen would do interesting work together in the future.

See also: *You Were Never Lovelier, Anchors Aweigh*; Rita Hayworth, Gene Kelly, Stanley Donen, Ira Gershwin, Jerome Kern biography boxes

FURTHER READING

Dick, Bernard, ed. *Columbia Pictures: Portrait of a Studio*. Lexington: University of Kentucky Press, 1991.
Furia, Philip. *Ira Gershwin: The Art of the Lyricist*. New York: Oxford University Press, 1997.
Hill, James. *Rita Hayworth: A Memoir*. New York: Simon & Schuster, 1983.

CAN'T HELP SINGING

Studio and release date: Universal; December 1944
Producer: Felix Jackson
Screenplay: Lewis Foster, Frank Ryan, based on the novel *Girl of the Overland Trail* by Samuel J. and Curtis B. Warshawsky
Songwriters: Jerome Kern (music), E. Y. Harburg (lyrics)
Director: Frank Ryan
Musical Directors: Hans J. Salter, Edgar Fairchild
Cinematographers: Woody Bredell, W. Howard Greene
Cast: Deanna Durbin, Robert Paige, Akim Tamiroff, Leonid Kinskey, David Bruce, Ray Collins, Thomas Gomez
Songs: "Can't Help Singing"; "Any Moment Now"; "Californ-i-ay"; "More and More"; "Elbow Room"; "Swing Your Sweetheart"

A frontier movie musical that captured the enthusiasm for land (there was even a rousing song celebrating "Californ-i-ay") and the pioneer spirit, many consider it Deanna Durbin's best film. The movie gave her a strong story, an excellent score, and presented her for the first (and only) time in Technicolor. The success of *Oklahoma!* on Broadway in 1943 prompted the studios to look for stories that might make effective frontier musicals. Universal found one in the novel *The Girl of the Overland Trail*, and there was no question who would play the "girl." Durbin, now 22 years old, was outgrowing teen roles but still looked too youthful to play mature leading ladies. So the young, determined heroine of the story was ideal for her.

Set in 1847, the plot followed the spunky Caroline (Durbin), the daughter of East Coast senator Frost (Ray Collins), who falls in love with an army officer. Her farther disapproves of the match and uses his political power to have the young man transferred far away—the farther the better. So the military sends the officer to California just as news of gold reaches the East Coast. Caroline ignores her father's threats and sets off across country with the hundreds who are heading to California. After traveling by train and steamboat, she joins a wagon train whose travelers include the cocky outdoorsman Johnny Lawlor (Robert Paige). The two do not get along at first but the audience was quick to realize that they are made for each other. By the time Caroline and Johnny reach California, the two are in love. Character actors Akim Tamiroff and Leonid Kinskey supplied the humor as the pair of European fortune hunters Prince Gregory and Koppa who are bumbling across the prairie. It was not a complex story but one that afforded solid characters, good opportunities for songs, and a lot of terrific scenery. Filmed on location in Utah and the California mountains, *Can't Help Singing* was beautiful to behold. It was also musically enthralling. Jerome Kern (music) and E. Y. Harburg (lyrics) provided the best original score of Durbin's career, mixing operetta and Broadway sounds in such songs as the rapturous ballad "Any Moment Now," the eager love song "More and More," and the waltzing title number. This last was first sung by Caroline as she drove a carriage through Washington, DC. It was reprised later in the film by Caroline and Johnny as they soaked in wooden outdoor bathtubs separated by a wall, their voices joining in a silly, romantic manner. Harburg's lyrics are particularly sly in numbers such as the dancing "Swing Your Sweetheart," the rousing "Elbow Room," and "Californ-i-ay," which praised the Western land with its tongue in its cheek.

Can't Help Singing gave Durbin the opportunity to show that she was more than a cute kid with an operatic singing voice. Her fans were pleased, and even moviegoers who were not endeared to the teenage Durbin liked her in this film. The musical was very popular, breaking some box office records in New York City and finding just as much appreciation in rural markets. The success of the movie also prompted other frontier musicals, most notably *The Harvey Girls* (1946). Unfortunately, *Can't Help Singing* was Durbin's last high-quality movie musical. The material and/or the songs in her six subsequent films were inferior and, just when Durbin should have

> **Deanna Durbin** (1921–2013)   A lively actress with a classically trained soprano voice, her career was short but memorable. She was born in Winnipeg, Canada, and raised in California where at a young age she showed a talent for singing. As a teenager, Durbin starred in such screen musicals as *Three Smart Girls* (1935), *One Hundred Men and a Girl* (1935), *Mad About Music* (1938), *That Certain Age* (1938), *Three Smart Girls Grow Up* (1939), *First Love* (1939), *It's a Date* (1940), *Spring Parade* (1940), *Nice Girl!* (1941), and *It Started With Eve* (1941). As she matured and her roles approached adulthood, Durbin remained popular with such musicals as *The Amazing Mrs. Holliday* (1943), *Hers to Hold* (1943), *His Butler's Sister* (1943), *Can't Help Singing* (1944), *Because of Him* (1946), *I'll Be Yours* (1947), *Something in the Wind* (1947), *Up in Central Park* (1948), and *For the Love of Mary* (1948). At the age of 27, Durbin left films and retired to France where for over 60 years she refused film offers and requests for interviews. She excelled at playing wholesome youths with a bubbly personality, was one of the top box office attractions for a time, and was a leader in record sales. Biography: *Deanna Durbin: Fairy Tale*, W. E. Mills (1996).

been moving into an exciting new phase of her career, her popularity dropped and she retired. All the same, *Can't Help Singing* is a kind of glimpse into the kind of movies Durbin should have graduated to had not Hollywood let her down.

See also: *One Hundred Men and a Girl*, *The Harvey Girls*; Deanna Durbin, Jerome Kern, E. Y. Harburg biography boxes

FURTHER READING

Fitzgerald, Michael G. *Universal Pictures: A Panoramic History*. Westport, CT: Arlington House, 1977.
Freeland, Michael. *Jerome Kern: A Biography*. New York: Stein and Day Publishers, 1981.
Mills, W. E. *The Deanna Durbin Fairy Tale*. New York: Images, Ltd., 1996.

MEET ME IN ST. LOUIS

Studio and release date: Metro-Goldwyn-Mayer; December 1944
Producer: Arthur Freed
Screenplay: Irving Brecher, Fred Finklehoffe, based on the *Kensington Avenue* stories by Sally Benson
Songwriters: Hugh Martin and others (music), Ralph Blane and others (lyrics)

Director: Vincente Minnelli
Choreographer: Charles Walters
Musical Director: George Stoll
Cinematographer: George Folsey
Cast: Judy Garland, Margaret O'Brien, Mary Astor, Lucille Bremer, Leon Ames, Tom Drake, Harry Davenport, Marjorie Main
Songs: "Have Yourself a Merry Little Christmas"; "The Trolley Song"; "The Boy Next Door"; "Meet Me in St. Louis, Louis"; "Under the Bamboo Tree"; "You and I"; "Skip to My Lou"

Rarely has American life of the past been captured so nostalgically as in this musical favorite. Audiences have been drawn to *Meet Me in St. Louis* for decades because it is sentimental without being maudlin. The nearly plotless movie celebrates domestic life, which was more precious than ever during World War II when the movie was first released. In the summer of 1903, all of St. Louis is excited because in one year the World's Fair will be held there. The Smith family of Kensington Avenue goes through the four seasons with anticipation, heartbreak, and, finally, joy. The eldest daughter Rose (Lucille Bremer) gets engaged, her sister Esther (Judy Garland) falls in in love with the boy next door (Tom Drake), and little Tootie Smith (Margaret O'Brien) has a Halloween adventure she'll never forget. When banker Mr. Smith (Leon Ames) is offered a higher position if he will move to the New York City office, his wife (Mary Astor) and family are in turmoil. Once father realizes how much their old house and old friends mean to them, he turns down the offer and the Smiths go off to the opening of the fair, officially called the Louisiana Purchase Exposition of 1904. The uneventful yet totally pleasing screenplay was based on a series of stories by Sally Benson, who grew up in a large family in St. Louis. Director Vincente Minnelli turned each section/season into a visual and emotional postcard, and choreographer Charles Walters staged the songs with a simple but thrilling joy, as in the famous "The Trolley Song." Yet many of the movie's memorable moments come from book scenes, such as the mischievous Tootie's bold confrontation with a "witch" on Halloween. The cast was splendid from the stars to the minor bit parts, each a vivid characterization that seemed to glow through the haze of nostalgia for an America long gone.

Some period songs were mixed in with new numbers by Hugh Martin and Ralph Blane, and it is a credit to their songs that all the musical numbers blend into a whole. The old favorites included the waltzing title song, the spirited "Skip to My Lou," and the jungle-flavored ditty "Under the Bamboo Tree," the last done as a charming parlor entertainment by Garland and O'Brien as they sang to guests and broke into a sprightly cakewalk step. "The Trolley Song" sounded like an old standard, the wistful "The Boy Next Door" had the simplicity of an early Tin Pan Alley ballad, and "Have Yourself a Merry Little Christmas"

The nostalgic *Meet Me in St. Louis* (1944) was a delectable piece of Americana that pleased moviegoers during the war years. It still manages to enthrall audiences today. Pictured is Judy Garland in the spirited "The Trolley Song" number written by Ralph Blane and Hugh Martin and directed with skill by Vincente Minnelli. (MGM/Photofest)

has proven its timelessness by remaining a holiday favorite for over seven decades. Of all the scores Martin and Blane wrote together and with others for Broadway and Hollywood, none approaches the warmth and emotional pull that this one has. Producer Arthur Freed later stated that *Meet Me in St. Louis* was his favorite of all the musicals he presented at MGM and it is not difficult to understand why.

Yet Freed was being nostalgic with his selected memory. In reality, *Meet Me in St. Louis* had an awful birth, with problems from start to finish. The film came about because MGM had access to a Technicolor movie camera for a limited amount of time and the studio was looking for a musical project that would best show off the dazzling color process. None of the scripts on file seemed right, so some writers were assigned the task of adapting Benson's stories. The trouble was that the stories were episodic incidents with no through line. The first script was a meandering mess so contract writers Irving Brecher and Fred Finklehoffe were told to come up with a new one. Finklehoffe left the project after a while and Minnelli helped Brecher fashion a serviceable screenplay that emphasized character over story. The studio had Garland in mind from the start, so imagine their chagrin when she hated the script and refused to play another teenager on-screen. She was also worried

Vincente Minnelli (1903–1986)   A top director of Hollywood musicals in the 1940s and 1950s, his films were known for their elegant style and painterly look. He was born in Chicago, Illinois, to a family of vaudeville entertainers and was onstage at the age of three. But young Minnelli preferred drawing, so he quit school as a teenager and worked painting billboards and as an apprentice at a photographer's studio. He eventually found recognition for designing large spectaculars at Radio City Music Hall and on Broadway. Hollywood hired him in 1940 for his design talents but soon he was directing films, including such notable musicals as *Cabin in the Sky* (1943), *Meet Me in St. Louis* (1944), *Yolanda and the Thief* (1945), *Ziegfeld Follies* (1946), *The Pirate* (1948), *An American in Paris* (1951), *The Band Wagon* (1953), *Brigadoon* (1954), *Kismet* (1955), *Gigi* (1958), *Bells Are Ringing* (1960), and *On a Clear Day You Can See Forever* (1970). Biographies: *Vincente Minnelli: Hollywood's Dark Dreamer,* Emanuel Levy (2007); *A Hundred or More Hidden Things: The Life and Films of Vincente Minnelli,* Mark Griffin (2010).

(rightfully so) that the pint-sized Margaret O'Brien would steal every scene that the two of them were in. It took a lot of encouragement on Brecher's part to convince Garland that the role of Esther was not like the teenagers she had played opposite Mickey Rooney, and that Minnelli would keep O'Brien under control.

There were also difficulties with the score, particularly with "Have Yourself a Merry Little Christmas." The original lyric was one of despair, stating that there will be no more Christmases if the family moves to New York. Garland refused to sing the song, saying it was depressing and not what an elder sister would sing to a child. The songwriters were forced to change the lyric to the more hopeful one that is famous today. Garland may have been right about that song but often during filming was wrong about other things. She disliked the script, her character, and some of the actors. It took a lot of coaxing by Minnelli but he eventually got her trust and a marvelous performance out of her. Soon after filming was complete, she married Minnelli.

With such a rocky production history, it is a miracle that *Meet Me in St. Louis* turned out so well. But many great movies had troubled births, and the turmoil behind the camera rarely shows up on the screen. *Meet Me in St. Louis* may have been born of fire, but for generations it is one of the warmest of all family musicals.

See also: *Babes in Arms, The Harvey Girls*; Judy Garland, Vincente Minnelli, Arthur Freed biography boxes

FURTHER READING

Bloom, Ken. *Hollywood Musicals: The 101 Greatest Song-and-Dance Movies of All Time*. New York: Black Dog and Leventhal, 2010.

Edwards, Anne. *Judy Garland: A Biography*. Lanham, MD: Taylor Trade Publishing, 2013.

Fordin, Hugh. *MGM's Greatest Musicals: The Arthur Freed Unit*. Boston: Da Capo Press, 1996.

Kaufman, Gerald. *Meet Me in St. Louis*. (BFI Film Classics). London: British Film Institute, 1994.

ANCHORS AWEIGH

Studio and release date: Metro-Goldwyn-Mayer; July 1945

Producer: Joe Pasternak

Screenplay: Isobel Lennart, based on the story *You Can't Fool a Marine* by Natalie Marcin

Songwriters: Jule Styne and others (music), Sammy Cahn and others (lyrics)

Director: George Sidney

Choreographer: Gene Kelly

Musical Director: George Stoll

Cinematographers: Robert Planck, Charles Boyle

Cast: Gene Kelly, Frank Sinatra, Kathryn Grayson, José Iturbi, Dean Stockwell, Pamela Britton, Carlos Ramirez, Leon Ames

Principal Songs: "I Fall in Love Too Easily"; "I Begged Her"; "The Charm of You"; "What Makes the Sunset?"; "Jealousy"; "All of a Sudden My Heart Sings"; "Waltz Serenade"; opera and classical orchestral selections

Frank Sinatra got his first starring role in this "sailors-on-leave" musical that also featured Gene Kelly as his costar. Sinatra was the shy sailor Clarence Doolittle and Kelly was the girl-chasing cad Joe Brady. While on leave in Hollywood, they run up against a little tyke (Dean Stockwell) who wants to run away from home and join the navy. Begrudgingly the two sailors bring the boy back home where he lives with his aunt Susan Abbott (Kathryn Grayson), a struggling opera singer. Clarence is smitten with Susan and talks Joe into giving him lessons on how to win over dames. Of course Joe and Susan start to fall in love and, in order to impress her, Joe tells Susan that Clarence is a friend of the famous maestro José Iturbi at Metro-Goldwyn-Mayer and that they can set up an audition for her. Much of the movie then concentrated on Joe and Clarence trying to find Iturbi, and it got pretty tedious except for the musical numbers. In the end, Susan gets a contract, Joe stops his philandering and wins her hand, and Clarence is more than happy with a girl

Frank Sinatra (1915–1998)   The blue-eyed recording star who remained popular for over 50 years, he also had an impressive career in movie musicals. He was born in Hoboken, New Jersey, the son of Italian immigrants, and began his professional singing career on the radio. Sinatra was a featured vocalist with the Harry James and Tommy Dorsey bands and went solo with great success, becoming the singing idol of young women in the 1940s. After playing himself in a few movie musicals, he graduated to character parts, usually young, shy juveniles who were hesitant with women but won them over with his singing, as seen in *Step Lively* (1944), *Anchors Aweigh* (1945), *It Happened in Brooklyn* (1947), *Take Me Out to the Ball Game* (1949), *On the Town* (1949), and *Strictly Dynamite* (1951). Sinatra moved into dramatic roles in the 1950s and played more mature roles in the musicals *Guys and Dolls* (1955), *High Society* (1956), *The Joker Is Wild* (1957), *Pal Joey* (1957), *Can-Can* (1960), and *Robin and the Seven Hoods* (1964). Sinatra's special way with a song and relaxed singing style made him a longtime favorite, but he also possessed a strong film presence and managed to be intriguing even when his vehicles were second rate. Biographies: *Sinatra: Behind the Legend*, J. Randy Taraborrelli (2015); *Frank Sinatra: The Man, the Music, the Legend*, Jeanne Fuchs, Ruth Prigozy (2007); *Frank Sinatra: An American Legend*, Nancy Sinatra [daughter] (1998).

(Pamela Britton), who hails from Brooklyn just like himself. *Anchors Aweigh* set a pattern for two other Kelly-Sinatra musicals—*Take Me Out to the Ball Game* (1949) and *On the Town* (1949)—in which Kelly played the wolf and Sinatra the girl-shy novice. The film, the first in which Kelly was principal choreographer, was a significant step in his development as a master actor-dancer-director-choreographer.

Between new songs and classical selections, there was a lot of music in *Anchors Aweigh*. Sinatra got to sing the enticing ballad "I Fall in Love Too Easily" by Jule Styne (music) and Sammy Cahn (lyrics), and his recording was very popular. The same songwriters wrote the pleasing ballad "The Charm of You," the questioning list song "What Makes a Sunset?," and the bragging "I Begged Her," which was followed by a vigorous tap number with Kelly and Sinatra leaping over beds in a servicemen'a dormitory. Pianist-conductor Iturbi presented selections by Liszt and Tchaikovsky, and Grayson sang the art songs "Jealousy (Jalouise)" and "All of a Sudden My Heart Sings." But it was the dance sections of the movie that one most remembers. There was a bombastic sequence in which Kelly wooed Grayson as he scaled the battlements and parapets of a castle, a lively "Mexican Hat Dance" routine with little Sharon McManus, and the brilliant dance duet "The King Who

Couldn't Dance" (also called "The Worry Song") with the cartoon character Jerry the Mouse. The last was a stunning combination of live-action dancing with an animated figure that took two months and $100,000 to animate and film. The studio wanted to use Mickey Mouse in the sequence, but Walt Disney was not willing to give permission. So MGM's own cartoon mouse was used. The dance required 10,000 drawings, which Kelly then coordinated into a seamless man-and-mouse *pas de deux*.

Anchors Aweigh was also an important film in Sinatra's career. The popular band singer, who broke away from the Big Band scene and went solo with success, was quite the rage in the early 1940s with his records and concert appearances. Hollywood was interested in putting the bobbysoxer favorite on-screen but in the film shorts and three features that Sinatra had appeared in, none were box office hits. It looked like the singer would not have a successful movie career. It was his performance in *Anchors Aweigh* that turned the tide. Sinatra was neither an actor nor a dancer so the production had to make concessions. Playing the naive Clarence was not too difficult, but for "I Begged Her," his one big dance number with Kelly, it took eight weeks of rehearsal and 72 takes before it was deemed satisfactory to choreographer Kelly. Despite all the work, Kelly teamed with Sinatra on two more musicals—*On the Town* (1949) and *Take Me Out to the Ball Game* (1949)—thereby solidifying Sinatra's budding film career.

See also: *On the Town, The Joker Is Wild*; Gene Kelly, Frank Sinatra biography boxes

FURTHER READING

Grant, Barry Keith. *The Hollywood Film Musical*. Hoboken, NJ: Wiley-Blackwell, 2012.
Thomas, Lawrence B. *The MGM Years*. New York: Arlington House, 1971.
Yudkoff, Alvin. *Gene Kelly: A Life of Dance and Dreams*. New York: Billboard Books, 2001.

STATE FAIR

Studio and release date: 20th Century Fox; August 1945
Producer: William Perlberg
Screenplay: Oscar Hammerstein, based on the 1933 film script by Sonya Levien and Paul Green, which was based on the novel by Philip Stong
Songwriters: Richard Rodgers (music), Oscar Hammerstein (lyrics)
Director: Walter Lang
Musical Directors: Alfred Newman, Charles Henderson

Cinematographer: Leon Shamroy

Cast: Jeanne Crain, Dana Andrews, Dick Haymes, Vivian Blaine, Charles
    Winninger, Fay Bainter

Songs: "It Might as Well Be Spring"; "It's a Grand Night for Singing"; "That's for
    Me"; "Isn't It Kinda Fun?"; "Our State Fair"; "All I Owe Ioway"

A warm and folksy tale that is a simple and loving look at Americana, this rural
musical was the only movie musical that the famous team of Richard Rodgers
(music) and Oscar Hammerstein (lyrics) wrote directly for the screen. After the
Broadway success of *Oklahoma!* (1943), Rodgers and Hammerstein received many
offers from Hollywood, but both had had unpleasant experiences with the studio
system in the 1930s and were reluctant to go back. Then 20th Century Fox asked
them to musicalize *State Fair*, a novel by Philip Stong that the studio had successfully filmed in 1933 as a nonmusical. It was similar to *Oklahoma!* in its Midwestern setting, rural characters, and rustic humor. So Rodgers and Hammerstein agreed
and came up with a movie classic.

The story is homespun and charming. As the Frake family prepares to leave their
farm for the Iowa State Fair, the father Abel (Charles Winninger) makes a bet with
a neighbor that his boar Blue Boy will win the top prize and that every family member will have a great time at the fair. His wife Melissa (Fay Bainter) is entering her
homemade mincemeat in the competition, son Wayne (Dick Haymes) is hoping
to win his prizes on the midway, and daughter Margy (Jeanne Crain) is looking
forward to getting away from her dull fiancé. At the fair, Wayne falls into a too-
casual romance with a band singer, Emily Edwards (Vivian Blaine), and Margy is
attracted to the news reporter Pat Gilbert (Dana Andrews) from the big city.
Although Blue Boy and the mincemeat both win ribbons, the younger Frakes are
less lucky in love. Emily realizes that she has no future with the naive Wayne,
and Pat rushes off when he learns of a job at a Chicago newspaper. Returning
home, Wayne happily goes back to his old girlfriend. Abel claims his bet and when
Margy hears from Pat that he wants to marry her, she is overjoyed. So the neighbor admits that all had a good time at the fair and pays up. The performances from
the leads to the character parts are excellent and the production values were top
notch, with Walter Lang directing with just the right touch of whimsy and romance.
Although there were only six songs, each number counted and all of them were
winners. The opening "Our State Fair" introduced the family as the song bounced
through the household, and the movie ended with the merry "All I Owe Ioway,"
a sillier version of the boastful song "Oklahoma." The numbers for the city
characters—the climbing ballad "That's for Me" and the jaunty "Isn't It Kinda
Fun?"—had a touch of swing and jazz, and Rodgers wrote one of his most infec-
tious waltz melodies for "It's a Grand Night for Singing," sung by most of the cast
at the fair's midway. The highlight of the score was the Oscar-winning "It Might As

Richard Rodgers and **Oscar Hammerstein**   The most famous songwriting team in the history of Broadway, they also contributed to original screen musicals, and most of their stage work together and with others have been filmed. Rodgers (1902–1979) was born into a middle-class Jewish family, the son of a physician, and before he even began school he had taught himself to play piano. He wrote music for student shows at Columbia University, then he met lyricist Lorenz Hart and the two immediately hit it off and started collaborating. The Rodgers and Hart musicals include some of the most popular Broadway shows of the 1920s and 1930s, including *The Garrick Gaieties* (1925), *Dearest Enemy* (1925), *A Connecticut Yankee* (1927), *Present Arms* (1928), *Heads Up!* (1929), *Jumbo* (1935), *On Your Toes* (1936), *Babes in Arms* (1937), *I'd Rather Be Right* (1937), *I Married an Angel* (1938), *The Boys From Syracuse* (1938), *Too Many Girls* (1939), *Pal Joey* (1940), and *By Jupiter* (1942). During the darkest days of the Depression, the team went to Hollywood and scored such notable musicals as *Love Me Tonight* (1932), *The Phantom President* (1932), *Hallelujah, I'm a Bum* (1933), and *Mississippi* (1935). Rodgers first collaborated with lyricist-librettist Oscar Hammerstein (1895–1960) on *Oklahoma!* (1943), the show that revolutionized the musical play. When Hart died in 1943, Rodgers worked exclusively with Hammerstein for the next 17 years. Hammerstein was born in New York City into a famous theatrical family; his grandfather was the colorful theater and opera impresario Oscar Hammerstein I, and his uncle, Arthur Hammerstein, was a prosperous Broadway producer. He was educated at Columbia University to become a lawyer, but his involvement in the campus theater productions convinced him to follow in the family profession. Hammerstein began his Broadway career in 1920, working with the top composers of the day on such musicals as *Rose-Marie* (1924), *Song of the Flame* (1925), *Sunny* (1925), *The Desert Song* (1926), *The New Moon* (1928), *Show Boat* (1927), *Sweet Adeline* (1929), *Music in the Air* (1932), and *Very Warm for May* (1939). He also turned to Hollywood during the Depression but found little success despite his excellent lyrics in *Viennese Nights* (1930), *Children of Dreams* (1931), *The Night Is Young* (1935), *High, Wide and Handsome* (1937), and *The Great Waltz* (1938). Hammerstein's career was revived by *Oklahoma!* and his musicals with Rodgers. For Broadway they wrote such beloved favorites as *Carousel* (1945), *South Pacific* (1949), *The King and I* (1951), *Flower Drum Song* (1958), and *The Sound of Music* (1959), all of which were made into successful Hollywood films. In 1945 they wrote their only original screen score for *State Fair*, and their 1957 television musical *Cinderella* also was popular. Hammerstein's death from cancer in 1959 was the end of an era but Rodgers continued on, scoring the Broadway musicals *No Strings* (1962), *Do I Hear a Waltz?* (1965), *Two By Two* (1970), *Rex* (1976), and *I Remember Mama* (1979) without much success. The contribution of Rodgers and Hammerstein to the American musical cannot be overstated. Rodgers' music employs enticing melody and harmony, endless variety, and the ability to capture a mood or a place or a character in a few notes. Hammerstein brought integrity to the stage libretto and lyricwriting, raised the level of truthfulness in musicals, created the serious musical play, and introduced the integrated musical. Autobiography (Rodgers): *Musical Stages* (1975); biographies: *Somewhere for Me: A Biography of Richard Rodgers*, Meryle Secrest (2001); *Richard Rodgers*, William Hyland (1998); *Getting to Know Him: A Biography of Oscar Hammerstein II*, Hugh Fordin (1977).

Well Be Spring," a tender character song that became the most famous of all the numbers. It was sung by Margy (Crain dubbed by Louanne Hogan) in her homey, feminine bedroom. Because of the old-fashioned look and temperament of *State Fair*, the film strikes some modern viewers as dated, but *State Fair* can still be enjoyed as a nostalgic example of a 1940s domestic musical in the manner of *Meet Me in St. Louis* (1944).

It is curious that Rodgers and Hammerstein never wrote an original movie musical again. They were certainly powerful enough that Hollywood would have backed any project the team was interested in. They did oversee the film versions of their Broadway successes and wrote eight more Broadway shows after *Oklahoma!* so perhaps they were just too busy to want to work in Hollywood again. Yet they found time to write the television musical *Cinderella* in 1957, but that was done in New York City. After Hammerstein's death in 1960, Rodgers did return to Tinseltown again. In 1962, Fox remade *State Fair* when many studios were remaking their old musicals. Producer Charles Brackett wanted a new, contemporary *State Fair* in wide-screen Cinemascope with a young cast that would appeal to the ever-younger moviegoing public. The new screenplay reset the tale in Texas to get away from corn-fed Iowa and padded the thin story to nearly two hours. The score was reorchestrated to make some of the numbers sound more up to date. When the studio asked for five new songs, Rodgers obliged and wrote both music and lyrics for the new numbers, "More Than Just a Friend," "Never Say No to a Man," "This Isn't Heaven," "Willing and Eager," and "It's the Little Things in Texas." While none came close to the quality of the original score, they served the plot and, as a 1960s pop musical, *State Fair* did very well at the box office. *State Fair* also showed up on Broadway in 1996 with some lesser-known Rodgers and Hammerstein songs from other shows added to the score. *State Fair* was not a box office hit on Broadway but today many theater groups, anxious for a "new" Rodgers and Hammerstein musical, produce the stage version with success.

See also: *Meet Me in St. Louis, Oklahoma!*; Richard Rodgers and Oscar Hammerstein biography box

FURTHER READING

Allvine, Glendon. *The Greatest Fox of Them All.* New York: Lyle Stuart, 1969.
Bloom, Ken. *Hollywood Musicals: The 101 Greatest Song-and-Dance Movies of All Time.* New York: Black Dog and Leventhal, 2010.
Mordden, Ethan. *Rodgers & Hammerstein.* New York: Abradale/Abrams, 1995.
Nolan, Frederick. *The Sound of Their Music: The Story of Rodgers and Hammerstein.* Montclair, NJ: Applause Theatre & Cinema Books, 2002.

ROAD TO UTOPIA

Studio and release date: Paramount; December 1945
Producer: Paul Jones
Screenplay: Norman Panama, Melvin Frank
Songwriters: James Van Heusen (music), Johnny Burke (lyrics)
Director: Hal Walker
Choreographer: Danny Dare
Musical Director: Robert Emmett Dolan
Cinematographer: Lionel Lindon
Cast: Bing Crosby, Bob Hope, Dorothy Lamour, Robert Benchley, Hillary Brooke, Douglass Dumbrille, Jack LaRue
Songs: "Personality"; "Put It There, Pal"; "It's Anybody's Spring"; "Sunday, Monday or Always"; "Goodtime Charlie"; "Welcome to My Dream"; "Would You?"

In the opinion of many, the best of the Bing Crosby-Bob Hope "Road Pictures" was this silly, tuneful comedy set in Alaska. All seven films were funny and popular then and, surprisingly, they still delight. Nothing dates as fast as topical comedy, but this series had a self-mocking sense of humor and was endlessly clever in the way that it reminded moviegoers that it was only a movie and not to be believed for a second. Paramount's original plan in 1940 was to make a "buddy" comedy called *Road to Mandalay* with actors Fred MacMurray and Jack Oakie. At the time Crosby and Hope each had a radio show, and they were getting laughs with a friendly "feud" between the two. Paramount dropped MacMurray, Oakie, and the title and signed up Crosby and Hope for a small-scale comedy now titled *Road to Singapore*. Since a movie with Crosby had to have a song or two, musical numbers were added though none were expensive production numbers. The formula for all seven of the "Road Pictures" was established in the first film. Crosby was the straight man, sang the ballads, and got the girl (Dorothy Lamour) in the end. Hope was the put-upon chump, always got into difficult straits because of Crosby, and invariably fell for Lamour but lost her or any other beautiful woman who came along. Besides being laughably predictable, the musical comedies were also filled with wisecracks and recurring gags, ridiculous plots, and even the occasional breaking of character. The two comics often spoke directly into the camera and made fun of Paramount, Hollywood, and their own careers. In *Road to Singapore*, Crosby played Joshua Mallon, the son of shipping millionaire Joshua Mallon IV (Charles Coburn), who doesn't want to marry high-society gal Gloria Wycott (Judith Barrett) so he runs off with his penniless friend Ace Lannigan (Hope) to the South Seas. There they rescue Mima (Lamour) from the sinister Caesar (Anthony Quinn) who makes his living whipping cigarette ends out of Mima's mouth. The songs were by Johnny Burke, James V. Monaco, and Victor Schertzinger (who also directed), the best being the rhythmic ditty "Sweet Potato Piper." Yet there was much to be said for the ballads "Too Romantic" and "The Moon and the Willow Tree." The movie was far from the best in the series but the Hope-Crosby-Lamour chemistry was magic and the picture was very popular.

The three stars were quickly reassembled for *Road to Zanzibar* in 1941, which was a better comedy all around. Con men Chuck Reardon (Crosby) and Hubert "Fearless" Frazier (Hope) have to skip town when they sell a phony diamond mine to an unhappy customer. They travel to Africa where they meet the con women Donna Latour (Lamour) and Julia Quimny (Una Merkel) on safari. In addition to spoofing every jungle picture ever made, the film offered two pleasing ballads by Burke and James Van Heusen (the two would score the rest of the *Road* musicals), "You're Dangerous" and "It's Always You." *Road to Morocco* in 1942 had fun ribbing *Arabian Nights* movies as the carefree bums Jeff Peters (Crosby) and Orville "Turkey" Jackson (Hope) are shipwrecked on the shore of North Africa and set off across the desert only to find themselves rescuing Princess Shalmar (Lamour) from the murderous chieftain Mullay Kasim (Anthony Quinn). One of the funniest of the entries, the film included a sequence in which Hope played his own Aunt Lucy. The movie also boasted a superb score headed by "Moonlight Becomes You," the biggest selling song to come out of the whole series. The other songs were the ballads "Constantly," the carefree "Ain't Got a Dime to My Name," and the funny title song.

The series reached a kind of comic peak with *Road to Utopia* in 1945. This time the story was told in flashback. Turn-of-the-20th-century vaudevillians Duke Johnson (Crosby) and Chester Hooton (Hope) head for the Klondike with a map showing the location of a lost gold mine. They team up with saloon singer Sal Van Hoyden (Lamour) and, pursued by a set of villains, set off on dog sleds for a series of merry misadventures. For a change, Hope wins Lamour when Crosby is set adrift on an ice-floe and is presumed dead. Jumping to the present, the older Chester and Sal complete the story just as Duke shows up, not too surprised to note that the couple's baby, Junior Hooton, is a spitting image of Crosby. The movie was narrated with wry charm by humorist Robert Benchley, who had pulled off this kind of humor in a series of comedy shorts in the 1930s and 1940s. Once again the songs were excellent, the most popular being the sassy and suggestive "Personality." Also enjoyable were the enticing ballad "Welcome to My Dream," the vaudeville soft-shoe number "Goodtime Charlie," and the optimistic "It's Anybody's Spring." The comedy in *Road to Utopia* is perhaps the most polished without losing the slaphappy spontaneity of the earlier movies. After four films, one might suspect that the series began to lose steam with *Road to Rio* in 1947 but Crosby, Hope, Lamour, and Paramount did not disappoint. Although a bit more conventional and perhaps a little less inspired, *Road to Rio* was still top-notch entertainment. When musicians Scat Sweeney (Crosby) and Hot Lips Barton (Hope) accidentally burn down the carnival where they work, the two hop aboard a boat for Rio de Janeiro. On the journey they meet Brazilian heiress Lucia Maria de Andrade (Lamour) who is being hypnotized by her evil Aunt Catherine (Gale Sondergaard) into marrying a fortune-hunting Brazilian she does not love. Once in Rio, the two musicians foil the crooks and stop the wedding in time. The Andrews Sisters joined in on the singing this time and the Burke-Van Heusen score included the hit ballad "But Beautiful" and the sly and peppy "You Don't Have to Know the Language." The popular song "Brazil" by Ary Barroso was interpolated in the score for atmospheric flavor.

Because of Crosby and Hope's busy radio and television activities, moviegoers had to wait five years for *Road to Bali* (1952). Some of the jokes were aging along with the stars but the movie was still delicious fun. Vaudevillians George Cochran (Crosby) and Harold Gridley (Hope) were once again on the run, the duo heading for the South Seas searching for hidden treasure but finding Princess Lal (Lamour) instead. The film included brief guest appearances by Humphrey Bogart, Bob Crosby, Jane Russell, and Hollywood's newest comedy team, Dean Martin and Jerry Lewis. The songs were not as memorable this time around, though Hope and Crosby had fun with the spirited "Chicago Style" and got to put on kilts and sing the Scottish parody "Hoots Mon." A decade went by with no new *Road* picture so audiences assumed that the series was over. When United Artists released *The Road to Hong Kong* in 1962, audience response was not overwhelming. The only film to add "the" to its title, it added nothing else and was an uninspired affair with the spirit of the series missing. Once again the two stars were con men. Harry Turner (Crosby) and Chester Babcock (Hope) try to sell rocket ships in Tibet but

Bob Hope (1903–2003)   The durable comedian who was a star for six decades, he appeared in many Hollywood musicals during his busy lifetime. He was born in Eltham, England, and came to America at the age of four and grew up in Cleveland. Hope worked as a clerk, newsboy, soda jerk, and even a boxer before going into show business as a song-and-dance man on the variety circuit. Hope was featured in some Broadway shows before going to Hollywood in 1937 and making a notable debut in *Big Broadcast of 1938* in which he sang "Thanks for the Memory." He first teamed up with Bing Crosby in *Road to Singapore* (1940), followed by six more "Road" pictures. Hope's other screen musicals include *College Swing* (1938), *Give Me a Sailor* (1938), *Thanks for the Memory* (1938), *Louisiana Purchase* (1941), *The Paleface* (1948), *Fancy Pants* (1950), *The Lemon Drop Kid* (1951), *Son of Paleface* (1952), *The Seven Little Foys* (1955), and *Beau James* (1957). He continued to make film comedies in the 1960s even as he was a familiar figure in television, concerts, and entertaining American troops during four wars. Hope's comedy was wisecracking and satirical, and his adequate singing voice was ideal for the kinds of songs written for him. He wrote several comic memoirs, including *They Got Me Covered* (1941), *Have Tux, Will Travel* (1954), *I Owe Russia $1,200* (1963), *The Last Christmas Show* (1974), *The Road to Hollywood: My 40-Year Love Affair With the Movies* (1977), and *Don't Shoot, It's Only Me* (1990). Biographies: *Bob Hope: A Life in Comedy,* William Robert Faith (2003); *Bob Hope: The Road Well-Traveled,* Lawrence J. Quirk (2000).

are run out of the country, travel to Hong Kong, and get involved with spies looking for a secret rocket fuel formula. Although the twosome briefly meet Lamour when they visit a nightclub where she performs, the woman they fight over this time is the agent Diane (Joan Collins). By the end of the story, the two comics are shot off into space where they come across fellow spacemen Frank Sinatra and Dean Martin. Van Heusen wrote the songs with Sammy Cahn this time and three of them—the buddy trio "Teamwork," the soothing ballad "Warmer Than a Whisper," and the romantic duet "Let's Not Be Sensible"—were delightful. Again there were cameo appearances, this time by David Niven, Peter Sellers, and Jerry Colonna, but it wasn't enough to disguise the lack of excitement. The *Road* pictures were products of their time yet are still very enjoyable. Various studios have tried to copy the formula over the years. *Ishtar* (1987) was an infamous failure, but the animated musical *The Road to El Dorado* (2000) was popular.

See also: *Going My Way*; Bing Crosby, Bob Hope, James Van Heusen and Johnny Burke biography boxes

FURTHER READING

Eames, John Douglas. *The Paramount Story*. New York: Crown Publishers, 1985.

Grudens, Richard. *Bing Crosby: Crooner of the Century*. Stony Brook, NY: Celebrity Profiles, Inc., 2002.

Mielke, Randall G. *The Road to Box Office: The Seven Film Comedies of Crosby, Hope and Lamour*. Jefferson, NC: McFarland Publishing, 1997.

Quirk, Lawrence J. *Bob Hope: The Road Well-Traveled*. Montclair, NJ: Applause Books, 2000.

THE HARVEY GIRLS

Studio and release date: Metro-Goldwyn-Mayer; January 1946

Producer: Arthur Freed

Screenplay: Edward Beloin, Nathaniel Curtis, Samson Raphaelson, based on a story by Samuel Hopkins Adams

Songwriters: Harry Warren (music), Johnny Mercer (lyrics)

Director: George Sidney

Choreographer: Robert Alton

Musical Director: Lennie Hayton

Cinematographer: George Folsey

Cast: Judy Garland, John Hodiak, Ray Bolger, Angela Lansbury, Virginia O'Brien, Kenny Baker, Marjorie Main, Cyd Charisse, Preston Foster

Songs: "On the Atchison, Topeka and the Santa Fe"; "It's a Great Big World"; "In the Valley Where the Evening Sun Goes Down"; "Wait and See"; "The Wild Wild West"; "Swing Your Partner Round and Round"

An outstanding frontier musical, this western adventure boasted a memorable score by Harry Warren (music) and Johnny Mercer (lyrics) and sparkling performances by Judy Garland and company. The easterner Susan Bradley (Garland) travels to Sandrock, New Mexico, in 1880 to work as a waitress in Frank Harvey's restaurant chain that promises good food and a genteel eating atmosphere in the rugged West. Susan and the other Harvey girls are pitted against the less wholesome gals in town, particularly at the Alhambra Saloon run by Ned Trent (John Hodiak) and presided over by the worldly wise Em (Angela Lansbury). The rivalry gets nasty (they even set fire to the Harvey restaurant) but Susan ends up in the arms of Ned thanks to a quick change of heart by Em. MGM intended to make a comedy-western out of Samuel Hopkins Adams' story with Lana Turner as Susan and Clark Gable as Trent. But when *Oklahoma!* opened on Broadway in 1943 and was such a smash, every studio was looking for a frontier story that could be musicalized. So *The Harvey Girls* became a musical and Garland, the MGM's reigning musical star, was cast as the female lead.

Ray Bolger (1904–1987)   Forever remembered as the rubber-jointed Scarecrow in the film classic *The Wizard of Oz* (1939), this versatile comic dancer and character actor had a long and varied career on Broadway, movies, and television. He was born in Dorchester, Massachusetts, and worked as a bank clerk and vacuum cleaner salesman even as he took dance lessons and got stage experience performing in summer stock. Bolger was later part of a dance act in vaudeville that led to his Broadway debut in 1926. He was featured in *Heads Up!* (1929) and in some stage revues before finding wide recognition in *On Your Toes* (1936) in which he got to perform in the "The Slaughter on Tenth Avenue" ballet. That same year he made his screen debut in *The Great Ziegfeld*, followed by many movie musicals over the next 40 years, including *Rosalie* (1937), *Sweethearts* (1938), *The Wizard of Oz*, *Sunny* (1940), *Four Jacks and a Jill* (1941), *Stage Door Canteen* (1943), *The Harvey Girls* (1946), *Look for the Silver Lining* (1949), *April in Paris* (1952), and *Babes in Toyland* (1961). Returning to Broadway on occasion, Bolger starred in *By Jupiter* (1942), *Where's Charley?* (1948)—which he reprised in the 1952 movie—and *All American* (1962). His later career included many television musical specials, series, and dramas.

Producer Arthur Freed wanted the film to be as integrated as *Oklahoma!*, with each song contributing to the plot. Mercer, who was known for his rustic, rural lyrics, was teamed with the chameleon-like composer Warren who could write any kind of music. Together they wrote 11 songs for *The Harvey Girls* but only 8 were used, each one a gem. Garland sang the yearning ballad "In the Valley (Where The Evening Sun Goes Down)" while riding through the twilight on a train; Lansbury led her saloon girls in the sly "Oh, You Kid"; and Garland, Marjorie Main, and Ray Bolger joined the Harvey girls in the contagious waltz "Swing Your Partner Round and Round." Garland and fellow waitresses Virginia O'Brien and Cyd Charisse lamented that "It's a Great Big World," and O'Brien sarcastically sang about "The Wild Wild West." But without question, the musical highlight of *The Harvey Girls* was the Oscar-winning song "On the Atchison, Topeka and the Santa Fe." As directed by George Sidney and choreographed by Robert Alton, it is arguably the best train number in movie musicals. The number is a complex musical scene involving several characters and locales and builds up gradually to a powerhouse finale. The sequence begins in a saloon where the train whistle is first heard. Porter Ben Carter announces the arrival of the train coming from Philadelphia and heading to California, then a group of cowboys on the station platform sing about the train. Soon engineers Vernon Dent and fireman Jack Clifford onboard are singing it along with the train passengers, including Ray Bolger and Virginia O'Brien. The number then moves to a middle section written by Roger Edens and Kay Thompson, allowing each of the arriving Harvey girls to sing about their origin and their hopes for a new life out West. The number then climaxes with Garland and Bolger leading the ensemble in a high-kicking dance as the steam surrounds them and the train pulls out of the station. Although "On the Atchison, Topeka and the Santa Fe" was not a ballad or love song, it became a major hit on radio and records and today is a perennial standard.

The Harvey Girls was not only a first-class frontier musical, it showed how Hollywood could turn out quality musicals on just about any subject. Movie musicals set in the country were not in fashion in the 1940s. Yet when Broadway's *Oklahoma!* demonstrated that war-weary audiences liked stories set in the American prairie and applauded all-American characters with a pioneer spirit, the studios took notice. The frontier movie musical was revived, and Hollywood sent its cameras out into the wilderness to film rural America. *The Harvey Girls* was shot on location in Utah, Arizona, and a ranch in California. A certain kind of authenticity shows up on the screen, yet it is always clear that this is a musical with colorful costumes to match the colorful characters. The same efforts would be taken if a musical took place in Spain or on Mars. Hollywood created its own musical reality no matter what the location. That is why movies from the Golden Age of musicals cannot be repeated or re-created today. The money and the imagination are no longer there. The studios were factories that manufactured magic. The factories are gone and so are musicals like *The Harvey Girls*.

See also: *High, Wide and Handsome, Can't Help Singing*; Judy Garland, Ray Bolger, Arthur Freed, Harry Warren, Johnny Mercer biography boxes

FURTHER READING

Clarke, Gerald. *Get Happy: The Life of Judy Garland*. Crystal Lake, IL: Delta, 2009.

Furia, Philip. *Skylark: The Life and Times of Johnny Mercer*. New York: St. Martin's Press, 2004.

Thomas, Tony. *Harry Warren and the Hollywood Musical*. New York: Lyle Stuart, 1975.

THE JOLSON STORY

Studio and release date: Columbia Pictures; September 1946
Producer: Sidney Skolsky
Screenplay: Stephen Longstreet, Sidney Buchman
Songwriters: Irving Berlin, George Gershwin, Ray Henderson, Walter Donaldson, Lewis Young, Joe Young, Jean Schwartz, B. G. DeSylva, Louis Silvers, Ion Ivanovici, Saul Chaplin, and others (music and lyrics)

Director: Alfred E. Green
Choreographers: Jack Cole, Joseph H. Lewis
Musical Directors: Morris Stoloff, Saul Chaplin
Cinematographer: Joseph Walker
Cast: Larry Parks, Evelyn Keyes, William Demarest, Ludwig Donath, Tamara
   Shayne, Scotty Beckett
Principal Songs: "Anniversary Song"; "April Showers"; "My Mammy"; "Toot
   Toot Tootsie"; "I'm Sittin' on Top of the World"; "Swanee"; "California, Here I
   Come"; "Waiting for the Robert E. Lee"; "You Made Me Love You"; "Avalon";
   "There's a Rainbow Round My Shoulder"; "Liza"

One of the most popular musical biographies of its time, this film may have
been filled with worn clichés and brash untruths but it remains an exuberant
piece of entertainment. By 1946 the great entertainer Al Jolson was no longer in
the public eye. He had played himself or bit characters in a few movies in the late
1930s and early 1940s, but a whole generation had grown up without knowing him
very well. Even his records no longer sold in large numbers, so Jolson went into a
kind of retirement. Columbia producer Sidney Skolsky thought that Jolson's life and
songs would make a good musical bio-pic along the lines of *Yankee Doodle Dandy*
(1942). In fact, he tried to get James Cagney, who had triumphed as George M.
Cohan in that movie, to play Jolson but the actor refused. Jolson, who was 66 years
old, could not play himself on-screen but he agreed to do the singing for whoever
portrayed him in the film. The role went to the up-and-coming actor Larry Parks. As
not to offend the often-egotistical Jolson, the screenplay was closer to the story of
The Jazz Singer (1929) than Jolson's real life. There was also the difficulty raised
when Jolson's ex-wife Ruby Keeler refused to let her name be used in the film. So
The Jolson Story ended up being fiction with a lot of show biz clichés at every turn.
But the movie was very authentic when it came to the music, the way Jolson delivered his songs, and the charisma the star was able to generate.

   In the screenplay, young Asa Yoelson (Scotty Beckett), the son of a cantor (Ludwig Donath), runs away from home to go on the vaudeville stage, changing his
name to Jolson. He is discovered by Steven Martin (William Demarest) who promotes him and becomes his lifelong friend. The adult Jolson (Parks) develops his
own unique singing style by going down on one knee and clutching his heart while
singing sentimental songs. He soon rises from vaudeville to Broadway, reveling in
his fame and tirelessly pushing himself to new heights, much to the dissatisfac-
tion of his wife Julie Benson (Evelyn Keyes). She finally gets Jolson to retire but on
the night that they celebrate his aged parents' wedding anniversary, they all go to
a nightclub where the patrons ask Jolson to sing. At first he refuses, then he launches
into one song after another, finding his life's blood in public adulation. Knowing
that he can never quit, Julie walks out of his life forever. *The Jolson Story* was

high-class melodrama with great songs. The real Jolson's egotism came across as enthusiasm and love for his public in the screen version, and the fading entertainer found a whole new audience to love him back. The recordings that Jolson made for the film became bestsellers and he was called upon to make other records as well. Rarely had one film provided such a comeback for a musical star.

The success of the movie can be attributed to many factors: Parks' dynamic performance, Jolson's singing, and the catalogue of songs that he had originally sung and made famous. There were over two dozen songs in the movie, all sung by Parks/Jolson. They included such favorites as "Toot, Toot, Tootsie," "You Made Me Love You," "Rock-a-Bye Your Baby With a Dixie Melody," "I'm Sittin' on Top of the World," and "Swanee." There was only one original number in the score, "Anniversary Song" by Jolson and Saul Chaplin based on an old waltz tune, which Parks/Jolson sang to his parents; the Jolson recording sold over a million records. *The Jolson Story* was a surprise hit, bringing in $8 million at the box office, so a sequel was inevitable. Columbia released *Jolson Sings Again* in 1949 and, while it may not have matched the earlier biography in quality, it had its merits all the same and again the bio-pic was very popular. Parks again played Jolson (with Jolson again providing the singing) who goes off to entertain troops in World War II. He suffers a physical collapse, is cared for and brought back to health by the nurse Ellen Clark (Barbara Hale) whom he later marries, and makes a big comeback at a Hollywood benefit show. It was no more truthful than the first film, but neither was it as engaging. The musical numbers remained the highlights, repeating some favorites from the first movie and adding plenty more, including "For Me and My Gal," "I'm Looking Over a Four Leaf Clover," "Sonny Boy," "Carolina in the Morning," and "Is It True What They Say About Dixie?" The most bizarre scene in *Jolson Sings Again* is when Jolson hears of the film they are making of his life and he goes to meet the actor who will portray him, with Parks playing both roles thanks to an effective double exposure technique. These two bio-pics encouraged Hollywood to make more musicals about entertainers. Over the next decade it seemed that every singer, dancer, songwriter, and band leader was the subject of a movie musical. Yet few were as satisfying as the two Jolson films.

See also: *The Jazz Singer, Yankee Doodle Dandy, Till the Clouds Roll By*; Al Jolson biography box

FURTHER READING

Dick, Bernard, ed. *Columbia Pictures: Portrait of a Studio*. Lexington: University of Kentucky Press, 1991.

Oberfirst, Robert. *Al Jolson: You Ain't Heard Nothin' Yet!* New York/London: Book Sales Inc., 1981.

TILL THE CLOUDS ROLL BY

Studio and release date: Metro-Goldwyn-Mayer; November 1946
Producer: Arthur Freed
Screenplay: Myles Connolly, Jean Holloway
Songwriters: Jerome Kern (music), Oscar Hammerstein, Otto Harbach, P. G.
    Wodehouse, Dorothy Fields, and others (lyrics)
Directors: Richard Whorf, Vincente Minnelli, George Sidney
Choreographer: Robert Alton
Musical Director: Lennie Hayton
Cinematographers: Harry Stradling, George Folsey
Cast: Robert Walker, Van Heflin, Dorothy Patrick, June Allyson, Judy Garland,
    Frank Sinatra, Kathryn Grayson, Lena Horne, Tony Martin, Caleb Peterson,
    Angela Lansbury, Virginia O'Brien, Ray McDonald, Dinah Shore
Principal Songs: "Till the Clouds Roll By"; "Ol' Man River"; "Look for the Silver
    Lining"; "Leave It to Jane"; "Cleopatterer"; "The Last Time I Saw Paris"; "All
    the Things You Are"; "Make Believe"; "Smoke Gets in Your Eyes"; "Who?";
    "Can't Help Lovin' dat Man"; "How'd You Like to Spoon with Me?"

Jerome Kern was considered the dean of American musical theater composers. His career stretched back to 1903 when his songs began being interpolated into Broadway shows. He scored nearly 40 stage shows and a dozen movies before leaving Broadway and settling in Hollywood in 1939. A biographical musical about his life and career could have dozens of memorable songs to choose from as well as scenes from such memorable Broadway shows as *Oh, Boy!* (1917), *Sally* (1920), *Sunny* (1925), *Show Boat* (1927), *Music in the Air* (1932), and *Roberta* (1933), and such films as *Swing Time* (1936), *Hide, Wide and Handsome* (1937), *You Were Never Lovelier* (1942), *Can't Help Singing* (1944), and *Cover Girl* (1944). What Kern's life did not have was an interesting plot. He was an industrious, exacting artist who worked steadily with various composers, was happily married, and had suffered no great tragedies along the way. When MGM producer Arthur Freed suggested to Kern a movie musical about his life, the composer said his life was so dull that the script would have to be fiction. So that is what the studio did. Ironically, the fictitious story that *Till the Clouds Roll By* told was even duller than Kern's actual life. Luckily this yawn of a tale was interrupted by over two dozen Kern songs and that was all that mattered.

The film begins in 1927 with the opening night of *Show Boat* and presents a 15-minute version of that landmark musical, featuring Kathryn Grayson, Tony Martin, Lena Horne, Virginia O'Brien, Caleb Peterson, and others. Then the plot jumps back to the young and struggling Kern (Robert Walker) as he gets advice from his teacher and mentor James Hessler (Van Heflin) to stop writing mindless ditties and compose great music for the theater. Kern takes his advice, struggles briefly to get his music heard, goes to England and meets his future bride Eva (Dorothy Patrick), and eventually becomes famous. The only conflict is when Hessler's daughter grows up to become a temperamental singer and has a hissy fit when a song Kern wrote for her goes to star Marilyn Miller (Judy Garland). Three different directors contributed to the film and none of them could breathe any life into it anytime the music stopped. Luckily it didn't stop very often because wonderful Kern songs were paraded by with professional panache. Garland sang "Who?" and "Look for the Silver Lining," a young Angela Lansbury got to do her own vocals with the coy musical hall ditty "How'd You Like to Spoon With Me?," Dinah Shore recalled "The Last Time I Saw Paris," Grayson performed the dreamy "Long Ago and Far Away," Martin did justice to the entrancing "All the Things You Are," and June Allyson showed a wry sense of humor with "Leave It to Jane" and "Cleopatterer." Robert Alton did the spirited choreography, the dance highlight being Allyson and Ray McDonald's vivacious version of the title song. The only number that failed to catch fire was Frank Sinatra in a white tuxedo perched on a white pedestal singing "Ol' Man River." Everything about the number seemed wrong and the film ends with a thud.

Kern was pleased with the finished film because the musical numbers were so well done and because the plot had nothing to do with his real life. MGM was also happy until the studio learned that copyright issues arose with some of the music publishers of Kern's songs, and legal hassles forced the studio to delay the release of *Till the Clouds Roll By* for nearly two years. During that time Kern had died of cerebral hemorrhage at the age of 60. MGM decided to make no changes in the movie and released it in 1946 with no mention of Kern's death in the story. Perhaps the studio thought it in poor taste to show Kern's demise on-screen. Regardless, the movie was well received by the press and the public and it remains one of the better musical bio-pics of the period.

In Hollywood's eagerness to make movie musicals about celebrated artists, it often dramatized the lives of songwriters. But, unlike George M. Cohan in *Yankee Doodle Dandy* (1942), most songwriters were not performers. So the songwriter was usually cast with a nonsinging actor, as with Walker in *Till the Clouds Roll By*, and the singing was left to others. Cary Grant was a nonsinging Cole Porter in *Night and Day* (1946), just as Robert Alda was as George Gershwin in *Rhapsody in Blue* (1944). Mickey Rooney sang a bit as lyricist Lorenz Hart in *Words and Music* (1948) but his composer-partner Richard Rodgers (Tom Drake) did not. All of these bio-pics were as fictitious as *Till the Clouds Roll By*. Sometimes the true story could not be filmed (as with Porter and Hart's homosexuality) but often the studio just preferred a cliché-ridden rags-to-riches tale than the real story. In each case, the biographical musicals pleased more for their musical numbers than for their biography. It was the way the studio wanted it and, probably, the way the moviegoers wanted it as well.

See also: Yankee Doodle Dandy, Show Boat; Jerome Kern, Arthur Freed biography boxes

FURTHER READING

Bordman, Gerald. *Jerome Kern: His Life and Music*. New York: Oxford University Press, 1980.

Fordin, Hugh. *MGM's Greatest Musicals: The Arthur Freed Unit*. Boston: Da Capo Press, 1996.

GOOD NEWS!

Studio and release date: Metro-Goldwyn-Mayer; December 1947
Producer: Arthur Freed
Screenplay: Betty Comden, Adolph Green, based on the 1927 stage script by Laurence Schwab, B. G. DeSylva
Songwriters: Ray Henderson and others (music), Lew Brown and others (lyrics)
Director: Charles Walters
Choreographer: Robert Alton
Musical Director: Lennie Hayton
Cinematographer: Charles Schoenbaum
Cast: June Allyson, Peter Lawford, Joan McCracken, Mel Tormé, Patricia Marshall, Ray McDonald, Robert Strickland
Songs: "The Best Things in Life Are Free"; "The Varsity Drag"; "Pass That Peace Pipe"; "Lucky in Love"; "Just Imagine"; "Good News"; "Be a Ladies' Man"; "The French Lesson"

The 1927 Broadway hit is considered one of the best of the college musicals and it was filmed in 1930 but with limited success. It is this 1947 version by MGM that is most known and admired today. *Good News!* was one of a handful of 1920s musicals with a college setting. It was the best book musical by the team of B. G. DeSylva (book and lyrics), Lew Brown (lyrics), and Ray Henderson (music) and it is still done today. The story was set at fictional Tait College and, as in most collegiate musicals, the plot revolved around football. The team's star player Tom Marlowe may not be able to play in the big game if he fails his astronomy exam. The brainy Connie Lane, who is in love with Tom but fears his affections lie elsewhere, agrees to tutor Tom. In the process he falls in love with Connie, passes the test, and wins the game. The predictable plot left lots of room for production numbers, and the songs and the dances were exhilarating as only a Roaring Twenties musical can be. Highlights of the stage score included the dreamy "Just Imagine," the swinging

Betty Comden and **Adolph Green.**   One of the longest songwriting partnerships in show business, the twosome contributed lyrics and scripts for Broadway and Hollywood over a period of 50 years. Comden (1917–2006) was born in Brooklyn and educated at New York University before entering show business as a singer in small clubs and cabarets. Green (1915–2002) was also a native New Yorker who started as a performer. The two first found success when they teamed up with composer Leonard Bernstein for the Broadway musical *On the Town* (1944). Later they had another hit with Bernstein in *Wonderful Town* (1953). Among the many other Broadway shows they contributed to are *Two on the Aisle* (1951), *Peter Pan* (1954), *Bells Are Ringing* (1956), *Do Re Mi* (1960), *Subways Are for Sleeping* (1961), *Fade Out—Fade In* (1964), *Hallelujah, Baby!* (1967), *Applause* (1970), *On the Twentieth Century* (1978), and *The Will Rogers Follies* (1991). Comden and Green first went to Hollywood in 1945 where they wrote the screenplay and/or the song lyrics for *Good News!* (1947), *Take Me Out to the Ball Game* (1949), *The Barkleys of Broadway* (1949), *On the Town* (1949), *Singin' in the Rain* (1952), *The Band Wagon* (1953), *It's Always Fair Weather* (1955), and *What a Way to Go* (1964). Their lyrics, stage scripts, and screenplays are usually in the conventional musical comedy tradition, but they have an energy and playfulness that keeps them from being dated. Autobiography: *Off Stage*, Comden (1995).

"Lucky in Love," the optimistic "The Best Things in Life Are Free," the foot-stomping "Varsity Drag," and the spirited title number. The Broadway success of *Good News!* prompted MGM to buy the rights, and in 1930 it released the first film version. The movie did not begin to capture the vitality and playfulness of the Broadway hit, and the studio, nervous about the public's growing disenchantment with movie musicals, cut two of the best songs ("The Best Things in Life Are Free" and "Lucky in Love") in order to shorten the picture. The screenplay did not stray too far from the stage script, but campus frivolity did not look as appealing in the early days of the Depression as it had in the prosperous 1920s. Yet there are moments to enjoy in the film, particularly the "Varsity Drag" and the title song choreographed with splash by Sammy Lee. There were a few new numbers ("Students Are We," "If You're Not Kissing Me," and "But I'd Like to Make You Happy") but the best things in the film were from the stage. As the studio feared, *Good News!* was not a box office success.

The same studio had much better luck 17 years later with this color version of the musical. At first MGM wanted to cast Mickey Rooney and Judy Garland as the college sweethearts but decided they were needed for *Strike Up the Band* (1940) so the project was delayed for six years. Producer Arthur Freed resurrected the idea of a new version of *Good News!* that would emphasize swing rather than 1920s

Charleston-like numbers. A slightly updated screenplay by Betty Comden and Adolph Green (in their first screen assignment) tightened up the plot. Tommy (Peter Lawford) is still a football hero at Tait College but he cannot pass French class so Connie (June Allyson) has to coach him, thereby falling in love with the thick-headed fellow. Competition comes in the form of the man-hungry Pat McCellan (Patricia Marshall) who pursues Tommy for much of the movie. Again the musical ends with Tommy winning the big football game and Connie as well. It was as predictable as ever, but the dialogue was a bit sharper in the new version and each of the production numbers were thrilling. Much of the stage score was used and it sounded better than ever. The ballads "The Best Things in Life Are Free" and "Just Imagine" were performed with charm by the principals but it was the vivacious "Varsity Drag," performed by the whole cast at a school dance, that stole the show. Two of the new numbers that were added to the score measured up to the old standards: the conversational duet "The French Lesson," by Roger Edens (music), Comden, and Green (lyric) and sung by Lawford and Allyson; and the contagious romp "Pass That Peace Pipe" by Edens, Hugh Martin, and Ralph Blane (music and lyrics) that Joan McCracken and Ray McDonald led in a campus ice cream parlor. The lively choreography was by Robert Alton and Charles Walters (who also directed) and this time MGM had a hit. The only drawbacks in the musical are Lawford's less-than-magnetic performance as Tommy and the fact that most of the principals and ensemble look far too old to be in college. But then *Good News!* is pure musical escapism; college is not, nor ever was, like this.

See also: Arthur Freed, Betty Comden and Adolph Green biography boxes

FURTHER READING

Bloom, Ken. *Hollywood Musicals: The 101 Greatest Song-and-Dance Movies of All Time*. New York: Black Dog and Leventhal, 2010.
Eames, John Douglas. *The MGM Story*. New York: Crown Publishers, 1975.

EASTER PARADE

Studio and release date: Metro-Goldwyn-Mayer; June 1948
Producer: Arthur Freed
Screenplay: Sidney Sheldon, Frances Goodrich, Albert Hackett
Songwriter: Irving Berlin (music and lyrics)
Director: Charles Walters
Choreographer: Robert Alton
Musical Director: Johnny Green

Cinematographer: Harry Stradling
Cast: Fred Astaire, Judy Garland, Ann Miller, Jules Munshin, Clinton Sundberg
Principal Songs: "Easter Parade"; "Better Luck Next Time"; "It Only Happens When I Dance with You"; "I Love a Piano"; "Shaking the Blues Away"; "A Couple of Swells"; "I Want to Go Back to Michigan"; "Steppin' Out with My Baby"; "When the Midnight Choo-Choo Leaves for Alabam'"; "Snookey Ookums"

In an odd but interesting casting move, the 48-year-old hoofer Fred Astaire was paired with Judy Garland, who was practically half his age and not known for her dancing abilities. But the resulting movie was an all-out hit, resurrecting Astaire's career (he had gone into semiretirement) and Garland surprising audiences with her dancing abilities. The dance team of Don Hewes (Astaire) and Nadine Hale (Ann Miller) is broken off in 1911 when Nadine dumps Don to accept a role in the *Ziegfeld Follies*. Determined to continue on without her, Don takes the rookie dancer Hannah Brown (Garland) as his new partner and vows to make her as popular as Nadine. Even though Hannah is not physically nor vocally like Nadine, Don tries to turn her into a copy of his former partner. Once he allows Hannah be herself, the new team becomes popular. The jealous Nadine tries to break up the twosome by dancing with Don at a nightclub and suggesting to Hannah that he is still in love with her. The wealthy New Yorker Johnny Harrow (Peter Lawford) has fallen in love with Hannah but she loves Don. By Easter Sunday, Hannah and Don are romantic as well as dancing partners and they stroll down Fifth Avenue in the Easter parade. The score consisted of both old and new Irving Berlin songs, all of them top drawer. The jaunty "A Fella With an Umbrella," the torch number "Better Luck Next Time," and the gliding ballad "It Only Happens When I Dance with You" were the quieter numbers while Miller did some furious tapping in "Shaking the Blues Away" and Astaire danced all over a toy shop in "Drum Crazy." In one of the most stunning dances of the 1940s, Astaire danced to "Steppin' Out with My Baby" in slow motion while the chorus behind him hoofed in real time. The comic highlight of the score was Garland and Astaire cutting loose as a duo of happy hobos in "A Couple of Swells." The title number, introduced on Broadway years before in the revue *As Thousands Cheer* (1933), was heard as couples strolled Fifth Avenue on Easter Sunday; the Berlin favorite became more popular than ever.

Easter Parade is a good example of how a movie musical changes in production depending on the casting. The film was set to begin filming with Gene Kelly and Garland as the leads, reuniting the couple from *For Me and My Gal* (1942) and *The Pirate* (1948). But Kelly sprained his ankle right before filming was to begin and production would have to be halted for several weeks. Kelly suggested to producer Arthur Freed that he ask Astaire to do the role. Two years earlier, Astaire had

Ann Miller (1923–2004)   A dark-haired, apple-cheeked singer-actress, she rarely played leading roles on-screen but was a recognized star because of her vivacious tap dancing. She was born in Chireno, Texas, but grew up in Southern California where she took dance lessons as a child. Miller was only a teenager when she was cast in B movie musicals before getting better roles in *True to the Army* (1942), *Priorities on Parade* (1942), *Reveille With Beverly* (1943), *What's Buzzin', Cousin?* (1943), *Carolina Blues* (1944), *Eadie Was a Lady* (1945), and *The Thrill of Brazil* (1946). Widespread fame came when she danced with Fred Astaire in *Easter Parade* (1948), followed by such films as *On the Town* (1949), *Texas Carnival* (1951), *Two Tickets to Broadway* (1951), *Lovely to Look At* (1952), *Small Town Girl* (1953), *Kiss Me, Kate* (1953), *Deep in My Heart* (1954), *Hit the Deck* (1955), and *The Opposite Sex* (1956). Throughout her career, Miller frequently performed in musicals on the stage, ranging from Broadway to summer stock, and she was still performing into the 1990s. Autobiography: *Miller's High Life*, with Norma Lee Browning (1972).

announced his retirement, saying he was getting too old (48) to play leading men opposite much younger women. Yet when Freed offered *Easter Parade*, the veteran dancer quickly accepted. He was bored and restless with retirement and was attracted to a project with Berlin songs and the chance to work with Garland. (Interestingly, Astaire and Garland had never met and had to be introduced to each other on the first day of filming.) Another casting change occurred at the same time when Cyd Charisse had to bow out of playing Nadine and she was replaced by Ann Miller. Finally there was a change in director. Vincente Minnelli was to direct *Easter Parade* but he was having marital problems with his wife, who happened to be Garland. Her psychiatrist suggested they not work together and so Charles Walters was assigned to direct. With songs and script already written, sets and costumes prepared, the dances and songs outlined, and the crew ready to start, it seemed that *Easter Parade* would be on schedule. But how could it? Kelly and Astaire are too very different kinds of dancers and Astaire was too old to do the athletic kind of hoofing that the younger Kelly could pull off. Also, Charisse was primarily a delicate ballet dancer while Miller was an exuberant tap dancer. So much of *Easter Parade* had to be reimagined and altered. Watching the film today, one cannot picture Kelly and Charisse in it. That is the sign of high artistry when a musical seems so perfect the way it is that anything different sounds wrong.

See also: *Holiday Inn*; Irving Berlin, Fred Astaire, Judy Garland, Arthur Freed biography boxes

FURTHER READING

Berrgreen, Laurence. *As Thousands Cheer: The Life of Irving Berlin.* Boston: Da Capo Press, 1996.

Hirschhorn, Clive. *The Hollywood Musical.* 2nd ed. New York: Crown Publishers, 1996.

NEPTUNE'S DAUGHTER

Studio and release date: Metro-Goldwyn-Mayer; June 1949
Producer: Jack Cummings
Screenplay: Dorothy Kingsley
Songwriter: Frank Loesser (music and lyrics)
Director: Edward Buzzell
Choreographer: Jack Donohue
Music Director: George Stoll
Cinematographer: Charles Rosher
Cast: Esther Williams, Ricardo Montalban, Red Skelton, Betty Garrett, Keenan Wynn, Xavier Cugat
Songs: "Baby, It's Cold Outside"; "My Heart Beats Faster"; "I Love Those Men"

All of the movies featuring swimming star Esther Williams, dubbed "America's Mermaid," found an audience but this lightweight romp was the most popular. It probably helped that the film has a better score than was usually found in Williams' watery vehicles. Also, the plot, a case of extended mistaken identity, was better structured than the stories Williams was usually handed. Ex-swimming champion Eve Barrett (Williams) runs a successful swimsuit manufacturing company and is throwing a big fashion show to be held at the New York Polo Club. When the Latin American polo star José O'Rourke (Ricardo Montalban) comes to town with his team, Eve's oversexed sister Betty (Betty Garrett) is anxious to meet the millionaire. She goes to the polo grounds where she mistakes the clubhouse masseur Jack Spratt (Red Skelton) for the famous sportsman and throws herself at him. Spratt, the kind of guy who never gets the girl, does not correct Betty's misunderstanding and the two fall in love. When Eve finds out about the relationship, she fears that Betty's heart will be broken when the polo team returns to South America. So she goes to José to persuade him to break it off with Betty, but instead she is smitten by the dashing Latino and he with her. Complications arise because Eve is afraid she is stealing Betty's sweetheart away from her, and it is not until the final reel that the mixup was cleared up and a double wedding was in the forecast. The film had only three songs, all by Frank Loesser, but there were also instrumentals by Xavier Cugat and his orchestra and, of course. Williams' swimming

Esther Williams (1921–2013)   Hollywood's best (and only) swimming star, she possessed singing and acting talents as well and was featured in several movie musicals. She was born in Los Angeles and by her teen years was already a champion swimmer. Williams studied at Los Angeles City College for a time while doing some modeling. A talent agent spotted her, and she was cast in a few Andy Hardy films before taking to the water on-screen for the first time in *Bathing Beauty* (1944). Williams was an immediate hit with the public so a series of films were written around her swimming, including *Thrill of a Romance* (1945), *Ziegfeld Follies* (1946), *Fiesta* (1947), *This Time for Keeps* (1947), *On an Island With You* (1948), *Take Me Out to the Ball Game* (1949), *Neptune's Daughter* (1949), *Duchess of Idaho* (1950), *Pagan Love Song* (1950), *Texas Carnival* (1951), *Skirts Ahoy* (1952), *Million Dollar Mermaid* (1952), *Dangerous When Wet* (1953), and *Jupiter's Darling* (1955). When she turned to dramatic, nonswimming roles, Williams lost her popularity so she retired to promote swimming competitions and exhibitions. She later appeared occasionally on television and at special events. Autobiography: *The Million Dollar Mermaid* (1999).

numbers were musicalized as well. *Neptune's Daughter* was the biggest hit of the swimming star's 18 movies.

Jack Donohue staged some spectacular water ballets for Williams, yet it is the delightful score by Frank Loesser that sticks in the memory, particularly the Oscar-winning duet "Baby, It's Cold Outside" which made no sense since the story took place in summer. The original song that Loesser wrote for the lovers was "On a Slow Boat to China" but the studio censor thought the lyric too suggestive so the song was rejected. Needing another duet in a hurry, Loesser offered the charming "Baby, It's Cold Outside," a song he wrote some years before that he and his wife had often sung at parties. Also in the score was the raucous "I Love Those Men" delivered by an oversexed Garrett and the warm ballad "My Heart Beats Faster" crooned by Montalban in his Latin-flavored style.

Like the skating star Sonja Henie, Williams had to have her movie musicals tailor made to work in her athletic talents. Just as a Henie film had to have a dazzling ice skating sequence or two, audiences expected Williams to take to the water. She was a unique Hollywood star. As a teenager she won many swimming competitions, but her screen career began when she was spotted by a Hollywood agent when she was working in a department store. At first cast as the pretty girl-next-door type (she got her first on-screen kiss from Mickey Rooney in an Andy Hardy film), her swimming talents were discovered later. Louis B. Mayer wanted MGM to have its version of Fox's Henie. When he could find no skating figure who he thought was photogenic enough, Mayer switched his plan to a swimming star and Williams was the obvious candidate. Special pools were constructed at MGM to film her aquatic numbers using custom-made underwater cameras. It seemed like a lot of extra expense for the studio but a Williams' movie usually paid its way and then some. *Neptune's Daughter* made over $3 million at the box office on its first release, a considerable sum in 1949. In the later 1950s, the public lost interest in on-screen swimming, or perhaps they lost interest in Williams, so she turned to dramatic roles in nonmusicals and had modest success. Williams retired from swimming in the 1960s and, as in *Neptune's Daughter*, went into the bathing suit and swimming pool business.

See also: *Sun Valley Serenade*; Esther Williams, Frank Loesser biography boxes

FURTHER READING

Loesser, Susan. *A Most Remarkable Fella: Frank Loesser and the Guys and Dolls in His Life*. New York: Donald I. Fine, Inc., 1993.
Thomas, Lawrence B. *The MGM Years*. New York: Arlington House, 1971.
Williams, Esther, and Digby Diehl. *The Million Dollar Mermaid: An Autobiography*. New York: Simon & Schuster, 1999.

ON THE TOWN

Studio and release date: Metro-Goldwyn-Mayer; December 1949
Producer: Arthur Freed
Screenplay: Betty Comden, Adolph Green, based on their 1944 stage script
Songwriters: Leonard Bernstein, Roger Edens (music), Betty Comden, Adolph Green (lyrics)
Directors/Choreographers: Gene Kelly, Stanley Donen
Musical Director: Lennie Hayton
Cinematographer: Harold Rosson
Cast: Gene Kelly, Frank Sinatra, Jules Munshin, Ann Miller, Betty Garrett, Vera-Ellen, Florence Bates, Alice Pearce
Songs: "New York, New York"; "Come Up to My Place"; "I Feel Like I'm Not Out of Bed Yet"; "Count on Me"; "On the Town"; "Prehistoric Man"; "Main Street"; "You're Awful"

Although it was based on a 1944 Broadway hit, this vigorous, high-flying musical dropped much of the outstanding score by composer Leonard Bernstein and lyricist-librettists Betty Comden and Adolph Green. Yet the screen version has many merits and remains a cinema favorite. If the movie resembles a modern ballet, that is because the idea for the musical was a ballet. Jerome Robbins choreographed a high-flying piece titled *Fancy Free*, which was set to music by Bernstein. The mini-ballet followed three sailors on leave in New York City and the adventures and romance they find there. Robbins and Bernstein expanded on the dance and, with a script by Comden and Green, it opened on Broadway in 1944 as *On the Town*. The show was a surprise hit because none of the creators had ever worked on Broadway before. The story was not much more complicated than the ballet. Sailors Ozzie, Chip, and Gabey, whose ship is docked at the Brooklyn Navy Yard, get 24-hour leave and explore New York City. Chip wants to see the sights but Gabey and Ozzie are more interested in romance. Gabey sees a poster of "Miss Turnstiles" in a subway station and is smitten with her. Her name is Ivy Smith and she is that month's cover girl for the city's transit system. While Gabey goes off in search of Ivy, Ozzie finds an oddball romance at the Anthropological Museum with anthropology student Claire de Loon. Chip hails a cab to take him to see the sights but the cabbie is the oversexed Hildy Esterhazy who is more interested in smooching than sightseeing. Gabey finds Ivy at Symphonic Hall taking voice lessons with the inebriated Madame Dily and she agrees to meet Gabey that night at Coney Island. She doesn't tell Gabey that she works as a cooch dancer on the boardwalk to earn money for her lessons. After touring a round of nightclubs, all three couples end up together on Coney Island. But the night of frivolity ends at dawn and the couples bid each other farewell as the three sailors return to their ship. It was not the most gripping or original of scripts but most of the show was danced and the dancing was sublime. The music the cast danced to was also outstanding, as were the songs. The vibrant "New York, New York" became the most popular song but the score was filled with wonderful numbers, such as the manic "I Get Carried Away," the torchy "Lonely Town," the quietly celebratory "Lucky to Be Me," the farcical "Come Up to My Place," the vivacious "You Got Me," the swinging "I Can Cook Too," and the poignant parting song "Some Other Time." *On the Town* was a hit and launched the careers of Robbins, Bernstein, Comden, and Green.

MGM paid a high price for the screen rights of *On the Town* then, with usual Hollywood logic, kept the thin story and discarded most of the splendid score. In fact, producer Arthur Freed didn't like Bernstein's music, finding it too modern and unusual for the general public's ear. He hired Comden and Green to write the screenplay and the lyrics to six new songs composed by Roger Edens. Of the Broadway score, only the opening "New York, New York," the comic "Come Up to My Place," the lullaby "I Feel Like I'm Not Out of Bed Yet," and sections of Bernstein's dance music were used. The screenplay was very similar to the stage script and again much of the musical was dance. As codirected and co-choreographed by Stanley Donen and Gene Kelly, those dances were so exciting that no one minded the predicable story. The movie was unique in the way it used on-location filming in New York City, the celebrated tourist sights becoming the background for the action. Not since *The Jazz Singer* (1927) had done some filming on the streets of

The first movie musical to be shot on location in New York City, *On the Town* (1949) turned the "Big Apple" into a major character in the film. Also on hand were Frank Sinatra (center), Gene Kelly (left), and Jules Munshin (right) as three sailors with twenty-four hours' leave to find fun and romance in the city. Kelly co-directed and co-choreographed the musical with Stanley Donen. (MGM/Photofest)

the Lower East Side had a musical gone on location in New York and the effect was thrilling. Another innovation in the dancing was the use of trained ballet dancers to substitute for some of the principals in the "Day in New York" ballet. They were not hidden doubles but clearly stylistic representations of the characters, something Agnes de Mille had done on Broadway in *Oklahoma!* six years earlier. Just as *On the Town* had opened doors for dance in the musical theater, the film version suggested new possibilities for movie dancing. These possibilities led to such later musicals as *An American in Paris* (1951) and *Singin' in the Rain* (1952).

The cast for *On the Town* was led by Kelly, who played Gabey, and he was joined by Frank Sinatra as Chip, Jules Munshin as Ozzie, Vera-Ellen as Ivy, Ann Miller as Claire, and Betty Garrett as Hildy. In some ways they gave the finest performances of their careers. Their delivery of the Bernstein songs was spot on and they even made the mediocre songs composed by Edens sound better than they were. Only the facial tribal number "Prehistoric Man" came close to the quality of the original songs. Yet *On the Town* was all about dance so a few lackluster songs did

> **Stanley Donen** (b. 1924)   A film director and choreographer who often worked with dancer Gene Kelly, he devised some notable innovations in how to film a musical. He was born in Columbia, South Carolina, and educated at the University of South Carolina before appearing as a dancer on Broadway in *Pal Joey* (1940). He befriended the show's star Gene Kelly and helped Kelly choreograph *Best Foot Forward* (1941) on Broadway before both headed to Hollywood and worked on *Cover Girl* (1944) together. Donen was solo choreographer for *Anchors Aweigh* (1945), *A Date With Judy* (1948), *Take Me Out to the Ball Game* (1949), and other movies before choreographing and codirecting *On the Town* (1949) with Kelly. It was the first musical shot on location in New York and was innovative in its quick-cutting montages and travelogue-like approach to location filming. The two men codirected and choreographed *Singin' in the Rain* (1952) and *It's Always Fair Weather* (1955), and Donen directed *Royal Wedding* (1951), *Give a Girl a Break* (1953), *Seven Brides for Seven Brothers* (1954), *Deep in My Heart* (1954), and *Funny Face* (1957). He turned to producing as well as directing with *The Pajama Game* (1957) and repeated both chores for *Damn Yankees* (1958), *The Little Prince* (1973), and *Movie Movie* (1978). He was responsible for some of the era's most unique musical sequences, such as Fred Astaire dancing on the ceiling in *Royal Wedding*, Kelly's dance with the cartoon Jerry the Mouse in *Anchors Aweigh*, and the wet title number in *Singin' in the Rain*. Biography: *Dancing on the Ceiling: Stanley Donen and His Movies*, Stephen M. Silverman (1996).

not much matter in the long run. The 1940s was filled with superior movie musicals but one of the best opened at the very end of the decade. *On the Town* remains a high point in a Golden Age.

See also: *Born to Dance, Anchors Aweigh, Singin' in the Rain*; Gene Kelly, Stanley Donen, Frank Sinatra, Ann Miller, Arthur Freed, Betty Comden and Adolph Green biography boxes

FURTHER READING

Fordin, Hugh. *MGM's Greatest Musicals: The Arthur Freed Unit*. Boston: Da Capo Press, 1996. Miller, Ann, and Norma Lee Browning. *Miller's High Life*. New York: Doubleday, 1972.

Silverman, Stephen M. *Dancing on the Ceiling: Stanley Donen and His Movies*. New York: Knopf, 1996.

THE 1950s: COMPETING WITH TELEVISION

For many Americans, the 1950s was a time of prosperity and the pursuit of the good life. The suburbs blossomed, the childbirth rate boomed, and the sale of cars and the building of highways made Americans more mobile than ever before. The cloud that hung over this idyllic existence was the Cold War and the threat of communism. This undeclared war between democracy and communism became uncomfortably real at the very start of the decade when the Korean War began in 1950. The conflict was resolved two years later, leaving a communist North Korea and a democratic South Korea. A civil war in Vietnam that started in 1954 would eventually escalate into the longest and most unpopular war in the history of the United States. In 1959, Fidel Castro and his communist forces took over the country of Cuba. Communism was now right next door to the United States. A more tangible threat was that of nuclear war, with both the United States and the Soviet Union building up atomic weapons. Bomb shelters and plans for surviving a nuclear attack were prevalent, adding a kind of paranoia to the happy lives of most Americans. The fear of communism within the United States led to a movement to root out "un-American" elements, most infamously the so-called witch hunts in which lives were destroyed if there was any suspicion of socialist activities in the present or the past. For many, the prosperous, conservative 1950s was a time of discontent. For example, the seed of the Civil Rights Movement began in 1955 when African American Rosa Parks refused to give up her bus seat to a white man. The bus boycott that followed was the beginning of a long struggle for justice for minority Americans. Much of the turmoil of the 1960s can be traced back to 1950s events such as this.

While the adult population in the 1950s might be classified as conservative, the younger generation was much less so. The birth explosion since the end of

World War II created a new and powerful force: the baby boomers. As this new generation of Americans grew into their teens, they not only outnumbered the adults but they became a financial powerhouse. They were the first teen generation to have money to spend, and these young consumers dictated what was popular. Their influence was felt most strongly in the music business. The music that teens listened to was not what their parents liked, and a musical generation gap was formed. Rock and roll was the new sound and teens embraced it passionately. The 1955 recording of Bill Haley and the Comets singing "Rock Around the Clock" has been pinpointed as the beginning of rock but, in reality, it grew out of "race music," the name given to a jazzy version of the blues developed by African American musicians. Once white teenagers started listening to such music, its name was changed to "rhythm and blues" (R&B) and the sound became a significant force in mainstream American music.

The 1950s saw many inventions and technical achievements. Jonas Salk developed an effective polio vaccine in 1953 and by the next year it was first administered to children, eventually eradicating the dreaded disease. That same year the molecular biologists James Watson and Francis Crick discovered DNA, and the so-called secret of life was uncovered. In 1957 the Russians launched Sputnik I, the first man-made object to orbit the Earth, thereby beginning the "space race" to put a man on the moon. At the end of the decade, Xerox Corporation introduced the first copier. But of all the inventions that came to fruition in the 1950s, none had such an impact on American life as television. Although television had been available to the public since 1945, it was not until the next decade that it became a mass media. Six million TV sets were in American homes in the year 1950; by 1960, that number was 66 million. Unlike radio, television was a visual medium and was considerable competition for the movies. At first the studios ignored television, calling it a novelty that could not replace the experience of going to the movies. As one apocryphal story has it, when a reporter asked a Hollywood executive if television was a threat to movies, he replied "People have kitchens—but they still go to restaurants to eat." But soon Hollywood was indeed threatened and the studios combated television by offering things that one could not get on a 15-inch black-and-white screen: color, spectacle, and even gimmicks like 3-D. Biblical epics and musicals offered plenty of opportunities for all three. Consequently the movie musicals of the 1950s tended to be large and colorful. Certain stars still had box office power, but often a musical was sold to the public for its lavish look on the wide screen. Sometimes these colorful musicals were big just for the sake of being big. Other times the wide-screen look enhanced the storytelling and revitalized the production numbers.

Because the 1950s was such a fruitful time for Broadway musicals, Hollywood benefited and often a stage hit was turned into a popular movie musical. The songwriting team of Rodgers and Hammerstein, for example, had four of their Broadway shows turned into successful films in the 1950s. *Oklahoma!* (1955), *The King and I* (1956), *Carousel* (1956), and *South Pacific* (1958) were brought to the screen with their stories, characters, songs, and even dances intact. Among the many other stage musicals to appear on-screen in the 1950s were *Annie Get Your Gun* (1950), *Show Boat* (1951), *Where's Charley?* (1952), *Call Me Madam* (1953), *Gentlemen Prefer Blondes* (1953), *Kiss Me, Kate* (1953), *The Student Prince* (1954), *Brigadoon* (1954), *Carmen Jones* (1954), *Guys and Dolls* (1955), *Kismet* (1955), *Silk Stockings* (1957), *The Pajama Game* (1957), *Pal Joey* (1957), *Damn Yankees* (1958), *Li'l Abner* (1959), and *Porgy and Bess* (1959). Some of these were filmed with the same directors, choreographers, and performers from the Broadway productions. So not only were they entertaining in themselves, the films also provided an archival record of a golden era of Broadway musicals.

An interesting development in original movie musicals was the emphasis put on dance. Hollywood musicals had always had dance sequences but in the 1950s these were turned into extended ballets. The idea came from the theater but on-screen these elaborate production numbers utilized modern dance, jazz dance, and traditional ballet to tell a story or to relate what a character was feeling. The lengthy ballet near the end of *An American in Paris* (1951) is considered by many to be the finest of these cinematic ballets. Also impressive were the ballets in *Singin' in the Rain* (1952), *The Band Wagon* (1953), *Oklahoma!* (1955), and *Carousel* (1956). Dance was also given a great deal of focus in other musicals that did not have ballets. The vigorous dancing during the barn-raising scene in *Seven Brides for Seven Brothers* (1954), Fred Astaire dancing on the ceiling in *Royal Wedding* (1951), the Sadie Hawkins Day chase dance in *L'il Abner* (1959), the crapshooters' dance in *Guys and Dolls* (1955), the "Small House of Uncle Thomas" narrative dance in *The King and I* (1956), and the baseball players' dance on the infield in *Damn Yankees* (1958) are all unforgettable movie musical moments from the decade.

In quite a different mode were the many 1950s musicals that not only didn't have dancing, they also didn't have jokes. These were the dark musical melodramas that were far from escapist. Some were bio-pics about celebrities who battled alcoholism, drugs, depression, or physical handicaps. Others were original tales that took a bleak point of view of life. Surprisingly, some of these films were able to find an audience. For example, Frank Sinatra played the singer-turned-comic Joe E. Lewis in *The Joker Is Wild* (1957). It was a grim, true story of crooner Lewis who ran afoul of some gangsters so they slashed his vocal chords and ended his singing career. So Lewis becomes a cynical comic who drinks, gambles, and abuses the women in his life. Lewis was not a likable character but Sinatra's performance made him a fascinating character. Other similarly somber movie musicals from the 1950s include *Young Man with a Horn* (1950), a thinly disguised bio-pic about jazz trumpet player Bix Beiderbecke (Kirk Douglas) who is a genius musician but a self-destructive figure who dies young. *With a Song in My Heart* (1952) was about band singer Jane Froman (Susan Hayward) who was in a plane crash while going to entertain U.S. troops in Europe. Her recovery and return to singing made for an inspiring movie. *The Glenn Miller Story* (1954) ended with a plane crash that killed the famous band leader who was also flying to perform for GIs in Europe. *The Country Girl* (1954) gave Bing Crosby one of his most challenging roles when he played an alcoholic singer trying for a comeback. Doris Day shone as singer Ruth Etting who battles an abusive husband (James Cagney) in *Love Me or Leave Me* (1955). *Pete Kelly's Blues* (1955) was a fictional account of the backstabbing world of speakeasies during Prohibition. Susan Hayward played another singer in *I'll Cry Tomorrow* (1956), this time the comic actress Lillian Roth who battled alcoholism, a tireless stage mother, and bad marriages. Such movies would not have been made in the 1940s but they were in the 1950s and were applauded for their honesty.

After being preoccupied with making propaganda and training films during the war and musical anthologies in the late 1940s, the Disney studio returned to the animated musical feature and presented a series of memorable films in the 1950s. *Cinderella* (1950), *Alice in Wonderland* (1950), *Peter Pan* (1953), *The Lady and the Tramp* (1955), and *Sleeping Beauty* (1959) have all become timeless favorites. Walt Disney and his staff still had no competition in the area of animated features. Also, Disney was shrewd enough to rerelease his films from the 1930s and 1940s at planned intervals so that each new generation of children could see them in a movie theater. With the seemingly endless supply of kids during the baby boom era, this meant that past movies could finance new projects, a concept the other studios failed to grasp. Disney was also smart in that he did not see television as the enemy. Instead he used his television shows *Disneyland* and *The Mickey Mouse Club* to promote not only his new and old movies but also his theme park. The whole package was tied together with Disney characters, such as Jiminy Cricket, to ensure that everyone was aware of his world of entertainment. While most moviegoers did not know or care which studio made which films, everyone knew and recognized a Disney product.

MGM made more musicals in the 1950s than any other studio. It also came up with a handful of classics. In addition to the already mentioned *Singin' in the Rain, The Band Wagon, An American in Paris, Seven Brides for Seven Brothers, Royal Wedding, Brigadoon, Silk Stockings, Annie Get Your Gun, Show Boat, The Student Prince, Love Me or Leave Me, Guys and Dolls, Kismet,* and *Kiss Me, Kate,* the studio released such beloved movie musicals as *Three Little Words* (1950), *Summer Stock* (1950), *The Great Caruso* (1951), *The Belle of New York* (1952), *Lovely to Look At* (1952), *High Society* (1956), *Funny Face* (1957), and *Gigi* (1958). The last was the most honored musical of the lot, winning nine Oscars including best picture. Perhaps *Gigi* represented the finest qualities of MGM and its celebrated Freed unit (musicals produced by Arthur Freed). But *Gigi* also represented the end of an era. Many consider it the last great musical of a Golden Age. The studio system was beginning to collapse because of different factors. A Hollywood studio could no longer own a string of movie houses because it was considered a monopoly by the government. Without the income of a theater owner, the studios suffered and had to appeal to independent movie house owners to distribute their products. A bigger factor facing Hollywood was the drastic drop in attendance at the movies because of television. Fewer Americans frequented the movies in the 1950s than in the last three decades, and hundreds of movie houses closed. Even some of the great movie palaces from the 1920s were torn down to make way for parking lots, a more lucrative business in urban areas. When the studios tried to combat television by offering wide screens, color, spectacular epics, and even 3-D features, the payoff was barely enough to offset the high cost. Musicals, being among the most expensive of genres to make, were considered poor business risks so fewer were made. But the quality of 1950s movie musicals was frequently very high even as the quantity diminished. Moviemaking would have to change in the 1960s and the musical would change with it.

ANNIE GET YOUR GUN

Studio and release date: Metro-Goldwyn-Mayer; April 1950
Producer: Arthur Freed
Screenplay: Sidney Sheldon, based on the 1946 stage script by Dorothy and Herbert Fields
Songwriter: Irving Berlin (music and lyrics)
Director: George Sidney
Choreographer: Robert Alton
Musical Director: Adolph Deutsch
Cinematographer: Charles Rosher
Cast: Betty Hutton, Howard Keel, Louis Calhern, J. Carroll Naish, Edward Arnold, Keenan Wynn
Songs: "There's No Business Like Show Business"; "They Say It's Wonderful"; "Anything You Can Do"; "You Can't Get a Man with a Gun"; "The Girl That I Marry"; "I Got the Sun in the Morning"; "Doin' What Comes Natur'lly"; "My Defenses Are Down"; "I'm an Indian Too"; "Colonel Buffalo Bill"

Faithfully based on the 1946 Broadway musical hit, the screen version of this frontier musical managed to become the top-grossing movie of the year. When hillbilly Annie Oakley (Betty Hutton) comes into town to sell some game she's shot, she meets up with members of Buffalo Bill's Wild West Show, in particular the dashing Frank Butler (Howard Keel) who is the show's prize sharpshooter and a bit of a ladies' man. When Buffalo Bill (Louis Calhern) sees how well Annie can shoot, he

Betty Hutton (1921–2007)   With an overpowering singing and speaking voice, the "Blonde Bombshell" excelled at broad comedy and raucous singing. She was born in Battle Creek, Michigan, and started singing in school. By the time Hutton was a teenager, she was a vocalist for local bands then for name bands. She made her film debut in a bit part in the musical *The Fleet's In* (1942) and was soon noticed. Although Hutton was usually cast in supporting roles in musicals and comedies, her exuberant personality always made her stand out, as in such musicals as *Star Spangled Rhythm* (1942), *Happy Go Lucky* (1943), *And the Angels Sing* (1944), *Here Come the Waves* (1944), *Duffy's Tavern* (1945), and *The Stork Club* (1945). She eventually played leading roles in the musicals *Incendiary Blonde* (1945), *The Perils of Pauline* (1947), *Annie Get Your Gun* (1950), and *Somebody Loves Me* (1952). Despite her unforgettable presence in comedies, such as the farcical *Miracle at Morgan's Creek* (1944), and her own television show in the 1950s, the oft-married Hutton soon fell out of favor and years later was discovered living on charity and battling mental illness.

hires her and soon she starts to eclipse Frank in the show even as she's falling in love with him. His masculine pride hurt, Frank leaves Buffalo Bill and works for another showman while Annie takes Europe by storm when her show goes on tour and she gets plenty of medals from counts and kings. Frank and Annie meet up again when she arrives back in the United States and it looks like they are going to get together until Annie dazzles him with all her prizes and still claims to be the better shot. A shooting match is arranged and, taking the advice of the wise old Chief Sitting Bull (J. Carroll Naish), Annie lets Frank win the match and thereby wins him. Songwriter Irving Berlin had the biggest Broadway success of his career with *Annie Get Your Gun* thanks in part to a score filled with hits, more than in any of his other stage works. Highlights include the ballads "They Say It's Wonderful" and "I Got Lost in His Arms," the sprightly character numbers "Doin' What Comes Natur'lly" and "You Can't Get a Man With a Gun," the vivacious "I Got the Sun in the Morning," the dreamy "Moonshine Lullaby," and the marching anthem "There's No Business Like Show Business." Rarely has a Broadway score produced so many standards.

The idea of a Broadway musical about Annie Oakley came from Richard Rodgers and Oscar Hammerstein, the renowned songwriters who also produced shows in New York. Tailor-made for Ethel Merman, *Annie Get Your Gun* was to have a score by Jerome Kern (music) and Dorothy Fields (lyrics) with a script by Fields and her brother Herbert. Kern had been in Hollywood for six years and was anxious to return to New York and work on a Broadway project. But soon after Kern arrived in Manhattan, he passed out on the street and later died of a cerebral hemorrhage. The theater community was in shock and it looked like the Annie Oakley project was finished. But the producers knew that Merman as Annie was bound to be a success so they approached popular songwriter Irving Berlin. Since the arrival of *Oklahoma!* in 1943, the Broadway musical had changed significantly and Berlin thought he couldn't write a show in the new style. Rodgers and Hammerstein convinced Berlin that he could do it, so after a few trial songs the 50-year-old Berlin agreed to *Annie Get Your Gun*. Because Berlin always wrote his own lyrics, Dorothy Fields stayed on as scriptwriter only. Anticipation for the show was high but when it opened, *Annie Get Your Gun* went beyond everyone's expectations and it was a triumph for all concerned.

MGM bought the screen rights for a record $650,000. Most of the stage songs were used in the movie and the script was very faithful to the original, but the Broadway star Ethel Merman was not considered for the screen version. Producer Arthur Freed contracted Judy Garland to play Annie, and she completed the vocal recordings and a few scenes before illness forced her to withdraw. Betty Hutton, who had always played comic supporting roles in film musicals, was given the plum role and she was not shy about grabbing it and giving it her all. Howard Keel, in his movie musical debut, was also in fine form as Frank Butler. There were other casting changes (Frank Morgan was to play Col. Buffalo Bill but he died after a few days of shooting and was replaced by Louis Calhern) and even a director change. Busby Berkeley shot a handful of scenes before he was replaced by George Sidney. One's appreciation of *Annie Get Your Gun* on-screen depends on your reaction to Hutton's broad, funny, full-voiced performance. She is in just about every scene and sings most of the songs so Hutton dominates the musical. The production values are top class throughout and Sidney moves the story along at a good pace. Robert Alton did the choreography, which included a Wild West Show as well as a comic tribal dance for "I'm an Indian, Too." This last number has proven to be offensive to modern audiences because it deals in stereotypic images of Native Americans. Chief Sitting Bull is a wise and sympathetic character in the movie but, because he is played by a white actor (J. Carroll Naish), it also offends some moviegoers. Very rarely were "Indian" characters played by Native Americans in Hollywood until the 1960s so one has to view *Annie Get Your Gun* with that perspective. MGM spent a bundle on the production, all of which it made back when the film was a box office smash.

See also: *The Harvey Girls, Calamity Jane*; Irving Berlin, Betty Hutton, Howard Keel, Arthur Freed biography boxes

FURTHER READING

Arceri, Gene. *Rocking Horse: A Personal Biography of Betty Hutton*. Albany, GA: BearManor Media, 2009.

Eames, John Douglas. *The MGM Story*. New York: Crown Publishers, 1975.

Jablonski, Edward. *Irving Berlin: American Troubadour*. New York: Henry Holt & Co., 1999.

THE GREAT CARUSO

Studio and release date: Metro-Goldwyn-Mayer; April 1951
Producer: Joe Pasternak
Screenplay: Sonia Levien, William Ludwig
Songwriters: Juventino Rosas, Irving Aaronson, Paul Francis Webster, and others (music and lyrics)
Directors: Richard Thorpe, Peter Herman Adler
Musical Directors: Peter Herman Adler, Johnny Green
Cinematographer: Joseph Ruttenberg
Cast: Mario Lanza, Ann Blyth, Dorothy Kirsten, Richard Hageman, Jarmila Novotna, Carl Benton Reid, Eduard Franz
Songs: "The Loveliest Night of the Year"; "'Tis the Last Rose of Summer"; opera selections

In this musical biography of the celebrated Italian tenor Enrico Caruso, the leading role was played by the equally celebrated Mario Lanza in his best and most successful film. As with most bio-pics, *The Great Caruso* fudged the facts and resembled just about every other rags-to-riches film. The boy Caruso (Peter Price) grows up in the slums of Naples and loves music, particularly opera. As an adult (Lanza), he struggles as a singer in the local cafés but no one seems to notice him. Caruso falls in love with the girl Musetta (Yvette Duguay) but her father (Nestor Paiva) does not approve of the relationship. Once Caruso's exceptional singing voice is discovered, he's off to New York where he sings at the Metropolitan Opera and falls in love with the high-society Dorothy Benjamin (Ann Blyth). Her father (Carl Benton Reid) also does not approve of the match but Caruso and Dorothy wed and are happy together as he climbs new heights in international acclamation. Always pushing himself, the 48-year-old Caruso collapses and dies onstage while singing in the opera *Martha*. It was another variation of the Cinderella tale and rarely came close to the truth. (Caruso had a common-law wife, some children, and many mistresses, and when he collapsed onstage he did not die until sometime later.) The temperamental Caruso was portrayed without warts in the movie and Lanza played it all beautifully. Blyth was also in top form as Dorothy, who got to sing the film's biggest hit, "The Loveliest Night of the Year," which Irving Aaronson and Paul Francis Webster adapted from an old Mexican waltz tune. Lanza sang opera selections from Verdi, Puccini, and Leoncavallo, and he was joined by some other notable opera singers.

MGM did not spend a lot of money on the film because the studio thought it would have limited appeal. It was dismissed by the studio as a high-brow musical that gave MGM some class. Imagine MGM's surprise when *The Great Caruso* ended up being one of the top-grossing movies of the year. Much of the success could be attributed to Lanza, who, in his third feature film, had found wide popularity. Also, it seemed moviegoers liked the scenes from the different operas, finding that—taken in small doses—opera was not so painful after all. It turned out that Lanza did more for opera in America than any other singer. The success of *The Great Caruso* prompted Hollywood to make more bio-pics of opera singers, and movie musicals about Marjorie Lawrence, Grace Moore, and Nellie Melba appeared later in the 1950s. Moore was among the handful of opera divas to make movies in the 1930s and 1940s, including Lily Pons, Gladys Swarthout, Lauritz Melchior, Rise Stevens, and Elio Pinza. But none of these created such excitement as Lanza did in his seven musical films.

If a movie about Lanza's life were made, it would resemble *The Great Caruso*. He loved opera as a child growing up in Philadelphia and quit school to pursue a singing career. Instead he ended up working in his grandfather's grocery business. In 1942 Lanza auditioned for conductor Serge Koussevitzky who featured the young singer at a summer concert at Tanglewood. Lanza started recording in the late 1930s and, after serving in World War II, became popular in concerts and opera houses. But when Hollywood beckoned, he went West and was starred in the musical *That Midnight Kiss* (1949). Moviegoers were as entranced as classical music lovers were and Lanza's subsequent musicals were international hits, among them *The Toast of New Orleans* (1950), *Because You're Mine* (1952), and *The Seven Hills of Rome* (1958). But the temperamental singer was difficult to work with, suffering from alcoholism and emotional insecurity, and when he put on too much weight, he was dropped from *The Student Prince* (1954) after recording the soundtrack; actor Edmund Purdom played the title role using Lanza's singing voice. When the great tenor's films did not do well at the box office, he moved to Europe where he made some foreign films and sang in concerts until his premature death by heart attack at the age of 38. It was a tragic life not unlike that of Caruso's. Lanza was different from other celebrated opera singers because he chose Hollywood over the opera world. He was handsome and photogenic, could act, and liked the prestige of being a movie star. But, like Caruso, he was self-destructive. Fortunately he made many records and seven films so we have dynamic evidence of his amazing talent.

FURTHER READING

Bloom, Ken. *Hollywood Musicals: The 101 Greatest Song-and-Dance Movies of All Time*. New York: Black Dog and Leventhal, 2010.

Farkas, Andrew, and Enrico Caruso, Jr. *Enrico Caruso: My Father and My Family*. Montclair, NJ: Amadeus Press, 2003.

Mannering, Derek. *Mario Lanza: Singing to the Gods*. Ramsbury, Wiltshire, GB: Robert Hale Press, 2011.

AN AMERICAN IN PARIS

Studio and release date: Metro-Goldwyn-Mayer; August 1951
Producer: Arthur Freed
Screenplay: Alan Jay Lerner
Songwriters: George Gershwin (music), Ira Gershwin and others (lyrics)
Director: Vincente Minnelli
Choreographer: Gene Kelly
Musical Director: Johnny Green
Cinematographers: Alfred Gilks, John Alton
Cast: Gene Kelly, Leslie Caron, Oscar Levant, Georges Guetary, Nina Foch
Songs: "I Got Rhythm"; "Embraceable You"; " 'S Wonderful"; "Love Is Here to Stay"; "By Strauss"; "I'll Build a Stairway to Paradise"; "Nice Work If You Can Get It"; "I Don't Think I'll Fall in Love Today"; "Liza"

An artsy musical about art and artists, the musical is visually stunning and, thanks to the George Gershwin compositions, musically a treat. Although Gershwin had died in 1937, his music shows up in many films, perhaps none more effectively than in *An American in Paris*. Alan Jay Lerner's original screenplay was concise and smart, leaving plenty of room for the music and for extended dance sequences. Ex-GI Jerry Mulligan (Gene Kelly) remains in Paris after World War II to pursue his dream of becoming an artist. He falls in love with the perfume counter salesgirl Lise Bourvier (Leslie Caron) but she is engaged to the older, dashing Henri Baurel (Georges Guetary), a music hall entertainer who had saved her life while they were fighting in the Resistance movement. Jerry, in turn, is pursued by the art patroness Milo Roberts (Nina Foch) who wants to set him up in his own studio and promote his work. Through a mutual friend, the sardonic pianist Adam Cook (Oscar Levant), Jerry and Henri become friends without knowing they love the same girl. Once Jerry thinks he has lost Lise forever, he imagines himself in a ballet with all of Paris swirling around him. When Jerry returns to reality, he finds that Henri has graciously stepped out of the way so Jerry and Lise can be together. Producer Arthur Freed gave Lerner only the premise of an American artist in Paris

Perhaps no other Hollywood musical is as painterly as *An American in Paris* (1951). Director Vincente Minnelli, who was a Broadway designer before he went to Hollywood, worked with actor-dancer-choreographer Gene Kelly (pictured) on recreating the look of different French artists for particular scenes. The work of Henri de Toulouse-Lautrec was used in this scene from the film's final ballet. (MGM/Photofest)

and told him to devise a screenplay using the music of Gershwin as the score, particularly the symphonic suite "An American in Paris" (1928). The result is a simple but effective story that allows for a variety of Gershwin songs as well as two of his concert pieces. Director Vincente Minnelli, who had started his career as an artist and stage designer, created an artist's view of Paris by filming the musical entirely in a studio and presenting each scene as a painting. This is particularly noticeable in the film's 17-minute "An American in Paris" ballet in which the look of each section is inspired by a different French artist, from Renoir and Utrillo to Dufy and Toulouse-Lautrec. *An American in Paris* looks like no other musical because Paris is seen only as Jerry Mulligan sees it. A variety of Gershwin songs were used, many with lyrics by his brother Ira, and the movie ended up being a salute to the versatility of the composer. Kelly's singing "I Got Rhythm" with a bunch of French kids or his romancing Caron along the banks of the Seine with "Love Is Here to Stay" are a delightful contrast, just as Guetary, Kelly, and Levant

Gene Kelly (1912–1996)   One of the giants of Hollywood musicals, the singer-actor-dancer-director-choreographer was known for his athletic style of dance and his continual experimenting with dance on film. He was born in Pittsburgh, the son of a sales executive and a former actress, and studied economics at Penn State and the University of Pittsburgh. Kelly had taken dance lessons as a child and as an adult worked as a dance instructor to support himself while he pursued acting jobs in New York. His performances in the drama *The Time of Your Life* (1939) and the musical *Pal Joey* (1940) brought wide recognition, and he was brought to Hollywood where he made his screen debut in the musical *For Me and My Gal* (1942), followed by one of the most impressive careers in movie history. Kelly is most remembered for the movies he both choreographed and danced in, such as *Cover Girl* (1944), *Anchors Aweigh* (1945), *The Pirate* (1948), *Words and Music* (1948), *Take Me Out to the Ball Game* (1949), *Summer Stock* (1950), *An American in Paris* (1951), *Brigadoon* (1954), and *What a Way to Go* (1964). He directed as well as choreographed and performed in *On the Town* (1949), *Singin' in the Rain* (1952), *It's Always Fair Weather* (1955), and *Invitation to the Dance* (1956) as well as directing *Hello, Dolly!* (1969). He also acted in nonmusical movies and made many television appearances over the years. Biographies: *Gene Kelly: A Life of Dance and Dreams*, Alvin Yudkoff (1999); *Gene Kelly: A Biography*, Clive Hirschhorn (1985).

clowning with "By Strauss" is balanced by Levant's earnest playing of the "Concerto in F." As for the dancing, many feel that Kelly's choreography and dancing in the film are the finest of his career. The numbers are inventive, stylized, and enchanting. The choreography (and the film itself) has less humor than, say *Singin' in the Rain* (1952), but there is a trancelike beauty to the dancing in this movie that is unforgettable.

The studio heads at MGM were worried about *An American in Paris* from the start. The biggest risk was the long "An American in Paris" ballet that ends the film. MGM didn't think moviegoers would sit still for 17 minutes of no singing or talking. Kelly and Freed argued that the British film *The Red Shoes* (1948) had included a long ballet and the film was a hit in both Britain and the United States. All the same, after filming was finished, MGM wanted to edit or completely cut Kelly's ballet, which had taken a month to film and cost $542,000. Again Freed and Kelly had to convince studio executives that without the ballet, the movie was just another musical romance set in Paris. The ballet remained, the movie received rave reviews, and *An American in Paris* won six Oscars, including best picture. Originally Kelly wanted to make the film in Paris but MGM thought it too expensive so, except for a few location shots that did not involve any of the characters, the movie was filmed on a sound stage. This limitation turned out to be a blessing because the movie is not a realistic view of Paris but an artist's perception. That's what makes *An American in Paris* unique and a one-of-a-kind film.

See also: On the Town, Singin' in the Rain, Funny Face; Gene Kelly, George and Ira Gershwin, Vincente Minnelli, Arthur Freed biography boxes

FURTHER READING

Bloom, Ken. *Hollywood Musicals: The 101 Greatest Song-and-Dance Movies of All Time*. New York: Black Dog and Leventhal, 2010.
Harris, Sue. *An American in Paris.* (BFI Film Classics). London: British Film Institute, 2015.
Levy, Emanuel. *Vincente Minnelli: Hollywood's Dark Dreamer*. New York: St. Martin's Press, 2009.
Pollack, Howard. *George Gershwin: His Life and Work*. Oakland: University of California Press, 2007.

SINGIN' IN THE RAIN

Studio and release date: Metro-Goldwyn-Mayer; March 1952
Producer: Arthur Freed
Screenplay: Betty Comden, Adolph Green
Songwriters: Nacio Herb Brown (music), Arthur Freed (lyrics)
Directors/Choreographers: Gene Kelly, Stanley Donen
Musical Director: Lennie Hayton
Cinematographer: Harold Rosson
Cast: Gene Kelly, Debbie Reynolds, Donald O'Connor, Jean Hagen, Millard Mitchell, Cyd Charisse, Rita Moreno
Songs: "Singin' in the Rain"; "You Were Meant for Me"; "Broadway Melody"; "All I Do Is Dream of You"; "Would You?"; "Make 'Em Laugh"; "I've Got a Feelin' You're Foolin'"; "Good Morning"; "Beautiful Girl"; "Fit as a Fiddle"; "Moses Supposes"

In the opinion of many, this is the best Hollywood musical from the Golden Age. It may or may not be the greatest, but it is probably more fun than any other. *Singin' in the Rain* can be seen as the culmination of what Gene Kelly and Stanley Donen had been experimenting with in their earlier films together. It is not a dance musical, although it has plenty of dancing and even a ballet, but is more plot and character driven. It is also a comic homage to the early days of the talkies,

Singin' in the Rain (1952) is near the top of everyone's list of favorite movie musicals. This tuneful satire about the early days of talking pictures is loaded with memorable scenes and songs. Gene Kelly (left), Donald O'Connor (right) and Debbie Reynolds sing the joyous "Good Morning" as they dance all over the furniture. Kelly co-directed and co-choreographed with Stanley Donen. (MGM/Photofest)

spoofing the era and, at the same time, being accurate about some of the problems Hollywood faced when sound came in. Finally, *Singin' in the Rain* is a musical comedy that is actually funny. There are no dull scenes or annoying plot devices used only to keep the story going. Both dialogue and musical numbers are equally entertaining, something that happens rarely in even the best musicals of the period.

The original screenplay concerns silent screen idol Don Lockwood (Gene Kelly) who meets the chorus girl Kathy Selden (Debbie Reynolds) who dreams of being a serious actress. She scoffs at Don's dashing but phony film performances but even she has to earn money by popping out of cakes at Hollywood parties. Each having deflated each other's ego somewhat, Don and Kathy fall in love. Suddenly *The Jazz Singer* opens and Hollywood rushes to make talking pictures. The silent film Don is making is to be reshot with sound but the studio is worried about what to do with the beautiful but nasal-sounding star Lina Lamont (Jean Hagen). Don and his dancing buddy Cosmo Brown (Donald O'Connor) come up with a solution: Kathy is hired to do Lina's dialogue and singing, and the track is used to

Debbie Reynolds (b. 1932)   A perky blonde actress-singer-dancer who was part of the last generation of stars during the Golden Age of Hollywood musicals, her career included stage, nightclubs, television, and nonmusical films. She was born in El Paso, Texas, and as a teenager won some beauty pageants, which led to a movie contract. Reynolds was noticed in her first screen musical, *The Daughter of Rosie O'Grady* (1950), followed by featured roles in *Three Little Words* (1950), *Two Weeks with Love* (1950), and *Mr. Imperium* (1951). She graduated to adult roles with *Singin' in the Rain* (1952), followed by *Skirts Ahoy* (1952), *Give a Girl a Break* (1952), *I Love Melvin* (1952), *Athena* (1954), *Hit the Deck* (1955), *Bundle of Joy* (1956), *The Unsinkable Molly Brown* (1964), and *The Singing Nun* (1966). Reynolds was still making films in the new century. Autobiographies: *Unsinkable*, with Dorian Hannaway (2013); *Debbie: My Life*, with David Patrick Columbia (1988).

replace the voice for Lina on-screen. The movie musical is made and at the premiere the audience cheers Lina's beautiful singing voice. When it is revealed that Kathy is the real voice, she gets a contract and stars in the studio's next film musical with her sweetheart Don. Betty Comden and Adolph Green wrote the satirical screenplay using the Nacio Herb Brown-Arthur Freed catalogue of songs as their inspiration. It is a splendid script that bounces along easily, each scene punctuated with a song. The difficulties in making early talkies were presented hilariously and accurately and the result was a good-natured spoof of Hollywood in general. Newcomer Reynolds was a sparkling revelation, Kelly was at his best being both silly and romantic, and Hagen gives one of the funniest supporting performances in Hollywood history as the nasty, irritating Lina. The plot found room for O'Connor to give his most nimble performance ever and for naughty flapper Cyd Charisse to make quite an impact in a sultry dance duet with Kelly.

Even without the musical numbers, this film would have been a comic treasure but the songs and dances are the crowning touch. There was a nonsense ditty "Moses (Supposes)" written by Comden, Green, and Roger Edens for the film and a new Brown-Freed number, "Make 'Em Laugh," for O'Connor to perform in one of the movie's most memorable scenes. The rest of the score was comprised of old Brown-Freed favorites that were so marvelously staged by codirector-choreographers Kelly and Donen that the songs are usually remembered for this film rather than their initial screen appearances. The title number was the most famous case in point. Kelly joyously splashing down the street in "Singin' in the Rain" is movie musical heaven. Although the song had been heard in a handful of movies since it was introduced in *Hollywood Revue of 1929*, it is Kelly singing and dancing in

Donald O'Connor (1925–2003)   An energetic and agile song-and-dance man who dazzled stage and screen audiences with his sprightly dancing, he lit up many movie musicals for 20 years. He was born in Chicago into a show business family and performed in vaudeville as a child. At the age of 12, O'Connor made his movie musical debut in 1937 then played juvenile roles in such nonmusicals as *Tom Sawyer Detective* (1938) and *Beau Geste* (1939). While still a teenager, O'Connor was featured in such musicals as *Sing You Sinners* (1937), *On Your Toes* (1939), *Private Buckaroo* (1942), *When Johnny Comes Marching Home* (1942), *Top Man* (1943), *Follow the Boys* (1944), *The Merry Monahans* (1944), and *Bowery to Broadway* (1944). With his ever-youthful looks, O'Connor was able to play young men for many years and, while he was cast in major roles in nonmusicals such as the *Francis the Talking Mule* series of comedies, he usually was in secondary roles in musicals. His most remembered performances were in *Singin' in the Rain* (1952), *I Love Melvin* (1952), *Call Me Madam* (1953), *There's No Business Like Show Business* (1954), and *Anything Goes* (1956). O'Connor made many television appearances, including his own series, and was on Broadway in *Bring Back Birdie* (1981) and the 1983 revival of *Show Boat*.

the rain that is unforgettable. Other memorable songs used include the sprightly dance number "The Wedding of the Painted Doll," the rhapsodic "Would You?," the dreamy "You Are My Lucky Star," the lively "Fit as a Fiddle," the flowing ballad "You Were Meant for Me," and the wistful "All I Do Is Dream of You." The big "Broadway Rhythm" ballet at the end was more playful than Kelly's usual long dance pieces and reaffirmed the satirical tone of the whole picture. Surprisingly, *Singin' in the Rain* was only moderately successful in its first release. Over the years it has achieved cult status and represents the finest hour of its stars and the whole Freed unit.

See also: *The Jazz Singer, Hollywood Revue of 1929, On the Town*; Gene Kelly, Stanley Donen, Debbie Reynolds, Donald O'Connor, Nacio Herb Brown, Arthur Freed, Betty Comden and Adolph Green biography boxes

FURTHER READING

Fordin, Hugh. *MGM's Greatest Musicals: The Arthur Freed Unit*. Boston: Da Capo Press, 1996.

Reynolds, Debbie, and Dorian Hannaway. *Unsinkable: A Memoir*. New York: William Morrow, 2013.

Silverman, Stephen M. *Dancing on the Ceiling: Stanley Donen and His Movies*. New York: Knopf, 1996.

Wollen, Peter. *Singin' in the Rain*. (BFI Film Classics). London: British Film Institute, 2008.

HANS CHRISTIAN ANDERSEN

Studio and release date: Goldwyn/RKO; November 1952
Producer: Samuel Goldwyn
Screenplay: Moss Hart
Songwriter: Frank Loesser (music and lyrics)
Director: Charles Vidor
Choreographer: Roland Petit
Musical Director: Walter Scharf
Cinematographer: Harry Stradling
Cast: Danny Kaye, Joey Walsh, Zizi Jeanmarie, Erik Bruhn, Roland Petit
Songs: "Wonderful Copenhagen"; "Anywhere I Wander"; "No Two People";
   "The Inch Worm"; "Thumbelina"; "The Ugly Duckling"; "I'm Hans Christian
   Andersen"; "The King's New Clothes"

There were so many factual errors in this musical biography of the beloved Danish storyteller that the country of Denmark insisted that a prologue be added saying the movie was a fairy tale version of Andersen's life. Independent producer Samuel Goldwyn had wanted to make a movie about the renowned storyteller for many years, commissioning over a dozen different screenplays over time. Having discovered Danny Kaye and bringing him to Hollywood, Goldwyn knew that he was the ideal actor to play Andersen. He then convinced noted playwright Moss Hart to write yet another screenplay tailored to Kaye's talents. Goldwyn then spent over $4 million on the production, $14,000 just on shoes. *Hans Christian Andersen* turned out to be one of Goldwyn's biggest hits, bringing in over $6 million on its first release. Yet the fairy tale–like movie doesn't feel like a Hollywood blockbuster. At times it has the tone of a European art film, such as *The Red Shoes* (1948). At the same time, there is also a Broadway quality to the movie because of the marvelous score by Broadway veteran composer Frank Loesser. *Hans Christian Andersen* is not like other bio-pics with the usual rags-to-riches plot. The fanciful tone of Andersen's stories seems to have rubbed off on the film's creators, making it unique in many ways.

   Shoe cobbler Hans (Kaye) is an unwanted distraction for the children in his little village, telling them stories when they should be in school. Some of the elders of the town like Hans but admit that he is a nuisance and try to stop Hans' storytelling. Preferring fiction to shoes, Hans and his young apprentice Peter (Joey Walsh) travel to the big city of Copenhagen. He finds work there making shoes for the famous ballerina Doro (Zizi Jeanmarie) and soon is in love with her. His affection is not returned because she still loves her husband, the temperamental Niels (Farley Granger), the two of them quarreling all the time. Doro stars in the ballet "The Little Mermaid" based on one of Hans' stories, but he doesn't get to see it because on opening Niels locks him in a closet to keep him away from Doro. The ballet is a big success and Doro and Niels are happily reunited. Realizing his

Frank Loesser (1910–1969)   A versatile songwriter who contributed to many film musicals in the 1940s without much recognition, he later found fame on Broadway. He was born in New York and grew up in a musical family, his father a piano teacher and his brother Arthur later became a respected concert pianist. Loesser wrote popular songs as a child then as an adult worked as a newspaper reporter before writing sketches and lyrics for vaudeville acts, radio shows, and summer resorts. He went to Hollywood in 1936 and wrote lyrics for such musicals as *College Swing* (1938), *St. Louis Blues* (1939), *Man About Town* (1939), *Destry Rides Again* (1939), *Buck Benny Rides Again* (1940), *Sis Hopkins* (1941), *Kiss the Boys Goodbye* (1941), *True to the Army* (1942), *Sweater Girl* (1942), *Seven Days' Leave* (1942), *Happy Go Lucky* (1943), and *Thank Your Lucky Stars* (1943). Loesser's music and lyric for the hit song "Praise the Lord and Pass the Ammunition" prompted him to write his own music, and he did so for the rest of his career. His Broadway shows, most of which were later filmed, are *Where's Charley?* (1948), *Guys and Dolls* (1950), *The Most Happy Fella* (1956), *Greenwillow* (1960), and *How to Succeed in Business Without Really Trying* (1961). Loesser continued his ties with Hollywood, writing songs for the musicals *Neptune's Daughter* (1949), *Red, Hot and Blue* (1949), and *Hans Christian Andersen* (1952). Loesser was an eclectic songwriter who seemed as inspired in slick Broadway musical comedy as in Italian opera and rustic folk music. Memoir: *A Most Remarkable Fella: Frank Loesser and the Guys and Dolls in His Life: A Portrait by His Daughter,* Susan Loesser (2000).

love for Doro was a fairy tale, Hans returns home and decides to write stories rather than make shoes. It may have been an unexciting story, but it had its charm and provided Kaye the chance to play a real character instead of the clown roles he was usually offered. Many consider it Kaye's finest performance.

Similarly, Loesser wrote his best screen score for *Hans Christian Andersen*. The movie is filled with memorable songs, such as the rousing waltz "Wonderful Copenhagen"; the dreamy "Anywhere I Wander"; the tuneful duet "No Two People"; the haunting "Inch Worm"; and some delightful story-songs based on Andersen's stories, such as "Thumbelina," "The Ugly Duckling," and "The King's New Clothes." Perhaps the musical highlight of the film was not a song but the elaborate, stylistic ballet "The Little Mermaid," choreographed by Roland Petit who also performed in it. The 17-minute sequence may have been inspired by Gene Kelly's ballets in *On the Town* (1949), *An American in Paris* (1951), and *Singin' in the Rain* (1952), yet Petit's ballet had its own distinctive look and feel. The sequence took weeks to film and cost $400,000, but Goldwyn's gamble paid off because it was a masterful piece of dance and the centerpiece of the movie.

Loesser's songwriting career moved in reverse order of most composers or lyricists. While just about all of America's popular songwriters started on Broadway then moved to Hollywood in the Depression, Loesser first found modest success in Tinseltown, writing lyrics for good songs in mostly B movies. By the 1940s he was regarded as a first-rate composer and lyricist, even winning an Oscar for his song "Baby, It's Cold Outside" in 1949. He went to Broadway in 1948 and scored a series of hits over a 20-year period. After the success of Loesser's *Where's Charley?* (1948) and *Guys and Dolls* (1950) on Broadway, Goldwyn brought him back to Hollywood for *Hans Christian Andersen*, but after it was made, Loesser returned to Broadway and scored no more films. Songwriters were treated better in New York than in Tinseltown, so Hollywood lost one of its best composer-lyricists to the stage.

See also: *An American in Paris, The Little Mermaid, Frozen*; Danny Kaye, Frank Loesser biography boxes

FURTHER READING

Berg, A. Scott. *Goldwyn: A Biography.* New York: Riverhead Books, 1998.
Koenig, David. *Danny Kaye: King of Jesters.* Irvine, CA: Bonaventure Press, 2012.
Loesser, Susan. *A Most Remarkable Fella: Frank Loesser and the Guys and Dolls in His Life.* New York: Donald I. Fine, Inc., 1993.

GENTLEMEN PREFER BLONDES

Studio and release date: 20th Century Fox; June 1953
Producer: Sol C. Siegel
Screenplay: Charles Lederer, based on the 1949 stage script and the 1925 novel by Anita Loos
Songwriters: Jule Styne, Hoagy Carmichael (music), Leo Robin, Harold Adamson (lyrics)
Director: Howard Hawks
Choreographer: Jack Cole
Musical Director: Lionel Newman
Cinematographer: Harry Wild
Cast: Marilyn Monroe, Jane Russell, Charles Coburn, Tommy Noonan, Elliott Reid, Taylor Holmes, George Winslow, Norma Varden
Songs: "Diamonds Are a Girl's Best Friend"; "A Little Girl from Little Rock"; "Bye Bye Baby"; "Ain't There Anyone Here for Love?"; "When Love Goes Wrong"

First a best-selling novel, then a silent film, then a play, then a Broadway musical, and finally a movie musical, *Gentlemen Prefer Blondes* has a long history. It also has a quintessential American comic character: gold digger Lorelei Lee. Anita Loos created Lorelei in 1925 and in some ways the flapper character epitomized the Roaring Twenties. The novel has remained in print ever since and Lorelei has captivated the public in just about every media. In 1926 she shone on Broadway in a play version and two years later was on the silent screen. In 1949 *Gentlemen Prefer Blondes* was musicalized on Broadway with success, making a star out of Carol Channing. Finally the 1953 screen version of the musical offered Marilyn Monroe as Lorelei, and the actress gave one of her most beguiling performances. Since the original novel consisted of a series of entries in Lorelei's journal, adapting the material for the stage and screen has been problematic. Also, the novel is episodic rather than linear, so each adaptation picks and chooses its own scenes and characters. But through it all, Lorelei is the main attraction.

The screenplay for the movie musical varies only slightly from the Broadway script. Lorelei (Monroe) and her pal Dorothy (Jane Russell) set off for Europe, all expenses paid by Lorelei's "daddy," the wealthy button manufacturer Gus Esmond (Tommy Noonan). On the ocean liner crossing the Atlantic, Lorelei is attracted to the stuffy Brit Henry Spofford (George Winslow) because of a diamond tiara of Mrs. Spofford's that she has her eye on. In Paris, wealthy Sir Beekman (Charles Coburn) hires the detective Ernie Malone (Elliott Reid) to keep Lorelei away from his son. The two girls get caught up in intrigues with lawyers and diamonds, but all ends happily when they perform together in a nightclub show and Gus forgives all of Lorelei's indiscretions. It was an efficient screenplay, but much of the flavor of the tale was lost when Fox decided to move the plot from the 1920s to the present. It is a very stylish, professional movie, but something seems missing when the setting was 1953. Only three of the stage songs by Jule Styne (music) and Leo Robin (lyrics) were used in the movie but they were splendid: the marching credo "Diamonds Are a Girl's Best Friend," the lullaby-like "Bye, Bye, Baby," and the sassy character number "A Little Girl From Little Rock." Two new songs by Hoagy Carmichael (music) and Harold Adamson (lyrics)—"Ain't There Anybody Here for Love?" and "When Love Goes Wrong (Nothing Goes Right)"—were also first rate. Jack Cole was the clever choreographer and Howard Hawks directed the Sol C. Siegel production. 20th Century Fox spent a fortune on the lavish film, but it turned out to be a box office diamond mine all its own.

The screen version of *Gentlemen Prefer Blondes* was built as a showcase for Monroe and she did not disappoint. Yet she was not the original choice for the film. The reigning blonde in Hollywood in the 1940s was Betty Grable and she was still a major star in 1953. She demanded a hefty $150,000 to play Lorelei and the studio was willing to pay it until the movie *Niagara* was released. This was a breakthrough performance for Monroe and, although she did not sing or dance in the melodrama, it was clear that she had the sex appeal and the screen presence to star in a musical. The Lorelei that ended up on-screen was more Hollywood's vision of Monroe than it was Loos' original character. Monroe never looked more glamorous or wore better clothes than she did in *Gentlemen Prefer Blondes* so for many this is the ultimate Monroe film. Fox planned to dub her singing with the voice of Marni Nixon, but Nixon thought Monroe's thin but expressive singing voice was ideal for Lorelei. Nixon convinced the studio to let her dub just a few high notes in "Diamonds Are a Girl's Best Friend" and allow Monroe to carry the rest of the score. It was a wise decision because Monroe's rendition of the songs is uniquely hers. Perhaps something was lost when *Gentlemen Prefer Blondes* went from a satiric musical comedy about the sexes to a Marilyn Monroe extravaganza, but what was gained in the transition is worth cherishing.

See Also: Gold Diggers of 1933

FURTHER READING

Spoto, Donald. *Marilyn Monroe: The Biography*. New York: Dansker Press, 2014.
Taylor, Theodore. *Jule: The Story of Composer Jule Styne*. New York: Random House, 1979.
Thomas, Tony, and Aubrey Solomon. *The Films of 20th Century-Fox*. Secaucus, NJ: Citadel Press, 1979.

THE BAND WAGON

Studio and release date: Metro-Goldwyn-Mayer; July 1953
Producer: Arthur Freed
Screenplay: Betty Comden, Adolph Green
Songwriters: Arthur Schwartz (music), Howard Dietz (lyrics)
Director: Vincente Minnelli
Choreographer: Michael Kidd
Musical Director: Adolph Deutsch
Cinematographer: Harry Jackson
Cast: Fred Astaire, Cyd Charisse, Oscar Levant, Nanette Fabray, Jack Buchanan, James Mitchell, Thurston Hall
Songs: "That's Entertainment"; "Dancing in the Dark"; "Triplets"; "By Myself"; "I Guess I'll Have to Change My Plan"; "A Shine on Your Shoes"; "I Love Louisa"; "Louisiana Hayride"; "Something to Remember You By"; "High and Low"; "New Sun in the Sky"

One of the most fondly remembered Broadway revues of the Depression was *The Band Wagon* (1931). Because it had no through plot, the show was never filmed. But songs by Howard Dietz (lyrics) and Arthur Schwartz (music) from that musical and their other Broadway shows provided the score for this stylish Fred Astaire musical. The movie is mostly satirical, poking fun at pretentious musical theater, backstage movie musicals, detective thrillers, and "let's put on a show" formula films. The screenplay by Betty Comden and Adolph Green has some of the same qualities of their script for *Singin' in the Rain* (1952). Also like that film, the writers were commissioned to concoct a musical using the catalogue of old songs by an established songwriting team. If the script and the songs in *The Band Wagon* are not quite as good as those in *Singin' in the Rain*, they come pretty close.

The song-and-dance man Tony Hunter (Astaire) is washed up in show business, getting older and the new style of shows passing him by. Needing a hit comeback vehicle on Broadway, he enlists his songwriter friends Lily (Nanette Fabray) and Lester Marton (Oscar Levant) to write a tuneful score that will highlight his talents. He also convinces the popular ballerina Gabrielle Gerard (Cyd Charisse) to be his leading lady and hires the temperamental but brilliant director Jeffrey Cordova (Jack Buchanan) to stage the show. But Cordova turns the piece into a ponderous musical based on the German *Faust* legend and the musical flops out of town. Once everyone realizes the importance of "entertainment," they rework the show into a light musical comedy revue and it's a smash. Comden and Green not only wrote in many show biz jokes, they patterned the characters of Lily and Lester after themselves. Producer Arthur Freed hired Dietz and Schwartz to write "That's Entertainment," the movie's only new song. The rest of the score came from various Broadway revues the team had scored in the 1930s and 1940s. Musical highlights include Astaire and Charisse gliding through a moonlit Central Park to the strains of "Dancing in the Dark," Buchanan and Astaire doing a debonair soft-shoe to "I Guess I'll Have to Change My Plan," Astaire and LeRoy Daniels tapping through a Times Square penny arcade to "A Shine on Your Shoes," and the hilarious "Triplets" with Astaire, Fabray, and Buchanan howling as three obnoxious infants. The musical climaxes with a modern mock ballet "The Girl Hunt" in which Astaire, speaking the sly first-person narration, plays a hard-boiled private eye caught up in a case of bad women and intrigue in a crime-ridden dive. The extended number not only spoofed the then-popular Mickey Spillane crime novels but was a wry commentary on the arty ballets Hollywood had recently given the public, such as those in *An American in Paris* (1951) and *Hans Christian Andersen* (1952). Michael Kidd was the film's expert choreographer, and the performances throughout were superb. Before *The Band Wagon*, Astaire had been considering retirement, feeling he was no longer able to keep up with Gene Kelly and the younger generation. The success of this film revitalized his career.

When the 1974 documentary *That's Entertainment* prompted interest in the MGM musicals of the Golden Age, the song "That's Entertainment" also became popular again. In fact, the sly musical commentary on show biz became the unofficial theme song for the Hollywood musicals of the past. Because *That's Entertainment* was released in movie theaters, many moviegoers saw scenes from these

> **Cyd Charisse** (1921–2008)   The long-legged dancer was featured in many movie musicals before she became a star. She was born in Amarillo, Texas, and as a child took ballet lessons. As a teenager, Charisse danced with the Ballet Russe and was spotted by Hollywood agents. After playing supporting roles or specialty numbers in such musicals as *The Harvey Girls* (1946), *Ziegfeld Follies* (1946), *Till the Clouds Roll By* (1946), *Singin' in the Rain* (1952), and *Deep in My Heart* (1954), she became a leading lady in such beloved musicals as *The Band Wagon* (1953), *Brigadoon* (1954), *It's Always Fair Weather* (1955), and *Silk Stockings* (1956). When less and less movie musicals were made in the 1960s, Charisse played dramatic roles in films and on television but was more successful appearing in nightclubs with her husband Tony Martin. Late in her career, Charisse turned to the stage, appearing in a 1972 Australian production of *No, No, Nanette* and on Broadway in *Grand Hotel* in 1990. Autobiography: *The Two of Us,* with Martin (1976).

great musicals on the big screen for the first time. Later in the 1970s, videotapes first became available and then later DVDs and movie lovers could rent or own their favorite films. But what was viewed on the home television was not what audiences saw in movie theaters in the past. So in some ways the new technology has made it more difficult to see old movies as they were meant to be seen.

See also: *An American in Paris, Singin' in the Rain, Hans Christian Andersen*; Vincente Minnelli, Arthur Freed, Fred Astaire, Cyd Charisse, Betty Comden and Adolph Green biography boxes

FURTHER READING

Bloom, Ken. *Hollywood Musicals: The 101 Greatest Song-and-Dance Movies of All Time*. New York: Black Dog and Leventhal, 2010.

Charisse, Cyd, and Tony Martin with Dick Kleiner. *The Two of Us*. New York: Mason/Charter, 1976.

Harvey, Stephen. *Directed By Vincent Minnelli*. New York: HarperCollins, 1990.

THE 5,000 FINGERS OF DR. T

Studio and release date: Columbia; July 1953
Producer: Stanley Kramer
Screenplay: Dr. Seuss, Allan Scott
Songwriters: Friedrich Hollaender (music), Dr. Seuss (lyrics)

Director: Roy Rowland
Choreographer: Eugene Loring
Musical Director: Morris Stoloff
Cinematographer: Franz Planer
Cast: Tommy Rettig, Hans Conreid, Peter Lind Hayes, Mary Healy, Jack
    Heasley, Noel Cravat
Songs: "Because We're Kids"; "Dressing Song"; "Dream Stuff"; "Ten Happy
    Fingers"; "Get-Together Weather"; "Terwilliker Academy"; "The Dungeon Song"

A one-of-a-kind movie that looks and feels like no other, this Dr. Seuss musical fantasy, once viewed, cannot be forgotten. Theodore Geisel, better known as Dr. Seuss, co-wrote the original screenplay about young Bartholomew Collins (Tommy Rettig) who is forced to practice the piano when he would rather be outside playing baseball. When the youth dozes off, he dreams that his piano teacher Mr. Terwilliker (Hans Conreid) becomes the diabolical Dr. T who has imprisoned 500 boys in his dungeon and forces them to play on long curling pianos that only Dr. Seuss could dream up. Also in the prison are non-piano musicians who have grown green and moldy and finally break out in song and dance and a pair of roller-skating twins who are attached by the same long beard. Dr. T kidnaps Bartholomew's widowed mother Heloise (Mary Healy) so the boy convinces the kindly plumber August Zabladowski (Peter Lind Hayes) to help rescue her. The day of the giant concert arrives, Dr. T dresses up to conduct the 500 boys but chaos breaks out, the boy pianists revolt, and August and Bartholomew escape with his mother. Then Bartholomew awakes from the dream to find that the plumber and his mother are in love. The very distinctive film doesn't always work, but Rudolph Sternad's optical illusion sets (inspired from the illustrated Seuss books), Conried's zany performance as Dr. T, and the tuneful songs by Friedrich Hollaender (music) and Geisel (lyrics) help one get through the weak spots. "Because We're Kids" is a quiet but poignant song about how children are neglected or dismissed by adults, "The Dressing Song (My Do-Me-Do Duds)" is a hilarious list song that Dr. T sings using delicious Seuss lyrics, the anthem "Terwilliker Academy" is an oddball pastiche of a school song, and "Ten Happy Fingers" is catchy in the distinct Seuss style.

In 1953 the children's books by Dr. Seuss were already very popular and several of them had already been turned into film shorts. The first one, *Put on the Spout,* was released back in 1931. Among the many subsequent shorts were *'Neath the Bababa Tree* (1931), *Horton Hatches an Egg* (1942), *The 500 Hats of Bartholomew Cubbins* (1943), *And to Think That I Saw It on Mulberry Street* (1944), and *Gerald McBoing-Boing* (1950). Yet his first feature film, *The 5,000 Fingers of Dr. T,* was not based on an existing story. Producer Stanley Kramer commissioned Seuss to write an original screenplay for a movie musical in the style of the famous books. All of the previous film versions had been animated, but Kramer wanted to bring Seuss' imaginative look to the screen with live actors, real sets and costumes, and songs. The result was a very expensive production with dozens of bizarre sets that defied logic and gravity. The costumes and makeup also were a challenge, especially since Kramer insisted that the movie be in color. The budget did not allow for 500 boy extras so 150 were hired and many days of chaotic confusion resulted when director Roy Rowland tried to shoot the scenes where the boys arrive, play the pianos, then break out in a riot. Waiting under the hot lights for hours, one of the boys vomited on the piano and the smell set off a chain reaction of upset and sick extras. Also problematic were some of the special effects, which could not be computerized in 1953. The intricate ballet performed by the mold-covered prisoners was another nightmare to film but it proved to be an oddball highlight of the film.

The 5,000 Fingers of Dr. T received mixed reviews when it opened and did not do well at the box office. Some audiences found the quirky film fascinating but, mostly, the public stayed away because the title was not that of a recognized Seuss story. One of the difficulties with the movie is the question of just who the movie is for. Much of it is too dark and confusing for young children, and even adults are baffled by the dark humor in the piece. Today such films are popular because of the screen adaptations of Roald Dahl's books. The musical *Willy Wonka and the Chocolate Factory* has a similar offbeat sensibility as *The 5,000 Fingers of Dr. T*, yet that 1971 movie was very popular. Geisel/Seuss was so discouraged with the reaction to his first feature film that for the rest of his movie and television career he stuck to adaptations of his well-known stories. Since the writer was so prolific, this was not a problem for future screen versions. To date there are over 70 movies and TV specials based on Seuss stories. Several of them are musicals, as with the 1966 classic *How the Grinch Stole Christmas*.

See Also: *Willy Wonka and the Chocolate Factory, The Nightmare Before Christmas*

FURTHER READING

Dick, Bernard, ed. *Columbia Pictures: Portrait of a Studio*. Lexington: University of Kentucky Press, 1991.

Morgan, Judith, and Neil Morgan. *Dr. Seuss and Mr. Geisel: A Biography*. Boston: Da Capo Press, 1996.

KISS ME, KATE

Studio and release date: Metro-Goldwyn-Mayer; October 1953
Producer: Jack Cummings
Screenplay: Dorothy Kingsley, based on the 1948 stage script by Bella and Sam Spewack
Songwriter: Cole Porter (music and lyrics)

Director: George Sidney
Choreographers: Hermes Pan, Bob Fosse
Musical Directors: André Previn, Sol Chaplin
Cinematographer: Charles Rosher
Cast: Kathryn Grayson, Howard Keel, Ann Miller, Tommy Rall, Keenan Wynn, James Whitmore, Bobby Van, Bob Fosse
Songs: "Too Darn Hot"; "Wunderbar"; "Brush Up Your Shakespeare"; "From This Moment On"; "Always True to You (in My Fashion)"; "So in Love"; "I Hate Men"; "We Open in Venice"; "Why Can't You Behave?"; "Tom, Dick or Harry"; "Where Is the Life That Late I Led?"; "I've Come to Wive it Wealthily in Padua"; "Were Thine That Special Face"

Cole Porter's best (and most successful) Broadway musical came to the screen with just about all of its score and story intact, making it the most faithful of all Porter films. *Kiss Me, Kate* boasts one of the best musical scripts ever written for Broadway. One might say *two* of the best scripts because the musical uses double plotting. While a musical version of Shakespeare's *The Taming of the Shrew* is performing in a Baltimore theater, the stars Fred Graham and Lilli Vanessi, who used to be married to each other, play Petruchio and Kate and battle both on and offstage. Also in the cast are sweethearts Lois Lane and Bill Calhoun who are plagued by Bill's gambling addiction. When Bill signs Fred's name to an IOU for some gangsters, two henchmen come to the theater to collect the money from Fred and end up helping him keep Lilli from walking out on the show. Just as Shakespeare's story comes to a happy ending, Fred and Lilli are reconciled by the finale of both shows. Bella and Sam Spewack wrote the brilliant script in which the modern story comments on the Shakespearean one, and the other way around as well. Even more accomplished, one gets the sense of having seen the whole Shakespeare tale when in effect only a few scenes/songs were shown. The writers also created backstage characters that are just as much fun as the Shakespearean characters. The Spewacks' two comic henchmen, with no direct parallels to the Elizabeth tale, are among the funniest supporting characters of the era, speaking in a genteel slang that foreshadows the type of comic gangsters in *Guys and Dolls* (1950).

Porter wrote two scores for *Kiss Me, Kate*; a pseudo-Elizabethan set of songs for the musical of *The Taming of the Shrew* that is taking place onstage and a contemporary score for the backstage story. The two scores are very distinct yet are all part of a whole because the *Shrew* songs are filled with anachronisms, as if Porter was making fun of what the musical theater does to the classics. Yet both scores have their serious and comic songs, their choral numbers, and their love songs. The way the two scores balance each other is one of the many remarkable aspects of *Kiss Me, Kate*. While numbers such as the ballad "So in Love," the jazzy "Too Darn Hot," and the waltzing "Wunderbar" have found success outside of the

Cole Porter (1891–1964)   The renowned American songwriter known for the sophistication in both his romantic and comic songs, he had equally successful Broadway and Hollywood careers. He was born into a wealthy family in Peru, Indiana, and was educated at Yale where his football fight songs and campus productions were legendary. Porter studied law at Harvard but he had always known that music would be his life. Some of his songs were interpolated into Broadway musicals in the 1910s, and he did not get much attention until his song "Let's Do It (Let's Fall in Love)" was heard in *Paris* (1928). Among his other notable stage works were *Fifty Million Frenchmen* (1929), *The New Yorkers* (1930), *Gay Divorce* (1932), *Anything Goes* (1934), *Jubilee* (1935), *Red, Hot and Blue!* (1936), *You Never Know* (1938), *Leave It to Me!* (1938), *DuBarry Was a Lady* (1939), *Let's Face It!* (1941), *Something for the Boys* (1943), *Kiss Me, Kate* (1948), *Can-Can* (1953), and *Silk Stockings* (1955). Although most of Porter's stage musicals were filmed, often the scores were abridged and songs by others were usually added. Yet he wrote some sparkling original scores for Hollywood, including *Born to Dance* (1936), *Rosalie* (1937), *Broadway Melody of 1940*, *You'll Never Get Rich* (1941), *The Pirate* (1948), *High Society* (1956), and *Les Girls* (1957). Porter's lyrics have a breezy elegance, a farcical wit, and sometimes a romantic yearning that is almost painful. His music tended toward the exotic and the Latin sound. Autobiography: *The Cole Porter Story, As Told to Richard G. Hubler* (1965); biographies: *Cole Porter*, William McBrien (2000); *Cole Porter: The Life That Late He Led*, George Eells (1967).

context of the show, the score is amazingly integrated with the script. This is particularly impressive when one considers that for 25 years Porter had been writing scores for musical comedies in which such integration was not necessary. After the change in musical structure, brought on by *Oklahoma!* (1943), Porter confessed that the theater had passed him by and he stuck to writing for the movies. But given an excellent script, Porter proved that he could write a score in the Rodgers and Hammerstein model and still have it sparkle like his old songs did. Critics immediately recognized the development in his work and cheered it. *Kiss Me, Kate* ran a happy 1,070 performances on Broadway, by far the biggest hit of Porter's stage career.

MGM did not tinker too much with the original when *Kiss Me, Kate* was filmed in 1953. The screenplay by Dorothy Kingsley added an awkward opening scene that took place away from the theater, giving Lois (Ann Miller) the chance to do a vigorous tap version of "Too Darn Hot." The rest of the film is set in the theater. MGM, like other studios, was coping with the predominance of television and embraced different gimmicks to compete with the small screen. So *Kiss Me, Kate* was filmed in 3-D and director George Sidney sometimes had characters tossing objects at the camera to get the three-dimensional effect. Soon the 3-D fad of the 1950s faded, and most moviegoers since then have never seen the 3-D version. The movie was cast effectively. Howard Keel and Kathryn Grayson were in full voice and full bluster as the battling couple onstage and offstage, Miller and Tommy Rall shone as the secondary couple, and the supporting cast was first rate, particularly Keenan Wynn and James Whitmore as the two gangsters. Hermes Pan was the choreographer but dancer Bob Fosse got to stage one new Porter number, "From This Moment On," which was added to the score. The best songs from Broadway made it to the screen. In addition to the already mentioned numbers, there was the comic duet "Brush Up Your Shakespeare," the clever "Where Is the Life That Late I Led?," the rousing "Another Op'nin', Another Show," and the sly "Always True to You in My Fashion." *Kiss Me, Kate* is one of those happy exceptions when a dazzling Broadway show was brought to the screen without losing its luster.

See also: *Broadway Melody of 1940, Oklahoma!*; Cole Porter, Howard Keel, Ann Miller, Hermes Pan, Bob Fosse biography boxes

FURTHER READING

Eells, George. *The Life That Late He Led: A Biography of Cole Porter*. New York: J. P. Putnam's Sons, 1967.

Keel, Howard. *Only Make Believe: My Life in Show Business*. Fort Lee, NJ: Barricade Books, Inc., 2005.

Thomas, Lawrence B. *The MGM Years*. New York: Arlington House, 1971.

CALAMITY JANE

Studio and release date: Warner Brothers; November 1953
Producer: William Jacobs
Screenplay: James O'Hanlon
Songwriters: Sammy Fain (music), Paul Francis Webster (lyrics)
Director: David Butler
Choreographer: Jack Donohue
Musical Director: Ray Heindorf
Cinematographer: Wilfred M. Cline
Cast: Doris Day, Howard Keel, Allyn Ann McLerie, Philip Carey, Dick Wesson, Paul Harvey, Chubby Johnson

Songs: "Secret Love"; "Just Blew in from the Windy City"; The Deadwood
   Stage"; Hive Full of Honey"; "The Black Hills of Dakota"; "A Woman's
   Touch"; "Keep It Under Your Hat"; "It's Harry I'm Planning to Marry";
   "Higher Than a Hawk"; "I Can Do Without You"; "Introducing Henry Miller"

A frontier musical about a gunslinging spitfire from the Wild West, it gave Doris
Day the opportunity to cut loose as she rarely was allowed to. *Calamity Jane* was
also Warner Brothers' attempt to come up with its version of the popular *Annie
Get Your Gun,* which had been a smash hit on Broadway in 1946 and as an MGM
film in 1950. While the plot and the score could not rival that Irving Berlin classic, *Calamity Jane* had a lot going for it. Martha Jane Canary, nicknamed Calamity
Jane, was a famous frontierswoman in the second half of the 19th century who
liked to dress in male attire and held masculine jobs, such as scout for wagon trains
and cargo wagons. She was such a good shot with a rifle that she later worked in
Buffalo Bill's Wild West Show (just as Annie Oakley did) and was a big success at
the Pan-American Exposition in 1901. She had many friends, including another
famous sharpshooter, Wild Bill Hickok, and was known for her sympathy for Native
Americans, although in her early years she fought alongside the military to quell
Indian skirmishes. Jane probably got her nickname because she was such a dare-
devil and often took risks that might well have turned into calamities.

When producer Jack Warner could not get the screen rights to *Annie Get Your
Gun,* he turned to this similar Western heroine, Calamity Jane, and commissioned
a script that would give Doris Day a chance to rough it up on-screen. He believed
that the former band singer was capable of much more than genteel leading ladies
on-screen; in fact, he had wanted Day to play Annie Oakley if he had gotten the
rights to *Annie Get Your Gun.* Screenwriter James O'Hanlon had plenty of dramatic
material to work with, but there was no romance in Jane's life and a musical needs
a love story. So he gave Jane not just one love interest but two and took a few
other liberties with history as well. In the movie, Jane works as a sharpshooter who
protects a stagecoach line as it travels through the Dakota hills. After she saves
the life of Lieut. Danny Gilmatin (Philip Carey), she is smitten with him but he
just sees Jane as a sharpshooter who can match any of the men in Deadwood.
Jane has a friendly rivalry with Wild Bill Hickok (Howard Keel) and, although they
enjoy quarreling with each other, there doesn't seem to be any romance there.
When Henry Miller (Paul Harvey), the owner of the Golden Garter Saloon, fails
to bring any female entertainment to town, it looks like the sex-starved men in
Deadwood are about to bust up his establishment. Jane boasts that she can get
the famous Chicago singer Adelaide Adams to come to Deadwood and perform. Taunted by Bill that she can't, Jane goes to Chicago to find Adelaide. Instead
she finds the eager singer Katie Brown (Allyn McLerie) and brings her back to
Deadwood to sing at the Golden Garter and she is a hit with the fellows. By this

time Jane realizes that she doesn't love Danny but Bill and, once he realizes it as well, the two are reconciled and hitched.

Calamity Jane has a surprisingly integrated score by Sammy Fain (music) and Paul Francis Webster (lyrics). It may not have boasted so many song standards as Berlin's score for *Annie Get Your Gun*, but there was a runaway hit with the rhapsodic "Secret Love," which won the Oscar and was oft recorded. Other highlights in the tuneful score include the lullaby-ballad "The Black Hills of Dakota," the raucous "Just Blew In From the Windy City," the bickering duet "I Can Do Without You," the silly ditty "It's Harry I'm Planning to Marry," and an extended opening sequence called "The Deadwood Stage," which was a marvel in musical exposition, introducing locales and characters in a lively manner. The movie was beautifully filmed in Technicolor on location at various ranches in California and directed in an efficient manner by David Butler. *Calamity Jane* also offered some spirited dances by Jack Donohue and a strong supporting cast, but the movie belongs to Day who sang just about every song, was in most every scene, and held the musical together with her vivacious performance. Years later, Day stated that of her 39 movies, *Calamity Jane* was her favorite.

See also: *Annie Get Your Gun*; Doris Day, Howard Keel biography boxes

FURTHER READING

Bingen, Steven. *Warner Bros.: Hollywood's Ultimate Backlot*. Lanham, MD: Taylor Trade Publishing, 2014.

Bloom, Ken. *Hollywood Musicals: The 101 Greatest Song-and-Dance Movies of All Time*. New York: Black Dog and Leventhal, 2010.

Hotchner, A. E. *Doris Day: Her Own Story*. New York: William Morrow & Co., 1975.

THE GLENN MILLER STORY

Studio and release date: Universal; January 1954
Producer: Aaron Rosenberg
Screenplay: Valentine Davies, Oscar Brodney
Songwriters: Harry Warren, Mack Gordon, Spencer Williams, Jerry Gray, Eddie DeLange, George and Ira Gershwin, and others (music and lyrics)
Director: Anthony Mann
Musical Directors: Joseph Gershenson, Henry Mancini
Cinematographer: William Daniels
Cast: James Stewart, June Allyson, Harry Morgan, Charles Drake, George Tobias, Frances Langford, Louis Armstrong, Gene Krupa, Irving Bacon, Kathleen Lockhart

Principal Songs: "Chattanooga Choo-Choo"; "Pennsylvania 6–5000"; "String of
Pearls"; "Basin Street Blues"; "Tuxedo Junction"; "Little Brown Jug";
"Moonlight Serenade"; "Stairway to the Stars"; "Bidin' My Time"

The Big Band era was fading in the 1950s but Hollywood's interest in musical biographies of the famous band leaders was not. This is perhaps the best of the lot, a sentimental but well-directed, well-acted film that is still very effective. Most of the Big Band stars of the 1940s appeared in movie musicals but, because few of them could act, they usually played themselves and were given little dialogue. Glenn Miller and his famous band appeared in three feature films, but his music can be heard in over 100 films and television shows. Miller was at the peak of his popularity in 1944 when the plane he was traveling in to entertain the troops in Europe went missing over the English Channel. With such a tragic ending, the screenplay could not help but be sentimental and patriotic. Yet it is an intelligently written script that uses the conventional rags-to-riches formula but has solid character development throughout. Trombone player Miller (James Stewart) is usually out of work and when he does get a gig he is forced to play bland foxtrot music. He often has to hock his trombone to make ends meet but he is not discouraged, striving to come up with a very particular sound that he experiments with. That sound, of course, is the Big Band sound, which he eventually develops and finds fame with. The romance in the story was the meeting, wooing, and wedding of Helen Berger (June Allyson) who helps him through tough times. When World War II breaks out, he is active in touring different military camps with his band. While the musicians wait for him in Paris, Miller makes some personal appearances in London. Then he sets off for the continent by military plane and is never heard from again. In the finale scene, the band plays in Paris without Miller while his wife listens to the radio broadcast at home.

Because the movie was not only a bio-pic but also a tribute to Miller, many of the musicians and singers who worked with him in the 1940s appeared as themselves in the film, giving *The Glenn Miller Story* an authenticity that few biographies could claim. Louis Armstrong, Gene Krupa, Ben Pollack, Frances Langford, the Modernaires, and others performed old favorites, and Harry Morgan, who had acted with Miller in *Orchestra Wives* (1942), played Miller's close friend Chummy MacGregor in the bio-pic. (The real MacGregor served as a consultant on the film.) Joe Yukl, who had been in the Miller band, did Stewart's trombone playing on the soundtrack and the most dedicated fans knew that the sound was authentic. In fact, the trombone Stewart used in the film was Miller's instrument, loaned to Universal by the Miller family. All of the Miller song favorites were heard—from "Basin Street Blues" and "In the Mood" to "Pennsylvania 6–5000" and "Chattanooga Choo-Choo." A particularly memorable musical moment was when Krupa jammed with Armstrong on "Basin Street Blues." The old standard "Little Brown Jug" was heard throughout the movie as Miller tried to turn the old song into a swing number. In the final scene, Helen listens to the completed swing version on the radio and the ditty turns into a poignant moment.

Audiences nostalgic for the previous decade were in bliss during *The Glenn Miller Story,* not only for the music but for an era that was being replaced by new kinds of music. Most of the Big Band leaders continued to perform far into the 1950s, and replacement musicians continued to play the old songs into the 1980s. Because *The Glenn Miller Story* was one of the most successful musicals of the 1950s, Hollywood produced a batch of Big Band bio-pics, including *The Benny Goodman Story* (1956) with Steve Allen as Goodman, *The Eddy Duchin Story* (1956) with Tyrone Power as the title character, *The Gene Krupa Story* (1959) with Sal Mineo as the famous jazz drummer, and *The Fabulous Dorseys* (1947) in which Tommy and Jimmy Dorsey played themselves. While these movies varied in quality and accuracy, the music was usually correct and that is what mattered. These bio-pics often hold up very well with modern audiences because the Big Band sound that Miller strived for is still very appealing to many.

FURTHER READING

Fitzgerald, Michael G. *Universal Pictures: A Panoramic History.* Westport, CT: Arlington House, 1977.

Grudens, Richard. *Chattanooga Choo-Choo: The Life and Times of the World Famous Glenn Miller Orchestra.* Stony Brook, NY: Celebrity Profiles Publishing, 2004.

SEVEN BRIDES FOR SEVEN BROTHERS

Studio and release date: Metro-Goldwyn-Mayer; June 1954
Producer: Jack Cummings
Screenplay: Frances Goodrich, Albert Hackett, Dorothy Kingsley, based on the Stephen Vincent Benét story *The Sobbin' Women*
Songwriters: Gene de Paul (music), Johnny Mercer (lyrics)
Director: Stanley Donen
Choreographer: Michael Kidd
Musical Director: Adolph Deutsch
Cinematographer: George Folsey
Cast: Jane Powell, Howard Keel, Jeff Richards, Russ Tamblyn, Tommy Rall, Marc Platt, Matt Mattox, Jacques d'Amboise
Songs: "Wonderful, Wonderful Day"; "Lonesome Polecat"; "Spring, Spring, Spring"; "When You're in Love"; "Goin' Co'tin' "; "Bless Your Beautiful Hide"; "Sobbin' Women"

The plot for this classic frontier musical is so outrageous that it is surprising that it works so well on-screen. But thanks to a smart and funny script, a soaring score by Gene De Paul (music) and Johnny Mercer (lyrics), and exuberant choreography by Michael Kidd, the whole package manages to be wholesome and sexy at the same time. Set in the mountains of Oregon in the 1850s, the story centers on the seven Pontipee brothers who are crude, brawling, ignorant, restless, and lonely for women. When eldest brother Adam (Howard Keel) goes into town and gets himself a wife by wooing the just-as-restless Milly (Jane Powell), the other siblings start hankering for wives too. Milly tries to teach the boys genteel manners but when they go into town to socialize, everyone breaks out in fist fights. Out of frustration (and a little encouragement from Adam), the six brothers sneak into town one night, steal six young unmarried women, and bring them back home to the cabin high in the mountains. They soon realize the error of their ways, but an avalanche blocks the pass back to civilization until spring. Milly, pregnant with her first child, sees that the girls are housed properly and that all proprieties are kept. During the long winter, the brothers have time to learn how to woo the ladies successfully. In the spring, Milly gives birth to her baby and the snow melts. The angry fathers of the girls arrive with vengeance in mind and refuse to let them marry their beaux. Then Milly's baby cries out and, because no one will admit to who the mother is, a shotgun wedding is planned for all six girls and the Pontipee brothers.

This unlikely plot for a musical was based on the Stephen Vincent Benét story *The Sobbin' Women*, which was an Appalachian folk version of the ancient episode by Plutarch known as the "Rape of the Sabine Women." The fact that the film is in good taste and still a lot of fun is a tribute to the fine writing. Like many classic movie musicals, *Seven Brides for Seven Brothers* did not have an easy time of it in preparation. MGM thought that, handled carefully, Benét's story could

Few frontier musicals are as much fun as *Seven Brides for Seven Brothers* (1954). Balancing all the lively shenanigans is the romance between Adam Pontipee (Howard Keel) and his new wife Milly (Jane Powell). Stanley Donen directed the offbeat musical with panache. (MGM/Photofest)

Howard Keel (1919–2004)   A virile leading man who charmed audiences with his powerful baritone singing voice, he starred in several film musicals in the 1950s and 1960s. He was born in Gillespie, Illinois, and grew up in California where he later worked as an aircraft salesman. Keel started singing in California stock theaters before appearing on Broadway in the late 1940s. He made a sensational screen debut as Frank Butler in *Annie Get Your Gun* (1950), followed by such movie musicals as *Show Boat* (1951), *Lovely to Look At* (1952), *Calamity Jane* (1953), *Kiss Me, Kate* (1953), *Seven Brides for Seven Brothers* (1954), *Rose Marie* (1954), *Deep in My Heart* (1954), *Jupiter's Darling* (1955), and *Kismet* (1955). Keel continued to sing on television, in clubs and concerts, and in stock revivals into the 1990s.

make a good frontier musical. But director-producer Joshua Logan had acquired the rights to the story and hoped to turn it into a Broadway musical. The project never materialized but MGM had to wait five years for the option on the story to run out, then the studio grabbed the rights. Producer Jack Cummings thought that the story called for existing American folk songs, and he spent months listening to dozens of recording before he realized that an original score was needed. The film was titled *The Sobbin' Women* in preparation but the studio thought it a terrible title for a musical. The project was then titled *A Bride for Seven Brothers* but the studio censor thought it too suggestive so it was changed to *Seven Brides for Seven Brothers*. Cummings hired Stanley Donen to direct because of the success of *On the Town* (1949) and *Singin' in the Rain* (1952). Both of those musicals had been codirected and co-choreographed with Gene Kelly, and Donen wanted to prove that he had talents of his own. In a brilliant move, the studio hired Michael Kidd as choreographer. Although he had gotten recognition on Broadway for doing the dances in *Finian's Rainbow* (1947), *Guys and Dolls* (1950), and a few other shows, Kidd had only choreographed one film, *Where's Charley?* (1952). With *Seven Brides for Seven Brothers* he became one of Hollywood's premiere choreographers. Once the movie was cast and production began, things went smoother and most of the creative talent later stated that *Seven Brides for Seven Brothers* was one of their best Hollywood experiences.

Donen directed the film with just enough brashness to make the crazy tale work, and the characters grew from cartoon types to engaging people in a cockeyed situation. It helped that Keel and Powell gave top-notch performances and that the supporting cast was also excellent. Most of the brothers were played by experienced ballet dancers so their singing had to be dubbed. Two of the brothers (Russ Tamblyn and Jeff Richards) were actors rather than experienced dancers so they were often hidden from view during the dance numbers. Ironically, Tamblyn

Jane Powell (b. 1929)   A wholesome teenager with an operatic soprano singing voice, she graduated to adult roles during the 1950s and retained her popularity. She was born in Portland, Oregon, and sang on the radio as a child. Powell was only 15 years old when she made her screen debut in 1944, playing vivacious and optimistic teens in musicals such as *Delightfully Dangerous* (1945), *Holiday in Mexico* (1946), *Three Darling Daughters* (1948), *Luxury Liner* (1948), *A Date With Judy* (1948), and *Nancy Goes to Rio* (1950). She got to mature into a leading lady with *Two Weeks with Love* (1950), *Royal Wedding* (1951), *Rich, Young and Pretty* (1951), *Small Town Girl* (1953), *Three Sailors and a Girl* (1953), *Athena* (1954), *Seven Brides for Seven Brothers* (1954), *Hit the Deck* (1955), and *The Girl Most Likely* (1957). When the Golden Age of Hollywood musicals ended, she continued to perform onstage and in TV musicals. Autobiography: *The Girl Next Door and How She Grew* (1988).

was an experienced acrobat and when Kidd found out, he added some impressive flips and turns for Tamblyn, giving the illusion that he was one of the principal dancers in the movie. The film was mostly shot in a studio, giving the tall-tale an artificial, folksy charm. Only a few location shots were added, such as the avalanche, which was filmed in Utah. Some difficulties during filming were solved in different ways. When the Pontipee brothers went to town and got into a brawl with the locals, it was hard to tell the men apart. The decision was made to dye all the brothers' hair red, thereby distinguishing the two groups. All the details aside, *Seven Brides for Seven Brothers* relied on a good score and superior dance. The songs De Paul and Mercer wrote were tuneful and varied. Highlights in the score include the vibrant ballads "Spring, Spring, Spring" and "Wonderful, Wonderful Day," the moaning lament "Lonesome Polecat," the narrative number "Sobbin' Women," and the silly wooing song "Bless Your Beautiful Hide." The most remembered musical number in the film was not sung but featured dancing, including the high-energy "House-Raising Dance," which Kidd choreographed with acrobatics, gymnastics, and vivid challenge dancing as the Pontipee brothers and the boys from town compete and try to impress the girls. Never before had dance been used so effectively in a wilderness setting. MGM was afraid that backwoodsmen dancing would look silly and even sissy, but once the studio executives saw clips of Kidd's brilliant choreography, they stopped worrying. The sequence is so well structured, telling a story as well and illustrating a character battle, that many rank the "House-Raising Dance" as one of the outstanding musical numbers of the 1950s. One would think that MGM knew it had a hit on its hands when filming and editing were complete but it was not the case. The studio sunk all its money into making and promoting *Rose Marie* (1954) and *Brigadoon* (1954), and *Seven Brides for Seven Brothers* was released as a B movie. MGM couldn't have been more wrong. *Rose Marie* and *Bridagoon* were critical and box office disappointments and *Seven Brides for Seven Brothers* turned out to be a cinematic masterpiece.

See also: *On the Town, Singin' in the Rain;* Jane Powell, Howard Keel, Johnny Mercer, Michael Kidd, Stanley Donen biography boxes

FURTHER READING

Casper, Joseph Andrew. *Stanley Donen*. Lanham, MD: Scarecrow Press, 1995.
Eskew, Glenn. *Johnny Mercer: Southern Songwriter for the World*. Athens: University of Georgia Press, 2013.
Powell, Jane. *The Girl Next Door . . . and How She Grew*. Belmont, CA: Untreed Reads Publishing, 2014.

WHITE CHRISTMAS

Studio and release date: Paramount; August 1954
Producer: Robert Dolan
Screenplay: Norman Krasna, Melvin Frank, Norman Panama
Songwriters: Irving Berlin (music and lyrics)
Director: Michael Curtiz
Choreographer: Robert Alton
Musical Director: Joseph J. Lilley
Cinematographer: Loyal Griggs
Cast: Bing Crosby, Danny Kaye, Rosemary Clooney, Vera-Ellen, Dean Jagger, Mary Wickes, Grady Sutton, Sig Rumann
Songs: "White Christmas"; "Count Your Blessings Instead of Sheep"; "Sisters"; "The Best Things Happen While You're Dancing"; "Snow"; "The Old Man"; "Love, You Didn't Do Right By Me"; "Choreography"; "Mandy"; "What Can You Do with a General?"; "Gee! I Wish I Was Back in the Army"; "Minstrel Show"

Perhaps the most frequently shown movie musical around Christmastime, the film capitalized on the enduring popularity of the 1942 title song by Irving Berlin and offered some memorable new tunes as well. Also, for many years the black-and-white *Holiday Inn* (1942) was not shown on television because some objected to the "Abraham" number. So the networks broadcast the color *White Christmas* instead. The idea for the musical came from Berlin who had an idea for a stage musical about a retired general who looks for a reason to keep living. Paramount heard about the idea and convinced Berlin to let the studio make a movie musical featuring a new Berlin score. Then the studio thought that a sequel to the very popular *Holiday Inn*, titled *White Christmas*, would be a winner. Paramount asked Bing Crosby and Fred Astaire, the stars of the earlier film, if they would reprise their characters in a new holiday movie. Neither liked the script and Astaire announced he was retiring. (He didn't.) Berlin talked Crosby into doing the movie and Donald O'Connor was cast in Astaire's role. Then O'Connor got sick from a fever he caught from his costar Francis the Talking Mule and he had to drop out. By the time Danny Kaye was signed, the idea of a sequel to *Holiday Inn* was dropped and a script with new characters was used. The only things from *Holiday Inn* that returned were Crosby, the song "White Christmas, and the old *Holiday Inn* setting, which was painted and reused as the general's inn. The role originally meant for Astaire involved a major amount of dancing, and Kaye was primarily a comic actor-singer. Yet the role was not changed and Kaye impressed the studio (and the public), doing more intricate dance than in any of his other films.

The rewritten screenplay was about army buddies Bob Wallace (Bing Crosby) and Phil Davis (Danny Kaye) and their love-hate relationship. Because Phil once saved Bob's life, he talks Bob, a noted performer before the war, into taking him on as a partner. The two go into show business together after they get out of the army and become famous. While performing in Florida, the two go to a nightclub to catch the sister act of Betty (Rosemary Clooney) and Judy Haynes (Vera-Ellen). Bob and Phil even help the sisters sneak out of the club when their landlord comes to collect damages to their apartment. The four travel up to Vermont where the girls have a booking to sing at a ski lodge but when the foursome arrive there is no snow and the lodge is like a ghost town. When the ex-GIs find out that their old commander, Major General Waverly (Dean Jagger), is the proprietor of the inn and is going bankrupt, Bob decides to rehearse and try out his Broadway-bound show at the lodge to attract business. Bob even goes on television to encourage former servicemen who served under the general to come to New England for the bash. Even though a romance is slowly beginning between Bob and Betty, it is thwarted when she mistakenly learns that Bob is using the general just to get some quick publicity for his show. Dozens of ex-GIs travel to Vermont to pay tribute to Gen. Waverly, the quarrel between Bob and Betty is resolved, and it starts to snow as everyone joyously sings the title song. What the script lacked in logic it more than made up for in charm. By the contrived happy ending, the audience is so caught up in the festivities that the nonsensical story seems to make sense.

Berlin wrote nine new songs for the film, and some joined the ranks of his beloved standards, including the tender lullaby "Count Your Blessings Instead of Sheep," the torchy "Love, You Didn't Do Right By Me," and the frivolous but catchy "Sisters," which was sung by Clooney and Vera-Ellen and then lip-synced by Crosby and Kaye in one of the movie's silliest but most beloved numbers. Actually,

Danny Kaye (1913–1987)   A popular comic actor-singer-dancer with a knack for singing rapid-fire songs, he shone in all areas of show business, including 20 films. He was born in Brooklyn, the son of a tailor, and left school as a teenager to perform as a comic in "Borscht Belt" nightclubs and then in vaudeville. Kaye found fame on Broadway in a supporting but memorable role in *Lady in the Dark* (1941) then starred in *Let's Face It!* (1941) before going to Hollywood where he was popular in movies, catering to his special talents for clowning, comic dancing, and vocal pyrotechnics. Among his best movie musicals were *Up in Arms* (1944), *Wonder Man* (1945), *The Kid From Brooklyn* (1946), *The Secret Life of Walter Mitty* (1947), *A Song Is Born* (1948), *The Inspector General* (1949), *On the Riviera* (1951), *Hans Christian Andersen* (1952), *White Christmas* (1954), *The Court Jester* (1956), *Merry Andrew* (1958), and *The Five Pennies* (1959). In the 1960s, Kaye was occupied mostly with concert tours, then he returned to Broadway in *Two By Two* (1970). He made many television appearances and was busy with charitable causes. Biographies: *Nobody's Fool: The Lives of Danny Kaye*, Martin Gottfried (1994); *Danny Kaye: King of Jesters*, David Koenig (2012).

the male version of "Sisters" was not in the shooting script. One day Kaye and Crosby were clowning around and imitating Clooney and Vera-Ellen and director Michael Curtiz liked it and put it in the movie. "The Best Things Happen While You're Dancing" was another commendable addition to the catalogue of Berlin dance songs, and "Gee, I Wish I Was Back in the Army" was a nostalgic soft-shoe in the grand manner. Other memorable numbers include the harmonizing "Snow"; the satiric "Choreography," which mocked modern dance; and of course the title song, which was heard at the beginning and the end of the movie. All four stars shone and gave outstanding performances. In the case of singer Rosemary Clooney, the movie gave her the best role of her career, and she gave her best screen performance. In the opinion of many, *White Christmas* was Danny Kaye's crowning performance. The supporting cast was solid, with Jagger providing the substance and Mary Wickes the comedy. *White Christmas* was the first movie in colorful Vistavision, which dazzled 1954 moviegoers. The effect is weakened on television and DVD today, though the vibrant color mostly survives. Curtiz directed the film at an efficient pace, and Robert Alton did the choreography, which ranged from old-time soft-shoe to satiric interpretive dance. *White Christmas* was the top-grossing movie of the year and its popularity remains high, returning each December as a holiday-time favorite.

See also: *Holiday Inn, Easter Parade*; Irving Berlin, Bing Crosby, Danny Kaye biography boxes

FURTHER READING

Eames, John Douglas. *The Paramount Story*. New York: Crown Publishers, 1985.

Gottfried, Martin. *Nobody's Fool: Danny Kaye*. New York: Simon & Schuster, 1994.

Nelson, Thomas. *Irving Berlin's White Christmas*. Nashville, TN: Thomas Nelson, Inc., 2004.

Prigozy, Ruth, and Walter Raubicheck, eds. *Going My Way: Bing Crosby and American Culture*. Rochester, NY: University of Rochester Press, 2007.

A STAR IS BORN

Studio and release date: Warner Brothers; September 1954

Producer: Sidney Luft

Screenplay: Moss Hart, based on the 1937 film script by Dorothy Parker, Alan Campbell, Robert Carson

Songwriters: Harold Arlen and others (music), Ira Gershwin and others (lyrics)

Director: George Cukor

Choreographer: Richard Barstow

Musical Director: Ray Heindorf

Cinematographer: Sam Leavitt

Cast: Judy Garland, James Mason, Jack Carson, Charles Bickford, Tommy Noonan, Grady Sutton

Principal Songs: "The Man That Got Away"; "Born in a Trunk"; "Gotta Have Me Go With You"; "Someone at Last"; "Here's What I'm Here For"; "It's a New World"; "Swanee"; "Lose That Long Face"

Many feel that Judy Garland gave her best performance in this, her last major movie musical. Some feel that it is the finest of all movie musical performances. As for the film itself, *A Star Is Born* ranks high, going into emotional territory that few musicals dared to consider. Some of this is due to Moss Hart's unsentimental screenplay, but much of the film's gritty power comes from Garland. The story line is not so complex as the characters. Band singer Esther Blodgett (Garland) meets alcoholic movie star Norman Maine (James Mason) at a Hollywood benefit where he literally stumbles into her act. After Norman hears Esther sing in a smoky little nightclub, he is determined to help her climb to stardom. The two marry but as Vicky Lester (as she is renamed by the studio) climbs to success, Maine descends until in despair he ends up drowning himself. The story was already familiar to movie audiences, the tale having been told as a nonmusical film in 1937 with Janet Gaynor and Fredric March as Esther and Norman. The idea of a movie musical originated with producer Sidney Luft, who was married to Garland at the time. Warner Brothers picked up the project then found itself making one of the most expensive movies of the 1950s. Garland's frequent illness caused shooting to run nearly 10 months, and the project went a couple of million dollars over budget.

Casting was also a problem. Just about every leading man in Hollywood turned down the role of Norman, not wishing to play a has-been actor on his way down. Luckily, Mason accepted the role and his performance provided the perfect foil for Garland's portrayal of Esther/Vicky. The huge production was directed by George Cukor who had never directed a movie musical before. It was also his first color film and was shot in CinemaScope, a process he was not familiar with. Yet Cukor ended up not only surviving the whole ordeal but coming up with a remarkable movie with strong performances throughout.

Warner Brothers was not happy with the first cut and, against the wishes of Cukor and the songwriters Harold Arlen (music) and Ira Gershwin (lyrics), the long "Born in a Trunk" sequence was added. The studio did not think that the Arlen-Gershwin songs were good enough so Warner Brothers had Roger Edens and Leonard Gershe write the medley using existing song standards. It is a first-class musical sequence showing the struggles of a young singer trying to make it in show biz, but it made the long movie even longer. The movie shown to preview audiences ran over three hours so, despite good audience reaction, the studio cut two scenes and two numbers to bring the running time to 154 minutes. The cutting did not help the structure of the film and it still seemed long without making sense at times. Some of the missing footage was restored and added to the 1983 rerelease and most felt the picture was improved by the additions. Warner Brothers was also wrong about the Arlen-Gershwin score. *A Star Is Born* has a superior set of songs, led by the indelible torch song "The Man That Got Away," which Garland sang in the empty nightclub after hours with some musician friends. Her recording of the song was one of her biggest hits. Another musical masterwork in the film is the extended "Someone at Last" song sequence, sung by Esther/Vicky to her husband, demonstrating the inane musical she is making at the studio. It's a comic *tour de force* that matches the earlier torch song in power. Also impressive was the swinging "Gotta Have Me Go With You" and the optimistic ballad "It's a New World." Cut from the film but restored in 1983 was the heartbreaking "Lose That Long Face," which provided a kind of theme for the whole movie. Musically, *A Star Is Born* is as rich and complex as the drama it has to tell. The backstage musical, going back to *The Broadway Melody* (1929) and *42nd Street* (1933), had come a long way.

Barbra Streisand, the reigning female Hollywood star of a later era, was the reason for the 1976 remake of *A Star Is Born*. A coproduction by Warner Brothers, Barwood, and First Artists, the film was produced by Streisand and Jon Peters with an eye on the youth market. Although the setting and the songs were very different, the plot was surprisingly similar. The ambitious pop singer Esther Hoffman (Streisand) rises to the top while her mentor and husband John Norman Howard (Kris Kristofferson) descends into drugs and suicide by crashing his Ferrari. Just as the earlier film sought to expose the hypocrisy of the show business of their day, the remake provided a very unglamorous view of rock singers and their world. Paul Williams and Streisand collaborated on the Oscar-winning song "Evergreen" (aka

Judy Garland (1922–1969)   Few movie stars had such an emotional connection with her fans as did this singer-actress who grew up on-screen. She was born in Grand Rapids, Minnesota, the daughter of vaudevillians, and was onstage at the age of three. Touring in a vaudeville act with her sisters called the Gumm Sisters Kiddie Act, Garland soon found recognition as the "little girl with the great big voice." As a young teen in Hollywood, she made some musical shorts before getting featured in the musicals *Pigskin Parade* (1936), *Broadway Melody of 1938* (1937), *Everybody Sing* (1938), *Listen, Darling* (1938), and *Love Finds Andy Hardy* (1938), her first teaming with Mickey Rooney. Her memorable performance as Dorothy in *The Wizard of Oz* (1939) was followed by a series of successful "let's put on a show" musicals with Rooney, such as *Babes in Arms* (1939), *Andy Hardy Meets Debutante* (1940), *Strike Up the Band* (1940). and *Babes on Broadway* (1941). Garland graduated to adult roles with *Ziegfeld Girl* (1941) and remained popular in musicals such as *For Me and My Gal* (1942), *Girl Crazy* (1943), *Meet Me in St. Louis* (1944), *The Harvey Girls* (1946), *Ziegfeld Follies* (1946), *Till the Clouds Roll By* (1946), *Words and Music* (1948), *The Pirate* (1948), *Easter Parade* (1948), and *In the Good Old Summertime* (1949). Her difficult life, her battle with pills and alcohol, and her failed marriages hurt her career in the 1950s, yet she shone in such musicals as *Summer Stock* (1950) and *A Star Is Born* (1954). Garland made several nonmusicals and appeared on many television programs, having her own variety show in the 1960s. Primarily a singer with an exceptional talent for interpreting a song, her acting and dancing talents were considerable and her persona on the screen was never less than magnetic. Memoir: *Me and My Shadows: A Family Memoir,* Lorna Luft [her daughter] (1999); biographies: *Heartbreaker,* John Meyer (2006); *Get Happy: The Life of Judy Garland,* Gerald Clarke (2001).

"Love Theme From *A Star Is Born*") and it was the best number in the score, though there was much to like in the rock-pop numbers "Queen Bee," "Woman in the Moon," and "I Believe in Love." The critics were not enthusiastic, but the new *A Star Is Born* was a resounding hit at the box office.

See also: *The Broadway Melody, 42nd Street*; Judy Garland, Harold Arlen, Ira Gershwin biography boxes

FURTHER READING

Bloom, Ken. *Hollywood Musicals: The 101 Greatest Song-and-Dance Movies of All Time.* New York: Black Dog and Leventhal, 2010.

Finch, Christopher. *Rainbow: The Stormy Life of Judy Garland.* New York: Grosset & Dunlap, 1975.

Rimier, Walter. *The Man That Got Away: The Life and Songs of Harold Arlen.* Champaign: University of Illinois Press, 2015.

LOVE ME OR LEAVE ME

Studio and release date: Metro-Goldwyn-Mayer; May 1955
Producer: Joe Pasternak
Screenplay: Daniel Fuchs, Isobel Lennart
Songwriters: Walter Donaldson, Gus Kahn, Irving Berlin, Ray Henderson, Lew Brown, B. G. DeSylva, Richard Rodgers, Lorenz Hart, and others (music and lyrics)
Director: Charles Vidor
Choreographer: Alex Romero
Musical Director: George Stoll
Cinematographer: Arthur Arling
Cast: Doris Day, James Cagney, Cameron Mitchell, Robert Keith, Tom Tully, Claude Stroud
Principal Songs: "Love Me or Leave Me"; "Ten Cents a Dance"; "Shaking the Blues Away"; "I'll Never Stop Loving You"; "You Made Me Love You"; "My Blue Heaven"; "Never Look Back"

One of the most accomplished torch singers of stage and nightclubs in the 1920s and 1930s, Ruth Etting had a troubled life and a turbulent marriage. Her husband was a small-time gangster who shot Etting's true love. But because the lover lived and the husband only went to jail, MGM saw a happy ending of sorts and commissioned a bio-pic about Etting using the many famous songs she sang. The studio wanted Ava Gardner for the role but she turned it down, not wanting to be dubbed again as she had in *Show Boat* (1951). Both Jane Russell and Jane Powell were considered, then James Cagney, who was to play the gangster-husband, suggested Doris Day to producer Joe Pasternak. Although she was often considered more a band singer than an actress, Day was cast as Etting for her singing and surprised everyone with her acting. The unsentimental movie also boasted another strong performance by Cagney (in his last gangster role) and the two played off each other superbly. In the MGM version of the truth, dance hall hostess Etting is discovered by small-time mobster "Gimp" Snyder (Cagney) who is not above using unethical means to further her career, even getting her into the *Ziegfeld Follies*. Snyder's jealousy, even after he marries Etting, is notorious and when she falls in love with pianist Johnny Alderman (Cameron Mitchell), Snyder finds out about it, stalks

Doris Day (b. 1924)   One of the top female stars in movies in the 1950s and 1960s, the singer-actress usually played wholesome, girl-next-door characters. She was born in Cincinnati and planned to be a dancer until a car accident ended her dreams of becoming a ballerina. Day started singing with bands when she was a teenager and eventually was the featured vocalist with Les Brown's Band. She became a screen star with her first movie, *Romance on the High Seas* (1948), and soon her records were high on the charts. Among Day's most memorable musicals are *It's a Great Feeling* (1949), *My Dream Is Yours* (1949), *Tea for Two* (1950), *West Point Story* (1950), *Lullaby of Broadway* (1951), *On Moonlight Bay* (1951), *I'll See You in My Dreams* (1951), *April in Paris* (1952), *By the Light of the Silvery Moon* (1953), *Lucky Me* (1954), *The Pajama Game* (1957), and *Jumbo* (1962). She got more dramatic roles in nonmusicals, but on occasion one of her musical roles gave her a chance to stretch her acting muscles, such as *Young Man with a Horn* (1950), *Calamity Jane* (1953), *Young at Heart* (1954), and *Love Me or Leave Me* (1955). Her later career in the 1960s included a series of coy sex comedies with Rock Hudson and a popular television show. Biographies: *Doris Day: Her Own Story* (1975); *Considering Doris Day*, Tom Santopietro (2007).

Johnny, then shoots him. Alderman survives, Snyder goes to jail, and in the film's only Hollywood concession, all three are reunited years later as Snyder, now out of jail, opens his new club. Cagney was as charismatic as ever but Day held her own in both the book scenes and in her interpretation of such Etting songs as "Ten Cents a Dance," "Shaking the Blues Away," "You Made Me Love You," and the title number. There were also two new torch songs for Day to sing, "Never Look Back" by Chilton Price and "I'll Never Stop Loving You" by Nicholas Brodszky (music) and Sammy Cahn (lyrics), which became a best-selling record for Day.

Although *Love Me or Leave Me* was filmed in color, it had a gritty, garish look that added to the melodrama. Charles Vidor directed with a taut flavor so the movie ended up being a drama with songs rather than a musical drama. This worried MGM, which prided itself on its polished, luscious musicals. MGM left the gritty musicals to Warner Brothers. But *Love Me or Leave Me* was a critical and popular success and was nominated for six Oscars. Oddly, Day was not even nominated, though Cagney was. Regardless, Day was taken much more seriously by Hollywood because of this film, and a variety of roles were offered to her. She even made several nonmusicals, some of them serious dramas. *Love Me or Leave Me* opened doors in other ways as well. The studios began making bio-pics that were far from the optimistic rags-to-riches formula. These "downers" were often about riches-to-rags celebrities and, while most ended hopefully, they were indeed serious. Eleanor Parker was the crippled opera singer Marjorie Lawrence in *Interrupted Melody* (1955), Susan Hayward played alcoholic movie actress Lillian Roth in *I'll Cry Tomorrow* (1955), Ann Blyth played self-destructive torch singer Helen Morgan in *The Helen Morgan Story* (1957), Frank Sinatra played tragic comic Joe E. Lewis in *The Joker Is Wild* (1957), Danny Kaye was the haunted musician Red Nichols in *The Five Pennies* (1959), and so on. The fictional *A Star Is Born* (1954) had demonstrated that musicals can be about tragic characters; *Love Me or Leave Me* showed that the stories could be true ones.

See also: *A Star Is Born, The Joker Is Wild*; Doris Day, James Cagney biography boxes

FURTHER READING

Irwin, Kenneth, and Charles O. Lloyd. *Ruth Etting: America's Forgotten Sweetheart.* Lanham, MD: Scarecrow Press, 2009.

McCabe, John. *Cagney.* New York: Knopf, 2013.

McGee, Garry. *Doris Day: Sentimental Journey.* Jefferson, NC: McFarland Publishers, 2010.

OKLAHOMA!

Studio and release date: Magna; October 1955

Producer: Arthur Hornblow Jr.

Screenplay: Sonya Levien, William Ludwig, based on the 1943 stage script by Oscar Hammerstein, which was based on the 1931 play *Green Grow the Lilacs* by Lynn Riggs

Songwriters: Richard Rodgers (music), Oscar Hammerstein (lyrics)

Director: Fred Zinnemann

Choreographer: Agnes de Mille

Musical Director: Jay Blackton

Cinematographer: Robert Surtees

Cast: Shirley Jones, Gordon MacRae, Gene Nelson, Gloria Grahame, Eddie Albert, Charlotte Greenwood, Rod Steiger, James Whitmore

Songs: "Oh, What a Beautiful Mornin' "; "People Will Say We're in Love"; "The Surrey With the Fringe on Top"; "Oklahoma"; "Kansas City"; "Out of My Dreams"; "I Cain't Say No"; "The Farmer and the Cowman"; "Pore Jud"; "Many a New Day"; "All er Nothin' "

A faithful screen adaptation of the very influential and long-running 1943 Broadway musical by Rodgers and Hammerstein, the movie is a polished frontier musical with top-notch production values. Yet *Oklahoma!* on-screen is just another quality musical, while *Oklahoma!* on Broadway was a landmark. Not only the most important of the Richard Rodgers (music) and Oscar Hammerstein (book and lyrics) musicals, it is also the single most influential work in the American musical theater. In fact, the history of the stage genre is divided into two periods: musicals before *Oklahoma!* and those after *Oklahoma!* Hammerstein's stage script was based on the 1931 rural comedy-drama *Green Grow the Lilacs* by Lynn Riggs. He fleshed out the characters and allowed song and dance to tell the story rather than interrupt it. The plot is rather straightforward. The Oklahoma territory is experiencing a land rush, which creates friction between the farmers and the cowmen. There is also friction between the cowboy Curly McLain and the farm hand Jud Fry over Laurey Williams, who lives with her Aunt Eller on the farm where Jud works. Although Laurey much prefers Curly, she agrees to go to the box social with Jud in order to punish Curly for taking her for granted. She immediately regrets her decision and has a nightmare in which she sees the sinister Jud intrude on her wedding to Curly and carry her away. At the box social, Curly outbids Jud for the picnic hamper that Laurey has prepared, even though he has to sell everything he owns to do it. Jud threatens Curly and Laurey so she fires him and Curly and Laurey confess they love each other. At their wedding celebration, a drunk Jud shows up with a knife and challenges Curly; in the scuffle, Jud falls on his own knife and dies. So that the newlyweds can leave on their honeymoon, Aunt Eller convinces the local judge to hold the trial immediately. Curly is acquitted and the couple leads the neighbors in a celebration of their new statehood as they leave on their honeymoon. The comic subplot also concerns a romantic triangle: the flirtatious Ado Annie Carnes is promised to Will Parker but is also drawn to the wily peddler Ali Hakim. Caught in a compromising position with Annie, Hakim is going to be forced into a shotgun wedding with her, but he arranges to buy Will's wedding presents at such inflated prices that Will has enough money to marry Annie himself. While all this may not seem very innovative, the way Rodgers and Hammerstein told the tale was. A cowboy musical would traditionally start with a barn dance or square dance (as suggested by the original title *Away We Go!*), but Rodgers and Hammerstein liked the quiet beginning of Riggs' play and opened their musical with Aunt Eller churning butter and Curly entering singing "Oh, What a Beautiful Mornin'." Hammerstein remained true to the characters when mapping out the story and the songs. Director Rouben Mamoulian approached the musical piece as a dramatic play, and choreographer Agnes de Mille took the same approach to the dances. The two ended up creating a seamless piece of musical drama. The innovative ballet that ended the first act was mostly de Mille's idea, as was her suggestion to illustrate Jud's naughty French postcards in Laurey's dream. By the time the musical opened on Broadway, it was retitled *Oklahoma!* because that song stopped the show each night.

Oklahoma! is the first fully integrated musical play, and its blending of song, character, plot, and even dance would serve as the model for Broadway shows for decades to follow. No song from the score could be reassigned to another character, no less another show, because each was drawn from the character so fully that it became an integrated piece of the character's development within the plot. By the time Curly has finished singing the seemingly casual "The Surrey With the Fringe on Top," the dramatic situation has altered. Every musical number became a little one-act play of sorts. The musical was also unique in other ways. Without waving a flag as George M. Cohan had done in his patriotic shows, *Oklahoma!* celebrated the American spirit, which was particularly potent in 1943 with the country deep in World War II. *Oklahoma!* also celebrated the rural life, whereas most musicals were decidedly urban. The characters in the story were not placed in the tragic circumstances of, say, *Show Boat* (1927), but they were fully developed all the same and the sincerity of their everyday emotions was refreshing after the slick, Broadway types that populated most Broadway shows. Even the so-called villain Jud is a complex creation, arousing conflicting emotions in the audience just as he confuses Laurey's feelings about him. Finally, *Oklahoma!* used dance as never seen before, the hoofing growing out of the characters and their emotions rather than from disjointed dance cues. Will Parker's lively retelling of life in "Kansas City" grew into a dance demonstrating what he'd seen in the big city and soon the stage was exploding with competitive cowboys doing the two-step. Laurey's indecision about her feelings for Curly and Jud led into the famous "Laurey Makes Up Her Mind" ballet, the American theater's first fully realized psychological dance piece. Even the rousing chorus number "The Farmer and the Cowman" is a challenge dance that echoes the conflicts between the two rival groups. The impact *Oklahoma!* had on the American musical theater cannot be overestimated. Even the silliest, least consequential musical comedies after 1943 were directly affected by the Rodgers and Hammerstein landmark show. No longer could the plot turn on a dime to reach its expected conclusion. No longer could a performer break out of character to sing a specialty number that had no relation to the rest of the show. And no longer could a musical be thrown together with the traditional elements of entertainment without the audience expecting some sort of cohesive logic to it all. Few Broadway products would accomplish what *Oklahoma!* did onstage, but all of them would be judged by the example set by the Rodgers and Hammerstein masterwork.

During the musical's five-year run on Broadway (a new record), Rodgers and Hammerstein would not allow a screen version of *Oklahoma!* to be made. Not until 1955, when the last touring company of *Oklahoma!* returned home, did they agree to a movie, and they retained complete control over the project. Both had been stung by Hollywood too many times in the past, seeing their Broadway shows altered and decimated on the screen. They chose the small, independent Magna company

Gordon MacRae (1921–1986)   A masculine, full-voiced baritone with a genial persona, he starred in a dozen movie musicals in the 1950s. MacRae was born in East Orange, New Jersey, the son of a toolmaker-singer and a concert pianist, and went to schools in Buffalo and Syracuse before becoming a band vocalist. After serving as a navigator in World War II, MacRae returned to singing, first on the radio and then on Broadway in the revue *Three to Make Ready* (1946). This appearance led to a movie contract and he made his screen debut in 1948 in *The Big Punch*. MacRae starred in such musicals as *Tea for Two* (1950), *West Point Story* (1950), *On Moonlight Bay* (1951), *By the Light of the Silvery Moon* (1953), *The Desert Song* (1953), and *Three Sailors and a Girl* (1953) before getting his best film roles in *Oklahoma!* (1955) and *Carousel* (1956). He played songwriter B. G. DeSylva in the bio-pic *The Best Things in Life Are Free* (1956), but with the waning of movie musicals in the 1960s, MacRae concentrated on concerts, summer stock, touring companies, and television where he had a show of his own and appeared in many specials.

and supervised every aspect of the production—from the casting to the locations. All of the players did their own singing. Such would not have been the case had James Dean or Paul Newman played Curly, Joanne Woodward was Laurey, and Eli Wallach as Jud; they had all tested for the film and were seriously considered. Jud's "Lonely Room" and Ali Hakim's "It's a Scandal! It's an Outrage!" were cut from the film but the rest of score was intact, beautifully conducted by Jay Blackton who had worked on the stage version. The waltzing cowboy ballad "Oh, What a Beautiful Mornin'," the evocative "The Surrey With the Fringe on Top," the dreamy "Out of My Dreams," the warm ballad "People Will Say We Are in Love," the comic numbers "I Cain't Say No" and "All er Nothin'," the exuberant "Kansas City," and the rousing title song all sounded better than ever. Interior scenes were shot in Hollywood, but for the exteriors a location was selected in Arizona where period farm houses were built and acres of corn were planted. The respected director Fred Zinnemann had never directed a musical before but was selected with the hope of making *Oklahoma!* not look like a Hollywood musical. In many ways the risk paid off, for the movie doesn't have the glossy look and feel of a backlot musical. Zinnemann got sincere and nicely nuanced performances from his cast: Gordon MacRae as Curly, Shirley Jones as Laurey, Charlotte Greenwood as Aunt Eller, Rod Steiger as Jud, Gloria Graham as Ado Annie, and Gene Nelson as Will. Agnes de Mille re-created her dances for the screen and they serve as a colorful record of her stage work, but even they seem less impressive in the movie. Filmed in a new wide-screen process called Todd-AO, the movie often seemed bigger than it had to be. The open prairie is well served by such an expansive look, but *Oklahoma!* has always been about characters, not scenery. Most of the reviews were complimentary and the picture was a box office hit. In 1956, 20th Century Fox rereleased the film in CinemaScope and that is the format that most have seen it in over the years. As enjoyable as the movie is, the screen version of *Oklahoma!* is more pleasant than momentous, more competent than exceptional.

See also: *Hide, Wide and Handsome, State Fair*; Richard Rodgers and Oscar Hammerstein, Gordon MacRae biography boxes

FURTHER READING

Carter, Tim. *Oklahoma!: The Making of an American Musical*. New Haven, CT: Yale University Press, 2007.

Mordden, Ethan. *Rodgers and Hammerstein*. New York: Abradale/Abrams, 1995.

Wilk, Max. *OK!: The Story of Oklahoma!* Montclair, NJ: Applause Theatre & Cinema Books, 2002.

GUYS AND DOLLS

Studio and release date: Goldwyn/Metro-Goldwyn-Mayer; November 1955
Producer: Samuel Goldwyn
Screenplay: Joseph L. Mankiewicz, based on the 1950 stage script by Abe Burrows, which was based on the stories by Damon Runyon
Songwriter: Frank Loesser (music and lyrics)
Director: Joseph L. Mankiewicz
Choreographer: Michael Kidd
Musical Director: Jay Blackton
Cinematographer: Harry Stradling
Cast: Marlon Brando, Frank Sinatra, Jean Simmons, Vivian Blaine, Stubby Kaye, Johnny Silver, B. S. Pully, Robert Keith, Sheldon Leonard
Songs: "Sit Down, You're Rockin' the Boat"; "Guys and Dolls"; "I'll Know"; "If I Were a Bell"; "The Oldest Established"; "Fugue for Tinhorns"; "Luck Be a Lady"; "Adelaide's Lament"; "Sue Me"; "Take Back Your Mink"; "Pet Me, Poppa"; "A Woman in Love"; "Adelaide"

After 60 years, *Guys and Dolls* remains one of the most popular of all Broadway musical comedies. Many consider it the best of the genre. Yet the screen version is oddly cast and the score is somewhat depleted, making the movie musical uneven even as it is often pleasing. Based on a series of stories and characters by Damon Runyon, *Guys and Dolls* was a perfect blending of story, songs, and dance when it opened on Broadway in 1950. Abe Burrows wrote the hilarious script, taking characters and situations from different Runyon tales and turning them into a tightly structured comedy masterwork. Gambler Nathan Detroit has enough on his mind, trying to find a new location for his famous floating crap game, when his longtime sweetie, the nightclub singer Adelaide, wants to know when they are finally going to get married. To raise the cash to secure a place for the big game, Nathan bets the slick lady-killer Sky Masterson that he can't get the prim Save-a-Soul Mission worker Sarah Brown to go to Havana with him. Sky wins the bet but, because he has fallen in love with Sarah, he reforms. Sarah helps Adelaide to take Nathan in tow and the musical ends with a double wedding. *Guys and Dolls* is unique in that the two romantic couples are equally interesting rather than one being major and the other secondary. It also has several supporting characters who are delightful and colorful, helping to create a Runyonesque landscape where whimsy and farce coexist. Frank Loesser wrote his most famous score for *Guys and Dolls*. Not only did the ballads become popular but the character songs are also familiar favorites. "Adelaide's Lament" is one of the funniest, cleverest, and most revealing character numbers ever written; the duets "Sue Me" and "Marry the Man Today" are ingeniously straightforward; the solos "If I Were a Bell" and "My Time of Day" are masterful examples of a character putting down his/her guard; and the revival-like "Sit Down, You're Rockin' the Boat" remains one of Broadway's best 11 o'clock numbers. Every song in the show is effective, even the quiet Irish-flavored "More I Cannot Wish You," providing a quaint touch of sincerity amidst all of the plotting and deceiving. A score this good could have hidden a weaker libretto but luckily it didn't have to. The original production was pure gold, with George S. Kaufman directing and Michael Kidd providing the nimble choreography. The original production ran 1,200 performances, followed by tours then mountings by every kind of theater group imaginable.

Eccentric producer Sam Goldwyn purchased the film rights for a record $1 million then proceeded to cast the movie with an eye toward disaster. Nonsinger Marlon Brando was cast as the singing Sky Masterson, while singer Frank Sinatra was contracted for the nonsinging role of Nathan Detroit. Joseph L. Mankiewicz, who had never directed a musical before, was hired to write and helm the $5 million production. Two of the stage score's biggest hits, "I've Never Been in Love Before" and "A Bushel and a Peck," were cut and replaced by the forgettable "A Woman in Love" and "Pet Me, Poppa" (also by Loesser). Also cut and not replaced were the tender "My Time of Day," the Irish ballad "More I Cannot Wish You," and the merry duet "Marry the Man Today." To give Sinatra more singing, the ballad "Adelaide" was added, surely the dullest song that Loesser ever wrote. Yet Goldwyn did some things right. He let Vivian Blaine reprise her hilarious Adelaide onscreen, hired Michael Kidd to restage his Broadway dances, and got stage designer Oliver Smith to create a cartoonish Runyonland in the studio. The result was a movie far better than most expected. Brando did his own singing and found a sincere charm in the con man Sky. Jean Simmons, also doing her own singing, was surprisingly effective as Sarah. The supporting cast was excellent, including the three bookies—Stubby Kaye, Johnny Silver, and B. S. Pully—who had sung "Fugue for Tinhorns" on Broadway. The movie has a stylized look that complements the material, and Kidd's production numbers were energetic and fun. Goldwyn's gamble paid off; the film was one of the top-grossing pictures of the year. *Guys and Dolls* is best enjoyed if one forgets the superior stage version. Since that version is being revived all the time, it is difficult to forget.

See also: Hans Christian Andersen; Frank Sinatra, Frank Loesser, Michael Kidd biography boxes

FURTHER READING

Breslin, Jimmy. *Damon Runyon: A Life.* Jefferson City, MO: Laurel, 1992.
Kaplan, James. *Sinatra: The Chairman.* New York: Doubleday, 2015.
Loesser, Susan. *A Most Remarkable Fella: Frank Loesser and the Guys and Dolls in His Life.* New York: Donald I. Fine, Inc., 1993.

THE KING AND I

Studio and release date: 20th Century Fox; March 1956
Producer: Charles Brackett
Screenplay: Ernest Lehman, based on the 1951 stage script by Oscar Hammerstein, which was based on the book *Anna and the King of Siam* by Margaret Landon
Songwriters: Richard Rodgers (music), Oscar Hammerstein (lyrics)
Director: Walter Lang
Choreographer: Jerome Robbins
Musical Director: Alfred Newman
Cinematographer: Leon Shamroy
Cast: Deborah Kerr, Yul Brynner, Rita Moreno, Martin Benson, Terry Saunders, Rex Thompson, Carlos Rivas, Patrick Adiarte, Alan Mowbray
Songs: "Hello, Young Lovers"; "Getting to Know You"; "Shall We Dance"; "We Kiss in a Shadow"; "I Whistle a Happy Tune"; "A Puzzlement"; "Something Wonderful"; "The Small House of Uncle Thomas"

A lavish and exotic musical about the Orient, this is arguably the finest film adaptation of any Rodgers and Hammerstein musical, perhaps even better than the more popular movie *The Sound of Music* (1965). Richard Rodgers (music) and Oscar Hammerstein (book and lyrics) based their 1951 Broadway hit on Margaret Landon's 1944 novel *Anna and the King of Siam*. The plot for the stage and screen versions is exactly the same. The Welsh widow Anna Leonowens (Deborah Kerr) and her young son Louis (Rex Thompson) arrive in Siam where she has been hired as a teacher for the king's son, Prince Chulalongkorn (Patrick Adiarte), and the many children the king has sired with his various wives. Right away Anna and the king (Yul Brynner) are at odds, he insisting on her living

Few Broadway musicals came to the screen as effectively as *The King and I* (1956). Yul Brynner (pictured) reprised his stage performance as the King of Siam and Deborah Kerr was the Englishwoman who tutors his many children. Here she teaches the King how to do a polka in the "Shall We Dance?" number. (20th Century Fox/Photofest)

in the palace when her contract calls for a separate house for her and Louis. Anna would leave immediately but she is charmed by the anxious and loving faces of the children and decides to stay. Also new to the court is the Burmese slave Tuptim (Rita Moreno) who is a "gift" for the king, but she and her emissary Lun Tha (Carlos Rivas) are in love and hope to escape together. While the tension between the king and Anna remains, they soon develop a healthy respect for each other and she helps the king and his wives prepare for a visit by foreign dignitaries to show that the Siamese monarch is not the barbarian that rumors say he is. At the state occasion, Tuptim and members of the court perform a version of *Uncle Tom's Cabin* that Tuptim has written, condemning slavery and ruthless monarchs. After the performance, Tuptim and Lun Tha flee the palace but are captured by the king's guards. The king tries to punish Tuptim by flogging her himself but he cannot, plagued by Anna's accusations and his doubts about his barbarism. Anna and Louis make preparations to leave Siam but she is called to the deathbed of the king who encourages the prince to rule as he sees fit. The king dies and Anna remains to guide the young king. Among the songs in the glorious score are the childlike ditty "Getting to Know You," the waltzing ballad "Hello, Young Lovers," the lyrical duet "We Kiss in a Shadow," the lively polka "Shall We Dance?," and the stirring "Something Wonderful." The Broadway version ran three years and has been revived in New York more than any other Rodgers and Hammerstein musical.

The movie version of *The King and I*, directed with skill by Walter Lang, is very faithful to the original. Some will go so far as to say that it is the only musical by the team that is actually better on the screen than the stage, since Ernest Lehman's screenplay trims the stage script, cuts three songs, and makes for a more compact and powerful show. Comparisons aside, it is safe to say that it is a beautifully directed, designed, acted, and sung movie and true to the Broadway show without seeming stage bound. Jerome Robbins re-created his choreography from the Broadway production, the highlight being the imaginative and exotic theater-dance piece "The Small House of Uncle Thomas." Yul Brynner got to reprise his stage portrayal of the king, so there is a vivid record of one of the greatest of all musical theater performances. The role of Anna on Broadway was played by Gertrude Lawrence but she died in 1952 so several Hollywood actresses were considered for the part, including Dinah Shore and Maureen O'Hara. It was Brynner who suggested the British actress Kerr and she gave an outstanding performance as Anna, balancing the character's icy British reserve with her temperamental Welsh wit. The rivalry between Brynner's king and Kerr's Anna hits all of the exciting levels of their relationship. Kerr's singing was dubbed by Marni Nixon but the two voices are perfectly matched, one of the best dubbing jobs in a Hollywood musical. The supporting cast is also first class, with Moreno's seething Tuptim a standout piece of acting. The Charles Brackett production was a box office hit and remains popular on DVD. After the somewhat disappointing screen versions of Rodgers and Hammerstein's *Oklahoma!* (1955) and *Carousel* (1956), the arrival of *The King and I* was a wonderful surprise, proving that the two masters of the Broadway musical stage could be as potent on the screen.

See also: *Oklahoma!, The Sound of Music*; Richard Rodgers and Oscar Hammerstein biography box

FURTHER READING

Allvine, Glendon. *The Greatest Fox of Them All*. New York: Lyle Stuart, 1969.

Bloom, Ken. *Hollywood Musicals: The 101 Greatest Song-and-Dance Movies of All Time*. New York: Black Dog and Leventhal, 2010.

Habegger, Alfred. *Masked: The Life of Anna Leonowens, Schoolmistress at the Court of Siam*. Madison: University of Wisconsin Press, 2014.

Nolan, Frederick. *The Sound of Their Music: The Story of Rodgers and Hammerstein*. Montclair, NJ: Applause Theatre & Cinema Books, 2002.

HIGH SOCIETY

Studio and release date: Metro-Goldwyn-Mayer; July 1956
Producer: Sol C. Siegel
Screenplay: John Patrick, based on the 1939 play *The Philadelphia Story* by
    Philip Barry
Songwriter: Cole Porter (music and lyrics)
Director/Choreographer: Charles Walters
Musical Director: Johnny Green
Cinematographer: Paul Vogel
Cast: Bing Crosby, Frank Sinatra, Grace Kelly, Celeste Holm, John Lund, Louis
    Calhern, Louis Armstrong
Songs: "True Love"; "You're Sensational"; "Now You Has Jazz"; "Well, Did You
    Evah?"; "Mind If I Make Love to You?"; "I Love You, Samantha"; "Who
    Wants to Be a Millionaire?"; "Little One"; "High Society Calypso"

Playwright Philip Barry's comedy of manners *The Philadelphia Story* was made into
a terrific movie in 1940 that was hard to beat, but this musicalization of the story is
able to make one (temporarily) forget the film, especially when the delectable Cole
Porter songs are performed by a sparkling cast. *The Philadelphia Story* opened on
Broadway in 1939 and proved to be one of the best comedies of manners of its era.
The comedy was not only a triumph for playwright Barry but also for Katharine Hepburn, who played the haughty, sensual heroine. Hepburn owned the movie rights so
she starred in the 1940 film version with Cary Grant and James Stewart, resulting in
one of the best of all Hollywood comedies. So making a musical of the piece was
problematic with moviegoers having such fond memories of the original. Hepburn
being such a distinctive actress, MGM thought the musical heroine should be a very
different kind of performer. Elizabeth Taylor was producer Sol C. Siegel's first choice
but she was fully booked making *Giant* (1956) and *Raintree County* (1957). Grace
Kelly, at the peak of her popularity, had just gotten engaged to the Prince Rainier
of Monaco but was willing to make one more film before retiring. The problem
was, Kelly was not a singer and the leading lady in a musical usually carried the
bulk of the score. But with Frank Sinatra and Bing Crosby in the cast, MGM decided to let them handle the singing, and Kelly just sang along in two numbers.
John Patrick's screenplay moved the action from Philadelphia to Newport, Rhode
Island, home to a famous jazz festival. This allowed for some song possibilities
and provided a spot for Louis Armstrong to perform. Retitled *High Society*, the production, under the direction of Charles Walters, went smoothly and resulted in a
first-class movie musical.

Despite all the changes made from the nonmusical film, *High Society* did not
stray too far from it when it came to the story. On the eve of her wedding to the
stuffy millionaire George Kittredge (John Kund), the spoiled heiress Tracy Lord

Louis Armstrong (1901–1971)   With his raspy singing voice and piercing trumpet playing, the African American musician-singer-songwriter was featured in two dozen Hollywood films, usually playing himself and always stopping the show. Armstrong was born in New Orleans and learned to play the bugle and clarinet as a boy, earning money playing for funerals, parades, and other gatherings. His professional career began with the Kid Ory Band and then the Creole Jazz Band. (He was nicknamed "Satchmo," short for Satchelmouth, which was slang for a brass musician.) Armstrong made his first of many recordings in 1923 and was popular enough in nightclubs that he was featured in the Broadway revue *Hot Chocolates* (1929). He made his feature film debut with *Pennies From Heaven* (1936) and did specialty spots in such musicals as *Artists and Models* (1937), *Doctor Rhythm* (1938), *Jam Session* (1944), *Atlantic City* (1944), *Hollywood Canteen* (1944), *New Orleans* (1947), *Carnegie Hall* (1947), *A Song Is Born* (1948), *Here Comes the Groom* (1951), *The Strip* (1951), *The Glenn Miller Story* (1954), and *When the Boys Meet the Girls* (1965). He also played characters in *Going Places* (1939), *Cabin in the Sky* (1943), *Glory Alley* (1952), *Paris Blues* (1961), and *A Man Called Adam* (1966). But Armstrong is most remembered on-screen for playing himself and joining celebrated stars in rousing duets, as with Bing Crosby in *High Society* (1956), Danny Kaye in *The Five Pennies* (1959), and Barbra Streisand in *Hello, Dolly!* (1969). A giant in the world of jazz, he composed several songs, made many television appearances over the decades, and toured internationally. Autobiography: *Satchmo: My Life in New Orleans*, 1986; biography: *Satchmo: The Genius of Louis Armstrong*, Gary Giddins (2001).

(Kelly) is visited in her Newport summer mansion by two men who give her second thoughts. One is her ex-husband, songwriter-singer C. Dexter Haven (Crosby), who is in town for the jazz festival and is still liked by Tracy's family, particularly her younger sister Caroline (Lydia Reed). The other man is the radical journalist Mike Connor (Sinatra) who has come with the wisecracking photographer Liz Imbrie (Celeste Holm) to cover the wedding. To avoid a scandal, the family pretends that Uncle Willie (Louis Calhern) is really Tracy's father because her real father is off philandering with a chorus girl in New York. Although Tracy and her riches represent everything he is against, Mike is drawn to her and the two go off for a midnight swim. George is shocked, breaks off the engagement, and Dexter rescues the day by offering to marry her once again since they obviously still love each other.

The score is arguably the finest set of songs Porter ever wrote for one movie—from the lyrical ballads "True Love" and "You're Sensational" to the tongue-in-cheek character songs "Who Wants to Be a Millionaire?" and "Well, Did You Evah?" This last number, written years earlier by Porter for the Broadway show *DuBarry Was a Lady* (1939), was added at the last minute when the studio realized that there was no song in the score for Crosby and Sinatra to sing together. Perhaps the highlight of this musical feast was Crosby and Louis Armstrong bringing down the house with "Now You Has Jazz." Singing and joking and making love, the cast is in superb form, and the chemistry between Kelly and both Crosby and Sinatra makes the triangle all the more intriguing. For a nonsinger, Kelly found herself on a platinum record when her duet version of "True Love" with Crosby from the movie sold over a million discs. There is very little dancing in *High Society* because the musical remains a comedy of manners. The sets and costumes were dazzling as only MGM could afford, and the bright, seaside feel of the movie was enchanting. It turned out that Kelly's last movie was as glamorous as she was.

See also: *Kiss Me, Kate*; Cole Porter, Bing Crosby, Frank Sinatra, Louis Armstrong biography boxes

FURTHER READING

Eames, John Douglas. *The MGM Story*. New York: Crown Publishers, 1975.
Grudens, Richard. *Bing Crosby: Crooner of the Century*. Stony Brook, NY: Celebrity Profiles, Inc., 2002.
Schwartz, Charles. *Cole Porter: A Biography*. Boston: Da Capo Press, 1979.

FUNNY FACE

Studio and release date: Paramount; March 1957
Producer: Roger Edens
Screenplay: Leonard Gershe
Songwriters: George Gershwin, Roger Edens (music), Ira Gershwin, Leonard Gershe (lyrics)
Director: Stanley Donen
Choreographer: Eugene Loring
Musical Director: Adolph Deutsch
Cinematographer: Ray June
Cast: Fred Astaire, Audrey Hepburn, Kay Thompson, Michel Auclair, Robert Flemyng
Songs: "Funny Face"; "How Long Has This Been Going On?"; "'S Wonderful"; "Clap Yo' Hands"; "He Loves and She Loves:'; "Think Pink"; "Let's Kiss and Make Up"; "Bonjour, Paris!"; "On How to Be Lovely"

Hollywood sometimes bought the screen rights to a Broadway musical only to discard everything but the title and the title song. Such is what happened to this 1927 musical with a superlative score by George (music) and Ira Gershwin (lyrics). Fred Astaire and his sister Adele starred in the original *Funny Face* on Broadway and there was talk of filming it with the two stage stars. But Hollywood decided otherwise and the musical was instead turned into the British movie *She Knew What She Wanted* (1936). Decades later, writer Leonard Gershe had an idea for a musical about the fashion photographer Richard Avedon. Titled *Wedding Day*, the project was tackled by various songwriters before it was dropped. A few years later, Gershe showed the script to songwriter Roger Edens who remembered the long-ago musical *Funny Face* and thought the Gershwin songs from the show would fit *Wedding Day* nicely. They interested Paramount in the idea, but the Gershwin songs were owned by Warner Brothers. Astaire was interested in playing the Avedon character but he was under contract to MGM, as was Stanley Donen who wanted to direct the musical. Since the leading lady in the tale was a top fashion model, the creators immediately thought of Audrey Hepburn, the most photogenic star in Hollywood. Hepburn was being wooed to play the title role in the movie musical of *Gigi* (1958), but when she was offered the chance to play opposite Astaire, she jumped at it. It took a lot of negotiations among Paramount, MGM, and Warner Brothers to make *Funny Face*, but it was worth it because the film turned out to be one of the most sophisticated and beautiful-looking musical of the 1950s.

Gershe's screenplay was sly and satiric, even as it was very romantic. Fashion photographer Dick Avery (Astaire) discovers the brainy Jo Stockton (Hepburn) working in a Greenwich Village bookstore and is determined to make a star model out of her. With the help of fashion magazine editor Maggie Prescott (Kay Thompson), who wants the women of the world to "think pink," he takes Jo to Paris for a shoot. Jo agrees only because she wants to meet the French philosopher Emile Flostre (Michel Auclair) whose Existentialist-like writings she so admires. When she finally meets Flostre, he turns out to be an unsavory wolf. But by that time Jo has succumbed to the charms of Dick Avery and the city of Paris. The two settle into a Parisian romance and Jo becomes a famous cover girl. Since the movie was about fashion photography, the celebrated photographer Richard Avedon served as consultant so the look of the film was unique. The on-site locations in New York City and Paris certainly helped as director Donen turned each sequence into a dazzling magazine spread. Eugene Loring and Astaire did the choreography, the most memorable moments being Astaire's solo "Let's Kiss and Make Up," in which a raincoat and umbrella become his partner, and a lyrical duet with Hepburn and Astaire dancing to "He Loves and She Loves" through a morning mist rising from a pond. The other Gershwin songs used included the rhythmic "Clap Yo' Hands," the wistful "How Long Has This Been Going On?," the stylish " 'S Wonderful," and the adoring title song. Edens (music) and Gershe (lyrics) added three new songs, which, while not on the level of a Gershwin tune, were a lot of fun. The celebratory "Bonjour, Paris!" was sung by Hepburn, Astaire, and Thompson at different Paris locations, including the Eiffel Tower. The harmonizing duet "On How to Be Lovely" was performed with tongue in cheek by Thompson and Hepburn, and Thompson was delightful as she sang to the woman of the world to "Think Pink!" Another musical highlight was Hepburn's satiric "Basal Metabolism" dance, which she did in a Paris bistro to the accompaniment of bongo drums. Just as impressive as the musical numbers were the fashion shoots in which the beautifully garbed Hepburn posed in various locations, the scenes freezing and becoming magazine covers. With Avedon in charge of these sequences, they are indeed stunning.

An unusual but satisfying aspect of *Funny Face* was the fact that the studio let Hepburn do her own singing. A thin but pleasing voice, she rendered both the Gershwin and Edens songs with class and playfulness. It was Hepburn's first musical and she loved doing all the singing and dancing that the role required. No wonder she was so disappointed seven years later when her singing in *My Fair Lady* (1964) was dropped and replaced by Marni Nixon's voice. The pairing of 58-year-old Astaire with Hepburn, who was 30 years his junior, may have looked suspect on paper but works on the screen. He is obviously too old to play the conventional leading man, but then Astaire never was the usual kind of star. As he grew older, his leading ladies remained much younger than him and no one minded, particularly those women who got to sing and dance with him.

See also: *An American in Paris, The Band Wagon, My Fair Lady, Gigi*; Fred Astaire, George and Ira Gershwin, Stanley Donen biography boxes

FURTHER READING

Astaire, Fred. *Steps in Time: An Autobiography*. New York: Dey Street Books, 2008.
Eames, John Douglas. *The Paramount Story*. New York: Crown Publishers, 1985.
Silverman, Stephen M. *Dancing on the Ceiling: Stanley Donen and His Movies*. New York: Knopf, 1996.

THE JOKER IS WILD

Studio and release date: Paramount; August 1957
Producer: Samuel Briskin
Screenplay: Oscar Saul, based on the Joe E. Lewis biography of the same title by Art Cohn

Songwriters: James Van Heusen, Sammy Cahn, Walter Donaldson, and others
   (music and lyrics)
Director: Charles Vidor
Choreographer: Josephine Earl
Musical Director: Walter Scharf
Cinematographer: Daniel Fapp
Cast: Frank Sinatra, Jeanne Crain, Mitzi Gaynor, Eddie Albert, Beverly Garland,
   Jackie Coogan
Principal Songs: "All the Way"; "I Cried for You"; "If I Could Be with You One
   Hour Tonight"; At Sundown"; "Out of Nowhere"; "Swinging on a Star"

Of the handful of downbeat musical bios that Hollywood made after the success
of *Love Me or Leave Me* (1955), this "melodrama with songs" was perhaps the most
uncompromising. It was directed by Charles Vidor, who had directed *Love Me or
Leave Me* with a grim, unsentimental feel that was practically oppressive. Given
the subject matter, the tragic singer-comic Joe E. Lewis, the movie could be little
else. The project would probably never have gotten off the ground had not Frank
Sinatra pushed for it to be made. He not only knew the story's seamy nightclubs
and hoodlum owners, Sinatra was a close friend of Lewis. *The Joker Is Wild* would
also give Sinatra the chance to stretch his wings and give a raw, powerful performance. Paramount backed the unlikely project and lost money. *The Joker Is Wild*
was perhaps too raw and powerful for mainstream audiences.

   Oscar Saul's screenplay, based on a biography of Lewis by Art Cohn, pulled no
punches. During Prohibition, crooner Lewis (Sinatra) decides to leave one mobster's nightclub to work for a rival hood. In retribution, he is attacked one night by
some thugs and his vocal cords are so damaged that he cannot sing again. So Lewis
becomes a raspy voiced stand-up comic, making jokes about his alcohol and gambling addictions and finding modest fame in less-than-glamorous clubs. Sinatra
found a harsh and gritty reality in the character that, though unlikable, was fascinating. Eddie Albert was Austin Mack, Lewis' long-time friend and accompanist,
Jeanne Crain played the Chicago socialite Letty Page, and Mitzi Gaynor was the
showgirl Martha Stewart, both of whom Lewis weds and divorces, never willing to
give either of them his love. Ironically, the hit song from the film, James Van Heusen and Sammy Cahn's "All the Way," was about the kind of affection Lewis was
not capable of. Also heard in the movie were several smoky standards, including
"I Cried for You," "At Sundown," and "If I Could Be With You One Hour Tonight."
Vidor directed perhaps too well, for the uncomfortable film was not a success at
the box office. Yet Sinatra got a best-selling record from the experience and the
movie was later reissued as *All the Way* to capitalize on it.

   Sinatra's movie career is an interesting one because it is filled with paradoxes.
Pampered, difficult, moody, and sometimes just plain lazy, Sinatra was far from

easy to work with. Even as a young singer getting his feet wet appearing in 1940s musicals, he found moviemaking annoying and time-consuming. As one of the most popular singing stylists of his time, he didn't need the movies. Yet he kept returning to Hollywood to act in musicals, melodramas, comedies, and even war films. Sometimes he couldn't bother with taking a film seriously; other times he took on challenging parts and pushed himself mercilessly. *The Joker Is Wild* is a case of Sinatra caring so much for a project that he pursues it even though he knows the result will not be popular with the public. Having won an Oscar for his performance in the drama *From Here to Eternity* (1953), he was probably hoping to wow the Academy with his searing performance as Joe E. Lewis. Oddly, Sinatra was not even nominated even though the consensus was that *The Joker Is Wild* offers his greatest performance. Hollywood loved him and hated him, yet he made 58 feature films and didn't seem to care. His movie musicals are highly ranked and his performances in them are consistently accomplished. In the case of *The Joke Is Wild*, he was much more than that.

See also: *Love Me or Leave Me*; *Anchors Aweigh*; Frank Sinatra biography box

FURTHER READING

Cohn, Art. *The Joker Is Wild: The Story of Joe E. Lewis.* New York: Random House, 1955.
Eames, John Douglas. *The Paramount Story.* New York: Crown Publishers, 1985.
Leigh, Spencer. *Frank Sinatra: An Extraordinary Life.* London: McNidder and Grace, 2015.

SOUTH PACIFIC

Studio and release date: Magna/20th Century Fox; March 1958
Producer: Buddy Adler
Screenplay: Paul Osborn, based on the 1949 stage script by Oscar Hammerstein and Joshua Logan, which was based on the 1947 novel *Tales of the South Pacific* by James Michener
Songwriters: Richard Rodgers (music), Oscar Hammerstein (lyrics)
Director: Joshua Logan
Choreographer: LeRoy Prinz
Musical Director: Ken Darby
Cinematographer: Leon Shamroy
Cast: Mitzi Gaynor, Rossano Brazzi, John Kerr, Ray Walston, Juanita Hall, France Nuyen, Russ Brown, Ken Clark
Songs: "Some Enchanted Evening"; "Younger Than Springtime"; "Bali Hai"; "There Is Nothin' Like a Dame"; "I'm Gonna Wash That Man Right Outa My

Hair"; "This Nearly Was Mine"; "A Wonderful Guy"; "A Cockeyed Optimist"; "Honey Bun"; "Bloody Mary"; "Twin Soliloquies"; "Dites-moi"; "Happy Talk"; "You've Got to Be Carefully Taught"; "My Girl Back Home"

The Richard Rodgers (music) and Oscar Hammerstein (book and lyrics) musical classic took nearly a decade to come to the screen but both critics and audiences agreed it was worth the wait. The film's plot follows that of the 1949 Broadway hit rather closely. During the Pacific campaign of World War II, the young nurse Nellie Forbush (Mitzi Gaynor) from Little Rock, Arkansas, falls in love with the older, gentlemanly Emile de Becque (Rossano Brazzi) who left France years ago to become a planter on an island where the allies are now stationed. The upper-class Lieutenant Joe Cable (John Kerr) from Philadelphia arrives on the island to prepare for a dangerous mission and falls for the beautiful Polynesian girl Liat (France Nuyen), the two young lovers brought together by Liat's crafty mother, the black-market operator Bloody Mary (Juanita Hall). When Nellie learns that Emile has had a Polynesian wife who died and left him two children, her prejudices force her to turn down Emile's proposal of marriage, just as Joe realizes he has no future with Liat and leaves her. The disillusioned Emile agrees to help Joe with his mission and the two depart for a remote island where they will radio news about the Japanese fleet. Joe is killed in the endeavor but Emile manages to return to the base where Nellie, who has learned to love Emile's two Eurasian children, is willing to conquer her prejudices and marry Emile. The comedy was provided by the conniving Luther Billis (Ray Walston) who operates his own laundry service on the island and sells and buys trinkets to whomever looks like a sucker. *South Pacific* is considered the most adult Rodgers and Hammerstein musical; its story is not dictated merely by romance but also by prejudice and fear. The plot and characters, taken from two sections of James Michener's 1947 novel *Tales of the South Pacific*, are both more thought-provoking and brutally honest than what one expected from a musical. The entire Broadway score was retained for the movie version, a rarity in Hollywood. Among the highlights were the popular ballad "Some Enchanted Evening," the haunting "Bali Ha'i," the romantic "Younger Than Springtime," the expansive "A Wonderful Guy," the frolicking "I'm Gonna Wash That Man Right Outa My Hair," the simple ditty "Happy Talk," the rollicking "Honey Bun," and the torch classic "This Nearly Was Mine." Most unusual of all is "You've Got to Be Carefully Taught," Joe's bitter accusation in which he is the accused one. The songwriters were pressured to cut the song on Broadway but argued that it was the theme of the whole musical. Hollywood also tried to cut the uncomfortable number but Rodgers and Hammerstein again held firm. Joe also sang "My Girl Back Home," a song written for the Broadway production but cut and then reinstated in the film. Joshua Logan, who had staged the Broadway version, directed the movie, which was filmed on location on the Hawaiian island of Kauai with its beautiful postcard vistas, but they are frequently ruined by Logan's decision to use color filters to denote mood.

Mary Martin, who had won acclaim as Nellie on Broadway, was considered too old (45 years old) for the film version so the studio considered Elizabeth Taylor, Doris Day, Judy Garland, Ginger Rogers, Audrey Hepburn, and even Patti Page for the role before casting Mitzi Gaynor. She is perky and appealing in the role; Gaynor was also one of the few cast members who did her own singing. Brazzi was dubbed by opera singer Giorgio Tozzi and some felt it was an awkward match, although Brazzi was very effective as Emile. He was clearly too young to play the middle-aged Frenchman and the gray touches in the hair fooled no one. Yet Brazzi had the charming, alluring quality that was needed to interest Nellie. The supporting cast is uneven but, Hall, who reprised her stage performance as Bloody Mary, is funny and crafty. Oddly, her singing also was dubbed because her voice had deteriorated some in the years since she appeared in *South Pacific* on Broadway. As enjoyable as the movie is, it never has the punch it did onstage. Perhaps all that gorgeous scenery took some of the bite out of the story. But *South Pacific* often works on the screen as well as it did on the stage, which is no small accomplishment.

See also: Oklahoma!, The King and I; Richard Rodgers and Oscar Hammerstein biography box

FURTHER READING

Lovensheimer, Jim. *South Pacific: Paradise Rewritten*. New York: Oxford University Press, 2010.

Masion, Laurence. *The South Pacific Companion*. New York: Touchstone, 2008.

Nolan, Frederick. *The Sound of Their Music: The Story of Rodgers and Hammerstein*. Montclair, NJ: Applause Theatre & Cinema Books, 2002.

GIGI

Studio and release date: Metro-Goldwyn-Mayer; May 1958
Producer: Arthur Freed
Screenplay: Alan Jay Lerner, based on the 1944 novella by Colette
Songwriters: Frederick Loewe (music), Alan Jay Lerner (lyrics)
Directors: Vincente Minnelli, Charles Walters
Musical Director: André Previn
Cinematographer: Joseph Ruttenberg
Cast: Leslie Caron, Maurice Chevalier, Louis Jourdan, Hermione Gingold, Isabel Jeans, Ava Gabor
Songs: "Gigi"; "Thank Heaven for Little Girls"; "I Remember It Well"; "The Night They Invented Champagne"; "I'm Glad I'm Not Young Anymore"; "The Parisians"; "Say a Prayer for Me Tonight"; "She Is Not Thinking of Me"; "It's a Bore"

Gigi (1958) does not have a traditional boy-meets-girl story. Gaston (Louis Jourdan) thinks of Gigi (Leslie Caron) as a fun-loving child and only after he falls in love with her does he realize she has grown up to be a woman. Vincente Minnelli directed the French-flavored musical with high style. (MGM/Photofest)

One of the most beautiful looking of all movie musicals, *Gigi* was the last great film musical of the 1950s and, in many ways, the last of the classic musicals that Hollywood had done so efficiently for decades. For some, the film was the climax as well as the end of a Golden Age. The story came from a 1944 novella by the French authoress Colette. During the end of the 19th century in Paris, the bored nobleman Gaston Lachailles (Louis Jourdan) scoffs at the carefree life of his *bon vivant* uncle Honoré (Maurice Chevalier) and the other Parisians and prefers spending his time with the tomboy Gigi (Leslie Caron), the granddaughter of the retired courtesan Madame Alvarez (Hermione Gingold). Gigi is being groomed by her Aunt Alicia (Isabel Jeans) to become a high-class courtesan someday, and as Gigi matures Gaston considers making her his mistress. But realizing he truly loves Gigi, he proposes marriage instead. The subject of grooming a courtesan was not typical musical fare in Hollywood but scriptwriter Alan Jay Lerner insisted on staying true to Colette's book and producer Arthur Freed backed him up before worried studio executives. The film was shot mostly in Paris by director Vincente Minnelli, using such famous landmarks as Maxim's restaurant, the Bois de Boulogne, and the Tuileries. Chevalier served as the musical's narrator and helped give the picture a French flavor that was much needed.

The score by Frederick Loewe (music) and Lerner (lyrics) is one of Hollywood's finest. The entrancing title song was the standout hit but also embraced were such character-based songs as the comic-wistful "I Remember It Well," the wryly philosophical "I'm Glad I'm Not Young Anymore," the sly "Thank Heaven For Little Girls," the tender "Say a Prayer for Me Tonight," and the celebratory trio "The Night

Alan Jay Lerner and **Frederick Loewe**   One of most successful and beloved Broadway songwriting teams of the post-World War II decades, most of their stage works were filmed with success, and they created a classic screen original with *Gigi* (1958). Lerner (1918–1986) was born into a wealthy New York family, the owners of a chain of retail clothing stores, and educated at Harvard, Juilliard, and Oxford Universities, writing librettos and lyrics for campus shows then working in radio as a scriptwriter. Loewe (1901–1988) was born in Berlin, Germany, to a musical family and was a child prodigy on the piano, playing with the Berlin Symphony at the age of 13. He studied with celebrated music teachers in Europe before immigrating in 1924 to America where he could not make a living with music and for 10 years worked as a boxer, a busboy, a cow puncher, and even a gold prospector. Loewe finally had some of his songs heard in a handful of Broadway shows before he met Lerner in 1942 and they began collaborating. Their first Broadway success was *Brigadoon* (1947), followed by *Paint Your Wagon* (1951), *My Fair Lady* (1956), and *Camelot* (1960). Lerner was also active in Hollywood, scoring the movie musical *Royal Wedding* (1951) with composer Burton Lane, writing the screenplay for the classic *An American in Paris* (1951), and scoring *Gigi* with Loewe. After Loewe retired in 1960, Lerner continued to write for the stage but few of the musicals succeeded. Loewe reteamed with him for the failed screen musical *The Little Prince* (1974). Loewe's music is rich in variety, has strong melodic lines, and blends the operetta and Broadway sound with very pleasing results. Lerner's librettos for his musicals vary in quality, though his lyrics are consistently literate, witty, and elegantly memorable. Autobiography: *The Street Where I Live* [Lerner] (1978); biographies: *Alan Jay Lerner*, Edward Jablonski (1996); *Inventing Champagne: The Worlds of Lerner and Loewe*, Gene Lees (1990).

They Invented Champagne." Even the less famous songs, such as the waltzing "She Is Not Thinking of Me," the petulant "It's a Bore," and Gigi's frustrated "(I Don't Understand) The Parisians" are ingenious numbers with sparkling lyrics and catchy French-flavored music. *Gigi* was the first musical project for Lerner and Loewe after their resounding triumph with *My Fair Lady* (1956) on Broadway. Fearful that whatever they did next in New York would pall by comparison, the songwriters turned to Hollywood. But MGM, which was losing money for the first time in decades, was very cautious and gave Lerner and Loewe all kinds of trouble. The subject matter was deemed too suggestive until Lerner convinced the studio that the script was moral because it condemned the mistress system of Belle Epoch period. Lerner and Minnelli insisted on filming the movie in Paris and MGM balked at the expense. Minnelli was powerful enough to get his way, but the studio pan-icked after a few weeks and insisted the crew return home and finish production in a studio. When the first cut of *Gigi* was shown to a preview audience, the reaction was very negative. MGM decided that the movie was hopeless and decided not to waste any more money and give it a minor release. Lerner convinced the studio to let a handful of scenes be reshot on a soundstage directed by Charles Walters because Minnelli was already involved with filming another movie. The revised scenes made all the difference and *Gigi* was a resounding hit when it opened, later winning all nine of the Oscars for which it was nominated. If *Gigi* signaled the end of an era never to be seen again, at least the era went out in a blaze of glory.

See also: *My Fair Lady*; Alan Jay Lerner and Frederick Loewe, Maurice Chevalier, Vincente Minnelli biography boxes

FURTHER READING

Chevalier, Maurice. *I Remember It Well*. New York: Macmillan & Co., 1970.

Lees, Gene. *Inventing Champagne: The Worlds of Lerner and Loewe*. New York: St. Martin's Press, 1990.

Lerner, Alan Jay. *The Street Where I Live*. New York: W. W. Norton & Co., 1978.

Levy, Emanuel. *Vincente Minnelli: Hollywood's Dark Dreamer*. New York: St. Martin's Press, 2009.

THE 1960s: MUSICALS DURING A REVOLUTION

The first few years of the 1960s were very much like those of the 1950s: conservative, prosperous, wholesome, and even patriotic. But after 1964 the country was shaken with a revolution of sorts. The Civil Rights Movement, the growing antiwar feelings over Vietnam, the ever-widening "generation gap," and the explosions in music, fashion, and even sex were all signs that America was changing. Many resisted the change. This led to a rivalry between the old and established ways and the radical new ideas. It was a restless decade filled with tragedy (assassinations) and triumph (man on the moon). There was so much noise that only looking back can one begin to sense what was revolutionary and innovative and what was just discontent and anger. One thing is for sure: America at the end of the 1960s was not the same place it was at the beginning of the decade.

The decade started on an optimistic note when John F. Kennedy was elected president and he represented a young, aggressive kind of spirit that was in contrast to the mild Eisenhower years of the 1950s. But by 1961 the United States started sending troops to Vietnam to aid the democratic side of the civil war. That same year the Berlin Wall was constructed in Germany, and in 1962 the Cuban Missile Crisis brought the Cold War close to American shores. The so-called Space Race between the United States and the Soviet Union paralleled the Cold War. In 1961, Russia sent cosmonaut Yuri Gagarin into space; soon after astronaut Alan Shepard became the first American in space. The optimism that space travel brought was crushed in 1963 when Kennedy was assassinated. His successor, Lyndon B. Johnson, had trouble maintaining the nationalism that Kennedy had created. By 1965 the war in Vietnam had escalated to the point where thousands of Americans were being drafted into a war that was far from popular with the younger generation. By the end of the decade, the older generation was coming to realize that Vietnam was a political, social, and international disaster. During the 1968 Democratic National Convention in Chicago, police clashed with protestors, and all of America watched on television the collapse of political unity in the nation. The antiwar movement was matched by the Civil Rights Movement. What Rosa Parks had started in 1955 was further ignited when the U.S. Supreme Court forced the University of Mississippi to allow African Americans to enroll for classes. When James Howard Meredith tried to register, a riot broke out in which two people were killed. During a march on Washington in 1963, Dr. Martin Luther King gave his celebrated "I Have a Dream" speech. The following year the Civil Rights Act of 1964 was passed, ensuring voting rights for African Americans and outlawed discrimination in housing and jobs. Just as it seemed progress was being made, Dr. King was assassinated in 1968 and the backlash involved riots in several cities. Clearly, true civil rights were yet to come. Two other movements were also born in the 1960s. The National Organization of Women (NOW) was founded in 1966 and began the long struggle for equal rights for American women. In 1969, the police raided the gay nightspot Stonewall Inn in Manhattan and prompted the beginning of the gay rights movement. The decade ended on a rare moment of optimism when American astronauts landed on the moon in 1969.

The cultural changes across the nation were often fueled by the arts. One could see the divided nature of the country by looking at literature, art, music, theater, and the movies. The aged but still potent Spanish artist Pablo Picasso finally found himself widely accepted by the masses, opening doors for avant-garde American artists Andy Warhol, Mark Rothko, Roy Lichtenstein, and others. Conservative art lovers were more content with Andrew Wyeth and Norman Rockwell. While American readers turned Harper Lee's *To Kill a Mockingbird* (1960) and Katherine Ann Porter's *A Ship of Fools* (1962) into bestsellers, others were more interested in such cutting-edge novels as Joseph Heller's *Catch-22* (1961), Ken Kesey's *One Flew Over the Cuckoo's Nest* (1962), and Kurt Vonnegut's *Slaughterhouse-Five* (1969). Among the appealing Broadway musicals of the decade were such popular works as *Bye Bye Birdie* (1960), *Oliver!* (1963), *Hello, Dolly!* (1964), *Fiddler on the Roof* (1964), *Mame* (1966), and *1776* (1969). More adventurous theatergoers applauded such disturbing musicals as *Cabaret* (1966) and *Hair* (1968). But it was in music that the national divide was most prevalent. The popular music of the early 1960s was a continuation of the 1950s' easy-listening music with some early rock and roll. But that changed once the Beatles arrived in America in 1964. After appearing on national television and touring the country, the British foursome made it clear what the youth of America wanted. Quickly, other American and British rock groups found recognition, including the Rolling Stones; Earth, Wind & Fire; Blood, Sweat & Tears; Led Zeppelin; and The Grateful Dead. Many African American singers and musicians also found a wide audience with soul music and rhythm and blues, such as Aretha Franklin, James Brown, Stevie Wonder, Jimi Hendrix, Ray Charles, and the artists of the Motown sound. Urban folk singers were perhaps the most vocal in their antiwar sentiments, as witnessed by the songs by Pete Seeger, Simon and Garfunkel, Arlo Guthrie, Joan Baez, Judy Collins, Bob Dylan, and Peter, Paul and Mary. The decade and the music scene climaxed in 1969 with the Woodstock Festival in upstate New York. Both a protest and a celebration, Woodstock was a vibrant symbol of the baby boomers' revolt against establishment America.

It was a difficult decade for Hollywood. Not only did moviegoing decrease further, the studios were not clear on just who they were making movies for. Most films were still aimed at middle America, meaning anyone who still liked westerns, action movies, romances, comedies, and musicals. Yet throughout the decade were films that were definitely meant for a younger and more eager audience, as with *Dr. Strangelove* (1964), *Who's Afraid of Virginia Woolf?* (1966), *Midnight Cowboy* (1969), and *Easy Rider* (1969). Television embraced the rock stars of the 1960s even as it held on to traditional entertainment like cheery sit-coms and nostalgic variety shows. Hollywood was reluctant to cater to young audiences at first but it was soon clear that a large proportion of moviegoers were teenagers and people in their early twenties. It was a minor studio, American International Picture, that first offered musicals for youth: the harmless Annette Funicello-Frankie Avalon "Beach" movies. The rest of Hollywood aimed for the older audience, as with *My Fair Lady* (1964), or to young children, as with *Mary Poppins* (1964). There were a few exceptions, such as the free-spirited Beatles musicals, *A Hard Day's Night* (1964), *Help!* (1965), and *Yellow Submarine* (1968). But by and large, the movie musicals of the 1960s were not very adventurous and far from cutting edge.

Most of the decade's movie musicals were based on successful Broadway shows. In fact, the 1960s top-grossing screen musicals came from the stage, such as *West Side Story* (1961), *The Music Man* (1962), *My Fair Lady*, *The Sound of Music* (1965), *Funny Girl* (1968), and *Oliver!* (1968). Only Disney's original musical *Mary Poppins* made the list. Other Broadway shows to make it to the screen in the 1960s include *Can-Can* (1960), *Bells Are Ringing* (1960), *Flower Drum Song* (1961), *Gypsy* (1962), *Jumbo* (1962), *Bye Bye Birdie* (1963), *The Unsinkable Molly Brown* (1964), *How to Succeed in Business Without Really Trying* (1966), *A Funny Thing Happened on the Way to the Forum* (1966), *Camelot* (1967), *Half a Sixpence* (1967), *Finian's Rainbow* (1968), *Sweet Charity* (1969), *Paint Your Wagon* (1969), and *Hello, Dolly!* (1969). While most of these were fairly faithful to the stage originals, only a few of them worked as well on the screen as they had on Broadway. Most of the original Hollywood musicals of the decade were costly misfires. *Mary Poppins*, as mentioned, was a major success. But the Disney studio failed to match its magic with its live-action musicals *Babes in Toyland* (1961), *Summer Magic* (1963), *The Happiest Millionaire* (1967), and *The One and Only, Genuine, Original Family Band* (1968). At least there was much to enjoy in the animated features *One Hundred and One Dalmatians* (1961), *The Sword in the Stone* (1963), and *The Jungle Book* (1967).

The other original movie musicals of the decade were a mixed bag indeed. For children and fantasy lovers, there was *The Wonderful World of the Brothers Grimm* (1962), *Doctor Dolittle* (1967), and *Chitty Chitty Bang Bang* (1968). For teens, there was *Beach Party* (1963), *Muscle Beach Party* (1964), *Bikini Beach* (1964), *Beach Blanket Bingo* (1965), and *How to Stuff a Wild Bikini* (1967). For Elvis Presley fans, young and old, there were 25 musicals during the 1960s, including such favorites as *GI Blues* (1960), *Blue Hawaii* (1961), *Kid Galahad* (1962), *Girls! Girls! Girls!* (1962), *Fun in Acapulco* (1963), *Kissin' Cousins* (1964), *Viva Las Vegas* (1964), *Roustabout* (1964), *Girl Happy* (1965), *Harum Scarum* (1965), *Frankie and Johnny* (1966), *Spinout* (1966), *Double Trouble* (1967), *Clambake* (1968), and *Live a Little Love a Little* (1968). That left *State Fair* (1962), *I Can Go on Singing* (1963), *Robin and the Seven Hoods* (1964), *Your Cheatin' Heart* (1965), *The Singing Nun* (1966), *Thoroughly Modern Millie* (1967), *Star!* (1968), *Goodbye, Mr. Chips* (1969), *Darling Lili* (1969), and the animated *Gay-Purr-ee* (1962) for the adults who liked their musicals with stars and non-rock music.

As with the previous decade, the Hollywood musicals during the 1960s were larger and more expensive than in earlier decades but there were also fewer of them. The studios reasoned that putting a lot of money into a blockbuster was smarter than making many modest-sized musicals. On a few occasions this was true, but most of these mega-musicals bombed at the box office and lost money on their initial release. The price tags for such expensive films as *Camelot*, *Doctor Dolittle*, *Star!*, *Paint Your Wagon*, *Hello, Dolly!*, and *Darling Lili* made musicals unprofitable. There was also a problem with personnel. Most of the directors, choreographers, musical directors, designers, and performers from the Golden Age of the Hollywood musical were retired or deceased by the mid-1960s. Gone also were the established music departments that each studio had maintained in the past. With fewer and fewer musicals being made, there were fewer and fewer artists who knew how to make them. *Hello, Dolly!* was fortunate to have on staff veterans from the old Freed unit at MGM, including director Gene Kelly, choreographer Michael Kidd, producer Roger Edens, costumer Irene Sharaff, and cinematographer Harry Stradling. Perhaps that is why *Hello, Dolly!* looked and sounded like a musical from the old days. But the finances were such that the expensive movie would not pay back its huge cost for several years. Such were the economics in Hollywood that a musical could make a killing, as with *The Sound of Music*, but it was just as likely to lose a bundle, quality notwithstanding. Kelly and Kidd and the other veterans who worked on *Hello, Dolly!* all retired by the 1970s and the last generation of superior musical craftsmen was gone. So was Walt Disney and other experienced producers. The 1960s was their last hurrah and they would be missed. So too would Kelly, Frank Sinatra, Bing Crosby, Debbie Reynolds, Fred Astaire, Jane Powell, Rex Harrison, Ginger Rogers, Audrey Hepburn, Elvis Presley, and even the Beatles, all of whom stopped making musicals in the 1960s. It would be up to

Julie Andrews, Barbra Streisand, and other new stars to carry on the Hollywood musical tradition. The question was: What kind of musicals, if any, would there be for them to star in?

WEST SIDE STORY

Studio and release date: Mirisch/United Artists; September 1961
Producer: Robert Wise
Screenplay: Ernest Lehman, based on the 1957 stage script by Arthur Laurents
Songwriters: Leonard Bernstein (music), Stephen Sondheim (lyrics)
Directors: Robert Wise, Jerome Robbins
Choreographer: Jerome Robbins
Musical Director: Johnny Green
Cinematographer: Daniel Fapp
Cast: Natalie Wood, Richard Beymer, Rita Moreno, Russ Tamblyn, George Chakiris, Simon Oakland
Songs: "Tonight"; "Somewhere"; "Maria"; "I Feel Pretty"; "Gee, Officer Krupke"; "America"; "Cool"; "One Hand, One Heart"; "Jet Song"; "Something's Coming"; "A Boy Like That"; "I Have a Love"; "Tonight Quintet"

One of the most powerful movie musicals of the 1960s was also one of the most admired, winning 10 Academy Awards including best picture. The musical updating of *Romeo and Juliet* was a risky undertaking in the theater, mixing harsh drama with music and modern dance. Telling such a tragic tale in the form of a movie musical was even more daring. *West Side Story* had been a modest success on Broadway, but the stage was better equipped to handle such stylistic ventures. Movies are a different medium and trickier when it comes to mixing reality and stylized presentation. For most moviegoers, *West Side Story* succeeded in balancing the two.

The plot for the film followed that of the stage work but a few of the songs were shifted around. The street rivalry between the gang of Puerto Rican immigrants known as the Sharks and the native-born New York gang called the Jets has intensified over the summer. The Jet leader Riff (Russ Tamblyn) tries to get Tony (Richard Beymer), who cofounded the gang with him, to get more involved but Tony is restless and is outgrowing street fighting. Riff plans to challenge the Sharks at the dance where the two gangs and their girls will be together, and it is there that Tony sees Maria (Natalie Wood), the newly arrived immigrant who is the sister of Bernardo (George Chakiris), the leader of the Sharks. The two are immediately drawn to each other, and that night they meet on the fire escape outside her bedroom window and profess their love for each other. A rumble between the two gangs is

Dance took on a powerful new meaning in *West Side Story* (1961) as frustration, bitterness, and even hatred were illustrated through dance. Pictured are members of the gang called the "Jets" as they sing and dance about how they proudly rule their turf. Robert Wise directed and Jerome Robbins provided the stunning choreography. (United Artists/Photofest)

planned, and when Maria hears of it she makes Tony promise he will try to stop it. When Tony attempts to do so, Bernardo stabs and kills Riff and in anger Tony kills Bernardo. While the police are looking for Tony, Maria sends her friend Anita to take a message to Tony through the Jets, but the gang taunts Anita and in anger she tells them that Maria has been killed by her jealous fiancé Chino (José De Vega). When Tony gets word of this, he goes looking for Chino, asking to be killed as well. Chino shoots Tony and he dies in Maria's arms, then she takes the gun and vents her anger on both gangs, accusing them and their rivalry for all that has happened. The 1957 Broadway production featured an outstanding score by Leonard Bernstein (music) and Stephen Sondheim (lyrics) with such memorable songs as the rhapsodic duet "Tonight," the light-headed "I Feel Pretty," the adoring ballad "Maria," the tearful "Somewhere," the sarcastic "Gee, Officer Krupke," the vivacious Latin number "America," the seething "Cool," and the operatic "A Boy Like That/I Have a Love." Also memorable was the "Tonight Quintet" in which five different melodies were sung by five groups of characters at the same time, a device only heard before in opera. Jerome Robbins' direction and choreography of the Broadway production were bold and exciting. The dancing was sometimes joyous but just as often was filled with tension and frustration. This was a landmark musical in many ways.

Robbins wanted to both direct and choreograph the movie version, but the producing Mirsch brothers were cautious because Robbins had never directed a film before. So they hired the distinguished Hollywood director Robert Wise even though he had never done a musical before. In order not to lose Robbins and his brilliant choreography, they made Robbins codirector and choreographer. Neither Carol Lawrence nor Larry Kert, who had played Maria and Tony on Broadway, was considered for the film. Wise wanted Audrey Hepburn and Elvis Presley for the romantic leads, and many other stars were considered before Natalie Wood and Richard Beymer were cast. Both had their singing dubbed, as did most of the cast. A few scenes, including the dynamic opening, were filmed in New York City but most of the movie was shot at studios in Hollywood. From the start, there were problems with Robbins. He insisted on three months of dance rehearsals before filming could begin, then he redid most of the choreography on the set so the movie was soon weeks behind schedule. After having filmed four dance numbers, Robbins was fired and Wise directed the rest of the film alone. Robbins never worked on a movie again. It took six months to complete principal photography and another seven months of mixing and editing before the movie could be released. The reaction by the critics and the moviegoers was overwhelming. The audience had no trouble with the mix of ballet and knife fights. What had been so bold and exciting on the stage was just as thrilling on the screen. Yet it was clear that *West Side Story* had some weak spots. The very non-Hispanic Wood played Maria effectively, but many considered Beymer a bland Tony and the love scenes never reached the heights that they had on Broadway. Also, many found the dubbing annoying, especially when Marni Nixon's singing voice did not match Wood's speaking voice. The supporting cast, on the other hand, was outstanding. Considering the acting, singing, and dancing demands of the gang members and their girls, it becomes clear that the movie works as well as it does because of them. And, of course, much of the success of *West Side Story* can be attributed to Robbins' electric choreography. He may not have had much say over how the film turned out, but the dances he taught the cast while he was still involved in the project are the highpoint in movie musical choreography. *West Side Story* was not only a movie hit, but its success made the Broadway version more popular. Before the film was released, *West Side Story* onstage was thought different and daring; after the movie, it joined the ranks of the Broadway classics.

See also: *Fiddler on the Roof*; Stephen Sondheim biography box

FURTHER READING

Acevedo-Muñoz, Ernesto R. *West Side Story as Cinema: The Making and Impact of an American Masterpiece*. Lawrence: University Press of Kansas, 2013.

Berson, Misha. *Something's Coming: West Side Story and the American Imagination*. Montclair, NJ: Applause Theatre & Cinema Books, 2011.

Bloom, Ken. *Hollywood Musicals: The 101 Greatest Song-and-Dance Movies of All Time*. New York: Black Dog and Leventhal, 2010.

THE MUSIC MAN

Studio and release date: Warner Brothers; April 1962

Producer/Director: Morton Da Costa

Screenplay: Marion Hargrove, based on the 1957 stage script by Meredith Willson, Franklin Lacey

Songwriters: Meredith Willson (music and lyrics)

Choreographer: Onna White

Musical Director: Ray Heindorf

Cinematographer: Robert Berks

Cast: Robert Preston, Shirley Jones, Buddy Hackett; Paul Ford; Hermione Gingold, Pert Kelton, Ronny Howard, Buffalo Bills

Songs: "Seventy-Six Trombones"; "Till There Was You"; "Goodnight, My Someone"; "Trouble"; "Shipoopi"; "Marian the Librarian"; "Gary Indiana"; "Being in Love"; "Lida Rose"; "Wells Fargo Wagon"; "The Sadder-but-Wiser Girl"; "Pick-a-Little, Talk-a-Little"; "Sincere"; "Piano Lesson"

The homespun 1957 Broadway musical was a delicious mixture of nostalgia and innovation that has not lost any of its charm over the decades. The screen version is a superior adaptation of a Broadway hit, made all the better by having Robert Preston reprise his dazzling stage performance. The creative force behind *The Music Man* was Meredith Willson, a conductor, an arranger, a musician, a composer, and a lyricist who worked in radio, on Broadway, and the in movies. Everyone in show business knew Willson from his many assignments over the years. Often he regaled friends and coworkers with his funny stories about growing up in a small town in Iowa at the turn of the 20th century. Songwriter Frank Loesser urged Willson to turn his childhood into a musical. Writing the songs came easily to Willson but he struggled with the script, writing many drafts and then enlisting the help of writer Franklin Lacey. Producer Kermit Bloomgarden took on the project but had trouble finding a leading man. After considering several top Broadway and Hollywood names, Bloomgarden hired Robert Preston, a film actor who had played supporting roles in many movies but whose career was stalled. *The Music Man* was a surprise hit, running nearly five years and becoming one of the most produced of all American musicals.

The plots for the Broadway and Hollywood version are almost identical. When the con man Professor Harold Hill (Preston) comes to the small Iowa town of River City, he points out the dangers of the new pool parlor in town and gets the citizens all excited about forming a boys' marching band to protect the youth from the evils of the world. With the help of his old pal Marcellus Washburn (Buddy Hackett), Hill collects money for instruments and uniforms even as he keeps the suspicious Mayor Shinn (Paul Ford) and the other authorities off balance. The unmarried piano teacher Marian Paroo (Shirley Jones) sees right through the phony "professor" and is about to expose his fraud to the mayor when the Wells Fargo wagon comes to town with the instruments and she sees the look of delight on the face of her shy little brother Winthrop (Ronnie Howard) when he receives his coronet. While Hill stalls, waiting for the uniforms to arrive, Marian falls in love with him. When he is found out, she even defends him, reminding her fellow citizens of all the joy he has brought to the town. When the boys enter and proceed to produce squawks and screeches from their instruments, the townspeople are thrilled and all is forgiven. In a nice cinematic touch, the film ends with the whole town magically transformed into a big parade led by Hill. Just about all of Willson's stage score made it to the screen. It is a unique set of songs, employing not only traditional musical theater songs but also barbershop quartets, square dance music, soft-shoe, patter songs, and even an early version of rap. Among the memorable numbers are the rhythmic "Rock Island" and "Trouble," the flowing ballad "Till There Was You," the harmonizing quartet "Lida Rose," the jaunty soft-shoe "Gary, Indiana," the comic seduction number "Marian the Librarian," and the popular march "Seventy-Six Trombones," which was slowed down and also became the wistful ballad "Goodnight, My Someone." Onna White re-created her stage choreography, and Morton Da Costa produced and directed the movie, which remains a screen favorite. It also preserves one of the American musical theater's legendary performances by capturing Preston's Harold Hill on film.

The Music Man seems like such a simple, old-fashioned musical that few audience members notice how innovative it is. Willson knew the formula for stage and screen musicals well, yet when he wrote the score for *The Music Man* he broke many of the rules and experimented with musical forms rarely, if ever, heard in a musical before. The opening number "Rock Island," for example, is presented by the male chorus with no accompaniment from the orchestra. Instead the number uses nonsinging voices set to the pattern of a train starting up, gaining speed, slowing down, and then stopping. The vocal phrases are not rhymed or even sung but delivered with a rapid sputter that foreshadows rap music. The duet "Piano Lesson" is a musical argument between mother and daughter that is set to the pattern and notes of a piano exercise, climbing and descending the scale as the young girl Amaryllis (Monique Vermont) practices her finger work. "Pick-a-Little, Talk-a-Little" is an ingenious song for the leading ladies of the town, their short, rapid phrases emulating the sounds of chickens squawking. As for the popular song "Seventy-Six Trombones," Hill's upbeat march melody is slowed down to become Marian's wistful lullaby "Goodnight, My Someone," the two very different characters linked musically even before they fall in love. The score for *The Music Man* is filled with such inspired touches, making the music in *The Music Man* so much more sophisticated than many realize.

FURTHER READING

Hirschhorn, Clive. *The Warner Bros. Story*. New York: Crown Publishers, 1979.

Skipper, John C. *Meredith Willson: The Unsinkable Music Man*. El Dorado Hills, CA: Savas Publishing Co., 2000.

Willson, Meredith. *But He Doesn't Know the Territory*. Minneapolis: University of Minnesota Press, 2013.

VIVA LAS VEGAS

Studio and release date: Metro-Goldwyn-Mayer; May 1964
Producers: Jack Cummings, George Sidney
Screenplay: Sally Benson
Songwriters: Doc Pomas, Mort Shuman, Sid Tepper, Red West, and others (music and lyrics)
Director: George Sidney
Choreographer: David Winters
Musical Director: George Stoll
Cinematographer: Joseph Biroc
Cast: Elvis Presley, Ann-Margret, Cesare Danova, William Demarest, Nicky Blair, Jack Carter
Principal Songs: "Viva Las Vegas"; "If You Think I Don't Need You"; "The Lady Loves Me"; "I Need Somebody to Lean On"; "Appreciation"; "My Rival"; "Yellow Rose of Texas"

An engaging chemistry between Elvis Presley and Ann-Margret made this vehicle for the rock-and-roll star more interesting than usual. Moviegoers must have thought likewise because *Viva Las Vegas* did the biggest box office of Presley's 31 films. Even though it follows the same formula of most of Presley's movies, this time around there are sparks between him and his costar. MGM must have sensed it early on because Presley and Ann-Margret recorded three duets together;

Elvis Presley (1935–1977)   The pioneering rock-and-roll star was so popular in the late 1950s and 1960s that Hollywood featured him in 33 movie musicals tailored to his image and his audience. He was born in Tupelo, Mississippi, and spent his teen years in Memphis, Tennessee, where he started singing and signed with a local record company. In 1955 RCA Records discovered him and soon he was changing the face of American pop music. Presley made his film debut in *Love Me Tender* (1956), followed by a series of movie musicals that may not have given the singer a chance to act or his fans a chance to see their idol as anything more than a star. Among his films are *Jailhouse Rock* (1957), *King Creole* (1958), *GI Blues* (1960), *Blue Hawaii* (1961), *Kid Galahad* (1962), *Fun in Acapulco* (1963), *Viva Las Vegas* (1964), *Roustabout* (1964), *Frankie and Johnny* (1966), *Spinout* (1966), *Easy Come, Easy Go* (1967), *Clambake* (1968), *The Trouble with Girls* (1970), and *Change of Habit* (1970). Presley left films in 1970 and concentrated on concerts, recordings, television specials, and nightclubs until his premature death at the age of 42. The throaty singer with the gyrating hips remains as popular today, if not more so, than when he was alive. Among the many film and television bio-musicals about the popular singer are *Elvis* (1979), *This Is Elvis* (1981), *Elvis* (1990), and *Elvis* (2005). Biographies: *Last Train to Memphis*, Peter Guralnick (2014); *Elvis Presley: The Man, the Life, the Legend*, Pamela Clarke Keogh (2004).

unfortunately, two were cut. Usually he just sang to girls and they worshipped him. In *Viva Las Vegas,* Presley seems to be as attracted to Ann-Margret as the fans are to him. The fact that Presley and Ann-Margret were having an affair during the shooting certainly helped. But on-screen chemistry is a delicate thing and unmistakable when it happens. It happens here. The uninventive story told how race car driver Lucky Jackson (Presley) comes to Las Vegas to enter the Grand Prix. His car is there but the engine is not; he needs cash to get it out of hock. Lucky raises the money easily but loses it just as easily. Having met the sexy redhead Rusty Martin (Ann-Margret) when her car breaks down, he is smitten with her and she plays it cool. When her car is fixed, Rusty drives off without giving her name or phone number. Lucky and his sidekick Shorty Fansworth (Nicky Blair) check out all the Vegas casinos looking for Rusty in the chorus lines, but it turns out she is a swimming instructor at the Flamingo Hotel. Lucky gets a job as a waiter at the hotel so he can be around Rusty and break down her reserve. Before you know it, she loosens up and the two have a romantic spree visiting the sights of the area. As Lucky prepares for the race, his racing rival Count Elmo Mancini (Cesare Danova) also gets interested in Rusty, providing a convenient romantic triangle. But it lasts only until Lucky wins the race and Rusty gets him. The screenplay held few surprises along the way but it was painless, stylish fun whenever Presley and Ann-Margret were on-screen together, which was, thankfully, most of the time.

The songs in *Viva Las Vegas* were by various songwriters but seemed to be cut from the same cloth. The catchy title song was a breezy rockabilly number that mixed the speed of racing with the sizzle of Las Vegas. Presley sang most of the songs, including the tearful ballads "I Need Somebody to Lean On" and "If You Think I Don't Need You," the vigorous "Come On, Everybody," and the rousing "Yellow Rose of Texas," which he sang to lead a bunch of drunk tourists out of a bar. Ann-Margret was an accomplished dancer so her songs usually involved a lot of movement. Her sunny, knowing duet with Presley, "The Lady Loves Me," was perhaps the musical highlight of the movie. Encouraged by his costar, Presley did more dancing than usual, and he did a decent job keeping up with the gyrating Ann-Margret. The supporting cast was solid, particularly William Demarest as Rusty's understanding father. David Winters did the spirited choreography, and George Sidney directed the movie with a light touch but a firm hand when it came to pace. Watching *Viva Las Vegas* today, one gets an accurate glimpse into what Vegas looked like in 1964. The movie was shot completely in and around the city, and many of the casino and nightspot scenes were filmed in the actual locations. But all the scenery that *Viva Las Vegas* needed was Presley and Ann-Margret and they were indeed the real thing.

Presley's movie career was relatively short (14 years) and, as popular as he was on-screen, it was a disappointing career. He had found fame in the mid-1950s with his records and television appearances but his manager, Colonel Tom Parker, wanted Presley to be a movie star. Parker got Paramount to sign Presley up for a hefty amount of money, then the studio didn't quite know what to do with the singer who had no acting experience. So he was loaned to different studios where Presley made a handful of successful movies, making him by 1957 the top box office star in Hollywood. It seemed that with such an impressive standing, Presley could make any kind of film he wanted. But the studios and Parker wanted the same Presley in every movie: a handsome free spirit in an exotic location surrounded by comely girls. So Presley went to Acapulco, Hawaii, New Orleans, the Florida beaches, the Old West, the Tennessee hills, the Middle East, and all over Europe, starring in movies that often went nowhere. If Presley was a limited actor, his roles were even more limiting. When offered meaty parts in musicals like *West Side Story* (1961) and *A Star Is Born* (1976), Parker said no. The Presley movie formula was so rigid that each film was as predictable as it was routine. That is why the better films, such as *Viva Las Vegas*, make one realize that Presley was capable of so much more.

See also: *Beach Blanket Bingo*; Elvis Presley biography box

FURTHER READING

Bloom, Ken. *Hollywood Musicals: The 101 Greatest Song-and-Dance Movies of All Time*. New York: Black Dog and Leventhal, 2010.

Guralnick, Peter. *Last Train to Memphis: The Rise of Elvis Presley*. New York: Little, Brown & Co., 2014.

Williamson, Joel. *Elvis Presley: A Southern Life*. New York: Oxford University Press, 2014.

A HARD DAY'S NIGHT

Studio and release date: United Artists; August 1964
Producer: Walter Shenson
Screenplay: Alun Owen
Songwriters: John Lennon, Paul McCartney (music and lyrics)
Director: Richard Lester
Musical Director: George Martin
Cinematographer: Gilbert Taylor
Cast: John Lennon, Paul McCartney, George Harrison, Ringo Starr, Wilfred Brambell, Victor Spinetti, Norman Rossington, Kenneth Haigh, Anna Quayle
Songs: "A Hard Day's Night"; "She Loves You"; "Can't Buy Me Love" "I Should Have Known Better"; "All My Loving"; "Tell Me Why"; "And I Love Her"; "I'm Happy Just to Dance with You"; "If I Fell"

Only a few months after the Beatles made their first appearance in America, Hollywood had a film featuring the Fab Four in movie theaters. It was low budget and quickly made (the film's purpose was more to gain the rights to the soundtrack album than to present anything of quality), but the many fans didn't care and the movie was a pleasing surprise. Director Richard Lester and scriptwriter Alun Owen took the opportunity to make a frenetic mock-documentary about a typical day in the life of the Beatles (Paul McCartney, John Lennon, George Harrison, and Ringo Starr), and the result was an original, freewheeling celebration of rock that was a forerunner to the later MTV videos. The movie, filmed in black and white to save money, had a newsreel quality that was very tongue in cheek as the foursome ran from hordes of females, took Paul McCartney's grandfather (Wilfred Brambell) on a train ride to a rehearsal, and ended the day performing in a theater full of screaming fans. What little plot there was concerned the foursome's attempts to get from their hometown Liverpool to London to record a television special. Incidents along the way were of little importance, but fans loved seeing the Beatles offstage and supposedly as themselves. How truthful this depiction is of the real Beatles is difficult to determine. Screenwriter Owen traveled with the foursome when they toured the United States and wrote down phrases and expressions that the boys used. He then wrote the script, using the material from the tour. But legend has it that several of the lines in the movie were ad-libbed by the four singers. Such improvisation, unheard of in Hollywood, is one of the reasons *A Hard Day's Night* seems so spontaneous.

As part of the deal with United Artists, the Beatles would write and perform seven new songs for the movie. Lennon and McCartney wrote them all, though it was Starr who suggested the phrase "A Hard Day's Night" and it was turned into the title song. Other hits to come from the movie include "And I Love Her," "Can't Buy Me Love," and "I Should Have Known Better." Previously recorded hits heard in the film include "All My Loving," "If I Fell," and "She Loves You." Many of these were performed during a rehearsal or at the concert. But it was the use of rock songs behind other scenes that was unique, turning pop music into a movie soundtrack. Also innovative about *A Hard Day's Night* was the inventive camera-work. Hand-held cameras and even camera operators running and leaping as they filmed gave the movie a kinetic look not seen before. During McCartney's singing of "And I Love Her," the camera pans around him until the bright light of an arc lamp causes the shot to go white. The studio thought it was a mistake and wanted the scene reshot; producer Walter Shenson explained that it was desired effect and took half a day to get it just right. Such camera techniques later became common in film and television, especially for rock concerts, but in 1964 it was a startling new look.

The immediate effect of *A Hard Day's Night* was a series of movies using other rock groups. The Dave Clark Five in *Catch Us If You Can,* also known as *Having a Wild Weekend* (1965), and Herman's Hermits in *Hold On!* (1966) were the most obvious copies. Also patterned closely after the Beatles' first film was the popular television show *The Monkees* (1966 to 1968), featuring a rock foursome who were created by NBC to sing and clown around in the style of *A Hard Day's Night.* The Beatles themselves ended up copying themselves in the 1965 movie *Help!* This time United Artists spent a lot more money on the movie, filmed it in color, and commissioned a script with a more conventional story. A mixture of James Bond spoof and Beatles music video, the film is silly but contagious fun. Again Lester directed with a loose style, but *Help!* was less spontaneous, more controlled. The farcical movie had the foursome caught up in a plot to blow up the world and a religious cult with a high priest (Leo McKern) chasing them about for a missing sacrificial ring that Ringo was wearing. The frolicking took place on ski slopes, a beach in the Bahamas, and on Salisbury Plain with tanks coming to the rescue. It all looked a bit forced, but the music was still classic rock and roll, including "Ticket to Ride," "You're Gonna Lose That Girl," "You've Got to Hide Your Love Away," and the exclamatory title song.

The Beatles did not get much satisfaction from moviemaking and turned down offers to do any more films, though in 1968 they did lend their singing voices to the animated *Yellow Submarine*. A winning combination of imaginative animation and top-notch Beatles' songs make this surreal fantasy a visual and musical treat. The good-versus-evil tale was set in Pepperland where the Blue Meanies overcome the peaceful, music-loving kingdom and place it under a frozen spell. The four Beatles leave their British homeland and travel in a yellow submarine through exotic, fantastical places before arriving in Pepperland, defeat the Meanies, and restore music to the land. Director George Dunning and the animators used plenty of psychedelic and pop-art design and there was nothing subtle about the drug-induced kind of imagination at work. Yet the movie is also a simple, wholesome fable with a straightforward appreciation of a merry tale. All of the songs were already hits from the group's albums, so it was probably the finest collection of Beatles songs ever heard in one film, including "Sgt. Pepper's Lonely Club Band," "When I'm Sixty-Four," "Nowhere Man," "Lucy in the Sky with Diamonds," "All You Need Is Love," "Eleanor Rigby," "All Together Now," and the title song.

See also: The Jungle Book

FURTHER READING

Glynn, Stephen. *A Hard Day's Night: British Film Guide*. London/New York: I. B. Tauris, 2005.
Morton, Ray. *A Hard Day's Night*. (Music on Film). Montclair, NJ: Limelight Editions, 2011.
Roberts, Michael J. *The Beatles on Film*. Portland, OR: BookBaby, 2014.

MARY POPPINS

Studio and release date: Disney/Buena Vista; September 1964
Producer: Walt Disney
Screenplay: Bill Walsh, Donald Da Gradi, based on the stories by P. L. Travers
Songwriters: Richard M. and Robert B. Sherman (music and lyrics)
Director: Robert Stevenson
Choreographers: Marc Breaux, Dee Dee Wood
Musical Director: Irwin Kostal
Cinematographer: Edward Colman
Cast: Julie Andrews, Dick Van Dyke, David Tomlinson, Glynis Johns, Ed Wynn, Karen Dotrice, Matthew Garber, Hermione Baddeley, Jane Darwell
Songs: "A Spoonful of Sugar"; "Chim-Chim-Cheree"; "Feed the Birds"; "Supercalifragilisticexpialidocius"; "I Love to Laugh"; "Jolly Holiday"; "Step in Time"; "Stay Awake"; "Let's Go Fly a Kite"; "Sister Suffragette"; "The Life I Lead"; "The Perfect Nanny"; "A Man Has Dreams"; "Fidelity Fiduciary Bank"

One of the most popular of all Hollywood musicals, the tuneful fantasy is superior in all its elements, from the screenplay and score to the performances and production values. In 1910 London, the stuffy banker Mr. Banks (David Tomlinson) lives on Cherry Tree Lane where his household is anything but calm. Mrs. Banks (Glynis Johns) is active in the women's suffrage movement and his two young children Jane (Karen Dotrice) and Michael (Matthew Garber) go through nannies as fast as they are hired. The arrival of Mary Poppins (Julie Andrews), an unconventional nanny who flies off a cloud and into the Banks house in answer to an advertisement in the paper, changes everything. With her magical ways, she makes everything, even cleaning a room or taking medicine, an adventure. With her pal Bert (Dick Van Dyke), the chimney sweep/sidewalk chalk artist, Mary and the children enter one of his pictures and have a merry day with carousel horses that go off on their own, dancing penguins, and nonsense songs with raucous street buskers. Mr. Banks, in his efforts to show his children the practical and serious side of life, takes them to his dour place of employment but the kids accidentally start a run on the bank and it looks like Mr. Banks will be fired and the family destitute. Yet the experience forces him to become a more understanding and even playful father. He gets his job back, the family is closer than ever, and Mary Poppins, her job done, flies off to new adventures.

Although the musical was based on P. L. Travers' children's books, it took plenty of liberties with various aspects of the popular series. Walt Disney had been trying to get the rights to the stories since 1938 but Travers always refused. Not until she was financially strapped in the late 1950s did she relent. But Travers hated the Disney-view of the world and gave him a hard time at every turn. Her stories are less sentimental, even dark and cruel in spots. The character of Mary Poppins is stern at times and her use of magical powers could be frightening. But Disney made the movie that he wanted and the public must have agreed with him because *Mary Poppins* was a giant hit. Although Julie Andrews had never made a movie, Disney thought her perfect after seeing her onstage in *My Fair Lady* (1956) and *Camelot* (1960). At the time Disney offered Andrews the part, she was pregnant and hoping to make the film version of *My Fair Lady* in the near future. Disney was willing to hold production up for two years just so she could play Mary. As it turned out, Andrews was not cast in the movie of *My Fair Lady* so, after giving birth to her son, she began work on *Mary Poppins*. Andrews made a "practically perfect" screen debut as Mary, finding charm in efficiency and playfulness even while maintaining a stiff upper lip. Dick Van Dyke was cast as the Cockney Bert even though many (including himself) didn't think he was right for the part. His suspect Cockney accent aside, it is a delicious performance. Van Dyke also played the caricatured old bank president Mr. Dawes; he pleaded with Disney, and even auditioned for the role of Dawes, which he felt was an actor's dream. The veteran comic Ed Wynn was a cartoon come alive as Bert's jolly Uncle Albert who can't help floating up in the air every time he laughs. The rest of the British and American

Among the many charms of *Mary Poppins* (1964) is the clever mixing of live action and animation in some of the production numbers. Mary (Julie Andrews) and Bert (Dick Van Dyke) are joined by two sheep during the famous "Jolly Holiday" sequence. Robert Stevenson directed, and the choreography was by Deedee Wood and Marc Breaux. (Walt Disney Pictures/Photofest)

cast gave jocular performances with the right touch of sincerity. The mixing of animation and live action was the most sophisticated and inventive yet seen and the decor for both the real and fantastical worlds was colorful and evocative.

Richard M. and Robert B. Sherman wrote their best film score for *Mary Poppins*. The variety is considerable yet all the songs seem to be part of one musical point of view. The Oscar-winning "Chim-Chim-Cheree" is easygoing yet mysterious. The other hit songs were the march "A Spoonful of Sugar," the slaphappy nonsense song "Supercalifragilisticexpialidocius," the rousing polka "Step in Time," and the expansive "Let's Go Fly a Kite." Yet equally as accomplished were the lullaby "Stay Awake," the contagious romp "Jolly Holiday," and the indelible ballad "Feed the Birds." Rarely has the music for a children's movie gone so many wonderful places. Yet *Mary Poppins* was one of the brothers' most difficult projects. They ended up writing some 30 songs for the film because Travers or Disney kept rejecting some and others were filmed but not used. Director Robert Stevenson had his hands full with the time-consuming special effects. The mechanical bird that sits on Mary's finger took months to design and build then involved many wires running up Andrews' sleeve. Also difficult was the scene with Uncle Albert in which five actors sitting on chairs are floating in the air. Today such effects are easily done with computers, but everything in *Mary Poppins* was done

Richard M. and **Robert B. Sherman**   Brother songwriters with many movie scores and songs, they are most known for their films with the Disney company. Richard M. Sherman (b. 1928) and Robert B. Sherman (1925–2012) were born in New York, the sons of Hollywood songwriter Al Sherman, and both were educated at Bard College. They had written some pop hits before Walt Disney hired them to provide songs for the nonmusicals *The Parent Trap* (1961) and *In Search of the Castaways* (1962). Soon the brothers became the studio's unofficial songwriters-in-residence, writing the scores for *Summer Magic* (1963), *Mary Poppins* (1964), *The Happiest Millionaire* (1967), *The One and Only Genuine Original Family Band* (1968), and *Bedknobs and Broomsticks* (1971) as well as the animated features *The Sword in the Stone* (1963), *The Jungle Book* (1967), *The Aristocats* (1970), and, years later, *The Tigger Movie* (2000). For other studios the Shermans scored *Chitty Chitty Bang Bang* (1968), *Charlotte's Web* (1972), *Snoopy Come Home* (1972), *Tom Sawyer* (1973), *Huckleberry Finn* (1974), *The Slipper and the Rose* (1976), and *The Magic of Lassie* (1978). The Shermans' songs can be buoyant, tender, silly, and contagious as well as popular. It is estimated that "It's a Small World (After All)," which they wrote for Disneyland, has been heard by many, many millions. Their lyrics are also memorable, particularly when they used made-up words such as "Higitus Figitus," "Fortuosity," "Gratifaction," and "Supercalifragilisticexpialidocius."

by hand. Despite all the problems, Stevenson directed the huge production with just the right tone that allowed reality and fantasy to coexist. Marc Breaux and Dee Dee Wood choreographed (the rooftop "Step in Time" number was particularly thrilling), and Peter Ellenshaw did the special effects, which were as wondrous as they were fun. A splendid combination of top talent, unforgettable songs, and an intriguing tale that appeals to different ages for different reasons, the movie was producer Disney's finest musical film and the best musical fantasy since *The Wizard of Oz* (1939). *Mary Poppins* was such a hit at the box office that for years after Disney tried desperately to copy the formula and repeat its success, never succeeding. Other studios tried as well, even hiring the Sherman brothers and Van Dyke for *Chitty Chitty Bang Bang* (1968), but it seems that the magic of *Mary Poppins* was not easily re-created and the film remains as unique as it does entertaining.

See also: *Chitty Chitty Bang Bang; Willy Wonka and the Chocolate Factory;* Walt Disney, Julie Andrews, Richard M. and Robert B. Sherman biography boxes

FURTHER READING

Maltin, Leonard. *The Disney Films*. 4th ed. Glendale, CA: Disney Editions, 2000.

Stirling, Richard. *Julie Andrews. An Intimate Biography*. New York: St. Martin's Press, 2008.

Thomas, Bob. *Walt Disney: An American Original*. Glendale, CA: Disney Editions, 1994.

Woodhouse, Horace Martin. *The Essential Mary Poppins*. Seattle: CreateSpace Publishing, 2014.

MY FAIR LADY

Studio and release date: Warner Brothers; October 1964

Producer: Jack L. Warner

Screenplay: Alan Jay Lerner, based on his 1956 stage script, which was based on George Bernard Shaw's 1914 comedy *Pygmalion*

Songwriters: Frederick Loewe (music), Alan Jay Lerner (lyrics)

Director: George Cukor

Music Director: André Previn

Choreographer: Hermes Pan

Cinematographer: Harry Stradling

Cast: Rex Harrison, Audrey Hepburn, Stanley Holloway, Wilfred Hyde-White, Jeremy Brett, Gladys Cooper, Mona Washburn, Theodore Bikel

Songs: "I Could Have Danced All Night"; "On the Street Where You Live"; "The Rain in Spain"; "Wouldn't It Be Loverly"; "I've Grown Accustomed to Her Face": "With a Little Bit of Luck"; "Without You"; "Get Me to the Church on Time"; "A Hymn to Him"; "I'm an Ordinary Man"; "Why Can't the English?"; "Just You Wait"; "Show Me"; "You Did It"; "Ascot Gavotte"

One of Broadway's most literate, romantic, and elegant musicals, its screen version was highly anticipated so there was some disappointment when it was finally released. Yet much of what made the 1956 stage musical so special managed to make it to the screen. *My Fair Lady* was the biggest Broadway hit of the 1950s, and many still consider it the finest of all American musicals. Yet the show was something of a surprise hit. Richard Rodgers, Oscar Hammerstein, Frank Loesser, and other notable songwriters tried to musicalize George Bernard Shaw's play *Pygmalion* but found that the comedy of manners did not fall into the standard musical format. Even Lerner and Loewe abandoned the project for a while until Lerner decided that this musical would have to be written in a new and different way. Since the story is about a speech teacher, some of the songs would have to be written as "talk songs" for the character. Also unusual about *My Fair Lady* is that it has very little dancing, no overt love story, and the tale is very British in temperament. Against such odds, *My Fair Lady* was a triumph when it opened on Broadway in 1956.

The story line follows *Pygmalion*, sometimes word for word, but Lerner opens up the story effectively. The London phonetics professor Henry Higgins observes the Cockney flower girl Eliza Doolittle selling her wares outside St. Paul's Church after the opera lets out and boasts that with proper training in speech he could pass her off as a duchess. Liza comes to Higgins' home asking for speech lessons, and he bets his fellow bachelor friend Colonel Pickering that he will turn the squawking, ignorant girl into a lady in six months. The training is rigorous and ruthless and after showing her off at the Ascot races, Higgins and Pickering bring her to an embassy ball where she not only comes across as a lady but charms the royal members present. The bet having been won, Eliza turns on Higgins, demanding to be treated like the lady he has made her and threatening to wed the youth Freddie Hill who has been courting her. Higgins denounces Liza as an ungrateful upstart, but after she walks out on him he realizes that he is rather fond of her and is more than pleased when she eventually returns to continue their relationship on more equal terms. The comic subplot concerns Eliza's father Alfred, a common dustman, who inherits a bundle of money and is forced to become respectable, much against his nature and sense of happiness. The sterling stage score by Lerner and Loewe was overflowing with superior music. The standout hits were the ballads "I Could Have Danced All Night" and "On the Street Where You Live," but few songs are as easily recognized as "The Rain in Spain." Other gems in the score include the wishful "Wouldn't It Be Loverly"; the raucous "Get Me to the Church on Time" and "With a Little Bit of Luck"; the vehement "Just You Wait" and "Show Me"; and the revealing character songs "I've Grown Accustomed to Her Face," "I'm an Ordinary Man," and "A Hymn to Him." Rex Harrison was not a strong singer but as Higgins he "spoke" his songs on pitch, creating a unique talk-sing style that other nonsingers later adopted when doing musicals. Julie Andrews shone brightly as Eliza and the low comedy was supplied by Stanley Holloway as Alfred Doolittle. *My Fair Lady* broke box office records on Broadway, running over six years.

Hollywood was immediately interested and there was a bidding war among the studios to get the rights to the screen version. Jack L. Warner paid a record-breaking $5.5 million for the rights and sought to protect his investment by casting recognized stars such as Cary Grant and Audrey Hepburn as Higgins and Eliza. Grant refused and pressure was put on the studio to let Harrison reprise his legendary stage performance. Andrews, who had never made a film, was not considered and Hepburn was cast as Eliza with Marni Nixon providing her singing on the soundtrack. Holloway got to repeat his Doolittle, and many of the creative talents from the Broadway version were hired for the film. Lerner adapted his stage script into a solid screenplay and, a rare case in Hollywood, every song in the Broadway score was used in the film. Warner spent a bundle on the production but the film was a major box office hit and turned a healthy profit. While it is an elegant and stylish movie, *My Fair Lady* on the screen is not as vivid and alive as onstage.

Harrison's Higgins is very polished if a bit more weary than is comfortable, and Hepburn makes a dazzling "lady" even if many think her Cockney performance is unconvincing. George Cukor directed with care and the film was filled with gorgeous sets and costumes. While *My Fair Lady* may not be a great film, it is a very faithful movie version of a great American musical.

See also: *Gigi, Mary Poppins*; Alan Jay Lerner and Frederick Loewe; Julie Andrews biography boxes

FURTHER READING

Lees, Gene. *Inventing Champagne: The Worlds of Lerner and Loewe*. New York: St. Martin's Press, 1990/2005.
Lerner, Alan Jay. *On the Street Where I Live*. Boston: Da Capo Press, 1994.
McHugh, Dominic. *Loverly: The Life and Times of My Fair Lady*. New York: Oxford University Press, 2012.

THE SOUND OF MUSIC

Studio and release date: 20th Century Fox; March 1965
Producer: Robert Wise
Screenplay: Ernest Lehman, based on the 1959 stage script by Howard Lindsey and Russel Crouse, which was based on the book *The Trapp Family Singers* by Maria Augusta Von Trapp
Songwriters: Richard Rodgers (music), Oscar Hammerstein (lyrics)
Director: Robert Wise
Choreographers: Marc Breaux, Dee Dee Wood
Musical Director: Irwin Kostal
Cinematographer: Ted McCord
Cast: Julie Andrews, Christopher Plummer, Peggy Wood, Eleanor Parker, Richard Haydn, Charmian Carr
Songs: "The Sound of Music"; "Climb Every Mountain"; "Do-Re-Mi"; "My Favorite Things"; "Edelweiss"; "Something Good"; "I Have Confidence in Me"; "Sixteen Going on Seventeen"; "So Long, Farewell"; "How Do You Solve a Problem Like Maria?"; "Lonely Goatherd"

Still the most popular movie musical ever made, it has been seen by more people around the world than any other. It is also a movie much loved, often parodied, and holds a major place in the American consciousness. Yet *The Sound of Music* is also one of the least American musicals, sometimes closer to European operetta than

Hollywood, and extremely proficient, highly polished, and beautifully filmed. The baroness Maria Von Trapp's book about her singing family was filmed in Germany in 1956 as *The Trapp Family* and it was so popular in Europe that a sequel, *The Trapp Family in America*, was released in 1958. Songwriters Richard Rodgers and Oscar Hammerstein thought the first film would make an appealing Broadway play with some Austrian folk songs added for flavor. But the project evolved into a full-scale musical with an original score by Rodgers (music) and Hammerstein (lyrics). With Mary Martin as the heroine, *The Sound of Music* was a resounding hit in New York and, later, London. 20th Century Fox bought the screen rights for a hefty sum, then realized there was no Hollywood star who seemed ideal for the role of Maria. Doris Day, Audrey Hepburn, and Romy Schneider were considered, but none had the youth and freshness the role required. Director Robert Wise had seen Julie Andrews onstage and thought her a good possibility but she had never made a film and no one knew how she would come across on-screen. Walt Disney let Wise and some Fox executives see some of the rough footage for *Mary Poppins* and Andrews got the job.

While the details in the story and the placement of the songs differ somewhat from the 1959 Broadway version, the film is very faithful to the stage work. The Mother Abbess (Peggy Wood) and her advisors at the Austrian Abbey at Nonnberg are not sure that the spirited postulant Maria Rainer (Andrews) is a good candidate for the religious order, so Maria is sent to serve as governess for the seven children of the widower Captain Georg Von Trapp (Christopher Plummer). The children are reluctant to like the new governess until she teaches them to sing, and she even manages to soften the stern exterior of their father. Although he is engaged to wed the sophisticated baroness Elsa Schraeder (Eleanor Parker), the captain finds himself attracted to Maria and breaks off the engagement. The captain and Maria wed but, on returning from their honeymoon, the Nazis have annexed Austria and the captain is ordered to serve in the German navy. Rather than bow to the Nazis, he and his family slip away during a musical festival in which they are performing and escape over the mountains to Switzerland and freedom. The stage version was more political (the captain and the baroness break off their engagement because they do not agree about the Nazis), and two songs with a sarcastic tone were cut for the movie. But what the movie lost in bite it gained in scope. Although Fox was on a budget-cutting campaign, the producers insisted that the movie had to have some location shooting in Austria. Someone must have sensed that Salzburg was the other star of the show. Ernest Lehman's screenplay opened up the stage musical as few musicals have ever been opened up for the screen. The story was played against a huge panoramic backdrop, yet the focus was still on the characters. Most of the famous stage score was used for the film, including such familiar favorites as the catchy children's number "Do-Re-Mi," the naive "Sixteen Going on Seventeen," the cheery "My Favorite Things," the yodeling ditty

Julie Andrews (b. 1935)   A much-loved British performer with a crystal-clear singing voice, precise diction, and ladylike demeanor, she has appeared in notable musicals on Broadway, in Hollywood, and on television. She was born in Walton-on-Thames, England, the daughter of entertainers, and sang on the stage as a young girl. Her surprisingly adult soprano voice made her an unusual attraction, and by the age of 12, Andrews was performing professionally in London concerts and pantomimes. She first performed on Broadway in 1954 in the British musical spoof *The Boy Friend* then scored a major triumph in *My Fair Lady* (1956). Andrews played the title role in Rodgers and Hammerstein's television musical *Cinderella* (1957), then in 1960 she shone again on Broadway in *Camelot* (1960). Andrews was not chosen to re-create her stage performance in the 1964 film version of *My Fair Lady*, but Walt Disney provided her screen debut as *Mary Poppins* (1964), beginning her remarkable Hollywood career. Andrews had her greatest screen success as Maria in *The Sound of Music* (1964). Her other film musicals include *Thoroughly Modern Millie* (1967), *Star!* (1968), *Darling Lili* (1969), and *Victor/Victoria* (1982). She returned to Broadway in the stage version of *Victor/Victoria* (1995). Andrews has appeared in many nonmusical films, television specials, and some TV dramas. Under the pen name Julie Edwards, she has written several children's books. Autobiography: *Home: A Memoir of My Early Years* (2008); biography: *Julie Andrews: An Intimate Biography*, Richard Stirling (2008).

"The Lonely Goatherd," the inspiring "Climb Ev'ry Mountain," the character number "Maria," the folk song "Edelweiss," and the joyous title song. Because Hammerstein had died in 1960, Rodgers wrote both music and lyrics for two new songs—the tender duet "Something Good" and the marching "I Have Confidence."

Wise directed the expansive musical and got outstanding performances from the cast, both stars and supporting players. *The Sound of Music* is also one of the most beautifully filmed of all movie musicals. Often criticized for its sentimentality, sweetness, and wholesomeness, the movie nevertheless is a high-quality, exceptional piece of work. The film opened to wildly mixed film reviews by the critics. Moviegoers didn't care about the reviews and ticket sales passed $79 million in 1965 dollars. As sometimes happens, the popularity of the movie made the stage musical more famous and there were more productions of *The Sound of Music* in theaters across the country than before the film opened. Although it has been available on video for several years, movie houses still present *The Sound of Music* on the big screen. By the end of the century, "sing-along" showings of the movie became a fad in Great Britain and then in the United States, the audience dressing up like the characters and singing the songs either from memory or from the lyrics projected on the screen. This sort of thing only happens to films such as *The Rocky Horror Picture Show*, but *The Sound of Music* is, in its own wholesome way, a cult film as well.

See also: *Mary Poppins*, *The Rocky Horror Picture Show*; Richard Rodgers and Oscar Hammerstein, Julie Andrews biography boxes

FURTHER READING

Arntz, James. *Julie Andrews*. Raleigh, NC: Contemporary Books, 1995.

Flinn, Caryl. *The Sound of Music*. (BFI Film Classics). London: British Film Institute, 2015.

Hirsch, Julia. *The Sound of Music: The Making of America's Favorite Movie*. New York: McGraw-Hill, 1993.

Maslon, Laurence. *The Sound of Music Companion*. London: Pavilion, 2015.

Nolan, Frederick. *The Sound of Their Music: The Story of Rodgers and Hammerstein*. Montclair, NJ: Applause Theatre & Cinema Books, 2002.

BEACH BLANKET BINGO

Studio and release date: American International Pictures; April 1965

Producers: James A. Nicholson, Samuel Z. Arkoff

Screenplay: William Asher, Leo Townsend

Songwriters: Jerry Styner and others (music), Guy Hemric and others (lyrics)

Director: William Asher

Choreographer: Jack Baker

Musical Director: Al Simms

Cinematographer: Jack Baker

Cast: Annette Funicello, Frankie Avalon, Deborah Walley, Harvey Lembeck, John Ashley, Jody McCrae, Donna Loren, Linda Evans

Songs: "Beach Blanket Bingo"; "It Only Hurts When I Cry"; "Follow the Leader"; "Fly Boy"; "These Are the Good Times"; "New Love"; "Cycle Set"; "I'll Never Change Him"; "I Think You Think"

The fourth "beach" movie musical starring Annette Funicello and Frankie Avalon, this film was perhaps the most enjoyable, which didn't mean that it made any more sense than the others. American International Pictures, a minor Hollywood studio, had a formula for success: make many movies, very cheaply, and if one in a dozen is a hit, you're home free. That formula hit pay dirt more than once in a dozen with the "beach" movies in the early 1960s. These harmless but highly appealing (to teenagers) flicks were set in California, where attractive teens surfed during the day and danced or snuggled around a campfire on the beach at night. They seemed to have no parents or any other responsible adults around, which made the lifestyle all the more attractive. When an adult dropped into the plot, it was usually an ineffectual police officer or a screwy beach bum way past his prime. The five beach movies were all popular and, since they were made on the cheap, the AIP formula worked like a charm.

The series started with *Beach Party* in 1963 and most of the sequels were patterned after it. The screenplay wanted the audience to believe that anthropology professor Robert Orwell Sutwell (Robert Cummings) and his secretary Marianne (Dorothy Malone) go to the beach to study the sex habits of the American teen in the 1960s. As they follow surfer Frankie (Avalon), his girlfriend Dee Dee (Funicello), and their beach buddies around, the researchers don't find much sex going on but a lot of surfing, singing, and dancing. The comic villain of the piece was biker Eric Von Zipper (Harvey Lembeck) and he was so delightfully ineffective that he returned in later films. The impetus behind *Beach Party* was to come up with a cut-rate product that would have a similar appeal to teens as the Elvis Presley films. AIP could not afford a big-name singer like Presley but they could get a lot of mileage out of lite-pop singer Avalon and comely Funicello, who had graduated from *The Mickey Mouse Club* on television and was anxious to have a movie career outside of the Disney studio. *Beach Party* was a surprise hit and the $350,000 production brought in over $4 million. Funicello and Avalon played the same characters in *Muscle Beach Party* (1964) and *Bikini Beach* (1964).

By the time *Beach Blanket Bingo* was released in 1965, audiences knew what to expect and were not disappointed. The convoluted plot involved a singing star Sugar Kane (Linda Evans) kidnapped by Von Zipper (Lembeck) and his motorcycle gang, two sky-diving surfers (Deborah Walley and John Ashley) involved in a publicity stunt, a publicity agent (Paul Lynde) who will stop at nothing, and a gang member named Bonehead (Jody McCrea) who falls in love with a mermaid (Marta Kristen). Funicello and Avalon seemed to enter the plot less and less with each film but they always sang and danced. In *Beach Blanket Bingo*, the songs, mostly by Jerry Styner (music) and Guy Hemric (lyrics), were more fun than usually found in the beach movies, and the two stars had their innocent, goofy, romantic delivery down pat. The title song enjoyed some popularity, but there was something to be said for such silly numbers as "It Only Hurts When I Cry," "He's My Fly Boy," and "These Are the Good Times." Sadly for their many fans, Avalon tired of the beach movies. In the next one, *How to Stuff a Wild Bikini* (1965), he only appears briefly, his character joining the naval reserves and off to other beaches. Dee Dee was left behind where she was courted by the advertising executive Ricky (Dwayne Hickman). In the most wacko plot of the five films, a witch doctor (Buster Keaton) uses his questionable magic to create a floating bikini then stuffs it with the provocative Cassandra (Beverly Adams) whose job is to lure Ricky away from Dee Dee. Also, biker Von Ripper (Lembeck) showed up one last time, a member of the beach family comes home again. *How to Stuff a Wild Bikini* must have had too much sand even for Funicello who gave up surfing and tried for a more substantial film career. She appeared in a handful of films and television shows into the 1980s but never found as much success as she had enjoyed with Disney or on the beach.

See also: *Viva Las Vegas*

FURTHER READING

Bloom, Ken. *Hollywood Musicals: The 101 Greatest Song-and-Dance Movies of All Time*. New York: Black Dog and Leventhal, 2010.

McGee, Mark Thomas. *Fast and Furious: The Story of American International Pictures*. Jefferson, NC: McFarland Publishers, 1984.

Shapiro, Marc. *Annette Funicello: America's Sweetheart*. New York: Riverdale Avenue Books, 2013.

THE JUNGLE BOOK

Studio and release date: Disney/Buena Vista; December 1967
Producer: Walt Disney
Screenplay: Larry Clemmons, Ralph Wright, Ken Anderson, Vance Gerry, based on the stories by Rudyard Kipling
Songwriters: Richard M. and Robert B. Sherman, Terry Gilkyson, (music and lyrics)
Director: Wolfgang Reitherman
Musical Director: George Bruns
Voices: Bruce Reitherman, Phil Harris, Sebastian Cabot, Louis Prima, George Sanders, Sterling Holloway, J. Pat O'Malley, Verna Felton
Songs: "The Bare Necessities"; "I Wanna Be Like You"; "Colonel Hathi's March"; "Trust in Me"; "That's What Friends Are For"; "My Own Home"

Thin on plot but rich in character and songs, this musical was the last animated film that Walt Disney personally produced. Fortunately, it is also one of the most musical of all his features, the songs by Terry Gilkyson and Richard M. and Robert B. Sherman often becoming the movie's highlights instead of pleasant diversions along the way. The screenplay was the simple tale of the "man-cub" Mowgli who is orphaned in the jungles of India when the plane carrying his family crashes. The infant is raised by a kind family of wolves but when Mowgli is a bit older and able to survive in the jungle, the wolves turn the boy over to the wise panther Bagheera that teaches the youth the ways of the jungle. But when the deadly tiger Shere Khan returns to the area, Bagheera knows that Mowgli is in danger and convinces the fun-loving bear Baloo to escort the boy to the "man-village." On the way there, Baloo and Mowgli encounter the predatory snake Kaa who tries to eat the boy, a herd of elephants under the leadership of the blustering Colonel Hathi, four vultures who anticipate Mowgli's demise with glee, and the wild ape King Louis who attempts to capture the youth but is distracted by Baloo in an ape disguise. When Shere Khan tries to kill Mowgli, Baloo fights the tiger and is severely wounded. But Baloo survives and brings the boy to the edge of the village. Mowgli would rather stay with Baloo in the jungle and refuses to part ways with the bear. Then a pretty Indian girl from the village comes to the river's edge to collect water and Mowgli sees her and is fascinated, never having seen a female human before. He bids Baloo goodbye and follows the girl to the village. Most of Mowgli's and Baloo's encounters during their journey led to a song, often in the form of a vaudeville turn. Baloo and Mowgli cut loose with the vivacious "The Bare Necessities," Kaa slithered through the hypnotic lullaby "Trust in Me," the vultures harmonized "That's What Friends Are For," and King Louis and the apes went wild with "I Wanna Be Like You." Rarely has a Disney animated film put so much focus on the music.

Rudyard Kipling's *Mowgli* stories had been filmed by Hollywood before but this was the first animated version. Disney thought the stories delightful fun and commissioned a script that would allow for tuneful songs. But Disney thought the score written by Gilkyson was too dark and rejected it, hiring the Shermans to write a more upbeat one. However, the animators urged Disney to keep one of Gilkyson's songs, the contagious "The Bare Necessities," and it remained in the movie, later getting nominated for the best song Oscar. Brian Epstein, the manager of the Beatles, wanted to get his clients in a Disney film and suggested that the foursome do the voices of the four vultures. The animators actually patterned the hairdos of the vultures after the Beatles' mop hairstyle. But it turned out the Beatles were not as interested in voicing a Disney movie as their manager was so the deal fell through. Ironically, Disney was not too upset. He thought the Beatles were just a passing fad and that their singing on the soundtrack would date the movie for future audiences. Instead the Shermans wrote a barbershop quartet number titled "That's What Friends Are For." In the planning of *The Jungle Book*, Disney reversed one of his rules from the past. He always insisted that the voice actors not be known to the public so that the moviegoers would not recognize the voice and think only of the character. But for *The Jungle Book*, he hired well-known actors and singers to voice some of the characters and instructed his animators to use physical aspects of the live performers in the character animation. For example, Shere Khan greatly resembles the actor George Sanders who voiced him. Popular singers Phil Harris and Louis Prima were also caricatured somewhat in animating Baloo and King

Louie. The Disney artists also shone in their re-creation of the Indian jungle. The background art is not only accurate (the artists studied the vegetation in India) but also very evocative. The animation of the characters is also first class, the facial gestures and the voices being superbly balanced.

Walt Disney died in 1966 during the preparation of *The Jungle Book* and it was released the next year. The musical was well received by the audiences and the critics, and the film was a box office success. It is very fortunate that it was a hit because the Disney company was in chaos after its founder's death and there was talk of eliminating the animation department. The success of *The Jungle Book* encouraged the studio to make more animated features. It is generally misconceived that the studio's films after Disney's death were inferior and unpopular until *The Little Mermaid* came along in 1989. It is true that many of the live-action comedies were far from inspired and do not hold up today, but the Disney studio produced some very fine animated movies during this period and most did well at the box office. *The Aristocats* (1970), *Robin Hood* (1973), *The Rescuers* (1977), *The Fox and the Hound* (1981), *The Great Mouse Detective* (1986), and *Oliver & Company* (1988) are not only commendable but sometimes very accomplished. Also, musically, they each offered some fine songs that have stood up well over time. The so-called Disney Renaissance was indeed a blossoming of superior animated musicals, but one must remember that what came before it was not a cinematic wasteland.

See also: *Mary Poppins, The Little Mermaid*; Walt Disney, Richard M. and Robert B. Sherman biography boxes

FURTHER READING

Maltin, Leonard. *The Disney Films.* 4th ed. Glendale, CA: Disney Editions, 2000.
Thomas, Bob. *Walt Disney: An American Original.* Glendale, CA: Disney Editions, 1994.

FUNNY GIRL

Studio and release date: Rastar/Columbia; September 1968
Producer: Ray Stark
Screenplay: Isobel Lennart, based on her 1964 stage script
Songwriters: Jule Styne and others (music), Bob Merrill and others (lyrics)
Director: William Wyler
Choreographer: Herbert Ross
Musical Director: Walter Scharf
Cinematographer: Harry Stradling

Cast: Barbra Streisand, Omar Sharif, Kay Medford, Walter Pidgeon, Tommy
Rall, Anne Francis, Mae Questel, Lee Allen
Songs: "People"; "Don't Rain on My Parade"; "My Man"; "Sadie Sadie"; "His
Love Makes Me Beautiful"; "I'd Rather Be Blue Over You"; "I'm the Greatest
Star"; "You Are Woman, I Am Man"; "Second Hand Rose"; "If a Girl Isn't
Pretty"; "The Swan"; "Funny Girl"; "Roller Skate Rag"

Just as the 1964 stage work made Barbra Streisand a Broadway star, the screen
version of *Funny Girl* made her a movie star. Her performance as the great
comedienne-singer Fanny Brice dominated both the Broadway and Hollywood versions, though both were also solid musicals on their own. Fanny Brice was a distinctive comedienne-singer because she made no attempt to disguise her Jewish
heritage and try to be a mainstream entertainer. Yet she became a star in vaudeville, on Broadway, and on radio and appealed to a wide audience. Brice also made
many records, many of them comic ditties, but there were torch songs as well. The
only medium she didn't conquer was movies. She appeared in eight movies but
rarely did they capture her special kind of comedy and her interaction with a live
audience. The idea of a Broadway musical about Brice's life came from producer
Ray Stark who was Brice's son-in-law. He wanted Ann Bancroft to play the great
comedienne but she backed out before the show went into rehearsal. Impressed
with Streisand's performances in a supporting role in the Broadway musical *I Can
Get It for You Wholesale* (1962), Stark auditioned her several times before taking
a risk and casting her. Streisand's recording of the ballad "People" was just starting to get recognition when *Funny Girl* opened on Broadway and she received raves
from the press and adulation from theatergoers. Since the character of Brice sang
most of the songs and appeared in just about every scene, Streisand carried the
show. She reprised her performance in London with great success and began a
series of legendary television specials that received high ratings. Yet as popular as
Streisand had become, Columbia didn't want to cast her in the movie of *Funny
Girl*. Because of her unusual look and the fact that she had never made a movie
before, Streisand was considered too great a risk. Columbia wanted to cast Shirley MacLaine in the role but Stark, who also produced the film, insisted on Streisand until the executives at Columbia gave in. The result was one of the most
stunning film debuts in the history of movie musicals.

As in the stage script, the screenplay followed the awkward, stage-struck Fanny
from her futile auditions to get on the stage to her discovery by Florenz Ziegfeld
(Walter Pidgeon) to her becoming a comic singing star of the *Ziegfeld Follies*. But
Fanny has less luck in keeping her husband, the gambling addict Nicky Arnstein
(Omar Sharif), and when he is convicted for an illegal bond scheme, he goes to jail
and Fanny is left only with her career. Jule Styne (music) and Bob Merrill (lyrics)

> **Barbra Streisand** (b. 1942) One of the very few female top box office movie stars in the last decades of the 20th century, the singer-actress-director began her career in musicals and has frequently returned to the genre in different media. She was born in Brooklyn and began her career singing in nightclubs before appearing on Broadway in *I Can Get It for You Wholesale* (1962) and *Funny Girl* (1964). She made a sensational screen debut in *Funny Girl* (1968), followed by such musicals as *Hello, Dolly!* (1969), *On a Clear Day You Can See Forever* (1969), *Funny Lady* (1975), *A Star Is Born* (1976), and *Yentl* (1983), directing the last and going on to direct nonmusical movies. Streisand starred in a series of musical specials on television that rank among the most popular and renowned of their kind—just as her many recordings through the decades are prized by her legion of fans—and her infrequent concert appearances quickly sell out. Biographies: *Barbra: The Way She Is*, Christopher Andersen (2006); *Streisand: The Intimate Biography*, James Spada (1995).

wrote the pleasing score that included the runaway hit "People" and other accomplished songs such as the mocking love song "His Love Makes Me Beautiful," the grasping "I'm the Greatest Star," the sly duet "You Are Woman," the old-fashioned number "Sadie, Sadie," and the propulsive "Don't Rain on My Parade." For the film, Styne and Merrill wrote a wistful title song, and some of Brice's actual songs from the past were added, most memorably the torch classic "My Man." William Wyler directed with skill and Herbert Ross staged the *Follies* numbers with wit and style. Yet it all really came down to Streisand, who was in every scene and sang just about every song. With the confidence of a veteran trouper, she turned her screen debut into a polished *tour de force*. With so much attention on Streisand/Brice, one forgets to notice how fine the movie itself is. The early years of the century are depicted with nostalgia and accuracy. *The Ziegfeld Follies* numbers are lavish and sparkling, but they actually look like they can take place on a stage. The supporting cast is very proficient, but most of the secondary characters from the play were reduced or eliminated in the movie because the studio wanted the focus to remain on Streisand. All the same, Kay Medford, for example, shines in the much-edited role of Mrs. Brice. *Funny Girl* is more than a one-woman show but, often, it seems like that is precisely what it is.

Five years later, Streisand returned to the character of Fanny Brice in the sequel *Funny Lady*, also produced by Columbia. The story picked up when Arnstein (Sharif) gets out of jail and Fanny dreams of a better future for their marriage. Instead he asks for a divorce and goes his own way. Fanny fights with and then marries songwriter-producer Billy Rose (James Caan) on the rebound, but his infidelities destroy the marriage and by the final reel Fanny is alone once again. *Funny Lady* was a rather disjointed affair and it was not very popular at the box office. All the same, Streisand was in top form, Caan gave a charming performance, and the 18 musical numbers were excellent. The old standards "Am I Blue?," "I Found a Million Dollar Baby in a Five-and-Ten Cent Store," "It's Only a Paper Moon," and "Great Day" were joined by some new songs by John Kander (music) and Fred Ebb (lyrics), including the breezy "How Lucky Can You Get," the plaintive "Isn't This Better?," and the affirming "Let's Hear It For Me."

See also: *The Great Ziegfeld*; Barbra Streisand biography box

FURTHER READING

Dick, Bernard. *Columbia Pictures: Portrait of a Studio*. Lexington: University Press of Kentucky, 1991.

Goldman, Herbert G. *Fanny Brice: The Original Funny Girl*. New York: Oxford University Press, 1993.

Spada, James. *Barbra Streisand: Her Life*. Bloomington, IN: Author & Company, 2013.

CHITTY CHITTY BANG BANG

Studio and release date: Warfield/United Artists; November 1968
Producer: Albert R. Broccoli
Screenplay: Roald Dahl, Ken Hughes, based on the book by Ian Fleming
Songwriters: Richard M. and Robert B. Sherman (music and lyrics)
Director: Ken Hughes
Choreographer: Marc Breaux, Dee Dee Wood
Musical Director: Irwin Kostal
Cinematographer: Christopher Challis
Cast: Dick Van Dyke, Sally Ann Howes, Heather Ripley, Adrian Hill, Lionel Jeffries, Gert Forbe, Anna Quayle, Benny Hill
Songs: "Chitty Chitty Bang Bang"; "Hushabye Mountain"; "Me Ol' Bamboo"; "Toot Sweet"; "Truly Scrumptious"; "Lovely Lonely Man"; "Posh!"; "Chu-Chi Face"

Leading man Dick Van Dyke, choreographers Marc Breaux and Dee Dee Wood, and songwriters Richard M. and Robert B. Sherman from *Mary Poppins* (1964) were featured in this big budget musical fantasy, so comparisons to the Disney classic were inevitable. The Disney studio tried to copy the success of *Mary Poppins* with *The Happiest Millionaire* (1967) and *Bedknobs and Broomsticks* (1971), so it is not so surprising that other studios did likewise. British movie producer Albert L. Broccoli, who found fame and high profits with the James Bond films, wanted to make his own fantasy musical for families, so he turned to Ian Fleming, the author of the Bond films. Fleming had written a children's book titled *Chitty Chitty Bang Bang* and it had found a following in Europe. Fleming had died in 1964, so Broccoli hired the famous children's books author Roald Dahl to write the screenplay with director Ken Hughes lending a hand. Their screenplay is rather convoluted with fantasy, flashbacks, and reality so jumbled that it was best not to think about it and enjoy the ride. Crackpot British inventor Caractacus Potts (Van Dyke) is always coming up with ideas and gismos but rarely do they work. For example, his edible candy whistle sounds like a good idea until the whistling sound produced by the candy product attracts all the dogs in the area and they destroy the candy factory. Potts finally comes up with something that works, a floating-flying car, that his two young children Jemina (Heather Ripley) and Jeremy (Adrian Hill) call Chitty Chitty Bang Bang. The Baron Bomburst of Vulgaria (Gert Forbe) sees the car in flight and wants it, so he has his henchmen steal Chitty and the children and take them to Vulgaria. It is a terrible place for children because the loathsome Child Catcher (Robert Helpmann) hates children and tracks them down much like a dog catcher, putting the kids in dark prison cells. Potts and his sweetheart Truly Scrumptious (Sally Ann Howes) travel to Vulgaria and, with help of the Toymaker (Benny Hill), they rescue the two kids, set free the other children in Vulgaria, and fly away in their magical car.

Determined to copy *Mary Poppins*, Broccoli commissioned the Shermans to write the score, their first screen assignments away from the Disney studio. He then approached Julie Andrews and Dick Van Dyke for the leading roles. Both refused but the insistent Broccoli kept offering Van Dyke so much money that the actor finally agreed on the condition that he did not have to use a British accent. For the female lead, Broccoli hired the next best thing to Andrews: the British singer-actress Sally Ann Howes who had replaced Andrews during the run of *My Fair Lady* on Broadway and in London. Broccoli then had dozens of sets built for the movie and sent the crew to Germany and France for some location shooting. No expense was spared in making *Chitty Chitty Bang Bang*. One musical number, "Toot Sweet," took three weeks to film and included dozens of singers, dancers, musicians, and even 100 dogs. The final production cost for the film was about $10 million. Broccoli only earned back about $8 million on the movie's first release, then eventually made a small profit with television rights and video/DVD sales. Although *Chitty Chitty Bang Bang* might be described as a vanity production for Broccoli, the British-American film is often entertaining and there is much to admire in the overproduced musical. Despite a personable cast and excellent production values, there were long stretches in the film that did not work, but the songs were mostly delightful, particularly the slaphappy "Me Ol' Bamboo," the whistling ditty

"Toot Sweet," the poignant lullaby "Hushabye Mountain," the merry "Truly Scrumptious," and the catchy title tune.

Chitty Chitty Bang Bang was a turning point in the screen career of writer Roald Dahl. Although he had scripted some television dramas and a few of his stories had been dramatized, he did not get involved with movies until Broccoli hired him to write the screenplay for the 1967 James Bond thriller *You Only Live Twice*. Dahl made many changes to Fleming's original story when he scripted *Chitty Chitty Bang Bang*. In fact, the whole idea of Vulgaria and the characters there were all Dahl's invention. Moviegoers, particularly Americans not very familiar with Dahl's books, were very uncomfortable with such a diabolical character as the Child Catcher in a family movie. (The same problem had beset Dr. Seuss' script for *The 5,000 Fingers of Dr. T* in 1953.) The rounding up of children and sending them to prison had obvious parallels to the Nazi persecution of Jews during the Holocaust. This was not what one expected in a family musical. Today we are more used to the very dark aspects of Dahl's stories and *Chitty Chitty Bang Bang* is easier to watch and understand. And there is plenty to appreciate in this oddball vanity production by Broccoli, who returned to making James Bond films and never attempted a musical again.

See also: *The 5,000 Fingers of Dr. T, Mary Poppins, Willy Wonka and the Chocolate Factory*; Richard M. and Robert B. Sherman biography box

FURTHER READING

Van Dyke, Dick. *My Lucky Life In and Out of Show Business: A Memoir*. New York: Random House, 2011.

OLIVER!

Studio and release date: Columbia; December 1968
Producer: John Woolf
Screenplay: Vernon Harris, based on the 1960 stage script by Lionel Bart, which is based on Charles Dickens' novel *Oliver Twist*
Songwriter: Lionel Bart (music and lyrics)
Director: Carol Reed
Choreographer: Onna White
Musical Director: Johnny Green
Cinematographer: Oswald Morris
Cast: Mark Lester, Ron Moody, Shani Wallis, Jack Wild, Oliver Reed, Harry Secombe, Hugh Griffith

Songs: "Consider Yourself"; "As Long as He Needs Me"; "Where Is Love?"; "I'd Do Anything"; "Who Will Buy?"; "Food Glorious Food"; "You've Got to Pick a Pocket or Two"; "Oom-Pah-Pah"; "Boy for Sale"; "Reviewing the Situation"; "It's a Fine Life"

Charles Dickens' classic novel *Oliver Twist* has found success on the stage since the 1840s and on-screen since the days of the early silents. When Lionel Bart's musical version *Oliver!* opened in London in 1960, it was such a hit that the show was brought to Broadway in 1963, becoming the longest-running British musical on the New York stage. Columbia bought the movie rights and then did something not often done in Hollywood: It hired a British director, screenwriter, and cast for the film. Evidently a Dickens tale, even in musical form, was something that should be left to the British. It was a wise decision because *Oliver!* may be a Hollywood product but it has an Englishness about it that is hard to fake. Much of Dickens' novel was covered in Vernon Harris' screenplay. The adventures of the orphan boy Oliver Twist (Mark Lester) take him from a rural workhouse to the teeming Victorian city of London. He is befriended by a band of pickpockets run by Fagin (Ron Moody) and soon finds himself on the wrong side of the law. Oliver eventually finds

His many troubles begin when little Oliver Twist (Mark Lester) asks the beadle (Harry Secombe) for another bowl of gruel in *Oliver!* (1968), the British musical based on Charles Dickens' literary classic. Director Carol Reed brought Victorian England to life in the acclaimed movie musical. (Columbia Pictures/Photofest)

his long-lost relatives but only after robbery, betrayal, and murder have been committed. Considering how dark the story was at times, most of the stage songs by Bart were cheerful music hall-like numbers, such as the mock etiquette number "I'd Do Anything," the sprightly "You've Got to Pick a Pocket or Two," the culinary anthem "Food, Glorious Food," the catchy singalong "It's a Fine Life," and the exuberant "Consider Yourself." Also in the score was the tender ballad "Where Is Love?," the plaintive torch song "As Long As He Needs Me," and the stream-of-conscience character number "Reviewing the Situation." All of them were used in the film directed by the distinguished British director Carol Reed and choreographed with panache by Onna White, the only American in the creative team.

Columbia did not cast any stars, even British stars, though it had tried to. Peter O'Toole, Albert Finney, Richard Burton, Laurence Harvey, and Peter Sellers were all considered for Fagin, but the studio ended up using the stage actor Ron Moody who had played Fagin in London. Elizabeth Taylor petitioned (unsuccessfully) to play Nancy and other names were considered but instead the plum role went to singer Shani Wallis who was little known in the United States. Some 4,000 boys were auditioned to play the title role, which went to unknown Mark Lester who could not sing. Not until 1988 was it revealed that Oliver's singing was dubbed by Kathe Green, the daughter of musical director Johnny Green. The supporting cast was uniformly excellent, from the creepy performance by Oliver Reed as Bill Sikes to the animated shenanigans by little Jack Wild as the Artful Dodger. The production values on-screen were impressive; some felt a bit too impressive. Some of the musical numbers were overproduced, involving plenty of extras and going on for too long. For example, the "Consider Yourself" number when Oliver is welcomed to London by Dodger required dancing policemen, vendors, shop girls, and hundreds of extras. For the "Who Will Buy?" sequence, it took six weeks to film the dozens of Londoners as well as a whole parade. The entire Shepparton Studio in London was entirely taken over by the *Oliver!* production in order to fit in all the sets and extras. Ironically, the scenes one remembers most fondly from the musical are the more intimate ones, including Fagin and the boys singing and dancing to "You've Got to Pick a Pocket or Two" in their cramped hideaway, Oliver singing "Where Is Love?" locked in the basement of the funeral parlor, and the quixotic Fagin arguing with himself as he fingers his possessions and sings "Reviewing the Situation." Movie musicals in the 1960s tended to be on a large scale and one can understand why Columbia took no risks and made *Oliver!* a big production piece.

Another difficulty with *Oliver!* onstage and on-screen is the awkward contrast between the dark story and the cheerful score. There is a joyous music hall quality to many of Bart's songs, something very common on the London musical stage. Yet this is a tale of child abuse, kidnapping, theft, and murder. Granted there are some sobering songs in the stage score but most of these did not appear in the movie, so this uncomfortable use of happy songs for a mostly unhappy story is disturbing.

Because no stage production of *Oliver!* could hope to be on such a large scale as the film, the intimacy of the drama onstage is not weakened by such bright and colorful production values. But even if some found *Oliver!* to be somewhat over-produced, it did not bother most audiences. *Oliver!* was a box office hit and won the Oscar for best picture. It is considered the last blockbuster of its time; 35 years would go by before another movie musical won the Oscar.

See also: *Hello, Dolly!, Willy Wonka and the Chocolate Factory, Les Misérables*

FURTHER READING

Hirschhorn, Clive. *The Columbia Story*. 2nd ed. Emeryville, CA: Hamlyn, 2001.
Napolitano, Mark. *Oliver! A Dickensian Musical*. New York: Oxford University Press, 2014.
Stafford, David, and Caroline Stafford. *Fings Ain't Wot They Used T' Be: The Lionel Bart Story*. London: Omnibus Press, 2011.

HELLO, DOLLY!

Studio and release date: 20th Century Fox; December 1969
Producer: Ernest Lehman
Screenplay: Ernest Lehman, based on the 1964 stage script by Michael Stewart, which was based on the 1955 comedy *The Matchmaker* by Thornton Wilder
Songwriter: Jerry Herman (music and lyrics)
Director: Gene Kelly
Choreographer: Michael Kidd
Musical Directors: Lennie Hayton, Lionel Newman
Cinematographer: Harry Stradling
Cast: Barbra Streisand, Walter Matthau, Michael Crawford, Marianne McAndrew, Danny Lockin, E. J. Peaker, Tommy Tune, Joyce Ames, Louis Armstrong, Fritz Feld
Songs: "Hello, Dolly!"; "Before the Parade Passes By"; "It Only Takes a Moment"; "Put on Your Sunday Clothes"; "So Long, Dearie"; "It Takes a Woman"; "Dancing"; "Love Is Only Love"; "Ribbons Down My Back"; "Just Leave Everything to Me"; "Elegance"

A great big Broadway musical hit became an even bigger Hollywood movie but it lost a bundle at the box office on its release and only later acquired many admirers. Yet there is something contagiously joyous about parts of *Hello, Dolly!* and the overproduced, over-budget film's saving grace was the miscast Barbra Streisand. Few American musicals have such a long ancestry. The character of the wily matchmaker was introduced in Moliere's 1668 comedy *The Miser*. An 1835 British comedy used the character in a tale about some rural hicks in London. An Austrian play about a matchmaker and her various schemes opened in Vienna in 1842. Thornton Wilder adapted the comedy in 1938, giving it an American setting and calling it *The Merchant of Yonkers*. The play failed on Broadway but in 1955 Wilder revised the work, gave it the title *The Matchmaker*, and it was a hit. When the film version of the play was released in 1958, Broadway producer David Merrick thought the tale would make a splendid musical comedy for the stage and so he bought the rights. Titled *Hello, Dolly!*, the show opened on Broadway in 1964 and was a rousing success, running six years and solidifying the stardom of Carol Channing who played the title role. 20th Century Fox purchased the movie rights for a hefty sum, then hired the best of the musical artists from the golden days of MGM, namely, Gene Kelly as director, Michael Kidd as choreographer, cinematographer Harry Stradling, costumer Irene Sharaff, scenic designer Jack Martin Smith, and Roger Edens as associate producer. The plan was to create a movie musical in 1969 that looked and felt like an MGM classic from the 1950s.

What Fox didn't have was any musical stars with screen experience and box office clout. It was to be a very expensive production and required a sure-fire star as Dolly. Channing was the obvious choice, but it was felt that she had little box office pull outside of New York even though she had been nominated for an Oscar for her supporting role in *Thoroughly Modern Millie* (1967). Elizabeth Taylor, Shirley MacLaine, Doris Day, and other stars were considered, but none were hot box office properties in 1969. In fact, only one woman made the Top Ten list in Hollywood at the time: Barbra Streisand. She was only 27 years old and had made only one film, *Funny Girl* (1968), in which she reprised her stage performance. Dolly in the story was a middle-aged widow who was Irish (her maiden name was Gallagher) but married the Jewish businessman Ephraim Levi. The finances of Hollywood declared that Streisand was the only person for the role, so the script would have to be adjusted to fit her. While the character of Dolly was made younger and more Jewish, Ernest Lehman's script was very close to the stage script until the last reel or so. When the Yonkers businessman Horace Vandergelder (Walter Matthau) hires matchmaker Dolly Levi (Streisand) to find him a wife, little does he suspect that Dolly has herself in mind. She also matches up the clerk Cornelius Hackl (Michael Crawford) with the milliner widow Irene Molloy (Marianne McAndrew), the woman Horace is thinking of marrying, and works things so that Horace's niece Ermengarde (Joyce Ames) gets to wed her sweetheart, the artist Ambrose Kemper (Tommy Tune). Despite a fiasco at the Harmonia Gardens Restaurant, where Horace loses his wallet and gets into a free-for-all on the dance floor, Dolly calms his anger and accepts his marriage proposal.

The title song was one of the few theater songs of the decade to climb the charts, but all of Jerry Herman's score is superior. The propulsive "Put on Your Sunday

Michael Kidd (1915–2007)   A dancer-turned-choreographer/director, his work onstage and on-screen is characterized by its energy and vitality. He was born in Brooklyn and began studying at New York City College for an engineering degree when he began to take ballet lessons and decided to pursue a dance career instead. He was a featured dancer with the American Ballet Theatre before making a dazzling choreography debut on Broadway in 1947 with *Finian's Rainbow*, followed by such stage hits as *Guys and Dolls* (1950), *Can-Can* (1953), *Li'l Abner* (1956), and *Destry Rides Again* (1959). Kidd also directed the last two productions and did both for such Broadway shows as *Wildcat* (1960), *Subways Are for Sleeping* (1961), *Ben Franklin in Paris* (1964), *The Rothschilds* (1970), *Good News!* (1974), and *The Music Man* (1980). He choreographed his first movie musical, *Where's Charley?*, in 1952, followed by notable work in *The Band Wagon* (1953), *Seven Brides for Seven Brothers* (1954), *Guys and Dolls* (1955), *Li'l Abner* (1959), *Star!* (1968), *Hello, Dolly!* (1969), and others. Kidd has also performed in films on occasion, as in *It's Always Fair Weather* (1954), *Smile* (1975), and *Movie Movie* (1978).

Clothes," the merry march "It Takes a Woman," the gentle "Ribbons Down My Back," the mock aria "So Long, Dearie," and the affirmative "Before the Parade Passes By" are among the musical gems from the stage to be used in the film. Perhaps the musical highpoint of the movie was when Louis Armstrong joined Streisand in the title song and the two created sparks that could rival the best moments from Hollywood's Golden Age. As intended, *Hello, Dolly!* did look like an MGM musical with vivacious choreography by Kidd, colorful period sets and costumes, and a lighthearted spirit of fun and musical adventure with Kelly's direction. As for Streisand, she made no attempt to age herself, tackled the humor with a Jewish flavor, and sang the songs with polish and style. The person playing Dolly is expected to carry the whole production; Streisand did that plus. With $25 million riding on her back, she seems undaunted and makes the whole film worth watching.

There were many criticisms when *Hello, Dolly!* was released about the size of the production. Every penny of the $25 million was on the screen and some thought it excessive. The "Before the Parade Passes By" number involved the largest set ever constructed in Hollywood since the silent days. Several blocks of 14th Street in the 1890s were re-created and thousands of extras hired for several weeks. The Harmonia Gardens Restaurant, consisting of three levels and room for hundreds of diners, dancers, and musicians, was one of the largest and most complex interior sets ever built. These were seen as excessive by many of the critics and some of the audience. Yet the year before, the movie *Oliver!* was nearly as excessive and few complained. Ironically, *Oliver!* is a musical melodrama; *Hello, Dolly!* is a musical comedy. Which genre would most logically employ such a bright and cheerful excess? When Merrick sold the movie rights to *Hello, Dolly!*, the deal stipulated that the movie could not be released until the Broadway show had closed. Fox began production in 1966, figuring that the stage version would close soon. But Merrick pulled a fast one on the studio. He recast the Broadway production of *Hello, Dolly!* with Pearl Bailey and an all-black cast, the show getting another round of raves and running until 1970. The screen version was completed and sat on the shelf for a full year. Fox had to pay Merrick additional funds to let it release the movie in 1969. It added substantially to the already over-budget musical. *Hello, Dolly!* did strong business when first released but it wouldn't pay back its $25 million until many years later.

See also: *Funny Girl, Oliver!*; Barbra Streisand, Gene Kelly, Michael Kidd biography boxes

FURTHER READING

Allvine, Glendon. *The Greatest Fox of Them All.* New York: Lyle Stuart, 1969.
Busa, Paul. *The Barbra Streisand Film Guide.* Seattle: CreateSpace Publishing, 2015.
Citron, Stephen. *Jerry Herman: Poet of the Showtune.* New Haven, CT: Yale University Press, 2004.

THE 1970S: STRUGGLING TO SURVIVE

The first few years of the 1970s were as explosive as the 1960s but as the decade wore on a kind of balance was achieved—the new ways coexisting with the traditional way of life. Antiwar temperament was high as the decade began and was fueled in 1970 when U.S. troops invaded Cambodia, increasing rather than decreasing American involvement in Southeast Asia. The new offensive spurred demonstrations across the country, particularly on college campuses. At the assembly of protestors at Kent State University, the Ohio National Guard opened fire on the crowd and killed four students, setting off another nationwide wave of protests. Yet the Vietnam War continued on for four more years. In 1975, Saigon fell to communist North Vietnam and American troops were quickly withdrawn from the country. It was America's longest and most unpopular war. Significantly, it was the only war the nation had ever lost. Returning GIs were not welcomed with parades and testimonials. Instead, Vietnam vets were ignored or even scorned, many of them having long-lasting issues with drugs and other postwar traumas. President Richard Nixon was no longer in office when the vets returned home. He had resigned the year before, facing impeachment on charges stemming from the Watergate scandal. Although Nixon had achieved some positive legislation and had even opened China to the West, his use of covert activities to win the election of 1972 had finally surfaced and for the first time in history a U.S. president resigned from office.

The Civil Rights Movement of the previous decade had turned from violence and anger to a more efficient system as African Americans finally began to make some headway into business, politics, higher education, and entertainment. The decade's new political force was the struggle for a Women's Equal Rights Amendment to the Constitution. Such a law did not come into being, but the voice of women was clearly heard for the first time and some improvements in equal pay and other rights were activated. Also encouraging was the space program that saw the first space station and space probes from the Soviet Union and the United States that brought back the first pictures of various planets. Altair put the first personal computer on the market in 1975, but its widespread use would not come until the next decade. The Concorde, the first supersonic passenger jet, began service in 1976, cutting travel time across the Atlantic by two-thirds.

The nation got more involved in the Middle East during the 1970s. President Jimmy Carter mediated an agreement between Egypt and Israel that removed Israeli troops from the Sinai Peninsula. It seemed that a truce, if not a peace, was possible in that volatile part of the world. Then the Shah of Iran was deposed and the country was ruled by a religious zealot, the Ayatollah Khomeini, who ordered an attack on the American Embassy and held dozens of Americans hostage for over a year. American-Russian relations improved earlier in the decade and when Leonid Brezhnev was named president of the Soviet Union in 1977. But when Russia invaded Afghanistan in 1979, tensions increased and, in protest, America withdrew from the upcoming 1980 Olympics in Moscow.

The "younger generation" of the 1960s matured into adult citizens in the 1970s. These "baby boomers," born during the two decades after World War II, were a significant force because of their large numbers. Many of them were raised in the suburbs, but as adults they returned to cities and many a metropolis enjoyed a kind of renaissance with urban neighborhoods "re-gentrified." Movies, television, publishing, fashion, art, and particularly music were all fueled by what appealed to the boomers; they were the majority and could not be ignored.

Hollywood tried to appeal to this new majority and offered a variety of movies that included everything from probing dramas like *Taxi Driver* (1976) to high-flying escapism such as *Star Wars* (1977) to journeys into the grotesque like *The Exorcist* (1973). Ironically, many of the boomers preferred "art house" films from foreign lands and Hollywood classics from the past. These were shown in "revival houses" in big cities and college towns and were often in conflict with what the studios were currently presenting. (This was before the introduction of videotapes and the concept of owning or renting movies; watching them at home was unheard of.) Because of this renewed interest in the past, film was finally considered an art form and was studied in colleges and written about by scholars. Movie musicals from the 1930s and 1940s were of particular interest to the boomers and they were not alone. The 1974 documentary *That's Entertainment!*, about the golden age of MGM musicals, was not an art house offering but a mainstream box office hit. (It did even better business than the 1970 documentary *Woodstock*.)

Television remained the strongest medium for news and entertainment. The most-watched films were not in theaters but on the smaller screen. TV movies and miniseries were prevalent, the most successful being the 12-hour series *Roots*, which broke ratings records in 1977. The development of cable systems meant more channels were possible, and the American viewership was divided into many fragmented groups. Broadway was similarly scattered about even as the number of productions and theatergoers decreased considerably. The number of plays and musicals that opened on Broadway in the 1970s fell to an all-time low. The theater district in New York was unsightly and unsafe, which added to Broadway's woes. Traditional theatergoers had the choice of a thin selection of comedies and musicals to attend, the most successful being *Applause* (1970), *No, No, Nanette* (1971), *Grease* (1972), *Pippin* (1972), *The Magic Show* (1974), *The Wiz* (1975), *Chicago* (1975), *Annie* (1977), *The Best Little Whorehouse in Texas* (1978), *Ain't Misbehavin'* (1978), and *Sugar Babies* (1979). The longest-running show of the decade was *A Chorus Line* (1975), which broke from tradition even as it satisfied a wide-range audience. The more adventurous theatergoers were interested in the demanding Stephen Sondheim musicals, such as *Company* (1970), *Follies* (1971), *A Little Night Music* (1973), *Pacific Overtures* (1976), and *Sweeney Todd* (1979). And there was a new force on Broadway that decade: the British musical. The success of *Jesus Christ Superstar* (1971) and *Evita* (1979) foreshadowed the British Invasion of the 1980s.

The movie musical continued to dwindle as the studios made fewer musicals and put their money into a handful of possible blockbusters rather than spreading out the money to diverse projects. Though the quantity was down, the quality was sometimes surprisingly high. Such hard-hitting and demanding musicals as *Cabaret* (1972), *Lady Sings the Blues* (1972), *Nashville* (1975), *New York, New York* (1977), and *All That Jazz* (1979) may have been uneven at times but they were serious efforts to redefine the movie musical in the 1970s. None were box office champs. For the big bucks, one had to turn to the youth-oriented musicals that managed to appeal to wide audiences. The two standout successes were *Saturday Night Fever* (1977) and *Grease* (1978), but similar in temperament were *Phantom of the Paradise* (1974), *The Rocky Horror Picture Show* (1975), *A Star Is Born* (1976), *The Buddy Holly Story* (1978), *FM* (1978), *American Hot Wax* (1978), *Sgt. Pepper's Lonely Hearts Club Band* (1978), *I Wanna Hold Your Hand* (1978), *Thank God It's Friday* (1978), *Rock 'n' Roll High School* (1979), and *The Rose* (1979). Fewer film versions of stage musicals were made during the decade and only *Grease* was a hit. *On a Clear Day You Can See Forever* (1970), *Song of Norway* (1970), *The Boy Friend* (1971), *Fiddler on the Roof* (1971), *Cabaret* (1972), *1776* (1972), *Man of La Mancha* (1972), *Godspell* (1973), *Jesus Christ Superstar* (1973), *Lost in the Stars* (1974), *A Little Night Music* (1977), and *Hair* (1979) were quality products but didn't appeal to mainstream audiences. *Mame* (1974) and *The Wiz* (1978), probably the two most expensive Broadway adaptations of the decade, were met with disdain by audiences and critics.

The Disney studio, still hoping to recapture the magic of *Mary Poppins* (1964), set its hopes on the live-action musicals *Bedknobs and Broomsticks* (1971) and

Pete's Dragon (1977), both costly ventures that did not make any money until they went to video in the 1980s. More satisfying were the Disney animated musicals *The Aristocats* (1971), *Robin Hood* (1973), and *The Rescuers* (1977). There were also the non-Disney animated musicals *Shinbone Alley* (1971), *Journey Back to Oz* (1972), and *Charlotte's Web* (1973), yet none of them did the kind of box office that the Disney products had done in the 1950s. A different sort of animation was successful with the public. *The Muppet Movie* (1979), with its humans and cloth puppet characters, was an immediate hit and inspired a series of other musicals featuring Jim Henson's Muppet characters. The fantasy musicals of the decade were quite a mixed bag. *Willy Wonka and the Chocolate Factory* (1971) was a first-class musical, and *Scrooge* (1970) was a pleasant holiday diversion. But the rest of the lot were disappointing, including *Pufnstf* (1970), *Lost Horizon* (1973), *The Little Prince* (1975), *The Blue Bird* (1976), and *The Slipper and the Rose* (1976).

Musical bio-pics returned in the 1970s, the best being the already mentioned *The Buddy Holly Story* and *Lady Sings the Blues*. Competently done but not successful with the critics or moviegoers were *The Great Waltz* (1942) about Johann Strauss, *Funny Lady* (1975) about Fanny Brice after *Funny Girl* (1969), *Leadbelly* (1976) about folk pioneer Huddle Ledbetter, *Scott Joplin* (1977), and *Elvis* (1979). The decade saw two Mark Twain musicals, *Tom Sawyer* (1973) and *Huckleberry Finn* (1974), and *Catch My Soul* (1974), a gospel version of Shakespeare's *Othello* set in the Wild West. There were two films that pastiched the musicals of the past but neither found an audience. *Movie Movie* (1978) was a double feature with a spoof of *42nd Street* (1933) that was accurate in its look and its music. *At Long Last Love* (1975) was an homage to the Cole Porter screen musicals of the 1930s. It received the worst reviews of the decades, even more scathing than those for *Mame* or *The Wiz*.

Liza Minnelli moved to the top of the short list of movie musical stars after her stunning performances in *Cabaret* and *New York, New York*. The two leading ladies of 1960s musicals, Julie Andrews and Barbra Streisand, had less success. Andrews gave a strong performance in the less-than-satisfying musical *Darling Lili* (1970), then spent the rest of the decade in film comedies. Streisand made three musicals in the 1970s and had a hit with the rock remake *A Star Is Born*. Despite her commendable performances in *On a Clear Day You Can See Forever* and *Funny Lady*, neither film found much of an audience. John Travolta became the significant male star of the Hollywood musical in the 1970s, based on his expert singing and dancing in the two youth hits *Saturday Night Fever* and *Grease*. Diana Ross impressed with her version of singer Billie Holiday in *Lady Sings the Blues*, but her career took a beating with *The Wiz*. Bette Midler made a sensational debut in *The Rose*. Had this been the Golden Age, each of these performers would be embarking on an exciting career in musicals. Instead the future held so few musicals that all of them concentrated on nonmusical movies in the 1980s and beyond. By the end of the

1970s, it looked like the movie musical was on its way to extinction. One had better go to *That's Entertainment!* and enjoy the nostalgia because, as Frank Sinatra said in the documentary's narration, "you're never gonna see anything like this again."

WOODSTOCK

Studio and release date: Warner Brothers; March 1970
Producers: Dale Bell, Bob Maurice
Director: Michael Wadleigh
Cinematographers: Malcolm Hart, Michael Margetts, and others
Cast: Joan Baez, Jimi Hendrix, Arlo Guthrie, Richie Havens, Sha-Na-Na, The Who, Joe Cocker, Santana, Sly and the Family Stone, Jefferson Airplane, Crosby, Stills & Nash
Principal Songs: "Woodstock"; "Freedom"; "Joe Hill"; "At the Hop"; "With a Little Help from My Friends"; "Rock and Soul Music"; "I'm Going Home"; "Wooden Ships"; "Going Up the Country"; "A Change Is Gonna Come": "Handsome Johnny"; "We're Not Gonna Take It"; "Summertime Blues"; "Coming Into Los Angeles"; "Purple Haze"

Just as the 1969 gathering in Bethel, New York, is the most famous of all rock festivals, this film about the "three days of peace and music" is the most famous rockumentary. The music festival was the idea of Michael Lang, John Roberts, Joel Rosenman, and Artie Cornfield, who had recently produced the Miami Pop Festival that played to about 25,000 fans. The new concert event was titled "An Aquarian Exposition" and plans were set to have the three-day event in the quiet town of Woodstock in the Catskill Mountains of New York State. The town officials vetoed the idea, as did the towns of Saugerties and Walkill. Because Lang and his associates were already booking acts, the necessity of finding a place grew as the August 15–17 festival dates got closer. Finally, dairy farmer Max Yager in Bethel, New York, agreed to rent his farm, which included a wide hill that made an ideal amphitheater. Lang assured the town of Bethel that no more than 50,000 spectators were expected. Tickets to the three-day event cost $18 in advance, $22 at the gate. Thirty-two acts were booked and continuous music was planned for the festival's three days. Although fences and ticket booths were erected, they could not handle the thousands of fans who descended on Bethel days before August 15. Fearful of riots, the promoters declared the festival a free event, and fans tore down the fences to settle in for the concert, which was still unofficially called Woodstock. By the time the first performer, Jimi Hendrix, took to the stage, an estimated 400,000 people were on the grounds. Despite rain, lack of food, poor sanitary conditions, and drug overdoses, Woodstock was a peaceful and often joyous event and long treasured by most of the thousands who attended and performed there. Lang and his investors lost a lot of money on the enterprise but were proud to have sponsored such a pivotal event in music, not to say a cultural milestone.

Weeks before the festival, film director Michael Wadleigh asked Lang and the other sponsors if they would like to invest in a film covering the concert. They foolishly refused. It turned out that the documentary *Woodstock* was the only profitable venture in the whole project. Wadleigh hired 100 technicians, cameramen, and interviewers to cover the three-day event, all of them working for a percentage of the eventual profit from the film. By the end of the festival, Wadleigh had 120 hours of footage of setting up the festival; interviews with patrons, performers, police, and even local farmers; exciting footage of the concert itself; as well as fascinating scenes backstage and in the crowd. When Wadleigh and his editors began to put the footage into a feature-length documentary, it was clear that the movie could not do justice to the actual concert and still capture the world of the festival. One of his editors, future film director Martin Scorsese, came up with a brilliant solution. He suggested splitting the wide movie screen into three sections at times, allowing the viewers to see the performers and, at the same time, showing the crowd reactions or the activity backstage. This technique, as well as dizzying montage, multipaneled images, and vibrant use of color, gave *Woodstock* a look like no other movie. Such revolutionary cinematic was later copied and used in other rockumentaries and, eventually, the split screen was used at live concerts with giant screens set up for all to see.

The 184-minute running time of *Woodstock* still could not include everything, and not all the artists who performed in the festival got on film. But a "director's cut" version was released in 1994, which added 40 more minutes of performance. Joni Mitchell, who did not perform at the festival, wrote the tribute song "Woodstock," which was recorded by Crosby, Stills, Nash & Young and used in the movie. The rest of the music came from the concert itself, and it was an impressive lineup of rock performers including Jimi Hendrix, Joe Cocker, Sly and the Family Stone, Joan Baez, Ten Years After, The Who, Arlo Guthrie, The Jefferson Airplane, Janis Joplin, Richie Havens, Sha-Na-Na, Canned Heat, Country Joe and the Fish, and Crosby, Stills & Nash. *Woodstock* is not only a record of a pivotal event but it seems to define and illustrate an era and a spirit as few documentaries have.

FURTHER READING

Evans, Mike, and Paul Kingsbury. *Woodstock: Three Days That Rocked the World*. New York: Sterling, 2010.
Lang, Michael. *The Road to Woodstock*. New York: Ecco, 2010.

WILLY WONKA AND THE CHOCOLATE FACTORY

Studio and release date: Wolper/Paramount; June 1971
Producers: David L. Wolper, Stan Margulies
Screenplay: Roald Dahl, David Seltzer, based on Dahl's 1964 book *Charlie and the Chocolate Factory*
Songwriters: Leslie Bricusse, Anthony Newley (music and lyrics)
Director: Mel Stuart
Choreographer: Howard Jeffrey
Musical Director: Walter Scharf
Cinematographer: Arthur Ibbetson
Cast: Gene Wilder, Peter Ostrum, Jack Albertson, Roy Kinnear, Julie Dawn Cole, Leonard Stone, Michael Bollner, Denise Nickerson, Paris Themmen
Songs: "Pure Imagination"; "The Candy Man"; "(I've Got a) Golden Ticket"; "Cheer Up, Charlie"; "Oompa-Loompa-Doompa-De-Do"; "I Want It Now!"; "Wondrous Boat Ride"

This first film version of Roald Dahl's dark, fantastical book *Charlie and the Chocolate Factory* may have softened and sentimentalized the original story a bit, but it made Dahl accessible to all and opened the door for several other movies based on his books. Although Dahl was English, *Charlie and the Chocolate Factory* was first published in the United States in 1964, then three years later in Great Britain. The book was inspired by Dahl's experience as a boy when the Cadbury chocolate company would send samples of its newest candy to area schools to get opinions from kids. Although the children's book was well reviewed when it was first published, it did not become a favorite until after the movie was released. Paramount bought the film rights and then made a deal with the Quaker Oats Company to license a new candy bar called a Wonka Bar. That is why the film version was retitled *Willy Wonka and the Chocolate Factory* so that the product was in the title. Although the movie was a hit, the Wonka Bar was not. There was an error in the formula and the bars melted even while still in the wrapper. The name was sold to the Sunline candy company, which found a way to make a better product. The casting of Willy Wonka for the film version was not easy. Joel Grey, Spike Milligan, Jon Pertwee, and Ron Moody were all considered but none seemed to have that needed combination of quirkiness, charm, and moody menace. Actors Jon Cleese, Graham Chapman, Eric Idle, Terry Jones, and Michael Palin—who were just finding fame on *Monty Python's Flying Circus* on British television—all expressed great willingness to play Willy Wonka but none had star power, especially in America. When Gene Wilder auditioned for director Mel Stuart, the offbeat actor immediately

The musical fantasy *Willy Wonka and the Chocolate Factory* (1971) is held together by Gene Wilder's enigmatic performance as the candy magician Willy Wonka. Wilder is both enticing and threatening in the film, which has its dark side as well. Mel Stuart directed the popular movie musical. (Paramount Pictures/Photofest)

impressed Stuart and coproducer David L. Wolper as ideal for the role.

The film stuck fairly close to the original book, centering on the English lad Charlie Bucket (Peter Ostrum) who is one of the lucky winners of a candy manufacturer's contest. Charlie and his grandfather (Jack Albertson) are invited, with four obnoxious kids and their parents from different parts of the globe, to tour the candy factory run by the eccentric Willy Wonka (Wilder). Inside the bizarre and fanciful factory, the guests are shown how the pint-sized Oompa Loompas made the chocolate. The tour turns out to be a test of character, which the other children fail miserably and for which they are punished in ghastly ways. But Charlie and his grandfather pass the test, inherit the factory, and go flying into the air in one of Wonka's many strange and wonderful contraptions. Dahl's book had verses in it that were chanted by the Oompa Loompas, but the lyrics were pretty much ignored and original songs for the movie were written by Anthony Newley and Leslie Bricusse, "The Candy Man" being the big hit. Even better was the enchanting lullaby "Pure Imagination." Wilder gave a bizarre, intriguing performance as Wonka, and the set decor was often stunning. Interestingly, both the location exteriors and the studio interiors for the musical were filmed in Germany. In fact, many of the Oompa Loompas were German extras who could not speak English. Sometimes maudlin, other times cruel, always fascinating, the movie took a while to gain the following it enjoys today on DVD. As for Dahl's original book, it has entered the list of the top 10 most read books by children.

In 2005, Dahl's book was filmed again, this time using the original title *Charlie and the Chocolate Factory* and featuring Freddie Highmore as Charlie and Johnny Depp as Willy Wonka. Some of Dahl's verses were put to new music but the movie was not really a musical. The Tim Burton-directed film was closer to the original book, perhaps even darker. Supposedly, Dahl was not happy with *Willy Wonka and the Chocolate Factory*. Legend has it that he so hated the musical version of his sobering tale that he refused permission for Hollywood to make a movie out of the sequel, *Charlie and the Great Glass Elevator*. Others say that Dahl never watched the whole movie but, in truth, he attended the opening and never publicly made a negative statement about the film. Dahl died in 1990 so it is conjecture to say what he might have felt about the more somber 2005 movie version. But it is safe to say that *Willy Wonka and the Chocolate Factory* has become a family film classic and one of the best fantasy musicals.

See also: *The 5,000 Fingers of Dr. T*

FURTHER READING

Cole, Julie Dawn. *I Want It Now! A Memoir of Life on the Set of Willy Wonka and the Chocolate Factory*. Longboat Key, FL: Oceanview Publishing, 2011.
Mangan, Lucy. *Inside Charlie's Chocolate Factory*. London: Puffin Books, 2014.
Stuart, Mel, and Josh Young. *Pure Imagination: The Making of Willy Wonka*. New York: St. Martin's Press, 2002.

FIDDLER ON THE ROOF

Studio and release date: Mirisch/United Artists; October 1971
Producer: Norman Jewison
Screenplay: Joseph Stein, based on his 1964 stage script, which was based on the story *Tevye's Daughters* by Sholom Aleichem
Songwriters: Jerry Bock (music), Sheldon Harnick (lyrics)
Director: Norman Jewison
Choreographer: Tom Abbott
Musical Director: John Williams
Cinematographer: Oswald Morris
Cast: Topol, Norma Crane, Molly Picon, Leonard Frey, Michele Marsh, Neva Small, Rosalind Harris, Paul Mann, Michael Glaser
Songs: "Sunrise, Sunset"; "Tradition"; "Matchmaker, Matchmaker: "If I Were a Rich Man"; "To Life"; "Far from the Home I Love"; "Do You Love Me?"; "Sabbath Prayer"; "Miracle of Miracles"; "Tevye's Dream"

A so-called Jewish musical whose universal themes made it a favorite around the world, it was brought to the screen faithfully with fine performances and its heartfelt score by Jerry Bock (music) and Sheldon Harnick (lyrics). *Fiddler on the Roof* was a surprise hit on Broadway in 1964. Its creators thought that their touching Jewish show would have limited appeal but were proud of it. They were all surprised when it became universally embraced and moved people of all religions and races. Joseph Stein wrote the tender, funny, and efficient stage script, based on Sholom Aleichem's stories, and let the simple charm of the characters carry the plot. Dairyman Tevye and his wife Golde are like all the other Jewish citizens of the Russian village of Anatevka, holding on to traditions that dictate how to do everything. His daughters start to break from the old ways, falling in love and finding spouses without the aid of a matchmaker. Even more upsetting, one daughter marries outside of the Hebrew faith. After some demonstrations of their distaste for the Jews living in their community, the Cossacks order the Jews to leave the village and it seems that the world is coming to an end. By the final curtain the villagers set off for new lives in the New World, bringing their traditions with them. By emphasizing the Jewish community from the beginning, the story took on a folktale-like quality and the village types were as familiar as they were endearing. Jerome Robbins directed and choreographed the Broadway production with a delicate touch, avoiding spectacle and cleverness and relying on traditional images, such as a family at prayer or the celebrants at a wedding. Even the choreography grew from the rustic lives of the people, and the bottle dance at the wedding took on a mythic feeling of ancient ritual.

So many of the songs from *Fiddler on the Roof* have become so familiar over the years that one forgets how daring it was to write a score that avoided slick jokes, overt emotion, and other forms of theatrics. Harnick's lyrics are marvels of simplicity and sincerity, the humor growing gently out of the characters and the emotions quietly expressed. Bock's music is ethnic sounding without being clichéd, and there is a richness in even the most uncomplicated melodies. "Sunrise Sunset" has become the most recognized song, helped no doubt by its use in weddings over the decades; "Matchmaker, Matchmaker" is the catchiest tune; and "If I Were a Rich Man," with its cantor-like chanting, is the most revealing of the many character numbers. Although it is mostly a quiet score, it has its moment of joy, as in the riotous "To Life" and the celebratory "Miracles of Miracles." The charm song "Do You Love Me?' may just be the most charming of that genre ever written.

Zero Mostel, usually cast in clowning roles, scored a triumph as Teyve onstage but he was not considered for the movie. The producing Mirish brothers offered the role to Orson Welles, Anthony Quinn, Marlon Brando, and others but were turned down. Instead they went not with a big star but to the Israeli actor Topol who had played Tevye on the London stage. While he did not have box office clout, Topol was a more authentic choice and his performance was less Broadway and more European art film. In fact, director Norman Jewison wanted the whole film to have the look of a classical European painting, in particular the French artist Jean-François Millet. Cinematographer Oswald Morris obliged, giving the film muted colors and a soft focus that was sometimes impressionistic. One might say the acting was also muted. Jewison discouraged broad humor or big emotions from his actors. Norma Crane underplayed the wife Golde; Rosalind Harris, Michele Marsh, and Neva Small played the eldest daughters with youthful reserve; and even scene stealer Molly Picon seemed subdued as the matchmaker Yente. Robbins' celebrated stage choreography was re-created by Tom Abbott for the movie. The famous "bottle dance" at the wedding celebration was the film's most memorable piece of choreography, but also well done was the vibrant "To Life" dance and the bizarre "Tevye's Dream," which used marvelous cinematic effects not possible on the stage. All but two of the Bock-Harnick songs from Broadway were used in the film and were beautifully rendered by the cast. Yet in some ways the musical highlight of the movie was Isaac Stern's superb violin solo heard over the opening credits. While all the elements in *Fiddler on the Roof* were individually excellent, the movie as a whole was somewhat disappointing. Jewison treated the material with respect and integrity, but the pace was slow. The overlong (180 minutes) movie rarely captured the spirit and exuberance of the Broadway production. In 1979 the film was rereleased in Dolby stereo with 32 minutes cut out, resulting in what many felt was an improved movie.

See also: *The Jazz Singer, West Side Story*

FURTHER READING

Isenberg, Barbara. *Tradition! Fiddler on the Roof: The World's Most Beloved Musical.* New York: St. Martin's Press, 2014.

Lambert, Philip. *To Life! The Musical Theatre of Bock and Harnick.* New York: Oxford University Press, 2010.

Solomon, Alissa. *Wonder of Wonders: A Cultural History of Fiddler on the Roof.* New York: Metropolitan Books, 2013.

CABARET

Studio and release date: ABC/Allied Artists; January 1972
Producer: Cy Feuer
Screenplay: Jay Presson Allen, based on Joe Masteroff's 1966 stage script and Christopher Isherwood's *Berlin Stories*
Songwriters: John Kander (music), Fred Ebb (lyrics)
Director/Choreographer: Bob Fosse
Musical Director: Ralph Burns
Cinematographer: Geoffrey Unsworth

Cast: Liza Minnelli, Joel Gray, Michael York, Helmut Griem, Marisa Berenson,
Fritz Wepper

Songs: "Cabaret"; "Wilkommen"; "Maybe This Time"; "Tomorrow Belongs to
Me"; "Mein Herr"; "Money, Money"; "Two Ladies"; "If You Could See Her"

A classic Broadway musical became a very different movie classic when this musical melodrama was reimagined for the screen. Rarely have the stage and screen
versions been so different and yet individually distinguished. *Cabaret* was one of
the boldest and most uncompromising Broadway musicals of the 1960s. Yet despite
its grim subject matter and brutally honest approach to that material, the 1966
musical was very popular and remains so on stages around the world. Although
based on John Van Druten's play *I Am a Camera* (1951), which was taken from
Christopher Isherwood's original stories about Berlin, Joe Masteroff's script for *Cabaret* was frequently original. The American writer Clifford Bradshaw goes to Berlin
on the eve of the Nazi takeover and is fascinated by the city, the decadent Kit Kat
Club, and British singer Sally Bowles. The two drift into a casual affair while the
Jewish fruit merchant Herr Schultz romances his landlady Fraulein Schneider. She

Director-choreographer Bob Fosse was inspired by German films of the 1930s when he
made *Cabaret* (1972). Liza Minnelli (pictured) performed an homage to Marlene Dietrich
in the "Mein Herr" number at the Kit Kat Klub. (Allied Artists/Photofest)

Liza Minnelli (b. 1946)   The high-energy yet vulnerable actress-singer-dancer has found stardom onstage and in movies, usually in musicals. She was born in Los Angeles, the daughter of Judy Garland and Vincente Minnelli, and educated at the Sorbonne in Paris before studying acting in New York. She appeared in summer stock as a teenager then was featured in musicals Off Broadway and later on Broadway. Minnelli made her adult screen debut in 1967 but became a full-fledged movie star with her first film musical, *Cabaret* (1972). Unfortunately, few screen musicals were being made in the 1970s so much of her career was on television, in concert, and on Broadway where she shone in *The Act* (1977) and *The Rink* (1984). Her screen musical *A Matter of Time* (1976) was a failure, but there was much to applaud in *New York, New York* (1977). While Minnelli has suffered from physical and mental ailments and has been tabloid fodder for decades, she remains a major star in the old-fashioned manner with fans who are as devoted to her as those for her mother. Biographies: *Under the Rainbow: The Real Liza Minnelli,* George Mair (1996); *Liza Minnelli: Born a Star,* Wendy Leigh (1994).

submits to his romantic intentions until worries about anti-Semitism force her to break off the engagement. Sally finds that she's pregnant, and Cliff offers to marry her and bring her back with him to America. Sally agrees but soon realizes that she would make a terrible wife and mother and prefers to continue living a carefree, decadent life in Berlin. The political situation worsens, Cliff leaves Berlin, and Sally goes back to the cabaret where everyone can continue to ignore what is happening around them. Both stories were framed by acts at the cabaret, supervised by the sleazy master of ceremonies, and the numbers often commented on the characters and their situation. It was a powerful musical and boasted two outstanding scores by John Kander (music) and Fred Ebb (lyrics), one for the plot and characters, another for the Kit Kat Club itself. Because of their chilly, distanced tone, all the numbers are of a whole. The love songs and the happy numbers hint at self-deception, the sexy ditties are tainted with self-disgust, and the title song itself a lie, no one (including Sally who sings it) believing a word of it. For this reason few of the songs in *Cabaret* "travel" well and have rarely been recorded because they are tied so tightly to the dark tone of the show. Kander and Ebb found plenty of variety even while working within this somber subtext. "Don't Tell Mama" has a British music hall flavor, Fraulein Schneider's solos "So What?" and "What Would You Do?" have a Kurt Weill-like temperament, "Meeskite" has an Eastern European Jewish quality, and "Tomorrow Belongs to Me" is a frightening Nazi anthem because it is so stirring and seemingly positive. The emcee's Kit Kat Club numbers were ironic and sometimes scathing including the ribald "Two Ladies," the

---

Bob Fosse (1927–1987)   The distinctive stage, film, and television choreographer-director, he had a jazzy style that was unique and easily identifiable. He was born in Chicago, Illinois, the son of a salesman, and as a teenager danced professionally in local nightclubs, burlesque houses, and vaudeville theaters. After appearing in the chorus of a handful of forgotten Broadway musicals, he had better luck in Hollywood, dancing in such musicals as *Kiss Me, Kate* (1953), *Give a Girl a Break* (1953), and *My Sister Eileen* (1955). Fosse then returned to Broadway as a choreographer and became famous for his work in *The Pajama Game* (1954), *Damn Yankees* (1955), *Bells Are Ringing* (1956), *New Girl in Town* (1957), and *How to Succeed in Business Without Really Trying* (1961) as well as directing and choreographing *Redhead* (1959), *Little Me* (1962), *Sweet Charity* (1966 and 1986), *Pippin* (1972), *Chicago* (1975), and *Dancin'* (1978). When he returned to the movies, it was to direct *Sweet Charity* (1968), *Cabaret* (1972), and *All That Jazz* (1979). Biographies: *All His Jazz: The Life and Death of Bob Fosse*, Martin Gottfried (1990/2003); *Razzle Dazzle: The Life and Work of Bob Fosse*, Kevin Boyd Grubb (1989).

---

trilingual welcome song "Wilkommen," and the oddball love song "If You Could See Her," which turns ugly at the end. The score remains Kander and Ebb's finest achievement.

Bob Fosse directed and choreographed the screen version of *Cabaret* and had definite ideas about how to reimagine the musical for the screen. He wanted all of the musical numbers to take place in the Kit Kat Club, which was now a small, sleazy dive with decadence everywhere. In Jay Presson Allen's taut screenplay, the story is now a melodrama with songs. The movie dropped characters and plot lines and added new ones, some going back to Isherwood's original stories. Liza Minnelli, in her first screen musical, lit up the screen as the eager, desperate-to-be-bad nightclub singer Sally Bowles (changed from a Brit to an American), and she was balanced by a calm, amused performance by Michael York as her bisexual lover (changed from an American to the British Brian). Joel Grey reprised his unforgettable stage performance as the emcee and Helmut Griem and Marisa Berenson were cast in the new subplot about a young Jewish couple whose dreams are thwarted by the growing Nazi party. The older couple Schneider and Shultz was dropped as was much of the Kander and Ebb score. Only five songs from the stage made it to the movie—"Wilkommen," "Two Ladies," "Tomorrow Belongs to Me," "If You Could See Her," and the title song—and the team wrote two new ones: the rapid-fire "Money Money" and the coolly seductive "Mein Herr." Interpolated into the screen score was the wishful ballad "Maybe This Time," written by Kander and

Ebb some years before. Although confined to a small space, the musical numbers were brilliantly staged and very effective using cheap lighting effects and interesting points of view from the audience. The only number not in the club was the chilling "Tomorrow Belongs to Me," which was set in an outdoor beer garden where the song built to a haunting climax as a young Nazi (Oliver Collignon) sang the seemingly innocent anthem. *Cabaret* was shot on various locations in Germany and, often, the cinematography was as active as Fosse's choreography. The movie was also edited in such a way that the frenetic world of Berlin in 1929 was viewed in bits and pieces through a smoky, alcohol-tainted dream. Rarely has the film version of a Broadway musical taken so many liberties with the script and score and ended up being as powerful as the original.

See also: South Pacific, Les Misérables; Liza Minnelli, Bob Fosse biography boxes

FURTHER READING

Garebian, Keith. *The Making of Cabaret.* 2nd ed. New York: Oxford University Press, 2011.

Leve, James. *Kander and Ebb.* New Haven, CT: Yale University Press, 2009.

Tropiano, Stephen. *Cabaret: Music on Film.* Montclair, NJ: Limelight Editions, 2011.

Wasson, Sam. *Fosse.* New York: Dolan/Houghton Mifflin Harcourt, 2013.

LADY SINGS THE BLUES

Studio and release date: Paramount; October 1972
Producers: Jay Weston, James White
Screenplay: Terrence McCloy, Chris Clark, Suzanne de Passe, based on Holiday's 1956 memoir
Songwriters: Billie Holiday, George and Ira Gershwin, Jimmy Sherman, Jimmy Davis, Roger Ramirez, Portere Grainger, Harry Woods, and others (music and lyrics)
Director: Sidney J. Furie
Musical Director: Gil Askey
Cinematographer: John Alonzo
Cast: Diana Ross, Billy Dee Williams, Richard Pryor, James Callahan, Paul Hampton, Sid Melton, Virginia Capers, Scatman Crothers
Principal Songs: "The Man I Love"; "Lover Man"; "Good Morning Heartache"; "Strange Fruit"; "God Bless the Child"; "What a Little Moonlight Can Do"; " 'Taint Nobody's Business If I Do"; "Love Is Here to Stay"; "Them There Eyes"; "Don't Explain"

The legendary jazz-blues singer Billie Holiday had a short and difficult life but left behind many recordings and a few film appearances. This biographical musical about her life was a long time coming and when it finally was made it seemed to be more about Diana Ross than Holiday. When Hollywood was making all those bio-pics about singers who hit bottom, as with *Love Me or Leave Me* (1955), *I'll Cry Tomorrow* (1955), and *The Joker Is Wild* (1957), they were afraid of doing one on Billie Holiday. Those movies offered some kind of self-reckoning and even hope at the end, but how do you make a musical about a singer who died of heroine poisoning at the age of 44? Also, the studios were cautious about movies featuring African American musicians and singers. Where were the bio-pics about Louis Armstrong, Count Basie, Duke Ellington, Bessie Smith, Ma Rainey, or Charlie Parker? It wouldn't be until the 1970s before some of them saw dramatizations, including this one about Holiday. Paramount had been considering a Holiday bio-pic for several years, and various African American singers were slated to play her, among them Dorothy Dandridge, Abbey Lincoln, Diana Sands, and Diahann Carroll. When the project was finally green-lighted and casting began, one of the top singers on the charts was Ross, who had just split from the Supremes. There were a few problems though: Ross had never played a character in a movie, she did not look anything like Holiday, and she certainly didn't sound like "Lady Day," as Holiday was nicknamed.

Holiday was born Eleanor Fagan in Philadelphia where she had a terrible childhood. She was raped at an early age and worked as a prostitute as an adult. But she could sing. Her low, even raspy singing voice was distinctive and her interpretation of blues and jazz, particularly torch songs, was compelling. Holiday worked in dives before getting a record contract and finding fame with her rendition of "What a Little Moonlight Can Do." More records, concerts, and even a few movies followed. But the self-destructive Holiday was plagued with bad health, drug problems, and three unsuccessful marriages. She wrote about it all in her memoir *Lady Sings the Blues* in 1956, the same year she performed at Carnegie Hall. To say Holiday was a trailblazer is an understatement. Although famous among jazz and blues fans when she was alive, Holiday's status as a legendary figure came after her death. By 1972, when this bio-pic was released, most moviegoers did not know what Holiday sounded like. But they certainly knew what Ross sounded like and that was enough for Paramount.

Perhaps the greatest irony about *Lady Sings the Blues* is that it resembles those old rags-to-riches bio-pics of two decades earlier. The screenplay distorted the facts and offered a plot that was as predictable as it was cliché ridden. Young Holiday from the streets of Harlem learns that the prostitutes dress better than menial laborers who clean out the whorehouses so she becomes a successful call girl. She finds the strength to quit and pursue a singing career but ends up dancing in a Harlem nightclub. Once her singing is recognized as something special, she breaks convention and gets a gig singing with the all-white band led by Reg Hanley (James T. Callahan). When the band tours, Holiday encounters prejudice wherever she goes and gets involved with drugs for the first time. With the help of her husband Louis McKay (Billy Dee Williams), she gets better and better engagements. But the marriage is a tempestuous one and her addiction starts to affect her singing. The movie climaxes with her concert at Carnegie Hall but it is undercut with photos and headlines illustrating her tragic future. While there were plenty of melodramatics, the film never explained or demonstrated what was so special about Holiday's talents. Also, many of the supporting characters were one-dimensional and uninteresting. Only Richard Pryor, as Holiday's co-addict and friend Piano Man, came to life, and it seemed like some of their scenes were improvised rather than written.

Many comparisons were made between *Lady Sings the Blues* and *Funny Girl*, another bio-pic about a struggling singer with a bad marriage. While Barbra Streisand did not impersonate Fanny Brice in that movie, she manages to capture the essence of Brice's comic talents. The fact that Streisand was a much more accomplished singer than Brice didn't seem to bother too many moviegoers. In *Lady Sings the Blues*, Ross is a very different singer than Holiday. Ross delivered the Holiday song hits in a smooth, velvety style that sounded more contemporary than the raw, aching voice of Holiday herself. The same incongruity could be found in the acting. Ross had so much class that her tough times seemed to be an annoyance rather than a tragedy. That said, Ross makes a masterful movie debut in *Lady Sings the Blues*, carrying the film as Streisand (in her screen debut) had to. The old standards were interpreted well by Ross, including "Strange Fruit," "Good Morning, Heartache," "The Man I Love," " 'Tain't Nobody's Bizness If I Do," "Lover Man," "God Bless the Child," and the title number. *Lady Sings the Blues* made Ross a movie star and rightfully so. The soundtrack album also sold well and introduced many listeners to Holiday's incredible repertory of songs, if not to the singer herself.

See also: *Love Me or Leave Me*, *Funny Girl*

FURTHER READING

Holiday, Billie. *Lady Sings the Blues*. Revised. New York: Broadway Books, 2011.
Szwed, John. *Billie Holiday: The Musician and the Myth*. New York: Viking, 2015.
Taraborelli, J. Randy. *Diana Ross: A Biography*. Secaucus, NJ: Citadel, 2014.

CHARLOTTE'S WEB

Studio and release date: Hanna-Barbera/Paramount; March 1973
Producers: Edgar M. Bronfman, Joseph Barbera, William Hanna
Screenplay: Earl Hammer Jr., based on the 1952 book by E. B. White
Songwriters: Richard M. and Robert B. Sherman (music and lyrics)
Directors: Charles A. Nichols, Iwao Takamoto
Musical Director: Paul DeKorte
Voices: Debbie Reynolds, Henry Gibson, Pamelyn Ferdin, Paul Lynde, Rex
    Allen, Martha Scott, Agnes Moorehead, Dave Madden, Danny Bonaduce,
    Don Messick, Herb Vigran
Songs: "Charlotte's Web"; "Mother Earth and Father Time: "A Veritable
    Smorgasbord"; "Chin Up"; "Zuckerman's Famous Pig"; "There Must Be
    Something More"; "Deep in the Dark"; "I Can Talk"; "We've Got Lots in
    Common"

An animated musical version of the beloved children's book by E. B. White, the
movie was faithful to the source material and boasted a fine score by Richard M.
and Robert B. Sherman (music and lyrics). It was also one of the very few animated
features of the 1970s not made by the Disney studio. White wrote *Charlotte's Web* in
1952 and it immediately became a favorite. Over 60 years later, it remains one of
the most-read children's books in English, probably because it has a delightful,
far-fetched plot that charms both young and adult readers. The piglet Wilbur is the
runt of the liter but is saved by eight-year-old Fern who takes him as her pet. Years
later, Wilbur has been forgotten by Fern and the word in the farmyard is that he is
going to become the Christmas dinner. But this time Wilbur is saved by Charlotte
the spider who spins out words over Wilbur's stall. The strange phenomenon makes
the pig famous, becomes a prizewinner at the fair, and is spared an early death.
Charlotte dies of old age but Wilbur takes care of her many offspring in remem-
brance of his spider friend who saved his life. The tale is populated by other lively
animal characters, most memorably the self-centered rat Templeton. Although the
idea of possible slaughter of Wilbur and the actual death of Charlotte would seem
to make the book too upsetting for children, White insisted that this darker side
of the story was important to its meaning. For decades children have enjoyed the
book and seem to deal well with the specter of death in the tale.

The 1973 screen version of *Charlotte's Web* was made by television cartoon spe-
cialists Joseph Barbera and William Hanna. They had presented many film shorts
and TV cartoon series before but *Charlotte's Web* was their first feature musical.
The animation department at Hanna-Barbera Studios could not compete with the
Disney artists so they didn't try to. The Hanna-Barbera cartoons were simply drawn
with basic backgrounds and uncomplicated movement. The studio's strength was

in its many memorable characters—from the Flintstones and Huckleberry Hound to Yogi Bear and the Jetsons. Therefore, one should not expect Disney-like animation in a Hanna-Barbera work. That is definitely true of *Charlotte's Web*, which has colorful, expressive animation on a simple scale. The script for the musical version remains faithful to the book in its plotting, but the spirit of the original is sometimes lost, particularly in the darker aspects of the story. Because *Charlotte's Web* is not a long book, it was possible to dramatize all the events and still have room for songs. The Sherman brothers' songs are Disney quality even if the animation isn't. Most of the numbers are character songs, giving the different animals a sincerity and depth not found in the usual Hanna-Barbera critters. Charlotte (voiced by Debbie Reynolds) sings the tender ballad "Mother Earth and Father Time" about the passing of the seasons and the birth and rebirth that occurs in nature. Charlotte also sings the optimistic number "Chin Up' and joins Wilbur (Henry Gibson), Ram (Dave Madden), and the other animals in the catchy "We've Got a Lot in Common." There is a merry march titled "Zuckerman's Famous Pig," and the chorus sings the title song while Charlotte spends the night weaving the message that will save Wilbur. Perhaps the song that viewers most remember is "A Veritable Smorgasbord," which is sung by Templeton (Paul Lynde) and the Goose (Agnes Moorehead) as they list all the garbage at the fair that is fit for eating. The song, like the movie itself, is unpretentious fun and still holds up well after all these years.

Because animation has been so associated with the Disney studios over the years, one forgets that there were other animated musicals made by other studios in the past. In 1939, just two years after Walt Disney released the first animated feature, *Snow White and the Seven Dwarfs*, the Fleischer Studios made Hollywood's second animated feature, *Gulliver's Travels*, released through Paramount Pictures. It was a jolly retelling of one section of Jonathan's Swift's classic fantasy novel and boasted a fine score by Ralph Rainger (music) and Leo Robin (lyrics). The love song from the film, "Faithful Forever," was nominated for an Oscar and recorded by many artists in the 1940s. But both Paramount and animator Dave Fleischer found that animated features were costly and not time-efficient so Fleischer returned to making cartoon shorts just like the other studios. Another memorable non-Disney animated musical was *Gay-Purr-ee*, which Warner Brothers released in 1962. The romance between two French cats was not a very riveting tale but the songs by Harold Arlen (music) and E. Y. Harburg (lyrics) were exceptional. Of course it helped that they were sung by Judy Garland and Robert Goulet. Most memorable were the delicate "Little Drops of Rain" and the torchy "Paris Is a Lonely Town." Again the costs were high and the box office low. A non-Disney animated musical that did make money was *Yellow Submarine*, a British movie that was released in the United States by United Artists in 1968. The fact that it was chock full of Beatles hit songs explains its popularity but the pop-art animation and the playful story add to the enjoyment. With the runaway success of Disney's

The Little Mermaid in 1989 and *Beauty and the Beast* in 1991, all the studios again considered making animated musicals, and some of them did.

See also: *Snow White and the Seven Dwarfs, A Hard Day's Night*; Richard M. and Robert B. Sherman, Debbie Reynolds biography boxes

FURTHER READING

Sherman, Robert B., and Richard M. Sherman. *Walt's Time: From Before to Beyond*. Santa Clarita, CA: Camphor Tree Publishers, 1998.
Sims, Michael. *The Story of Charlotte's Web*. London: Walker Books, 2011.

NASHVILLE

Studio and release date: ABC/Paramount; June 1975
Producer: Robert Altman
Screenplay: Joan Tewkesbury
Songwriters: Richard Baskin, Keith Carradine, Henry Gibson, Ronee Blakley, Karen Black (music and lyrics)
Director: Robert Altman
Musical Director: Richard Baskin
Cinematographer: Paul Lohmann
Cast: Keith Carradine, Ned Beatty, Lily Tomlin, Henry Gibson, Ronee Blakley, Keenan Wynn, Karen Black, Shelley Duval, Geraldine Chaplin, Barbara Harris, Gwen Welles, David Hayward, Timothy Brown, Michael Murphy, Allen Garfield, Jeff Goldblum, Barbara Baxley
Principal Songs: "I'm Easy"; "It Don't Worry Me"; "My Idaho Home"; "Keep-a-Goin'"; "200 Years"; "For the Sake of the Children"; "Tapedeck in His Tractor"; "Memphis"; "Rolling Stone"

Although it is not often thought of as a musical, this intriguing, unique film by director Robert Altman has more songs (23) than just about every other Hollywood tuner. Also, the songs in *Nashville* were all performed on-screen by characters rather than just heard on the soundtrack. Most of the songs are pastiche of country western numbers, but the score also includes some folk, blues, rockabilly, and gospel. The complicated plot followed 24 distinct characters in the Tennessee music capital during a couple of days while a presidential campaign is going on. Part documentary and part satire, the intricate movie was a collage of characters and themes taking place onstage, backstage, and everywhere else in the city. Among the many stories being told include: The untalented Sueleen Gay (Gwen Welles) longs to be a country singer but the only singing job she gets involves stripping at a political fundraising "smoker"; the gospel singer Linnea Reese (Lily Tomlin) with a husband Delbert (Ned Beatty) and two deaf children has a brief affair with the much younger folk singer Tom Frank (Keith Carradine); popular but emotionally fragile country singer Barbara Jean (Ronee Blakley) gets herself so worked up she has a breakdown onstage at Opryland; the selfish L. A. Joan (Shelley Duval) comes to Nashville to visit her dying aunt but instead takes in the nightlife, irritating her distraught uncle (Keenan Wynn); popular country star Hamilton Haven (Henry Gibson) is apolitical until campaign manager John Triplett (Michael Murphy) convinces him to support candidate John Phillip Walker who will help Hamilton become governor; the wacky would-be singer Albuquerque (Barbara Harris) is chased all over Nashville by her redneck husband (Allan F. Nicholls); the country star Connie White (Karen Black) is jealous of her rival Barbara Jean and doesn't try to hide it; and the lonely drifter Kenny Fraiser (David Hayward) has a mother complex and ends up shooting Barbara Jean while she is performing at a political rally. The stories as well as the characters overlap over the three days, creating a complex mosaic of a plot not like any other.

Joan Tewkesbury wrote the screenplay with help from the cast (sections of dialogue and some scenes are clearly improvised), who also penned most of songs in the movie. These songs, ranging from hillbilly parodies to bluegrass to folk to light rock and roll, gave the film its tempo and verve. Among the many memorable musical moments were Blakley's heartbreaking rendition of "Dues," Gibson in the studio recording the blindly patriotic "200 Years," Gibson and Blakley's harmonizing on the duet "One, I Love You," Black's too-casual singing of the torch song "Rollin Stone," Tom's folk trio performing the rhythmic "Since You've Gone," Harris' stylistic interpretation of "It Don't Bother Me," and Tom's nightclub performance of the ballad "I'm Easy," which won the Oscar for best song. None of the songs were prerecorded but instead were performed on the set with Nashville musicians. The whole movie was filmed on location in Nashville using real locations rather than studio sets. Also unusual is that *Nashville* was shot pretty much in sequence, the last scene filmed being the outdoor political rally at the Parthenon. While the movie was being filmed, the van promoting the campaign for John Phillip Walker drove up and down the streets of the city and most residents thought Walker was an actual person.

Nashville had a limited budget (about $2 million), and many of the famous actors worked for less than usual because they wanted to be in an Altman film. Citizens of Nashville were used for the many crowd scenes, often working for free. By the time filming was completed, Altman had miles of footage and the first cut ran over four hours. Turning the footage into two movies, *Nashville Red* and *Nashville Blue*, was considered, but Paramount, the film's distributor, vetoed the idea, and *Nashville* was edited down to 159 minutes. This explains why in the released version some stories have gaps and others don't resolve themselves completely. Yet *Nashville* is such a complex montage of a movie that one can barely take it all in, much less notice such details in one viewing. On a few occasions, the four-hour version has been shown and many of these loose ends are completed. Many consider *Nashville* to be Altman's best film. It is certainly his most ambitious. He directed the sprawling giant of a movie with cockeyed affection for the country music business and the American character itself. Musical or not, *Nashville* is a one-of-a-kind film.

FURTHER READING

Caso, Frank. *Robert Altman: In the American Grain*. London: Reaktion Books, 2016.
Stuart, Jan. *Nashville Chronicles: The Making of Robert Altman's Masterpiece*. Montclair, NJ: Limelight Editions, 2004.

THE ROCKY HORROR PICTURE SHOW

Studio and release date: 20th Century Fox; September 1975
Producer: Michael White
Screenplay: Jim Sharman, Richard O'Brien, based on the 1973 stage script *The Rocky Horror Show* by Richard O'Brien
Songwriter: Richard O'Brien (music and lyrics)
Director: Jim Sharman
Choreographer: David Toguri
Cinematographer: Peter Suschitzky
Cast: Tim Curry, Meat Loaf, Barry Bostwick, Susan Sarandon, Richard O'Brien, Patricia Quinn, Nell Campbell, Jonathan Adams, Peter Hinwood, Charles Gray, Jeremy Newsom, Hilary Farr
Songs: "Time Warp"; "Sweet Transvestite"; "Wild and Untamed Thing"; "Dammit Janet"; "Science Fiction/Double Feature"; "The Sword of Damocles"; "Over at the Frankenstein Place"; "I Can Make You a Man"; "Hot Patootie— Bless My Soul"; "Eddie"; "Rose Tint My World"; "Planet, Schmanet, Janet"; "Touch-a, Touch-a, Touch-a, Touch Me"; "I'm Going Home"; "Super Heroes"; "Don't Dream It"

A musical spoof of science fiction, porno, and rock films, the London stage hit failed on Broadway but finally found success as a film-theater experience. Richard O'Brien's script concerned the innocent, naive couple Janet and Brad who have just gotten engaged. When their car breaks down on a "dark and stormy night," the couple takes refuge in a castle-like mansion where they are greeted by the creepy butler Riff-Raff and his two assistants, Magenta and Columbia. The castle is the domain of the transvestite Frank-N-Furter who has used different body parts to create the perfect man, the stud Rocky. Also living in the castle are assorted freaks and ghouls. Frank has sexual designs on both Janet and Brad but the couple is rescued by Dr. Scott who knows that all of the house's inhabitants come from outer space. It turns out that Riff-Raff is the mastermind of the whole operation. When Frank and Rocky get too cocky, Riff-Raff destroys them and the rest of the aliens disappear in a puff of smoke. The nonsense plot line was not what the show was all about. *The Rocky Horror Show* was a musical revolt, not unlike *Hair* was onstage in 1967. Rock music and outlandish characters were used to make fun of just about everything, the aim being to shock the conventional audience member but entertain the younger spectators. O'Brien also wrote the hard-driving, sarcastic rock score, which included "Sweet Transvestite," "What Ever Happened to Saturday Night," "Time Warp," "Charles Atlas Song," "Once in a While," and "The Sword of Damocles," all of which would become memorized favorites by the show's many fans.

The Rocky Horror Show was a campy stage success in London, where it eventually ran over five years in a dilapidated old theater. When it opened on Broadway in 1975, it captured little of the same tawdry atmosphere even though the Belasco Theatre was turned into a cabaret for the production. The oddball but likable musical only managed to run 32 performances and did not become popular in the United States until long after the 1975 film version. Retitled *The Rocky Horror Picture Show*, the movie was given a traditional release in theaters and attracted little or no attention. It looked like the show was going to bomb in America once again. Then slowly the movie was catching on in college towns. It spread to big cities until it became the ultimate cult film in the decade following its release. In both American and British movie theaters, patrons dressed up, brought props, and participated in the screenings, usually held at midnight. Different lines or songs in the film prompted audience members when to throw rice, ignite cigarette lighters, blow a whistle, squirt water pistols, or toss toast at the screen. Singing along to all the songs was also expected and most patrons knew them by heart. In some cities, showings of *The Rocky Horror Show* have continued on for decades. The Museum Lichtspiele Cinema in München, Germany, has shown the movie weekly since 1977. In South Africa, the film was banned by the nation's censor, yet *The Rocky Horror Picture Show* has still become a cult favorite with private screenings all over the country. Few films have risen above a cinema viewing and become a cultural phenomenon.

Viewing the movie away from these cult happenings reveals a clever and carefree piece of filmmaking. Because of its London stage success, 20th Century Fox agreed to make a movie of the stage show. The studio wanted familiar American stars for the leading roles and offered a big budget for the fantastical sets and costumes. O'Brien and director Jim Sharman wanted to use Curry and members of the London cast and to shoot most of the film on one set. Fox agreed but cut the budget and insisted on two American actors for Brad and Janet. With a budget of only, $1.2 million, Sharman and O'Brien shot the film on the sets of some old horror movies made by Hammer Films in England. Most of the costumes came from the London stage production and filming conditions were Spartan. Actress Susan Sarandon actually caught pneumonia from the damp and drafty studio. O'Brien's screenplay is close to the original, but the word "picture" was added to the title to make it clear that this was a film and not a copy of the stage performance (although basically it was). Tim Curry (in his screen debut) repeated his bizarre, hilarious Dr. Frank-N-Furter from the Broadway production, and the young couple was played by unknowns Barry Bostwick and Sarandon, who both became famous because of the movie. The action of the play is opened up somewhat by director Sharman, and the production numbers are staged inside the castle with cinematic flair. There is tawdriness to the movie that echoes the original London show. The eventual popularity of the film prompted some revivals of the stage version (including a 2000 Broadway mounting that ran nearly a year) but for devotees, the only real *Rocky Horror* experience is in a movie house filled with costumed, singing spectators.

See also: *Hedwig and the Angry Inch*

FURTHER READING

Bloom, Ken. *Hollywood Musicals: The 101 Greatest Song-and-Dance Movies of All Time*. New York: Black Dog and Leventhal, 2010.

Piro, Sal, and Larry Viezel. *The Rocky Horror Treasury: A Tribute to the Ultimate Cult Classic Musical*. Philadelphia: Running Press, 2004.

SATURDAY NIGHT FEVER

Studio and release date: Paramount; December 1977
Producer: Robert Stigwood
Screenplay: Norman Wexler, based on an article *Tribal Rites of the New Saturday Night* in *New York Magazine* by Nik Cohn
Songwriters: Barry, Robin, and Maurice Gibb (music and lyrics)
Director: John Badham
Choreographer: Lester Wilson
Cinematographer: Ralf D. Bode

Cast: John Travolta, Karen Lynn Gorney, Barry Miller, Donna Pescow, Joseph
   Cali, Paul Pape, Bruce Ornstein, Val Bisoglio
Principal Songs: "Staying Alive"; "How Deep Is Your Love?"; "More Than a
   Woman"; "Night Fever"; "If I Can't Have You"; "You Should Be Dancing"

This is not only the movie that made John Travolta a screen star, it also helped
popularize disco dancing in America. Disco was a fad that did not survive into the
1980s but when it was hot it was indeed hot. So was Travolta who was well-known
to television viewers from the series *Welcome Back, Kotter*. The inspiration for the
film was an article in *New York Magazine* in which writer Nik Cohn wrote about
the tough street kids of Brooklyn who turned to disco dancing at the 2001 Odyssey
disco club on Saturday nights. (Years later Cohn admitted that he fabricated the
whole article.) Record producer Robert Stigwood thought that the article would
make a good movie and commissioned his clients the Bee Gees (Barry, Robin, and
Maurice Gibb) to write some disco music for the film. Since the *New York Magazine*
article had no plot, screenwriter Norman Wexler came up with a tale about the aim-
less Brooklyn youth Tony Manero (Travolta) who has a dead-end job working in a
paint store by day and getting into trouble with gangs and girls at night. Yet on Saturday nights he puts on a silk shirt and a white leisure suit and transforms into a
dance sensation at the local disco club where he finds some fleeting joy and meaning to his life. The story followed Tony's ambiguous relationship with the ambitious
Stephanie Mangano (Karen Lynn Gorney) who degrades his lifestyle but serves as
his dancing partner so that they can win a couples' contest at the disco. They win
but, Tony, having watched his equally dissatisfied pal Bobby (Barry Miller) jump off
a bridge in frustration, realizes that his Saturday night's glory is not the answer.
Saturday Night Fever showed that the crudest of society's discontents can achieve
ecstasy on the dance floor. The plot may have resembled a 1950s urban melodrama
but Travolta's magnetic performance and the Bee Gee's pounding disco music on
the soundtrack made it all seem new and exciting. Lester Wilson staged the vibrant
disco dancing, and John Badham's direction went right to the nerve. None of the
characters sang, but such hit numbers as "Staying Alive," "More Than a Woman,"
and "How Deep Is Your Love?" made it one of the most musical films of the 1970s.
It was also one of the most popular, the $3 million production bringing in a stagger-
ing $94 million. The movie's soundtrack album was also the biggest selling movie
LP to date. The inevitable sequel, *Staying Alive* (1983), also with Travolta, was a
critical and box office dud.

   The success of *Saturday Night Fever* was something of a turning point for Hollywood musicals. Here was a musical in which no characters sang and the songs on
the soundtrack had nothing to do with character or plot. The sweet singing sound of
the Bee Gees did not even match the gritty, raw melodrama that surrounded the

John Travolta (b. 1954)   The handsome Italian-Irish actor who has matured from a teen idol to a versatile screen performer, he has some impressive musical credits. He was born in Englewood, New Jersey, and dropped out of school at the age of 16 to pursue a career in musicals in summer stock. Travolta eventually got on Broadway as a replacement in *Grease* in 1972 and was featured in *Over Here!* (1974) before finding stardom in 1975 as a cute but dense high schooler in the television sit-com *Welcome Back, Kotter.* He secured his fame on-screen with his disco dancing in *Saturday Night Fever* (1977) and his singing and dancing in *Grease* (1979). He then suffered an up-and-down career with a series of hits and flops, such as the musical *Staying Alive* (1983). By the 1990s Travolta established himself as a durable film actor in a variety of genres, including the musical *Hairspray* (2007). Biographies: *John Travolta, King of Cool,* Wensley Clarkson (2005); *Fever! The Biography of John Travolta,* Douglas Thompson (1997).

many dance numbers. In fact, the songs were written with no knowledge of the story. And Travolta and the cast danced to canned music from the archives, the two not put together until the editing process. Yet *Saturday Night Fever* feels like a musical, just not the conventional kind of film musical. Some critics found this development more than a little disconcerting. The combination of acting, singing, and dancing—the very backbone of the musical form—was invalid in movies like *Saturday Night Fever*. Other versions of the new kind of nonsinging movie musicals followed, such as *Flashdance* (1983), *Footloose* (1984), and *Dirty Dancing* (1987). Some felt that the success of films like these meant the end of the movie musical. Of course, it wasn't the end. But it was the start of something different. One aspect of *Saturday Night Fever* did adhere to the traditional model and that was the dancing itself. Although disco was new and different, the way dance was filmed was very conventional. Travolta trained for weeks and endured endless dance rehearsals before filming began. Yet when the scenes were edited, the camera seemed to only see faces, expressions, and flashing lights. Travolta rightfully complained to Badham that the entire body should be seen when dancing, something Fred Astaire had also argued for in his movies four decades earlier. Travolta was probably afraid that audiences would think a double was hired for the difficult dancing because the way the dances were edited made it look like that. Balham agreed and allowed Travolta to work with the film editors to redo the footage and give the dancing (and dancers) its due.

See also: *Grease, Footloose*; John Travolta biography box

FURTHER READING

Echols, Alice. *Hot Stuff: Disco and the Remaking of American Culture*. New York: W. W. Norton & Company, 2010.

Scoll, Nathan. *Saturday Night Fever and the Contemporary Dance Film*. Saarbucken, Germany: LAP Lambert Academic Publishing, 2011.

GREASE

Studio and release date: Paramount; June 1978

Producers: Robert Stigwood, Allan Carr

Screenplay: Bronte Woodard, based on the 1972 stage script by Warren Casey, Jim Jacobs

Songwriters: Warren Casey, Jim Jacobs, and others (music and lyrics)

Director: Randal Kleiser

Choreographer: Patricia Birch

Musical Director: Bill Oakes

Cinematographer: Bill Butler

Cast: John Travolta, Olivia Newton-John, Stockard Channing, Jeff Conaway, Didi Conn, Barry Pearl, Jamie Donnelly, Michael Tucci, Kelly Ward, Frankie Avalon, Eve Arden

Principal Songs: "Grease"; "We Go Together"; "Hopelessly Devoted to You"; "Born to Hand Jive"; "Summer Nights"; "Freddie, My Love"; "You're the One That I Want"; "There Are Worse Things I Could Do"; "Look at Me, I'm Sandra Dee"; "Beauty School Dropout"; "Sandy"; "Greased Lightning"; "It's Raining on Prom Night"; "Blue Moon"; "Those Magic Changes"

Few American musicals have remained so popular for so long as this youthful pastiche of the 1950s. Both onstage and on-screen, it is a perennial favorite. Jim Jacobs and Warren Casey wrote the songs and the 1972 stage script about the "greasers" at Rydell High School in Chicago in the 1950s. Danny Zuko has fallen in love with the virtuous Sandy Dumbrowski instead of one of the streetwise Pink Ladies led by Betty Rizzo, and peer pressure seems to be against the couple. But Sandy learns to conform to more sluttish ways and thereby ends up in Danny's arms. Many of the songs have become popular favorites, such as "We Go Together," "Summer Nights," "Freddy, My Love," "Greased Lightnin'," "Look at Me, I'm Sandra Dee," "It's Raining on Prom Night," "Beauty School Dropout," and "Born to Hand-Jive." The Broadway version ran 3,388 performances, breaking the record for the longest-running musical at the time. National tours and hundreds of school productions followed. Record-movie producers Allan Carr and Robert Stigwood

The most popular movie musical of the 1970s, *Grease* (1978) was a nostalgic and playful look back to the 1950s. Most of the millions of moviegoers who saw it were too young to remember that era, but it didn't keep them from enjoying *Grease*. Olivia Newton-John and John Travolta (pictured) were the stars of the film but it was the 1950s look and musical sound that was the source of the fun. (Paramount Pictures/Photofest)

bought the screen rights to *Grease* and didn't wait for the Broadway show to close to go ahead and make a film of the musical. In fact, after the film came out, the stage show was still running and saw a burst of box office activity because moviegoers wanted to see the original. The producers wanted television actor Henry Winkler as Danny because he was so popular as the greaser Fonzi in the television series *Happy Days*. Winkler, not wanting to be typecast, refused. So they turned to another TV idol, John Travolta, who found fame on *Welcome Back, Kotter*. Travolta was still making his first movie, *Saturday Night Fever*, which Stigwood produced. The footage from that film convinced Paramount that Travolta would soon be even more popular as a movie star so he was cast as the hero (of sorts) of *Grease*. Very popular on the music charts in the 1970s was the Australian singer Olivia Newton-John and, although she had only appeared in two unseen Australian movies, she was offered the female lead. Newton-John felt secure about her singing but not her acting so she insisted on making a screen test. The footage demonstrated that, while not the next Oscar-winning actress, she was perfect for the innocent Sandy. Also inexperienced was director Randal Kleiser who had only directed in television. He had worked with Travolta on the TV movie *The Boy in the Plastic Bubble* (1976) and the two had got on well.

For the movie version, Sandy was changed to an Australian exchange student so that Newton-John's strong Aussie accent could be explained. She was 30 years old, not quite high school age, but none of the cast could pass even for college kids. Stockard Channing, who played the sour Rizzo, was 34 years old, and even the most obtuse moviegoers wondered how many years she must have been held back from graduating high school. The supporting cast, including Didi Conn (Frenchy), Jeff Conaway (Kenickie), and Dinah Manoff (Marty), were also a bit too mature, but all turned in youthful performances so all was forgiven. The producers decided to include several cameos in *Grease*, casting performers only the older generation would recognize. But veterans such as Eve Arden, Sid Caesar, Dody Goodman, Edd Byrnes, Joan Blondell, and Alice Ghostly were mostly wasted on bit parts and comic bits that weren't funny. The 1960s heartthrob Frankie Avalon, from the "beach" movies with Annette Funicello, fared better, playing the singing Teen Angel in one fantasy sequence. Most of the stage score was used and some new songs, by various tunesmiths, proved to be just as popular: A title song was written by Barry Gibb, and it was sung over the opening credits by another past favorite, Frankie Valli. Other new numbers include the rhythmic "You're the One That I Want" and the ballad "Sandy." The soundtrack was filled out with old recordings from the fifties, such as Sha-Na-Na singing "Blue Moon," "Hound Dog," and "Tears on My Pillow"; Jerry Lee Lewis rocking with "Whole Lotta Shakin' Goin' On"; and Ritchie Valens racing through "La Bamba." After the film was finished, the producers thought that Sandy's character was not as well established as it should be, so they commissioned John Farrar to write a new song for her. Newton-John returned to the studio to record and film "Hopelessly Devoted to You," which became one of her biggest hits.

Grease was so popular at the box office ($100 million by its 10th anniversary and a hit all over again when it was rereleased in theaters in 1998) that Hollywood was convinced a musical could make money only if it was a youth product. Several imitations followed, including Paramount's *Grease 2* (1982), but few were as much fun (or as successful) as the original. This was not a good omen for the future of musicals. If such movies were made to appeal only to young people, both the subject matter and the music would be very limited. Yet the studios found success with such musicals as *The Buddy Holly Story* (1978), *The Rose* (1979), *Flashdance* (1983), *Footloose* (1984), and *Dirty Dancing* (1987) that their theory seemed to be correct. This left fewer movie musicals for older generations. In the case of *Grease*, many of that aging generation enjoyed the nostalgic look back to the 1950s. But it is safe to say that *Grease* was (and remains) popular because it appeals greatly to moviegoers who never lived through that long-past time.

See also: *Beach Blanket Bingo, Saturday Night Fever, Footloose;* John Travolta biography box

FURTHER READING

Clarkson, Wensley. *John Travolta: Back in Character*. New York: Overlook Press, 1996.
Tropiano, Stephen. *Grease: Music on Film*. Montclair, NJ: Limelight Editions, 2011.

THE BUDDY HOLLY STORY

Studio and release date: Columbia; July 1978
Producer: Freddy Bauer
Screenplay: Robert Gittler, based on the 1975 biography *Buddy Holly: His Life and Music* by John Goldrosen
Songwriters: Buddy Holly, Norman Petty, Jerry Allison, and others (music and lyrics)
Director: Steve Rash
Musical Director: Joe Renzetti
Cinematographer: Stevan Larner
Cast: Gary Busey, Charles Martin Smith, Don Stroud, Maria Richwine, Conrad Janis, Amy Johnson, Dick O'Neil
Principal Songs: "That'll Be the Day"; "Chantilly Lace"; "Peggy Sue"; "It's So Easy"; "Well All Right"; "Oh Boy"; "Rock Around the Ollie Vee"; "Maybe Baby"; "Mockin' Bird Hill"; "Words of Love"

Gary Busey's performance as the early rock-and-roll star Buddy Holly was more authentic than most Hollywood musical biographies, and the film itself was less cliché-ridden than the average rags-to-riches backstager. The film was made nearly 20 years after Holly's death, but over that time he had become a cult figure and was recognized as one of the most important pioneers of rock and roll. Born Charles Hardin Holley in Lubbock, Texas, he was a fan of gospel, folk, country, and "race" music, the name used before "rhythm and blues" was coined in the 1940s. There was no such thing yet as rock and roll, so Holly experimented with these various forms and came up with a new sound all his own. With three other musicians, the guitar-playing songwriter formed the band Buddy Holly and the Crickets and they played in minor clubs. One time they were mistakenly booked into a Harlem venue when the proprietor thought that the band was African American; the black audience liked the new sound as well. Holly and the band got a record contract with Decca Records and their recognition soared, appearing on *The Ed Sullivan Show* and other television programs. With several songs on the charts, Holly was at the peak of his popularity when he died in a plane crash at the age of 22. Many later rock stars have stated that Holly was a major inspiration to them. Four Liverpool lads were so impressed with Holly that they copied his Crickets idea and called themselves the Beatles.

Making a movie about Holly's life had been attempted by a couple of studios, but the estate was in the name of his widow Maria Elena Holly, who would not give permission. When John Goldrosen's biography of Holly was released in 1975, interest in the singer was revived and Columbia was allowed to make a bio-pic with Mrs. Holly's supervision. This is probably why the screenplay for *The Buddy Holly Story* is more accurate than most movie biographies. Mrs. Holly insisted that no major star be cast as Buddy because attention would be drawn away from Holly. She also wanted the actors playing Buddy and the Crickets to do their own singing and play their own instruments. Such restraints made casting very difficult, but producer Freddy Bauer found the solution in the part-time musician/actor Gary Busey. The gangly, buck-toothed actor had appeared in a number of television shows and a handful of forgettable movies so he was not a familiar face to the public. Busey played the guitar well but still had to work on getting Holly's vocal sound correct. The Crickets (reduced to two musicians for the movie) were played by Dan Stroud and Charles Martin Smith, who also did their own singing and instrument playing. (Because the three surviving Crickets would not give permission to use their names, the musicians were given fictitious names in the film.) Director Steve Rash, in his feature film debut, added another level of authenticity to the movie by having the actors sing and play their instruments on the set rather than prerecording the tracks as was usually done. The screenplay followed the young Texan as he forms his band, struggles for recognition, meets and marries the Latina Maria Elena (Maria Richwine), and eventually becomes the first white performer to sing at Harlem's Apollo Theatre. Holly's tragic death in a plane crash in 1959 while touring with Ritchie Valens and the "Big Bopper" was, oddly, not included in the film. His death was announced in titles at the end of the movie.

The facts were correct but, more importantly, the character and musical sound of Holly were accurate. Busey's performance was far from romantic. Shy, gawky, nervous, and something of a geek, Holly was portrayed warts and all by Busey in a way that was sometimes off-putting. As for the singing, it was so close to Holly's voice that many moviegoers thought Busey was lip-syncing to the original Holly recordings. Nearly 20 songs from the period were heard on the soundtrack and Busey sang most of the Holly standards, including "That'll Be the Day," "Chantilly Lace," "Peggy Sue," "Rock Around With Ollie Vee," "It's So Easy' " and "Oh Boy." A whole generation discovered Holly's music when the film was released and was a box office success. Made on a modest budget, *The Buddy Holly Story* earned a lot of money and encouraged other films about early rock and roll, including *American Hot Wax* (1978), *I Wanna Hold Your Hand* (1978), *Elvis* (1979), and *La Bamba* (1987). Not directly based on the film but sharing the same subject was the Broadway musical *Buddy* (1990), which ran less than a year in New York; the same show ran over 20 years in London. The British have always loved Buddy Holly's music.

See also: *La Bamba*

FURTHER READING

Dick, Bernard. *Columbia Pictures: Portrait of a Studio*. Lexington: University of Kentucky Press, 1991.

Goldrosen, John. *Buddy Holly: His Life and Music*. Johannesburg, South Africa: Quick Fox, 1975/1979.

Lehmer, Larry. *The Day the Music Died: The Last Tour of Buddy Holly, The Big Bopper, and Ritchie Valens*. New York: Schirmer Trade Books, 2012.

Norman, Philip. *Rave On: The Biography of Buddy Holly*. New York: Simon & Schuster, 2014.

THE MUPPET MOVIE

Studio and release date: Henson Associates/ITC; May 1979
Producer: Jim Henson
Screenplay: Jerry Juhl, Jack Burns
Songwriters: Paul Williams, Kenny Ascher (music and lyrics)
Director: James Frawley
Musical Director: Ian Freebairn-Smith
Cinematographer: Isidore Mankifsky
Voices: Jim Henson, Frank Oz, Jerry Nelson, Dave Goelz, Richard Hunt
Cast: Charles Durning, Austin Pendleton, Milton Berle, Paul Williams, Steve Martin, Madeline Kahn, Dom DeLuise, Mel Brooks, Bob Hope, James Coburn, Orson Welles
Principal Songs: "The Rainbow Connection"; "I'm Going to Go Back There Someday"; "Movin' Right Along"; "I Hope That Somethin' Better Comes Along"; "Never Before, Never Again"; "Can You Picture That?"; "The Magic Store"

The famous cloth puppets called Muppets were very popular on American and British television in the 1970s so it was understandable that they would graduate to the big screen. The serviceable screenplay for the Muppets' first film followed Kermit the Frog (operated and voiced by Jim Henson) as he leaves the swamp and heads to Hollywood with his friends Miss Piggy, Fozzie Bear, Rowlf the Dog, and others, voiced by such talents as Frank Oz, Jerry Nelson, Richard Hunt, and Dave Goelz. Although he doesn't know it, Kermit is being hunted down by entrepreneur Doc Hopper (Charles Durning), who wants the singing-dancing green fellow to be spokesman for his fast-food chain of fried frogs' legs. Along the way the Muppets meet up with guest stars in cameo roles, from veterans Bob Hope, Milton Berle, and Edgar Bergen, to more recent celebrities such as Steve Martin, Richard Pryor, and Madeline Kahn. Paul Williams and Kenny Ascher wrote an agreeable set of songs, most memorably "The Rainbow Connection," which became a hit and Kermit's signature song. Also pleasant were the jaunty "Movin' Right Along" and the wistful "I'm Going to Go Back There Some Day." It was a risk in putting the Muppets, who have only appeared on television, on the big screen. The producers were concerned that the artificiality of puppetry would not work when blown up so big. Henson made several screen tests with some Muppet characters and they were used to convince British producer Lew Grade to go ahead with the project. Henson wanted the movie to contain technical advances not seen on television, such as showing Kermit's whole body when riding a ride. The biggest challenge was the movie's finale in which 250 puppets, operated by 137 puppeteers, sang a reprise of "The Rainbow Connection." Puppet operators from a dozen states were hired for the scene, which was shot in one day.

The Muppet Movie was one of the top box office champs of the year. Over the years there have been other Muppet features, most of them musicals. With stronger story lines and better production numbers, they were sometimes more satisfying than this original. Universal's *The Great Muppet Caper* in 1981, for example, cast Kermit and Fozzie as newspaper reporters who go to London and get involved with the investigation into who stole the valuable jewels belonging to Lady Holiday (Diana Rigg). Joe Raposo, who had written many songs for the Muppets on *Sesame Street*, provided nine new songs for the comedy, including "The First Time It Happens," "The Muppet Fight Song," and "Steppin' Out with a Star." The production numbers were especially clever and enjoyable. *The Muppets Take Manhattan* in 1984 was perhaps the most sentimental of the series but even it had some satirical moments. Kermit and friends try to conquer Broadway with their musical show *Manhattan Melodies* and, after complications that included amnesia on Kermit's part, they succeed. Jeff Moss wrote several songs for the plot and the show-within-a-show but few of them found much life outside the movie. In many ways the most satisfying Muppet film was *The Muppet Christmas Carol*, presented by the Disney studio in 1992, in which Michael Caine (Scrooge) and a handful of other human actors performed effectively with the cloth characters. The familiar tale by Charles Dickens was given a few playful twists, such as the ghost Jacob Marley turned into the geriatric duo of Marley and Marley played by the complaining Statler and Waldorf. Gonzo played Dickens and narrated the tale with snide comments by Ratso, while Kermit and Miss Piggy were the Crachits. The excellent production values were matched by the tuneful songs by Paul Williams. The poignant "Thankful Heart" and "When Love Is Gone" contrasted nicely with the more upbeat "One More Sleep 'til Christmas" and "It Feels Like Christmas." Jim Henson had died in 1990, and this was the first Muppet movie in which he did not actively participate. But the direction by his son Brian Henson minted the playful spirit of the earlier Muppet projects.

Another film with a strong story line was Disney's 1996 *Muppet Treasure Island*, loosely taken from the Robert Louis Stevenson classic adventure tale. While Long John Silver (Tim Curry) and Jim Hawkins (Kevin Bishop) were very human and beautifully performed, the cloth characters provided the comedy and some of it was quite farcical. The castaway Ben Gunn was played by Miss Piggy as Benjamina Gunn, who shone in a ridiculous production number titled "Boom Shakalaka." Barry Mann and Cynthia Weil wrote the nine songs, the best being the rousing "Sailing for Adventure" and the wishful "Something Better." Again Brian Henson directed and the movie looked great, realistic in details but oversized in effect. Less accomplished but still enjoyable is *Muppets from Space*, which Columbia made in 1999. It had a scattered plot and fewer musical moments that took flight. Gonzo becomes convinced that he is an alien from space and attempts to join his interstellar family. A government agent (Jeffrey Tambor) is also convinced that Gonzo is an extraterrestrial and hunts him down while the Muppet gang works to keep Gonzo earthbound. Most of the score consisted of preexisting songs ranging from Stephen Foster's "Camptown Races" to "Shining Star" by Earth, Wind & Fire.

After a dozen-year hiatus, the Muppets returned to the screen with a musical movie simply titled *The Muppets*. Disney made it in 2011, and old and new fans of the cloth characters made it a hit. The main character in this nostalgic tale was not a human or a familiar Muppet but a cloth youth named Walter (voiced by Peter Linz) who idolizes Kermit and gets his human brother Gary (Jason Segel) to bring him to Hollywood to meet his hero. But the Muppet Theatre is in ruins and the Muppets scattered about and forgotten. In order to save the old theater from being bought up by mogul Tex Richman (Chris Cooper) who wants to drill for oil on the site, Kermit and both the human and cloth characters reunite to put on a big show. The movie was more serious than the other Muppet entries, several of the songs by various songwriters being wistful laments. The interesting duet "Man or Muppet" was catchy enough to win the Oscar. More fun was the Cold War spy spoof *Muppets Most Wanted* in 2014. Kermit is kidnapped by two Russian agents, the cloth frog Constantine (voice of Matt Vogel) and the human Nadya (Tina Fey), and put in a prison camp. Constantine then impersonates Kermit and plans the heist of the century. Despite a hilarious Russian accent, Kermit's friends do not catch on to the switch. Luckily, the truth comes out and the Muppets rescue Kermit from the Russian gulag. None of the songs by Bret McKenzie were serious this time around but instead were farcical satires of Broadway, folk, ethnic, and classical music. From the silly "We're Doing a Sequel" to the oppressive "The Big House," the score was as delightful as the shenanigans going on in the story. Again the Disney film was popular so we have not seen the last of the Muppets on the big screen.

See also: *Little Shop of Horrors*

FURTHER READING

Finch, Christopher. *Jim Henson: The Works—The Art, the Magic, the Imagination*. New York: Random House, 1993.

THE 1980s AND 1990s: LOOKING FOR NEW FORMS FOR MUSICALS

The 1980s resembled the 1950s in that these were prosperous times for those with money but not a good era for those left behind. Much of the decade consisted of the Reagan Era, eight years of conservative thinking, a strong economy, and a mellowing of the American spirit. It was a decade that was later mocked for its self-absorbed temperament and its concentration on success. Clearly, the boomers were getting older. There was progress and there were setbacks in several areas. American-Soviet relations seemed to improve during the 1980s, yet the Russians boycotted the Los Angeles Olympics in 1984 in response to the Americans' boycott of the 1980 Moscow Olympics. In 1981 the first American space shuttle, *Columbia*, was successfully launched. But in 1986, all seven astronauts aboard the space shuttle *Challenger* died when their ship exploded just after takeoff. Worldwide protests against nuclear weapons grew during the decade, as witnessed by a crowd of nearly one million who gathered in New York's Central Park in 1982. Yet the next year President Reagan budgeted millions of dollars to develop a Strategic Defense Initiative (nicknamed Star Wars). Remarkable advances were made during the decade in developing artificial human organs, such as a mechanical heart. At the same time a mysterious new disease was discovered that destroyed the body's immune system. It was named acquired immune deficiency syndrome but by the end of the decade it was well known as AIDS.

The 1990s took on a different light during the Clinton Era, a looser eight years symbolized by the first baby boomer president. It was a decade of optimism in several ways. The Soviet Union collapsed early in the decade and countries such as Poland, Hungary, Lithuania, and Latvia won their independence from the Soviet

Bloc. East and West Germany were reunited and, Czechoslovakia, a nation created after World War I, was turned into Slovakia and the Czech Republic, as befit their cultures. The imprisoned African leader Nelson Mandela was freed and eventually became the president of a reformed South Africa with an end to apartheid. But tensions in the Middle East were not much relieved. The Persian Gulf War in 1991 pitted the United States against Iraq, and Americans were mixed in their support of the conflict. Yugoslavia was the scene of a bloody civil war in 1992 that resulted in the country being divided up into several small nations. Racial strife resurfaced in the United States when riots broke out in Los Angeles in 1992 after white police officers were acquitted in the beating of the African American motorist Rodney King even though the entire incident had been videotaped by a bystander. In 1995 the federal building in Oklahoma City was bombed, and the next year a bomb went off in Atlanta. It was the beginning of an era in which Americans experienced terrorism on the home front, a threat that would increase in the years to come. A different kind of threat was recognized in 1999 when two teens at Columbine High School in Colorado murdered 13 fellow students and teachers. Similar events in schools would follow and plague schools and colleges into the new century. The approach of the millennium was a reason for celebration and also alarm. Massive computer glitches were predicted, and it was feared that a "Y2K bug" would wreak havoc on computer systems worldwide. But the new century arrived without incident and the world celebrated its coming with festivities on a mammoth scale. It was a heady time that would come crashing to the ground early in the new century.

By the 1980s, music, television, theater, literature, and the movies were so dispersed that it was getting difficult to measure what was popular. The music business, for example, had so many different charts that it was impossible to say "what was the top" anything. Even rock music had divided into heavy metal, acid rock, fusion rock, punk, hip-hop, and so on. Music stars Michael Jackson, Madonna, Bruce Springsteen, Garth Brooks, Linda Ronstadt, Harry Connick Jr., Whitney Houston, Billy Joel, Lionel Richie, Olivia Newton-John, Willie Nelson, and Bette Midler seem to have nothing in common except their popularity. Broadway slowly recovered from the lean 1970s and got healthier in the 1980s and early 1990s thanks to a series of London musicals. Labeled the "British Invasion" by Americans, it included such shows as *Cats* (1982), *Song and Dance* (1985), *For Me and My Girl* (1986), *Les Misérables* (1987), *Starlight Express* (1987), *The Phantom of the Opera* (1988), *Aspects of Love* (1990), *Miss Saigon* (1991), *Blood Brothers* (1993), and *Sunset Boulevard* (1994). Yet there were several successful home-grown musicals during that same period, including *42nd Street* (1980), *Dreamgirls* (1981), *Little Shop of Horrors* (1982), *La Cage aux Folles* (1983), *Big River* (1985), *Grand Hotel* (1989), *City of Angels* (1989), *Crazy for You* (1992), *Kiss of the Spider Woman* (1994), *Beauty and the Beast* (1994), and *Rent* (1996). Broadway enjoyed a rebirth of sorts in the later 1990s. With money from Disney and city government, Times Square and 42nd Street went from a sleazy, drug-infested thoroughfare to a slick, tourist mecca with new and restored theaters. It started in 1997 when Disney refurbished the long-abandoned New Amsterdam Theatre on 42nd Street and opened *The Lion King*, a stage version of its 1994 animated film. Other theaters and other productions followed and by the end of the century Broadway had more theaters and was playing to more people than it had in decades.

Moviegoing changed in the 1980s because now a film had two lives: its initial release in cineplexes and its subsequent life on videotape and later DVD. Many a film that failed at the box office later became a long-term favorite in the home. As for the movie musical, it seemed that the genre had just about disappeared. Not only were very few musicals made, the studios no longer had the staff to make them. Gone were the in-house conductor, choreographer, musical director, songwriter, and even the director. It seemed that every time a studio put together a musical, it was starting from scratch, hiring people from the theater or MTV or wherever. The very idea of what constituted a film musical was also starting to change. In the traditional musical, the characters sang and danced. But the Hollywood musicals of the 1980s and 1990s offered films in which none of the characters sang—the music was on the soundtrack only. *Flashdance* (1983), *Footloose* (1984), and *Dirty Dancing* (1987) managed to find a wide audience with their dazzling choreography and propulsive soundtracks, but some questioned if they were indeed musicals. Audiences didn't worry and neither did the studios. Perhaps this was the musical for a new generation of moviegoers.

While the forecast was dismal for the traditional movie musical, there was one genre that was reborn and blossomed in the 1990s: the animated musical. This rebirth was prompted by Disney's *The Little Mermaid* (1989), which was a beautifully told fairy tale but, most importantly, a musical with a full score by musical theater songwriters. What followed was a succession of Disney animated musicals that were very successful, some of them reaching the status of a classic: *Beauty and the Beast* (1991), *Aladdin* (1992), *The Lion King* (1994), *Pocahontas* (1995), *The Hunchback of Notre Dame* (1996), *Hercules* (1997), and *Mulan* (1998). Other studios jumped on the band wagon with *The Swan Princess* (1994), *Thumbelina* (1994), *A Troll in Central Park* (1994), *Cats Don't Dance* (1996), *Anastasia* (1997), *The Prince of Egypt* (1998), and *The Road to El Dorado* (2000), but it was clear that the Disney studio was the impetus and champ in the animated musical genre. Many of these films were better than most Broadway musicals so it was not surprising when several of them ended up onstage. This was a new development in the 1980s and 1990: movie musicals being turned into Broadway shows. In addition to Disney's *Beauty and the Beast* and *The Lion King*, theatergoers had their choice of *42nd Street* (1980), *Seven Brides for Seven Brothers* (1982), *Singin' in the Rain* (1985), *Meet Me in St. Louis* (1989), *Victor/Victoria* (1995), *State Fair* (1996),

Footloose (1998), and *Saturday Night Fever* (1999). Very few of these were hits, but it seemed that desperate Broadway producers needed new material so they turned to Hollywood. As far as the usual pattern—Broadway musicals turned into films— there were very few during the last two decades of the century. *Little Shop of Horrors* (1986) and *Evita* (1996) were expert adaptations, but *Annie* (1982) and *A Chorus Line* (1985) were financial and critical disasters.

The original movie musicals in the 1980s and 1990s were certainly diverse. Period pieces like *Victor/Victoria* (1982), *Yentl* (1983), *The Cotton Club* (1984), *For the Boys* (1991), *Newsies* (1992), and *That Thing You Do* (1996) had much to recommend but none was successful at the box office. Youth-oriented musicals, such as *Fame* (1980), *The Commitments* (1991), and the already mentioned *Footloose, Flashdance,* and *Dirty Dancing,* varied in quality but that didn't keep most of them from turning a large profit. The musical bio-pics during this period were quite accomplished. *Coal Miner's Daughter* (1980), in which Sissy Spacek portrayed country singer Loretta Lynn, was powerful moviemaking. So too was *La Bamba* (1987), about pioneer rocker Ritchie Valens, and *Bird* (1988), about jazz musician Charlie Parker. Jim Morrison was played by Val Kilmer in *The Doors* (1991) with success. Then there were those musicals that were so unusual that they define labeling. *Pennies from Heaven* (1981) had its actors lip-syncing old recordings of old song standards. *Everyone Says I Love You* (1997) has a cast of mostly nonsingers delivering old songs in their own voice. *Dick Tracy* (1990) was a live-action cartoon in which the action didn't stop for the songs so most of them were lost. And *Xanadu* (1980) was a fantasy musical that mixed disco numbers with Big Band songs.

Such offbeat musicals bring one back to the question: What constitutes a movie musical? It was clear in the 1980s and 1990s that Hollywood didn't know for sure so the studios tried just about anything. There were no rules or even guidelines. What was successful was correct; what didn't sell was wrong. Of course by this time the concept of a Hollywood studio had changed so much that it didn't seem like anyone was in charge. Most studios were just brand names owned by banking companies and other corporations. Individual producers initiated projects then went to the studio for funding. The sound stages in Los Angeles were still used but they were no longer factories. The studios were places that were rented out to whoever was willing to pay. Performers, directors, and the rest of the staff were not on contract but were hired for each individual project. Sometimes a company was formed just to produce one movie, the participants parting ways after the money was made or lost. Often it took two or more companies to come up with enough funding to make a movie. Musicals, still an expensive item, depended on so many resources that the finished film sometimes looked like a committee decision. Other times the producing companies left a talented director alone to do his or her work without interference. When millions of dollars were at stake, this was rare. But it did happen on occasion.

The reason movie musicals in the 1980s and 1990s did not look or feel like films from earlier decades is because they were not made the same way. Also, they were not made by people who had experience specifically with musicals. British actor-director Richard Attenborough, who had made the surreal antiwar film *Oh! What a Lovely War* (1969) that had some songs, was chosen to direct the American show biz tribute *A Chorus Line*. Renowned American director John Huston, known for his iconic dramas, directed *Annie*. Neither man had ever directed a full musical before. This never would have happened in the old studio system. When the factory is out of business, it seems that anyone can go in and make something. One shouldn't wonder why so many poor musicals were made at this time, but rather marvel that some fine ones managed to be made at all.

COAL MINER'S DAUGHTER

Studio and release date: Universal; February 1980
Producer: Bernard Schwartz
Screenplay: Tom Rickman, based on Loretta Lynn's 1976 autobiography *Coal Miner's Daughter* with George Vecsey
Songwriters: Loretta Lynn, Shel Silverstein, Don Gibson (music and lyrics)
Director: Michael Apted
Musical Director: Owen Bradley
Cinematographer: Ralf D. Bode
Cast: Sissy Spacek, Tommy Lee Jones, Beverly D'Angelo, Levon Helm
Songs: "Coal Miner's Daughter";"Honky-Tonk Girl"; "You're Lookin' at Country"; "One's on the Way"; "Sweet Dreams of You"; "You Ain't Woman Enough"; "Back in Baby's Arms"; "I Fall to Pieces"; "Crazy"; "Walking After Midnight"; "There He Goes"; "The Titanic"; "Blue Moon of Kentucky"; "Satisfied Mind"; "Walking the Floor Over You"; "It Wasn't God Who Made Honky Tonk Angels"

An unsentimental film about country singer Loretta Lynn, it rose above a routine "rags to riches" biographical musical about a celebrity because of a solid, truthful script and an enthralling performance by Sissy Spacek. Lynn is considered the most durable and endearing of all female country music singers, dubbed the "First Lady of Country Music" and the "Queen of Country." Her 60-year-plus career has brought her numerous awards as well as many hit records. Lynn was also very political, writing and singing songs about spousal abuse, birth control, unfaithful husbands, and the Vietnam War draft. Making a movie about a living legend was not usually done, but when Lynn wrote her autobiography *Coal Miner's Daughter* in 1975 with the help of George Vecsey, her story called out to be filmed. Universal bought the screen rights and considered Meryl Streep for the title role. But Lynn, who supervised many aspects of the production, thought Sissy Spacek was ideal for the role even though she did not look like her. Spacek didn't think she could imitate the living legend and tried to turn off the producers by saying she insisted on doing her own singing. Universal and Lynn thought it a good idea, and Spacek was talked into accepting the part. In preparation for filming, Spacek went on tour with Lynn and studied her mannerisms, vocal inflections, and even her walk. Lynn urged the director Michael Apted to film the movie close to her hometown of Butcher Hollow in the hills of Kentucky. Some scenes were shot there, the rest in nearby Wise, Virginia. With Lynn on the set to ensure authenticity, the furniture, props, and clothes were all approved of by her so the movie has a very un-Hollywood look. As done in *The Buddy Holly Story* (1978), the singers and musicians performed live on the set rather than lip-syncing to a prerecorded soundtrack. Apted also broke from tradition by watching the actors rehearse on their own then setting up each scene based on what he saw rather than planning out each scene beforehand.

With the movie based on Lynn's autobiography and her being directly involved in the production, one might suspect that *Coal Miner's Daughter* was a sugar-coated version of the truth. Instead, the screenplay by Tom Rickman is very honest with a warts-and-all approach to Lynn's story. Born into poverty in the backwoods of Kentucky, Lynn is one of eight children and at the age of 13 is married off to the World War II vet Doolittle Lynn (Tommy Lee Jones). She is a disappointment as a wife, afraid of sex and unable to run a household. When "Doo" buys Lynn a guitar as an anniversary present, she teaches herself to play and is soon writing original songs about her life and her home in the hills. Even though she is busy with her four children, Lynn perseveres, and when she is 18, Doo promotes her at the local radio station. Lynn's rise to fame in Nashville was handled with unromantic realism, as were her bouts with depression and a nervous breakdown right onstage. (Lynn was the inspiration for the character of Barbara Jean, who also had a breakdown onstage in the 1975 movie musical *Nashville*.) When she learns that her friend Patsy Cline has died in a plane crash, the news contributes to Lynn's downfall. Songs by Lynn and others were heard in the film, including such popular favorites as "Honky-Tonk Girl," "You're Lookin' at Country," "Sweet Dreams of You," and the title number. *Coal Miner's Daughter* was superior in all aspects, but it is Spacek's performance that holds the film together. Convincing as a 13-year-old bride, a weary mother of four, a struggling singer, and a polished star, Spacek also managed to sing Lynn songs accurately and with passion. Jones was magnetic as her overzealous husband, Beverly D'Angelo was convincing as Cline, and the supporting cast was also first rate.

Coal Miner's Daughter was a surprise hit, becoming one of the top box office attractions of the 1980s. It was also the first major film about a country music personality. Hollywood learned that the movie appealed to a much wider audience than just country music lovers, so some other bio-pics about Nashville stars were made. Jessica Lange played Patsy Cline in *Sweet Dreams* (1985), Joaquin Phoenix and Reese Witherspoon portrayed Johnny Cash and June Carter in *Walk the Line* (2005), and Waylon Payne was guitarist Hank Garland in *Crazy* (2007). These movies were all well received, so it is surprising that more bio-pics about country stars haven't been made.

See also: *Nashville*, *The Buddy Holly Story*

FURTHER READING

Lynn, Loretta, and George Vecsey. *Loretta Lynn: Coal Miner's Daughter*. New York: Vintage, 2010.

FAME

Studio and release date: Metro-Goldwyn-Mayer; April 1980
Producers: David DeSilva, Alan Marshall
Screenplay: Christopher Gore
Songwriters: Michael Gore and others (music), Dean Pitchford and others (lyrics)
Director: Alan Parker
Choreographer: Louis Falco
Musical Director: Michael Gore
Cinematographer: Michael Serecin
Cast: Irene Cara, Lee Curreri, Laura Dean, Barry Miller, Gene Anthony Ray, Antonia Franceschi, Albert Hague, Paul McCrane, Anne Meara, Maureen Teefy, Debbie Allen
Songs: "Fame"; "I Sing the Body Electric"; "Out Here on My Own"; "Red Light"; "Is It Okay If I Call You Mine"; "Hot Lunch Jam"; "Dogs in the Yard"

A film that wavered between a gritty, realistic look at show business and a romanticized "let's put on a show" musical, *Fame* could be seen as the *Babes in Arms* (1939) for the 1980s, just as the *High School Musical* TV movies and the series *Glee* would be for the first decade of the 21st century. Mickey Rooney, Judy Garland, and their fellow teens were passionate about performing; so were the young characters in *Fame*. The difference lies in the way the teenagers were portrayed. The "babes" in *Babes in Arms* were wholesome, optimistic, and usually perky with puppy love. The teens in *Fame* are mostly damaged, confused, frustrated, or angry. The "babes" put on their show in the barn and it is a hit, bringing a happy ending to the plot. The teens in *Fame* attend a performing arts school, which is a high-pressure academic version of the outside world, and they will face further difficulties after they graduate. The title *Fame* is meant to be ironic; these kids do not get a happy ending. The setting for the movie is the Fiorello LaGuardia High School of the Performing Arts in Manhattan, a public school for gifted students in the arts. Competition to get in is great and competition once inside is even greater. Christopher Gore's screenplay follows a group of teens from when they apply to get into the school up until graduation. During the four years the young hopefuls struggle through auditions, classes, rehearsals, setbacks, family troubles, and sexual anxiety, every once in a while bursting into song and dance everywhere from the school cafeteria to the street. The plot was episodic and the emphasis was on the characters, seven teens in particular. The talented Coco (Irene Cara) is a strong singer but comes on too strong in her personal life and makes many mistakes. Bruno (Lee Curreri) wants to be a composer of synthesized music, while the angry, illiterate African American Leroy (Gene Anthony Ray) wants to be a dancer. The class clown Ralph (Barry Miller) wants to be a stand-up comic and lies about his dysfunctional Puerto Rican family. The confused homosexual Montgomery (Paul McCrane) wants to be an actor but is not tough enough to handle criticism. The mousy Jewish princess Doris (Maureen Teefy) is a late bloomer who surprises herself when she finally blossoms. The snobbish Hilary (Antonia Franceschi) is determined to be a prima ballerina and already has a prima donna attitude. They were not a lovable bunch of kids but they held one's interest.

Most of the songs were written by Michael Gore (music) and Dean Pitchford (lyrics) and they were highly charged, joyfully noisy, and very engaging for younger moviegoers. The exuberant title song proclaimed "I'm gonna live forever!" and, as performed by the talented young cast, one almost believed it. The number was given a memorable staging in the movie. The song, supposedly written by the student Bruno, is broadcast on a loudspeaker from his father's taxicab then sung by Coco and picked up by the other students, who sing and dance to it on the street and the rooftops of cars stuck in a traffic jam. Also given an energetic staging was the driving rock number "Hot Lunch Jam," which was presented as a competitive singing and instrumental jam session in the school cafeteria. Coco's ambitious streak was demonstrated with the rebellious song "Out Here on My Own" while the whole class cut loose at graduation singing the fervent "I Sing the Body Electric" whose lyric was taken from a Walt Whitman poem. *Fame* was one of the first films to employ digital audio on the soundtrack, and it was recorded onto a compact disc, two years before CDs were introduced. Matching the vivacious score was the propulsive choreography by Michael Serecin; when the young cast danced, it did indeed seem like they were destined to be famous.

What Hollywood hoped with each of its youth-oriented movie musicals was a best-selling soundtrack album. *Fame* did not disappoint. Also, for the first time in its history, the Academy nominated two songs from *Fame*—"Out Here on My Own" and the title song—and Irene Cara had hit singles with both songs. *Fame* was also the first Hollywood musical to inspire a popular television series. The music-drama show was first broadcast in 1982 and ran for six seasons. Debbie Allen and Albert Hague, who had supporting roles as teachers in the movie, were featured in the series, and Gene Anthony Ray reprised his Leroy for the television show. It seemed like *Fame* itself would live on forever, but in 2009 the movie was updated and remade by MGM. Once again titled *Fame*, it also followed some students over the period of their four years at the same school, but this time around the dramatic situations seemed less potent and even the musical numbers failed to catch fire. There were many more songs than in the original, ranging from rap to classical, and the title song from the 1980 film was reprised. The new *Fame* was not popular with the critics or the public.

See also: *Babes in Arms*

FURTHER READING

Gonthier, David F., Jr. *The Films of Alan Parker.* Jefferson, NC: McFarland Publishers, 2015.
Hirschhorn, Clive. *The Hollywood Musical.* 2nd ed. New York: Crown Publishers, 1983.

FOOTLOOSE

Studio and release date: Indie Productions/Paramount; February 1984
Producer: Lewis Rachmil, Craig Zadan
Screenplay: Dean Pitchford
Songwriters: Tom Snow, Kenny Loggins, Dean Pitchford, and others (music and lyrics)
Director: Herbert Ross
Choreographer: Lynn Taylor-Corbett
Musical Director: Becky Shargo
Cinematographer: Ric Waite
Cast: Kevin Bacon, Lori Singer, John Lithgow, Dianne Wiest, Christopher Penn, Sarah Jessica Parker, Elizabeth Gorcey
Songs: "Holding Out for a Hero"; "Footloose"; "Let's Hear It for the Boy"; "Almost Paradise"; "Dancing in the Streets"; "Never"; "The Girl Gets Around"; "I'm Free"; "Somebody's Eyes"; "Hurts So Good"; "Bang Your Head"

So many moviegoers bought the prereleased soundtrack album for this dance-oriented musical that they went *into* the theaters singing the songs. Dean Pitchford's screenplay had an interesting premise: Dancing has been outlawed in the small midwestern town of Beaumont. Newcomer Ren McCormack (Kevin Bacon) arrives from the big city and is scorned by his fellow students for his big city ways. But he eventually wins his classmates over and routs the restless teens to battle the local minister Rev. Moore (John Lithgow), who is the strength behind the antidancing law. It seems that the Reverend's son died after a local dance so it has been his crusade to keep the town safe from such exhibitions. Ren and the teens win the fight, and he also wins the heart of the minister's daughter Ariel

Dancing was considered a dangerous social pastime in *Footloose* (1984), a film about a town which has outlawed dancing. Kevin Bacon (pictured) is the new kid in town who upsets the authorities by introducing the local teens to the joys of modern dance. Choreographer-turned-director Herbert Ross directed the movie and Lynn Taylor-Corbett staged the vivacious dancing. (Paramount Pictures/Photofest)

(Lori Singer). As contrived as the story may sound, it was based on a real incident. The conservative, religious town of Elmore City, Oklahoma, had an old law on the books for 90 years that made dancing illegal. A bunch of teenagers finally got it overturned in 1978. Pitchford built his story on this event, creating the city kid Ren, who doesn't fit in at first but eventually charms the youth of Beaumont. Paramount wanted John Travolta, fresh from his success in *Saturday Night Fever* (1977) and *Grease* (1978), to play Ren but he turned it down. The studio then tried to enlist Tom Cruise, his career just starting after *Risky Business* (1983), and then newcomer Rob Lowe from *Class* (1983), but both were unavailable. Director Herbert Ross was so taken with Kevin Bacon's performance in *Diner* (1982) that he convinced the studio to hire him, even though Bacon had little box office clout. Bacon took the role very seriously. The film was scheduled to be shot in various towns in Utah, so 24-year-old Bacon went to the principal of Payson (Utah) High School and arranged to attend the school as a transfer student from the East. Using the name Ren McCormack, he dressed in a slick, big-city manner and mixed with the locals. The students treated him with suspicion and scorn just as in the script. The ordeal was so upsetting, Bacon left after one day. Bacon was not a highly trained dancer, so a double was used for some of the more complicated dancing. The dance scenes, staged by theater choreographer Lynn Taylor-Corbett in her film debut, often looked like the kind of dancing that high schoolers would do. It helped that Ross was a Broadway choreographer before he turned to directing, because the whole movie moves like a musical.

Like *Saturday Night Fever*, none of the songs in *Footloose* were sung by the characters but only heard on the soundtrack. In fact, only the title song was written before filming began. The cast danced to archival music, and the rest of the score was written and recorded after *Footloose* was filmed and edited. Different songwriters contributed to the score, which included four hits: "Let's Hear It for the Boy," "Almost Paradise," "Holding Out for a Hero," and the title number. Paramount released the soundtrack months before *Footloose* opened in order to generate interest in the film. It certainly worked because both album and movie were giant hits. *Footloose* cost a little over $8 million to make and ended up earning $80 million. Once again Hollywood was convinced that a movie musical in the 1980s could only succeed if it was youth oriented. The decade had several conventional (meaning adult) musicals but few made any money: *Pennies From Heaven* (1981), *Annie* (1982), *Victor/Victoria* (1982), *The Cotton Club* (1984), and *A Chorus Line* (1985) all lost money on their first release. On the other hand, the youth musicals *The Blues Brothers* (1980), *Fame* (1980), *Flashdance* (1983), *Footloose*, *La Bamba* (1987), and *Dirty Dancing* (1987) all did well at the box office. It was looking more and more like the adult movie musical was on its way out.

Seventeen years after *Footloose*, the story was remade for a new generation of moviegoers, but this time the film failed to become a hit. The 2011 Paramount film, also titled *Footloose*, set the story in a small Tennessee town but most of the plot remained the same. Kenny Wormald was Ren, Julianne Hough was Ariel, and Dennis Quaid was the staunch minister. Again the soundtrack was filled with songs but the new ones were not very impressive; even the favorites from the original movie were rearranged to the point where they failed to please. This time the soundtrack CD was not a bestseller. *Footloose* also showed up on Broadway in 1998. The critics dismissed it but audiences kept the show running for nearly two years.

See also: *Saturday Night Fever, Fame, La Bamba*

FURTHER READING

Eames, John Douglas. *The Paramount Story*. New York: Crown Publishers, 1985.
Grant, Barry Keith. *The Hollywood Film Musical*. Hoboken, NJ: Wiley-Blackwell, 2012.
Scoll, Nathan. *Saturday Night Fever and the Contemporary Dance Film*. Saarbucken, Germany: LAP Lambert Academic Publishing, 2011.

LITTLE SHOP OF HORRORS

Studio and release date: The Geffen Company/Warner Brothers; December 1986
Producer: David Geffen
Screenplay: Howard Ashman, based on his 1982 stage script, which was based on the 1960 screenplay by Charles B. Griffith, Roger Corman
Songwriters: Alan Menken (music), Howard Ashman (lyrics)
Director: Frank Oz
Choreographer: Pat Garrett
Musical Director: Bob Gaudio
Cinematographer: Robert Paynter
Cast: Rick Moranis, Ellen Greene, Vincent Gardenia, Steve Martin, Tichina Arnold, Trisha Campbell, Michelle Weeks
Songs: "Somewhere That's Green"; "Suddenly Seymour"; "Little Shop of Horrors"; "Feed Me"; "Dentist!"; "Skid Row (Downtown)"; "Grow for Me"; "Suppertime"; "Don't Feed the Plants"; "Mean Green Mother from Outer Space"; "Some Fun Now"; "The Meek Shall Inherit the Earth"

The long-running Off-Broadway musical was brought to the screen with most of the 1960s pastiche songs and all of its wacko dark humor. *Little Shop of Horrors* is a science fiction spoof that was offbeat enough to be different and yet engaging enough to be appealing to a wide audience. It also introduced a new genre of Off-Broadway musical: the camp pulp musical. Shows had satirized movies and cheap fiction before, but never had a musical walked the line between satire and homage as this one did. The 1960 cult film on which the show is closely based was a low-budget feature with cheesy effects, amateurish acting, and an illogical but interesting premise. Howard Ashman, who wrote the stage adaptation as well as the lyrics, improved the movie plot, fleshed out the characters, and gave the dialogue a stilted yet sincere style that was refreshing. The 1960 film was enjoyable because it was so bad; the stage version was so delightful because it was so well done. Alan Menken's early 1960s pastiche music established the time period and the songs enhanced the cockeyed story in a way that made *Little Shop of Horrors* a tightly integrated musical treat.

The nerdy botanist Seymour Krelbourn, who works in the floundering flower shop of Mr. Mushnik and silently loves the sensual salesgirl Audrey, comes upon a mysterious plant that brings him fame and fortune as long as he feeds it human blood. As the plant continues to grow, so do its demands until Seymour is feeding it body parts from Audrey's sadistic dentist boyfriend Orin. Eventually the plant devours Seymour, Audrey, and everyone on planet Earth, even threatening the audience. Such a cartoonish plot could only sustain itself for so long, but the characters were developed to the point that one was caught up in the people, something that rarely happens in science fiction. Seymour is an awkward klutz, yet, like Audrey, we like him and find ourselves willing to accept him. Audrey is not just a blonde birdbrain but a weak-willed child who has vivid hopes for the future despite her dreary and abusive present. The Jewish caricature Mr. Mushnik finds a spark of self-worth when he grows to think of Seymour as his son, and even the one-joke sadomasochist Orin sees his abnormal behavior as a healthy zest for life. There are also three urchins acting as a Motown-flavored Greek chorus who not only comment on the action but often take the viewpoint of a specific character for whom they become back-up singers. One only has to see how little of all this cohesiveness is in the original B movie to appreciate Ashman's brilliant libretto.

Yet any musical stands on its score and the songs for *Little Shop of Horrors* are, each and every one of them, a marvel. "Skid Row (Downtown)" sets the scene by being both complaining and uplifting. Audrey's heartbreakingly funny solo "Somewhere That's Green" is one of the American theater's finest "I am" songs. "Mushnik and Son" is a dandy vaudeville turn, the kind of number Mushnik would fondly remember, while the numbers by the three urchins have the sound and attitude of the "girl group" songs of the early 1960s. The voice of the plant provides the sinister, sci-fi tone of the genre, yet its songs, such as "Feed Me" and "Suppertime," are so rhythmically intoxicating that the plant sometimes comes across like a revival preacher. Orin's proud solo "Dentist!" is a comic treasure with an Elvis-like flair. Seymour gets to sing the most telling numbers, from his pathetic plea "Grow for Me" to his resolve in "Now (It's Just the Gas)." The score climaxes with the oddball but very affecting love duet "Suddenly Seymour," which soars in such a way that the cartoon facade of the characters falls away. By the time the cast is singing the propulsive finale "Don't Feed the Plants," the audience has come full circle and feels like it has become part of the circus itself. Ashman directed the small but ingenious production that used cleverness rather than special effects to convey the science fiction aspect of the piece. The plant was portrayed at various stages by a series of puppets; not quite high tech but neither were the cheap effects in the film.

Little Shop of Horrors came to the screen with minimal changes, but some of the absurdism of the piece was lost when played on realistic (though artificial) sets and the plant was a high-tech monster. Much of the fun of the original movie and the stage version was the cheesy look of the tale. The movie musical had a polish that works against its tawdry material. Frank Oz, one of the top artists behind television's *The Muppet Show* and *Sesame Street,* directed the film with an understanding of how puppets can come alive. But the focus in *Little Shop of Horrors* is on the human characters and not the cleverly re-created plant. That said, Oz got outstanding performances from the cast. Rick Moranis exudes a goofiness and sincerity that works beautifully for Seymour. Ellen Greene, reprising her stage performance as Audrey, takes a breathy, sexy, yet clueless approach to the role, making her funny and pathetic at the same time. Warner Brothers must have been a little nervous about the musical's ending with the plant devouring everyone. The studio convinced Ashman to change his script and it is a more audience-friendly conclusion. Seymour kills the plant and he and Audrey survive to live happily ever after. Yet there was a cautionary epilogue of sorts that was typical of 1960s sci-fi films: new sprouts popped up in the garden and winked at the audience. Menken and Ashman wrote a new number for the plant, "Mean Green Mother from Outer Space," which was as silly and accurate as the rest of the score. The Off-Broadway musical was not an easy thing to put on film, but the filmmakers by and large pulled it off with a gleeful grin.

See also: *The 5,000 Fingers of Dr. T*; Howard Ashman and Alan Menken biography box

FURTHER READING

Shepherd, Marie. *Everything You Need to Know About Alan Menken*. Apsley, Australia: Emereo Publishing, 2014.

LA BAMBA

Studio and release date: Columbia; July 1987
Producers: Taylor Hackford, Bill Borden
Screenplay: Luis Valdez
Songwriters: Ritchie Valens and others (music and lyrics)
Director: Luis Valdez
Musical Directors: Miles Goodman, Carlos Santana
Cinematographer: Adam Greenberg
Cast: Lou Diamond Phillips, Esai Morales, Rosana DeSoto, Elizabeth Peña, Danielle Von Zerneck, Rick Dees, Joe Pantoliano, Los Lobos, Marshall Crenshaw

Principal Songs: "All My Love, All My Kisses"; "Little Darlin' "; "Come On, Let's Go"; "La Bamba"; "Donna"; "Baby, Baby"; "Rock All Night"; "Who Do You Love?"; "Saturday Night"; "You're Mine"; "Summertime Blues"; Rip It Up"; "Goodnight My Love"; "I Got a Gal Named Sue"

A vivacious musical biography about the young Chicano singer Ritchie Valens, the movie was mostly free of the usual clichés of the genre. More importantly, *La Bamba* was one of the earliest movies to examine Latino characters and culture. Born Richard Valenzuela in Southern California with Mexican American ancestry, he did not speak Spanish but grew up listening to Mexican folk songs. Valens taught himself to play the guitar and soon was writing his own songs and performing them at his high school and local gathering places. While still in school, his reputation traveled and soon he was recording his songs for Del-Fi Records. Valens quit high school to tour, to make more records, and, eventually, to appear on national television shows. He was only 17 years old when he died in a plane crash in 1959 with Buddy Holly and the "Big Bopper." Perhaps no other pop artist had such a short yet influential career. Valens mixed the new rock sound with traditional Latin forms and started the Chicano rock movement. He is also considered one of the pioneers of rock and roll and his recordings are still popular, alongside those by another pioneer, Buddy Holly.

The biggest difficulty in making a film about Valens' life was the lack of conflict. He was born into a poor but happy family, he met little resistance in his quest to make his own kind of music, he found fame quickly, and he died young. The respected Latino playwright and director Luis Valdez had the task of making a dramatic movie out of this rags-to-riches-to-early-death tale. In his screenplay, Valdez makes the Valenzuela family fatherless and shows them laboring in the fruit fields of California with no future except a life of drudgery. Valens' half-brother Bob (Esai Morales) comes on the scene and makes trouble with his petty crimes and drugs. He also steals Valens' girlfriend Rosie (Elizabeth Peña) and makes her miserable. When high schooler Valens (Lou Diamond Phillips) is smitten with the blonde Donna Ludwig (Danielle von Zerneck), her father objects to her having a Latino boyfriend. Perhaps Valdez came up with too much conflict. The character of Bob was so annoying that moviegoers couldn't begin to understand why Valens looked up to him. Just before Valens gets on the plane on that fatal night, he phones Bob and the two are reconciled somewhat. Some viewers were not interested. The movie ends with the aftermath of the tragic news, showing the effect it has on Bob, Donna, Rosie, and the rest of the family and the community. One device that Valdez handles well is Valens' fear of flying. It was true that when Valens was a young boy playing on the school playground, two airplanes collided with each other and came crashing down, killing some of his classmates. Valdez uses this image at the beginning and throughout the film as sober foreshadowing and to illustrate Valens' lifelong fear of flying.

The musical aspects of *La Bamba* are first rate. The Filipino actor Phillips had appeared in a few television programs and in small parts in two forgotten films. He was 25 years old when he played Valens and was convincing as a teenager and a singer even though his singing was dubbed by David Hidalgo. The re-creation of the Valens hits was excellent and the decades-old songs sounded better than ever. Highlights in the score include "All My Love, All My Kisses," "Baby, Baby," "Come On, Let's Go," "Little Darlin'," "Saturday Night," and the title number. This last was actually an old Mexican folk song that Valens reworked into a rock song, combining his Latino roots with the new rock sound. *La Bamba* may have strayed from the facts in order to be more dramatic, but it ended up being a powerful movie about Hispanic Americans. It remains one of the few Hollywood films ever shot in both English and Spanish so as to reach a wide Latino audience as well as traditional moviegoers. And it did just that. The low-budget musical made over $50 million just in the United States and found enthusiastic applause around the world.

See also: The Buddy Holly Story, Coal Miner's Daughter

FURTHER READING

Dick, Bernard. *Columbia Pictures: Portrait of a Studio*. Lexington: University of Kentucky Press, 1991.

Lehmer, Larry. *The Day the Music Died: The Last Tour of Buddy Holly, The Big Bopper, and Ritchie Valens*. New York: Schirmer Trade Books, 2012.

Mendheim, Beverly. *Ritchie Valens: The First Latin Rocker*. Tempe, AZ: Bilingual Review Press, 1987.

THE LITTLE MERMAID

Studio and release date: Buena Vista/Disney; November 1989
Producers: Howard Ashman, John Musker
Screenplay: John Musker, Ron Clements
Songwriters: Alan Menken (music), Howard Ashman (lyrics)
Directors: John Musker, Ron Clements
Musical Director: Alan Menken
Voices: Jodi Benson, Samuel E. Wright, Pat Carroll, Buddy Hackett, Kenneth Mars, Rene Auberjonais, Ben Wright
Songs: "Under the Sea"; "Kiss the Girl"; "Part of Your World"; "Poor Unfortunate Souls"; "Daughters of Triton"; "Les Poissons"; "Fathoms Below"

The Disney renaissance in animated musicals in the 1990s began with this exceptional movie musical. The film offered a classic story, superb animation, vibrant characters, and a Broadway-like score full of memorable songs. Based on a Hans Christian Andersen story, the screenplay took many liberties with the original. This has been true for just about every Disney animated feature starting with *Snow White and the Seven Dwarfs* (1937). In the case of *The Little Mermaid*, the story stays close to Andersen's 1837 fairy tale until the ending. In the screenplay, the mermaid Ariel is not happy in her underwater world, even though she is the daughter of King Triton. She has often swum to the surface and observed humans, even collecting the objects from their world that have sunk into the sea. Despite the arguments of the crab Sebastian that life under the sea is the best of all existences, Ariel yearns to be human, especially when she sees and falls in love with Prince Eric. After a fight with her father, Ariel makes a pact with the sea witch Ursula to exchange her beautiful voice for human legs. The deal involves Ariel getting Eric to kiss her or else she becomes the slave of the witch. Ursula tricks Eric by appearing as a beautiful woman with Ariel's voice, and he plans to marry the impostor. But the deception is discovered just in time, Eric slays the sea witch, and Ariel becomes a mermaid again. Triton, seeing how much his daughter loves Eric, uses his powers to make Ariel human once again, and she is reunited with Eric. In the original tale, the prince is forced to marry another princess, and Ariel can only save herself by killing the prince and letting his blood drip onto her feet. But Ariel still loves the prince so she returns to the sea where she is turned into foam and vanishes. In a later edition of the story, Ariel's spirit rises out of the water and flies about the earth for 300 years. In Andersen's version, Ariel's confidante is her grandmother who counsels her and warns her about the sea witch. As the Disney studio had done so well in the past, the writers created an array of colorful new characters, such as Ariel's fearful pal Flounder, the cockeyed seagull Scuttle, and the disapproving music-master crab Sebastian. Also a tradition, the villainess had her henchmen, two slithering, demonic eels named Flotsom and Jetsom. *The Little Mermaid* may have been a Disneyfied version of the Danish original but it was superior filmmaking in all aspects.

Songwriters Alan Menken (music) and Howard Ashman (lyrics) had found some success in the theater, mostly with *Little Shop of Horrors* (1982), and were invited to Disney when Walt's nephew Roy Disney wanted to build up the animation department at the studio. The glorious score Mencken and Ashman wrote for *The Little Mermaid* reminded audiences of what a top-notch Broadway score used to sound like. Not only were the musical numbers tuneful and imaginative, they also were marvelous character pieces that moved the story along effectively. Ariel's wistful "Part of Your World," the Oscar-winning calypso number "Under the Sea," the bombastic aria "Poor Unfortunate Souls," and the romantic Caribbean-flavored "Kiss the Girl" were more than musical diversions; they were the heart of the movie.

Howard Ashman and **Alan Menken.**   Although they worked together for only a dozen years, this songwriting team had a major impact onstage and on-screen musicals, particularly starting a wave of superb Disney animated musicals with *The Little Mermaid* (1989). Writer and lyricist Ashman (1950–1991) was born in Baltimore, the son of an ice cream cone manufacturer, and educated at Goddard College and Indiana University. He wrote sketches and lyrics for some Off-Off-Broadway revues before teaming up with composer Menken in 1979. The twosome's most famous stage work was the long-running Off-Broadway hit *Little Shop of Horrors* (1982). Seven years later they were at the Disney studio where they scored *The Little Mermaid*, revitalizing the animated musical. After the team wrote *Beauty and the Beast* (1991), Ashman died from complications due to AIDS. He finished half of the score for *Aladdin* (1992) before his early death. Menken (b. 1949) continued to write with various lyricists and has gone on to become one of the most successful, awarded, and versatile of Hollywood composers. He was born in New Rochelle, New York, the son of a dentist, and studied at New York University before writing music for television's *Sesame Street* in the late 1960s. His screen musicals after the death of Ashman include *Newsies* (1992), *Pocahontas* (1995), *The Hunchback of Notre Dame* (1996), *Hercules* (1997), *Home on the Range* (2004), *Enchanted* (2007), and *Tangled* (2010). Menken has returned to Broadway on occasion, providing new songs for such musicals as *A Christmas Carol* (1994), *Beauty and the Beast* (1994), *The Little Mermaid* (2008), *Sister Act* (2011), *Newsies* (2012), *Leap of Faith* (2012), and *Aladdin* (2014). His music is very tuneful and captures the flavor of the period and locations, which vary widely from one musical to another.

The Little Mermaid was a box office hit and opened the door for an exciting decade of musical animation from the Disney studio. The movie was popular enough to inspire a cartoon series on television, some made-for-video sequels, and a Broadway show in 2007.

The Little Mermaid was the first Disney animated feature based on a fairy tale since *Sleeping Beauty* in 1959. Many feel that the film was a return to the kind of movie musicals the studio did so well in the distant past. The Disney studio had been eyeing the Andersen tale for 50 years. Walt Disney wanted the story to be used in one of his Silly Symphony cartoons in the 1930s but it never materialized. In 1940 Disney wanted to make an animated feature of *The Little Mermaid* and even planned on using the original tragic ending. But with America involved with World War II, the studio's resources were being used for propaganda and training films and the project was abandoned. When writer-animator Ron Clements reread the story in 1985, he tried to get the studio interested in making an animated movie of *The Little Mermaid*. But the studio had just released the live-action comedy *Splash* in 1984 and didn't like the idea of a second mermaid film. It was producer Jeffrey Katzenberg who changed his mind and allowed Clements and John Musker to pursue the project. What was at first perceived to be a "girly" movie, *The Little Mermaid* grew into a very promising project. The studio spent more money on the film than they had on any other since the 1960s. The animation was so complex that the work was farmed out to studios in Glendale, California, and Orlando, Florida. Because it was the last animated movie to use hand-painted cells and the story required over a million cells, work was also sent to a studio in Beijing, China. In fact, when the Tiananmen Square protests broke out in China, thousands of completed cells were trapped in a vault before peace was restored and the cells could be shipped to the United States. The resulting animation makes *The Little Mermaid* one of the most visually dazzling of all Disney films. The background art was colorful and fairy tale-like and the animation was buoyant and playful. Since much of the story takes place under water, the artists strove to create bubbles, light seen through water, and other underwater effects with meticulous detail. They would have made Walt Disney proud.

See also: *Little Shop of Horrors, Beauty and the Beast*; Howard Ashman and Alan Menken biography box

FURTHER READING

Hochman, Stephen. *The Music Behind the Magic: The Musical Artistry of Alan Menken, Howard Ashman, and Tim Rice*. Glendale, CA: Disney Editions, 1994.

Maltin, Leonard. *The Disney Films*. 4th ed. Glendale, CA: Disney Editions, 2000.

BEAUTY AND THE BEAST

Studio and release date: Buena Vista/Disney; November 1991
Producer: Don Hahn
Screenplay: Linda Woolverton, based on the 1756 story by Jeanne-Marie Leprince de Beaumont
Songwriters: Alan Menken (music), Howard Ashman (lyrics)
Directors: Gary Trousdale, Kirk Wise
Musical Director: Alan Menken

Voices: Paige O'Hara, Robbie Benson, Richard Wright, Jerry Orbach, Angela Lansbury, David Ogden Stiers, Bradley Michael Pierce, Jesse Corti, Rex Everhart, JoAnne Worley

Songs: "Beauty and the Beast"; "Be Our Guest"; "Belle"; "Something There"; "Gaston"; "The Mob Song"

An animated classic that stands with the best of the Disney movies of the past, this is still the only animated musical film ever nominated for the Academy Award for best picture. *Beauty and the Beast* also showed that the success of *The Little Mermaid* two years earlier was not a lucky accident; the Disney studio was embarking on a dazzling new era of animation. As with *The Little Mermaid*, the new film was again based on a classic fairy tale. There are many variations of *Beauty and the Beast* dating back to the French Renaissance, but a 1756 version by Jeanne-Marie Leprince de Beaumont is the one that is most read and known around the world. The Disney version is based on Beaumont's tale and, unlike *The Little Mermaid*, the musical does not alter the plot or the ending. The story is embellished with original characters in the Disney manner but they do not detract from one of the world's great love stories. Linda Wolverton's screenplay emphasizes the French setting, just as songwriters Alan Menken (music) and Howard Ashman (lyrics) rely on French music. In a French provincial village, the young Belle is considered odd because she likes to read books and does not fawn over the muscular huntsman Gaston like all the other unmarried girls. Also an outcast of sorts is her father, Maurice, a crackpot inventor. On his way to a country fair to show off his latest contraption, he gets lost in the forest and stumbles onto a gloomy castle inhabited by enchanted objects that serve a bitter and fearsome beast. Maurice is made prisoner in the castle, and when Belle comes looking for him, she makes a bargain with the beast: if he will let her father go, she will remain and be his prisoner. The beast agrees and he tries to act civil toward Belle, but his excitable anger gets in the way. With the help of the enchanted candlestick Lumiere, the clock Cogsworth, the teapot Mrs. Potts, and others in the castle, Belle starts to have feelings for the beast. He lets her go to tend to her sick father only to have Gaston and the villagers, who have heard about the beast from Maurice, attack the castle. The enchanted objects drive the horde away but the beast is mortally wounded. Before he dies Belle tells him that she loves him, which removes the curse placed on the beast and he is transformed back into a prince and lives to marry Belle.

The film is a moving drama that still allows for farcical business and comic characters to fill out the story. Directors Gary Trousdale and Kirk Wise gave the film a soft and romantic rendering, and the superior animation and background art evoked a fantastical existence that could be both soothing and frightening. The climactic scene, when the beast is transformed back into a human because of Belle's love, may be one of the most affecting in all Disney cinema. Another memorable scene was when Belle and the beast dance in the castle's ballroom. The fusion of hand-drawn figures and computerized camera movement is stunning in a new and yet traditional manner. The writers solved the problem of exposition at the beginning of the movie by using stained glass windows to illustrate how the prince became a beast. The stylized glass images introduced the beast without actually showing him. *Beauty and the Beast* may have been conventional in its storytelling yet there were a few modern touches. Belle, for example, is a strongwilled heroine who is not out to get a prince. She loves to read, which makes her a freak to the villagers, and she doesn't need a husband to make her life complete. Gaston is also a new kind of villain. He is comic and oafish at first, seeming to be harmless and silly. Yet he develops into one of Disney's most fiendish human villains by the final scene. Not in the original tale but so effective in the animated musical is the device of the castle's staff being turned into enchanted objects.

An outstanding cast of theater performers provided the speaking and singing voices, including Paige O'Hara (Belle), Robby Benson (Beast), Angela Lansbury (Mrs. Potts), Jerry Orbach (Lumiere), David Ogden Stiers (Cogsworth), and Richard White (Gaston). The score by Menken and Ashman has a French flavor throughout yet is clearly in the Broadway mold. The opening musical sequence, "Belle," in which characters are introduced and the situation is revealed, is superb musical storytelling. "Be Our Guest" has a delightful *Follies Bergere* feel to it, "Gaston" is a slaphappy drinking song, "Something There" is a poignant character number, and the Oscar-winning title song is a simple narrative ballad raised to a warm and emotional level. Another song, "Human Again," was sung by the enchanted objects and was recorded and animated. But it was felt that the movie was running too long so it was cut. The very French waltzing number was restored when *Beauty and the Beast* was rereleased in 2002. It was not a coincidence that the voice cast chosen for *Beauty and the Beast* came from Broadway. The directors wanted the film to have a Broadway quality in both the songs and the voices. That is perhaps why the musical later fared so well on Broadway. *Beauty and the Beast* was praised by the movie critics when it opened and was an immediate hit with the public. Much awarded and dearly loved, the movie represented a high point for the new Disney era of animation in the 1990s. In 1994 it was turned into the first Disney Broadway production, running over 14 years, followed by hundreds of school and regional productions. On the horizon is a live-action screen version of the musical using the Menken-Ashman songs.

See also: *The Little Mermaid*; Howard Ashman and Alan Menken biography box

FURTHER READING

Bloom, Ken. *Hollywood Musicals: The 101 Greatest Song-and-Dance Movies of All Time*. New York: Black Dog and Leventhal, 2010.

Hochman, Stephen. *The Music Behind the Magic: The Musical Artistry of Alan Menken, Howard Ashman, and Tim Rice*. Glendale, CA: Disney Editions, 1994.

Maltin, Leonard. *The Disney Films*. 4th ed. Glendale, CA: Disney Editions, 2000.

ALADDIN

Studio and release date: Buena Vista/Disney; November 1992
Producer: R. S. Vander Wende
Screenplay: John Musker, Ron Clements, Ted Elliott, Terry Rossio
Songwriters: Alan Menken (music), Howard Ashman, Tim Rice (lyrics)
Directors: John Musker, Ron Clements, Ted Elliott, Terry Rossio
Musical Director: Alan Menken
Cast: Scott Weinger, Brad Kane, Robin Williams, Linda Larkin, Lea Salonga, Jonathan Freeman, Gilbert Gottfried, Frank Welker, Douglas Seale
Songs: "A Whole New World"; "Prince Ali"; "A Friend Like Me"; "Arabian Nights"; "One Jump Ahead"

The familiar tale of the youth Aladdin and his magic lamp was turned into one of the funniest entries in the Disney animated catalogue. It also made for three giant hits in a row for the studio, *Aladdin* earning critical and public praise similar to that for *The Little Mermaid* (1989) and *Beauty and the Beast* (1991). Like the last film, the story of Aladdin has many versions told in many countries. It is believed that the tale originated in the Middle East, but several versions set the story in China. The Disney studio took a risk by retaining the Middle East setting even though that had been and continued to be a hotbed of controversy. As the opening song "Arabian Nights" suggests, the story told is fanciful fiction and avoids any reference to modern-day countries. In the original version, there are two genies, two evil sorcerers, and Aladdin has two magical tools (the lamp and a special ring). He weds the sultan's daughter earlier in the tale and it is his wife who foolishly gives away the lamp to a peddler. A major character in the story is Aladdin's mother, someone the Disney screenwriters included in the plot during the early stages of development but later dropped. The production of *Aladdin* was actually begun before *Beauty and the Beast*, but the script was so problematic that the project was put aside temporarily and the studio concentrated on *Beauty and the Beast*. Howard Ashman, who wrote the lyrics for both *The Little Mermaid* and *Beauty and the Beast*, completed several songs for *Aladdin* with composer Alan Menken before Ashman died in 1991. When the Aladdin project was revived, British lyricist Tim

Tim Rice (b. 1944)   A British lyricist who has found success with different composers, he has written several stage and screen musicals. He was born in Amersham, England, and educated at Lansing College before beginning his career in music broadcasting and recording. Collaborating with composer Andrew Lloyd Webber, Rice wrote the lyrics for a trio of successful pop-rock musicals that were hits in both England and America: *Joseph and the Amazing Technicolor Dreamcoat* (1968), *Jesus Christ Superstar* (1971), and *Evita* (1979). While his shows with Webber were either made into movies or filmed for video, Rice wrote lyrics directly for the screen with the animated musicals *Aladdin* (1992), *The Lion King* (1994), and *The Road to El Dorado* (2000). Of his other London musicals, only *Chess* (1988) reached Broadway, but he was well represented in America with the lyrics he contributed to the stage versions of *Beauty and the Beast* (1994), *The Lion King* (1997), and *Aladdin* (2014) as well as the original musical *Aida* (2000) with composer Elton John. Autobiography: *Oh, What a Circus* (1999).

Rice was hired to finish the score with Menken. The scriptwriters solved the story problems, and Aladdin ended up being a fast-paced *Arabian Nights* farce that only occasionally slowed down for romance, as in the Oscar-winning song "A Whole New World." Aladdin is a lone "street rat" in this version, and Princess Jasmine is a spunky heroine who flees the palace to see what the real world is like. It isn't long before she is in trouble and is helped by Aladdin and his monkey sidekick Abu. When the palace guards find Jasmine and return her to the sultan, Aladdin is thrown into prison. The evil vizier Jafar, who controls the sultan through sorcery and wishes to take over the kingdom of Agrabah, uses Aladdin to try and get the magic lamp out of the Cave of Wonders. Aladdin ends up with the lamp but trapped in the cave until he rubs the lamp and the Genie appears with a flourish. He tells Aladdin that he gets three wishes, so Aladdin uses them to get out of the cave and to disguise himself as Prince Ali in order to woo Jasmine. Jafar strikes back with a series of magical tricks, eventually gets the lamp from Aladdin, and takes over the kingdom. Aladdin outwits Jafar by claiming that a genie is the most powerful force on earth, so Jafar wishes to be a genie and is then imprisoned in his own lamp. *Aladdin* has more plot than most Disney musicals but the action is swift, the jokes come fast, and the tender moments are well placed.

The comic highlight of the film was Robin Williams' Genie who was a visual and vocal explosion of lines and sounds, much of his text improvised in the recording sessions. It is arguably the funniest performance ever given by a Disney voice artist. Jonathan Freeman voiced Jafar with diabolical glee and he was supported by Gilbert Gottfried as Jafar's sidekick, the complaining parrot Iago. The rest of the voice cast was splendid, as was the expert score by Menken, Ashman, and Rice. In addition to the high-flying ballad "A Whole New World," the most memorable songs were the satirical parade "Prince Ali," the jazzy "One Jump Ahead," the chant-like "Arabian Nights," and the vaudeville showstopper "Friend Like Me." Ron Clements and John Musker, the talents behind *The Little Mermaid*, codirected the animated musical with a focus on comedy. Yet *Aladdin* is also very romantic in a somewhat realistic way. Jasmine is not a helpless female and Aladdin is not the usual dashing prince. Just as many of the jokes are modern and anachronistic, the love story is also very contemporary in tone. Once again the Disney artists came up with visually exotic backgrounds and engaging animated movement. The animation for the genie was based on the expressive line drawings of artist Al Hirschfeld and rarely has animation been so frenetic and funny. *Aladdin* was the top-grossing film of 1992. It also inspired made-for-video features and a television cartoon series. A stage version of Disney's *Aladdin* opened on Broadway in 2014 and it was a hit all over again.

See also: *The Little Mermaid, Beauty and the Beast*; Howard Ashman and Alan Menken biography box

FURTHER READING

Culhane, John. *Disney's Aladdin: The Making of an Animated Film*. Glendale, CA: Disney Editions, 1992.

Hochman, Stephen. *The Music Behind the Magic: The Musical Artistry of Alan Menken, Howard Ashman, and Tim Rice*. Glendale, CA: Disney Editions, 1994.

THE NIGHTMARE BEFORE CHRISTMAS

Studio and release date: Touchstone/Disney; October 1993
Producer: Tim Burton, Denise Di Novi, Kathleen Gavin
Screenplay: Caroline Thompson, Michael McDowell, based on the illustrated poem by Tim Burton
Songwriter: Danny Elfman (music and lyrics)
Director: Henry Selick
Musical Director: Steve Bartek
Cinematographer: Peter Kozichik
Voices: Chris Sarandon, Danny Elfman, Catherine O'Hara, William Hickey, Ken Page, Paul Reubens, Glenn Shadix, Ed Ivory
Songs: "What's This?"; "Jack's Lament"; "Oogie Boogie's Song"; "Sally's Song"; "This Is Halloween"; "Making Christmas"; "Jack's Obsession"; "Kidnap the

Sandy Claws"; "Town Meeting Song"; "Doctor Finklestein/In the Forest";
"Poor Jack"; "Nabbed"

A visual and musical treat from the creative mind of Tim Burton, this imaginative
animated musical was both bizarre and intriguing. *The Nightmare Before Christmas* uses stop-motion animation, one of the most difficult and time-consuming of
all filmmaking methods. Also called claymation, the characters and sets are three-
dimensional and are filmed one frame at a time, the figures moving slightly with
each shot. The process goes all the way back to silent European films and was
perfected in Hollywood with such movies as *King Kong* (1933) and *Jason and the
Argonauts* (1963). Stop-motion animation reaches a new level in *The Nightmare
Before Christmas*, which was directed with a flair by Henry Selick. The screenplay
was adapted from Burton's illustrated poem, which is very short. Writers Caroline
Thompson and Michael McDowell added new characters and filled out the story.
Danny Elfman wrote 10 songs for the film and provided the singing voice for Jack
Skellington, the central character. Jack is known as the "Pumpkin King" of Hallow-
eentown and he rules over Halloween each year. But he is getting bored with the
same scary goings-on year after year and wonders if there is more to life (and death).
Then he discovers Christmastown and the holiday of Christmas and gets excited
once again, creating his own frightening version of the merry holiday. His enthusiasm runs away with him as he has Santa Claus kidnapped and Jack tries to take
over his job, only to be feared by the rest of the world and shot down from the sky.
Jack returns to Halloweentown, rescues his sweetheart Sally from the clutches of
the monster Oogie Boogie, and returns to being a Halloween hero. The story was
populated with bizarre and fascinating supporting characters, such as the evil
Dr. Finkelstein, the frustrated Mayor, and the three mischievous sidekicks Lock,
Shock, and Barrel.

The idea for the movie goes back to Burton's childhood when he saw a store window being changed from a Halloween display to a Christmas one. Seeing characters and images from the two holidays together was decidedly weird and inspired
Burton years later to write the poem. He was also greatly influenced by the stop-
motion animation of Ray Harryhausen, as in *The Seventh Voyage of Sinbad* (1958),
Jason and the Argonauts, and *Clash of the Titans* (1981). Years later, after he had
established himself as a top director of action films and offbeat movies such as
Beetlejuice (1988) and *Edward Scissorhands* (1990), Burton approached the Disney
studio about making a feature-length film of his illustrated poem. Disney agreed but
as the movie took shape, the studio thought it too dark and scary for young children.
Instead of releasing *The Nightmare Before Christmas* under the Disney name, it
became a product of Touchstone Pictures, Disney's division for more adult movies.
Production on the odd musical was slow and laborious. Over 100 artists, cameramen, and animators worked for three years before *The Nightmare Before Christmas*

There is an eerie kind of beauty in the stop-action animated musical *The Nightmare Before Christmas* (1993). Even the muted romance between Sally and Jack, the Pumpkin King, is strangely moving. Henry Selick directed the mesmerizing fantasy based on a tale by Tim Burton. (Touchstone/Photofest)

was finished with a price tag of $18 million. The Disney studio was rightfully nervous, wondering if there was a big enough audience for such a special, unusual film. Happily, both the critics and the moviegoers applauded the movie and it paid back its cost several times over. Some consider *The Nightmare Before Christmas* a cult film; if so, it is a very large cult. The odd and even puzzling aspects of the story and the characters appeal to a wide audience.

Although Burton had little to do with the actual production of *The Nightmare Before Christmas*, the movie is in the same style as the live-action and animated shorts that he directed. But director Selick and his artists are the ones who turned a poem and some drawings into such a unique movie. The decor for the film was as stunning as the creatures that inhabited it, and so much is going on in some scenes that one cannot fully comprehend the film on one viewing. Also adding a great deal is Elfman's score, which was both disarming and exciting. The ponderous march "This Is Halloween," the gleeful "Making Christmas," the reflective "Jack's Lament," the touching "Sally's Song," the explosive "What's This?," and the rollicking "Oogie

Boogie's Song" were among the musical numbers, each one staged with mesmerizing style. Chris Sarandon provided the speaking voice of Jack, and also heard in the film were Catherine O'Hara, Ken Page, William Hickey, Glenn Shadix, and Paul Reubens, each giving a funny-wacko vocal performance. *The Nightmare Before Christmas* was released for Halloween of 1993 but it also became a Christmastime favorite. As dark and bizarre as it is, children seem to enjoy it as much as adults.

Burton and Elfman joined forces again in 2005 for *The Corpse Bride*, another stop-action horror tale that was also visually compelling. The Victorian gentleman Victor Van Dort is engaged to wed the innocent Victoria Everglot, but the day before the wedding he goes into an enchanted wood to practice his vows and mistakenly gets married to the Corpse Bride. Trapped in the world of the dead, Victor has to struggle to return to life before Victoria marries Lord Barkis. It was a dark tale told with too little humor and the characters were less fascinating than in the earlier film. Johnny Depp, Helen Bonham Carter, Emily Watson, Tracey Ullman, Paul Whitehouse, Albert Finney, Richard E. Grant, and Christopher Lee were among the distinguished actors who voiced the characters. Elfman again wrote the score and it included some interesting songs such as "Remains of the Day," "The Wedding Song," and "Tears to Shed." One watched the fanciful movie in a detached way and it did not share the success of *The Nightmare Before Christmas*.

See also: *The 5,000 Fingers of Dr. T*

FURTHER READING

Bloom, Ken. *Hollywood Musicals: The 101 Greatest Song-and-Dance Movies of All Time*. New York: Black Dog and Leventhal, 2010.

Thompson, Frank. *Tim Burton's Nightmare Before Christmas: The Film, the Art, the Vision*. Glendale, CA: Disney Editions, 2002.

THE LION KING

Studio and release date: Buena Vista/Disney; June 1994
Producer: Chris Sanders
Screenplay: Irene Mecci, Jonathan Roberts, Linda Woolverton
Songwriters: Elton John (music), Tim Rice (lyrics)
Director: Roger Allers, Rob Minkoff
Musical Director: Hans Zimmer
Voices: Matthew Broderick, James Earl Jones, Rowan Atkinson, Robert Guillaume, Jeremy Irons, Niketa Calame, Jonathan Taylor Thomas, Whoopi Goldberg, Jim Cummings, Cheech Marin

Songs: "Circle of Life"; "Can You Feel the Love Tonight"; "Hakuna Matata"; "I Just Can't Wait to Be King"; "Be Prepared"

Most Disney animated films are based on a preexisting book or fairy tale so it is surprising that the studio's most successful animated movie featured an original story. *The Lion King* broke all box office records and went on to become the biggest-selling DVD of all time. Ironically, the Disney studio put most of its resources and top animators on *Pocahontas* (1995) and considered *The Lion King* of secondary importance. The screenplay by Irene Mecchi, Jonathan Reynolds, and Linda Woolverton may have borrowed generously from *Hamlet* and the studio's own *Bambi* (1942), but the story and characters were solid, engaging, and lent themselves to an often serious musical film. The lion patriarch King Mufasa rules over all the animals on the African savanna from his den on Pride Rock. The birth of his son Simba is celebrated by all the creatures in the movie's stirring opening. Young Simba grows to be a playful but impatient cub who eagerly looks forward to being the lion king someday. During a stampede of wildebeests, Mufasa is pushed into the path of the herd and is trampled to death. Simba is convinced by his evil uncle Scar that the cub was responsible for the death of his father, when it was

There is a mythic quality to Disney's *The Lion King* (1994), even though it is not based on a classic story. Near the opening of the film, the mandrill Rafiki presents the newborn cub Simba to the animal kingdom as the baby's parents, King Mufasa and Queen Sarabi, proudly look on. (Walt Disney Pictures/Photofest)

Elton John (b. 1947)   Arguably the most durable British rock star of all time with a career spanning five decades, the singer-pianist-composer turned to stage and screen musicals in the 1990s. He was born in Pinner, England, and educated at London's Royal Academy of Music. Since 1970 he has been an internationally famous rock singer and composer with record-breaking albums and sold-out concerts around the world. His usual lyricist for his albums is Bernie Taupin, but he teamed with Tim Rice to write the scores for the animated movie musicals *The Lion King* (1994) and *The Road to El Dorado* (2000). On Broadway he wrote new songs with Rice for the 1997 stage version of *The Lion King*, and the two teamed up for an original score for *Aida* (2000). John had a giant hit on the London stage with *Billy Elliott* (2005) with book and lyrics by Lee Hall arriving on Broadway in 2008. John is as popular a performer as a composer and has appeared on television specials and in a handful of films, including the musical *Tommy* (1989) in which he played the Pinball Wizard. Biography: *Elton*, David Buckley (2013).

Scar himself who murdered his brother in order to take over the pride. Simba runs away and grows up under the "no worries" philosophy of the meerkat Timon and the warthog Pumbaa. Scar proves to be a neurotic, ineffective king, and his allies, the hyenas, are starting to turn against him. Simba is encouraged by the wise old baboon Rafiki to return home and avenge his father's death, and in the battle that follows the truth of who really murdered Mufasa is revealed. Scar is destroyed, Simba mates with his childhood sweetheart Nala, and the animals once again come to pay homage when the couple presents their newborn cub to the pride.

No animated film had taken on so many heavy issues, met them head on, and succeeded like *The Lion King*. The stampede in which Mufasa died was as powerful as any live-action adventure, yet the comedy of Timon and Pumbaa had the heart and soul of vaudeville. Directors Roger Allers and Rob Minkoff captured not only the look and feel of the African savanna but also the kinship of community that drives the plot. The depiction of the many different kinds of animals that are connected to the pride is both lyrical and stunning, like a ballet of nature enfolding before our eyes. The background art and animation are equally as evocative. The film may be the visual masterpiece of the renaissance in Disney animation that began with *The Little Mermaid* (1989). Elton John (music) and Tim Rice (lyrics) wrote the pop score, which sometimes bordered on the fervent—especially in the opening number "The Circle of Life," which combined music, animation, and ritual in a way rarely seen on the screen before. The other songs are Timon and Pumbaa's freewheeling "Hakuna Matata," Scar's Fascist creed "Be Prepared," young Simba's ambitious "I Just Can't Wait to Be King," and the Oscar-winning ballad "Can You

Feel the Love Tonight?" used behind the romantic scenes between adult Simba and Nala. The superb musical background score by Hans Zimmer gave the movie an authentic-sounding African rhythm not found in the songs, particularly the choral section arranged and conducted by African maestro Lebo M. Since most of the singers were Broadway veterans, there was a polished show biz quality to the singing. This was in contrast to the tribal chanting on the soundtrack. Never before had moviegoers been so enthralled by the musical sounds of Africa. The soundtrack recording was very popular and some of the songs quickly entered the league of Disney's most recognized tunes. As for the film itself, it was the biggest sleeper hit in the history of the Disney studios. From a totally unknown entity came the top-grossing animated movie of all time. The 1997 Broadway version of *The Lion King* was equally successful. Director-designer Julie Taymor rethought the movie in ritual and theatrical terms and the result was a dazzling display of musical celebration that pleased even the most adamant anti-Disney critics. Like the movie, the Broadway production has broken records and continues to fascinate both young and old theatergoers.

See also: *Beauty and the Beast, Pocahontas, Frozen*; Elton John, Tim Rice biography boxes

FURTHER READING

Buckley, David. *Elton John: The Biography*. London: Carlton, 2013.
Maltin, Leonard. *The Disney Films*. 4th ed. Glendale, CA: Disney Editions, 2000.
Rice, Tim. *Oh, What a Circus: The Autobiography*. London: Coronet Books, 1999.

POCAHONTAS

Studio and release date: Buena Vista/Disney; June 1995
Producer: James Pentecost
Screenplay: Carl Binder, Susannah Grant, Philip LaZebnik, Andrew Chapman
Songwriters: Alan Menken (music), Stephen Schwartz (lyrics)
Director: Mike Gabriel, Mike Goldberg
Musical Director: Alan Menken
Voices: Irene Bedard, Judy Kuhn, Mel Gibson, David Ogden Stiers, John Kassir, Russell Means, Linda Hunt, Christian Bale, Danny Mann, Billy Connolly, Joe Baker, John Pomeroy
Songs: "Colors of the Wind"; "Just Around the Riverbend"; "Listen with Your Heart"; "Mine, Mine, Mine"; "If I Never Knew You"; "Steady as a Beating Drum"; "The Virginia Company"; "Savages"

A rare animated film that dealt with American history, this love story was beautifully told but it ended up rather too low-key for a children's movie. In fact, many children were bored. None of the animals talked, there was no fantasy or magic save a little conjuring by Grandmother Willow, the issues were mature ones (ecological awareness, racial intolerance, the evils of imperialism), and at the end the lovers are separated. Also, the score had no show-stopping number like "Under the Sea" or "Be Our Guest" to provide spectacle and thrills. During test screenings, kids got so restless during the love duet "If I Never Knew You" that the studio cut the scene and played the song during the end credits. (It was later restored in the rereleased version and on DVD.) With so much out of the reach of children, it is no wonder that adults found more to savor in *Pocahontas* than kids. And savor it they did. Many consider *Pocahontas* the most mature, thought-provoking, and moving of the Disney animated features. But without the kids in the theater seats, the movie was a box office disappointment. Ironically, the studio thought *Pocahontas* would be the blockbuster and that *The Lion King*, in production at the same time, would be a modest success. They could not have been more wrong. Yet *Pocahontas* was a labor of love, a desire to do things in an animated movie that were usually left to live-action movies. Every aspect of the film, from the script and score to the movement and background art, was coordinated to create a poignant and meaningful drama.

The historical Pocahontas has been portrayed onstage and on-screen many times, rarely accurately. The same is true with the Disney version. Since the movie is a love story, the scriptwriters made Pocahontas a full-grown woman rather than the young preteen she actually was when the British arrived in Virginia. In history she wed her Native fiancée Kocoum after the wounded John Smith returned to England. Pocahontas later went to England with her second husband, Englishman John Rolf, and converted to Christianity. She died there at the age of 22. The famous episode, in which Pocahontas saves John Smith's life by putting herself between Smith and his executioner, has never been verified. Smith himself wrote about Pocahontas' bravery, but there is no historical proof that it happened as legend has it. The idea that Pocahontas and Smith were in love with each other is also suspect, but the Disney writers built the whole movie around this possibility. The screenplay is intelligently written and purposely breaks away from the stereotypes of both the Native Americans and the English explorers. The Patawomacks are portrayed as a peaceful tribe who are in harmony with nature. Any hostility shown comes from the infringement of the Europeans. Some of the English explorers, such as John Smith, have lofty ideas about a new world but Governor Ratcliffe is only interested in finding gold. Although some felt that the Disney version bent over backwards to reverse the clichéd portrayals of Indians from the past, the script is actually very balanced with good and evil characters on both sides.

Stephen Schwartz (b. 1948)   A multitalented songwriter with some long-run hits and admirable misses on Broadway, his songs have been heard in a handful of movie musicals. He was born in New York and raised on Long Island and was educated at Juilliard and Carnegie-Mellon University, where he wrote original musicals before embarking on a career as a record company executive and producer. While still in his early twenties, Schwartz had three New York musical hits to his credit: *Godspell* (1971), *Pippin* (1972), and *The Magic Show* (1974). Although his *The Baker's Wife* (1976), *Working* (1978), and *Rags* (1986) were not successful, they have much-admired scores. Schwartz finally had another Broadway triumph with *Wicked* (2003). *Godspell* is his only stage work so far to be filmed, but he wrote an original score for *The Prince of Egypt* (1998) and the lyrics for *Pocahontas* (1995) and *The Hunchback of Notre Dame* (1996). Schwartz's music and lyrics are imaginative and varied, using rock, vaudeville soft-shoe, gospel, pop, and romantic operetta. Biography: *Defying Gravity: The Creative Career of Stephen Schwartz*, Carol de Giere (2008).

The screenplay begins by showing the Englishmen sailing to the New World to found a settlement in the name of King James. John Smith looks upon the venture as a new and exciting chapter in his life but the greedy Governor Ratcliffe wants to find gold in Virginia, just as the Spaniards have in other parts of the New World. On land, the Chief of the Powhatan tribe wishes his daughter Pocahontas to wed the brave warrior Kocoum but she does not love him. When Pocahontas consults her deceased grandmother (who has taken the form of a willow tree), the spirit warns the girl that big changes are coming to the tribe. The change, of course, is the arrival of the English, who land with pomp and immediately start cutting down trees to build the walls of Jamestown. Ratcliffe sends men out to dig for gold but none is found, much to the governor's anger. When Smith and Pocahontas meet, they are fascinated and attracted by how different the other is. Pocahontas trusts Smith enough to take him to Grandmother Willow, and both swear to bring the tribesmen and the Englishmen together in peace. But when the jealous Kocoum sees Smith and Pocahontas kissing, he tries to kill the Englishman. Before he can, the colonist Thomas kills Kocoum and the Chief declares war on the Englishmen. Smith is captured by the Powhatans and is to be executed the next day. Pocahontas intercedes and pleads for Smith's life, convincing her father that not all the Englishmen are evil. But Ratcliffe arrives on the scene, attempts to shoot the Chief, but ends up wounding Smith instead. Ratcliffe is arrested by his own men and sent back to England on the same boat that is to transport the wounded Smith to medical help in Europe. The lovers part tearfully and the Chief tells Smith that he is welcome to return to Virginia where Pocahontas waits for him.

The production team for *Pocahontas* approached the project with thoroughness and dedication. The background artists studied the landscape near Jamestown and created a verdant depiction of nature. Because there were no exaggerated, cartoonish characters (except perhaps Ratcliffe), the animators took special pains to make human movement both natural and flowing. Native American actors were hired to voice the tribesmen so that the vocals would not slip into stereotype. The two animal characters, Flit the hummingbird and Meeko the lap dog, were originally given dialogue, but during production it was decided to make them more realistic. They still have lively personalities but their movements and sounds are those of animals. The score by Alan Menken (music) and Stephen Schwartz (lyrics) is tuneful but restrained, closer to operetta than musical comedy. Some of the songs took an inspirational tone, especially with the Oscar-winning "Colors of the Wind." Yet equally impressive was the reflective "Just Around the Riverbend," the rhythmic "Mine, Mine, Mine," and the lovely duet "If I Never Knew You." Mike Gabriel and Eric Goldberg directed with care and all the elements in *Pocahontas* were balanced and effective. The movie was successful enough to make a handsome profit but its real success was what one saw on the screen.

See also: The Lion King, Anastasia; Alan Menken, Stephen Schwartz biography boxes

FURTHER READING

de Giere, Carol. *Defying Gravity: The Creative Career of Stephen Schwartz*. Montclair, NJ: Applause Theatre & Cinema Books, 2008.
Shepherd, Marie. *Everything You Need to Know About Alan Menken*. Apsley, Australia: Emereo Publishing, 2014.

EVITA

Studio and release date: Hollywood Pictures; December 1996
Producers: Robert Stigwood, Alan Parker, Andrew G. Vajna
Screenplay: Alan Parker, Oliver Stone, based on the 1978 stage script by Tim Rice
Songwriters: Andrew Lloyd Webber (music), Tim Rice (lyrics)
Director: Alan Parker
Musical Director: David Caddick
Cinematographer: Darius Khondji

Cast: Madonna, Antonio Banderas, Jonathan Pryce, Jimmy Nail, Victoria Sus
Principal Songs: "Don't Cry for Me, Argentina"; "On This Night of a Thousand
    Stars"; "High Flying Adored"; "I'd Be Surprisingly Good for You,"; "Rainbow
    High"; "A New Argentina"; "Another Suitcase in Another Hall"; "You Must
    Love"; "Oh, What a Circus"; "And the Money Kept Rolling In"; "Buenos Aires"

Nearly 20 years after it took Broadway by storm, *Evita* was finally filmed. It was
the only big-budget film musical made in the 1990s, and every penny showed up
on the screen. Yet there was much more than spectacle involved, and the screen
version was as emotionally enthralling as it was visually stunning. The infamous
Eva Peron was an odd subject for a musical, which is why it appealed to young
songwriters Andrew Lloyd Webber (music) and Tim Rice (lyrics). Born into poverty, Eva Duarte rose to fame first as a radio and film actress then as a powerful
political force when she married Juan Peron and helped him become president of
Argentina. Much loved by her fellow citizens but scorned by the upper classes,
Evita (as she was affectionately known) was an enigmatic figure. Although she and
her husband were corrupt and self-serving, they also instilled confidence among
the Argentines in the late 1940s. Evita also worked for women's suffrage and
improving the conditions of the country's poor. She was running for vice president
when she died of cancer at the age of 33. Because she was an international celebrity, Eva Peron is viewed differently by different nations. England saw her as an
opportunist, so it was interesting that the British songwriters were drawn to musicalize her life.

Evita, like the same songwriters' earlier *Jesus Christ Superstar*, began as a concept album. In order to keep the narrative clear, a narrator was needed. Webber
and Rice gave the role to the radical Che Guevara who was a student in Argentina
during the reign of the Perons. The two-record recording was nonstop music that
ranged from Latin folk to rock. Intended as a stage piece, *Evita* needed a dynamic
staging to work in a theater. American director Harold Prince staged the 1978 London production with multimedia effects, German "alienation" techniques, and even
stylized Russian "biomechanics" to raise the gossipy subject matter to high art. The
authors seemed to be ambivalent about their feeling toward Eva Peron, for she is
depicted as both saint and whore, and Prince's chilly, detached presentation gave
the show a documentary feel that let the audience draw its own conclusions. The
plot started with Evita's funeral and the nationwide mourning that accompanied it.
Then Che steps out of the crowd and paints a different picture of the cherished
"Spiritual Leader of the Nation." The story then goes back to show the ambitious,
15-year-old Evita using the singer Augustin Magaldi to get to Buenos Aires where
she sleeps her way to the top of the Argentine entertainment business. When she
meets the politically ambitious General Juan Peron, Evita seduces him, marries
him, and aids him in his rise to the top. She also endears herself to the people by

forming the Eva Peron Foundation even as she and Juan help themselves to large chunks of the cash. When Evita does a grand "Rainbow Tour" of Europe to cement international relations, she receives a mixed reception. Although her health is failing, Evita prepares to run for vice president but she dies before the election. Throughout the musical, Che Guevara returns to give a sociopolitical point of view to the proceedings.

Evita boasted what was arguably the best score either Webber or Rice ever wrote. The standout hit song was the passionate "Don't Cry for Me, Argentina," but the score was filled with thrilling numbers, such as the sly duet "I'd Be Surprisingly Good for You," the crooning love song "On This Night of a Thousand Stars," the plaintive "Another Suitcase in Another Hall," the soaring ballad "High Flying Adored," the sarcastic "And the Money Kept Rolling In," the pulsating "Buenos Aires," and the rousing "A New Argentina." The musical was a triumph in London, and in 1979 it opened on Broadway to equal acclaim. There was immediately talk of a film version but, despite many attempts, it did not happen until 1997. Over the years many actresses were rumored to be cast in a screen version of *Evita*. Patti LuPone (who had played Evita on Broadway to wide acclaim), Elaine Paige (who originated the role in London), Barbra Streisand, Meryl Streep, Liza Minnelli, Bette Midler, Michelle Pfeiffer, Jennifer Lopez, Mariah Carey, and Gloria Estefan were all seriously considered. But the project seemed stalled for years and some contenders grew too old to play the young heroine. Director Alan Parker had wanted to make a movie of *Evita* from the start, approaching producer Robert Stigwood soon after the show opened in London. He tried again after *Evita* opened on Broadway but was again turned down. Stigwood did not seriously pursue a screen version until the 1990s but had trouble getting a studio to finance what would be a very expensive movie. Building on a screenplay written earlier by Oliver Stone, Parker and Stigwood started putting together a production but all the studios wanted to know was who was a big enough box office star to play Evita. The pop singer Madonna, who had already made 15 movies, campaigned for the part, even making a video of herself singing some of the songs. She may not have been box office gold, but Madonna was one of the most popular singers in the world, and Hollywood Studios wagered that she might be able to carry the movie financially. Because Madonna had a scandalous reputation and was seen as a sex symbol, fans of the musical feared that her Eva Peron would be little more than a singing slut.

Parker envisioned a huge movie filmed in the places where the story actually happened. The crew did get permission to film some scenes at the Casa Rosada, the president's palace, in Buenos Aires but most of the movie was shot in Budapest, Hungary, and in studios in London. *Evita* was indeed huge. Some scenes, such as the funeral, called for thousands of extras. Hundreds of costumes were made, including 85 just for Madonna, a cinema record. *Evita* onstage was sung through with very little dialogue. Parker made the bold choice to keep that format for the

Andrew Lloyd Webber (b. 1948)   The most successful songwriter in modern popular music, only three of his stage works have come to the screen so far. He was born in London into a family of classically trained and distinguished musicians. Webber studied classical music at Oxford University but turned to rock and other popular forms when he first collaborated with lyricist Tim Rice on *Joseph and the Amazing Technicolor Dreamcoat* in 1968. The young songwriters rose to prominence with their rock opera *Jesus Christ Superstar*, which was a successful album and later a stage hit in London and then in New York in 1971. This was followed by the team's very popular *Evita* (1979). With various lyricists, Webber has scored a number of musicals of diverse subject matter, most of which played on Broadway and none more successful than *Cats* (1982) and *The Phantom of the Opera* (1988). His other New York credits include *Song and Dance* (1985), *Starlight Express* (1987), *Aspects of Love* (1990), *Sunset Boulevard* (1994), *By Jeeves* (2001), *The Woman in White* (2005), and *School of Rock* (2015). While *Jesus Christ Superstar* (1973), *Evita* (1996), and *The Phantom of the Opera* (2004) were filmed, some of his other works were made into videos. Although he is rarely a critics' favorite, Webber is very popular with theatergoers on three continents and has been instrumental in bringing modern musical idioms to the theater. Biographies: *Andrew Lloyd Webber,* John Snelson (2004); *The Musicals of Andrew Lloyd Webber: His Life and Works,* Keith Richmond (2000).

film. Only a few stage songs were dropped or condensed, and Webber and Rice wrote a new number for the movie, the ballad "You Must Love Me," which won the Oscar for best song. The stage character of Che was turned into a series of Argentines who appeared in each scene, all played by Antonio Banderas with a smooth but seething presence. After months of filming and more of editing, *Evita* was completed with a price tag of $55 million. It opened to mostly favorable notices, and business was brisk if not overwhelming. *Evita* proved that the big movie musical was not dead and gone forever, but the picture did not make a profit on its first release and the studios once again shied away from screen versions of Broadway hits for several years. Just as Madonna surprised audiences with a commendable performance, so too the movie was more accomplished than many were expecting. Whereas *Evita* onstage was stylized and innovative, the movie was spectacular and engaging. But in both versions, Eva Peron is still an enigmatic character who fascinates whether one sees her as a saint or a seductress.

See also: *Les Misérables;* Tim Rice, Andrew Lloyd Webber biography boxes

FURTHER READING

Fraser, Nicholas, and Marsa Navarro. *Evita: The Real Lives of Eva Peron*. London: Andre Deutsch, 2013.

Parker, Alan. *The Making of Evita*. New York: HarperCollins, 1996.

Snelson, John. *Andrew Lloyd Webber*. New Haven, CT: Yale University Press, 2009.

Victor, Barbara. *Goddess: Inside Madonna*. New York: HarperCollins, 2013.

ANASTASIA

Studio and release date: Fox Animation Studios; November 1997

Producers: Don Bluth, Gary Goldman

Screenplay: Susan Gauthier, Bruce Graham, Bob Tzudiker, Noni White, based on the 1954 play by Marcelle Maurette, Guy Bolton

Songwriters: Stephen Flaherty (music), Lynn Ahrens (lyrics)

Directors: Don Bluth, Gary Goldman

Musical Director: Doug Besterman

Voices: Meg Ryan, Liz Callaway, John Cusack, Jonathan Dokuchitz, Kelsey Grammer, Bernadette Peters, Christopher Lloyd, Jim Cummings, Andrea Martin, Rick Jones, Lacey Chabert

Songs: "Journey to the Past"; "Once Upon a December"; "Paris Holds the Key (to Your Heart)"; "In the Dark of the Night"; "Learn to Do It"; "A Rumor in St. Petersburg"; "At the Beginning"

Of the many non-Disney animated features that were made after the success of *The Little Mermaid* (1989), this Fox musical is arguably the best. A classy animated musical with an unlikely subject matter, it was quite accomplished in many ways and compares favorably to the Disney movies of its era. The legend of Anastasia, the missing daughter of Czar Nicholas II and the Empress Alexandra, has fascinated the public for nearly 100 years. Books, plays, films, and TV movies have been made about her, and all of them differ because there are few facts and lots of conjecture. During the Russian revolution, the communists captured the czar and his family and imprisoned them. In 1918 the entire Romanov family was assassinated, but the body of the youngest daughter, Princess Anastasia, was believed missing. Years later several young women in Europe came forward and claimed to be the surviving princess. Since the dowager empress was alive and living in Paris, these impostors would be presented to the old woman, but she recognized none of them as her granddaughter. One Polish woman, Anna Anderson, who claimed to suffer from amnesia, convinced many that she was the lost princess, but the surviving members of the Romanov family did not believe. It was this Anna who

378 Musicals in Film

inspired several of the different dramatizations about the princess, Anastasia. In 2007, long after the collapse of communism in Russia, the burial site of the royal family was identified and, through DNA testing, it was determined that Anastasia's remains were with those of the other Romanovs.

The screenplay for *Anastasia* is a fanciful tale built on the assumption that the young princess escaped from Russia in 1918. The teenage Anya cannot remember her past, but the audience knows that she is the surviving Russian Princess Anastasia Romanov who miraculously survived when her family was murdered in the revolution. Anya is discovered by the enterprising Dimitri and his sidekick Vladimir who bring her from St. Petersburg to Paris to present her to the dowager empress as her long lost granddaughter. Dimitri's aims are mercenary, but when he falls in love with Anya, he changes his tune and helps her battle the back-from-the-grave Rasputin who has vowed to kill all the Romanovs. Much of the tale was far from children's fare, such as a sequence showing the Russian revolution and the capture of the Romanovs. But the studio put in some lovable Disney-like characters, such as Rasputin's wacky henchman Bartok the Bat and the life-affirming Parisian Sophie who brought a Broadway splash to the story. The superior score was by Broadway songwriters Stephen Flaherty (music) and Lynn Ahrens (lyrics), and the songs were as varied as they were tuneful. There was a warm and evocative lullaby "Once Upon a December" that was sung at different points in the film and was heard on a music box that was crucial to the story. Also in the score was the warm character song "Journey to the Past," the creepy conjuring number "In the Dark of the Night," the catchy ditty "Learn to Do It," and the rousing "Paris Holds the Key (To Your Heart)." Movie actors Meg Ryan, John Cusack, and Christopher Lloyd voiced Anastasia, Dmitri, and Rasputin, respectively, but the singing on the soundtrack was by Broadway performers, including Angela Lansbury as the dowager empress and Bernadette Peters as Sophie.

20th Century Fox created a whole new division in 1994 to make animated films, Fox Animation Studio, and *Anastasia* was the first project on the boards. It was far from a simple movie to make for a new studio, but coproducer and codirector Don Bluth had a long track record with animated films. He had been one of Disney's top animators before branching out on his own and directing such popular animated features as *An American Tale* (1986), *The Land Before Time* (1988), and *All Dogs Go to Heaven* (1989). Bluth insisted on as much accuracy as possible, even though the actual story was fiction. The Russian palace settings, the royal family's clothes, and even the music box were exact replicas of the real thing. In the scenes in Paris, famous personalities were glimpsed—from Maurice Chevalier and Sigmund Freud to Claude Monet and Charles Lindbergh. There were plenty of action scenes, including the revolution and a train wreck, and many special effects, particularly with the ghastly spirit of Rasputin. *Anastasia* was an ambitious first-time movie, but thanks to Bluth it looked very polished and highly professional. The venture cost Fox $53 million, so it took a long time for the movie to pay for itself. Perhaps not as beloved as the better Disney films, *Anastasia* has its many fans and is still being discovered by new generations.

See also: *Little Mermaid, Pocahontas*

FURTHER READING

Deneroff, Harvey. *The Art of Anastasia*. New York: HarperCollins, 1997.
Meyer, Carolyn. *Anastasia: The Last Grand Duchess*. New York: Scholastic, 2013.

Musicals since 2000: A Rebirth of Sorts

The celebrations and optimism that greeted the new century were dampened on September 11, 2001, when the nation was attacked by terrorists on a scale never experienced before. The destruction of the World Trade Center and a section of the Pentagon brought the country to a shocked standstill. A kind of paranoia, not felt since the Cold War of the 1950s, returned as Americans realized that the strongest nation on earth could be so vulnerable. Although new laws and security measures were quickly put in place, many knew that the world was never going to be such a safe place again. More American civilians died in the World Trade towers than in World War II, the Korean War, and the Vietnam War combined. The fact that the enemy was not easily or clearly defined added to the paranoia. America's international relations got more complicated in the wake of 9/11. At the same time, and probably related to this, a major economic recession hit the United States and several countries around the world. It would take more than a decade until the financial picture in America made significant improvements, while in some European countries, in particular Greece, matters got even worse. How such a small nation as Greece could have such an impact on the rest of Europe showed how complex the world's finances were.

Race relations and gay rights were frequently in the news in the new century. The election of the first African American president in 2008 was a landmark in the long history of Civil Rights. Barack Obama embarked on a crusade to improve health care and the economy. Despite a Republican Congress that consistently opposed him, Obama was able to make improvements in both areas. But racial conflict was still to be found in America, as witnessed by the 2014 riots in Ferguson, Missouri, when a black teenager was killed by a white policeman, who was acquitted on the plea of self-defense. The Gay Rights Movement made some advances in the first decades of the century. The military started accepting openly gay personnel in 2010, and in 2015 the Supreme Court made gay marriage legal in all 50 states. Shootings within the country and a bombing during the 2013 Boston Marathon made it clear that Americans had much to fear on the domestic front. International conflicts continued, fueled by the United States' invasion of Afghanistan soon after the destruction of the World Trade towers. Allied forces invaded Iraq in 2003, and missiles were used against Libya in 2011. U.S. troops captured the deposed Iraqi president, Saddam Hussein, in 2003 and terrorist leader, Osama bin Laden, in 2011, but worldwide terrorism continued. America after 9/11 was not the same place it was before the twin towers collapsed.

The computer and the World Wide Web continued to affect all aspects of daily life. Facebook was introduced in 2004; it was at the time the newest form of communication in a rapidly growing field. E-mail and the Internet were the most accepted means of buying, selling, getting information, and communicating. Cell phones became iPhones and, in many cases, texting replaced e-mail. The computer and the Internet played a major role in changing the face of entertainment. More and more, various kinds of computer technology were replacing television watching, DVD rentals, CD purchases, and attendance at cineplexes. There were so many new ways to enjoy music, movies, and television that the entertainment industry was often more concerned with format than content. Yet movies were far from passé and Hollywood came up with several blockbusters, including *Spider-Man* (2002), *Avatar* (2009), *The Hunger Games* (2012), *Jurassic World* (2015), and the Harry Potter series of fantasy adventures (2001 to 2011). Television programing became so complex and accessible that the first broadcast of a show was overshadowed by DVR recordings, streaming, and on-demand viewings. It got to the point that some movies never played in theaters but were made and released directly to one of these alternative forms of entertainment. Music was downloaded more often than it was purchased on a CD. Determining what the "top albums" were was tricky because the public tended to download songs rather than collections of songs. Even the art world was affected by the computer as video artists created kinetic and laser works of art that ran off computer programs.

It seemed that theater and dance were the only art forms not changed by the computer. Broadway continued to recover in the new century with over two dozen active playhouses and a rich variety of offerings. Many of the musicals were escapist fun, especially after 9/11. Among such diverting entertainment were *The Producers* (2001), *Mamma Mia!* (2001), *Hairspray* (2002), *Monty Python's Spamalot* (2005), *Shrek: The Musical* (2008), *The Addams Family* (2010), *Something Rotten* (2015), and *School of Rock* (2015). This last was one of several shows to have rock or pop scores. *Movin' Out* (2002), *Wicked* (2003), *Jersey Boys* (2005), *Spring Awakening* (2006), *In the Heights* (2008), *Billy Elliot* (2008), *Rock of Ages* (2009), *Next to Normal* (2009), *American Idiot* (2010), *Matilda: The Musical* (2013), and *Hamilton* (2015) varied greatly in their tone but all departed from the traditional music of old Broad-way. The Disney company continued to be a significant force on Broadway with the screen-to-stage musicals *Mary Poppins* (2006), *Tarzan* (2006), *The Little Mermaid* (2008), *Newsies* (2012), and *Aladdin* (2014). Other non-Disney films were also turned into musicals with success, notably *Thoroughly Modern Millie* (2002), *Chitty Chitty Bang Bang* (2005), *Xanadu* (2007), *White Christmas* (2009), and *An American in Paris* (2015). Happily there was still room on Broadway for darker, offbeat, or more demanding musicals, as witnessed with *Urinetown* (2001), *Avenue Q* (2003), *The Light in the Piazza* (2005), *The Color Purple* (2005), *Book of Mormon* (2011), and *Fun Home* (2015).

With Broadway on the comeback, there were more musicals for Hollywood to buy. But the studios were still hesitant. There had not been a successful movie musical in so long that the studios thought it best to concentrate on other genres. But back in 1996 a revival of the 1975 musical *Chicago* opened on Broadway for a long run and there was enough interest to finally get a movie version made. The 2002 screen adaptation of *Chicago* was a surprise hit, won the Oscar for best picture, and forced Hollywood to reconsider the movie musical. So a handful of musical adaptations were made. Unfortunately, *The Phantom of the Opera* (2004), *The Producers* (2005), *Rent* (2005), *Mamma Mia!* (2008), *Nine* (2009), and *Jersey Boys* (2014) all failed at the box office. All had been long-run hits on Broadway, but most of these film versions were botched in the transition from stage to screen. It seemed as if Hollywood had forgotten how to make a musical even when the material had proven to be popular. Luckily some musical adaptations were made that did find an audience or the studios would have given up entirely on bringing Broadway shows to the screen. *Dreamgirls* (2006), *Hairspray* (2007), *Sweeney Todd* (2007), *Les Misérables* (2012), and *Into the Woods* (2014) were modest successes at the box office, making enough money that Broadway adaptations were still worth doing. The fact that the four musicals mentioned were expertly done certainly helped.

Original musicals were far and few between in the new century. The surprise success of *Moulin Rouge!* (2001) forced Hollywood (and moviegoers) to reconsider just what a movie musical was. *Moulin Rouge!* had nonsingers who sang, some dynamic dancing filmed like a music video, and a quirky style that was not at all like the traditional musical. The preexisting songs came from everywhere—from opera to Elton John. Young audiences particularly loved the fast-paced, quick-cutting, even chaotic musical. Perhaps this was the new way to make a Hollywood musical. That was the style of the cutting-edge, transgender film *Hedwig and the Angry Inch* (2001) as well. The modest but memorable little musical was not a mainstream hit like *Moulin Rouge!* but it has found its own devout followers. Similarly, the low-budget but potent youth musical *Camp* (2003) found ardent admirers once it was released on DVD. The British dance film *Billy Elliot* (2000) and the small-scale Irish musical *Once* (2006) also managed to find interested American moviegoers, and both ended up as hits on Broadway and in London. *Billy Elliot* recalled the dance films of the 1980s in which there were no songs except on the soundtrack. *Once* had songs that were performed on the street or in a pub without any production embellishments. American studio executives, looking at *Once* and *Billy Elliot*, wondered if perhaps small musicals with big profits was the way to go.

Disney made five musicals in the first 13 years of the new century and had two surprise hits. *Enchanted* (2007) was a modern fairy tale that mixed animation and live action in a clever and appealing way. Its box office went beyond its modest expectations. But the bigger surprise was the animated *Frozen* (2013), which captured the imagination of moviegoers, in particular young girls who identified with the two princesses in the tale. The musical broke box office records for an animated film and produced a best-selling CD. Plans are in the works for a Broadway version of *Frozen* and a movie sequel. Disney's three other animated musicals were top-notch films but none sold as well as expected. *Home on the Range* (2004), *The Princess and the Frog* (2009), and *Tangled* (2010) boasted fine scores and superior animation. They are still being discovered on DVD and streaming. The non-Disney animated *The Road to El Dorado* (2000) kept its Elton John-Tim Rice songs on the soundtrack rather than in the mouths of the characters. DreamWorks planned for the movie to be the first in a series of "Road to" musicals, in the spirit of the popular "Road" movies starring Bing Crosby and Bob Hope in the 1940s. But *The Road to El Dorado* did disappointing business and plans for the sequels were abandoned.

Three musical bio-pics from this era were notably effective. Jamie Foxx played singer-musician-composer Ray Charles in *Ray* (2004), and both actor and film were highly praised. Country singers Johnny Cash and June Carter were portrayed by Joaquin Phoenix and Reese Witherspoon in *Walk the Line* (2005), and they also were well received. British actor Tom Hiddleston was surprisingly adroit as pioneering country singer Hank Williams in *I Saw the Light* (2016). Williams' life and music had been dramatized in 1964 in the bio-pic *Your Cheatin' Heart* with George Hamilton as the singer. The movie showed Williams' drinking problem but not his drug addiction. *I Saw the Light* was one of the new generations of bio-pics where such warts were clearly exposed. It is likely that in the future Hollywood will remake other old bio-pics with more accuracy and honesty. The future will also have more youth musicals. Television found that teen-oriented musicals, such as *Glee* and the *High School Musical* series, could mean high ratings and Hollywood took notice. *High School Musical 3* (2008) was released in movie theaters, and it is more than likely that we shall see similar kinds of musicals on the big screen.

In the year 2015, the earliest baby boomers started turning 70 years old. In numbers, they were still a powerful group. But how much do American movies, television, theater, and music cater to this sizable part of the population? There are many radio stations that play only "classic rock," meaning the 1960s and 1970s. There are television stations that broadcast old TV shows from the same time period. Stage musicals featuring songs from the baby boomers' past do well on Broadway, as with the long-running *Mamma Mia!, Smokey Joe's Cafe, Jersey Boys, Rock of Ages, Movin' Out, Tommy,* and *Beautiful: The Carole King Musical.* But what of the Hollywood musical? It seems that the studios have written off the boomers as inconsequential: better to make a musical for high schoolers and play it safe. The only film musical since 2000 that was meant to appeal directly to the children of the 1950s and 1960s was the antiwar movie *Across the Universe* (2007). It was set in the late 1960s and was filled with dozens of Beatles songs. For whatever reasons, the movie was not picked up and championed by the baby boomers. In fact, the audience members who were most taken with *Across the Universe* were under-30-somethings, some of whom were discovering the Beatles' music for the first time. So maybe the future of the Hollywood musical lies in the interests of the young. And perhaps that is the way it should be, for they are the future.

MOULIN ROUGE!

Studio and release date: Bazmark/20th Century Fox; June 2001
Producers: Baz Luhrmann, Fred Baron, Martin Brown
Screenplay: Baz Luhrmann, Craig Pearce
Songwriters: Marc Bolan, Marius DeVries, Jacques Offenbach, Eden Ahbez, Elton John, and others (music and lyrics)
Director: Baz Luhrmann
Choreographer: John O'Connell
Musical Director: Marius DeVries
Cinematographer: Donald McAlpine
Cast: Nicole Kidman, Ewan McGregor, John Leguizamo, Jim Broadbent, Richard Roxburgh, Garry McDonald, Jacek Koman, Matthew Whittet, Kerry Walker
Principal Songs: "Nature Boy"; "Children of the Revolution"; "Rhythm of the Night"; "Your Song"; "Meet Me in the Red Room"; "Come What May"; "Like a Virgin"; "Fool to Believe"; "Gaite Parisienne"

Young audiences particularly loved this frenetic musical extravaganza in which music, broad performances, and hyperactive camerawork often bombarded the audience. Director Baz Luhrmann and Craig Pearce wrote the screenplay about the young Englishman Christian (Ewan McGregor) who goes to Paris in 1899 to become a poet and ends up being a drinking pal of Toulouse-Lautrec (John Leguizamo) and other bohemian artists. They write a show for producer Harold Zidler (Jim Broadbent) who runs the famous Moulin Rouge nightspot. Christian falls in love with the sultry star of the club, Satine (Nicole Kidman), but their romance is thwarted by the wealthy Duke (Richard Roxburgh) who will support the financially strapped Moulin Rouge if Satine can be his. The duke tries to have Christian killed and when the plan fails, he himself tries to destroy his rival. Christian survives but leaves Satine until Lautrec encourages him to forgive her and love her. Satine is suffering from tuberculosis but before she dies she and Christian profess their love together. In the epilogue, it is one year later, the Moulin Rouge is closed, and Christian is writing the story of his love affair with Satine. The screenplay borrowed heavily from three operas: Puccini's *La Boheme* (1896), Offenbach's *Orpheus in the Underworld* (1858), and Verdi's *La Traviata* (1853). Sometimes the music used on the soundtrack reflected these operas as well. Surely the characters were larger than life and, also like an opera, expressed themselves in song rather than just dialogue. Yet *Moulin Rouge!* could never be mistaken for a conventional opera. The style was more MTV than opera house and the movie was filmed with modern cinema techniques so the period piece seemed right up to date.

Luhrmann took a bold and unconventional approach to the musical form. Whereas musicals from the Golden Age were romanticized versions of the real

Although they were not trained singers, Nicole Kidman and Ewan McGregor did their own singing in *Moulin Rouge!* (2001) and pulled it off nicely. Director Baz Luhrmann created a surreal Paris of the 1890s that was visually and musically frenetic and very appealing to many moviegoers. (20th Century Fox/Photofest)

world, *Moulin Rouge!* offered a kinetic, dreamlike reality in which logic and reason are replaced by colorful images and exaggerated characters. The setting for the film may have been 1899 but the temperament was the computer age. Costumes and sets reflected the past but the way they were filmed made everything look like a rock concert. The colorful circus of a movie was fast paced, the camera zooming in and out of locales with breakneck speed, and the editing so fervent that it made most music videos look static. The songs came from various sources and time periods, again fusing the past and the present. The music was sometimes so reconfigured that an old standard was barely recognizable. In some cases, this was refreshingly exciting; at other times it was annoying. The songs, sung by cast members as well as other artists on the soundtrack, were given a high-pressure treatment that matched the frantic camera work. Musical numbers as diverse as "Nature Boy," "Your Song," "Come What May," "Like a Virgin," "Lady Marmalade," and "El Tango de Roxanne" all seemed to explode on the screen. Although not cast with singers, the movie was surprisingly well sung. The two stars, Nicole Kidman and Ewan McGregor, surprised audiences with their vocals, although it was clear that there was a lot of mixing done to give them a highly electronic sound. The vigorous choreography by John O'Connell broke from conventional musicals by only showing body parts, a quick facial gesture, and a series of rapid cuts rather than revealing the dancer's whole body. While this added to the energy of the film, it also diminished the talent of the performers. One wondered if the actor dancing was actually doing the steps or if we were seeing a montage of dance positions. Some audience members (as well as some of the creative team) felt cheated. In fact, when *Moulin Rouge!* was released on DVD, the bonus features included footage of the dances before they were edited. Some preferred this view of the performers even though it lacked the dazzling presentation of the edited movie.

Critical reaction to *Moulin Rouge!* was mixed although most applauded the stylized look of the film. Some viewers thought the movie was the most innovative, exciting musical in decades; others wanted to run out of the theater in panic. Regardless, box office was surprisingly strong and the expensive film managed to pay off its $52 million cost and then some. If *Moulin Rouge!* opened doors to a new kind of movie musical, there have not been many artists to venture through those doors. Luhrmann returned to the opera world and staged some nontraditional pieces but none of his subsequent films have been musicals. The quick cutting in *Moulin Rouge!* has probably influenced the way other musicals have been filmed, most notably *Hedwig and the Angry Inch* (2001) and *Chicago* (2002). But the style that worked so effectively in *Moulin Rouge!* is not appropriate for most musicals. Perhaps the future will prove otherwise. In the meantime, *Moulin Rouge!* remains a unique, possibly "one-of-a-kind," musical experience.

See also: *Hedwig and the Angry Inch, Chicago*

FURTHER READING

Luhrmann, Baz, and Catherine Martin. *Moulin Rouge! The Splendid Book That Charts the Journey of Baz Luhrmann's Motion Picture*. New York: Newmarket Press, 2001.

HEDWIG AND THE ANGRY INCH

Studio and release date: New Line; August 2001
Producers: Pamela Koffler, Katie Roumel, Christine Vachon
Screenplay: John Cameron Mitchell, based on the 1998 stage script by Mitchell and Stephen Trask
Songwriters: Stephen Trask and others (music and lyrics)
Director: John Cameron Mitchell
Musical Director: Stephen Trask
Cinematographer: Frank G. DeMarco
Cast: John Cameron Mitchell, Miriam Shor, William Pitt, Maurice Dean Wint, Andrea Martin
Principal Songs: "The Origin of Love"; "Wicked Little Town"; "Tear Me Down"; "Sugar Daddy"; "Angry Inch"; "Freaks"; "The Long Grift"; "Midnite Radio"; "Hedwig's Lament"; "Wig in a Box"; "Exquisite Little Town"

An Off-Broadway cult hit along the lines of *The Rocky Horror Show*, this dazzling little rock musical was the most audacious, most daring, most in-your-face show New York had seen in a long time. Much was lost when it became a movie, but the best things remained, particularly John Cameron Mitchell's compelling performance. Onstage, the offbeat musical took the form of a concert with Hedwig (Mitchell) narrating his/her tale between songs. Young Hansel was born in East Berlin the year the Wall went up and grows into a confused transsexual. He marries an American GI to get to the United States but has to have a sex change operation to qualify. The operation is botched and Hedwig is left with an inch of undetermined sexual embarrassment. Once in America, she is dumped by the GI and has an affair with a military brat named Tommy Gnosis who becomes a rock star using Hedwig's songs, then he too abandons her. Left singing rock-and-roll dirges in third-class dives, Hedwig continues on, searching for a personal and sexual identity. The idea for the 1998 musical came when actor Mitchell and composer-musician Stephen Trask put together a drag show featuring the transgender character of Hedwig. The bewigged, heavily made up Mitchell told the story with Trask joining him for the songs. It was very unusual for a drag performance to have a plot, and it was suggested that the piece might make a full musical. Only one other performer was added to the cast, and the musical remained a concert but this time it was part of a tour Hedwig is making across America. Much of the story was narrated rather than acted out, but *Hedwig and the Angry Inch* was far from static onstage. Mitchell was mesmerizing, singing the rock score by Stephen Trask, telling his/her story with a phony German accent, and exuding a strange sensuality that was sexy without knowing which sex it was. Songs such as "Origin of Love," "Angry Inch," "Wicked Little Town," and "Tear Me Down" made no pretense of sounding like theater numbers; they were undiluted rock and fierce in their sound and ideas. *Hedwig and the Angry Inch* originated Off-Off Broadway and was too outrageous to be ignored. The contracts were rewritten as an Off-Broadway entry and the musical rocked Greenwich Village for over two years.

No major studio was interested in making a movie out of *Hedwig and the Angry Inch*, but the small, independent company Killer Films thought it was ideal material for a potent alternative movie and made a deal with New Line Cinema to release it. Mitchell rightfully wanted to maintain control of his little musical and, although he had never directed a film before, he convinced the producers to let him direct the musical for the screen. There was no question that Mitchell should reprise his electric stage performance and to write the screenplay with Trask. The two reworked the stage script, opening up the story and showing much of what was only described in the stage version. One actually saw the various characters who Hedwig encountered as well as the places where he/she met them. What was left to the imagination in the theater was clearly shown on the screen and some felt that this weakened the musical. Mitchell's direction was energized and used a lot of MTV techniques but, sometimes, the film got bogged down in the cinematic tricks and the bizarre story line was not always clear; consequently, the characters rarely seemed as interesting as they had in the theater. But the things that made *Hedwig and the Angry Inch* rock onstage were still there: the propulsive score, the weird concept, and Mitchell's astonishing performance.

Hedwig and the Angry Inch was made for a reasonably modest cost that didn't affect the quality of the product. Unfortunately, Fine Line must not have had much faith in the movie or was too strapped for cash because the promotion for the film was weak and the distribution rather puny. Only nine screens across the country showed the movie on its opening weekend. It took several months before *Hedwig and the Angry Inch* earned back its $6 million cost. The film did better on DVD, though most of the public was not even aware of its existence. Even many fans of the stage version did not know there was a film version. After its Off-Broadway run, *Hedwig and the Angry Inch* received many regional productions, and the challenging little musical started to catch on, though it never became a mainstream favorite. Then in 2014, the stage-television star Neil Patrick Harris played Hedwig in a Broadway version of the musical and it was very popular, running a year and a half. The revival finally brought the show the recognition it deserved and more attention was given to the movie version. *Hedwig and the Angry Inch* will always be a challenging musical and not one for all tastes. It has the audacious quality of *The Rocky Horror Picture Show*, but it will never have such a large following because it is more disturbing and closer to reality. That makes the movie version all the more valuable.

See also: *The Rocky Horror Picture Show, Moulin Rouge!*

FURTHER READING

Otterwell, Jessica. *Like a Fork Shoved on a Spoon: Notions of Gender Identity Within Hedwig and the Angry Inch*. Seattle: Amazon Digital, 2013.

Wollman, Elizabeth Lara. *The Theatre Will Rock: A History of the Rock Musical, From Hair to Hedwig*. Ann Arbor: University of Michigan Press, 2009.

CHICAGO

Studio and release date: Miramax; January 2003
Producer: Martin Richards
Screenplay: Bill Condon, based on the 1975 stage script by Fred Ebb, Bob Fosse, which was based on the 1926 play by Maurine Dallas Watkins
Songwriters: John Kander (music), Fred Ebb (lyrics)
Director/Choreographer: Rob Marshall
Musical Director: Doug Besterman
Cinematographer: Dion Beebe
Cast: Renée Zellweger, Catherine Zeta-Jones, Richard Gere, Queen Latifah, John C. Reilly, Christine Baranski, Taye Diggs
Songs: "All That Jazz"; "Cell Block Tango"; "When You're Good to Mama"; "All I Care About"; "Nowadays"; "Mister Cellophane"; "Razzle Dazzle"; "Roxie"; "I Can't Do It Alone"; "Funny Honey"; "I Move On"; "We Both Reached for the Gun"

Not only was this vibrant, satirical movie musical a major accomplishment in many ways, its box office success opened the doors for more musicals in Hollywood where most studios had given up on the genre. *Chicago* began as a comedy on Broadway in 1926 when it spoofed the sensational murder trials of the day. The play by Maurine Dallas Watkins introduced the character of Roxie Hart who revels in sensationalism. It was a very timely work because in the 1920s the newspapers were very powerful and made celebrities out of anyone they wished, including murderesses. *Chicago* was filmed twice, as a silent in 1927 and as *Roxie Hart* in 1942. In 1975 it was turned into a jazzy Broadway musical that used the techniques of vaudeville to tell its wildly improbable tale of sin and insincerity. The jazz score was by John Kander (music) and Fred Ebb (lyrics) who also cowrote the script with director-choreographer Bob Fosse. The musical retained much of the plot of the original play. In 1920s Chicago, Roxie Hart shoots her lover when he tries to walk out. She gets big-time lawyer Billy Flynn to defend her and, more important, keep her name on the front page. Roxie even goes so far as to announce that she is pregnant in order to gain the sympathy of the public. Throughout it all, her ineffectual husband Amos is a pawn in the scheme planned by Roxie and Flynn. Also in the Chicago women's jail, run by the motherly but corrupt matron Mama Morton, is fellow murderess Velma Kelly who is worried about her own publicity and is Roxie's rival for attention. When both Velma and Roxie are pushed out of the limelight by a new murder and a new celebrity murderess, the two end up doing a double act together in vaudeville.

The stage musical took the form of a variety show with each musical number announced by an emcee and each song echoing a particular 1920s song or song type. The vibrant opening number "All That Jazz" became the show's most popular song but also first rate were the smooth soft-shoe number "Nowadays," that Latin-flavored "Cell Block Tango," the dishonest "All I Care About (Is Love)," the sour duet "Class," the red-hot number "When You're Good to Mama," the pitiful lament "Mister Cellophane," and the sizzling "Razzle Dazzle." Although Gwen Verdon (Roxie) and Chita Rivera (Velma) were the stars of Chicago, it was Fosse who got most of the attention with his delicious stylized choreography. The dark musical spoof received good notices and ran for 898 performances in New York then was little heard of for 20 years. A Broadway revival opened in 1996 in which Ann Reinking played Roxie and re-created Fosse's choreography in a slimmed-down production with no scenery and simple costumes. Both critics and playgoers thought the satiric musical more timely than ever and embraced its dark humor. Chicago has gone on to become the longest-running revival in Broadway history.

The popularity of this stage production encouraged Hollywood to finally make a screen adaptation of Chicago. But there were problems. The vaudeville aspects of the stage work would be difficult to sustain on-screen. A movie that takes place entirely inside a vaudeville theater would be too confining. Yet putting the musical into realistic locales around Chicago would detract from the satiric, stylized aspects of the show. Rob Marshall, a Broadway and film choreographer, went to Miramar with his solution: change the "vaudeville" musical into a period piece in which the heroine Roxie imagines everyone and everything around her as a vaudeville act. The concept opened up all kinds of possibilities for screenwriter Bill Condon and allowed director-choreographer Marshall to film the songs unrealistically. The concept worked with Roxie watching others in musical acts and even imagining herself performing on a stage. A few songs from the stage score were cut and one character was radically changed. Onstage, the "sob sister" reporter Mary Sunshine was

Rob Marshall (b. 1960)   A dancer-turned-choreographer-turned-director, he has an impressive track record onstage and on-screen during a relatively short period of time. He was born in Madison, Wisconsin, and grew up in Pittsburgh where he was educated at Carnegie-Mellon University. Marshall began his career performing in a touring production of *A Chorus Line,* followed by some jobs in Broadway musicals. He started to choreograph regionally, then did the dances for the Broadway musicals *She Loves Me* (1993), *Kiss of the Spider Woman* (1993), *Damn Yankees* (1994), *The Petrified Prince* (1994), *Company* (1995), *Victor/Victoria* (1995), and *A Funny Thing Happened on the Way to the Forum* (1996). Marshall made his directorial debut co-staging with Sam Mendes the highly praised 1998 revival of *Cabaret,* then directed and choreographed the revival of *Little Me* (1998). His Hollywood career took off as director and choreographer with the lauded movie version of *Chicago* (2003), followed by *Nine* (2009) and *Into the Woods* (2014). His dances are in the traditional Broadway mode but often his direction is unique and resourceful.

played by a male in drag who sang in a soprano voice, fooling the audience until his male identity was revealed near the end of the show. In the film, Mary was played by Christine Baranski and the role edited down to a minor character. Although Marshall had never directed a feature film before, he had very specific ideas about how each scene should be filmed. Taking some ideas from *Moulin Rouge!,* Marshall cut the dances up into rapid shots of close-ups, rarely showing the dancer's entire body. There was also some dizzying camera work and MTV-like editing that some felt distracted rather than added to the musical.

It seemed that every female star in Hollywood under the age of 40 was considered for the twin leading roles of Roxie and Velma. Although Renée Zellweger had no previous dancing or singing experience, she was cast as Roxie and her character did not dance as much as the character had onstage. Catherine Zeta-Jones, who had musical theater experience, was cast as Velma and she was given most of the dancing chores. Both stars surprised moviegoers and critics with their strong performances. Actor Richard Gere (Flynn), pop singing star Queen Latifah (Mama Morton), and character actor John C. Reilly (Amos) were also commendable but, once again, it was Marshall's choreography that often stole the show. Although it was not an exact copy of the Fosse stage choreography, the dancing was certainly in the jazzy style of Fosse.

Kander and Ebb wrote a new number for the film, "I Move On," which was heard over the final credits. The movie was the sleeper of the year, winning the

Best Picture Oscar and opening doors for subsequent film musicals based on Broadway shows.

See also: Moulin Rouge!; John Kander and Fred Ebb, Rob Marshall biography boxes

FURTHER READING

Bloom, Ken. *Hollywood Musicals: The 101 Greatest Song-and-Dance Movies of All Time*. New York: Black Dog and Leventhal, 2010.
Leve, James. *Kander and Ebb*. New Haven, CT: Yale University Press, 2009.

RAY

Studio and release date: Anvil/Universal; October 2004
Producers: Stuart Benjamin, Howard Baldwin, Karen Elise Baldwin, and others
Screenplay: James L. White, Taylor Hackford
Songwriters: Ray Charles, Herbert Lawson, Lowell Fulson, Sam Sweet, and others (music and lyrics)
Director: Taylor Hackford
Choreographer: Vernel Bagneris
Musical Director: Craig Armstrong
Cinematographer: Pawel Edelman
Cast: Jamie Foxx, Kerry Washington, Regina King, Clifton Powell, Harry Lennix, Bokeem Woodbine, Aunjanue Ellis, Sharon Warren, C. J. Sanders, Curtis Armstrong
Principal Songs: "Georgia on My Mind"; "The Midnight Hour"; "I Got a Woman"; "Mary Ann"; "Night Time Is the Right Time"; "Hit the Road Jack"; "I Can't Stop Loving You"; "Born to Lose"; "Bye Bye Love"; "Rock This House"; "Straighten Up and Fly Right"; "What'd I Say"

The celebrated African American singer Ray Charles was the subject of this bio-pic, and its star, Jamie Foxx, gave such a masterful performance that the movie was much better than many of Hollywood's romanticized "rags-to-riches" musical biographies. Charles was such an all-encompassing artist that he is considered a musical giant in soul, gospel, country, blues, and jazz. He was born in Albany, Georgia, and grew up in Greenville, Florida, where he showed a capacity for tinkering with mechanics and playing the piano. Charles started going blind at the age of four and was completely without sight by the time he was seven. He attended the Florida School for the Deaf and Blind in St. Augustine where he received a classical music education and started performing blues and jazz at social gatherings and on local radio. After several years of writing and performing songs and struggling to he heard, Charles was signed to Atlantic Records and his remarkable career was launched. He won numerous awards and near the end of his life wrote his autobiography, which was published soon after his death in 2004. Director Taylor Hackford secured the rights to Charles' life story in 1987 but couldn't find a major studio to finance it, so the movie was eventually made as an independent feature by Anvil Films and released through Universal. Hackford wrote the screenplay with James L. White, and they decided to end the movie when Charles was 49 years old because the next two decades were mostly filled with success and acceptance with too little conflict. The writers also made the risky decision to include scenes dealing with Charles' drug addictions, his two marriages, and his 12 children by 9 different women. Since Charles was still alive during preparation and was somewhat involved in the project, this was a bold move on the filmmaker's part. The result was a truthful yet inspiring bio-pic.

The film's story begins in 1948 when Charles is 18 years old and traveling to Seattle to try and break into the music business. His early jobs, his first tour in which he gets hooked on heroin, and his troubled relationship with women are all shown. More importantly, the film illustrates how Charles develops his particular form of music. Throughout the story, flashbacks reveal Charles' childhood in poverty, the death of his brother, his losing his sight, and the way his strong-willed single mother Aretha encouraged him in his music. Despite Jim Crow laws in the South and more subtle racial discrimination in the North, Charles breaks onto the charts with his records. He tours Europe many times and becomes a major force in rhythm and blues, jazz, gospel, and even country music, breaking boundaries by sometimes mixing two of the sounds together. Yet his weakness for drugs and women starts to deteriorate his personal life and only after he turns himself around and defeats his own demons does he feel like a winner. The narrative concludes in 1979 when the Georgia legislature honors Charles by making his "Georgia on My Mind" the official state song.

When Denzel Washington turned down the offer to play Charles on-screen, the role went to Jamie Foxx, a television and film actor with many credits but still mostly unknown to the public. In preparation for the role, Foxx toured with Charles and watched his gestures, the way he played the piano, and other physical characteristics. Although Charles provided the singing on the soundtrack, Foxx did his own piano playing. In addition to piano lessons, Foxx took classes at the Braille Institute, learning to read braille. For filming, he wore eye prosthetics so that he was "blind" for many hours each day he was filming. Yet it was Foxx's acting that most mattered and he gave a riveting, multifaceted performance that was rewarded with an Oscar. The supporting cast was uniformly excellent, in particular Sharon

Washington as his mother Aretha, Kerry Washington as Charles' long-suffering wife Dela Bea, and Regina King as his mistress Margie Hendricks. With Charles doing the singing vocals, *Ray* is musically authentic and exciting. Among the many Charles favorites heard in the film were "Georgia on My Mind," "I Can't Stop Loving You," "I Got a Woman," "Unchain My Heart," "Hit the Road Jack," and "Let the Good Times Roll."

Charles got to hear the first edited version of the film before he fell ill. Postproduction dragged on and, by the time *Ray* was released, Charles had died of liver failure four months earlier. The movie was a surprise hit. As popular as Charles was, Universal did not think a film about him would have such a wide appeal. Perhaps the recent death of the music legend prompted more interest in the movie than it otherwise might have gotten. But it is just as likely that the quality of the bio-pic and the strong audience reaction contributed even more to its success. *Ray* was nominated for six Academy Awards including best picture, the first time an African American bio-pic had been nominated. The film certainly changed the direction of Foxx's career. Among his subsequent movies was the musical *Dreamgirls*.

See also: *Dreamgirls*

FURTHER READING

Charles, Ray, and David Ritz. *Brother Ray: Ray Charles' Own Story*. Boston: Da Capo Press, 2004.
Lydon, Michael. *Ray Charles: Man and Music*. London: Routledge, 2004.

DREAMGIRLS

Studio and release date: Dreamworks/Paramount; December 2006
Producer: Laurence Mark
Screenplay: Bill Condon, based on the 1981 stage script by Tom Eyen
Songwriters: Henry Krieger (music), Tom Eyen (lyrics)
Director: Bill Condon
Choreographer: Donald Barrett
Musical Director: Matt Sullivan
Cinematographer: Tobias A. Schliessler
Cast: Jamie Foxx, Beyoncé Knowles, Jennifer Hudson, Eddie Murphy, Danny Glover, Anika Noni Rose, Sharon Leal, Keith Robinson, Hinton Battle, Mariah Iman Wilson, Ken Page
Principal Songs: "Dreamgirls"; "And I Am Telling You I'm Not Going"; "One Night Only"; "When I First Saw You"; "Family"; "I Am Changing"; "I Meant

You No Harm"; "Takin' the Long Way Home"; "Fake Your Way to the Top"; "I Love You I Do"; "Move"; "Cadillac Car"; "Steppin' to the Bad Side"; "Listen"

A backstage musical loosely based on the real-life Motown trio The Supremes, it was dramatically and musically enthralling and just as powerful as the 1981 Broadway show it was based on. Of the many musical talents that Detroit record producer Berry Gordy introduced in the 1950s and 1960s, perhaps none was more popular than Diana Ross and the Supremes. The African American singing trio had a series of hits in the 1960s, and their glamorous clothes and stylish hairdos became a fashion icon during that decade. The backup members of the group changed because of backstage friction and it was this conflict that inspired *Dreamgirls*. Tom Eyen's script for the Broadway musical changed names and details, but there was no doubt that the singing trio The Dreams was The Supremes. In the plot, three African American singers—Deena Jones, Effie White, and Lorrell Robinson—climb the show biz ladder with the help of their ruthless manager Curtis Taylor Jr., who is not above discarding one of the trio (and his former lover) and replacing her when he thinks it's good for business. With success come heartaches and damaged relationships with friends, family, and spouses. Yet the women triumph in the end by being true to themselves and their personal dreams. The songs by Henry Krieger (music) and Eyen (lyrics) captured the Motown sound in both the character numbers, such as "Family," "And I'm Telling You I Am Not Going," "I Am Changing," and "When I First Saw You" as well as the onstage pop songs like "One Night Only," "Steppin' to the Bad Side," and the title number. The score also managed to cross over from one music chart to another as the girls sang soul, gospel, pop, and blues. The gritty yet sparkling Broadway musical was given a stunning production by director-choreographer Michael Bennett, and the show enjoyed a long run.

A screen version of *Dreamgirls* was on the planning boards for years but not until the success of the film version of *Chicago* (2002), which Bill Condon wrote, was the project green-lighted with Condon as writer and director. Because Bennett's stage production moved in and out of different places and switched from the audience's point of view to that of the actors', the show seemed cinematic already. Condon built on Bennett's ideas and jumped from location to location even during one song, giving the film a vibrant if sometimes dizzying feeling. Condon also made many minor changes but the story essentially stayed the same. The cast was not only excellent but also full of surprises. Newcomer Jennifer Hudson triumphed as Effie, the amiable Jamie Foxx gave a vicious performance as Curtis, and Eddie Murphy as the fading star James Thunder Early revealed a whole new side to his many talents. The other Dreams were played by Beyoncé Knowles and Anika Noni Rose, and the splendid supporting cast included Danny Glover, Keith Robinson, Hinton Battle, Sharon Leal, and Loretta Devine, who had been in the Broadway production 25 years earlier. Everyone did their own singing and it was riveting to hear them. The Kreiger-Eyen score was well served by the movie, with most of the songs retained, and some new numbers ("I Love You I Do," "Patience," and "Listen") were added.

The integration of music and scenes was particularly effective. Bennett's Broadway staging was notable for the way he changed locations right in front of the audience's eyes. Of course the same effect is much easier to do in the movies, so *Dreamgirls* on the screen did not seem as innovative. Yet the movie was edited in such a way that was just as exciting. With its many locations and swift cross editing, the film was well paced and the energy was maintained throughout. *Dreamgirls* was probably influenced by the editing in *Moulin Rouge!* (2001) and *Chicago* (2002). Because the original Broadway production was so theatrical, some feared that such a stunning theater piece would lose a great deal on the screen. But most critics and moviegoers applauded the well-crafted, beautifully performed musical. It was nominated for eight Oscars (though not best picture) and more than paid back its $7 million cost. The Broadway show that fans feared would never come to the screen finally arrived and it was worth the wait.

See also: Moulin Rouge!, Chicago, Ray

FURTHER READING

Bordman, Gerald. *American Musical Comedy: From Adonis to Dreamgirls*. New York: Oxford University Press, 1982.

Ribowsky, Mark. *The Supremes: A Saga of Motown Dreams, Success and Betrayal*. Boston: Da Capo Press, 2009.

Woll, Allen. *Black Musical Theatre: From Coontown to Dreamgirls*. Boston: Da Capo Press, 1991.

HAIRSPRAY

Studio and release date: New Line; July 2007
Producers: Neil Meron, Craig Zadan
Screenplay: Leslie Dickson, based on the 2002 stage script by Mark O'Donnell, Thomas Meehan, which was based on the 1988 film script by John Waters
Songwriters: Marc Shaiman (music), Scott Wittman, Marc Shaiman (lyrics)
Director: Adam Shankman
Choreographer: Adam Shankman
Musical Director: Paul Broucek
Cinematographer: Bojan Bazelli

Cast: Nikki Blonsky, John Travolta, Zac Efron, Michelle Pfeiffer, Christopher Walken, Queen Latifah, Amanda Bynes, James Marsden, Brittany Snow, Elijah Kelley, Allison Janney

Songs: "You Can't Stop the Beat"; "Without Love"; "Welcome to the 60s"; "Good Morning Baltimore"; "It Takes Two"; "Mama, I'm a Big Girl Now"; "The Nicest Kids in Town"; "Big, Blonde and Beautiful"; "The New Girl in Town"; "(You're) Timeless to Me"; "Breakout"; "Run and Tell That"; "Tied Up in the Knots of Sin"; "I Know Where I've Been"; "(The Legend of) Miss Baltimore Crabs"; "Boink Boink"; "Cooties"; "Trouble on the Line"; "I Can Hear the Bells"; "Come So Far (Got So Far to Go)"; "Ladies' Choice"; "(It's) Hairspray"

A cult movie from 1988 that became a mainstream hit musical 14 years later, *Hairspray* was a satire even as it was nostalgic for the past. Just as *Grease* found popularity in spoofing and finding charm in the late 1950s, so this tuneful musical had fun with teenagers in the early 1960s. And just as *Little Shop of Horrors* had been inspired by a tacky low-budget movie, so too was *Hairspray*, which was based on a small campy film with cheesy production values. The creator behind it all was maverick filmmaker John Waters who made a series of outrageous films in the 1970s and 1980s that aimed to shock with bad taste but were usually very funny. A handful of them featured the transvestite Divine who matched Waters in crude humor. Waters' 1988 comedy *Hairspray* was a bit more conventional than his other projects, and even Divine was toned down to the point where her character was actually very human. Divine played the overweight, frumpy mother of the heroine and, though still a travesty of a woman, was quite touching at times. *Hairspray* also proved to be Waters' most popular movie, appealing to mainstream audiences more than his previous works. Without making too many changes to the story, *Hairspray* was turned into a very successful Broadway show in 2002. Hefty high schooler Tracy Turnblad lives in Baltimore in 1962 and dreams of appearing on the Corny Collins dance show on local television. When the program sponsors an open contest for Miss Teenage Hairspray, Tracy enters with high hopes. But because "Negroes" are excluded from the competition, Tracy organizes a protest with the reluctant help of her mother, the overabundant Edna. Despite the efforts of the conniving Velma Von Tussle and her ambitious daughter Amber, Tracy wins the contest and the heart of handsome teen Link Larkin as well as striking a blow for desegregation. The musical was fun, tuneful, and actually very wholesome. The only true Waters touch was having Edna played by the gravel-voiced Harvey Fierstein who turned drag into a fine art. The 1960s were evoked by the colorful costumes, exaggerated hairdos, and the delightful pastiche songs by Marc Shaiman (music and lyrics) and Scott Wittman (lyrics). Some of the most catchy numbers included the rocking "You Can't Stop the Beat," the uptempo "Good Morning, Baltimore," the

The full-figured heroine of *Hairspray* (2007) is Tracy Turnblad (Nicole Blonsky), a high school girl who turns Baltimore upside down in 1962 by her dancing and by striking a blow for civil rights. Here she performs on the local *Corny Collins* television show. Adam Shankman directed and choreographed the film, which did for the 1960s what *Grease* had done for the 1950s. (New Line/Photofest)

charm song "Timeless to Me," the defiant "Mama, I'm a Big Girl Now," and the rhythmic love song "Without Love."

Hairspray ran seven years on Broadway. It was still running when the movie version was released in 2007. Director-choreographer Adam Shankman made some minor changes in the story and one major one: The contest is not won by Tracy (Nikki Blonsky) but by the African American youth Inez (Taylor Parks). Since she was a minor character, this was surprising to audiences familiar with the original movie and the stage musical. The score remained mostly intact, and the film had the bright, colorful 1960s look of the Broadway show. Shankman's approach to the character of the heavyweight Edna differed greatly from the first movie and the stage version. John Travolta was cast as Edna and he was fitted with a specially designed fat suit and endured silicone face prosthetics to look more feminine. Travolta also used a tiny, sweet voice for Edna, making her a shy, shrinking violet of a mother. This was in direct contrast to Divine and Fierstein's masculine-looking, grotesque Edna with a deep voice and bold delivery. Some moviegoers saw this as an original interpretation of the character; others thought it was a cop-out and removed the tacky quality that was pure Waters. Michelle Pfeiffer dominated much of the movie for the role of Velma had been built up some, yet newcomer Blonsky made a commendable screen debut as Tracy. Zac Efron was a personable Link, and there were fine performances in supporting roles played by Amanda Bynes, Queen Latifah, Christopher Walken, Elijah Kelley, Brittany Snow, and James Marsden. Because the stage musical was so well-known, the movie version of *Hairspray* was eagerly anticipated and the film quickly became a financial hit.

As in *Grease*, the nostalgia created in watching *Hairspray* was rather artificial. Neither film gives an accurate depiction of the eras they pastiche. Also, most of the moviegoers who enjoy *Grease* and *Hairspray* were not born before the late 1950s or the early 1960s. These two movies do not strive to rise above clichés, which is why they are so much fun. At the same time, they conjure up a fantasy world that is as unreal as the bizarre Gold Digger musicals of the 1930s and the South American musicals of the 1940s. For those who did live through the 1950s and 1960s, films like *Hairspray* bring back memories because they sound like the music of those eras. Yet when the early days of the Civil Rights Movement are presented as a tuneful joke, as in *Hairspray*, this manufactured nostalgia seems in poor taste. While both *Grease* and *Hairspray* were intended as harmless pieces of entertainment, some audiences might question this rose-colored version of recent history.

See also: *Grease, Little Shop of Horrors;* John Travolta biography box

FURTHER READING

Clarkson, Wensley. *John Travolta: King of Cool.* London: John Blake Books, 2005.
Landau, Diane. *Hairspray.* San Rafael, CA: Insight Editions, 2007.

LES MISÉRABLES

Studio and release date: Universal; December 2012
Producers: Tim Bevan, Eric Fellner, Debra Hayward, Cameron Mackintosh
Screenplay: William Nicholson, Alain Boublil, Claude-Michel Schönberg, based on Boublil and Schönberg's 1985 stage script, which was based on the 1862 novel by Victor Hugo
Songwriters: Claude-Michel Schönberg (music), Alain Boublil, Herbert Kretzmer (lyrics)
Director: Tom Hooper
Choreographer: Liam Steel
Musical Director: Claude-Michel Schönberg
Cinematographer: Danny Cohen

Cast: Hugh Jackman, Russell Crowe, Anne Hathaway, Amanda Seyfried, Sacha Baron Cohen, Helena Bonham Carter, Eddie Redmayne, Aaron Tveit, Samantha Barks, David Huttlestone

Principal Songs: "Do You Hear the People Sing?"; "One Day More!"; "I Dreamed a Dream"; "Master of the House"; "Empty Chairs at Empty Tables"; "Castle on a Cloud"; "On My Own"; "At the End of the Day"; "Who Am I?"; "Suddenly"; "A Heart Full of Love"

Thirty years after this French musical first burst on the scene, a screen version was made with most of the plot, characters, and songs in place. An international sensation, *Les Misérables* had many ardent fans and most were pleased with the long-awaited screen version. Victor Hugo's 1862 novel was one of the great sociopolitical works of the 19th century. It is a work of fiction, but the squalid conditions of the poor and the 1832 rebellion in Paris were historically accurate. Even though the novel is long and has many characters, *Les Misérables* has long been a favorite on the stage, screen, and television. This musical version has a long history also. In the early 1960s, the French author Alain Boublil saw the musical *Oliver!* on the London stage and was enthralled with the way a great novel could become a very accessible musical. The young character of the Artful Dodger in that musical reminded him of the streetwise Gavroche in *Les Misérables* and he started outlining how Hugo's massive novel might become a musical. Boublil enlisted the help of the composer Claude Schönberg, and the two of them wrote and recorded a concept album in 1980. (Andrew Lloyd Webber and Tim Rice's musicals *Jesus Christ Superstar* and *Evita* had also originated as concept albums.) The album was popular in France, selling thousands of copies. That same year *Les Misérables* was staged as a pageant-like event in the Palais des Sports in Paris and was so popular that it ran 100 performances, playing to over 500,000 spectators. British producer Cameron Mackintosh thought that the musical would appeal to English-speaking audiences as well. He commissioned British writer Herbert Kretzmer to translate, adapt, and even rewrite the French text into a musical and then, in 1985, interested the Royal Shakespeare Company in London in producing it for a limited engagement. Codirectors Trevor Nunn and John Caird made further changes, shaping the long, ungainly piece into a cohesive musical drama. The show ran a little over three hours but audiences were enthusiastic and the engagement sold out. Mackintosh then moved the production to the West End where it has run over 25 years. The Broadway version of *Les Misérables* opened in 1987 and ran over 17 years. National and international tours covered much of the globe, making it the most successful musical worldwide.

Plans for a screen version of *Les Misérables* began in the late 1980s when directors such as Alan Parker and Bruce Beresford were attached to the project. An agreement to film the musical was announced in 1992 but that project fell through.

Not until 2005 did plans for the movie resurface, and it was 2012 before production actually began. Mackintosh was one of the movie's producers and made sure that no radical changes were made to his very popular property. The stage musical is sung through without dialogue, and it was felt that the film should use the same format. There were precedents for this. The sung-through stage musicals *Jesus Christ Superstar* (1973) and *Evita* (1996) had been filmed that way with success. William Nicholson wrote the screenplay, tightening the plot enough to get the musical down to two-and-a-half hours. The director, Tom Hooper, and Mackintosh made a bold decision regarding the score. Instead of prerecording the songs in a studio and having the actors lip-sync to their own voices, all the singing was done on the set. This technique was not new; it was the way the earliest movie musicals were made. But the decision created many difficulties in sound recording and balancing voices. Also, the performers sang to a recorded piano track and the orchestra was added later in the editing and mixing process. Although few experienced singers were cast, just about all of the performers in the movie did their own singing. Even though the action is set in Paris and various French locales, the movie was filmed entirely in England, both in a studio and in various towns with architecture that resembled Paris of the early 19th century. Despite cold weather and many on-site problems, *Les Misérables* came in on schedule and on budget ($61 million).

Since the stage work was a musical pageant of sorts, audiences and critics wondered how the big, emotional, spectacular musical would play on the screen. Rather than diminish the piece, the film version made it grander. Also, the sung-through format caused no difficulty and the movie told the long story with clarity. The determined Jean Valjean (Hugh Jackman) is sentenced to jail for stealing a loaf of bread in 19th-century France, escapes, and over the next 17 years is hounded by the obsessed police officer Javert (Russell Crowe). Other characters involved in the plot include the tragic Fantine (Anne Hathaway), her daughter Cosette (Amanda Seyfried) whom Jean adopts, the student Marius (Eddie Redmayne) who loves Cosette, the despicable couple the Thenardiers (Sacha Baron Cohen and Helena Bonham Carter), and their love-torn daughter Eponine (Samantha Barks). Most of the popular score was heard in the film, including the fervent "I Dreamed a Dream," the pleading "Bring Him Home," the character number "Who Am I?," the rousing "One Day More," the lamenting "Empty Chairs at Empty Tables," the ribald "Master of the House," and the lullaby-like "Castle on a Cloud." The performers in the film were mostly very skilled and several turned in superior performances, in particular Jackman and Hathaway. The screen version was on a massive scale and went in for gritty realism even though the premise was that of a sung-through opera. There were some complaints about the uneven singing and the overuse of close-ups but for most *Les Miz* fans, this is the movie they had been waiting and hoping for since the 1980s.

See also: Evita

FURTHER READING

Antinoff, Steve. *Les Misérables for Musical Movie Lovers Who Have Not Read Victor Hugo's Novel.* University Media, 2012.
Morrison, John. *To Love Another Person: A Spiritual Journey through Les Misérables.* Allentown, PA: Zossima Press, 2012.
Vermette, Margaret. *The Musical World of Boublil and Schönberg.* Montclair, NJ: Applause Theatre & Cinema Books, 2007.

FROZEN

Studio and release date: Disney; November 2013
Producer: Peter Del Vecho
Screenplay: Jennifer Lee, based on the 1845 story *The Snow Queen* by Hans Christian Andersen
Songwriters: Robert Lopez, Kristen Anderson Lopez (music and lyrics)
Directors: Chris Buck, Jennifer Lee
Musical Director: Robert Lopez
Voices: Kristen Bell, Idina Menzel, Jonathan Groff, Josh Gad, Santino Fontana, Alan Tudyk, Ciarán Hinds, Chris Williams, Stephen Anderson
Songs: "Let It Go"; " "Love Is an Open Door"; "For the First Time in Forever"; "Do You Want to Build a Snowman?"; "In Summer"; "Fixer Upper"; "Frozen Heart"; "Reindeer(s) Are Better Than People"

A surprise hit from the Disney studio, the animated musical fantasy has captured the hearts of young girls who can't seem to get enough of the songs and characters. After the success of musicalizing Hans Christian Andersen's *The Little Mermaid* (1989), it was only a matter of time before the Disney studio returned to the Danish author for another animated movie musical. Yet it is surprising that they turned to the 1845 tale of *The Snow Queen* because it is one of Andersen's longest, most complicated, and most allegorical stories. If the writers for *The Little Mermaid* had to fill out the story for the screen, the writers for *Frozen* had to carefully select which characters and episodes to use. The Andersen tale is actually seven stories that draw on native folk traditions, supernatural mythology, and Christian philosophy. The main plot centers on the youth Kai who is entrapped by the evil Snow Queen. She has turned his heart to ice and transformed him from a fun-loving boy into a calculating man of cold reason and mathematics. His childhood playmate Gerda is determined to find Kai, travels to the Snow Queen's castle, and

As in the Hans Christian Andersen tale it was based on, Disney's animated musical *Frozen* (2013) has a very dark subtext. Princess Elsa (top) has magical powers but sometimes they seem misguided to her sister Anna (foreground). Chris Buck and Jennifer Lee co-directed the popular fantasy musical. (Walt Disney Studios Motion Pictures/Photofest)

saves him, her tears of sympathy melting his frozen heart. This basic story is surrounded by many other characters (including animals and trolls) and episodes, the complete tale resembling a mini-epic poem. Despite its complexity, *The Snow Queen* has intrigued artists who have used the tale to create songs, operas, ballets, orchestral suites, animated shorts and features, and even video games. It is commonly believed that C. S. Lewis was greatly inspired by the Andersen story when writing *The Lion, the Witch and the Wardrobe* (1950).

The Disney studio set out to make a musical based on *The Snow Queen*, but the more they worked on it, the more the story departed from Andersen's original. In fact, they dropped Andersen's title because the shooting script barely resembled his original tale. Several of Disney's top writers labored over finding a way to adapt the story and most gave up. In codirector Jennifer Lee's screenplay, the Scandinavian kingdom of Arendelle has been put into a state of endless winter by the princess Elsa who has taken refuge in a faraway ice palace. Her younger sister Anna sets out to find Elsa and get her to bring a long-awaited spring. Joining Anna on her journey is the woodsman Kristoff, his faithful reindeer sidekick Sven, and a lively snowman named Olaf. Added to the mix are Prince Hans who is wooing Anna, various court intrigues, and the rigors of the frozen countryside. (If one was looking for some tribute to Andersen, one had to put together the characters' names: Hans Kristof Anna Sven.) The songs and the added characters helped fill out this simple tale, but the plot was full of holes and unexplained complications. In fact, the more one examines the movie, the less sense it makes. Yet this didn't stop hoards of moviegoers, particularly young ones, from embracing *Frozen*. One might credit the stunning Nordic look of the movie, the dazzling animation, and even the tuneful songs by Robert Lopez and Kristen Anderson-Lopez (music and lyrics) as reasons for the film's popularity. But a more likely explanation is less artful. Most Disney movies have a beautiful but struggling princess who little girls love to admire, imitate, and dress up like. *Frozen* had two such icons and both fascinated the young female moviegoers.

Frozen is as finely crafted as the best Disney animated musicals, particularly in its look and movement. The creation of the ice palace before our eyes was particularly ingenious. As for the score, the runaway hit was the catchy soaring ballad "Let It Go" but also enjoyable were the comic wish song "In Summer," the childlike ditty "Do You Want to Build a Snowman?," the jaunty duet "Love Is an Open Door," and the anticipation number "For the First Time in Forever." Idina Menzel voiced Elsa's speaking and singing and gave a superb performance. Others providing voices include Kristen Bell (Anna), Jonathan Groff (Kristoff), Santino Fontana (Hans), and Josh Gad (Olaf), and they could not be faulted for the lack of logic or consistency in their characters. No one was more surprised by the runaway success of *Frozen* than the Disney studio. Aiming to make a child-friendly movie with strong princess appeal, it created a box office juggernaut. *Frozen* was its biggest sleeper since *The Lion King* and just as profitable. While the income from the recent (and superior) *The Princess and the Frog* (2009) and *Tangled* (2010) was disappointing, the profits from *Frozen* were unexplainably high. Even the soundtrack recording broke records. Instead of worrying over why all this happened, the Disney studio is doing the obvious: a movie sequel and a Broadway version are in the works.

See also: *Hans Christian Andersen, The Lion King*

FURTHER READING

Andersen, Hans Christian. *The Complete Fairy Tales and Stories*. Translated by H. B. Paull. Chicago: Centaur, 2013.
Solomon, Charles. *The Art of Frozen*. San Francisco: Chronicle Books, 2015.

INTO THE WOODS

Studio and release date: Disney; December 2014
Producers: Rob Marshall, Marc Platt, John DeLuca, Callum McDougall
Screenplay: James Lapine, based on his 1987 stage libretto
Songwriter: Stephen Sondheim (music and lyrics)

Director: Rob Marshall
Musical Director: Paul Gemignani
Cinematographer: Dion Beebe
Cast: Meryl Streep, James Corden, Anna Kendrick, Emily Blunt, Lilla Crawford, Daniel Huttlestone, Tracey Ullman, Johnny Depp, Christine Baranski
Principal Songs: "No One Is Alone,"; "Children Will Listen"; "Giants in the Sky"; "Agony"; "It Takes Two"; "On the Steps of the Palace"; "Hello, Little Girl"; "I Know Things Now"; "The Last Midnight"; "Rapunzel's Song"; "Into the Woods"

One of Stephen Sondheim's most popular stage works with hundreds of productions every year, the movie version was also popular and will probably remain so for some time. James Lapine's 1987 stage script is set in a fairy tale forest where characters from old and new children's tales meet and help each other achieve their happy endings. While many of the fairy tale characters are familiar (Cinderella, Rapunzel, Little Red Riding Hood, Jack of bean stock fame, etc.), the story is held together by an original fairy tale. A humble baker and his wife cannot have children because a witch has put a curse on his family. The only way to break the spell is to find certain specific items (a white cow, a red cape, some golden yellow hair, and a glass slipper) and give them to the witch before the "last midnight." The search for these items allows the baker and his wife to encounter famous fairy tale characters once they go into the woods. The first act of the musical ends happily with the curse lifted, the giant killed, and Cinderella marrying her prince. But in the second act the same characters are called to account for their actions, such as killing a giant and marrying a prince one hardly knows, and they strive to reach a more mature recognition of their wishes. Some characters die and others are transformed before the second happy ending, which is more bittersweet than joyous. Among the many outstanding Sondheim songs were the lullaby "Children Will Listen," the expansive "Giants in the Sky," the comforting ballad "No One Is Alone," the comic duet "Agony," the reflective "Moments in the Woods," the fine character number "On the Steps of the Palace," the sultry "Hello, Little Girl," and the catchy title number.

Although *Into the Woods* was a hit on Broadway (765 performances) and the musical became a favorite with schools and other producing groups, Hollywood was not interested in making a movie of the very theatrical show. Not until after the success of the film version of *Chicago* in 2002 was its director Rob Marshall able to stir up interest in a screen version of the Sondheim musical. It took a dozen years before the film was finally made, and it opened to strong reviews and respectable business. Lapine adapted his own stage script, leaving out some characters and plot sequences in order to concentrate on the baker and his wife. Just about all of the Sondheim stage score was retained for the film, and it was sung by a suburb cast of new and familiar performers. In particular, Meryl Streep was a fascinating witch, James Corden an engaging Baker, Anna Kendrick a thoughtful Cinderella, David Huttlestone a winsome Jack, and Lilla Crawford a vivacious Little Red Riding

Before she became a movie star, Meryl Streep appeared in Broadway musicals. In the film *Into the Woods* (2014), Streep returned to singing when she played the Witch in the complex musical. Rob Marshall directed the dark fantasy with a magical touch. (Walt Disney Studios Motion Pictures/Photofest)

Hood. Marshall directed *Into the Woods* with the right blend of fantasy and empathy, and the unreal sets and costumes were cinematic rather than stage bound. In some ways, *Into the Woods* recalled the golden days when a Hollywood musical had a special, magical look.

Because many of the ideas and observations from the Broadway show made it to the screen, the movie is one of the more intriguing of Hollywood musicals. Although it is certainly entertaining, *Into the Woods* is also disturbing and unsettling in a way few film musicals are. Such themes as taking responsibilities for one's actions and finding happiness without highly romantic ideals are all the more interesting when put into the context of a complicated fairy tale. Sondheim had been offering audiences such thought-provoking musicals for decades but rarely did they make it to the screen. Perhaps the 2007 film version of his 1979 musical thriller *Sweeney Todd: The Demon Barber of Fleet Street* is the only other opportunity movie-goers have had to experience the complex and fascinating world of a Sondheim

Stephen Sondheim (b. 1930)   Broadway's most innovative composer and lyricist of the second half of the 20th century, his songs have been heard in many screen musicals. He was born in New York City, the son of a prosperous businessman, and grew up in Manhattan and rural Pennsylvania where he befriended Oscar Hammerstein who served as the youth's mentor. After studying at Williams College, Sondheim wrote radio scripts and crossword puzzles, finally making his Broadway writing debut as the lyricist for *West Side Story* (1957). He also penned the lyrics for *Gypsy* (1959) before Broadway heard its first Sondheim score—music and lyrics—in the popular *A Funny Thing Happened on the Way to the Forum* (1962). Although his *Anyone Can Whistle* (1964) failed to run, wide recognition came with *Company* (1970), followed by such adventurous works as *Follies* (1971), *A Little Night Music* (1973), *Pacific Overtures* (1976), *Sweeney Todd, the Demon Barber of Fleet Street* (1979), *Merrily We Roll Along* (1981), *Sunday in the Park With George* (1984), *Into the Woods* (1987), *Assassins* (1991), *Passion* (1994), *Bounce* (2003), and *The Frogs* (2004). Because of the highly theatrical nature of his musicals, less than half of them have been turned into films, which include *West Side Story* (1961), *Gypsy* (1962), *A Funny Thing Happened on the Way to the Forum* (1967), *A Little Night Music* (1978), *Sweeney Todd* (2007), and *Into the Woods* (2014). Sondheim has written original songs for a handful of movies, including *Dick Tracy* (1990) and *The Birdcage* (1996). While Sondheim's tough, ingenious, and sometimes abrasive scores might not have wide appeal, there is an uncompromising quality and an acute sense of dedication that ties him with Oscar Hammerstein. Biography: *Stephen Sondheim, A Life*, Meryle Secrest (1998).

musical. One can only hope that, with the success of *Into the Woods*, some of his other stage works will eventually arrive on the big screen.

See also*: West Side Story, Chicago*; Stephen Sondheim, Rob Marshall biography boxes

FURTHER READING

Gordon, Joanne. *Art Isn't Easy: The Theatre of Stephen Sondheim*. Boston: Da Capo Press, 2009.

Gordon, Robert. *The Oxford Handbook of Sondheim Studies*. New York: Oxford University Press, 2014.

Zadan, Craig. *Sondheim & Company*. Boston: Da Capo Press, 1994.

BIBLIOGRAPHY

Acevedo-Muñoz, Ernesto R. *West Side Story as Cinema: The Making and Impact of an American Masterpiece*. Lawrence: University Press of Kansas, 2013.

Allvine, Glendon. *The Greatest Fox of Them All*. New York: Lyle Stuart, 1969.

Altman, Rick. *The American Film Musical*. Bloomington: Indiana University Press, 1987.

Andersen, Hans Christian. *The Complete Fairy Tales and Stories*. Translated by H. B. Paull. Chicago: Centaur, 2013.

Andrews, Julie. *Home: A Memoir of My Early Years*. Glendale, CA: Hyperion, 2008.

Antinoff, Steve. *Les Misérables for Musical Movie Lovers Who Have Not Read Victor Hugo's Novel*. University Media, 2012.

Arceri, Gene. *Rocking Horse: A Personal Biography of Betty Hutton*. Albany, GA: BearManor Media, 2009.

Armstrong, Louis. *Satchmo: My Life in New Orleans*. Boston: Da Capo Press, 1986.

Arntz, James. *Julie Andrews*. Raleigh, NC: Contemporary Books, 1995.

Astaire, Fred. *Steps in Time: An Autobiography*. New York: Dey Street Books, 2008.

Aylesworth, Thomas G. *Broadway to Hollywood*. New York: Gallery Books, W. H. Smith Publishers, 1985.

Balio, Tino. *United Artists*. Madison: University of Wisconsin Press, 1976.

Barrett, Mary Ellen. *Irving Berlin: A Daughter's Memoir*. Montclair, NJ: Limelight Editions, 2004.

Barrios, Richard. *A Song in the Dark: The Birth of the Musical Film*. 2nd ed. New York: Oxford University Press, 2010.

Barrios, Richard. *Dangerous Rhythm: Why Movie Musicals Matter*. New York: Oxford University Press, 2014.

Bawden, Liz-Anne. *The Oxford Companion to Film*. New York: Oxford University Press, 1976.

Berg, A. Scott. *Goldwyn: A Biography*. New York: Riverhead Books, 1998.

Bergman, Andrew. *We're in the Money: Depression America and Its Films*. New York: Harper & Row, 1971.

Bergren, Laurence. *As Thousands Cheer: The Life of Irving Berlin*. Boston: Da Capo Press, 1996.

Berson, Misha. *Something's Coming: West Side Story and the American Imagination*. Montclair, NJ: Applause Theatre & Cinema Books, 2011.

Bingen, Steven. *Warner Bros.: Hollywood's Ultimate Backlot*. Lanham, MD: Taylor Trade Publishing, 2014.

Bloom, Ken. *Hollywood Musicals: The 101 Greatest Song-and-Dance Movies of All Time*. New York: Black Dog and Leventhal, 2010.

Bogle, Donald. *Heat Wave: The Life and Career of Ethel Waters*. New York: HarperCollins, 2011.

Bordman, Gerald. *Jerome Kern: His Life and Music*. New York: Oxford University Press, 1980.

Bordman, Gerald. *American Musical Comedy: From Adonis to Dreamgirls*. New York: Oxford University Press, 1982.

Bordman, Gerald. *Days to Be Happy, Years to Be Sad: The Life and Music of Vincent Youmans*. New York: Oxford University Press, 1982.

Bradley, Edwin M. *Unsung Hollywood Musicals of the Golden Era*. Jefferson, NC: McFarland & Co., 2016.

Breslin, Jimmy. *Damon Runyon: A Life*. Jefferson City, MO: Laurel, 1992.

Bret, David. *Maurice Chevalier*. London: Robson Books, 2003.

Buckley, David. *Elton John: The Biography*. London: Carlton, 2013.

Busa, Paul. *The Barbra Streisand Film Guide*. Seattle: CreateSpace Publishing, 2015.

Cagney, James. *Cagney By Cagney*. New York: Knopf Group, 2010.

Canfield, Stephen. *Jerome Kern*. New Haven, CT: Yale University Press, 2006.

Cantor, Eddie. *My Life in Your Hands*. New York: Copper Square Press, 1928/2000.

Cantor, Eddie. *Take My Life*. New York: Copper Square Press, 1957/2000.

Cantor, Eddie. *As I Remember Them*. New York: Duell, Sloan & Pearce, 1962.

Carter, Tim. *Oklahoma!: The Making of an American Musical*. New Haven, CT: Yale University Press, 2007.

Caso, Frank. *Robert Altman: In the American Grain*. London: Reaktion Books, 2016.

Casper, Joseph Andrew. *Stanley Donen*. Lanham, MD: Scarecrow Press, 1995.

Charisse, Cyd, and Tony Martin with Dick Kleiner. *The Two of Us*. New York: Mason/Charter, 1976.

Charles, Ray, and David Ritz. *Brother Ray: Ray Charles' Own Story*. Boston: Da Capo Press, 2004.

Chevalier, Maurice. *The Man in the Straw Hat*. New York: Crowell, 1949.

Chevalier, Maurice. *With Love*. Boston: Little, Brown & Co., 1960.

Chevalier, Maurice. *I Remember It Well*. New York: Macmillan & Co., 1970.

Citron, Stephen. *Jerry Herman: Poet of the Showtune*. New Haven, CT: Yale University Press, 2004.

Clarke, Gerald. *Get Happy: The Life of Judy Garland*. Crystal Lake, IL: Delta, 2009.

Clarkson, Wensley. *John Travolta: Back in Character*. New York: Overlook Press, 1996.

Clarkson, Wensley. *John Travolta: King of Cool*. London: John Blake Books, 2005.

Cohan, Steven. *Hollywood Musicals, The Film Reader*. New York: Routledge, 2002.

Cohn, Art. *The Joker Is Wild: The Story of Joe E. Lewis*. New York: Random House, 1955.

Cole, Julie Dawn. *I Want It Now! A Memoir of Life on the Set of Willy Wonka and the Chocolate Factory*. Longboat Key, FL: Oceanview Publishing, 2011.

Comden, Betty. *Offstage*. New York: Simon & Schuster, 1995.

Coppula, Christopher A. *Jimmy Van Heusen: Swinging on a Star*. Nashville, TN: Twin Creek Books, 2014.

Croce, Arlene. *The Fred Astaire-Ginger Rogers Book*. New York: Dutton, 1987.

Crosby, Bing, and Pete Martin. *Call Me Lucky*. Boston: Da Capo Press, 2001.

Crosby, Gary, and Ross Firestone. *Going My Own Way*. New York: Doubleday, 1983.

Crosby, Kathryn. *Bing and Other Things*. New York: Meredith Press, 1967.

Crowther, Bosley. *The Lion's Share: The Story of an Entertainment Empire*. New York: E. P. Dutton & Co., 1957.

Culhane, John. *Disney's Aladdin: The Making of an Animated Film*. Glendale, CA: Disney Editions, 1992.

de Giere, Carol. *Defying Gravity: The Creative Career of Stephen Schwartz*. Montclair, NJ: Applause Theatre & Cinema Books, 2008.

Decker, Todd. *Show Boat: Performing Race in an American Musical*. New York: Oxford University Press, 2012.

Deneroff, Harvey. *The Art of Anastasia*. New York: HarperCollins, 1997.

Denkirk, Darcia. *A Fine Romance: Hollywood and Broadway*. New York: Watson Guptill Publications, 2005.

Dick, Bernard, ed. *Columbia Pictures: Portrait of a Studio*. Lexington: University of Kentucky Press, 1991.

Druxman, Michael B. *The Musical From Broadway to Hollywood*. New York: Barnes, 1980.

Eames, John Douglas. *The MGM Story*. New York: Crown Publishers, 1975.

Eames, John Douglas. *The Paramount Story*. New York: Crown Publishers, 1985.

Echols, Alice. *Hot Stuff: Disco and the Remaking of American Culture*. New York: W. W. Norton & Company, 2010.

Edwards, Anne. *Judy Garland: A Biography*. Lanham, MD: Taylor Trade Publishing, 2013.

Eells, George. *The Life That Late He Led: A Biography of Cole Porter*. New York: J. P. Putnam's Sons, 1967.

Elder, Jane Lenz. *Alice Faye: A Life Beyond the Silver Screen*. Jackson: University Press of Mississippi, 2002.

Eskew, Glenn. *Johnny Mercer: Southern Songwriter for the World*. Athens: University of Georgia Press, 2013.

Evans, Mike, and Paul Kingsbury. *Woodstock: Three Days That Rocked the World*. New York: Sterling, 2010.

Faith, William Robert. *Bob Hope: A Life in Comedy*. Boston: Da Capo Press, 2003.

Farkas, Andrew, and Enrico Caruso, Jr. *Enrico Caruso: My Father and My Family*. Montclair, NJ: Amadeus Press, 2003.

Feuer, Jane. *The Hollywood Musical*. Bloomington: Indiana University Press, 1982.

Finch, Christopher. *Rainbow: The Stormy Life of Judy Garland*. New York: Grosset & Dunlap, 1975.

Finch, Christopher. *Jim Henson: The Works—The Art, the Magic, the Imagination*. New York: Random House, 1993.

Fitzgerald, Michael G. *Universal Pictures: A Panoramic History*. Westport, CT: Arlington House, 1977.

Flinn, Caryl. *The Sound of Music*. (BFI Film Classics). London: British Film Institute, 2015.

Fordin, Hugh. *Getting to Know Him: A Biography of Oscar Hammerstein II*. Boston: Da Capo Press, 1977/1995.

Fordin, Hugh. *M-G-M's Greatest Musicals: The Arthur Freed Unit*. Boston: Da Capo Press, 1996.

Franceschina, John. *Hermes Pan: The Man Who Danced with Fred Astaire*. New York: Oxford University Press, 2012.

Fraser, Nicholas, and Marsa Navarro. *Evita: The Real Lives of Eva Peron*. London: Andre Deutsch, 2013.

Freedland, Michael. *Jerome Kern: A Biography*. New York: Stein and Day Pub., 1981.

Freedland, Michael. *Jolson: The Story of Al Jolson*. London: Virgin Books, 1995.

Fuchs, Jeanne, and Ruth Prigozy. *Frank Sinatra: The Man, the Music, the Legend*. Rochester, NY: University of Rochester Press, 2007.

Furia, Philip. *Ira Gershwin: The Art of the Lyricist*. New York: Oxford University Press, 1997.

Furia, Philip. *Skylark: The Life and Times of Johnny Mercer*. New York: St. Martin's Press, 2004.

Gabler, Neal. *Walt Disney: The Triumph of the American Imagination*. New York: Vintage Press, 2006.

Garebian, Keith. *The Making of Cabaret*. 2nd ed. New York: Oxford University Press, 2011.

Geduld, Harry M. *The Birth of the Talkies*. Bloomington: Indiana University Press, 1975.

Gehring, Wes D. *Irene Dunne: First Lady of Hollywood*. 2nd ed. Lanham, MD: Scarecrow Press, 2006.

Giddins, Gary. *Stachmo: The Genius of Louis Armstrong*. Boston: Da Capo Press, 2009.

Giles, Sarah. *Fred Astaire: His Friends Talk*. New York: Doubleday, 1988.

Glynn, Stephen. *A Hard Day's Night: British Film Guide*. London/New York: I. B. Tauris, 2005.

Goldman, Herbert G. *Fanny Brice: The Original Funny Girl*. New York: Oxford University Press, 1993.

Goldman, Herbert G. *Banjo Eyes: Eddie Cantor and the Birth of Movie Stardom*. New York: Oxford University Press, 1997.

Goldrosen, John. *Buddy Holly: His Life and Music*. Johannesburg, South Africa: Quick Fox, 1975/1979.

Gonthier, David F., Jr. *The Films of Alan Parker*. Jefferson, NC: McFarland Publishers, 2015.

Gordon, Joanne. *Art Isn't Easy: The Theatre of Stephen Sondheim*. Boston: Da Capo Press, 2009.

Gordon, Robert. *The Oxford Handbook of Sondheim Studies*. New York: Oxford University Press, 2014.

Gottfried, Martin. *All His Jazz: The Life and Death of Bob Fosse*. Boston: Da Capo Press, 1990/2009.

Gottfried, Martin. *Nobody's Fool: Danny Kaye*. New York: Simon & Schuster, 1994.

Grant, Barry Keith. *The Hollywood Film Musical*. Hoboken, NJ: Wiley-Blackwell, 2012.

Green, Stanley. *Encyclopedia of Musical Film*. New York: Oxford University Press, 1981.

Green, Stanley, and Barry Monush. *Hollywood Musicals Year by Year*. 3rd ed. Milwaukee: Hal Leonard Publishing Corp., 2010.

Griffin, Mark. *A Hundred or More Hidden Things: The Life and Films of Vincente Minnelli*. Boston: Da Capo Press, 2010.

Grubb, Kevin Boyd. *Razzle Dazzle: The Life and Work of Bob Fosse*. New York: St. Martin's Press, 1989.

Grudens, Richard. *Bing Crosby: Crooner of the Century*. Stony Brook, NY: Celebrity Profiles, Inc., 2002.

Grudens, Richard. *Chattanooga Choo-Choo: The Life and Times of the World Famous Glenn Miller Orchestra*. Stony Brook, NY: Celebrity Profiles Publishing, 2004.

Guralnick, Peter. *Last Train to Memphis: The Rise of Elvis Presley*. New York: Little, Brown & Co., 2014.

Habegger, Alfred. *Masked: The Life of Anna Leonowens, Schoolmistress at the Court of Siam*. Madison: University of Wisconsin Press, 2014.

Halliwell, Leslie. *Halliwell's Film Guide*. 7th ed. New York: Harper & Row, Publishers, 1989.

Harmetz, Aljean. *The Making of The Wizard of Oz*. Chicago: Chicago Review Press, 2013.

Harris, Sue. *An American in Paris*. (BFI Film Classics). London: British Film Institute, 2015.

Harvey, Stephen. *Directed By Vincent Minnelli*. New York: HarperCollins, 1990.

Haskins, James, and N. R. Mitgang. *Mr. Bojangles: The Biography of Bill Robinson*. New York: William Morrow & Co., 2014.

Henie, Sonja. *Wings on My Feet*. Upper Saddle River, NJ: Prentice-Hall, 1940.

Hill, James. *Rita Hayworth: A Memoir*. New York: Simon & Schuster, 1983.

Hirsch, Julia. *The Sound of Music: The Making of America's Favorite Movie*. New York: McGraw-Hill, 1993.

Hirschhorn, Clive. *The Warner Bros. Story*. New York: Crown Publishers, 1979.

Hirschhorn, Clive. *The Hollywood Musical*. New York: Crown Publishers, 1981.

Hirschhorn, Clive. *The Universal Story*. New York: Crown Publishers, 1981.

Hirschhorn, Clive. *The Hollywood Musical*. Revised 2nd ed. New York: Crown Publishers, 1983.

Hirschhorn, Clive. *Gene Kelly: A Biography*. New York: St. Martin's Press, 1985.

Hirschhorn, Clive. *The Columbia Story*. 2nd ed. London: Hamlyn Press, 2001.

Hischak, Thomas S. *Film It With Music: An Encyclopedic Guide to the American Movie Musical*. Westport, CT: Greenwood Press, 2001.

Hischak, Thomas S. *Through the Screen Door: What Happened to the Broadway Musical When It Went to Hollywood*. Lanham, MD: Scarecrow Press, 2004.

Hischak, Thomas S. *The Oxford Companion to the American Musical: Theatre, Film, and Television*. New York: Oxford University Press, 2008.

Hoberman, J. *42nd Street*. (BFI Film Classics). London: British Film Institute, 1993.

Hochman, Stephen. *The Music Behind the Magic: The Musical Artistry of Alan Menken, Howard Ashman, and Tim Rice*. Glendale, CA: Disney Editions, 1994.

Holiday, Billie. *Lady Sings the Blues*. Revised. New York: Broadway Books, 2011.

Hotchner, A. E. *Doris Day: Her Own Story*. New York: William Morrow & Co., 1975.

Hyland, William G. *Richard Rodgers*. New Haven, CT: Yale University Press, 1998.

Hyland, William G. *George Gershwin: A New Biography*. New York: Praeger, 2003.

Irwin, Kenneth, and Charles O. Lloyd. *Ruth Etting: America's Forgotten Sweetheart*. Lanham, MD: Scarecrow Press, 2009.

Isenberg, Barbara. *Tradition! Fiddler on the Roof: The World's Most Beloved Musical*. New York: St. Martin's Press, 2014.

Jablonski, Edward. *Harold Arlen: Happy With the Blues*. Boston: Da Capo Press, 1986.

Jablonski, Edward. *Alan Jay Lerner*. New York: Henry, Holt & Co., 1996.

Jablonski, Edward. *Irving Berlin: American Troubadour*. New York: Henry Holt & Co., 1999.

Jacobs, Lewis. *The Rise of the American Film*. New York: Harcourt, Brace & Co., 1939.

Jewell, Richard B., and Vernon Harbin. *The RKO Story*. New York: Arlington House, 1982.

Kaplan, James. *Sinatra: The Chairman*. New York: Doubleday, 2015.

Kasson, John F. *The Little Girl Who Fought the Great Depression: Shirley Temple and 1930s America*. New York: W. W. Norton & Co., 2014.

Katz, Ephraim. *The Film Encyclopedia*. 3rd ed. New York: Harper-Perennial, 1998.

Kaufman, Gerald. *Meet Me in St. Louis*. (BFI Film Classics). London: British Film Institute, 1994.

Kaufman, J. B. *Snow White and the Seven Dwarfs: The Art and Creation of Walt Disney's Classic Animated Film*. San Francisco: Walt Disney Family Foundation Press, 2012.

Kaufman, J. B. *Pinocchio: The Making of the Disney Epic*. San Francisco: Walt Disney Family Foundation Press, 2015.

Keel, Howard. *Only Make Believe: My Life in Show Business*. Fort Lee, NJ: Barricade Books, Inc., 2005.

Kennedy, Matthew. *Roadshow! The Fall of Film Musicals in the 1960s*. New York: Oxford University Press, 2014.

Keogh, Pamela Clarke. *Elvis Presley: The Man, the Life, the Legend*. New York: Atria Books, 2004.

Kniffel, Leonard. *Musicals on the Silver Screen: A Guide to the Must-See Movie Musicals*. Chicago: Huron Street Press, 2013.

Knight, Arthur. *Disintegrating the Musical: Black Performance and the American Musical Film*. Durham, NC: Duke University Press, 2002.

Koenig, David. *Danny Kaye: King of Jesters*. Irvine, CA: Bonaventure Press, 2012.

Konigsberg, Ira. *The Complete Film Dictionary*. 2nd ed. New York: Penguin, 1997.

Kreuger, Miles. *Show Boat: The Story of a Classic American Musical*. Boston: Da Capo Press, 1990.

Lambert, Philip. *To Life! The Musical Theatre of Bock and Harnick*. New York: Oxford University Press, 2010.

Landau, Diane. *Hairspray*. San Rafael, CA: Insight Editions, 2007.

Lang, Michael. *The Road to Woodstock*. New York: Ecco, 2010.

Lasky, Betty. *RKO: The Biggest Little Major of Them All*. Englewood Cliffs, NJ: Prentice-Hall, 1984.

Leaming, Barbara. *If This Was Happiness: A Biography of Rita Hayworth*. New York: Viking Press, 1989.

Lees, Gene. *Inventing Champagne: The Worlds of Lerner and Loewe*. New York: St. Martin's Press, 1990.

Lees, Gene. *Portrait of Johnny: The Life of John Herndon Mercer*. Montclair, NJ: Hal Leonard, 2006.

Lehmer, Larry. *The Day the Music Died: The Last Tour of Buddy Holly, The Big Bopper, and Ritchie Valens*. New York: Schirmer Trade Books, 2012.

Leigh, Spencer. *Frank Sinatra: An Extraordinary Life*. London: McNidder and Grace, 2015.

Leigh, Wendy. *Liza Minnelli: Born a Star*. New York: Dutton, 1994.

Lerner, Alan Jay. *The Street Where I Live*. New York: W. W. Norton & Co., 1978.

Lertzman, Richard A., and William J. Birnes. *The Life and Times of Mickey Rooney*. New York: Gallery Books, 2015.

Leve, James. *Kander and Ebb*. New Haven, CT: Yale University Press, 2009.

Levin, Alice. *Eleanor Powell: First Lady of Dance*. Las Vegas, NV: Empire Publishers, 1998.

Levy, Emanuel. *Vincente Minnelli: Hollywood's Dark Dreamer*. New York: St. Martin's Press, 2009.

Loesser, Susan. *A Most Remarkable Fella: Frank Loesser and the Guys and Dolls in His Life*. New York: Donald I. Fine, Inc., 1993.

Louvish, Simon. *Monkey Business: The Lives and Legends of the Marx Brothers*. New York: Thomas Dunne Books, 2000.

Lovensheimer, Jim. *South Pacific: Paradise Rewritten*. New York: Oxford University Press, 2010.

Luft, Lorna. *Me and My Shadows: A Family Memoir*. New York: Gallery Books, 1999.

Luhrmann, Baz, and Catherine Martin. *Moulin Rouge! The Splendid Book That Charts the Journey of Baz Luhrmann's Motion Picture*. New York: Newmarket Press, 2001.

Lydon, Michael. *Ray Charles: Man and Music*. London: Routledge, 2004.

Lynn, Loretta, and George Vecsey. *Loretta Lynn: Coal Miner's Daughter*. New York: Vintage, 2010.

Magee, Jeffrey. *Irving Berlin: American Musical Theatre*. New York: Oxford University Press, 2012.

Mair, George. *Under the Rainbow: The Real Liza Minnelli*. Secaucus, NJ: Birch Lane Press, 1996.

Maltin, Leonard. *The Disney Films*. 4th ed. Glendale, CA: Disney Editions, 2000.

Mangan, Lucy. *Inside Charlie's Chocolate Factory*. London: Puffin Books, 2014.

Mannering, Derek. *Mario Lanza: Singing to the Gods*. Ramsbury, Wiltshire, GB: Robert Hale Press, 2011.

Marx, Groucho. *Groucho and Me*. Boston: Da Capo Press, 1959/2009.

Marx, Groucho. *Memoirs of a Mangy Lover*. Boston: Da Capo Press, 1964/2008.

Marx, Groucho, with Hector Arce. *The Secret Word Is Groucho*. New York: Putnam, 1976.

Marx, Harpo, with Rowland Barber. *Harpo Speaks*. Montclair, NJ: Limelight Editions, 1961/2004.

Maslon, Laurence. *The South Pacific Companion*. New York: Touchstone, 2008.

Maslon, Laurence. *The Sound of Music Companion*. London: Pavilion, 2015.

Mast, Gerald. *A Short History of the Movies*. Indianapolis: Pegasus, 1971.

Mast, Gerald. *Can't Help Singin': The American Musical on Stage and Screen*. Woodstock, NY: Overlook Press, 1987.

Matthew-Walker, Robert. *Broadway to Hollywood: The Musical and the Cinema*. London: Sanctuary Publishing, 1996.

McBrien, William. *Cole Porter*. New York: Vintage Press, 2011.

McCabe, John. *Cagney*. New York: Knopf, 2013.

McGee, Garry. *Doris Day: Sentimental Journey*. Jefferson, NC: McFarland Publishers, 2010.

McGee, Mark Thomas. *Fast and Furious: The Story of American International Pictures*. Jefferson, NC: McFarland Publishers, 1984.

McGee, Tom. *Betty Grable: The Girl With the Million Dollar Legs*. New York: Welcome Rain Publishers, 1995/2009.

McGuire, Patricia Dubin. *Lullaby of Broadway: The Life of Al Dubin*. Secaucus, NJ: Citadel, 1983.

McHugh, Dominic. *Loverly: The Life and Times of My Fair Lady*. New York: Oxford University Press, 2012.

McLean, Adrienne L. *Being Rita Hayworth: Labor, Identity, and Hollywood Stardom*. Brunswick, NJ: Rutgers University Press, 2004.

Mendheim, Beverly. *Ritchie Valens: The First Latin Rocker*. Tempe, AZ: Bilingual Review Press, 1987.

Meyer, Carolyn. *Anastasia: The Last Grand Duchess*. New York: Scholastic, 2013.

Meyer, John. *Judy Garland: Heartbreaker*. Secaucus, NJ: Citadel, 2006.

Mielke, Randall G. *The Road to Box Office: The Seven Film Comedies of Crosby, Hope and Lamour*. Jefferson, NC: McFarland Publishing, 1997.

Miller, Ann, and Norma Lee Browning. *Miller's High Life*. New York: Doubleday, 1972.

Mills, W. E. *The Deanna Durbin Fairy Tale*. Baltimore: Images, Ltd., 1996.

Mordden, Ethan. *The Hollywood Musical*. New York: St. Martin's Press, 1982.

Mordden, Ethan. *The Hollywood Studios*. New York: Alfred A. Knopf, Inc., 1988.

Mordden, Ethan. *Rodgers & Hammerstein*. New York: Abradale/Abrams, 1995.

Mordden, Ethan. *Ziegfeld: The Man Who Invented Show Business*. New York: St. Martin's Press, 2008.

Morgan, Judith, and Neil Morgan. *Dr. Seuss and Mr. Geisel: A Biography*. Boston: Da Capo Press, 1996.

Morley, Sheridan. *Shall We Dance: The Life of Ginger Rogers*. New York: St. Martin's Press, 1995.

Morrison, John. *To Love Another Person: A Spiritual Journey through Les Misérables*. Allentown, PA: Zossima Press, 2012.

Morton, Ray. *A Hard Day's Night*. (Music on Film). Montclair, NJ: Limelight Editions, 2011.

Mundy, John. *The British Film Musical*. Manchester, UK: Manchester University Press, 2007.

Myerson, Harold, and Ernie Harburg. *Who Put the Rainbow in The Wizard of Oz?* E. Y. Harburg, Lyricist. Ann Arbor: University of Michigan Press, 1995.

Napolitano, Mark. *Oliver! A Dickensian Musical*. New York: Oxford University Press, 2014.

Nelson, Thomas. *Irving Berlin's White Christmas*. Nashville, TN: Thomas Nelson, Inc., 2004.

Nolan, Frederick. *The Sound of Their Music: The Story of Rodgers and Hammerstein*. Montclair, NJ: Applause Theatre & Cinema Books, 2002.

Norman, Philip. *Rave On: The Biography of Buddy Holly*. New York: Simon & Schuster, 2014.

Oberfirst, Robert. *Al Jolson: You Ain't Heard Nothin' Yet!* New York/London: Book Sales Inc., 1981.

Otterwell, Jessica. *Like a Fork Shoved on a Spoon: Notions of Gender Identity Within Hedwig and the Angry Inch*. Seattle: Amazon Digital, 2013.

Parish, James Robert. *The Jeanette MacDonald Story*. New York: Mason/Charter, 1976.

Parker, Alan. *The Making of Evita*. New York: HarperCollins, 1996.

Piro, Sal, and Larry Viezel. *The Rocky Horror Treasury: A Tribute to the Ultimate Cult Classic Musical*. Philadelphia: Running Press, 2004.

Pollack, Howard. *George Gershwin: His Life and Work*. Oakland: University of California Press, 2007.

Porter, Cole. *The Cole Porter Story, As Told to Richard G. Hubler*. Wenatchee, WA: World Publishing Co., 1965.

Powell, Jane. *The Girl Next Door . . . and How She Grew*. Belmont, CA: Untreed Reads Publishing, 2014.

Prigozy, Ruth, and Walter Raubicheck, eds. *Going My Way: Bing Crosby and American Culture*. Rochester, NY: University of Rochester Press, 2007.

Quirk, Lawrence J. *Bob Hope: The Road Well-Traveled*. Montclair, NJ: Applause Books, 2000.

Reid, John Howard. *Hollywood Movie Musicals: Great, Good and Glamorous*. 2nd ed. Raleigh, NC: Lulu Press, 2010.

Reynolds, Debbie, with David Patrick Columbia. *Debbie: My Life*. New York: William Morrow, 1988.

Reynolds, Debbie, with Dorian Hannaway. *Unsinkable: A Memoir*. New York: William Morrow, 2013.

Ribowsky, Mark. *The Supremes: A Saga of Motown Dreams, Success and Betrayal*. Boston: Da Capo Press, 2009.

Rice, Tim. *Oh, What a Circus: The Autobiography*. London: Coronet Books, 1999.

Rich, Sharon. *Sweethearts: The Timeless Love Affair . . . Between Jeanette MacDonald and Nelson Eddy*. 3rd ed. New York: Bell Harbour Press, 2014.

Richmond, Keith. *The Musicals of Andrew Lloyd Webber: His Life and Works*. London: Virgin Publishing, 2000.

Rimier, Walter. *The Man That Got Away: The Life and Songs of Harold Arlen*. Champaign: University of Illinois Press, 2015.

Roberts, Michael J. *The Beatles on Film*. Portland, OR: BookBaby, 2014.

Robinson, Mark A. *The World of Musicals: An Encyclopedia of Stage, Screen, and Song*. Santa Barbara, CA: ABC-CLIO Greenwood, 2014.

Rodgers, Richard. *Musical Stages*. Boston: Da Capo Press, 1975/2009.

Rogers, Ginger. *Ginger: My Story*. New York: Harper/It Books, 1991/2008.

Rooney, Mickey. *i.e.: An Autobiography*. New York: Putnam, 1965.

Rooney, Mickey. *Life Is Too Short*. New York: Villard Books, 1991.

Rosenberg, Deena Ruth. *Fascinating Rhythm: The Collaboration of George and Ira Gershwin*. Ann Arbor: University of Michigan Press, 1998.

Rubin, Martin. *Showstoppers: Busby Berkeley and the Tradition of Spectacle*. New York: Columbia University Press, 1993.

Rushdie, Salman. *The Wizard of Oz*. (BFI Film Classics). London: British Film Institute, 2012.

Santopietro, Tom. *Considering Doris Day*. New York: St. Martin's/Griffin, 2007.

Schwartz, Charles. *Cole Porter: A Biography*. New York: Dial Press, 1977.

Scoll, Nathan. *Saturday Night Fever and the Contemporary Dance Film*. Saarbucken, Germany: LAP Lambert Academic Publishing, 2011.

Secrest, Meryle. *Stephen Sondheim: A Life*. New York: Vintage, 1998.

Secrest, Meryle. *Somewhere for Me: A Biography of Richard Rodgers*. Montclair, NJ: Applause Theatre & Cinema Books, 2001.

Sennett, Ted. *Warner Brothers Presents*. Secaucus, NJ: Castle Books, 1971.

Shapiro, Marc. *Annette Funicello: America's Sweetheart*. New York: Riverdale Avenue Books, 2013.

Shepherd, Marie. *Everything You Need to Know About Alan Menken*. Apsley, Australia: Emereo Publishing, 2014.

Sherman, Robert B., and Richard M. Sherman. *Walt's Time: From Before to Beyond*. Santa Clarita, CA: Camphor Tree Publishers, 1998.

Shipman, David. *The Story of Cinema*. New York: St. Martin's Press, 1982.

Silverman, Stephen M. *Dancing on the Ceiling: Stanley Donen and His Movies*. New York: Knopf, 1996.

Sims, Michael. *The Story of Charlotte's Web*. London: Walker Books, 2011.

Sinatra, Nancy. *Frank Sinatra: An American Legend*. New York: Readers Digest Assn, 1998.

Skipper, John C. *Meredith Willson: The Unsinkable Music Man*. El Dorado Hills, CA: Savas Publishing Co., 2000.

Snelson, John. *Andrew Lloyd Webber*. New Haven, CT: Yale University Press, 2009.

Solomon, Alissa. *Wonder of Wonders: A Cultural History of Fiddler on the Roof*. New York: Metropolitan Books, 2013.

Solomon, Charles. *The Art of Frozen*. San Francisco: Chronicle Books, 2015.

Spada, James. *Barbra Streisand: Her Life*. Bloomington, IN: Author & Company, 2013.

Spergel, Mark. *Reinventing Reality: The Art and Life of Rouben Mamoulian*. Lanham, MD: Scarecrow Press, 1993.

Spivak, Jeffrey. *Buzz: The Life and Art of Busby Berkeley*. Lexington: University Press of Kentucky, 2010.

Spoto, Donald. *Marilyn Monroe: The Biography*. New York: Dansker Press, 2014.

Stafford, David, and Caroline Stafford. *Fings Ain't Wot They Used T' Be: The Lionel Bart Story*. London: Omnibus Press, 2011.

Stirling, Richard. *Julie Andrews. An Intimate Biography*. New York: St. Martin's Press, 2008.

Stuart, Jan. *Nashville Chronicles: The Making of Robert Altman's Masterpiece*. Montclair, NJ: Limelight Editions, 2004.

Stuart, Mel, and Josh Young. *Pure Imagination: The Making of Willy Wonka*. New York: St. Martin's Press, 2002.

Szwed, John. *Billie Holiday: The Musician and the Myth*. New York: Viking, 2015.

Taraborelli, J. Randy. *Diana Ross: A Biography*. Secaucus, NJ: Citadel, 2014.

Taraborelli, J. Randy. *Sinatra: Behind the Legend*. New York: Grand Central Pub., 2015.

Taylor, Theodore. *Jule: The Story of Composer Jule Styne*. New York: Random House, 1979.

Temple, Shirley. *Child Star.* New York: McGraw-Hill, 1998.

Thomas, Bob. *The Man, the Dancer: The Life of Fred Astaire.* New York: St. Martin's Press, 1987.

Thomas, Bob. *Walt Disney: An American Original.* Glendale, CA: Disney Editions, 1994.

Thomas, Lawrence B. *The MGM Years.* New York: Arlington House, 1971.

Thomas, Tony. *The Busby Berkeley Book.* New York: New York Graphics Society, 1973.

Thomas, Tony. *Harry Warren and the Hollywood Musical.* New York: Lyle Stuart, Inc., 1975.

Thomas, Tony. *The Dick Powell Story.* Burbank, CA: Riverwood Press, 1992.

Thomas, Tony, and Aubrey Solomon. *The Films of 20th Century-Fox.* Secaucus, NJ: Citadel Press, 1979.

Thompson, Douglas. *Fever! The Biography of John Travolta.* London: Trafalgar Square Publishing, 1997.

Thompson, Frank. *Tim Burton's Nightmare Before Christmas: The Film, the Art, the Vision.* Glendale, CA: Disney Editions, 2002.

Traubner, Richard. *Operetta: A Theatrical History.* Garden City, NY: Doubleday & Co., 1983.

Tropiano, Stephen. *Cabaret: Music on Film.* Montclair, NJ: Limelight Editions, 2011.

Tropiano, Stephen. *Grease: Music on Film.* Montclair, NJ: Limelight Editions, 2011.

Turk, Edward Baron. *Hollywood Diva: A Biography of Jeanette MacDonald.* Oakland: University of California Press, 2000.

Van Dyke, Dick. *My Lucky Life in and Out of Show Business: A Memoir.* New York: Random House, 2011.

Vermette, Margaret. *The Musical World of Boublil and Schönberg.* Montclair, NJ: Applause Theatre & Cinema Books, 2007.

Victor, Barbara. *Goddess: Inside Madonna.* New York: HarperCollins, 2013.

Warren, Doug. *Betty Grable: The Reluctant Movie Queen.* New York: St. Martin's Press, 1981.

Wasson, Sam. *Fosse.* New York: Dolan/Houghton Mifflin Harcourt, 2013.

Waters, Ethel, and Charles Samuels. *To Me It's Wonderful.* New York: Harper & Row, 1972.

Waters, Ethel, and Charles Samuels. *His Eye Is on the Sparrow: An Autobiography.* Boston: Da Capo Press, 1992.

Wilk, Max. *OK!: The Story of Oklahoma!* Montclair, NJ: Applause Theatre & Cinema Books, 2002.

Williams, Esther, and Digby Diehl. *The Million Dollar Mermaid: An Autobiography.* New York: Simon & Schuster, 1999.

Williamson, Joel. *Elvis Presley: A Southern Life.* New York: Oxford University Press, 2014.

Willson, Meredith. *But He Doesn't Know the Territory.* Minneapolis: University of Minnesota Press, 2013.

Winer, Deborah Grace. *On the Sunny Side of the Street: The Life and Lyrics of Dorothy Fields.* New York: Schirmer Books, 1997.

Wlaschin, Ken. *Opera on Screen.* Los Angeles: Beachwood Press, 1997.

Woll, Allen L. *The Hollywood Musical Goes to War.* Chicago: Nelson-Hall, 1983.

Wollen, Peter. *Singin' in the Rain.* (BFI Film Classics). London: British Film Institute, 2008.

Wollman, Elizabeth Lara. *The Theatre Will Rock: A History of the Rock Musical, From Hair to Hedwig.* Ann Arbor: University of Michigan Press, 2009.

Woodhouse, Horace Martin. *The Essential Mary Poppins.* Seattle: CreateSpace Publishing, 2014.

Yudkoff, Alvin. *Gene Kelly: A Life of Dance and Dreams.* New York: Watson-Guptil Publications, 1999.

Zadan, Craig. *Sondheim & Company.* Boston: Da Capo Press, 1994.

Zoglin, Richard. *Bob Hope: The Entertainer of the Century.* New York: Simon & Schuster, 2014.

Index

Page numbers in **bold** indicate main entries in this volume.
Page numbers in *italics* indicate photos.

ABOUT THE AUTHOR

Thomas S. Hischak is an internationally recognized author and teacher in the performing arts. He is the author of 24 nonfiction books about theater, film, and popular music, including *The Oxford Companion to the American Musical, The Rodgers and Hammerstein Encyclopedia, Broadway Plays and Musicals, Through the Screen Door, The Tin Pan Alley Encyclopedia, Off-Broadway Musicals Since 1919, The Disney Song Encyclopedia, Broadway Lyricists, American Literature on Stage and Screen, Theatre as Human Action,* and *The Oxford Companion to American Theatre.* He is also the author of 33 published plays performed throughout the United States, Canada, Great Britain, and Australia. Hischak is a Fulbright scholar who has taught and directed in Greece, Lithuania, and Turkey.

Since 1983 he has been Professor of Theatre at the State University of New York at Cortland, where he has received such honors as the 2004 SUNY Chancellor's Award for Excellence in Scholarship and Creative Activity and the 2010 SUNY Outstanding Achievement in Research Award. Four of his books have been cited as Outstanding Non-fiction Books by the American Library Association, and *The Oxford Companion to the American Musical* was cited as an Outstanding Reference Work by the New York City Public Library in 2008. His playwriting awards include the Stanley Drama Award (New York City) for *Cold War Comedy* and the Julie Harris Playwriting Award (Beverly Hills, California) for *The Cardiff Giant.*